PERGAMON INTERNATIONAL LIBRARY
of Science, Technology, Engineering and Social Studies

The 1000-volume original paperback library in aid of education,
industrial training and the enjoyment of leisure

Publisher: Robert Maxwell M.C.

Anatoly Karpov:
Chess is My Life

PERGAMON RUSSIAN CHESS SERIES

General Editor
David N. L. Levy

Executive Editor
Martin J. Richardson

Related books of interest:

Anatoly Karpov: Chess is My Life

by

ANATOLY KARPOV

and

ALEKSANDR ROSHAL

Translated by
KENNETH P. NEAT

PERGAMON PRESS

OXFORD · NEW YORK · TORONTO · SYDNEY · PARIS · FRANKFURT

U.K.	Pergamon Press Ltd., Headington Hill Hall, Oxford OX3 0BW, England
U.S.A.	Pergamon Press Inc., Maxwell House, Fairview Park, Elmsford, New York 10523, U.S.A.
CANADA	Pergamon of Canada, Suite 104, 150 Consumers Road Willowdale, Ontario M2J IP9, Canada
AUSTRALIA	Pergamon Press (Aust.) Pty. Ltd., P.O.Box 544, Potts Point, N.S.W. 2011, Australia
FRANCE	Pergamon Press SARL, 24 rue des Ecoles, 75240 Paris, Cedex 05, France
FEDERAL REPUBLIC OF GERMANY	Pergamon Press GmbH, 6242 Kronberg-Taunus, Pferdstrasse 1, Federal Republic of Germany

English Translation Copyright © 1980 K. P. Neat.

First edition 1980

British Library Cataloguing in Publication Data

Karpov, Anatolii Evgenievich
Anatoly Karpov. — Chess is My Life (Pergamon Russian Chess Series)
1. Karpov, Anatolii Evgenievich 2. Chess players–Russia–Biography
I. Roshal, Aleksandr
794.1'092'4   GV1439. K37   78-41215

ISBN 0-08-023118-7 hardcover
ISBN 0-08-023119-5 flexicover

Printed in Hungary by Franklin Printing House

Contents

Acknowledgements

The following games are reproduced with permission from *Karpov's Collected Games*, edited by David N. L. Levy and published by Robert Hale.

	page		page
Karpov–Tseitlin	55	Karpov–Gligorić	92
Karpov–Browne	90	Karpov–Spassky	117

The translator is grateful to Mrs. Y. Clarkson and Dr. R. C. Lane of Durham University for advice on a few points of translation.

Foreword

Confessional books by great players from the past used to disappear instantly from book-shop counters, and have long since become bibliographic rarities. One could, for instance, cite the book by Alexander Alekhine *Auf dem Wege zur Weltmeisterschaft*, which was written soon after Alekhine, who was then over thirty, had deprived Capablanca of the world crown. Delving into our memories, we can no doubt find other examples... But it has to be agreed that genuine chess literature is becoming more and more rare, although the total number of sheets printed has without doubt grown enormously. Regarding the reproaches addressed to grandmasters on this account, the author of the foreword to this book is prepared to take them as referring to himself. Of the top grandmasters in recent years, only Robert Fischer and Bent Larsen, who have produced collections of their games—with their own annotations—have to some extent begun to pay off the debt owed by the grandmaster clan to readers.

When writing a book, one would like not only to show some games, but also to say something of interest. But today players barely have time to compete—and for relating their experiences (sincerely, and in detail) there is simply not the time. And while constant over-the-board play, during which we calculate variations and think up plans, makes it easier and quicker to write subsequent annotations, to bring ourselves to describe competitive, to say nothing of real-life situations, is much more difficult. It is for this reason, perhaps, that there is a lack of frank discussions between grandmaster and reader, and that we do not see any real chess writing (but not the work of dabblers—of that there is sufficient), illustrated by games which are annotated by a top player, not only from the viewpoint of the accomplished theorist, but also, as one might say, "for the people"—in a general, intelligible and instructive manner. Instead one has to wait until a grandmaster "retires", and finds time for his literary endeavours.

In contrast to us, our colleague Anatoly Karpov has found an *alter ego*—a "second self"— a person who has known him since childhood, who has watched him closely over the years, a journalist with whom he is extremely frank and whom he trusts completely. Thus this book has two authors:

Anatoly Karpov. 28-year-old World Champion, a chess player who drew attention to himself right from his early years, and whose chess career since then has been very much open to view. At the age of eighteen he became World Junior Champion, a year later—a grandmaster, and within a further year was performing brilliantly in the most imposing of international tourna-ments. There have been no failures in his chess biography, and his successes grow with each new event. Every day the name of Karpov becomes more and more popular, and his constant victories, strange as it may seem, become ever more puzzling and difficult to explain.

Aleksandr Roshal. Chess master, honoured trainer of the Russian Republic, from under whose "wing" have developed a number of players, who are known far beyond the bounds of the Soviet Union. He is a professional journalist, being an active worker not only for the world's top chess weekly *64*, for which he is Chief Secretary, but also in many other publications, literary and general-political, in particular *Izvestiya*, for which he is the regular chess correspondent.

I see the present book as an interesting attempt at collaboration between two quite different authors. The young, quick-tempered (which you would never think, seeing the rational way he plays) World Champion Anatoly Karpov, and the experienced, critical and even sceptically-inclined Aleksandr Roshal. Strictly speaking, the number of authors of this book is considerably greater... Karpov, when appearing in events, does not of course play there alone. On the pages of this book his opponents and rivals give their opinions on the young player. Their points of view are expressed openly, in plain terms, and in everyday language. The journalist in question has been present at numerous tournaments, he is very well acquainted with many of the top players, and has interviewed probably all the leading grandmasters in the World. And now we can distinguish, as if by ear, one chess player from another. It is gratifying to note that the journalist has not attempted to group them all under the same standard, and now this book, while it talks mainly about Karpov, will also tell the attentive reader something about other players, and about the highly complex and confused situations in the chess world. Here we have remarks made before the start of tournaments and matches, as well as after the finish of nerve-racking events. Some of the opinions included here are highly subjective. These are normally accompanied by an analysis, soberly carried out after an elapse of time, when passions have died down, and when everything is in its place. And this is all very, very interesting.

The book has an unusual lay-out, its "geometry" is not altogether normal. Of course, Karpov is not just an isolated specimen—he grew up together with a large group of contemporaries. His elders passed on to him their experience, while those of the same age would battle against him "to the last drop of blood", and then immediately sit down to analyse the game just finished, and in a friendly atmosphere prepare together for future battles.

Since we have been talking about the "geometry" of the book, it should be remarked that the chapter which unobtrusively describes the biography of the new World Champion, is called "Karpov's Vertical" (a fully justified name, which in itself is something of a find). Here are extracts from Karpov's life, which as yet has lasted all of twenty-eight years. But, as it turns out, this has already contained a great deal. Here are his childhood years, and his school, which he concluded with distinction, and we find that it is not just his chess results that have been excellent. There is a great deal about the Champion's unusual character, about his inclinations and pastimes.

In this book there is much that is appearing for the first time. Chess fans will read this with interest, and I also believe that journalists will find it useful.

The final result of any chess game, whatever its course, can be expressed in one of three numerical measurements—1, $\frac{1}{2}$ or 0. But these figures must not remain bare, they must without fail be accompanied by a detailed and gripping account of the most memorable events and games.

It is here that we encounter a device which is original in chess literature—we hear two authors, who rarely speak "with one voice", but more often appear independently, or else hold a sort of dialogue. And it is here that we hear the maturity, scepticism, and occasional irony of the journalist (on which I remarked earlier), and the opinions of our young Champion—interesting, at times sharp and categorical, but always authentically reflecting his point of view. And this refers not only to moves on the chess board, but also to important steps taken in life. Karpov, it turns out, is capable of the apparently most unexpected actions. From his very first steps he became accustomed to listening carefully to the opinions of the experts, extracting from them everything possible, but... But then acting only in the way that he considered correct. This is confirmed both by his chess playing, and by his life. Take for instance his moving from Moscow to Leningrad, which he was categorically "recommended" not to do by "the great" Botvinnik. Karpov is a chess player, an excellent chess player, but—I trust the reader will excuse the banality of this remark—he is first and foremost a person, with all his human qualities, his strong and weak points. These qualities are disclosed in his contacts with his surroundings, with the people close to him. In this book I was particularly pleased to come across the names of various kind and clever people, with whom I too have long had friendly relations.

The choice of the games in this book is rather unusual. I have already remarked that the most important part of Karpov's chess biography has been open to general view, and chess players from round the World know many more of their Champion's games than have found their way into this book. But the selection of games reveals to a certain extent the approach of Karpov to the game of chess itself. In practice he has chosen only games he has won.* Karpov considers that chess is first and foremost a sport. This is his point of view, and it can be accepted completely or only partially, but this is the World Champion's point of view. And since Anatoly's play is logical, and is subjected, so to speak, to classical laws, according to which White has the advantage, in the overwhelming majority of cases Karpov wins when he has the white pieces. Perhaps those who like sharp conflicts would have wished to see in the book more combinative fireworks, and tactical sacrifices by both sides. There are, incidentally, quite a few such games played by Karpov, but the point is that it is not this that he sees as the essence and beauty of chess. And this chess style, which is typical of Karpov today, has as yet changed very little. His first games as a master, played when Anatoly had just turned fifteen, in direction and key do not differ significantly from those played today.

I should like to reinforce this idea with some comments "presented" to me from Roshal's extensive journalist's note-book. During a visit to the United States, Karpov was presented with a book containing opinions of famous masters on chess. Karpov's impulsive reactions to the reading of various aphorisms were quite unusual.

Tarrasch: "The threat is stronger than the execution".—"That's very true!", was Karpov's reply.

Or:

Teichmann: "Chess consists of 99 per cent tactics".—Karpov: "What rubbish..."

The reader should take my word for it that I do not completely agree with Karpov's assessment of the rôle of tactics in chess, but... this is what he thinks.

And here is another extract from the same journalist's note-book. In 1970, on returning from Venezuela from his first grandmaster tournament, Karpov set out the pieces, so as to show his future co-author some of his games. "Well, and how did you manage to defeat the experienced Hungarian grandmaster Barcza?" asked Roshal. "Very simply", replied Karpov. "I quickly exchanged off his knights, and they are his favourite pieces".

One cannot help but recall remarks from Botvinnik's diary, such as the following: "Euwe likes to make long moves with his queen...".

* In order to illuminate the narrative, a few lost or drawn games have been included in the English Edition (K.P.N.)

One thing which I must mention is the enormous benefit which Karpov gained from his collaboration with Semion Furman, one of the most erudite chess players of our time. It is significant that this benefit worked both ways, and most likely it was this collaboration which led to Furman's practical improvement as a grandmaster—take for instance the rivalry between teacher and pupil in the battle for first prize at Madrid in 1973. In short, in the words of the poet: "Artist, educate a pupil, so that you then have someone to learn from..."

An examination of the list of Karpov's victims in this book will reveal the names of many of the top players of our time. The author of this foreword is pleased to note that his name does not yet appear there, although Anatoly and I have played several games together, which have given us much to remember. I, for instance, recall our meeting in the 1971 Alekhine Memorial, the first tournament where Karpov forced those who mistrusted his junior and "foreign" results to treat him with respect. My game with Anatoly lasted 114 moves! And all this time I very much wanted to win. After twenty moves I thought that I would achieve my goal easily and quickly. But all it needed was for me to relax for a second, and my young opponent began to seek microscopic drawing chances with devilish ingenuity. At the time of the first adjournment there was possibly still a win, but after seventy-odd moves the game was again adjourned, and there was no longer a theoretical win. Something similar occurred in the Leningrad Interzonal Tournament, when international master Zuckerman, one of Fischer's advisers, who was present in Leningrad, stated that if Karpov could save a position such as he had against Tal, he must be practically invincible. A possibly over-emotional pronouncement, but one which turned out to be almost prophetic.

The Candidates' Matches are also described here. And described, essentially, for the first time in such detail, with accounts of the circumstances, and assessments by the players themselves and by the watching experts. Some of the pronouncements are so frank as to take one's breath away.

In the section where Fischer's growing conflict with the rest of the chess world is described, the reader will find both excellent chess fiction, and also real chess journalism...

However, we will not exhaust the reader by re-telling the whole of the book, the reader can see for himself the results of the fruitful co-operation between the firm of "Karpov, Roshal & Co." And the "Company" of these two authors is highly imposing and well-qualified. Here are the voices of Max Euwe, Mikhail Botvinnik, Tigran Petrosian, Lyev Polugayevsky, Robert Byrne, Semion Furman, and—forgive me my immodesty—Mikhail Tal, and many, many other grandmasters. And so, here is a book which is equally as unusual as the chess style of World Champion Anatoly Karpov, or the journalistic style of his co-author Aleksandr Roshal.

I am sure that I am recommending to the reader one of those rare books, for which chess fans the world over have been waiting so long.

MIKHAIL TAL

CHAPTER 1

Karpov's Vertical

Crystal chandeliers sparkled in the white-marbled Hall of Columns. Muscovites and visitors to the Soviet Capital, the envoys of many countries, were celebrating the fact that the laurel wreath had just been placed on the shoulders of the twelfth World Champion in the history of chess.

Not long before this, after the victory in the Final Candidates' Match, thunderous applause had drowned the following words, spoken by the President of the International Chess Federation, Dr Max Euwe:

"When I was celebrating my fiftieth birthday, I could never have guessed that within three days—on 23rd May 1951—a chess genius would be born. Now this is obvious to everyone. The only players to have obtained the official right to a match for the World Championship at the age of twenty-three have been Tal and Karpov. Karpov has had a brilliant chess career. What can I wish him? If it be the title of Champion, he is very close to that, and we hope that he will be the best World Champion of all time".

Anatoly Karpov was then presented with prizes and flowers, and cordial speeches were made. Cameras were directed at him and an interview, or at least his autograph, was sought not only by professional journalists, but also by his fellow-grandmasters. President Euwe very much wanted to be photographed with Karpov, "in memory of the occasion", and he then took a youth journal from one of the fans, and on a colour photograph wrote right across the cover in neat lettering: "This is the portrait of a chess genius"...

In the midst of all this splendour and activity, only two persons remained unmoved. From time to time they looked at each other with slightly moistened eyes, and, hunching up their shoulders still more, would retire even further into their shell. Then, when someone 'betrayed' them, Karpov's parents were immediately surrounded by journalists. Their replies were rather terse. The father: "You should always believe in your son". The mother: "He's got thinner again..."

There was much for them to remember on that day...

Yevgeny Stepanovich Karpov and Nina Grigorievna, née Sokolova, were natives of the Urals. They met at the factory, where twenty-two-year-old Yevgeny Karpov was working as a foreman after finishing technical college, and to which twenty-year-old Nina had come after a managerial course. Also living in Zlatoust were Yevgeny Stepanovich's mother and step-father (his own father had died seven months after the birth of the son in 1918). Yevgeny Karpov had a difficult childhood, and as a result he became accustomed to hard work at an early age. He was independent in nature, with a hard, at times even stern, character. Yevgeny Karpov was a good worker, was promoted at the factory, and they even wanted to make him Deputy Chief Engineer of the Machine Engineering Works. But for this he was required to further his education. He could not manage to do this by correspondence, and he could not allow himself to study in another town, since by that time the Karpovs already had two children—a daughter Larisa, and little Tolik*. But, although after the birth of her son Nina Grigorievna was not working, she insisted that her husband should go to Moscow to further his education in an advanced Technical College. So that in 1953 two of the Karpov family started learning: Larisa began her first year at school, and father—his first year at the Institute. It was a difficult time for them all, especially since little Tolya was constantly ill. One of the doctors even doubted whether the puny little child would live. He was fed on milk, and his mother and sister, with whom he was always exceptionally close, literally did not leave his bedside.

But the Karpovs endured all this, their Ural nature proved stronger than any of life's difficulties and illnesses. Yevgeny Stepanovich successfully completed his course, and obtained his Mechanical Engineer's Diploma. (Incidentally, persistence in the attainment of a goal, and an aptitude for science, are family traits. Both Larisa and Anatoly always obtained top marks at school.) It was just at this time that Tolya first became interested in chess. At roughly the age of four he began eagerly watching the chess battles between his father and his friends. Despite the persistent appeals of the lad, Yevgeny Stepanovich was in no hurry to teach his son seriously, and he explained the rules, of which the latter was already more or less aware, only when Tolya was nearer five. Tolik was terribly upset whenever he lost a game, but he was restrained from tears by his father's warning: "Someone has to lose, and if you start crying I won't play with you at all". Thus for probably the first time Anatoly Karpov made the acquaintance of a highly important law of chess: the threat is stronger than the execution. Soon he fell ill again, and his mother took the chess pieces away from him.

"But then I became frightened, and gave them back to him myself", says Nina Grigorievna, trying as if to justify herself. "I saw how he was looking up at the ceiling, and, really, I could see the knights jumping about in his mind. He was always good at counting up in his head, even when a little boy. In children's billiards it would sometimes happen that there were five balls lined up, and we would have paper ready so as to write down the scores and add them up. We would pot the balls, and he would very quickly fish them out from the pockets; the adults would get angry, saying that they hadn't managed to count up, and in reply Tolik would give them the correct sum.

"I was fortunate", Anatoly said later. "At that time Mikhail Tal had made a brilliant entry into big-time chess, and it seemed that everyone knew this name, everyone supported Tal—the young star!—and very many became interested in chess. In Zlatoust in those years we had something of a chess epidemic. In the Pioneers' Palace nearly all the lads knew how to play chess; for a time it supplanted all other games, and, after ensconcing ourselves on the steps, we would spend whole days playing chess. When I started in the first class at school, the lads from the block where I lived, who were older than me but with whom I played on equal terms, persuaded my parents to let them take me to the Sports Club of a metallurgical factory, where there was a chess room and where tournaments were held. Following this my friends asked the director of the Club, Aleksey Ivanovich Pak, to include me in a tournament where third category rating could be attained, since each of them was already playing in it, and I, they said, was not inferior to them..."

---

* Tolik and Tolya are diminutive forms of Anatoly (K.P.N.)

In the lives of many chess players there have been older friends, with whom they initially played on equal terms, and who in some way or other helped them to make the first steps along the difficult path. Anatoly Karpov frequently recalls in the kindest terms Sasha Kolishkin, who lived in the same block as the Karpovs, and who was in the same class as Larisa Karpov.

... Sasha was six years older than Tolik, but this did not stop them being friends. It is possible that the maturity of Karpov's character was noticeable even at such an early age. (It is significant that, even much later, amongst the people close to Anatoly there were, and to this day are, hardly any of his own age.) Sasha Kolishkin particularly began to "respect" his young neighbour, when he discovered that the latter played chess. There began between them a series of endless battles, which gradually revealed the superiority of the younger player. Tolya mercilessly defeated his friend in several games, and lost to him only at... gorodki*, a game where physical strength and dexterity are of primary importance. It is interesting that Sasha Kolishkin not only persuaded Tolya to join the chess club, but also "infected" him with another passion, which Karpov still maintains, the passion of collecting. At that time they collected matchbox labels, while now Anatoly has a most imposing stamp collection—he is an enthusiastic philatelist.

The present World Champion remembers literally all of the best players from Zlatoust and the regional centre—Chelyabinsk, with whom he happened to play in his early years. And they remember him. When he was already a Candidate for the World Championship, Karpov, at a simultaneous display in the editorial office of the paper 'Komsomolskaya Pravda', met a player from Chelyabinsk, who passed on to him a letter from Tamara Kalashnikova, with an invitation to visit the region where he was born. This was the same Tamara Kalashnikova, about whom Karpov's mother used to say: "I would go to the metallurgist's club in the evening for Tolik, and they would say to me that Kalashnikova had already taken him home".

It is true that there was an occasion when Nina Grigorievna, Karpov's mother, was "deceived". Tolya, as usual, was playing lightning chess in the club, according to the traditional rule: the loser is replaced, and the winner continues playing with the next contender. No one could make him give up his seat. And they only just managed to warn him that his mother had come looking for him. Little Tolik darted away under a table, while Sasha Kolishkin, blushing, informed Nina Grigorievna that her son had already gone home. However, they decided not to make such a deception again...

It is significant that the first visit Karpov made as World Champion was to his native Zlatoust, where he cut the ribbon at the opening of a new chess club, and where, true to his character, he immediately gave a simultaneous display, and took his revenge against all those who at some time had beaten him, even if only once, in the first years of his infatuation with chess. (For instance, he 'got even' with Semion Ginzburg, many-time Champion of the town.) But with Sasha Kolishkin, now the bearded father of a family, Anatoly Karpov, of course, played a draw...

There were not all that many who defeated him in those early games. At the first attempt he, a seven-year-old, attained the third category norm. It is curious that all the other chess barriers —even the very highest ones—fell to Karpov at the very first attempt. Anatoly was not yet ten years old when he attained the first category norm, although formally he was awarded this rating only several months later, at the junior championship of the Russian Republic in the

* A game similar to skittles (K.P.N.)

town of Borovichi. Of course, even in this junior tournament he was the youngest. Tolya was small in stature, and to make him equal with his older opponents they gave him a footstool, and placed a cushion on his chair. But sometimes, so as to see the board better, Karpov would play almost an entire game 'on his feet', standing at the chess table. He began this event—for the only time in his life—with two noughts, then scored $3\frac{1}{2}$ points in the next four games, and then suffered another defeat—at the hands of a big lad from the Krasnodarsk region. He couldn't contain himself, but rushed out of the hall and burst out crying. Then he took himself in hand, and concluded the tournament in a fitting manner.

That was Karpov's first trip outside his own district; before that his regular chess route had been the short train journey from Zlatoust to Chelyabinsk. From the regional centre he went off with an adult team to matches against a team from the famous giant Chelyabinsk tractor factory, and to individual tournaments. There Karpov met Leonid Gratvol, an excellent teacher, who put all his heart into teaching his pupils (it is thanks to this trainer that there have grown up in Chelyabinsk a number of young, but well-known players, such as grandmaster Yevgeny Svyeshnikov, and international masters Gennady Timoshchenko and Aleksandr Panchenko, while Gratvol also assisted in the development of Anatoly Karpov).

There is hardly any point in listing all the numerous events which Karpov took part in as a schoolboy. But the Championship of the Chelyabinsk region, which concluded in January 1963, is worth recalling. In view of Karpov's present popularity, it is not surprising that articles have begun periodically appearing in the press, recalling his early games. Anatoly happened to come across one of these articles, which told of his concluding encounter in the regional championship against Gratvol. In the last round, according to the author, eleven-year-old A. Karpov could attain the candidate master norm if he won, while L. Gratvol, if he took the point, would become regional Champion.

"...Dozens of fans surrounded the chess table where this dramatic encounter was taking place. Tolya was playing White. For a long time the position on the board was roughly equal, and when it became clear that Black had no chance of winning, Gratvol suggested to his young opponent that they agree a draw.

It is difficult to imagine what went on in the lad's heart at that moment. He seemed to be confused, and didn't know what to reply. Then he quickly made a move, and... darted away from the board. Gratvol shrugged his shoulders in bewilderment, as if to let those watching know that in such a position (which to everyone seemed level) he couldn't see any point in playing on.

But Tolya was playing to win! And what is most interesting is that the move made by the young player was the start of a forcing manoeuvre, which led to victory... That was how the youngest candidate master in our country emerged..."

Karpov carefully read through this note about an event which had occurred many years earlier. Then he made the following correction:

"No, at that point Gratvol no longer had any chance of becoming regional champion: the author is worried in case the reader should think that my teacher and, you might say, curator at that time, had fallen in with my wishes and deliberately given me the point. But everything else is correct."

And so, a candidate master at the age of eleven. Even Boris Spassky, who learned chess so early, had not managed that!

Great attention was devoted to Karpov, and in November 1963, together with five other talented youngsters, he set off for Moscow to the first session of the chess school of Mikhail Botvinnik, which had just been started. Here is what Karpov has to say about the time he spent there:

"During the school holidays I travelled three times to Moscow, and Botvinnik went through the games played by myself and the other lads. We analysed together, and looked at the best games played by grandmasters at that time. Botvinnik's approach to chess, and of course his direct comments regarding my play and my quite artless handling of the opening—all this made an impression on me. I began reading chess books, since, before my acquaintance with Botvinnik, my only book—it is true that I had read it from cover to cover—had been a book of Capablanca's selected games. I came across this book quite by chance: I saw it one day in a kiosk, and bought it. And it is perhaps the games of Capablanca which have left their stamp on my style of play, although I think that a player's style finally takes shape at a later age, say between twenty-six and twenty-seven, or even later, when he is in his prime.

In short", Karpov continues, "it was Botvinnik who changed my attitude to chess, but not to such an extent that I began to study it very seriously. Even without any knowledge of theory I could compete on equal terms with my opponents, by relying on my intuition and natural ability. It was an instance of the excessive self-confidence of young players!"

The reader would no doubt be highly interested to know what the Ex-World Champion thought at that time about his new acquaintance. This is what Botvinnik had to say:

"Karpov did not make much of an impression at that time: in a simultaneous display with clocks, I blundered away my queen against him in a won position, but nevertheless managed to draw the game".

It is amusing that Karpov should have a somewhat different account of this game. When Anatoly saw that Botvinnik had blundered away his queen, he asked the master who was assisting Botvinnik to point this out, and to suggest that the move be taken back. The Ex-World Champion declined, and then Karpov, not wishing to gain an "unlawful" point, deliberately made an oversight in reply, which led to the game being drawn.

While we are talking about simultaneous displays, it may be of interest to point out that Anatoly first came up against a grandmaster when he met two of them at once in 1965: Spassky and his trainer Bondarevsky gave a tandem simultaneous display against the Russian junior team. Here it should be added that Karpov very much enjoyed studying under Igor Bondarevsky, who had an intelligible way of explaining to the schoolboys the peculiarities of many typical middlegame positions.

"Simultaneous displays by well-known masters", says Anatoly Karpov, "are exceptionally valuable. Especially in those regions where there are no strong players, where it is not easy to obtain educational literature, and where it is difficult to improve one's game unassisted. But such displays should be utilized correctly. Thus once I permitted myself a highly typical 'infringement' of the ethics of the game, when a certain master came to Zlatoust to give a simultaneous display. Since I was small in stature and pretty inconspicuous, I ran from board to board and helped those taking part in the display. And after all, I already had the rating of candidate master, and it was wrong for me to act like that. My mother put a stop to it when she suddenly appeared in the hall, and forcibly took me home to bed. It is true that even more serious infringements can occur. For instance, after the 1970 Championship of the Russian Republic in Kuybishev, I gave a simultaneous display on a large number of boards, about thirty-five. One lad, in transposing into an ending, "stole" some three tempi from me, and when I attempted to make him admit he was wrong, he began to argue, and claimed that I was mistaken. I asked his mother to stay beside her son for a while, and when all the other games were finished, repeated the whole of this game, so as to show that my opponent had tried to pull a trick. Of course, to recall from my memory all the moves was not easy, (right in the opening the lad had lost a piece, and the remainder of the game had been lacking in all logic), but it was necessary to do so for pedagogical reasons, and for the sake of my prestige".

...On reading all this one might gain the impression that from a very early age all Karpov did was to travel from one chess event to another. Of course, all this demanded of Anatoly a great deal of effort and time, but he always scored top marks at school, as can be seen in the progress reports, carefully preserved in his "mother's archives", for all his years at school. After the difficult Junior Tournament of the Republic, which we have already mentioned, he was sent on holiday to the All-Union Pioneers' Youth Camp, where Anatoly won the honour to be photographed at the unfurling of the camp's Red Flag. Two years later he was a prize-winner at a festival held in Artek, at an All-Union Pioneers' Sanatorium on the Black Sea. Then in the seventh class of the Zlatoust secondary school No.3 he received a certificate, on which it was written that from then on he was an honoured pupil of the school, and that this would be recorded in the annals (now only pupils who score top marks are allowed to sit at the Karpov desk). Anatoly Karpov successfully took part in various academic competitions, and finished school with a gold medal in the town of Tula, to where his father had been posted in 1965, as chief engineer of a factory.

The teachers at school No.20 in Tula still speak with astonishment about the pupil who frequently distinguished himself in competitions, but never took advantage of his position as an already well-known sportsman, avoided any indulgence, and was even offended if anyone tried to be lenient with him, since this would have been a sign of weakness. The class in which Karpov studied was an exceptionally strong one specializing in mathematics, but he contrived to not only not fall behind the others, but to establish himself among the very best! They were fond of Anatoly there. When he had left Tula, they would constantly ask: "He hasn't got any thinner, has he?", "I hope he doesn't get too tired with all that chess playing", "He shouldn't go to tropical Manila, he was physically rather weak when he was here..." But how proud they are there of his successes!

And he is proud of that school in Tula, which became his home town. Normally not talka-tive, Anatoly relates with enthusiasm how the Fascist armies were stopped outside Tula in the Second World War, how the former estate of the great writer Lyev Tolstoy was rebuilt at "Yas-naya Polyana", which is twenty kilometres from the town. Karpov would always gladly travel to Tula, where until recently his mother and father lived (now Anatoly's parents have moved to Leningrad), where his sister Larisa lives with his adorable little niece Natasha ("She has a little snub nose", says Anatoly with undisguised pride, "and she already knows the names of all the chess pieces!").

Every time he comes to Tula he goes without fail to his school, meets the teachers, talks about himself, and shares his plans for the future. They are proud of Karpov. Only the mathematics teacher is a little unhappy. She grumbles all the time that it would have been better if he had been a mathematician—so well could he find his way through the most unfamiliar of problems, so logical was his thinking.

"But what was I to do?", says Karpov, as if asking himself. "In my way of thinking I am indeed a mathematician. After school I entered the Faculty of Mathematics and Mechanics at

Moscow University, virtually without any additional special preparation. I studied for a year, and saw that chess and mathematics were incompatible. The point was that I frequently went away to chess events, but mathematics is in the main a practical subject. I took my text books with me, so that I shouldn't fall behind on the theory, but for the practical side there wasn't enough time. And I was faced with a choice: mathematics or chess . . . "

Karpov was fortunate—he encountered a science which he found highly interesting, and which at the same time allowed him to combine it with chess (true, with enormous difficulty, and with constant time-trouble, which he never has at the board, but has more than enough of in everyday life). This science, his new fascination, was economics. He became a student in the Economics Faculty.

But soon life faced him with yet another problem. The point was that around that time he at last found himself a proper trainer—the Leningrad grandmaster Semion Abramovich Furman, and it so happened that it was in Leningrad that most of his friends lived, including his best friend Alik Bakh. And also . . . It has to be admitted that, in Moscow it seemed to Karpov that he was not paid as much attention as he already deserved. And so, he came to a decision, and it has to be said that Karpov does not often change his mind; his character is firm and not at all mild.

Spassky once admitted: "All great chess players are difficult characters. Difficult in their uniqueness, their peculiarity, and in the necessity always to be a fighter and a man." And Karpov remembers this. Although he admires the romantic poems of Lermontov, his behaviour is cool and composed. While happy to listen to light jazz music for hours, he remains serious beyond his years. Passionately interested in philately, he spends a great deal of money on stamps, but at the same time he is practical, thrifty and economical. Although basically he believes only himself, he shows great respect and attention towards other people. He always listens to the opinions of those around him, but only acts in the way that he considers correct.

However, Anatoly's mother knows another side of him: "He only appears to be like that, really he's very affectionate. He comes into the kitchen and stands around. What do you want, I ask him. And he's come in, simply to give me a kiss".

So there he is, a loving, thoughtful son, but by no means a "mother's little boy" . . . Thus his parents very much wanted him to continue his education in Moscow, Botvinnik too insistently advised him to do this, but Anatoly decided to do his further studying in Leningrad. Already in the immediate future the correctness of his decision was confirmed.

Here is a another little "educational episode" . . . Professor Sergey Borisovich Lavrov understands perfectly well how difficult it is for sportsmen to combine serious training and frequent appearances in competitions with study at university. He once admitted that he couldn't have brought himself to fail Tolya Karpov in an exam. "But on the other hand", the professor immediately added, "I could not imagine that he would come to an exam unprepared. When he went off to his first USSR Championship in Riga, what I was most afraid of was that he would have bits of work left unfinished."

A few days before his departure, Karpov, on scoring only four out of five, got terribly angry. He sat down with his books. He didn't sleep. He appeared once more at the University, and asked to be examined again. The astonished and consequently very strict teacher asked the "athlete" difficult questions for a good hour. The persistent student answered faultlessly and confidently. Thus without having to give up chess, he got rid of his "four" . . .

No, it was not for his sporting successes alone that the student from the Economics Faculty of Leningrad University, grandmaster Anatoly Karpov, was elected delegate to the 17th Congress of the Comsomol, and then made a member of the Central Committee!

In connection with this, it would be very interesting to hear the opinions expressed by the Prorector of Leningrad University L. Selesniev, at a celebration in honour of Karpov becoming World Champion:

"Leningrad University is fortunate with its chess players. Its students have included several top grandmasters, and now there is Karpov! Not at all bad for one University! Karpov is noted for his terrific sense of purpose, capacity for hard work, and self-discipline. These are qualities that are needed by young people, and Anatoly's example is both necessary and useful. Futurologists call Economics the science of the 21st century, and I hope that Karpov, who at the beginning of the next century will be at the height of his creative powers, will also achieve significant success in science".

And Karpov intends to do post-graduate work. For him Economics is a serious business.

Before discussing his education, we touched slightly on the world of his pastimes. Of course, first place among them is taken by philately. For a long time Karpov has had a passion for stamps; in his collection there are now tens of thousands of specimens, and about each stamp he knows literally everything. Collecting on such a scale not only provides a rest from chess, but also broadens his general outlook. If it were just the "chess" or "Olympic" series this wouldn't mean very much; it would be natural, since he is a sportsman. But for a long time Karpov has been a collector, for instance, of the "art" series. (He, incidentally, is in general very interested in paintings, and so he happily takes any opportunity to visit different types of exhibitions. You should have seen the interest shown by Karpov in the pictures from the New York Metropolitan Museum, when they were displayed in the Hermitage, or how during his stay in Italy in 1975 he eagerly visited the art galleries in Rome and Florence.)

It has already been said that in character Anatoly is exceptionally independent. And to such an extent that he infects others with his interests, as it were drawing them into the orbit of his pastimes. Here is a significant admission by Tigran Petrosian, a person who is normally also highly independent:

"I am afraid that my association with Karpov in San-Antonio may 'cost me dearly'. It turns out that Anatoly is a passionate philatelist. I have never been seriously interested in collecting stamps. Sometimes as a present I would send stamps on chess themes to some friends, and would keep one of each as a souvenir, nothing more. My association with Karpov, a passionate and knowledgeable collector, has changed my indifference to the hobby. At any rate, on returning from San-Antonio, I began to regard the stamps I had as a collection, and for the first time it would seem, called several stamps, bought for friends, duplicates..."

Between Petrosian and Karpov there began something of a competition in stamp collecting. In Paris, for instance, on returning from the Olympiad, Petrosian bought an extremely rare and valuable stamp, and proudly declared that no doubt Karpov wouldn't have it. Anatoly smiled and countered by saying that he had bought this stamp a long time ago, and much more cheaply. But he was seriously concerned when he heard that Petrosian had gone to Riga on business. "Oh, there's a certain old man there with a fine collection! I'm afraid that this time he may forestall me", said Karpov in genuine alarm.

One could talk for a long time about music, which he likes and which is almost always playing in his room, and one could mention that he tries not to miss any interesting drama productions.

But there is a risk that we may forget that Karpov is first and foremost a chess player. So let us therefore return again to chess.

Napoleon, before promoting one of his commanders, asked him whether the fates were kind to him, whether he was lucky. While Turgenev stated that good fortune is like health: when you have it, you don't notice it. The same is true of youth.

Karpov has been favoured by fortune. But there is some logic in this. When he entered big-time chess, general interest was directed towards the winning of the World Junior Championship. Very soon his name began to be associated with the much-desired wish to return the world chess crown to the Soviet Union. Yes, not without good reason is it said that every fame, apart from the wings visible to the world, also has a hidden reason for coming into being. Fame has the ability to promote its chosen one...

No doubt Karpov has been favoured by fortune. But this does not mean that things have always been so easy for him. Remember his "rough" childhood, when as a lad he was plagued by constant illnesses... And when he took up chess there were no books, and he had no constant highly-qualified trainer. Then such a trainer appeared. And however relations between them develop in the future, and however the situation changes, the rôle played by grandmaster Semion Abramovich Furman, one of the top Soviet chess theorists, in the development of Karpov as we know him, has without doubt been exceptionally important.*

Spassky, who at different times worked with different trainers, always knew what he was lacking, and what he had to obtain from his assistant. Karpov also knows exactly what he needs to take from a man who, at the most important points in their careers has helped both Botvinnik and Petrosian. It is interesting to observe the way in which Petrosian sometimes looks at Karpov's games. Pointing his finger, Furman-like, at the most important square on the board at that moment, and picturesquely forming his lips into a tube, the former World Champion concludes in the singing voice of the Leningrad grandmaster: "Furman's influence".

Coaching does not mean teaching someone how to think, but what to think about. Here there was no question of coaching, for Karpov since early childhood had been able to think independently; he merely swallowed information, digesting it in his own way, highly efficiently. At first Furman, like a talking book, took the place of voluminous opening guides, and helped him to find his way through the mass of opening variations. He generously showed Karpov numerous ideas of his own, adding with a smile: "The opponents must be surrounded by innovations, like wolves by red flags".

Semion Furman considerably shortened Karpov's path to the top.

"We worked hard and tried to iron out Karpov's deficiencies", was how Furman disclosed the 'secret' of success. "I happen to have helped a number of top players, but I have never obtained such satisfaction as from my association with Karpov. There is also the point, of course, that my other 'charges' were already fully-fledged grandmasters, and I was unable to influence their development to any great extent. With Tolya it is a totally different matter—he develops before my very eyes. At the same time I always tried to ensure that this growth and development was in accordance, as far as possible, with his creative individuality."

The career of the present World Champion can without exaggeration be called meteoric. He is recognized and is popular throughout the whole world. In conferring the "Chess Oscar" in 1973, 1974, 1975 and 1976, almost all the journalists gave their votes to Karpov. And yet...

---

* Semion Furman died in 1978 (K.P.N.)

Even a person so apparently favoured by fortune as Karpov does not have an easy life in chess. He is a person without complexes, he is not tormented by doubts, and other peoples' opinions interest him only to the extent that they may prove useful. And although, I repeat, Karpov is a person without complexes, for a long time he had to defend himself, and even almost justify himself. Why, for what reason? Many do not like his independent, stern and hard character. But the main point is that Karpov has time and again, and not only at the board, had to try to vindicate his views on the game, and his chess style. He once said:

"Not only many fans, but even certain grandmasters, do not understand (or do not wish to understand) my approach to chess. But in fact, I do not make any secret of this. For me, chess is first and foremost a struggle. The opponent has to be defeated, and this is what I aim for in practically every game".

He never, or at least very rarely, plays for a draw, but normally he does not try to extract from the position more than is justified. And certain critics take this realistic approach to be a sign of peaceableness.

"If you have to choose between a combinative path, from which you can expect a big advantage, and an ending with only slight winning chances, which do you prefer?".

Karpov replies to this question as follows:

"I assess the tournament situation. I consider how I feel on the particular day, how my mind is working. Finally, I take into account the player who is sitting opposite me. And only then do I come to a decision... But if I see only one correct path, then I follow it, whoever my opponent is".

At times Karpov becomes irritated by these endless uninformed discussions on his chess style, and then he is liable to cut short the questioner, by saying that, whatever the latter has heard about this 'style' of his, he plays the sort of chess that he likes, and which he wants to play!...

To some journalists writing on chess topics, Tigran Petrosian once put it this way:

"Every grandmaster is a rather complicated individual, and the impression people have of him does not always correspond to reality. Tal is not only 'sacrifices', Fischer—not only 'an electronic computer', and Petrosian—not only 'caution'."

But, it would appear, the Ex-World Champion's efforts were in vain—the apology for a critic does not accept the existence of half-tints, and paints the portraits of top grandmasters in one colour only. His views merely scratch the surface, since on account of a lack of knowledge of the subject he is afraid to "dig" deeper.

Incidentally, much is determined by the general trend of modern chess thinking. And in this, as Karpov states, what is characteristic is the tendency right through the 1970s—the growth of competitiveness.

"It is this that explains", the World Champion says, "a certain dissatisfaction on the part of 'aesthetes', supporters of 'pure art', who like only combinative games, containing, without fail, a certain degree of 'spice'. But combinations and sharp attacks are good only if they are the consequence of carefully thought-out, and technically correct play, and not the consequence of blunders and oversights. With high-class play, genuine beauty is hidden considerably more deeply than the eyes of lovers of sharp sensations can normally penetrate".

When observing Karpov's play or playing against him, one cannot help feeling that all his pieces are linked by invisible threads. This net moves foreward unhurriedly, gradually covering the enemy squares, but, amazingly, not relinquishing its own. His actions are easy and unconstrained, he does not make awkward movements, and avoids breaking the linking threads.

Grandmaster Igor Zaitsev waves his arms in bewilderment: "Do you understand? I don't. We all seem to play disjointedly, and only Karpov plays somehow collectively. It's like some sort of continuous vector diagram!"... Such a talent is more deep than a normal positional gift, and is found much more rarely than sharp combinative vision. Combinative talent normally develops of its own accord, but on the perfecting of their positional and strategical ability, some players have worked for twenty years or more.

Talent can take on opposing forms—such as Tal and anti-Tal. These are different natural talents of commensurable magnitude. For a long time Mikhail Tal was incomprehensible on account of his great complexity. Anatoly Karpov is incomprehensible on account of his simplicity, his unobtrusive evenness. At first sight this may seem paradoxical, but if one wishes one can even pick out a certain similarity in appearance between Karpov and Tal. Neither is built like a Hercules, both have prominent, intelligent eyes, with a characteristic slightly aggressive profile. But how they differ from each other, in their approach to chess, and to life in general. One is all aggravation, with the other everything is well thought-out and harmonious. Even at his mature age Tal has no intention of accepting the golden mean—he is either Caesar or no one! (It was once said to him that if his attitude to life had been the same as Botvinnik's, he would still have been World Champion today. But he replied that he would prefer to live a month "à la Tal" rather than a whole lifetime "à la Botvinnik", otherwise he would not have remained true to himself.)

Karpov, while at heart admiring Tal's ability to make dashing and reckless attacks, is nevertheless content with his "sober-minded" approach (this is how he put it, while not yet a grandmaster).

"Mikhail Tal once said that my faith is in chess realism. He is probably right. Risky play in the style of chess musketeers appeals to those who like sharp conflicts, but it is not to my taste", Anatoly admits. "I attempted to assess my possibilities soberly, and not to rack my brains. I enjoyed looking at Tal's games, but I always knew that his style was not for me. I wanted to find in chess something of my own".

Many call him a strictly positional player. Yes, he respects the laws, and considers chess to be a wonderfully logical game. But at the same time Karpov calculates variations brilliantly, and more and more of his games provide examples of excellently conducted attacks. He has to his credit a number of points attained by purely tactical means. How many brilliant victories did he gain at the 1972 Olympiad in Yugoslavia! One of his games, where there were numerous sacrifices, was judged to be the best from the Interzonal Tournament in Leningrad. Some of Karpov's wins from the 1974 Candidates' Matches were justifiably called the most interesting (and again—the most beautiful!). Paradoxical again, wouldn't it seem? Yes, but only at first sight.

He is against "risky play in the style of chess musketeers", but if his varied chess life nevertheless forces him sometimes to don the clothes of a musketeer, for a time he becomes d'Artagnan, with his Gascon quickness and cunning, and sometimes Athos, noble, but somehow unearthly, and therefore slightly vulnerable.

"This player has practically no weak points...", said Tal in surprise, when he became more closely acquainted with Karpov.

Here it is—the answer to many questions! Not allowing the opponent his type of game, but obtaining the positions which he himself likes—this is his favourite method—and this means that he has to be able to operate in any key, since the opponents he encounters are highly diverse.

Strangely enough, Karpov's universal rationalism does not antagonize young players, of whom he is the acknowledged leader. Dissatisfaction with him is expressed only by romantics of the older generation: "The practicalness of our century is a reproach to God on earth!" But Karpov's practical approach lies not in grandmaster draws, but in rejecting superfluous "fantasy", and in a complete and almost disdainful repudiation of "pure art".

Karpov loves to analyse the most varied positions. While doing this he keeps repeating: "I go here, he goes there... But perhaps first move the king away, so that it doesn't get in the way...", and his green eyes search and search the board, and his slender, expressive fingers, like those of a sorcerer, do not stay still for a moment. He attained great mastery in analysis a long time ago, and many turn to him for help. Karpov is an indispensible assistant to the trainers in team events. One recalls, for instance, how in the 1971 USSR Team Championship he startled everyone with his assessment of an adjourned position from a game between two lady players. R. Bilunova, a lady player from the Armed Forces team, for which Karpov was appearing on the junior board, adjourned her game against a representative of the "Lokomotiv" team. World Champion Spassky, at that time leader of "Lokomotiv", quickly assessed the position as drawn. But Karpov did not "believe" this, and set to to try to find a win. A day later, playing at the start of the adjournment session according to his recommendation, Bilunova gained a winning position, but then blundered, and the game nevertheless ended in a draw. It is difficult to convey the lady player's despair, as she exclaimed in fear: "What am I going to say to Anatoly?! He spent the whole of his free day on the analysis of my adjourned position, and then I go and let him down like that!". And they then said jokingly to Karpov: "Aren't you ashamed of yourself, reducing a woman to tears..."

Anatoly does not like talking about women on an intimate level, but with regard to chess—by all means.

It is ironic that this instance of "women's tears" is not the only one in his chess life. When he won the final game against Spassky in the Candidates' Semi-Final Match, one of the country's strongest lady players Valentina Kozlovskaya, the wife of Spassky's trainer Igor Bondarevsky, was also unable to restrain herself, and burst out crying. On learning of this, Karpov remarked: "This isn't the first time that Kozlovskaya has cried on account of me. That was back in 1963, when as a twelve-year-old I kept beating her at blitz..."

Lightning chess... Blitz! A duel between two players. At first a crackle of firing, and then the pieces are clattering like a machine-gun. You evade a dangerous thrust, and immediately reply, coolly and insidiously. And again you evade, so as to then make an attack. Meanwhile the ten steps or minutes (five each) between the opponents are fast disappearing, and the dénouement is inevitable.

Chess players love five-minute games. However, there are exceptions. Botvinnik, for example. He is virtually the only one of the top players who does not approve of lightning chess. Tal, on the other hand, is the opposite extreme: even during his illnesses, under his pillow he concealed from the doctors a chess clock, and, burning with impatience, waited in his hospital ward for new visitors, among whom, as I remember, was the young master Karpov, who was brought to the Ex-World Champion by their mutual friend Bakh. Before Karpov's departure to the 1969 World Junior Championship, a match between them (true, Tal was ill) ended in a draw—10–10, whereupon the grandmaster said: "He's in very good shape, he can go there with confidence!"

There was a time when the present World Champion was also passionately fond of blitz. His friend and present-day assistant Yuri Razuvayev describes in highly picturesque terms how at the first session of Botvinnik's special school they played five-minute games right through the night. Karpov, not satisfied with this, arranged a "medley" of games: dominoes, draughts, chess... And invariably emerged the winner. Even earlier, in his childhood, Anatoly won numerous lightning tournaments in Zlatoust, where at the age of nine or ten he easily defeated all the adults. In general, those who from their early years are good at lightning chess are normally very talented. This has been shown by numerous examples, and here is another one.

Korchnoi was on holiday with his family on the outskirts of Leningrad, and shortly before the World Junior Championship, Furman brought along his "charge" on a visit. It had long since grown dark, but the grandmaster was still playing five-minute games with the lad. Furman grew quite concerned, and warned Anatoly in a whisper: "If you lose, we'll have thirty kilometres to travel goodness knows how, but if you manage to win, perhaps he'll let us have his car..." Korchnoi, who is not in the habit of pampering children, unsmilingly threw open the door of his car to the visitors... And a week later, he, one of the top specialists in lightning chess in the world, paid Karpov a return visit, but failed to gain his revenge...

"Well, blitz is interesting enough", says Karpov now. "But I would say that it doesn't pay to get too distracted by it, or spend too much time, because it can engulf you like a swamp. One curious fact is that when I am well prepared for a serious tournament, I play really badly at lightning chess. And vice versa. Formerly I often used to play five-minute games during average sort of events, but now I have forbidden myself to do this."

Even in his amusements he is rational, and sticks to the same "golden mean". But once he is "switched on" he becomes irrepressible. In 1972, after the first cycle of the All-Union lightning tournament, in which virtually all the strongest players in the country took part, Karpov was a long way behind the leader, grandmaster Vladimir Tukmakov. Everyone was tired—there was a large number of competitors—but in the second cycle the lean figure of Karpov developed an unprecedented pace, and caught up with the leader. They shared first and second places, but the main prize was nevertheless awarded to Tukmakov. This exhausting tournament killed Karpov's taste for blitz for a long time, but he did not forget his failure, as for some reason he considered it. When he happened once to be in Odessa, he took the opportunity to meet Tukmakov in a match of several five-minute games. When the score reached 0–13 his opponent surrendered...

Pride—this is perhaps the main thing which strikes you about Karpov, if you observe him carefully and for a long time. No, not an unhealthy vanity, but a conscious pride. A defeat torments him, he seeks revenge without fail, and does not rest content until he gains it. By nature Karpov is a player in the best sense of the word (after all, in the end every game is to some extent a sport).

But do you know how he plays? No, not chess, but, say... billiards, or some other game. Amazingly seriously. And if you win and start mocking him a little, he can be quite offended. Before you is a black storm-cloud, where just a minute ago there was a placid little cloudlet. He doesn't leave the table, but if he does indeed prove to be weaker, he will try to find a spare hour, so as to practice a little and gain his revenge. He improves rapidly, soaking everything in like a sponge. And what is surprising in all this is that, although he is extremely angry with himself and with you, he plays using his head, without losing his self-control, resourcefully, quick-wittedly. So that it is not simply competitive fervour, but something qualitatively different. In general he has a startling knowledge of himself, and of his intrinsic possibilities. This is no doubt a natural gift, characteristic of a person who wishes to be (and is used to being!) always first.

Once during a game of the same billiards he knocked one of his fingers.

"Never mind. Heroes always get wounded..."

"...But it stops them carrying out heroic deeds", was Karpov's immediate counter.

But the sober philosopher continued playing with undiminished energy.

In the majority of games where one has to count and think, in these he has practically no equal. Who knows, perhaps it was this passion of a player who religiously believes in his own powers that called him to seek a match with Robert Fischer, called him even when it became clear that the American grandmaster was proposing unacceptable conditions. It is significant that, even after he had been awarded the title of World Champion, Anatoly Karpov publicly announced that he was ready and wished to do battle with the former champion. He wanted to play! And this was not at all because Karpov was afraid that, without a victory over Fischer, some might not believe in his right to be Champion. Since childhood he had been swiftly leaping ever higher up the steps of the chess ladder, and was not bothered by the lone voices of the sceptics, who said that he had taken the title "out of order". It was a matter of character. International grandmaster Yuri Razuvayev says with a laugh: "Those who come from the Urals are like that... During a simultaneous display in Zlatoust I offered some lad a draw in an equal position, and do you know, he didn't even favour me with a reply!"

The great ballerina Galina Ulanova, on looking in at one of the games from the Final Candidates' Match, was astonished by the natural confidence of movement which she suddenly saw in Karpov, who was calmly walking about on the stage. At the same time she noticed the amazing degree of self-absorption of the future Champion: it appeared that nothing existed for him, apart from the chess board and his opponent. It is said of Alexander Alekhine that, if at a time of utmost concentration he was suddenly torn away from the board, he was unable to answer the most elementary of questions, so totally was he engrossed in the position. Such an ability is to be found in other top players. And Anatoly Karpov also becomes exceptionally engrossed in the position, he is all attentiveness and concentration, and yet... If you ask him at such a point about something extraneous, or about that which you were discussing with him a few days earlier, he readily joins in the conversation, as if he had only just stopped in mid-sentence. He notices whereabouts in the hall his friends are sitting, and what they are doing. At one of the Olympiads the playing hall was at least as big as a football pitch, and around Karpov's table there was a crowd of fans. After the game he suddenly asked: "And what were you talking about for a good ten minutes with Smyslov's wife?"

His temperament is concealed from outside view. But he is given away by his eyes, which Dmitri Donskoy, who is constantly photographing him, calls the mirror of Karpov's soul. "Those eyes", remarks the well-known actor Rostislav Plyatt, "they are heavier than they should be. Perhaps they are the eyes of a genius!".

Those eyes... It is not easy to endure his probing and piercing glance for long. At such a time even an extraneous observer can become disconcerted. Grandmaster Pál Benkő, playing against Tal some time ago, demonstratively put on a pair of dark glasses, and now Korchnoi, during the Final Match with Karpov, did exactly the same.

"Yes, I know that I have this habit", Anatoly admits. "Everyone thinks, no doubt, that I am trying to find something out. Perhaps. But now Tal, for instance, wishes to instill something with his stare, but I wish—merely to find something out..."

Chess is played by living people. They study each other. They are subject to their feelings. Their experiences are shared by hundreds, thousands, even millions of those who repeat their moves. And this includes those who know nothing of the secrets of this world of chess.

Victory and defeat are inseparable. What one player loses the other one gains... It is a peculiar unity of opposites. It means that there is constant contact. It means that there is an inner sensing of the opponent. It means that the chess board does not separate the opponents, but, like a highly sensitive conductor, transmits an extremely high current from one to the other. This current flows along the lines of the board. These lines, which in separating, unite the opponents, in chess are called files. It is they which one tries most often to open, so as to break into the enemy position with one's heavy or major pieces. On the eight files the pieces make their mistakes. On the eight visible files.

But where do the two personalities come into collision? This file is sensed only by the two players. This ninth line, the character line, is perhaps the most important. It is along this that the fiercest battle rages. Victory here more often than not signifies the start of an offensive over the whole board.

Along this invisible front Karpov deploys enormous forces, and he is always ready to call up new reserves from the depths of his fighting nature. Here he dominates, and therefore he is victorious.

Words and concepts can have many meanings. In everyday life, away from chess, we normally think of a vertical as being a line which stretches upwards, straight upwards, without any deviation. Napoleon (who was a student of the mathematician Laplace, and perhaps for this reason loved precision) stated that a soldier could become a real commander only if his military capabilities formed a distinctive square: with his natural talent along the vertical axis, and along the horizontal—the strongest qualities of character.

So what is it that emerges? It turns out that the ninth file or vertical of the chess board, about which we have just been talking, is equivalent to the projection of a chess player's character "à la Napoleon"...

Karpov's natural talent is such that his vertical appears to be amazingly high. His career in the sport of chess confirms this: on the line extending upwards we see only high tournament places, we see victories which grip the heart. This line does not fluctuate—it is not a 'success curve', but a vertical.

And so, the two verticals merge into one. Karpov's vertical!

CHAPTER 2
Ever Higher...

...That evening, at Karpov's supreme moment, when he was crowned with the Champion's laurels, it was like a rustling again of the pages of his short, but already striking chess biography.

Karpov was called a representative—or more accurately, a forefather of the Ural school of chess (after all, he came from Zlatoust), and also a representative of Tula from Central Russia (there he had attained the level of master, and had finished school); in Leningrad they insisted that it was this student from their University who had corrected that annoying 'zig-zag of history', and had returned the chess crown to the motherland...

But Karpov now belongs to the entire chess world. Thus Max Euwe remarked that it was in Holland, and the European Junior Championship of 1967/68, that Karpov's road to big-time chess had begun. But a guest from Czechoslovakia, Jaroslav Šaitar, did not agree with this. He too was present to see Karpov's victories in the 1969 World Junior Championship, and the Student Olympiads of 1971 and 1972, but the first victory in an International Tournament, Šaitar recalls, was gained by Anatoly over the New Year of 1967 in the town of Czech metallurgists, Trinec.

Yes, junior victories soon gave way to successes in major adult events.

Karpov became a grandmaster in distant Caracas in 1970, and a year later, at the Alekhine Memorial Tournament in Moscow, the small number of strongest holders of the highest chess title accepted him into their ranks. Karpov then won the Interzonal Tournament, and became a Candidate for the World Championship. In 1973, he, as the top grandmaster, was awarded the 'Chess Oscar'. "We had absolutely no doubt that we would again be awarding Karpov this international prize in the following year", said the Spanish journalist Jordi Puig, handing the Soviet grandmaster the 'Chess Oscar 1974' at a memorable evening in the Hall of Columns. He received this prize because he had defeated all the other Candidates.

And then a moral victory, when all the world could see: Karpov wants to play Fischer, but Fischer does not want to play Karpov.

Excelsior! Ever higher and higher!... The chess ladder he has climbed has always been vertical. He has climbed quickly, but has remembered much. And so today we can have no better guide along this courageous path than Karpov himself.

And so, let's be off along Karpov's "chess vertical"!

MASTERS AGAINST CANDIDATES, LENINGRAD 1966

Some time ago the USSR Chess Federation used to arrange special tournaments between candidate masters and masters on the so-called 'Scheveningen' system (after the name of the Dutch town where it was first tried). Under such a system the masters did not play against each other, but only against each of the candidates in turn—it was something of a team event. If the candidate successfully passed the examination (i.e. achieved a norm established beforehand), his classification was raised, and he became a master. In order to provide a stimulus for the masters of sport participating in such a tournament, a special norm was also established, by which they could 'confirm' their title, which under the sporting classification system then in operation in the USSR was quite important. But the number of new masters began to grow too quickly, and this gave rise to the idea of a certain lessening in severity on the part of the 'old' examining masters. Gradually the Scheveningen system began to be used only for genuine team events (e.g. it received general recognition in the traditional matches between the USSR and Yugoslavia).

The 'mistrust' expressed regarding events between masters and candidates does not apply to the tournament which was held in the summer of 1966 in the Leningrad city chess club. It does not apply, because the master title was gained by only one of the candidates who participated, who in doing so surpassed the norm by two points(!), and did not suffer a single defeat. This was Anatoly Karpov, who a month earlier had celebrated his fifteenth birthday.

"Playing in the tournament was easy for me", relates Karpov. "The masters outplayed all the other candidates, who on this occasion did not demonstrate any great practical strength. (Incidentally, in the future too, only Mikhail Mukhin from among them was to become a relatively well known player.) The advice of my second in this event, the master Anatoly Matsukevich from Tula, did much to promote my successful play. The point was that, until the time of the Leningrad 'Scheveningen', I had not played at all against any really strong players— this was the first tournament where I played against masters on equal terms. However, as it turned out I was already of master strength, and my result was the third best in the whole event, although I had to compete against the masters, while they, in their turn, played... only against the candidates."

One of the strongest Soviet masters, Igor Zaitsev, had the best overall result in Leningrad; he has subsequently become an International Grandmaster, and frequently acts as second for Ex-World Champion Tigran Petrosian. This is what he had to say:

"To be honest, I did not take the young candidate masters altogether seriously, and realized that they were growing up only when I noticed that... they were interested in the girls who were working in the vicinity. Of course, this aspect of life did not yet bother Tolya Karpov, who was the youngest and also the smallest. But as a chess player he was fully developed, he played endings better than most of the adults, and he was also an excellent defender. I remember how in one of the games I gave him a good 'fright', and even sacrificed my queen, but he managed to create a perpetual check. We played a number of friendly games together in the hotel (I remember how he was offended when I first picked up a piece, and then took the move back), and I sensed his enormous strength. But many of the masters underestimated Karpov; Chistyakov, for instance, remarked at the end of the tournament that it was unfair that the event should be held over an odd number of rounds, since some players would have less Whites than Blacks... In principle the master was right, but everyone realised that he was referring to his allegedly undeserved failure in his games with Karpov."

"In fact it was with Black that I won a pretty good game against Chistyakov", said Karpov, laughing. "And what especially pleased me was that I won by outplaying in complications a prominent representative of combinational-style players.

Chistyakov–Karpov
Queen's Gambit Declined

1 P–Q4 N–KB3 2 P–QB4 P–K3 3 N–QB3 P–Q4 4 B–N5 B–K2 5 B×N B×B 6 P×P P×P 7 P–K3 0–0 8 B–Q3 P–B4 9 P×P P–Q5 10 N–K4 P×P 11 P×P B×P 12 R–N1 B–B3 13 N–KB3 B–R5+ 14 P–N3 B–K2 15 0–0 B–R6 16 R–B2 N–Q2 17 N–Q4 P–KN3 18 R–B2 R–B1 19 N–B2 (Diag.) 19 ... B–N4 20 R–K2 N×P 21 B×P RP×B 22 N×B N–K5 23 N–N5 Q–K2 24 N×B N×N 25 Q–Q5 KR–Q1 26 Q–N2 R–Q6 27 N×P R–B2 28 P–K4 Q–B4+ 29 K–R1 Q×N

30 P–KR4 N–K3 31 R–KB1 Q–R6 32 K–R2 R(2)–B6 33 Q–B2 R–B6 34 Q–K1 R×P 35 R(2)–KB2 R–R6+ 36 K–N1 Q–B4 37 Resigns

Another victory which I recall was gained over Grigory Ionovich Ravinsky, an honoured trainer of the USSR, and a well-known teaching specialist and theorist. Ravinsky had enormous experience in playing typical positions from the Ruy Lopez, but I outplayed him as Black, by advancing my Q-side pawns, and transposing into a typical ending, which frequently results from such positions..."

Ravinsky–Karpov
Ruy Lopez

1 P–K4 P–K4 2 N–KB3 N–QB3 3 B–N5 P–QR3 4 B–R4 N–B3 5 0–0 B–K2 6 Q–K2 P–QN4 7 B–N3 P–Q3 8 P–B3 0–0 9 R–Q1 N–QR4 10 B–B2 P–B4 11 P–Q4 Q–B2 12 P–KR3 R–K1 13 P×KP P×P 14 QN–Q2 R–Q1 15 N–B1 R×R 16 Q×R P–B5 17 B–N5 B–K3 18 Q–K2 N–N2 19 N–N3 P–N3 20 R–Q1 R–Q1 21 R×R+ B×R 22 Q–K3 N–Q2 23 B×B N×B 24 Q–R6 P–B3 25 Q–K3 P–QR4 26 P–KR4 P–N5 27 P–R5 K–N2 28 B–Q1 N–B2 29 RP×P RP×P 30 N–Q2 N–B4

31 P–N3 BP×P 32 RP×P Q–N3 33 N(3)–B1 N–Q3 34 P–QB4 Q–B3 35 B–B2 P–R5 36 P×P B×P 37 N–KN3 B–B2 38 P–R5 Q–N4 39 P–B4 Q×P 40 P×P Q–R8+ 41 K–B2 Q×P 42 N–B3 Q–N7 43 Q×N P–N6 44 N–Q4 P×B 45 Resigns

Karpov again smiles:

"The tournament was held right at the time of the football World Cup, and all the players tried to finish their games as quickly as possible, so as to get to the TV screen in time. I remember how in a game against one of the masters I reached an ending: knight and two pawns against knight. My advantage was obvious, but my opponent didn't resign, so I began thinking in terms of adjourning the game, so as to resume it in the following session. Just in case, I asked the chief controller about the theoretical possibility of adjourning the game (since the playing session still had some time to run, and I wasn't too well up in these subtleties). The controller brought me an envelope for the sealed move, but I said to him: 'No, I won't seal a move yet, I was only interested in whether I had the right to.' Then my opponent called the controller over: 'If he doesn't want to adjourn the game, then I'll seal a move—I'm also in a hurry.' To everyone's amusement the controller explained to the experienced master that he had played too slowly, and that now, according to the rules of chess, only one of us had the right to adjourn the game, and that was me. True, it didn't come to that: the master soon resigned...

FIRST INTERNATIONAL TOURNAMENT, TRINEC 1966/67

This was a most curious story... From Czechoslovakia to the USSR invitations were sent to an International Tournament. Either the conditions of the tournament were given incorrectly in the telegram, or else something got mixed up, but for some reason it was decided that the tournament would be a junior one, and the players sent to Czechoslovakia were fifteen-year-old Anatoly Karpov, a schoolboy from Tula, and a first-year student from Minsk University, Viktor Kupreichik. When the youths arrived, they discovered that all the members of the Czech national team, with the exception of the grandmasters, were participating, and that the tournament was by no means a junior one, but very much for adults. What were they to do, go back home?!

"We were received very warmly by the Czech metallurgical town", writes Anatoly. "However, at the start we were too involved with the tournament to take part in any excursions. The point was that, on top of everything else, we were slightly late for the start, and initially we had to play even two games a day. Strange as it may seem, it was in these early rounds that the quality of my play was fairly high. In the very first round I managed to outplay Jan Šmejkal, the brightest prospect in Czechoslovakian chess, and I went on from there... Kupreichik was eager to stop me: as the older member of our 'delegation', he very much wanted to make the highest score. The game between us was fairly interesting, and I nevertheless succeeded in 'cheating' Viktor.

When the question of first place was already essentially decided", continues Karpov, "my opponents could in no way adjust to my style of play and my 'simple' opening repertoire; I was particularly successful then with the unfashionable Closed Variation of the Sicilian Defence, and the Ruy Lopez. With a round to go I was already assured of first place. In addition, I did not lose a single game. To be honest, I did not especially want to win my last game against a likeable engineer from a local factory by the name of Rutka, and I went along intending to draw. But he unexpectedly threw himself at me so furiously, that I was forced, willy-nilly, to pull out all the stops. After this game too had ended in a win for me, I learned that my opponent had needed the point to attain some classification norm. A great pity, but that's sport...

Rutka–Karpov
Ruy Lopez

1 P–K4 P–K4 2 N–KB3 N–QB3 3 B–N5
P–QR3 4 B–R4 N–B3 5 P–Q3 P–QN4
6 B–N3 B–K2 7 P–B3 0–0 8 QN–Q2 P–Q3
9 N–B1 N–QR4 10 B–B2 P–B4 11 P–KR3
Q–B2 12 P–KN4 R–Q1 13 Q–K2 B–N2 14
N–N3 P–Q4 15 P–N5 P×P 16 P×P N–Q2
17 N–B5 B–KB1 18 P–KR4 P–B5 19 P–R5
N–B4 20 P–N6 N–Q6+ (Diag.)
  21 B×N P×B 22 P×RP+ K–R1 23 Q–K3
N–B5 24 Q–N5 B×P 25 P–R6 P–B3 26

P×P+ Q×P 27 Q–R5 Q–Q2 28 Q–N4
B–B4 29 Q×B P–Q7+ 30 B×P N×B 31
N(3)–R4 B×P+ 32 Resigns

After the finish of the tournament, which coincided with my first, but by no means last New Year abroad, Kupreichik and I were given the opportunity to get to know Czechoslovakia. I especially remember simultaneous displays and appearances in the town of Melnik, where we were most warmly received, and to this day my parents have kept a newspaper article about a cordial meeting with some lads from a technical college. This paper was sent to Tula by an unknown woman, and alongside the article was written in red letters: 'Hearty greetings from Czechoslovakia', and signed for some reason 'Mama'...''

...When the two young players returned to Moscow, Iakov Neishtadt, one of the editorial staff of the journal *Shakmaty v SSSR*, approached Anatoly Karpov in the Central Chess Club, and asked him to quickly annotate for the journal one of his games, and to write a paragraph on the tournament just finished. About an hour and a half later, on returning to the room where he had left Karpov, Neishtadt found a school exercise book with notes to an interesting game, written in a childish handwriting, but in perfectly professional chess language. This game was prefaced by a short paragraph, and before this, at the very top, was written in the same childish hand: "Tolya Karpov's Victory"—this was the simple heading that the author gave to his first chess article.

Joking apart, the victory by the 15-year-old master was most convincing. Karpov scored eleven points out of a possible thirteen, and finished a point and a half ahead of Kupku and Kupreichik. Fourth came Šmejkal, followed by E. Novak, Sikora and the other strongest Czech masters. His international debut had been wonderfully successful!

Kupreichik–Karpov
Ruy Lopez

1 P–K4	P–K4
2 N–KB3	N–QB3
3 B–N5	P–QR3
4 B–R4	N–B3
5 Q–K2	

Since we used to mix frequently with our contemporaries from Georgia, we were always prepared for the variations which they usually employed. In the present instance their example is followed by the master from Minsk, the Capital of Byelo-Russia, Viktor Kupreichik.

5 ...	P–QN4
6 B–N3	B–B4

The best rejoinder to the variation chosen by White.

7 P–B3	0–0
8 P–Q3	P–R3
9 0–0	P–Q3
10 P–KR3	R–N1

But this is incomprehensible... More logical is the simple 10 ... R–K1 or 10 ... B–N3.

11 R–Q1	R–K1
12 QN–Q2	N–KR4?!

With the dubious idea of transferring the knight to KB5. After the exchange of this knight White acquires a strong and mobile pawn centre, which is in no way compensated for by Black's two clumsy bishops.

13 N–B1	N–B5
14 B×N	P×B
15 P–Q4	B–R2
16 P–QR4	P–N5
17 B×P+ ?	

A mistake. Viktor fails to anticipate my rather amusing reply. 17 Q–B4 similarly achieved nothing after 17 ... B–K3 18 P–Q5 N–R4. Best was the simple 17 B–B4.

17 ...	K×B
18 Q–B4+	

18 ...	P–Q4!

This is the point! On 19 Q×N there follows 19 ... B–N2. and the queen is trapped.

19 KP×P	N–R4
20 Q–Q3	Q×P

Everything would appear to be settled. But the amazing ingenuity with which Kupreichik conducts the game, although a piece down, seriously complicates my task.

21 R–K1	B–N2

21 ... Q–KB4 was also worth considering.

22 Q–R7	N–B5
23 P–QN3	N–Q3

Threatening, for the second time in this game, to trap the white queen, only this time ... by exchanging.

24 R–K5	Q×NP
25 N(1)–Q2	Q×BP

Engaging in my favourite pursuit.

26 QR–K1	B×P
27 N–N5+	P×N
28 Q–R5+	P–N3
29 Q–R7+	K–B3

Here the king is perfectly content.

30 R–K7	B×BP+

The same sacrifice on the same square...

31 K–B1	Q–Q6+
32 R(1)–K2	B×P+

33 K×B(B2)	Q–KN6+
Resigns	

EUROPEAN JUNIOR CHAMPIONSHIP, GRONINGEN 1967/68

The event in question was only in the following year, 1968/69, officially called the European Junior Championship, when the International Master title was awarded to the winner. Earlier it was called the Niemeyer Cup Competition (after the name of the tobacco firm which subsidised this tournament for the strongest European juniors). It would be more accurate to call the majority of the participants students, rather than juniors, since it was possible for fairly experienced players to play in Groningen—those who on 1st September of the year in which the tournament started (in this case—1967) were not yet 21. In short, the lads appearing here were already quite grown-up, and 16-year-old Anatoly Karpov was younger than many...

"I associate this tournament with a most amusing story", says Karpov with a cheerful smile. "At that time I did not know any English (or any other language) at all, and I was sent abroad all on my own. In order that I, such a little lad, should not accidentally lose my way, I was given a special 'accompanying' letter, on which it was written that I, a Soviet chess player, was travelling to the town of Groningen to an International Tournament, and that it was requested that I be helped to find my way. I was happy enough until I sat down in the train, when I suddenly thought: "That's all very well, I'll show the letter, but how will I understand what people reply?". There was also an added complication, in that I first had to travel to the Dutch town of Ammersford, and then change trains before going on directly to Groningen.

Fortunately I was met in Ammersford by a Mr Withuis, a well-known editor of chess literature. I was all on my own in the train, but at that station few people had left the platform, when there remained only one young lad, whom he approached. We had a drink of coffee, and then I caught a suburban train to Groningen, in which my kind genie sat me down, after first asking the conductor to look after this child, so that nothing should happen to him... And then in Groningen things were more difficult, because there the tournament organizers did not go onto the platform. Anyone meeting a train there has to buy a special ticket to be admitted onto the platform. I waited and waited, and eventually decided to go out into the town, but, when giving up my ticket at the exit from the platform (there you have to return it for some reason), I met up with my hosts, who had been waiting for me there. After this, things were simpler...

The Semi-Final was a seven-round Swiss Tournament. I consider this system to be ideal for selecting the Final group in such an event: as a rule, all the strongest players reach the Final, and only occasionally is someone lost 'on the way', quite by chance. I played rather quietly in the Semi-Final, apart from the unforeseen complications which almost arose in the penultimate round in the game with Jan Timman, the future Dutch grandmaster.

In this preliminary stage I scored four and a half points out of seven, winning my first two games, and drawing the remainder without much trouble (with the exception, as I have already said, of the penultimate game). I shared second to sixth places, and thus fulfilled the first part of my task—I got through to the main final. First place in the Semi-Final was taken by András Jocha, a Hungarian player who later appeared under the name of Adorján, and who is now a fairly well known grandmaster. I managed to exact my first 'revenge' from him on the last day of 1967: in a lightning tournament, held on 31st December (the only rest day), I took first place with $13\frac{1}{2}$ points out of 16, then came Jocha with $12\frac{1}{2}$, the Pole Lewi—12, Timman—$10\frac{1}{2}$, etc. Incidentally, the results of the lightning tournament predicted exactly the final placings in the top section of the tournament proper.

The first move in my first semi-final game (with Schaufelberger) was made by the idol of the Dutch chess public, Ex-World Champion Dr Max Euwe. First he asked me what to move, and when I pointed to my king's pawn, he played 1 P–K4...

Jumping ahead, I should say that on 24th April 1974, at the enthronement of the twelfth World Champion in the history of chess, Max Euwe, now President of FIDE, was to joke that, during the last few years of his active chess appearances, Karpov had made not 3,000 moves, as the meticulous statisticians had calculated, but only... 2,999, and that he had become World Champion by following his, Euwe's, example.

We lived", continues Anatoly, "in the comfortable 'Terminus Nord' Hotel, adjacent to the 'Martini Hall', where the tournament was held. Everything was fine, except that in the playing hall there was always an acrid smell of tobacco. We were later presented with packets of this tobacco, and I hope I will not offend my hosts by saying that I never tried smoking it, and I was really shocked to see young lads (still children) who sometimes visited the tournament, rolling enormous cigarettes of their own, and lighting up.

After three rounds Timman was leading with 100%, and I was half a point behind," Karpov continues. "In the fourth round we met. Over such a short distance (only seven rounds) this encounter proved decisive: on the following days Timman was dispirited and suffered two further defeats, whereas I went on to the end of the tournament, feeling absolutely confident of the final result, and even Jocha, who took the second prize, did not make any serious attempt to catch me."

To the reader, Anatoly Karpov's tactics in this event (especially in the semi-final stage) might appear excessively cautious, and might even provoke antipathy on the part of 'tournament romantics'. But the dissatisfied critics should remember that the event was very much of an official nature, that the Soviet player wanted to finish first only, without fail, and that the short tournament distance dictated its own conditions. Let us hear Mikhail Botvinnik, who, as is well known, was always distinguished for his uncompromising approach to chess: "Karpov was an easy winner in the traditional tournament of European junior champions in Groningen. As a clever sportsman he always knows when to play for a win, when it is necessary to agree a quick draw. In chess circles in the West he was even criticised for a series of short draws in the Groningen tournament. In itself, of course, this was not very good, but it is surprising and worthy of recognition that a sixteen-year-old master should be able to adopt competitive tactics, characteristic of a mature grandmaster".

Karpov–Timman
English Opening

1 P–QB4	P–K3
2 N–QB3	N–KB3
3 N–B3	B–N5
4 Q–N3	P–B4
5 P–QR3	B–R4

The bishop is badly placed at ... QR4, and the whole of White's subsequent play is built on exploiting this circumstance. I consider that Black should have taken the knight, and then played ... N–B3, ... P–Q3 and ... P–K4.

6 P–K3	0–0
7 B–K2	P–Q4
8 0–0	N–B3

Of course, 8 ... P–Q5 is bad on account of 9 N–QR4, with advantage to White.

9 N–QR4

White begins playing actively. His plan is simple: as long as the enemy bishop is at ... QR4, Black cannot play ... P–QN3, and this means that the QBP is difficult to defend.

| 9 ... | Q–K2 |
| 10 Q–B2 | N–Q2 |

If 10 ... P–Q5, then 11 N×BP P×P (11 ... Q×N fails to 12 P–QN4 N×P 13 P×N B×P 14 P×P, while if 12 ... B×P 13 P×B N×P, then 14 Q–N3 P×P 15 B–R3 winning a piece) 12 BP×P Q×N 13 P–QN4 N×P (13 ... B×P 14 P×B N×P again fails to 15 Q–N3 and B–R3) 14 P×N B×P 15 P–Q4. White is a pawn down, but his position is highly promising.

11 P–Q4

White at last plays P–Q4. Black is poorly developed, and White's pieces occupy active positions.

| 11 ... | QP×P? |

Black's position was inferior, but of course it was not necessary to blunder away a pawn. He could have played 11 ... BP×P 12 KP×P P×P, although after 13 B×P the advantage remains with White.

12 P×P	P–K4
13 P–K4	N–Q5
14 N×N	P×N
15 B×P	N–K4
16 P–QN4	

An inaccuracy. With the game almost won, White goes wrong. He should have played 16 B–Q5.

| 16 ... | B–B2 |
| 17 B–Q5 | P–Q6? |

Black misses an excellent chance of compli-

cating matters: 17 ... N–B6+ 18 P×N Q–R5 19 P–K5 B×P 20 P–B4 P–Q6.

| **18 Q–Q1** | **B–N5** |

On 18 ... N–N5 there would have followed 19 P–B4 Q–R5 20 P–R3. If here 19 ... Q–B3, then 20 R–R2.

| **19 P–B3** | **B–R4** |
| **20 R–R2** | |

Now all Black's hopes of an attack disappear. In some cases White himself can launch an offensive on the K-side.

20 ...	**K–R1**
21 P–N4	**B–KN3**
22 P–B4	

22 R–KN2 followed by B–N2 and N–B3 would have been safer.

22 ...	**N×P**
23 Q×N	**P–B4**
24 P×P	**QB×P**
25 Q–B3	**QR–Q1**
26 N–B3	

The bishop has to be defended again, so as to deprive the opponent of tactical chances.

26 ...	**Q–B3**
27 R–KN2	**Q–Q5+**
28 K–R1	**R–B3**

29 B–Q2

29 B–N2 was better, but being short of time I decided for safety's sake to blockade the QP.

29 ...	R–R3
30 Q–B2	

In the time scramble I overlooked that my opponent could capture the bishop. Fortunately the win was still there.

30 ...	R×B
31 R–K1	R–K3
32 N×R	Q×N
33 R×R	B×R

34 K–N1	Q–N6

35 B–B3 was threatened.

35 Q–K1	K–N1?

35 ... P–KN3 was comparatively better.

36 P–B5	B–B2
37 B–R6	P–KN3
38 Q–R1	B–K4
39 Q×B	Q–Q8+
40 K–B2	Q–B7+
41 K–N3	Resigns

MOSCOW UNIVERSITY CHAMPIONSHIP, 1968/69

In Moscow on the Lenin Hills is situated the State University (MGU)—the major educational establishment in the Soviet Union, with tens of thousands of students. The university occupies an enormous area, and is almost equivalent to a complete small town. (Not without reason is it called the "town of five continents": living and studying here are envoys from practically all the countries of the world.) In the centre of this "town within a town" towers a fine sky-scraper, inside which there are not only libraries, roomy auditoria and ultra-modern laboratories, but everything else too: post and telegraph offices, refectories and snack bars, shops and various commercial and everyday repair establishments, sports halls and swimming baths, theatrical stages... Here also there are comfortable students' hostels, and in one of these rooms Anatoly Karpov lived from the Autumn of 1968, as a first year student in the Faculty of Mechanics and Mathematics.

Moscow University is without doubt the strongest, in the chess sense, educational establishment in the USSR, and its student team has on many occasions won the most imposing of events. In 1968 several masters and strong candidate masters took part in the MGU Championship —the tournament was so strong that it was even possible to set up a master norm for the young candidate masters. It was interesting to see how Karpov would fare, playing for the first time in a master tournament in the capital.

The tournament was held, as is customary, without any interruption of normal studies (or work). This meant that the students and lecturers were unable to play more than two, and sometimes even one, round a week. Such tournaments normally drag on for a long time, and this MGU Championship was no exception. In the University chess club the tournament table was on the wall for several months, being only gradually filled in. Anatoly Karpov was forced to break off, not only from his study in the very difficult Faculty of Mechanics and Mathematics, but also from his play in the MGU Championship, in order to travel to Riga for the USSR Team Championship...

The sports and academic heads of the University, and especially the heads of his faculty, were unhappy about Karpov's prolonged absence. Also unhappy about the 'postponement' taken by Karpov in the MGU Championship were the other players in the tournament. In particular, in an article devoted to this event, Yevgeny Gik, who shared second and third places, wrote that Karpov's departure to Riga had placed the other competitors in a comparatively unfavourable situation, since they were forced to 'play on ahead', not knowing how their main rival would fare. In itself the MGU Championship is a highly important event, and to be its winner is an enormous honour for any player. But for Karpov it was no less important to gain the right to play in the World Junior Championship (the USSR Team Championship was one of the elimination events). Nowadays Gik remembers with a smile how he preached at the future World Champion, and is very proud of the game which he lost to Karpov in that memorable university tournament.

Karpov–Gik
Sicilian Defence

1 P–K4 P–QB4 2 N–KB3 P–Q3 3 P–Q4 P×P 4 N×P N–KB3 5 N–QB3 P–KN3 6 B–K3 B–N2 7 P–B3 0–0 8 B–QB4 N–B3 9 Q–Q2 Q–R4 10 0–0–0 B–Q2 11 P–KR4 N–K4 12 B–N3 KR–B1 13 P–R5 N×RP 14 B–R6 B×B 15 Q×B R×N 16 P×R Q×BP 17 N–K2 Q–B4 18 P–N4 N–KB3 19 P–N5 N–R4 20 R×N P×R 21 R–R1 Q–K6+ 22 K–N1 Q×BP 23 R×P P–K3 24 P–N6 N×P 25 Q×P+ K–B1 (Diag.) 26 R–KB5 Q×B+

27 RP×Q P×R 28 N–B4 R–Q1 29 Q–R6+ K–K1 30 N×N P×N 31 Q×P+ K–K2 32 Q–N5+ K–K1 33 P×P R–B1 34 Q–N8+ K–K2 35 Q–N7+ K–Q1 36 P–B6 Resigns

One round before the finish Karpov was assured of first place. In the last round he had to meet his friend Volodya Skvortsov, who was a student in the same faculty. Skvortsov needed a win to reach the norm of master of sport. This game naturally provoked great interest. Skvortsov attacked recklessly, and the tournament leader appeared to be in great danger. Some of the spectators began to say that this was to be expected: Karpov, for whom this game was of no significance, was 'presenting' his friend with the necessary point. But then the attack was repulsed, and Karpov attained an absolutely won position. Any minute now, and he'll gain yet another win. Finally, with a sour look on his face, Skvortsov extends his hand to his opponent. But what's this? On the scoresheets there appears the word 'draw'! It turned out that before the game Karpov had warned his opponent that he had no intention of losing, but that he would agree to a draw at any time—which meant that the latter could pull out all the stops and play as boldly as possible.

As we have seen, even at the age of 17 Anatoly Karpov appreciated the value of his defeats, and perhaps even then he foresaw that within a few years each of his defeats would be considered a chess statistic. We now know that the number of defeats he has suffered so far has been extremely small. Incidentally, in that MGU Championship Anatoly Karpov did not lose a single game, and scored ten points out of thirteen. At the same time the tournament showed that he could already beat the 'average' master without difficulty. And this is very important before one takes the following step up the competitive ladder.

ON THE WAY TO THE WORLD JUNIOR CHAMPIONSHIP

The Soviet representative in the World Junior Championship is 'elected' in a specially organised elimination event. Sometimes, it is true, he is named without such a tournament being held, if he has already achieved major successes in important junior and adult events, and is clearly superior to his rivals (as it was, for instance, with Spassky in 1955).

When the All-Union Chess Federation was considering how to determine the most worthy representative for the World Junior Championship in 1969 (before the start of the event the participants had to be less than 20 years old), those whose chances were rated most highly were Mikhail Steinberg from Kharkov, Rafael Vaganian from Yerevan, and Anatoly Karpov, who had by then entered Moscow University. It has to be admitted that the general preference at that time was for Steinberg, the possessor of a record result—at the age of fourteen he became a master of sport, a feat which earlier no one had been able to achieve. Mikhail played excellently in the mass USSR Championship conducted on the Swiss system, and, what was quite unique at such an age, won there the prize 'for the best ending'. This success was confirmed in the Championship of the strong sports society 'Spartak', where the young Kharkov player came second only to grandmaster Suetin, and ahead of two other holders of the highest title (Simagin and Lilienthal), as well as a group of well-known masters.

Steinberg, who was born in January 1952, was the youngest of the three favourites.

Rafael Vaganian (born at the end of 1951) had taken third place in one of the USSR Championship Semi-Finals. And this says everything, since these tournaments are rated very highly: here the battle for a 'place in the sun' between the strongest players is especially fierce, and the results of such a battle are trusted completely.

It should be added that all three main contenders for the place in the World Junior Championship had been successful in the unofficial European Junior Championship in Holland (1966/67—Steinberg, 1st place; 1967/68—Karpov, 1st place; 1968/69—Vaganian, 1st–3rd place).

It so happened that the elimination event between these lads was preceded by the USSR Team Championship in Riga in December 1968.The team of each sports society included five men (in addition there was one reserve, who could replace any other team member), two juniors, two ladies, and one girl—altogether ten players.

By this time Anatoly Karpov had switched from 'Trud' to the Army Sports Society, and was ready to appear for the Armed Forces Team. It was then that an event occurred, which was to play an important rôle in the whole of his future life—he found for himself a genuine and permanent trainer, instead of just a temporary one. The trainer, in his turn, found a pupil of the type one normally only dreams about, and the work with him became his most important occupation.

"I first met Anatoly Karpov at the end of 1968, just before the USSR Team Championship. The army team held a training session, in which Anatoly took part, and he was invited to play on the first junior board", grandmaster Semion Furman later related.

...In this story, in fact, there is one inaccuracy: the future companions met for the first time much earlier, back in 1963, but soon forgot about this meeting. Furman, who had frequently acted as second to many top grandmasters, on account of his subtle understanding of the game and his vast opening knowledge, was invited to help Mikhail Botvinnik. When one of the games from the World Championship Match between Botvinnik and Petrosian was adjourned in a complex and unclear postion, Furman 'dared' to give his capricious master advice which disagreed with the latter's opinion. Botvinnik overestimated his chances, whereas his cautious second, foreseeing serious dangers, recommended that he take a draw, this being the best he could hope for. Just at this time, on the outskirts of Moscow, the sports society 'Trud', of which Botvinnik was a member, was holding its training session; its organizers were very much in need of well-qualified lecturers. And so Botvinnik sent his angered second 'into exile', to read lectures to players who had gathered from various corners of Russia. (In fact, within a couple of days Furman was again summoned to Moscow, since the then World Champion, who had failed to heed his advice, lost the adjourned game.) In the Karpovs' family archives is a yellowing snap-shot, where Semion Abramovich Furman is depicted reading a lecture in a small auditorium. Above one of the tables one can just make out the head of little Tolya Karpov, who along with his older colleagues is attentively listening to the words of the Moscow celebrity. This was in the summer of 1963, but Furman thinks that they met for the first time only five and a half years later. Here is how the trainer describes his further acquaintance with Karpov:

"He was a thin, pale lad, apparently rather phlegmatic. It even seemed difficult for him to move the chess pieces. Surely such a boy couldn't be capable of great competitive achievements"

When grandmaster Eduard Gufeld first saw Anatoly, he said: 'This lad will never be a grandmaster—he is too thin'. To which Efim Geller (also a grandmaster from the Armed Forces Team), who was standing near, remarked to Gufeld with some irony: 'Well, of course, everyone has his own yardstick. You, for instance, Edik, became a grandmaster when your weight reached 100 kilos...'

"Yes, Nature did not endow Anatoly Karpov with a powerful physique", Furman explains, "but it did give him a rare chess talent and strength of spirit. And in addition: modesty and a capacity for hard work. When I began working with Karpov, I immediately realized that he was a highly talented chess player, with great promise. And I was not mistaken. From this time onwards I, as trainer to the army players, took Anatoly under my constant wing, and helped him to prepare for events".

Karpov was excellently prepared for the USSR Team Championship, and it was not his fault that the Armed Forces Team took second place, behind the student team 'Burevestnik'. These two strongest teams met in the final round, and 'Burevestnik' scored a convincing victory. However, in this match the numerous spectators were concerned not only about the overall score, but also about the result on the first junior board between Anatoly Karpov and Ilya Miklyaev, a talented master from Kharkov (a compatriot and friend of Steinberg). Up till this point both had splendid results (nine points out of ten), and when Karpov defeated his rival in excellent style, his performance became quite outstanding—nine wins and two draws, without defeat—the best overall score in the whole Championship.

Karpov–Miklyaev
Ruy Lopez

1 P–K4 P–K4 2 N–KB3 N–QB3 3 B–N5 P–QR3 4 B–R4 P–Q3 5 P–B3 B–Q2 6 0–0 P–KN3 7 P–Q4 B–N2 8 P–KR3 N–B3 9 QN–Q2 0–0 10 R–K1 R–K1 11 B–B2 P–R3 12 P–R3 K–R2 13 N–B1 P–QN4 14 N–N3 N–QR4 15 P–N3 P–B4 16 P–Q5 P–B5 17 P–N4 N–N2 18 B–K3 Q–B2 19 N–R2 P–QR4 20 Q–Q2 R–R3 21 R–KB1 R(1)–QR1 22 QR–B1 P×P 23 RP×P N–N1

24 P–B4 P–B3 25 P–R4 B–K1 26 N–N4
P–R4 27 N–R2 P×P 28 B×P N–Q1 29 Q–Q1
K–R1 30 N–K2 N–B2 31 P–N4 N–K4
32 P×P P×P 33 N–N3 Q–B2 34 N–B3
N–N5 35 N–Q4 B–R3 36 Q–Q2 B×B 37

Q×B N(1)–R3 38 N(3)–B5 N×N 39 N×N
Q–B1 40 B–Q1 N–K4 41 R–QB2 R–R7
42 R×R R×R 43 N–N3 Q–N2 44 Q×P
Q×Q 45 R×Q R–R8 46 R–B1 R–B8 47
N–K2 R–R8 48 N–Q4 K–N1 49 N–B5
R–R3 50 K–B2 B–N3 51 K–K3 B×N 52 P×B
R–R7 53 K–Q4 R–R8 54 B–K2 R–R7 55
B×RP R–R7 56 R–B4 R–Q7+ 57 K–K4
R–Q6 58 P–B6 R×BP 59 K–B5 R–K6 60
R–B1 N–Q2 61 R–N1+ K–B1 62 R–QR1
R–K4+ 63 K–N6 R–K1 64 R–R7 R–Q1
65 R–B7 K–N1 66 K–N5 K–R1 67 B–N6
K–N1 68 P–R5 K–R1 69 P–R6 P–B6 70 R×P
R–KB1 71 P–B7 Resigns

Unfortunately, since then Miklyaev has not achieved any marked success, but has gradually and then altogether moved away from 'big-time chess'. Jumping ahead by several years, I can state that after Karpov was proclaimed World Champion in April 1975, he unexpectedly passed me one of the numerous congratulatory telegrams, and asked simply: 'Do you remember?'. I read the name at the bottom: 'Miklyaev, master of sport, kandidat in medical science'. It is surprising that Steinberg, who had already achieved some major successes and a considerable reputation, also virtually gave up appearing in serious tournaments. Here the main rôle was clearly not played by science, as in the case of Miklyaev... In the team tournament, Steinberg, who had just returned from some trip, replaced Vaganian in the 'Spartak' team, the latter having left to play in the Niemeyer Cup in Holland. Steinberg did not play badly, but he was highly offended when, at the closing ceremony of the championship in Riga, Botvinnik said that he considered the main Soviet contender for the place in the World Junior Championship to be Anatoly Karpov. Aleksandr Belyavsky (later World Junior Champion and adult Champion of the USSR), who was sitting next to Steinberg, heard him mutter angrily: 'Well we'll see about that!'. Nevertheless, after the 1969 World Junior Championship, the postman brought the following telegram to Karpov's parents' home in Tula: 'Congratulations on your brilliant victory. Misha Steinberg'.

In order to be sent numerous such congratulations, Anatoly Karpov had to first win the elimination match-tournament, before setting off for Stockholm. Karpov thinks that at that time he was still regarded with some mistrust, and that when after the third, and then the fourth cycle of the match-tournament he went ahead of his rivals by a significant margin, two more cycles were added to the event, so as to 'test' him, i.e. Karpov, more thoroughly. Aleksandr Belyavsky, as schoolboy champion of the USSR, was given the fourth place in the match-tournament, but for some reason at the last minute he failed to arrive in Leningrad. It was then that the decision was taken: Steinberg, Vaganian and Karpov should play not just four cycles (as would have been the case with Belyavsky competing), but six. Anatoly's victory in the match-tournament swept aside any last doubts, and he was named the USSR representative for the 1969 World Junior Championship.

"We played", Karpov recalls, "in a splendid building of the Leningrad Pioneers' Palace, where we were overlooked by portraits of now famous pupils from the chess club of this palace—grandmasters Spassky, Taimanov and others. Unfortunately, Misha Steinberg never became a grandmaster... Rafik Vaganian quite accidentally failed in the following World Junior Championship, to which he was sent without any preliminary elimination event. However Rafik managed to cope with his difficulties, played excellently in other tournaments, and gained the grandmaster title, and I once again see him as one of my future rivals, only this time in the battle for the title of 'adult' World Champion."

Vaganian–Karpov
Queen's Indian Defence

1 P–Q4 N–KB3 2 P–QB4 P–K3 3 N–KB3 P–QN3 4 P–K3 B–N2 5 B–Q3 B–K2 6 0–0 P–B4 7 N(1)–Q2 N–B3 8 P–QR3 P×P 9 P×P P–Q4 10 P×P Q×P 11 B–B4 Q–Q3 12 N–N3 0–0 13 Q–K2 P–KR3 14 R–Q1 KR–Q1 15 B–K3 QR–B1 16 QR–B1 N–Q4 17 B–Q2 P–QR4 18 R–B2 Q–N1 19 N–B1 N–B5 20 B×N Q×B 21 R(2)–Q2 B–B3 22 N–Q3 Q–B2 23 N(Q3)–K5 N×P 24 R×N R×R 25 N×R Q×(K4) 26 N–N5 Q×NP 27 N–Q6 Q×Q 28 B×Q R–B2 29 N×B R×N 30 P–QR4 R–B2 31 B–N5 R–B7 32 P–R3 P–N3 33 R–Q6 R–B8+ 34 B–B1 R–R8 35 R×N R×P 36 P–N3 B–Q5 37 R–N8+ K–N2 38 B–K2 R–R7 39 K–B1 P–R5 40 R–N4 P–K4 41 R–N7 P–R6 42 R×P+ K–R1 43 R–B8+ K–N2 44 R–B7+ K×R 45 B–B4+ K–B3 46 B×R

46 ... P–N4 47 P–B3 P–R4 48 K–K2 P–K5 49 P×P P–N5 50 P×P P×P 51 B–N3 B–K4 52 K–B2 K–K2 53 K–K3 B×P

54 K–Q4 B–K4+ 55 Resigns

Steinberg–Karpov
English Opening

1 P–QB4 P–K3 2 P–KN3 N–KB3 3 B–N2 P–B4 4 N–KB3 N–B3 5 0–0 P–Q4 6 P×P N×P 7 P–Q4 B–K2 8 P×P B×P 9 N–N5 B–K2 10 N–K4 0–0 11 QN–B3 N×N 12 N×N Q–N3 13 R–N1 R–Q1 14 Q–R4 B–Q2 15 B–K3 Q–N5 16 Q×Q B×Q 17 N–K4 B–K1 18 P–QR3 B–K2 19 KR–Q1 P–QN3 20 B–B4 R×R+ 21 R×R R–Q1 22 R×R N×R 23 B–B7 B–QB3 24 P–QN4 P–QN4 25 B–N8

25 ... P–B4 26 B–Q6 B×N 27 B×B(K7) N–B3 28 B×B P×B 29 B–B5 P–QR3 30 K–N2 N–K4 31 B–K3 K–B2 32 B–B1 N–B5 33 K–B1 K–B3 34 K–K1 K–B4 35 P–R3 P–KR4 36 K–Q1 P–N4 37 P–B3 P–K6 38 P–N4+ P×P 39 RP×P+ K–K4 40 K–B2 K–Q5 41 K–N3 and White resigned

WORLD JUNIOR CHAMPIONSHIP, STOCKHOLM 1969

For fourteen long years we waited and hoped... What did it matter, one might think, for a country whose representatives had gained all the highest chess honours, that the World Junior Championship was missing from this collection?! And yet... Time after time young Soviet masters set out to the Junior Championships, only to finish behind their rivals. They just couldn't win the gold medal, and there was a constant feeling of disappointment and a certain bewilderment in chess circles in the Soviet Union. How was it that, in this enormous chess country, a young talent couldn't be found, capable of repeating the success of Boris Spassky, who in 1955 demonstrated convincingly his superiority over his foreign rivals?

And how many famous child prodigies had there been, who flashed like meteors, and then equally quickly disappeared from the chess horizon at the first serious test?! Karpov, fortunately, was not one of them. There were many who believed that he would be successful. And Boris Spassky made this direct statement on the eve of Karpov's departure to Stockholm: "I am convinced that Karpov will repeat my success of fourteen years ago, and become World Junior Champion".

When Anatoly Karpov returned, he said:

"I am very glad that I have been able, at last, to show that the strongest junior player lives in the USSR. After all, for a long time our lads have simply been unlucky. But now I am sure that, for example, my comrades Misha Steinberg and Rafik Vaganian are at least as strong as those I had to play against in Stockholm.

All the time I believed in my ultimate success, although, of course, I was at first hindered somewhat by the psychological barrier resulting from the constant failures of my predecessors. However, I already had the experience of successful appearances abroad, in particular, in Holland, in the tournament for the strongest European juniors. I considered my main rivals to be the Hungarian Andras Adorjan, and the Swede Ulf Andersson, but when at the last moment the Puerto-Rican former Junior World Champion Julio Kaplan appeared, I began to think that it was he who would be my main rival. But Kaplan was too keen to come ahead of me, and as a result... did not even take second place.

At first things didn't go too well. True, I won my first game, but afterwards it turned out that this was a weak player—he lost to everyone. And then in the second round I was unable to overcome the Swiss player Werner Hug...

The third game in the Semi-Final was a hard and dramatic fight, which essentially turned out to be my most important game in the whole event. I had caught a cold, and couldn't manage to calculate long variations. Besides, I clearly underestimated the exceptional strength of the Filipino Eugenio Torre. The struggle was sharp, with the chances constantly changing sides. At first I had the better of it, then I accepted a pawn sacrifice, and came under attack. I thought for some forty minutes. I saw that Torre was nervous, and kept walking up and down the room... And then another factor came into it. On our clocks at home the flag starts to rise roughly three minutes before the hour, but on their's, in Sweden—about a minute. First of all I for some reason forgot about this, and then in my haste made a bad move. I came out a pawn down. I could have held on to a strong passed pawn, but I decided to give it up and create a fortress on the other wing, but the fortress did not materialise... Then I blundered away another pawn, and my position became hopeless. During the first adjournment session Torre made several mistakes, and for some reason began chasing my rook with his king;

the game was adjourned for the second time now with chances of a draw, which I successfully managed to attain.

Torre–Karpov
Ruy Lopez

1 P–K4 P–K4 2 N–KB3 N–QB3 3 B–N5 P–QR3 4 B–R4 N–B3 5 0–0 B–K2 6 P–Q4 P×P 7 P–K5 N–K5 8 P–QN4 N–B6 9 N×N P×N 10 P–QR3 0–0 11 Q–Q5 P–QN4 12 B–N3 P–QR4 13 B–K3 B–N2 14 QR–Q1 P×P 15 Q×QP Q–B1 16 P–K6 P×KP 17 P×P K–R1 18 B×P Q×Q 19 R×Q B–B1 20 R×P B×B 21 R×N B–B5 22 R–N1 B–R7 23 R–Q1 B×P 24 P–R3 KR–B1 25 R×R+ R×R 26 R–R1 B–B5 27 N–K5 B–Q4 28 R–N1 B–R6 29 R×P B–K5 30 B–Q4 P–R3 31 R–N3 B–N7 32 N–Q3 B–R8 33 R–R3 B×N 34 R×B B×P 35 R–R7 (Diag.) 35 ... R–KN1 36 P–R4 K–R2 37 B×BP P–R4 38 P–B3 B–B4 39 K–B2 K–N3 40 K–K3 B–K3 41 K–K4 B–B1 42 R–QB7 R–K1+ 43 B–K5 B–B4+ 44 K–B4 B–K3 45 R×P+ K–R3 46 P–N4 P×P 47 P×P R–KB1+

48 K–N3 R–B2 49 R–N5 R–QR2 50 B–Q4 R–R6+ 51 K–B4 R–R5 52 K–K5 B–N6 53 R–R5+ K–N3 54 R–N5+ K–R3 55 K–B6 R–R3+ 56 K–B5 R–R4+ 57 B–K5 B–B7+ 58 K–B6 R–R3+ 59 K–K7 R–R2+ 60 K–Q6 R–R3+ 61 K–B5 R–R5 62 R–N8 B–R2 63 R–N5 B–B7 64 B–B3 B–Q8 65 B–N4 B–K7 66 R–R5+ K–N3 67 R–K5 B–B6 68 P–R5+ K–N2 69 R–K6 K–B2 70 R–KN6 B–K7 71 R–N5 R–R1 72 K–Q5 R–KN1 73 R–B5+ K–N2 74 B–B3+ K–R3 75 R–B6+ K–N4 76 P–R6 R–Q1+ 77 R–Q6 **Drawn**

Between the adjournment sessions of this game I managed to win against the Austrian player. My nervousness passed, although I was still not completely on form. The last two rounds in the Semi-Final went well: while I was drawing with the Scot McKay, all my other rivals were fighting it out amongst themselves, and, irrespective of my result in the final round, I was already assured of a place in the top final group. (This last game I won, and thus took first place in the Semi-Final.)

It is not by accident that I have outlined these events from the Semi-Final in such detail. Such short elimination tournaments play on the nerves of the competitors, and sometimes prevent the strongest players from reaching the final. I consider the ideal selection system to be that which was adopted in the European Junior Championship in Holland—a general tournament on the Swiss system. After all, there is also the point that it is practically impossible to determine with any accuracy the relative strengths of junior players, and therefore it is not possible to arrange for the preliminary tournaments to be of equal strength. I, for instance, was of the possibly subjective, but firm conviction that 'my' Semi-Final was the most difficult one. It is revealing, with regard to this, that the 'delegate' from our sub-section, Torre, was the winner of the final 'B' section.

The deciding game in this second final was won by Torre against the American Rogoff. It is amusing that it should be representatives of the Philippines who cause the Americans so much trouble in chess events. Thus at the Lugano Olympiad (in 1968), and at the Students'

Olympiad in Dresden, the score in the matches USA—Philippines was equal—2–2. And on this occasion the two juniors were, as it were, settling the argument—who in fact is stronger?

Returning to the final", continues Anatoly Karpov, "I can honestly say that I found it much easier, I was more composed, than in the Semi-Final. It is interesting that, at the start of the tournament, it was said about me that I was not such a strong player. But then certain persons even asserted that I had played weakly in the Semi-Final on purpose, and that this was all 'cunning on the part of the Russians'. But in fact everything can be explained by the fact that my self-confidence and frame of mind improved during the course of the event.

During the Stockholm Tournament I made the closer acquaintance of Spassky, who had arrived for some exhibition games with Bent Larsen. The World Champion played with the famous Danish grandmaster a couple of demonstration games, which were later shown on Swedish television, and also visited our tournament. Spassky and I walked about the town, and had dinner together. Such 'trifles' can sometimes have a favourable effect on one's mood . . . There was also another episode, at first sight insignificant, which gave me a further supply of cheerfulness. Normally I used to arrive three or four minutes before the start of the round, and sit down at my board. Once during those minutes I was wrapped up in my own thoughts, when suddenly I heard: "Anatoly". My name is rarely pronounced abroad without any accent, and here it was being spoken in a pure Russian tongue! I looked round, but couldn't see anyone I knew. Then I heard the voice again. It turned out to be an elderly man, who had ended up in Scandinavia before the First World War, and who was desperately keen for me to win. Not wishing to disgrace myself in front of a compatriot, I managed to play quite a good game against the Swedish competitor.

There is hardly any point in talking about all the games from the World Junior Championship Final. I will add only that for my composure and good preparation I was greatly indebted to grandmaster Semion Abramovich Furman, an excellent trainer and person, who greatly helped me in understanding many of the secrets of chess, and who showed me how to build up a well-balanced system for studying the game. Perhaps he, as my faithful helper, should describe how the entire course of the 1969 World Junior Championship appeared to him."

And so, over to Semion Furman:

"The preparation for the World Championship was conducted along several lines. In the first instance it is very important for a chess player to know himself. This is not so simple, especially at a youthful age. In working with Karpov, we succeeded in detecting the strong and weak points in his game, and in fully assessing his capabilities. Thus, for instance, it turned out that Anatoly was not too well up on opening theory. This even pleased me; such a deficiency could be easily remedied, and we fairly quickly eliminated it. It is true that Karpov's opening repertoire was still rather limited, but we did not attempt to widen it. At the time our chief task was to obtain success in a specific event, and I did not try to deepen Karpov's knowledge of certain opening schemes.

I was delighted by the natural characteristic of Karpov's chess talent—his subtle positional understanding, that special intuition which always distinguishes great players. I also noted the mastery with which Karpov played endings, and also the technical accuracy with which he conducted a game.

But how were we to utilize most efficiently these strong aspects of Karpov's play in the coming event?

In studying the games of Karpov's future opponents, I gained the impression that the foreign juniors were in the main good tacticians, but weak strategists. They would normally seek a convenient moment to strike a tactical blow, and were rarely concerned about the strategical completeness of a game. Therefore we decided that Karpov should choose those openings, and those schemes of development, such that his opponents were not given the opportunity to complicate the game without running a risk. Jumping ahead, it should be said that this method of play proved to be the most expedient, and justified itself completely.

Attention also had to be paid to Anatoly's physical preparation. He was prescribed a daily course of morning exercises. During his training course Anatoly frequently played badminton and table tennis, and went boating. At first we relaxed on the outskirts of Moscow, and then moved near to Leningrad, to Zelenogorsk, with its almost Scandinavian climate. Such a change of scene proved most useful, since the World Junior Championship was to be held in Stockholm, and Anatoly needed to acclimatise.

Were we confident of ultimate success?

I must be frank and admit that I was not one hundred per cent confident that Karpov would win. I was not very well acquainted with the play of Anatoly's future opponents, and besides the final composition of the tournament became known only just before the first round. It is true that I was perfectly aware of Karpov's strength, and knew what he was capable of. But then everything is relative, and can only be found out by comparison.

Regarding Anatoly himself, he in general knows his true worth. I think that before Stockholm his confidence of victory harmonised with his strength.

We arrived in Sweden several days before the start of the Championship, so as to acclimatise as well as possible, and to become acquainted with the conditions. We were shown the tournament hall, to reach which we had to make our way through scaffolding and step ladders. We were not even sure that all the reconstruction work would be completed for the start of the tournament. But our fears were groundless: the Swedes did their best not to disappoint us with any deficiencies.

The building had been acquired not long before by the Stockholm Chess Federation from the city authorities. Money for the reconstruction was given by chess patrons. The building was sufficiently spacious for a club, but was clearly inadequate for the holding of a major event. There was no big hall, and in the oblong rooms, where the Junior Championship was held, it was very cramped, especially for the spectators. Of course, playing under such conditions would have been much more difficult for adults, but the youngsters did not complain. It is true that by the end of the event many of the lads were pretty tired, but I think that the severe schedule was responsible for this.

Adjourned games were played off in the mornings, and only one free day during an entire month was no help to anyone. The one consolation was the weather. The Swedes themselves said that they couldn't remember the last time there had been such a fine summer.

The 1969 World Junior Championship attracted a record number of participants. Thirty eight juniors from thirty seven countries contended for the title (as the host country the Swedes were allowed to put in two players).

All the competitors were divided into six Semi-Final groups, and two winners from each group made up the main final.

Of course, no one could have foreseen that in the Final Karpov would succeed in winning eight games in a row. No one set him such a target, and he himself never reckoned on such a series of wins. And even so, this was no accident. We managed to determine precisely the tactics

Anatoly should adopt in order to achieve the maximum success. Karpov proved to be an exceptionally capable student. He was able to develop at the board things which he had learned during his preparation for the tournament. Even those ideas which did not emanate from a given particular opening, Karpov utilized in a different situation.

I have already mentioned that the main strength of the foreign juniors was in tactical play. Therefore Karpov was faced with the task of obtaining positions in which the tactical trickery of his opponents would be doomed to failure. This meant that the position had to be sound, and that the plan of play should logically result from the demands of the position itself.

Nevertheless, certain of the players would sometimes manage to complicate the game, and 'drag' Anatoly into a tactical battle. But then they found themselves in an unfavourable situation, since they had acted anti-positionally.

From these games one can also form an opinion about Karpov's tactical ability. Therefore the 'course in solidity' was taken not on account of the weakness of Karpov's combinational vision, but rather with the aims of expediency and safety.

Karpov's excellent play and modest behaviour won him the respect and sympathy of Swedish chess fans. The local inhabitants wished him success, and then offered their congratulations. During the Championship Anatoly caught a cold. The Swedes were most concerned, and literally showered him with various medicines, while someone from Stockholm brought to Anatoly's hotel a thermos of hot tea. Anatoly quickly recovered. And I think that his recovery was helped not so much by the hot tea, as by the warm sympathy of his hospitable hosts.

The Swedish press, radio and television gave wide coverage to the Championship. The Swedes naturally supported their own Ulf Andersson, without doubt a highly talented player. When Ulf was still in with a chance, it was impossible to get through to the table where he was playing. Later the interest of the Stockholm public switched to Karpov. I even remember an instance when, under the pressure of spectators who had climbed onto a window-sill to get a better view of Anatoly, a radiator collapsed. A repair team had to be summoned urgently...

The closing ceremony took place in a park by the picturesque Lake Skansen. The Deputy Mayor of Stockholm arranged a banquet for all the competitors. There too the prizes were awarded.

And so, Anatoly Karpov won the title of World Junior Champion. In accordance with the FIDE rules, he would be awarded the International Master title. But what then? How would the young player's career develop? Many recognized grandmasters had in the past been Junior Champion. Would Karpov join their ranks?"

...When Semion Furman said all this, he was already convinced that Anatoly Karpov had a big, very big chess future. It is interesting that other competitors in the Stockholm World Junior Championship have subsequently also had considerable success. The names of Andersson, Torre, Adorjan, Rogoff, Kaplan, Vogt, Hug, and certain others, are widely known in the chess world today. And incidentally, it was not only Anatoly Karpov who arrived in Stockholm in 1969 with a personal trainer. The Hungarian Adorjan was accompanied by grandmaster Bilek, the Argentinian Sumiacher—by Julio Bolbochan, while the Yugoslav grandmaster Trifunovic had under his wing... Makropoulos of Greece...

Of course the Swedish organizers utilized the opportunity offered to arrange several simultaneous displays and lightning tournaments with the participation of the guests.

In the first of these Karpov conceded first place to Adorjan. The Hungarian scored 10½ out of 11, Karpov 9, Andersson 7½, Kaplan 7 etc. Then in the town of Vellinge the strongest of a series of lightning tournaments was held, with the participation of the adult guests. First place was taken by Furman—10½ out of 11, with Karpov half a point behind, then Adorjan and Andersson with 9, etc. In general Anatoly is a brilliant lightning player, but nevertheless, during serious events he normally avoids such games. But here it was impossible to refuse the hospitable hosts...

And here is another pronouncement by Karpov, which allows us to view from a rather unexpected angle the great significance for him of having won the title of World Junior Champion:

"In winning the World Junior Championship, I received the title of International Master —and thus overcame a colossal barrier which stands in the way of any talented master. In the USSR we have very many good players, but as yet, unfortunately, insufficient international tournaments, so that the opportunities for obtaining the international master title are limited. And this title alone assures one of a hearty welcome by the organizers of tournaments abroad. And when I succeeded at the first opportunity in overcoming this barrier, the road to international events immediately opened before me."

Karpov–Andersson
Ruy Lopez

1 P–K4	P–K4
2 N–KB3	N–QB3
3 B–N5	P–QR3
4 B–R4	N–B3
5 0–0	B–K2
6 R–K1	P–QN4
7 B–N3	0–0

Andersson and I met in the third round of the final. In a game against a strong opponent, I was happy that the opening should be a Ruy Lopez. At that time my opening repertoire was still highly limited, whereas I had been playing the 'Lopez' both as White and as Black since early childhood. I thus felt confident about the outcome of this game too (in the two preceding rounds I had won).

8 P–B3	P–Q3
9 P–KR3	N–QR4
10 B–B2	P–B4
11 P–Q4	Q–B2
12 QN–Q2	B–N2

One of the oldest continuations in the Chigorin Variation; nowadays this move is rarely played. When it is played, it is normally after the preliminary moves 12 ... BP×P 13 P×P, so as to gain counter-play along the opened QB–file. Now, however, White immediately closes the centre, and the black bishop has to waste a further couple of tempi in order to reach Q2, to where it could have gone straight away. It is fallacious to argue that in closed positions the loss of tempi is of no great significance. Of course, in open positions chess time (i.e. tempi) is more precious, but here too Black should not have wasted it unnecessarily.

13 P–Q5	B–B1
14 N–B1	B–Q2
15 P–QN3	

The aim of this move is to restrict the black knight. Generally speaking, in a number of openings Black experiences difficulties over the development of this or that piece. It is sufficient to recall the 'restricted' black bishops in the French Defence and in the Benoni Defence. In the given instance we are dealing with the 'ugly Spanish knight', which is quite unable to make itself useful. For the moment it is denied the square QB5, while if Black should advance his QBP, then after the reply P–QN4 the knight will have to retreat to QN2, where it again will have no favourable prospects (incidentally, something similar happens to this same queen's knight in the so-called Yugoslav Variation of the King's Indian Defence, so that this idea is by no means new).

15 ...	N–N2

Nevertheless, Black should probably have played 15 ... P–B5, so as after 16 P–QN4 N–N2 to be able to fight for the QR-file by ... P–QR4.

16 P–B4	KR–N1
17 N–K3	B–KB1

Normally Black tries not to allow the enemy knight in at KB5, and plays ... P–KN3. But here, having wasted time on the Q-side, he quite justifiably fears the typical sacrifice: P–KN4, K–R2 and N–B5, when the attack along the KN-file may become rather strong.

18 N–B5	N–Q1

Of course, ... B×N is unfavourable, since White's possession of his K4 square and the possibility of a K-side pawn storm give him total domination of the position. Therefore Andersson tries to set up a 'fortress' (by N–Q1, N–K1, P–B3, N–B2 and P–N3), and

on the other side of the board opens the QN-file for his rooks.

19 N–R2

The attack by P–B4 will probably be more effective than the convential P–KN4, K–R2 and R–KN1. One of the main defects of Black's position is that his bishop at Q2 takes away an important square from his knight, which from there could support his very important K4 square. It is this square that will come under attack after White's subsequent P–B4.

19 ...	N–K1
20 P–KR4	

This is not contradictory to the idea of P–B4. For the moment White intends to seize a little more space. In turn, 20 ... P–N3 is not good in view of 21 N–R6+, when the knight will play strongly on the enemy king's nerves.

20 ...	P–B3

A consequence of Black's cramped position is that, in order to bring one knight into play, he at the same time has to take squares away from the other with his pawns.

21 P–R5	N–B2
22 R–K3	

On the third rank the rook will be ideally placed for being switched to either flank. In general, rooks, like minor pieces, should be brought into play as quickly as possible.

22 ...	N–N4

In the present situation this is probably the only possibility of setting up, if not a fortress, then at least some advanced fortifications. Behind these the other pieces (in particular the black-squared bishop) are ready to come into play when White mounts a direct attack.

23 N–R4	Q–Q1
24 R–N3	N–QB2
25 N(R2)–B3	P–R3
26 N–N6	

Thus White has achieved all, or at least nearly all of his aims. For 'complete satisfaction' he still has to exchange the white-squared bishops, after first defending his pawns at QB4 and K4, when the opponent will have nothing with which to defend the weakened squares in his position. This is White's overall strategic plan. But to carry it out he still has to overcome a number of difficulties, and take account of numerous tactical subtleties.

26 ...	P–R4

Black starts his counter-play, and by the further advance of this pawn would like to open up two files straight off—the QR- and QN-files. Two files, not one, and this must be prevented.

27 P–R4!

The weakening of QN4 is unimportant— the transfer of a knight to this square does not threaten anything.

27 ...	P×BP
28 P×P	N–R3
29 Q–K2	R–R2
30 B–Q2	R(2)–N2
31 B–B3	

It is essential to keep under control all the possible entry squares of the enemy rooks.

31 ...	N–N5

An 'empty' move. Here the knight merely blocks the only open file. On this square Black should have sacrificed the exchange by ... R–N5. White's following, apparently rather intricate manoeuvres are directed towards both the effecting of his main strategical plan, as well as towards preventing any activity on Black's part.

32 B–Q1	N–R3
33 N–Q2	N–N5
34 R–K3	B–K1
35 N–B1	Q–B1
36 N–N3	B–Q2
37 Q–Q2	N–R2
38 B–K2	K–B2
39 Q–Q1	B–K2
40 N–B1	

40 ... P–B4 only favours White, and so this knight can calmly make first for KR2, so as to assist the exchange of bishops.

40 ...	B–Q1
41 N–R2	K–N1
42 B–N4	

At last... Incidentally, 42 ... B×B 43 N×B N–B7 fails now to 44 N×RP+.

42 ...	N–N4
43 B×B	Q×B
44 N–B1	

White has carried out his plan, and now intends by the manoeuvre N–N3–B5 followed by the pawn storm P–N3 and P–B4 to launch a decisive attack. Andersson attempts to escape from the vice.

44 ...	P–B4
45 P×P	Q×BP
46 N–N3	Q–B2

46 ... Q–B7 is answered by the terrible 47 P–B4, when 47 ... P×P fails to 48 R–K8+, mating.

47 Q–K2!

Again threatening the thematic P–B4.

| 47 ... | B–B3 |
| 48 R–KB1! | |

White is about to open files on the K-side for the intrusion of his heavy pieces, and meanwhile the black knights continue to play an ineffective rôle.

| 48 ... | Q–Q2 |

49 P–B4	P×P
50 R×P	B×B
51 R×B	R–K1

This, of course, is not an attack on the queen (52 ... R×Q 53 R–B8+ K–R2 54 R–KR8 mate), but rather an attempt to neutralize White's pressure down the K-file.

| 52 R–K3 | R(2)–N1 |
| 53 Q–KB2 | |

Threatening 54 R–K7!. The game is decided.

53 ...	N–R2
54 N–B5	R×R
55 Q×R	N–KB3
56 N(6)–K7+	K–R1

56 ... K–R2 loses to the same move 57 N×RP, while on 56 ... K–B2, 57 Q–KN3 is sufficient. The game concluded:

57 N×RP	R–K1
58 N–B7+	K–R2
59 R–K4!	R×N
60 R×R	Resigns

CHAMPIONSHIP OF THE RUSSIAN REPUBLIC, KUYBISHEV 1970

As soon as a player gains the title of World Junior Champion, the following question automatically arises: and when will he become a grandmaster? The point is that the majority of Junior Champions go on to establish themselves fairly securely on the approaches to the adult Olympus, to coin a phrase. And it's natural that princes should becomes kings. But how much time does this require? "Anyone can become a grandmaster", runs the rather gloomy joke, "but not everyone lives long enough..."

Karpov, the World Junior Champion, was faced by a new problem—to surmount the grandmaster barrier. "Anatoly will without doubt be a grandmaster", said Furman. "When? I think within two years. But this depends not only on his preparedness, but also on the opportunity he has for taking part in strong events. The sooner Anatoly begins meeting players of extra-class, the sooner he will become a grandmaster".

The reader may be surprised that we should begin here talking about Karpov's pursuit of the grandmaster title, when the Championship of the Russian Republic is not a tournament in which one can gain this distinguished title. The point is that the experience of events in the Soviet Union has shown that victory in the Championship of such a vast country as the Russian Republic is equivalent in difficulty to attaining the grandmaster norm. This was also realized, or rather, known, by Karpov. To the question, when did he intend to seriously go for the higher chess title, Anatoly replied:

"I don't like forecasting. But, if you really want to know, everything depends on the Championship of the Russian Republic in Kuybishev. What concerns me more than anything is whether I can get through to the USSR Championship Final, and compete alongside experienced players".

And so, in that year the Championship of the Russian Republic was at the same time a Semi-Final of the next USSR Championship, to which four winners of the Kuybishev tournament went through. It should be added that competing in the event were grandmasters Krogius, Antoshin, and the late A. Zaitsev.

Anatoly's play resembled a well-tuned clockwork mechanism, and he was always well ahead of the other players. He did not suffer a single defeat. The one who came nearest to defeating the leader was A. Zaitsev, the grandmaster from Vladivostok. But when Anatoly nevertheless succeeded in tipping the scales in his favour, the question of the tournament winner was practically decided. For, as is well known: "fortune always favours the stronger player".

Karpov–Krogius
French Defence

1 P–K4 P–K3 2 P–Q4 P–Q4 3 N–Q2 P–QB4 4 KN–B3 N–QB3 5 KP×P KP×P 6 B–N5 B–Q3 7 0–0 N–K2 8 P×P B×BP 9 N–N3 B–N3 10 R–K1 0–0 11 B–K3 B–N5

12 B×B Q×B 13 B×N N×B 14 Q×P N–N5 15 Q–K4 B×N 16 P×B P–QR4 17 P–QR3 N–B3 18 Q–K3 Q–N4 19 P–QR4 Q–R4 20 Q–K4 Q–KN4+ 21 K–R1 Q–B3 22 N–B5 QR–Q1 23 P–B3 P–QN3 24 N–Q3 P–R3 25 P–KB4 R–Q2 26 R–K3 KR–Q1 27 R–QN1 N–K2 28 N–K5 R–Q8+ 29 R–K1 R×R(K8)+ 30 R×R N–B4 31 N–N4 Q–N3 32 N–K5 Q–R4 33 Q–B3 Q–R5 34 N–B4 Q–B3 35 P–R3 N–R5 36 Q–K4 N–N3 37 P–B5 N–R5 38 N–K3 K–R1 39 R–K2 Q–N4 40 K–R2 P–R4 41 P–KB4 Q–R3 42 K–N3 P–KN4 43 P×P e.p. N×P 44 N–B5 Q–B1 45 Q–B3 K–N1 46 Q×P R–Q6+ 47 K–N4 Q–R1 48 N–Q4 R–Q8 49 N–B3 R–Q4 50 N–N5 Q–QB1+ 51 K–N3 R–KB4 52 Q–R7+ K–B1 53 Q–R6+ K–N1 54 N–K6 **Resigns**

Karpov–A. Zaitsev
Caro Kann Defence

1 P–K4 P–QB3 2 P–Q4 P–Q4 3 N–QB3 P×P 4 N×P N–Q2 5 N–KB3 KN–B3 6 N×N+ N×N 7 N–K5 B–B4 8 P–QB3 P–K3 9 P–KN4 B–N3 10 P–KR4 B–Q3 11 Q–K2 P–B4 12 P–R5 B–K5 13 P–B3 P×P 14 Q–N5+ N–Q2

15 N×P B–N6+ 16 K–K2 P–Q6+ 17 K–K3 Q–B3 18 K×B Q×N 19 R–R3 P–QR3 20 Q–N5 P–R3 21 Q–K3 P–K4 22 K×P B–B5 23 Q–N1 0–0–0 24 K–B2 B×B 25 R×B Q×QRP 26 R–R2 KR–B1 27 R–Q2 Q–R5+ 28 K–N1 Q–B3 29 B–Q3 K–B2 30 B–K4 Q–QN3 31 Q–R2 QR–K1 32 R(1)–Q1 N–B3 33 B–N6 R–K2 34 R–K1 Q–N4 35 R(2)–K2 N–Q2 36 B–B5! R×B 37 P×R Q–Q6+ 38 K–R1 Q×P(B4) 39 Q–R4 N–B3 40 Q–QB4+ K–Q1 41 Q–B5 N–Q2 42 Q–Q5 K–B1 43 R–K4 P–QN4 44 Q–B6+ K–Q1 45 Q×QRP Q×RP 46 P–KB4 Q–B4 47 Q–R8+ K–B2 48 Q–R5+ K–B3 49 P–B4 P–N5 50 Q×NP R–K3 51 P×P K–B2 52 Q–R5+ K–N2 53 Q–N5+ R–N3 54 Q–Q5+ K–B2 55 K–N1 Q–B7 56 R(4)–K2 Q–KB4+ 57 Q–K4 Q×Q+ 58 R×Q N–B4 59 R(4)–K3 N–K3 60 K–B2 P–N4 61 K–B3 P–R4 62 P–N4 R–R3 63 P–B5 R–R6+ 64 K–B4 R×R 65 R×R P–R5 66 P–N5 K–Q1 67 P–N6 K–Q2 68 R–Q3+ K–B1 69 R–Q6 P–R6 70 R×N P–N5 71 R–KR6 Resigns

THE GRANDMASTER NORM: CARACAS 1970

This was the first big tournament to take place in Venezuela, and it was held under the personal patronage of the President of the Republic, who was present at the opening ceremony. And yet not long before, chess had been considered here a game of chance, and the importation of pieces had been subject to a heavy duty, by the kilogram. During the time of the tournament chess enjoyed great popularity, second only to football. But during one of the rounds a chorus of car horns could be heard. The players were reassured: there was no point in paying any attention to the car drivers, since they were unlikely to quieten down: they were celebrating the victory by Brazil in the football World Cup.

Before the tournament in Caracas Karpov had managed to play all of five games with grandmasters—with Gipslis, Krogius, A. Zaitsev, and twice with Antoshin. And although he could not complain about the overall score in these games (two wins, one defeat and two draws), the young player admitted that at first he experienced a certain lack of confidence when faced by one of the holders of the higher chess title.

Karpov cheered up markedly when, at the formal opening of the tournament, when the draw took place, he picked the same number six which had been so lucky for him in the Championship of the Russian Republic. He was not particularly upset when he missed a win after the adjournment in his first round game with the American grandmaster Bisguier, since he immediately defeated the highly experienced Hungarian grandmaster Barcza. Then came a further encounter with a grandmaster, Parma, (incidentally, a former World Junior Champion), the win against whom Anatoly considers his best creative achievement in this tournament.

Barcza–Karpov
English Opening

1 N–KB3 P–QB4 2 P–B4 P–KN3 3 P–KN3
B–N2 4 B–N2 N–QB3 5 N–B3 P–K4 6 P–Q3
KN–K2 7 0–0 0–0 8 N–K1 R–N1 9 N–B2
P–QR3 10 R–N1 P–Q3 11 P–QN4 B–K3
12 P×P P×P 13 N–K3 P–N3 14 N(3)–Q5
B–Q2 15 B–Q2 N×N 16 N×N N–K2 17
Q–B1 N×N 18 B×N B–R6 19 R–K1

19 ... P–QN4 20 P–R3 Q–Q3 21 B–KB3
B–K3 22 P×P P×P 23 B–K3 KR–B1 24
Q–Q2 P–N5 25 P×P P×P 26 B–R7 R–N4
27 KR–QB1 R×R+ 28 Q×R P–N6 29
Q–B6 Q×Q 30 B×Q R–R4 31 B–K3 R–R7
32 B–QN5 P–N7 33 K–N2 P–K5 34 P–Q4
B–N6 35 Resigns

Karpov–Parma
Nimzo-Indian Defence

1 P–QB4 N–KB3 2 N–QB3 P–K3 3 P–Q4
B–N5 4 Q–B2 0–0 5 N–B3 P–B4 6 P×P N–R3

7 B–Q2 N×P 8 P–K3 P–QN3 9 B–K2 B–N2
10 0–0 P–Q3 11 KR–Q1 P–QR3 12 P–QN3
P–K4 13 P–QR3 B×N 14 B×B Q–K2 15
N–K1 QR–B1 16 QR–B1 N(3)–K5 17 P–QN4
N×B 18 Q×N N–K3 19 Q–Q3 KR–Q1
20 B–B3 B×B 21 N×B P–N3 22 N–Q2 N–B2
23 N–K4 N–K1 24 Q–Q5 K–N2 25 P–R3
N–B3 26 N×N K×N 27 Q–K4 K–N2 28
R–Q5 Q–B2 29 P–B4 R–K1 30 P×P P×P
31 P–B5 R–K3 32 Q–Q3 P×P 33 P×P
Q–B3 34 R–N1 Q–B2 35 R–KB1 R–B1 36
K–R1 Q–B3 37 R–QN1 Q–B2 38 P–K4
R–QN1 39 R–KB1 R–N2 40 Q–QB3 R–N4
41 P–QR4 R–N1 42 R–B1 R–QB1 43 R–QN1
K–N1 44 R(1)–Q1 Q–K2 45 R–KB1 R–B2
46 P–R5 R(3)–QB3 47 R–B1 P–B3

48 Q–Q2 K–B2 49 K–R2 K–K1 50 R–Q6
R–Q2 51 R–Q1 R(3)×R 52 P×R Q–K3 53
Q–Q3 Q–R7 54 Q×P Q–QB7 55 Q–R8+
K–B2 56 Q–Q5+ K–N2 57 R–Q2 Q–B6
58 R–R2 P–R4 59 R–Q2 P–R5 60 R–Q1
Q–B7 61 P–R6 Q–R5 62 Q–Q3 P–N4 63
R–QN1 P–B4 64 R–N7 P–N5 65 RP×P
P×NP 66 Q–K2 Resigns

He now had 2½ points after three games with grandmasters! Then he defeated Slujssar.
A number of Russian émigrés live in Caracas, and one of them presented the future grandmaster with an Indian bow and arrow, wishing him a steady hand and a keen eye. Incidentally,
Slujssar's father was Russian, which, however, was sufficient only for two draws from the whole
tournament. The only consolation for the home country was that this representative of Venezuela was young, of the same age as Karpov.

After this the Soviet player had 4½ out of 5, 5 out of 6... In the seventh round he defeated
yet another grandmaster—the Belgian O'Kelly. Anatoly became the leader with 6 out of 7!
The participants looked with astonishment at the table, which was headed by the youngster.
For the first time the most ambitious hopes arose (and then immediately disappeared).

Karpov–O'Kelly
Ruy Lopez

1 P–K4 P–K4 2 N–KB3 N–QB3 3 B–N5
P–QR3 4 B–R4 N–B3 5 0–0 B–K2 6 R–K1
P–QN4 7 B–N3 P–Q3 8 P–B3 0–0 9 P–KR3
N–N1 10 P–Q4 QN–Q2 11 QN–Q2 B–N2
12 B–B2 R–K1 13 N–B1 B–KB1 14 N–N3
P–N3 15 P–QR4 B–N2 16 B–Q3 P–Q4 (Diag.)

17 B–N5 P×KP 18 B×KP B×B 19 N×B
P×QP 20 N×P P–B4 21 B×N N×B 22
N×BP R×R+ 23 Q×R P–N5 24 R–B1 P×P
25 P×P Q–Q4 26 N(4)–N3 B–B1 27 Q–Q1
Q×Q+ 28 R×Q R–B1 29 N×P R×P

30 R–N1 B–Q3 31 R–Q1 B–B1 32 R–N1
N–Q2 33 P–R5 R–B3 34 R–Q1 N–K4
35 R–Q5 N–B5 36 N–N8 R–B1 37 N–Q7
B–K2 38 N–N6 R–B3 39 N×N R×N 40
P–R6 R–QR5 41 R–QR5 Resigns

When Karpov and Stein were one day walking about the town, they happened to run into Ivkov. "Already a grandmaster!" the Yugoslav exclaimed amicably. But on the following day Ivkov was paired with Karpov, and after sacrificing a pawn against him... immediately offered a draw. Karpov declined, but after this offer he was unable to gear himself up for a fight, his mind worked sluggishly, and he made some passive moves. His opponent, on the other hand, threw himself into the attack, preparing one sacrifice after another—he had nothing to lose!

...At that time Karpov used to dream about Spassky's universal style, and had a very simple explanation for why he wanted to play similarly: it would enable him to avoid losing. The ability to play the game in any key allows one, without visible effort, to change the register of the game of chess—be it the serene melodies of positional manoeuvring, or the dramatic chords of combinations. At that time such a change would sometimes lead to false notes, which used to cause him great concern. Once Mozart, on hearing a trumpeter in an adjacent room playing out of tune, fainted. Karpov possessed perfect chess pitch, but his technical ability was far from perfect. In his game with Ivkov he himself suddenly began to sense the false notes in his own performance, he began to torment himself with remorse, and then he suffered a genuine 'chess faint'...

It was even more vexing and disheartening for Karpov after the game, when Ivkov showed his young opponent how he could have not only saved the game, but even obtained an excellent position. The resourceful Karpov would of course have seen this possibility, if the register of the game had not switched so unexpectedly to wild combinational play, and if his perfect chess pitch had not reacted so painfully to his poor performance. His 'fainting state' did not pass immediately. The following day he just managed to hold out against the Argentinian Panno, he then lost to Kavalek, and drew with difficulty against the young and highly talented Icelandic player Sigurjonsson...

He got a grip on himself only towards the finish, when he had to defeat three outsiders and draw his three other games. True, against all the rules, his last round opponent, the American Addison, was allowed to play this game in advance. One day Stein and Karpov, exhausted by the heat, were sitting in their room just in their swimming trunks, playing a card game they had devised. There was a knock at the door, and Addison walked in, all dressed up in dark suit and tie. They were very pleased to have another player, and wanted to teach him their game there and then.

But Addison apologized, said that he had to fly home urgently, and asked whether Karpov would mind if their game from the last round was played earlier. Karpov agreed, the tournament controller gave his permission, the game ended in a draw, and thus the Soviet player attained the grandmaster norm even ahead of schedule.

Anatoly recalls that, in general, relations between the players were most friendly. Although, of course, there were inevitably one or two exceptional cases, in view of the fact that the majority of the controllers were insufficiently highly qualified, and that certain of the players lacked experience of major events. Thus the Ecuador player Yepez, on making his fortieth move, did not manage to press his clock in time. Karpov's position was in any case won, but why should he play on if his opponent's flag had fallen. Anatoly correctly asked that he be awarded the point, but unexpectedly both the controller and his opponent protested. Only the immediate intervention of several experienced players, including Panno, who enjoys an unquestionable authority amongst South Americans, enabled this amusing 'conflict' to be settled.

Incidentally, Panno also rendered the Soviet players another service during this tournament. Oscar invited them to his place, and on noticing how they looked round his splendidly spacious room, (the one in which Stein and Karpov were living together was considerably smaller), he suggested that they change hotels. They gratefully and with pleasure took up Panno's suggestion, who later joked that they had 'exchanged possession of the light central square e4 for the dark corner square h8'. Adjacent to Karpov and Stein's new room was a restaurant and swimming pool...

It so happened that, on account of this very swimming pool, Karpov genuinely fainted—he got sun stroke. The tournament was already coming to an end, and Karpov, after bathing rather incautiously in the sun, went off to relax before a large simultaneous display which all the tournament competitors were to give. Anatoly felt ill, but considered that he did not have the right to decline to play in the display. (Karpov relates how he was astonished by the enthusiasm for the display shown by the local residents, who arrived at the square with their own chess boards. It started to rain, and the grandmasters and masters hurried into shelter, but to a man all the participants in the simultaneous stayed in their places, so that they wouldn't lose them to others who wished to do battle with the guest celebrities.)

"At one point I went up to one of the tables, thought, and on making the first move which came to hand, suddenly quite literally toppled over. It was fortunate that someone managed to get me onto a chair. I did not come round straight away, and was then taken to the hotel", Anatoly related after that memorable tournament.

From Caracas he returned very tired, but very happy to have become the youngest grandmaster in the world.

38TH USSR CHAMPIONSHIP, RIGA 1970

Anatoly Karpov:

"To be perfectly honest, I have to admit that the first USSR Championship in which I took part was not an outstanding tournament. And this despite the fact that it is customary—normally quite justifiably—to think of all USSR Championships as being highly interesting events. But this particular Championship, which was held in winter in Riga, was a somehow 'sullen', and by no means festive tournament. Mikhail Tal was not allowed in: he, it was stated, had not taken part in the qualifying events, and at that time some had begun to have doubts about the playing strength of the Ex-World Champion. If Tal had been playing in his home town, the tournament would have been more interesting, entertaining, and festive... Also not appearing was a whole group of other strong players, whose participation would without doubt have enhanced the event. But nevertheless the Championship of the Soviet Union remained a very serious schooling, and a severe test, and I was prepared beforehand for a not very high place. The main difference between the Championship Finals of our Country, and International Tournaments, is that in the latter one always finds some weak opponents, whereas in our Championships there are no real outsiders.

It has to be said that to some extent that Championship Final justified in my eyes the claims which had been made on its behalf, but at the same time it did not prove to be such a severe examination. In short, it wasn't as bad as in the frightening tales told me by my older colleagues. And the fact that I began my appearances in the Final with one which was by no means the strongest or most difficult of such tournaments, was not at all a bad thing.

In 1970 I had been playing fairly frequently in tournaments, and from the very start of the Championship I felt overtaxed and fatigued. A lack of confidence in my ability gave rise to a certain degree of caution; I tried not to take risks, and even agreed several short draws. I was heavily criticized for this, but everyone forgot that this was my first Championship, and that I had a certain justification for such play".

...Yes, Anatoly Karpov was indeed heavily criticized during this Championship. At that time there had appeared in the Soviet chess arena a whole group of masters, who were soon to become grandmasters—Vladimir Tukmakov, Yury Balashov, Rafael Vaganian... None of them had such reproaches to endure as did Anatoly. Grandmasters, in contrast to the journalists, attempted to find an explanation. Tal, for instance, suggested that Karpov had too much respect for his opponents, and inwardly felt a certain timidity when confronted by them. The result was caution and constraint, so that he was unable to play his own game. Semion Furman attempted to defend his 'charge':

"In his present situation it is difficult for him to experiment. He is obliged to make a good score, and achieve success from the competitive point of view. He therefore has to restrain his emotions and his creative impulses, and play rather drably. A path, which, frankly speaking, is far from ideal. After all, if we were working with a real eye to the future, it would be better if Tolya were to play not very well competitively, but fruitfully in the creative sense"...

On all this Anatoly Karpov has his own point of view. This is how he expresses it today:

"Yes, somewhere inside of me I still experienced a certain timidity, and for this reason I acted with extreme care, and tried to play soundly; I did not hope for a great deal, but at the same time I did not want to be a failure. I set myself the task of losing as few games as possible. At that time this was not easily done, since as regards the opening I was still quite inadequately prepared, and as Black frequently got into difficult positions. But my opening knowledge had always been poor since childhood, (it is only recently that I have eliminated this deficiency), and perhaps this was how I acquired the resourcefulness and tenacity which I display in difficult positions. As one says, life forced it on me, or 'every cloud has a silver lining'.

At the level of the Championship Final of the country (even such an unimposing one as that in 1970) my knowledge of chess theory was markedly inferior to that of many of the contestants. And it was this that gave rise to my tactics. But I must admit that I rather over-did things, and at the start of the tournament scored eight draws in succession. In addition, things were especially difficult for me in my games with grandmasters—against all of them, except Vladimir Antoshin, the draw had given me the black pieces. And against Viktor Korchnoi in the ninth round I also had Black; this was the first game in my life against one of the top players. Here I found myself in a difficult position right from the opening.

Here I should like to make an important observation. Without wishing to offend my trainer Semion Abramovich Furman, to whom I owe a great deal, it nevertheless has to be said that, in my games against Korchnoi, I always got poor positions from the opening when I blindly followed Furman's advice. Korchnoi had studied Furman very well, since earlier they had worked together for a long time. And now Korchnoi would often cunningly exploit this circumstance, by guessing the moves that Furman would suggest to me. And it was only later, on realizing this, that I began to listen carefully to the advice of my trainer (here we are talking only about preparing for games against Korchnoi), but then nevertheless to go my own way. Without wishing to boast, I would say that when I operated in this way, Korchnoi could no longer achieve anything against me in the opening. But at that time, in Riga, I was still an insufficiently independent player.

In a difficult position I defended well, and had almost completely equalized when, evidently worn out by the constant defending, I failed to exploit an opportunity, and in the end suffered a defeat. The tension was terrific, and I had not yet become accustomed to such stress. In the twelfth round I at last gained my first win, and then another... I began to pluck up courage, but was promptly crushed by Oleg Dementiev, True, it all ended quite favourably—I finished with ' +3', and this fairly high score enabled me to share fifth to seventh place: not at all bad for a first appearance. Besides, the 1970 Championship showed me that it was possible to save difficult positions against very strong players (although, of course, it is better not to get into such positions in the first place). In short, this tournament reassured me".

Karpov–I. Zaitsev
Ruy Lopez

1 P–K4 P–K4 2 N–KB3 N–QB3 3 B–N5 P–QR3 4 B–R4 N–B3 5 O–O B–K2 6 R–K1 P–QN4 7 B–N3 P–Q3 8 P–B3 O–O 9 P–KR3 Q–Q2 10 P–Q4 B–N2 11 QN–Q2 QR–K1 12 N–B1 B–Q1 13 N–N3 P–R3 14 B–B2 K–R1 15 P–N3 N–KN1 16 P–Q5 N(3)–K2 17 P–B4 P–QB3 18 QP×P Q×BP 19 P×P P×P 20 P–N4 B–N3 21 B–Q3 P–Q4 22 B–N2 N–N3 23 P×P Q×P 24 B–K4 Q×Q 25 QR×Q B×B 26 N×B R–R1 27 P–R3 P–B4 28 N–Q6 P–K5 29 N–Q4 B×N 30 R×B N–B5 31 N×NP N–Q6 32 R–N1 KR–N1 33 N–Q6 N×B 34 R×N R×RP 35 N×BP N–B3 36 P–N5 R–R8+ 37 K–R2 R–R4

38 N–Q6 R–N3 39 R–B2 R–R1 40 R–B6 R(1)–QN1 41 R(4)–B4

41...R×P 42 N×R R×N 43 R–B2 K–R2 44 R–B7 R–Q4 45 R–K7 R–KN4 46 R–R2 N–Q4 47 R–K8 N–B3 48 R–QN8 P–R4 49 P–N3 R–KB4 50 K–N2 P–N4 51 R–N6 P–N5 52 P–R4 K–N3 53 R–R7 R–B6 54 R–K7 K–B4 55 R–N5+ K–N3 56 R–N5+ **Resigns**

Karpov–Vaganian
Grunfeld Defence

1 P–QB4 N–KB3 2 N–QB3 P–Q4 3 P×P
N×P 4 N–B3 P–KN3 5 Q–N3 N–N3 6 P–Q4
B–N2 7 B–N5 B–K3 8 Q–B2 N–B3 9 R–Q1
0–0 10 P–K3 N–N5 11 Q–N1 P–QR4 12
B–K2 P–R5 13 0–0 P–R3 14 B–R4 P–QB3
15 P–KR3 N(5)–Q4 16 R–B1 P–R6 17 N×N
B×N 18 P–QN3

18 ... P–KB4 19 B–N3 N–Q2 20 B–QB4 N–B3
21 B–K5 K–B2 22 B×B+ Q×B 23 KR–Q1
KR–Q1 24 N–K1 N–Q2 25 B×B K×B 26
R–B3 Q–Q3 27 P–QN4 N–N3 28 N–B2 N–Q4
29 R–N3 R–R5 30 N×P R(1)–QR1 31 N–B4
Q–K3 32 R–Q2 R(1)–R3 33 N–K5 Q–Q3
34 N–Q3 P–N3 35 R–B2 P–K3 36 P–N5 P×P
37 R×P R–R2 38 R(5)–N2 R–R6 39 N–K5
R–B6 40 R×R N×R 41 R×P Q–Q4 42
Q–N3 Resigns

Karpov–Mikenas
Alekhine's Defence

1 P–K4 N–KB3 2 P–K5 N–Q4 3 P–Q4
P–Q3 4 N–KB3 B–N5 5 B–K2 N–QB3 6 P×P
KP×P 7 P–B4 N–B3 8 0–0 B–K2 9 P–KR3
B–R4 10 P–Q5 B×N 11 B×B N–K4 12
B–K2 0–0 13 N–B3 N(4)–Q2 14 B–K3
P–QR4 15 Q–B2 N–B4 16 P–R3 N(3)–Q2
17 P–QN4 P×P 18 P×P R×R 19 R×R
N–R3 20 Q–Q2 N×P 21 R–N1 N–R3 22
R×P N(3)–B4 23 R–R7 Q–N1 24 N–N5
B–Q1 25 Q–R2 Q–N3 26 R–R8 P–QB3
27 N×P P×P 28 N–B8 Q–N2 29 B–B3
N–K5 30 P×P N–B6 31 Q–R6 Q×Q 32
R×Q B–B3 33 R–R8 N–K4 34 B–B5 R–Q1
35 B–N6 N×B+ 36 P×N R–B1 37 B–B5
R–Q1

38 B–K7 R–K1 39 P–Q6 B×B 40 P–Q7
K–B1 41 P×R–Q+ K×Q 42 N–Q6+ K–Q2
43 N×P K–K3 44 N–Q8+ K–Q2 45 N–N7
N–K7+ 46 K–R2 K–K3 47 R–R4 B–B3 48
N–B5+ K–B4 49 N–Q3 K–N4 50 R–R5+
K–R3 51 P–B4 K–N3 52 K–N2 P–R3 53
K–B3 N–Q5+ 54 K–N4 K–B2 55 R–R7+
K–K3 56 P–B5+ K–Q3 57 R–R6+ K–K2
58 N–B4 K–B2 59 R–R7+ K–N1 60 N–R5
Resigns

39TH USSR CHAMPIONSHIP, LENINGRAD 1971

"I appeared in my second USSR Championship after winning one of the Semi-Finals in the
Latvian town of Daugavpils. That qualifying tournament had shown that I was clearly superior
to the semi-final level, and was no longer a novice grandmaster, but a real, fully-fledged one.
In addition, I had behind me a secret training match with Korchnoi. A match, which had ended
in a draw, and shown me that things were not as difficult as might have been expected.

Karpov–Klovan
Ruy Lopez

1 P–K4 P–K4 2 N–KB3 N–QB3 3 B–N5
P–QR3 4 B×N QP×B 5 0–0 P–B3 6 P–Q4
P×P 7 N×P N–K2 8 B–K3 N–N3 9 N–Q2
B–Q3 10 P–QB3 0–0 11 Q–N3+ K–R1 12
N–B5 B×N 13 P×B N–R5 14 Q×P Q–Q2
15 Q–N3 N×BP 16 N–B4 KR–K1 17 QR–Q1
QR–N1 18 Q–B2 Q–K3 19 P–QN3 N×B
20 N×N R–N4 21 KR–K1 R–K4 22 P–N3
K–N1

23 N–N2 R–K7 24 R×R Q×R 25 R–Q2
Q–B6 26 K–B1 R–K4 27 Q–Q3 Q×Q 28
R×Q K–B2 29 N–K3 K–K2 30 N–B4 R–KR4
31 P–KR4 B–B4 32 N–N2 R–B4 33 R–Q2
K–K3 34 N–Q3 B–Q3 35 R–K2+ K–Q2 36
R–K3 P–N4 37 P–QB4 P–B4 38 K–N2
P–B3 39 P–B3 P×P 40 P×P B–B5 41 R–K4
B–Q3 42 P–B4 Resigns

Karpov–Korchnoi
French Defence

1 P–K4 P–K3 2 P–Q4 P–Q4 3 N–Q2 P–QB4
4 KN–B3 N–QB3 5 KP×P KP×P 6 B–N5
B–Q3 7 P×P Q–K2+ 8 Q–K2 B×BP
9 N–N3 B–N3 10 N–K5 K–B1 11 B–KB4
Q–B3 12 B–N3 P–KR4 13 P–KR4 KN–K2
14 0–0–0 N×N 15 B×N Q×BP 16 B×P+
K×B 17 Q×N B–KB4 18 Q–K5+ P–B3
19 Q–K7+ K–N3

20 R–Q2 B–K6 21 R–B1 B×R+ 22 N×B
Q–Q5 23 R×B K×R 24 B–Q3+ K–B5
25 Q–Q6+ Q–K4 26 Q–N4+ P–Q5 27
N–K4 K–B4 28 Q×NP K–N5 29 B–K2+
K×P 30 P–KN3+ K–R6 31 N–B2+ K–R7
32 Q–R1+ K×P 33 N–K4+ K–B5 34 Q–B3
Mate

And so, before the 1971 Championship I was already entertaining the most ambitious of hopes. It is true that on this occasion the tournament was very strong. Among those playing were Mikhail Tal, Vasily Smyslov, Leonid Stein, Lyev Polugayevsky, Efim Geller... Altogether twenty-two contestants. Who was it who thought up such a marathon event?! A terrible idea! A normal tournament is one with sixteen to eighteen players. After more than seventeen rounds a player simply becomes 'glassy-eyed', and grows inordinately tired. In addition, the schedule adopted was really gruelling: three rounds, adjournments, two rounds, again adjournments, and only then a free day. Nowhere else in our country do they have to work like this— seven working days in a row. At the end of such an event, all a player its left with is arrogance and quick-temper—anything except the necessary desire to play.

On the whole I didn't play badly, but I was dogged by ill luck. After defending successfully against Smyslov, I weakened slightly and lost; against Vaganian I overlooked a simple combination. In an overwhelming position against Vladimir Savon (and with him in time-trouble!)

I missed a winning continuation, and then analysed the adjourned position poorly, and failed to utilize the chances still remaining—my opponent managed to draw. Incidentally, it was this that to a great extent pre-determined Savon's overall win in the Championship. We met in the eleventh round, and by the time the game was finished after the adjournment, the players had got through thirteen or fourteen games. Savon is the type of player who, after a defeat, normally 'cracks up', but here, on receiving such a 'stimulant', he began playing with great verve and overall did not lose a single game. I suffered other frustrations too. For instance, I didn't manage to win a technically won position against Balashov, where I had a mighty knight against his bad bishop.*

How do you explain that in the 1971 Championship (and also later, in the 1973 Premier League) no one 'made me a present' of even half a point—no one allowed me to save a lost position, and no one allowed me to win a drawn one? The opposite has also happened. Apart from the natural explanation (competitors in the Championship Finals are exceptionally strong and evenly-matched), there is also a semi-psychological one, if one can express it thus. It is not possible that fortune should smile on a chess player throughout his whole life, or that he should always be dogged by ill luck. But in individual complete tournaments this can happen. Take for instance Vladimir Tukmakov. This grandmaster rarely finishes in the middle—either his game is successful, everything goes well, and he takes one of the top places in the tournament, or else nothing works out, his pieces can literally do nothing right, and then he slides rapidly down the tournament table. With me, of course, it doesn't occur in such exaggerated form. But it so happened that those two USSR Championships (I have in mind those in 1971 and 1973) were events where I was not particularly lucky. But on the whole I cannot complain of being fated by ill luck in chess tournaments, and in other events—apart from USSR Championships—it is as if a certain compensating takes place. The reader may of course take all this 'pseudo-scientific' explanation as a joke, but after all, in every joke there is some degree of truth. But speaking quite seriously now, I have no wish at all that this long list of my misfortunes in the Leningrad Championship should be taken as a complaint about my luck in the tournament. Simply, that is what happened..."

This is what Mikhail Tal had to say after the finish of the Championship:

"Karpov is very talented, sober-minded beyond his years, and, I would say, over-modest at the board. Here is a little example. In the last round he had Black against Polugayevsky, for whom the Championship had not been very successful. It was soon clear that victory would give the Leningrad player one of the medals. But it was obvious that he had no real intention of playing for a win. I can definitely say that I (at his age!) would have taken risks. But Karpov played accurately and carefully for a draw, and contented himself with fourth place..."

We have already talked, and will have some more to say, about Anatoly Karpov's attitude to chess, but for the moment we will merely hear what he had to say after the 1971 USSR Championship:

"If the results had been different in the last round, I could have hoped for an even higher place, but as it was Tal and Smyslov agreed a draw together practically without any play, whereas I gained a draw with Black against Polugayevsky, which in itself is not at all simple... Yes, before the tournament I set myself the goal of finishing in the first three, so as to be ad-

* This description doesn't quite tie up with the game score (K.P.N.)

mitted into the following Zonal Championship without having to qualify. But if someone had said to me beforehand that I would take fourth place, I would not have been disappointed. Now, after analysing my games, I see that I could have done better. Too many chances were missed..."

We should add, jumping ahead, that Anatoly Karpov had no need to be disappointed that he did not finish in the first three (and therefore go straight into the 1972 USSR Zonal Championship). On the results of his subsequent brilliant performances, he was included by the International Chess Federation, by-passing the zonal stage, straight into the 1973 Interzonal Tournament!

Karpov–Taimanov
Sicilian Defence

1 P–K4 P–QB4 2 N–KB3 P–K3 3 P–Q4 P×P 4 N×P N–QB3 5 N–N5 P–Q3 6 B–KB4 P–K4 7 B–K3 N–B3 8 B–N5 B–K3 9 N(1)–B3 P–QR3 10 B×N P×B 11 N–R3 N–K2 12 N–B4 P–Q4 13 P×P N×P 14 N×N B×N 15 N–K3 B–B3 16 B–B4 Q×Q+ 17 R×Q R–B1 18 B–Q5 B×B 19 R×B K–K2 20 K–K2 K–K3 21 KR–Q1 P–B4 22 P–KN3 P–B5 23 P×P P×P 24 N–N2 R×P+ 25 K–B3 B–B4 26 N×P+ K–B3 27 N–Q3 R–QB1 28 R–Q7 P–N4 29 R–K1 K–N2 30 R–K4 R–B5 31 N–K5 R×R 32 K×R K–N1 33 P–B4 B–B1 34 N×P R–B7 35 N–N5 B–R3 36 N–K6 R×RP 37 K–B5

37 ... B×P 38 K×B R×P 39 R–KN7+ K–R1 40 R–R7 P–KR4 41 R×P P–N5 42 N–Q4 R–N7 43 K–B3 R–Q7 44 K–K3 R–QN7 45 K–B4 R–Q7 46 N–B5 R–QN7 47 K–N5 P–N6 48 R–R6+ K–N1 49 K–B6 Resigns

Karpov–Tseitlin
Ruy Lopez

1 P–K4	P–K4
2 N–KB3	N–QB3
3 B–N5	P–B4
4 N–B3	N–Q5?!

Premature activity.

5 B–R4	

5 B–B4 isn't bad, e.g. 5 ... P×P 6 N×N P×N 7 N×P or 5 ... N–KB3 6 P–Q3.

5 ...	N–KB3
6 N×P	P×P

After the game Tseitlin admitted that this move was bad and suggested the improvement 6 ... Q–K2 7 P–B4 P–QN4!? 8 N×NP N×N 9 B×N P×P with some initiative for the sacrificed pawn. But instead of 7 P–B4 White can play 7 N–B3 N×N+ 8 Q×N P×P 9 Q–N3, e.g. 9 ... P–B3 10 0–0 P–QN4 11 B–N3 P–Q4 12 R–K1 followed by P–Q3 with advantage to White.

If 6 ... B–B4 then 7 N–Q3 B–N3 8 P–K5 with a big initiative.

7 0–0	B–B4

Possibly 7 ... B–Q3 8 N–B4 (if 8 N–N4 0–0) 8 ... B–K2 was more solid but after

9 P–Q3 P×P 10 Q×P N–K3 11 N–K5 White still maintains his advantage.

8 N×KP

Korchnoi suggested 8 P–Q3 as being stronger.

8 ...	N×N
9 Q–R5+	P–N3
10 N×NP	N–KB3?

Correct was 10 ... Q–N4 11 Q×Q N×Q 12 N×R P–N4 (not 12 ... N–K7+? 13 K–R1 N–K5 14 P–Q3 N×P+ 15 R×N B×R 16 B–R6 winning) 13 B–N3 N×B 14 RP×N B–Q5 15 P–B3 B×N 16 P–Q4 with a slight advantage.

After the text the game ends in a hurricane.

11 Q–K5+!	**B–K2**
12 N×R	

Also strong is 12 R–K1 N–B6+ 13 P×N R–KN1 14 Q×B+ Q×Q 15 R×Q+ and White stays two pawns ahead.

12 ...	P–N4
13 Q×N(4)	P×B

The rest is carnage.

14 R–K1 K–B1 15 P–Q3 R–N1 16 Q–K5 N–N1 17 Q–KR5 K–N2 18 N–B7 Q–K1 19 B–R6+ N×B 20 Q×N+ K×N 21 Q×P+ K–B1 22 R–K3 R–N3 23 R–N3 Resigns

Karpov–Tukmakov
Sicilian Defence

1 P–K4 P–QB4 2 N–KB3 P–K3 3 P–Q4 P×P 4 N×P N–QB3 5 N–N5 P–Q3 6 P–QB4 N–B3 7 N(1)–B3 P–QR3 8 N–R3 B–K2 9 B–K2 0–0 10 0–0 P–QN3 11 B–K3 B–N2 12 R–B1 N–K4 13 Q–Q4 N(4)–Q2 14 P–B3 P–Q4 15 KP×P B–B4 16 Q–Q2 B×B+ 17 Q×B P×P 18 KR–Q1 R–K1 19 Q–B2 R–QB1 20 R–B2 Q–K2 21 B–B1 Q–Q3 22 R(2)–Q2 P–QN4 23 N×QP N×N 24 P×N N–B3 25 B–Q3 B×P 26 B–K4 R–K4 27 B×B R×B 28 R×R N×R 29 Q–Q4 Q–QN3 30 Q×Q N×Q

31 R–Q6 R–N1 32 R–QB6 K–B1 33 N–B2 R–QB1 34 R×R+ N×R 35 N–N4 P–QR4 36 N–B6 P–R5 37 K–B2 K–K1 38 K–K3 K–Q2 39 N–K5+ K–K3 40 K–Q4 P–B3 41 N–Q3 K–Q3 42 N–B4 P–N3 43 N–Q5 P–B4 44 P–KN4 N–R2 45 N–N4 P×P 46 P×P N–B1 47 N–Q3 N–K2 48 N–K5 K–K3 49 P–QR3 N–Q4 50 N–Q7 K–Q3 51 P–N5 N–K2 52 N–B8 N–B3+ 53 K–B3 N–K4 54 N×RP N–B6 55 K–N4 Resigns

ALEKHINE MEMORIAL TOURNAMENT, MOSCOW 1971

In the long history of chess there have been very few tournaments of such high class as the Alekhine Memorial, which took place in November to December 1971. There gathered in Moscow eighteen grandmasters—only grandmasters!—among whom were four who at various times had held the title of World Champion. Karpov was invited to take part in this tournament not only as a representative of the 'new wave', but also as a young grandmaster who had already achieved a number of good results...

There was, however, one drawback to this prestigious invitation, which Anatoly explained as follows:

"In the first half of 1971 I practically didn't play at all. Then from June onwards I hardly ever got away from the board. June—USSR Championship Semi-Final, July—Student Olympiad, August—two Team Championships (of the country and of the Armed Forces), September and October—USSR Championship Final. If the Alekhine Tournament had not been so outstanding and tempting, I would have had to decline the invitation".

One can understand Karpov—even of your favourite occupation you can become tired. The tiredness, it is true, can be compensated for by something else... The late virtuoso violinist David Oistrakh was a very strong chess player, and, despite his heavy commitments, took every opportunity to watch chess events; he was well acquainted with many grandmasters and masters. And at that Alekhine Memorial Tournament, Oistrakh made this very accurate comment: "The more often a creative person appears in front of a large audience, the better they understand him, and the greater the success he is assured of".

However, at that time it was by no means everyone who understood Karpov. When at the opening ceremony Anatoly couldn't manage to open his wooden souvenir doll, in which his tournament number was concealed, one of the spectators joked: "He isn't very strong. How is he going to last out to the end of such a difficult event?!" But he not only coped with all his difficulties, but even created one of the greatest sensations of 1971.

"Before the start of the tournament", Karpov relates, "a friend of mine said he hoped I would finish in the first ten. I thought to myself then that I could do better, and reckoned that I could finish in the top five. I was not happy with the draw, which necessitated an energetic start, whereas I did not feel any great desire to play. There was something not quite right. All the time I wanted more, but nothing definite would emerge, and I found it difficult to put my game together..."

The Central Railwaymen's Club in Moscow is situated on the square of the three rail terminals, and its auditorium is always overcrowded (it is perhaps for this reason that chess players very much like playing in this comfortable building, where the USSR Championship has often been held). However, it has to be said that the chess public is always very strict and exacting, and demands fighting and uncompromising play. In particular, an excessive number of short draws at the start of the Alekhine Memorial provoked dissatisfaction in the auditorium, and I remember how one of the more effusive spectators even shouted from his seat to the chief controller (an unprecedented occurrence at a chess tournament): "Comrade Kotov, won't you ban, once and for all, these draws!". The controller, himself an experienced grandmaster, became confused, which with him does not often happen, and instead of severely reprimanding, as would be usual, the disturber of the 'code of silence', helplessly spread his hands. By about the tenth round the play in the tournament had become more 'bloody'—either it was the influence of the spectators, or else the journalists, demanding that the grandmasters satisfy the desires of chess fans, but at any rate the number of draws became markedly lower. Imagine, in such a situation, the mood of Karpov, who after defeating early on a relatively weak participant—Lengyel of Hungary—had contrived in his other nine games to score only draws. The young twenty-year-old rationalist heard reproaches being directed his way. And he decided before the eleventh round:

"It's all or nothing! There are seven games left. I have the white pieces today, and there are some very difficult opponents to come. I can no longer go on retreating (or more correctly, standing still)."

5

Anatoly Karpov defeated Vlastimil Hort, and this game became for him the turning point in the Alekhine Tournament, and perhaps not only there.

Yes, this game was a success both in the competitive, and in the creative sense. Karpov's spirits immediately rose. In the end he even managed to win the special prize for the best finish, and together with Leonid Stein he became the winner of the Memorial Tournament. And what is most astonishing is that Karpov did not deviate in the least from the tactics which he had adopted from his very first tournament appearances. The sobriety in his play had not been transformed into scepticism (and according to one of the precise aphorisms of the writer Felix Krivin: "Scepticism is an intoxicated form of sobriety.") After the game with Hort, i.e. after his "reviving stimulant", the newcomer to tournaments of extra class inflicted an instructive defeat on the highly experienced David Bronstein. In that game the younger player "seized" a pawn almost in the opening, and above the noise of the press-centre the slow, quiet voice of Semion Furman could be heard saying: "When Tolya is ahead in material, he wins. About this I have no qualms". In the last round Karpov also defeated the then USSR Champion Vladimir Savon.

Karpov–Bronstein
Sicilian Defence

1 P–K4 P–QB4 2 N–KB3 P–Q3 3 P–Q4 P×P 4 N×P N–KB3 5 N–QB3 P–QR3 6 B–K2 P–K4 7 N–N3 B–K3 8 P–B4 Q–B2 9 0–0 QN–Q2 10 P–B5 B–B5 11 P–QR4 B–K2 12 B–K3 0–0 13 P–R5 P–QN4 14 P×P e.p. N×NP 15 K–R1 KR–B1 16 B×N Q×B 17 B×B R×B 18 Q–K2 R–N5 19 R–R2 P–R3 20 R(1)–R1 B–B1 21 R–R4 R–B1 22 R×R Q×R 23 Q×P

23 ... R×N 24 P×R Q×KP 25 Q–Q3 Q–KB5 26 R–KB1 Q–KR5 27 N–Q2 P–K5 28 Q–N3 Q×Q 29 P×Q P–Q4 30 R–QN1 B–Q3 31 K–N1 B×P 32 K–B1 B–B5 33 K–K2 N–R4 34 N–B1 B–K4 35 N–K3 B×P 36 R–N8+ K–R2 37 N×P N–N6+ 38 K–B2 B–Q5+ 39 K–K1 N×P 40 R–N4 N–K6+ 41 K–K2 B–B4 42 R–N5 N×N 43 R×B N–B5+

44 K–B2 K–N3 45 P–N3 N–K3 46 R–Q5 P–B4 47 P–B4 P–B5 48 P–B5 P–K6+ 49 K–B3 P×P 50 K×NP P–R4 51 P–B6 P–K7 52 K–B2 K–B3 53 R–Q7 Resigns

Karpov–Savon
Ruy Lopez

1 P–K4 P–K4 2 N–KB3 N–QB3 3 B–N5 P–QR3 4 B–R4 N–B3 5 0–0 N×P 6 P–Q4 P–QN4 7 B–N3 P–Q4 8 P×P B–K3 9 P–B3 B–QB4 10 QN–Q2 0–0 11 B–B2 B–B4 12 N–N3 B–KN3 13 N(B3)–Q4 B×N 14 P×B P–QR4 15 B–K3 N–N5 16 B–N1 P–R5 17 N–Q2 P–R6 18 Q–B1 R–R3 19 P×P R–QB3 20 Q–N2 N–B7 21 R–B1 N×B 22 R×R N×BP

23 N–B1 Q–Q2 24 N×N Resigns

After the tournament, comfortably ensconsed in an enormous room in the "Leningrad" Hotel, the same Semion Furman said to me:

"For me personally Tolya's success is no surprise, if only because over the last few years his results have been consistent, and have improved with every tournament. Of course, I did not think that he would share first place, but I guessed approximately the number of points he would score. I reckoned that he would score '+4' or '+5' (in chess language this is the difference between the number of wins and losses). The place in a tournament is not always determined by the points ratio, it all depends on how the battle for the leadership develops. But the even strength of the competitors meant that such a score would guarantee a very high place.

Caution, or circumspection", the trainer went on, "is his characteristic trait. This particularly pleased me even on our first acquaintance: it is not often that one comes across this valuable quality in a young player. But for subsequent, higher achievements, a healthy degree of risk and greater aggression are required. Yes, in order to attain more distant goals, there will have to be some experimenting. But this cannot be done in elimination events. There, as grandmaster Uhlmann puts it: 'There are no tricks!'."

Semion Furman said that, in the chess sense, Anatoly was on the whole a very attentive pupil. Perhaps that is how it was to start with, but then the pupil's judgement, and his point of view regarding his chess style, became more independent. Here is how Karpov viewed this question at that time:

"I still have a rather narrow opening repertoire—the consequence of the fact that I have little free time for working on expanding it. Of course, it would be nice to play sharper and more modern set-ups, but in my opinion this bears no direct relation to one's style. At any rate, I am happy with my style, and at present there is no point in changing it. Sacrifice a piece? Why not sacrifice, if, of course, it is correct. Only I do not intend to burn my boats, as some do—burning boats is not my speciality.

I am asked why it is that I play quickly (can it be, they say, that I am never in doubt as to what to play?), and why my games frequently end in draws... The rapidity of my play is not at all, as some think, due to the fact that everything is clear to me. Simply I don't wish to get into time trouble. So far this has happened to me two or three times in my life, and I realize that sometimes it is better to restrict oneself simply to a good move and not seek the very strongest, rather than suffer the dissatisfaction of defeat. Regarding draws, I normally go along simply to play chess, without thinking beforehand in terms of a draw. Half-points suit me if I do not get the sort of game I want, or if these half-points enable me to attain a desired result in the event. In general one has to learn not to lose, and wins will then come of their own accord.

Now everyone will no doubt be waiting for me to repeat this success, so as to demonstrate its legality, as it were. It is even said that one grandmaster is ready to lay a bet... But I never make bets on anything. And for the moment I do not feel pressure on me to demonstrate anything. I have to learn how to play. After all, in the end absolutely all the chess players in the world are engaged in learning how to play better".

When Botvinnik heard by telephone that Karpov had become one of the winners of the Alekhine Memorial, he exclaimed, according to the person who informed him: "Remember this day, 18th December 1971. A new chess star of the first magnitude has risen".

And a few days later, in a big article "What has the Old Year given us?", another Ex-World Champion, Tigran Petrosian, wrote:

"In view of the formidable strength of the participants in the Memorial Tournament, Karpov's success is especially remarkable. It is gratifying that he no longer simply creates hopes, but also justifies them. One tires of reading and hearing about young players who show they are excellent players, but... Excellent play is a rather relative concept. One cannot for ever remain a 'blue-eyed boy', showing 'creative promise', but constantly having too few points in the tournament table. Good play must be accompanied by good results. And now today, speaking about Karpov, I can say that I like the points he scores, I like his attitude to chess, his competitive character, and the way he husbands his resources. I liked the way that, towards the finish of the tournament, he raised his speed, having evidently reckoned beforehand that, thanks to his youth, he would have greater stamina than the older players, and with a burst overtook many of us, as if we were standing still.

I think that today it is Karpov who represents our chief hope, and perhaps it is he who in the coming years will become the most serious obstacle to Western players in search of the world chess crown".

Karpov–Hort
Sicilian Defence

1 P–K4	P–QB4
2 N–KB3	P–Q3
3 P–Q4	P×P
4 N×P	N–KB3
5 N–QB3	P–K3
6 P–KN4	

The enduring weapon devised by Keres. The desire to drive back the knight from KB3 and to create the conditions for an attack on the K-side is supported on tactical grounds.

6 ...	N–B3

6 ... P–KR3 is more of a hindrance to White's plan, but in this case too Black has his difficulties.

7 P–N5	N–Q2
8 B–K3	

A very sharp game with good prospects for White results after 8 N(4)–N5 N–N3

9 B–KB4 N–K4 10 Q–R5 P–N3 11 Q–R3, but we will not now embark on a discussion of opening theory.

8 ...	P–QR3
9 P–B4	

Nowadays I would possibly have preferred 9 R–KN1.

9 ...	B–K2

On 9 ... P–R3 my opponent was probably afraid of the move I was intending to make—10 N×P (strictly speaking, there is no alternative, since 10 P×P and 10 P–N6 are simply unfavourable on account of 10 ... Q–R5+). Boundless complications could then have arisen—10 ... P×N 11 Q–R5+ K–K2 12 B–R3 Q–K1 13 Q–R4—with consequences difficult to assess. It was just this that my tournament position demanded.

10 R–KN1	**N×N**

Normally Black is in no hurry to make this exchange, but here it is difficult for him to find an alternative. 10 ... Q–B2 looks too slow; it is not easy to decide on 10 ... 0–0, straight into the attack, and 10 ... N–B4 11 N×N P×N 12 B×N gives White a clear advantage.

11 Q×N	**P–K4**
12 Q–Q2	**P×P**
13 B×BP	**N–K4**

Bad for Black, of course, was 13 ... Q–N3 14 R–N3 Q×P 15 R–QN1 Q–R6 16 N–Q5.

14 B–K2	**B–K3**

Black cannot make the active move 14 ... Q–R4, since the resulting endgame is clearly advantageous to White: 15 N–Q5 Q×Q+ 16 K×Q B–Q1 17 QR–Q1 B–K3 18 K–B1.

15 N–Q5

Immediately! Otherwise the enemy queen takes up an active position (15 0–0–0 Q–R4!).

15 ...	**B×N**

16 P×B

Normally one tries to occupy the blockading square with a piece, and indeed, 16 Q×B would have left me with an advantage, since Black's QP would all the time need to be defended. But then my KP would in some instances also have required guarding, which could have cramped my white-squared bishop. Now, however, this bishop is unrestricted in its movements, especially since its black opposite number has already left the board.

16 ...	**N–N3**

Black's position is markedly inferior, and so Hort looks for a tactical solution to the problems facing him. He would have been condemned to passive defence after castling short, or after 16 ... Q–B2 and then 17 ... 0–0–0.

17 B–K3	**P–R3!?**

It is difficult to know what kind of mark to attach to this move—so great is the significance, not merely chess-wise, which is contained in it. It shows fighting spirit, and the desire to give the game a tactical turn. It also shows an accurate assessment of the position, with a clear understanding of its drawbacks. In short, it is a move which is risky for both sides!

18 P×P	**B–R5+**
19 K–Q1	

The white king is not embarrassed by the loss of castling. At the same time, right to the end of the game Black's king has such a possibility open to it, but does not manage to utilize it.

19 ...	**P×P**
20 B×KRP	**B–B3**

20 ... Q–B3 probably did not appeal to Black, since his bishop's mobility would then be severely reduced. Hort has planned an

ideal arrangement for his forces, but in chess there are two sides, and I in my turn was able to take appropriate counter-measures.

21 P–B3   B–K4

It would appear that Black has achieved his aim—he threatens 22 ... Q–R5, while after 22 B–KN5 Q–N3 23 B–K3 Q–B2 White has achieved very little. But White finds a very strong rejoinder.

22 R–N4!

No one is concerned (for the moment!) about the KRP. At present what is most important is not to allow the enemy queen to take up an active position on the K-side, where White's pieces are nevertheless slightly 'hanging'.

22 ...   Q–B3

22 ... B×RP was comparatively best, re-establishing material equality. But one can understand the Czech grandmaster—he wanted to complete his development.

23 P–KR4!

Now Black cannot play 23 ... N×P?—24 B–N7. And in general, it will soon be difficult to win back this pawn, which until quite recently was so helpless, but which now gradually acquires formidable strength. 23 ... 0–0–0 also fails, to 24 B–KN5.

23 ...   Q–B4

By defending against the threat of 24 P–R5, Black hopes to castle Q-side.

24 R–N4!

An excellent square for the rook! As before, 24 ... 0–0–0 is impossible—25 B–N4, and meanwhile the QNP is attacked.

24 ...   B–B3
25 P–R5   N–K2

Of course, this is a less respectable square than K4, but here such pseudo-activity on Black's part could have cost him a piece (after 26 R–KB4). In passing, it should be noted that all this time Black has had no opportunity to sacrifice the exchange by ... R×B.

26 R–KB4   Q–K4

27 R–B3

The rook, at times such an awkward piece, in the given position displays miraculous powers of manoeuvre. It creates one threat after another, and operates efficiently not only in attack, but also in defence. Thus Black achieves nothing now by 27 ... Q×RP 28 R×B Q–R8+ 29 B–B1 (the rook defends both bishops) 29 ... N–N1 30 Q–K1+, and White wins.

27 ...   N×P
28 R–Q3   R×B

There is nothing better—on 28 ... N–K2 there follows 29 B–B4.

29 R×N	Q–K5

Black appears to have everything under control, but...

30 R–Q3!

That rook again! A player is accustomed to all his pieces working hard, but I think that one would agree that, as regards rooks, this applies mainly to the endgame.

30 ...	Q–R8+

Black is forced to go in for this far from equivalent exchange.

31 K–B2	Q×R
32 Q×R	B–K4
33 Q–N5	

Preventing Q-side castling, and creating irresistible threats against Black's stranded king.

In this hopeless position Hort overstepped the time limit. The game was voted the best in the Alekhine Memorial, while the Yugoslav 'Informator' named it as one of the best creative achievements of the 1971 chess year. I must admit that I too am very fond of this game...

HASTINGS 1971/72

While the Alekhine Memorial Tournament had merely introduced Karpov into the family of top grandmasters, the 1971 Christmas International Tournament at Hastings, which opened ten days after the grandiose event in Moscow, once and for all "confirmed" Anatoly as a full member of this small family of players of extra-class... Indeed, if one moves ahead a little in time, and looks at this tournament from the end, say, of 1973, we see here all the winners of the coming Interzonal battles.

On New Year's Eve 1971, the newspaper "Soviet Sport" decided to seek an interview with Karpov, who was then in England. Getting hold of the telephone number in England proved to be rather a difficult matter. Then someone had a bright idea: "We must ask grandmaster Flohr, he always knows everything". Solomon Mikhailovich was as if expecting that they would turn to him for help—just before holidays it was always to him that one turned with requests and for reminiscences—but the unusual question caught even him unawares:

"Where could they be staying in Hastings?.. The chess Festivals have been held there since 1895, and I first played in one of the supporting tournaments, let's see, in 1930. Ah yes, now I remember that chess players who were mere mortals were always accomodated in the Waverley Hotel. Only the chess kings Capablanca and Alekhine were taken straight from the station to the Queen's Hotel, and the rest, who included me, had to demonstrate at the board their right to this privilege. In the end I was able to join the 'kings' after I had several times taken first prize at Hastings. Now it is more difficult to do this: in each of the tournaments, which have been held there for so many years, outstanding grandmasters take part. It is sufficient to recall the names of Botvinnik, Euwe, Smyslov, Spassky, Keres... No no, I don't like this listing of names—I am bound to forget someone and thereby offend them".

We phoned the Queen's Hotel, and straight to the phone came Anatoly Karpov:

"This is the third time that I will be seeing in the New Year abroad. The first time this happened was in Czechoslovakia in 1967, and then in Holland I celebrated New Year 1968. On each of those occasions I was fortunate, and took first place. Whether this will happen here, where, apart from Korchnoi and myself, those taking part include grandmasters Byrne, Gligoric, Najdorf, and Unzicker, and well-known masters Andersson, Mecking, Pfleger, Keene and others, I wouldn't dare to say...

We arrived in England via the route Moscow–Stockholm–Oslo–London. At the airport of the Swedish Capital we met Andersson, who was booked on the next flight (however, for some reason he arrived an hour earlier than us). From London we went on by train. During this short journey—a little less than an hour and a half—I had time to gain a mass of non-chess impressions. It was very strange, for instance, to see decorated Christmas trees surrounded not by snow, as at home, but by green grass: the temperature was plus nine degrees! (In shop windows and on advertisements the Father Christmases were amusing—just like people of my own age, and without any beards.)*

On 31st December and 1st January we play chess. If a game held on the last day of the Old Year has to be adjourned, we sit down to resume it at exactly nine o'clock in the evening local time, just when in Moscow it will be striking midnight. Of course I will remember my home, my relatives and friends, but... much will depend on the position I am in. The Christmas Festival, during which it is customary to be pleasant to each other here, has already passed, and I can't count on receiving any presents..."

Later Karpov went on:

"The Hastings International Tournament has for a long time normally comprised ten players. In recent years this formula has become obsolete. Over the short distance the players avoided taking risks, since even just one defeat could have a fatal effect on the final result. The tournament tables became studded with draws, and the element of fight was reduced to the minimum. Such a situation did not suit either the players, or the tournament organizers. The English therefore decided that it was necessary to break with tradition, and to increase the number of competitors. This year sixteen players have been invited to take part in the main tournament.

I came to Hastings straight after the Alekhine Memorial, and felt fatigued. An 'echo' of the Moscow Tournament unexpectedly sounded when the draw was being made.

To everyone's amusement I picked 'my' number fourteen, which I played under in Moscow! How I found it, I don't know, but I certainly wasn't displeased. It is true that it gave me Black against nearly all my main rivals, but every cloud has a silver lining: against the weaker players I had the white pieces, and it was easier to beat them.

The conditions in the tournament hall, although it was quite adequate in size, proved to be very difficult. Our tournament was held alongside a master tournament, and there was a pretty large number of players and spectators. The public was only some two or three yards away, and all their conversations and remarks carried to us.

The tournament began well for me. After drawing in the first round with Pfleger, I won three games in a row, and after another draw again scored three victories. Here I sensed that my strength was on the wane. Over the last eight months I had played about a hundred games, and to be honest I was simply worn out.

---

* I can't imagine what Karpov is referring to! (K.P.N.)

The question of first place was decided in my game against the Englishman Markland. By incredible efforts I managed to overcome my opponent, and thus shared first place.

Karpov–Markland
French Defence

1 P–K4 P–K3 2 P–Q4 P–Q4 3 N–QB3 B–N5 4 P–K5 P–QB4 5 P–QR3 B×N+ 6 P×B Q–B2 7 N–B3 N–K2 8 P–QR4 P–QN3 9 B–QN5+ B–Q2 10 B–Q3 QN–B3 11 0–0 P–KR3 12 R–K1 N–R4 13 Q–Q2 R–QB1 14 P–R4 0–0 15 Q–B4 P–B4 16 P×P e.p. R×P 17 Q×Q R×Q 18 P×P P×P 19 N–K5 B–B1 20 P–QB4 N(4)–B3 21 B–N2 N–N5 22 P–QR5 R–B1 23 B–R3 P×P 24 N×P R–B5 25 N–Q6 N×B 26 P×N R×RP 27 N–K4 R–R4 28 KR–QB1 B–N2 29 N×P B–Q4 30 P–B3 R–B4 31 P–R6 R–B2 32 N–K4 N–B4 33 B–B5 R–QB1 34 B–B2 R(2)–B2 35 R×R R×R 36 R–N1 N–K2 37 R–N8+ K–R2 38 K–R2 N–N3 39 N–B5

R–B3

40 R–Q8 R–B2 41 R–Q7 R×R 42 N×R B–B3 43 N–N8 B–N4 44 B×P N–K2 45 B–N6 N–B1 46 B–B5 K–N3 47 P–R7 N×P 48 B×N P–K4 49 P–Q4 P×P 50 B×P K–B2 51 P–B4 52 P×P P×P 53 K–N3 K–N3 54 K–B3 K–B4 55 P–N3 **Resigns**

It was a particularly difficult game, remembering that only three rounds earlier I had been 1½ points ahead, and that now I was behind. It is curious that six months later at the Student Olympiad I defeated the same Markland without the least difficulty.

The battle for third place was between Byrne and Mecking. Success went to the Brazilian player, or more correctly, not success, but fortune. Thus Pfleger, in a superior position against Mecking, forgot to make his fortieth move, and lost on time. There was a very ugly incident in the Mecking–Botterill game. The players were in time trouble, with some two or three minutes left for eight moves. Mecking placed his hand on the clock, and would not allow the Englishman to press it. This unnerved Botterill, and two moves later he lost the game. Everyone was extremely angry".

Karpov–Byrne
Sicilian Defence

1 P–K4	P–QB4
2 N–KB3	N–QB3
3 P–Q4	P×P
4 N×P	N–KB3
5 N–QB3	P–Q3
6 B–KN5	B–Q2
7 Q–Q2	R–B1
8 0–0–0	N×N
9 Q×N	Q–R4

A well-known theoretical position has been reached.

10 P–B4

The alternative is 10 Q–Q2.

| 10 ... | P–KR3 |

10 ... P–K3 11 P–K5 P×P 12 P×P B–B3 used to be played here.

| 11 B–R4 | P–KN4 |
| 12 P–K5 | |

This position too is not new. A game from a certain Yugoslav tournament continued 12 ... B–N2, which led to great complications. The variation 13 B–K1 N–R4 14 N–Q5 Q×P 15 N×P would appear to be in White's favour, but I think that Black's idea is worth analysing.

12 ...	P×B
13 P×N	P–K3
14 B–K2	

A good move. Depending on the situation, the white-squared bishop can be moved to KB3 or KR5, from where it will control important squares.

14 ...	B–B3
15 KR–K1 ·	R–KN1
16 B–B3	

It wasn't easy for Black to decide on his next move, and it was no accident that Byrne thought for 20 minutes here.

| 16 ... | K–Q2 |

Black plans to evacuate his king to the Q-side. I managed to find a path leading to a clear positional advantage.

17 R–K5!	Q–N3
18 Q×Q	P×Q
19 B–R5	

Black cannot now defend his KBP. A forcing variation begins, with each side attempting to 'eat' as many of the opponent's pawns as possible.

19 ...	R×P
20 B×P	R×RP
21 B×P+	K–B2
22 R–K3	

White's position is better, since his pawns on the KB-file are more dangerous than Black's on the rook's file. In addition, Black's king's bishop is shut out of the game. Black now has a problem—to which square should he move his rook? Perhaps he should have moved it to QR1, but it wasn't easy to decide on this, since the black king is making for QN1.

22 ...	R–Q1
23 N–Q5+	B×N
24 R×B	

In spite of the opposite-coloured bishops, White's position is clearly superior, since Black has some very weak pawns.

| 24 ... | R–B7 |

By provoking the advance of the pawn at KB4, Black prepares to bring out his bishop to KR3.

| 25 P–B5 | P–R4 |
| 26 R–QB3+ | K–N1 |

27 P–R4

I am not altogether convinced about the correctness of this plan of attacking the king. Possibly I should have dealt with the enemy passed pawns, but that seemed to me too lengthy a way.

27 ...	R–B5
28 P–R5	P×P
29 R×RP	R–KN5
30 R(3)–QR3	K–B2
31 R–N5	

Black's QNP is in danger, and cannot be defended. His one means of counter-play is the continuation 31 ... R–N8+ 32 K–Q2 B–R3+. Byrne, however, begins with the second check, and allows the white king to calmly hide at QR2.

31 ...	B–R3+
32 K–N1	R–N6
33 R–R7	R–QN1
34 B–Q5	R–N8+
35 K–R2	R–KB8
36 R(7)×P+	R×R
37 R×R+	K–Q1
38 B–K6	P–R6

The last chance...

39 R–Q7+

In time trouble, Byrne noticed that in the event of 39 ... K–B1 40 R–KR7+ K–Q1 41 R×B P–R7 White manages to stop the pawn by 42 B–Q5. And so he played

39 ...	K–K1

but after

40 R–QB7

Black resigned in view of inevitable mate.

Karpov–Mecking
Sicilian Defence

1 P–K4	P–QB4
2 N–KB3	P–Q3
3 P–Q4	P×P
4 N×P	N–KB3
5 N–QB3	P–QR3
6 B–K2	

I frequently employ this system, and know it quite well. White avoids the heavily-analysed forcing continuations associated with 6 B–KN5.

6 ...	P–K4

6 ... P–K3 leads to the Scheveningen Variation.

7 N–N3	B–K3
8 P–B4	Q–B2
9 P–QR4	

An essential part of White's plan. He not only prevents 9 ... P–QN4, but also aims to blockade Black's Q-side pawns by P–R5. In reply Black normally plays 9 ... B–K2 or 9 ... QN–Q2. But Mecking was unhappy about something, and he thought for a long time before choosing a continuation which, though new, was by no means the strongest.

9 ...   N–B3?!

A dubious move. Black prevents 10 P–R5, but at a high price: he is now forced to exchange his bishop, and this allows his opponent the opportunity to dominate on the white squares.

10 P–B5   B×N
11 P×B   Q–N3

If White should manage to castle K-side and post his bishop at QB4, his advantage will be overwhelming. Mecking attempts to hinder this plan.

12 B–KN5   B–K2
13 B×N   B×B
14 N–Q5   Q–R4+
15 Q–Q2   Q×Q+
16 K×Q   B–N4+
17 K–Q3   0–0
18 P–KR4   B–Q1

On KR3 the bishop might have found itself in a dangerous position (after P–KN4).

19 QR–QB1

For the moment the white knight cannot be 'smoked out' of Q5, since on 19 ... N–K2 there follows 20 N×N+ B×N 21 R–B7. If on the other hand 19 ... N–Q5, then 20 P–QN4.

19 ...   P–QR4
20 K–Q2   R–N1
21 P–KN4

White's plan is clear—a K-side pawn storm, which after B–B4 will become highly dangerous. Realizing this, Mecking seeks salvation in an ending with opposite-coloured bishops.

21 ...   N–N5
22 B–B4   N×N
23 B×N

The position has stabilized. White has a big advantage, with his opponent completely deprived of counter-play. Mecking pinned great hopes on his next move, thinking that he would manage to blockade White's K-side pawns and halt their advance.

23 ...   P–KN4
24 P×P e.p.   RP×P
25 K–Q3   K–N2
26 P–R5   B–N3

26 ... B–N4 27 R–B7 is no better.

27 R–R3

So as after exchanges on KN6 to seize the KR-file.

27 ...   B–B4
28 R–B1   P–B3

Forced. The threat was 29 P–R6+.

29 P×P	**K×P**
30 R(1)–KR1	**QR–K1**
31 R–R7	**K–N4**

Mecking was in time trouble, and was afraid of the mating threats after R(1)–R5.

32 K–K2	**K–B5**

Here a 'murderous' idea came into my head, and I played

        33 R(1)–R3

My opponent did not notice the threat, and replied

33 ...	**B–Q5**

But even on the best defence—33 ... K×P 34 R–R1 R–KN1 35 B×R and 36 R–KB1—White wins easily.

        34 R–N7

Mecking lost on time, although he could have also resigned in view of the inevitable mate.

STUDENT OLYMPIADS, PUERTO RICO 1971 AND GRAZ 1972

World Student Team Championships, or, as they are also called, "little Olympiads", are held on exactly the same basis as "adult" Nations' Tournaments—each team has four main players and two reserves. However, it would be incorrect to separate completely these youth events from those "adult" Olympiads, since even "dads" of up to twenty-seven years have the right to appear for the students. It is no accident, therefore, that the teams here are often very strong, and for some teams famous grandmasters appear—the same participants as in the World Olympiads. But even so, when the 1971 Soviet Student Team arrived in Mayagüez (a relatively small town in Puerto Rico), everyone was surprised and even a little afraid to see as many as three grandmasters among them.

"We decided once and for all the question of who should play on which board", Karpov later related. "The main criterion both then and in the future was taken to be the results in the USSR Championship Finals. On top board for us was Vladimir Tukmakov, then came Yury Balashov, and then me—that was the order in which we finished in the previous Championship of the country. The team also included the very strong masters Mikhail Podgayets, Gennady Kuzmin, and Yury Razuvayev. I am quite convinced that if the bottom boards on our team had suddenly played at the top, and vice versa, the overall result of the winners would not have changed—so strong and evenly-balanced was our team. We came ahead of the second prize winners by eight clear points, and each member of our team also took first place on his own board.

We managed to break this record a year later in the Austrian town of Graz, where we finished now nine points ahead of our nearest rivals. By that time there had been some changes in our team (one more grandmaster had been added), and the first three boards were now in reverse order. Thus our team in 1972 was: Karpov, Balashov, Tukmakov, Vaganian, and the masters Podgayets (from Odessa) and Yury Anikayev (from the Siberian town of Novokuznietsk). I will always remember the Student Olympiads for their friendly atmosphere, and for the excellent 'climate' within the team... But why am I talking about them in the past tense? Perhaps I'll still have the opportunity to play..."

Anatoly Bikhovsky, the permanent trainer of the USSR youth teams, recalls with particular relish the Student Olympiads of 1971 and 1972:

"We have had, and will again have, excellent teams, but those I will remember for ever. It is no accident that these lads now battle for the highest places in any tournament, while regarding their interrelations, it is characteristic that Balashov, for instance, has frequently advised Karpov on opening problems, and that Razuvayev became one of Karpov's trainers after the latter had won the title of World Champion.

Incidentally", Bikhovsky continues, "those two Student Olympiads really 'revealed' Karpov to me. Take for instance this curious detail. Before the last round in Puerto Rico, Karpov had seven points out of seven! And suddenly he quite calmly agreed to a draw with a relatively weak player from Columbia... I didn't immediately understand this decision—surely this can't be lack of ambition, was my first thought. It was only later that I realized that what was important to Karpov was the overall result, the victory of his team, and that a striving for cheap, showy effects was foreign to his nature. Even then, in 1971, the ease and elegance of his play left an indelible impression on me. He was normally the first to finish his game, after spending not more than an hour on his clock. After losing to him, his opponents appeared somehow confused, it seemed that they could not quite understand the young grandmaster's ideas and moves. In my opinion, Karpov has such an original style of play that it is even difficult to name his predecessor as a chess player—and this is always a sign of real talent. I repeat, I was simply staggered by my discovery of Karpov...

I must mention one other characteristic of Karpov", the USSR youth team trainer adds. "He became the real leader of our group, everyone turned to him for advice, all asked for his help in the analysis of adjourned positions (and in this he is a genuine virtuoso!), and Karpov worked like a Trojan for the team.

I recall how in Graz in 1972 he came up against the West German grandmaster Robert Hübner. We always had a difficult match against the West German team, and here, in addition, Hübner was leading Karpov in the battle for the best result on first board. This was the same Hübner who had lost in the Candidates' Match by only the minimum margin to Ex-World Champion Petrosian (and the same Hübner who, soon after the Student Olympiad, was to again play brilliantly in the World Olympiad at Skopje). This was in every respect a vital encounter, it was to determine, as it were, the relative strengths for years to come, and to show how Karpov appeared in comparison with the leading young Western grandmaster. Anatoly showed that his positional understanding was both deeper, and more subtle".

Karpov–Rogoff
English Opening

1 P–QB4 P–K4 2 N–QB3 N–KB3 3 P–KN3 B–N5 4 B–N2 0–0 5 P–Q3 P–B3 6 Q–N3 B–R4 7 N–B3 P–Q4 8 0–0 P–Q5 9 N–QR4 QN–Q2 10 P–K3 P×P 11 B×P R–K1 12 P–QR3 B–B2 13 QR–Q1 B–Q3 14 P–Q4 P×P 15 N×P B–B1 16 Q–B3 Q–K2 17 KR–K1 Q–K4 18 P–QN4 Q–KR4 19 P–R3 N–N3 20 N×N P×N 21 P–N4 Q–N3 22 B–B4 B–Q2

23 N–B3 R×R+ 24 R×R N–K1 25 Q–Q2 R–Q1 26 N–R4 **Resigns**

Karpov–Hübner
Sicilian Defence

1 P–K4 P–QB4 2 N–KB3 P–K3 3 P–Q4 P×P 4 N×P P–QR3 5 B–Q3 B–B4 6 N–N3 B–R2 7 0–0 N–QB3 8 Q–K2 P–Q3 9 B–K3 B×B 10 Q×B N–B3 11 P–QB4 0–0 12 R–Q1 Q–B2 13 N–B3 N–K4 14 QR–B1 P–QN3 15 B–K2 B–N2 16 P–B4 N–N3 17 P–N3 KR–Q1 18 P–QR3 QR–B1 19 N–Q4 B–R1 20 P–N3 N–K2 21 B–B3 R–N1 22 P–QR4 Q–B4 23 R–Q3 P–K4 24 N(4)–K2 P×P 25 P×P Q×Q+ 26 R×Q N–N3 27 R–Q1 K–B1 28 R(3)–Q3 N–K1 29 K–B2 R(Q1)–B1 30 K–N3 N–K2 31 N–Q4 R–B4

32 R(1)–Q2 B–N2 33 N–B2 P–KN4 34 P×P R×NP+ 35 K–B2 N–N3 36 B–R1 R–B1 37 R–N3 R(1)–B4 38 N–K3 N–K2 39 B–B3 R×R 40 P×R R–K4

41 P–KN4 P–QR4 42 R–Q1 B–B3 43 N(B3)–Q5 N–B1 44 N–B5 B×N 45 BP×B N–K2 46 N–K3 N–N1 47 N–B4 R–K2 48 N×NP R–N2 49 N–B4 R×P 50 R–QR1 N(N1)–B3 51 N×RP R–N7+ 52 K–K3 N–Q2 53 N–B6 R–N6+ 54 K–B4 N–K4 55 N×N P×N+ 56 K–N3 N–Q3 57 K–B2 R–N7+ 58 K–N1 R–N2 59 P–R5 R–R2 60 P–R6 K–K2 61 K–B2 K–Q2 62 K–K3 N–B5+ 63 K–Q3 N–N3 64 B–K2 K–Q3 65 K–K3 N–Q2 66 R–R1 N–B1 67 R–R6+ K–K2 68 P–Q6+ K–Q1 69 B–N5 R–R1 70 R–R5 P–B3 71 R–R6 R–N1 72 B–B6 R–N6+ 73 K–Q2 R–QR6 74 R×PB R–R7+ **and Black resigned**

20TH OLYMPIAD, SKOPJE 1972

In the USSR Central Chess Club there is a special glass case for the exhibiting of prizes. Among the numerous trophies won by Soviet players, perhaps the most valuable is the large gold Hamilton–Russell Cup. An English Lord established this award for the strongest team in the World in 1927, when the first Chess Olympiad was held in his country.

Since then the International Chess Federation (FIDE) has staged the Olympiad, or, as it is also called, "Tournament of Nations", once every two years. It is held under the motto of the FIDE: "We are all one family", and the only time that chess players were unable to meet together was during the years of the Second World War, and immediately after it. In 1950, after a break of eleven years, this wonderful tradition was revived.

In 1952 at Helsinki, a team from the Soviet Union competed for the first time, and the Hungarians (twice former winners of the Olympiad), Germans, Yugoslavs, even the Americans —four-time winners, as well as the other favourites, had to concede victory to them. Since then the life of the Cup has become much quieter—it has a permanent residence permit in Moscow, from where it departs only with its owners to the "Tournament of Nations", and each time on its golden rim is inscribed one and the same name—"USSR".*

The popularity of Chess Olympiads is enormous. While in the first of them sixteen teams took part, to the 20th, Jubilee Olympiad in the Yugoslav town of Skopje, the representatives of sixty-three states arrived.

The town of Skopje has twice been born. It appeared some two thousand years ago, when the first Macedonian settlements were made on the banks of the river Vardar. After a terrible earthquake in 1963, Skopje, like the Phoenix, rose from the ashes. People from throughout the world extended a helping hand to the Yugoslav town, which became a symbol of international solidarity. And now only a memorial—the ruined building of the old railway station, with a clock stopped at the moment of the first underground tremor—reminds one of this terrible catastrophe.

However the special preparations for the Olympiad (which began two years before the event) demanded additional efforts, and great capital investment. New hotels were constructed: the stylish "Continental" in the centre of the town, where wealthy tourists and the majority of the delegates were accomodated, and, like a comfortable Alpine hotel, the "Panorama", situated outside the town, close to the mountains, where only a few teams stayed, including that from the USSR. Before the start of the Olympiad, an Olympic village was also built, and three buildings of what is now a permanent trade fair came into operation—it was here, in these splendidly light and spacious halls, that the two events were held (the Ladies' Olympiad was held simultaneously in Skopje). Chess tables were placed around the edge of the main hall, and the spectators were accommodated on the multi-tier "slopes" of an enormous cone, which was erected inside this circular hall. From the flat, truncated summit of this "hillock" picture,s of the boards with the most interesting games were transmitted by closed-circuit television to monitors set up in the press centre. The Olympiad was served by a variety of eleven special service agencies. Several hundred people worked in these: one hundred translators, eighty demonstrators, seventy controllers, one hundred game copiers, fifty technicians, two hundred drivers, as well as doctors and transport officials. The service personnel were dressed in an unusual uniform, and before the start of the round each competitor was handed a packet of chocolates and waffles. All this gave the event a particularly festive nature.

The Olympiad occupied a prominent place in the everyday life of Yugoslavia. On the one free day a special plane took a large delegation of players to Belgrade, where they were received by President Tito. The Marshall stood in the middle of a large hall, and a long chain of famous chess players filed past him. He shook hands with each of them, and with some exchanged a few words. Then Tito was photographed with a group of Champions. Straight from the Presidential Palace the players were taken again to the airport, from where they returned to Skopje.

The sixty-three teams were divided into eight semi-final groups. In making this division, account was taken of the average rating of each team according to the system devised by the American Professor Árpád Élő, which was worked out from the individual ratings of the members of each team. The formula by which this rating is evaluated depends both on the number of games played, and on the strength of the opponents that a player meets. All the mathematical operations at the Olympiad were carried out by several young men and a single computer. It made forecasts, and predicted almost faultlessly the results of the semi-finals.

---

* This was obviously written before the 1978 Buenos Aires Olympiad! (K.P.N.)

The average rating of the USSR team was, of course, the highest — 2625 (it is normally considered that 2600 is the "threshold" of extra-class). There followed: Yugoslavia—2527, Hungary —2509, West Germany—2498, Czechoslovakia — 2483, East Germany—2460, Bulgaria — 2449, USA — 2446 (the team was not only without Fischer, who had demanded an extra appearance fee, but also Evans and Lombardy, and had the eighth highest average rating in the Olympiad).

Each team consists of four main players and two reserves, although such a division is quite arbitrary, since—at any rate in the Soviet team—the load falls equally on practically all members of the team, and depends only on their form, and on how they feel at a particular time. To be frank, the selection of the USSR Olympic team is a far from painless process: it is a great honour to be in the team, and many wish, and have the right, to be granted this honour. At the ten Olympiads held since 1952, only fourteen Soviet grandmasters had been included in the team, and for the Olympiad in Skopje they were joined by Anatoly Karpov and Vladimir Savon, as first and second reserves respectively. The final composition of the USSR team to be sent to Skopje was settled only a few days before the flight to Yugoslavia. The names of five grandmasters were known, but as for the sixth... The return of the Soviet delegation from Reykjavik was awaited. Could Spassky lead the team following his extremely difficult World Championship Match? Alas, on his return from Iceland it was clear that the Ex-World Champion was very tired, and could not take part in the Olympiad. At the last moment the USSR Champion Savon was included in the team.

I (as correspondent for "*Soviet Sport*" and the weekly "*64*") shared a room with Mikhail Tal, while Karpov and Savon were in the adjacent room. Incidentally, all the hotels and the Olympic village, in which some of the players were living, were especially strictly guarded at that time, since the event in Skopje came soon after the bloodshed at the Olympic Games in Munich. The security was in evidence even in the vicinity of the Panorama Hotel, along a road leading to the hills, where many players went for a constitutional, the first to discover this path having been Ex-World Champion Botvinnik, an honoured guest at the Olympiad.

Petrosian and Tal, who made their debuts in the 1958 Olympiad, told Karpov and Savon in humorous terms about their "mishaps" as reserves, so as to prepare the young players for the fact that, by tradition, the USSR would field its "main" team for the first match.

"Do you remember, Misha", said Petrosian, "how the 'old men' ill-treated us. We worked away at the board for a whole week, but when the football match between the Soviet Union and England was televised, we weren't granted our day off."

"That's right", joined in Tal in the same cheerful tone. "I was always ready to play chess. But that day was an exception. But what can you do: a player making his debut has a difficult rôle, especially if formally he is listed as a reserve. And weren't you also a reserve, Tigran, in 1960? What a difficult schooling you had to go through!"

"It was psychological preparation", came the swift reply, and the young lads' spirits improved still further when they remembered that both Tal, only two years after his first Olympiad, and Petrosian, within five years, had become World Champion...

Beginning with the second round, Karpov and Savon were included in the team, but... with different results. Savon was too nervous, played badly, and as result was forced to spend the greater part of his time, as footballers say, "on the substitutes' bench". Karpov's appearance, on the other hand, was one of the brightest happenings in the Olympiad. It is interesting to note that on this occasion Anatoly did not operate in his now customary circumspect manner, but much more diversely and sharply. He avoided exchanging pieces, and later, explaining his strategy, said that he feared that exchanges would bring nearer the endgame, and with it the possibility of a draw. The USSR team had an untroubled passage through the Semi-Final, apart from when the first "alarm signal" sounded during the match with Cuba, when at first the Soviet grandmasters found themselves in difficulties. However, this does not apply to Anatoly Karpov, who on that day played an excellent game against the most experienced player in the Cuban team. Straight from the opening E. Cobo came under heavy positional pressure from the young grandmaster. He spent great efforts on carrying out a pseudo-freeing manoeuvre on the Q-side, while Karpov, in the meantime, had directed all his pieces against Black's K-side. The offensive was begun by the swift advance of a white pawn...

Botvinnik gives the following advice: "If Tal sacrifices a piece—take it, if I do—check the variations, and if it is Petrosian—decline the sacrifice". In stating this, our old Champion, a subtle psychologist, evidently wished to emphasize the difference in attitude to risk on the part of representatives of different playing styles. Positional players check everything most carefully, and therefore their rare sacrifices normally bring accurately calculated dividends within a few moves. Karpov, although he differs from Petrosian, is also close (at any rate, that's how it was in 1972) to the fraternity of positional players. At any event his opponent Cobo, without thinking, declined the piece sacrifice offered, but even this did not save the Cuban.

The Olympiad provided much work for the statisticians. They even discovered, among other things, who weighed less—Anatoly Karpov, or his contemporary from Sweden, Ulf Andersson, who had just become a grandmaster. It was somehow calculated that in the first half of the Olympiad the greatest number of autographs was signed by Mikhail Tal; he was followed by the Belgrade grandmaster Ljubomir Ljubojevic, and only a little behind them was Anatoly Karpov. However, it must be said that Karpov soon began to threaten quite seriously Tal's popularity, which formerly was unsurpassed in Yugoslavia (the Ex-World Champion would be recognized on any street of the Old Town, where youngsters would march after him, and his appearance in the press centre would, as if by order, bring reporters to their feet, armed with microphones and cameras). The same journalists became more and more interested in Karpov, and tried to persuade me, as a compatriot of the popular grandmaster, to make arrangements regarding an interview, which was "absolutely essential" for their publication. Soon Karpov had to be shielded from the journalists, almost as had been the case with Fischer. But what could one do—new stars were wanted. And it was not just the reporters. The veteran chess master and patron I. Turover, who had arrived from the USA, did not take his eyes off the young Soviet grandmaster, and said that he saw him as a rival to Fischer. He was not mistaken...

Anatoly Karpov himself takes up the story:

"And so, the Soviet team approached the final in good spirits. We were a little disconcerted by Savon's uncertain play, but nevertheless reckoned that everything would go well.

The first round pairings brought us up against the Hungarian team, which was strong, young and promising, and offered a serious danger in the battle for the highest places. Our trainers decided to field our full side. I was of the opinion that such an arrangement was not the most effective in a match against the Hungarians. And this is why. Petrosian normally plays badly against Portisch, and is unlikely, so I thought, to manage to win here. The other player with the white pieces is Smyslov, who nowadays rarely 'calculates variations', but relies in the main on his intuition and experience. But without concrete calculation he has little chance of success against such a solid positional grandmaster as Forintos.

Therefore the main weight of responsibility regarding the outcome of the match lies on the shoulders of those playing Black... But my reasoning ran counter to established tradition —that of playing the main team in the first round. Unfortunately, my worst fears were confirmed... All our misfortunes developed suddenly during the fifth hour of play. And what surprised me more than anything during the Olympiad was that these 'misunderstandings' in the match with the Hungarians did not prove to be accidental phenomena. At Skopje we managed to mess up more than one match which was at first going well for us. We lost this one by the score of 1½–2½.

Defeats are always unpleasant, especially against one's main rivals. Nevertheless, the following day we set off in cheerful mood for our match with West Germany. On the top board a crucial game was expected between the recent opponents in the Candidates' Match, Hübner and Petrosian.

The match with the West Germans proceeded with a marked advantage to the Soviet team, although the Germans have long been considered difficult opponents for us. And it was only a genuinely dramatic incident in Petrosian's game which prevented us from achieving a big score. What happened was this. From the opening Petrosian got into a difficult position, but defended with amazing tenacity, and, as in the good old days, emerged with honour from a fierce battle. For his last seven moves he left himself with five minutes, in a position where a draw was becoming more and more obvious.

After his difficult defence, one could understand Petrosian's desire to force a draw as quickly as possible, by making the strongest possible moves. And on his next four moves he used up... all his remaining time.

The Olympiad organizers, with the idea of helping players in time trouble, had ordered clocks with a flag which fell at the point when the minute hand was half way along it. The second half of the flag indicated the time remaining by figures, inscribed on the dial in small print. This was only in theory convenient, since a player who is short of time has no opportunity to read figures, but determines the time remaining by the position of the flag.

Tigran Petrosian had no suspicion of this peculiarity of his clock. On glancing at it (as it later turned out, some two to three seconds before the control), he thought that he still had sufficient time, and calmly continued thinking over his move. Almost immediately a controller came up and announced that he had lost on time. Angry and confused, Petrosian got up slightly from his chair, picked up the clock, looked closely at the flag, and went up to Keres, the team captain, demanding that a protest be registered. But what protest can be made when you have lost on time?! In the evening, at dinner, one of the Yugoslavs informed Petrosian that the whole incident had been shown on television, to which the Ex-World Champion replied: 'If I had known about that, I would have smashed the clock'. This was the first time in Petrosian's career that he had over-stepped the time limit. To the end of the Olympiad he was unable to forget this game, although by then he could joke about it ironically.

Then came the match with Holland—and a further unpleasantness: Savon lost. In the end we gained a victory, but only by the minimum margin.

The match with the Bulgarian team was also not easily forgotten. The Bulgarians normally play tenaciously, and we needed points at any price. We were already two points behind the Hungarians, and two and a half behind the Yugoslavs. The match against Bulgaria began well, and a good result seemed a possibility. But we returned to the hotel with one draw by Petrosian, and three unclear adjourned positions.

The following day Tal managed to win what at first appeared to be a drawn ending with opposite-coloured bishops. Korchnoi received an unusual present—in the envelope there was neither the scoresheet, nor the sealed move, of his opponent Tringov. Later the victim described how it had all happened. After writing down his move, he stopped the clock and sank into thought. At this point his opponent came up, and they began heatedly discussing the game. Mechanically the Bulgarian grandmaster placed the scoresheet with the sealed move in his pocket, sealed the empty envelope, and gave it to the controller.

And now regarding my game with Padevsky. It was to a certain extent significant, in that it was the last game which our team lost at the Olympiad. From very early on Padevsky as White obtained a slightly inferior position. I was seized by an over-strong desire to 'punish' my opponent for such passive tactics. I wasted much time in search of a forced winning continuation, ran short of time and lost my advantage. However, I did not wish to offer a draw from an inferior position, although I sensed that my opponent would have agreed to it at any point. Also, I didn't know what the outcome of the other games would be, and so I played on. Our analysis of the adjourned position was far from perfect, and after a sleepless night I failed to put up a fitting resistance, and thereby lost this game which had cost me so much effort.

Before the match against East Germany in round five we had the poor score of 9 out of 16, and were now three(!) points behind the Yugoslav team, and 2½ behind the Hungarians.

During the discussions to decide what team to field against the East Germans, Petrosian observed that each of the previous four rounds had been unfortunate for a new member of our team. The points lost by the Soviet team had already become an object of ridicule. Thus I, for instance, was asked by the Polish international master Bednarski: 'Have you drawn lots yet to decide who is going to lose today?' I replied that if it should happen again that day, then for the match with Poland we would have to omit the one member of the Soviet team who was still undefeated."

Karpov, you will notice, only mentions in passing the "discussions to decide what team to field against the East Germans". But in fact there was a pretty stormy and forthright argument within the USSR team. No one escaped criticism, and that included the team's highly experienced trainers, grandmasters Paul Keres, Vladimir Antoshin and Semion Furman. Karpov spoke out particularly sharply, criticizing the poor preparation for the various matches, and especially the careless and poor-quality analysis of adjourned positions. I happened to be present at that memorable meeting of the USSR team, and I saw with what unfeigned astonishment the veterans of the team observed the behaviour of the young debutant; in the eyes of some of them you could read: "The young people nowadays!..."

In order to understand fully the atmosphere reigning that day in the "headquarters" of the Soviet team, it should be remembered that, not long before this, a defeat for one of the members of the team had been considered something of an event. And here our leading players had lost one after another. The grandmasters were joking: "Who is next!". But after such ironical jokes the players decided in all seriousness to stick to the old rule of team events: no one must lose, and in such a strong team a winner is bound to emerge. The end of the Olympiad was reached without either Smyslov or Tal losing a game, and the team gained greatly in confidence. Here I again hand over to Karpov:

"The match against the East Germans went simply splendidly. From the leaders we were now but a step away, and before the ninth round our team was in second place, half a point behind the Yugoslavs.

It was proposed that the outcome of our encounter with the Czechs should be decided by Korchnoi and myself, who were playing White. Our opponents Šmejkal and Jansa defended with all their might, fully conceding the initiative and space, but erecting barricades along the back ranks. My opponent Jansa played splendidly in terrible time trouble (one minute for ten moves), and I did not manage to increase my advantage. As I was considering my sealed move, our team captain Keres came up and recommended that we consider the two draws offered by our opponents. After looking at Korchnoi's position (he appeared to be in some danger), I replied that I did not object, but asked our trainers to confer again. Soon the captain informed me of the decision to accept the two draws. On arriving at the hotel, we discovered that we had been wrong not to try to exploit the winning chances in my game . . .

Somewhat surprisingly, it was Smyslov who gained us our victory in the match with Yugoslavia. After all, he was playing Black! By either the sacrifice or the loss of a pawn he confused Ljubojevic, whereupon the latter made a mistake, and was forced to part with the exchange. The remainder was, as they say, a matter of technique, of which Smyslov is a master.

We set off for the match against the Americans with the most serious intentions. The Hungarians, a point behind, were meeting the weakened Spanish team, and did not conceal their high hopes. I managed to defeat Bisguier . . . Interest was provoked by the game between Tal and Benkő, whose chess acquaintance has a rich history. Back in the 1959 Candidates' Tournament, Benkő, who had lost three times to Tal, declared that the Riga grandmaster was hypnotizing him, and appeared for their last game in dark glasses. Many years had passed since then. Benkő had had to exchange his dark glasses for ordinary ones, but in Skopje even they did not save the American grandmaster from misfortune. After losing once again to Tal, Benkő refused to sign his scoresheet—this had to be done by the American team captain.

Three rounds before the finish the USSR and Hungarian teams were level, but this did not concern us unduly, since two of our remaining matches were against outsiders—Spain and Argentina. First we managed to beat the Spaniards by a big score, and gain a lead of one point. The Hungarians defeated the Rumanians with difficulty. At this point we all decided that the matter was settled—first place was assured, and all we had to do was to 'go along and collect our points from the Argentinians'.

And so, USSR v Argentina. All the unpleasantness began with my game. I decided to 'play quietly' that day, but unexpectedly came under a very strong attack. After beating off the first wave, I managed to offer a draw, which was accepted. Korchnoi engaged in intricate manoeuvring, and obtained . . . an even worse position. Petrosian changed his style, and decided to go in for active play with an isolated pawn. He was unable to attack at his leisure, as he prefers to, and with such a weak pawn one doesn't win by simple manoeuvres. Only Smyslov attained a technically won position, but in the fifth hour of play he overlooked a simple stroke, and to avoid the worst offered a draw. And at the same time the Hungarians were winning by a big score against Holland. But Forintos, sensing that the fate of the team depended on his game, grew nervous and overlooked a mate in two. After this Keres accepted the Argentinian captain's offer of two draws, and our match ended in a score of 2-2.

Before the last round the Hungarians were only half a point behind us, and for the Soviet team a share of first place would be equivalent to losing the Olympiad".

Karpov was too occupied during the last round, and so instead of an account by him I give here an extract from my report, which was sent at the time to Moscow by telephone.

"After a discussion regarding the composition of the team, the USSR players set off for the last round. The only one who wished unreservedly to play was Karpov... It was then that the decision was taken: to stand firm against the Rumanians as Black, and attempt to put on the pressure with White. These tactics were dictated by the assumption that the Hungarians should not be able to beat West Germany by a big score (up till then the Germans had lost only one match in the entire Olympiad—against the USSR by $1\frac{1}{2}$–$2\frac{1}{2}$). On the way to their boards, the Soviet players stopped involuntarily by the demonstration boards of the Hungary–West Germany match, and noticed that grandmasters Hübner and Darga were not in the German team. This strained their nerves even further—surely the other players weren't seeking a sensation, which is what the failure of the Soviet players to take first place would be?

Fortunately, there was no such evil intent. Grandmaster Lothar Schmid (who had been controller of the World Championship Match in Reykjavik, which had fatigued him and strained his nerves, for which reason he was not included in his West German Olympiad team) explained: Hübner was already assured of first place on top board, and did not wish to risk it, while Darga had vacated his place to Pfleger, who thus gained a chance to obtain the grandmaster title. But our players did not yet know this, and their task in the match with Rumania seemed extra-difficult. This is how the battle proceeded.

Petrosian as Black declines the draw immediately offered by Gheorghiu: as usual the latter is 'testing' an eminent opponent. Korchnoi sits there frowning, he is angry about his previous games and with everyone in general, but on this occasion he makes his moves quickly, energetically, almost thumping down the pieces. Tal, cigarette in hand, strolls like a commander across the carpeted route to the boards of the Hungary–West Germany match, and then back, then once again—there and back... Practically all the time Karpov stands beside his chair, looking first down—at his board, and then up—at the demonstration boards, where one after another the West German players get into difficult positions. (True, there the game Hecht–Bilek soon ends in a draw.)

It is as if there are not two matches on each of four boards, but just one match on eight. The points count both ways: everything that the West German team loses, the Soviet team must win back.

Ribli obtains a rook, bishop and knight against Kestler's lone queen. Those who are following the USSR–Rumania match do not see this. They merely hear the applause when the Hungarian player wins his side a point. But immediately, as if competing with the spectators on the other stand, 'our' spectators give an ovation to the young Soviet grandmaster Karpov, who with a fine stroke levels the score in this indirect contest with the Hungarians."

In the evening Anatoly Karpov sits, and for a long time ponders over which game to submit for the brilliancy prize. And then he gives a crafty, rather childish smile:

"Well, I don't think I played badly in the Olympiad, did I?"

And Mikhail Tal admitted to me:

"To be perfectly frank, it is only now, here in Skopje, that I realize that Karpov is indeed capable of the highest achievements. Earlier too he has had excellent results, but in the creative sense I was not impressed by his play. Here I have been quite carried away by several of Karpov's games. He alone has played almost as many such games as all the other members of the team put together. If we were asked today to show something interesting from what we played at Skopje, we would have difficulty in finding suitable examples, whereas Anatoly would have a different problem—he would be unable to decide which of his games was the best".

However, let us sum up the results of the 20th Chess Olympiad. Thus the Hungarians could not maintain their challenge, and in the end nevertheless fell behind. But the reasons for the Soviet team's difficulties lay not so much in the competitive situation, as inside the complex organism of the team. The computer operating in the press centre made scientifically-based forecasts, and predicted a gap of some five to six points between the Soviet grandmasters and their "pursuers". And if the computer was wrong, it was one of its few mistakes, and once again shows the influence of factors which cannot be included in a computer program.

There is one further conclusion, prompted by the results of the Olympiad, which should be mentioned. I have in mind the appearance in a number of countries of young, talented grandmasters, about whom we have already spoken when discussing the Student Olympiads, and who markedly strengthened the "adult" teams of their countries. In contrast, the only representative of the new wave to establish himself firmly in the Soviet team was Karpov.

Here, incidentally, is how Karpov himself summed up the results of the 20th Olympiad:

"A few words about why our players, who at one time won practically all International Tournaments (to say nothing of World Team Tournaments), are finding victory more and more difficult to come by.

The point would seem to be that the many years of chess supremacy, during which all the highest titles have been won by our grandmasters, have given certain leaders of the Soviet sports movement the impression that victories will continue to follow one after another. They have begun to be less concerned with chess, whereas in fact chess requires constant attention. Thus for many years in succession there was not a single addition to the corps of Soviet grandmasters.

As long as the 'old guard' continues to battle and to maintain its positions, we fail to take the impending crisis seriously. But what will things be like in five years' time? After all, a drastic renovation of a team rarely takes place without a decline. There is probably only one conclusion to be drawn: young players must be afforded greater opportunities for participating in strong tournaments".

And now a short postscript to this account of the 20th World Chess Olympiad... Why has this event been given such a prominent place in the book? It is true that, as a chess player, Karpov by that time was already superior to his opponents on the bottom boards of the other teams, and it would seem that encounters with them were of less significance than battles with famous grandmasters in strong individual tournaments. But what was noticeable was the style of Karpov's victories in the Olympiad, and the fact that from this time, Autumn 1972, in the majority of the events in which he took part, it was Karpov's games which were judged to be the best, and that he, more often than other players, was awarded special prizes for his high-quality games. We have already spoken about the importance for each Soviet grandmaster of an appearance in the USSR Olympiad team. I think also that the reader will be interested in the many assessments given by Anatoly Karpov himself on the course of the various matches, and in his frank opinions on the many questions arising here.

Karpov–Cobo
Sicilian Defence

1 P–K4	P–QB4
2 N–KB3	P–Q3
3 P–Q4	P×P
4 N×P	N–KB3
5 N–QB3	P–QR3
6 P–B4	

One of the possibilities here, along with 6 B–K2, 6 B–KN5 and 6 B–QB4. In certain variations it transposes into the 6 B–K2 line.

6 ...	P–K3
7 B–K2	Q–B2
8 0–0	N–B3
9 K–R1	B–Q2

The position reached is characteristic of the Scheveningen Variation, rather than the Najdorf Variation with which the game began. There is perhaps one slight drawback to Black's position—his queen has moved out to B2 a little early.

10 P–QR4	B–K2
11 N–N3	0–0
12 B–K3	

There was no point in trying to cramp Black's Q-side by 12 P–R5, since he manages to 'slip out' by 12 ... P–QN4. But now 13 P–R5 is an unpleasant threat.

12 ...	N–QN5

Black ignores his opponent's plan. 12 ... P–QN3 was essential, and only then N–QR4 or N–QN5. The immediate 12 ... N–QR4 gives White a slight advantage after 13 P–K5 N–K1 14 N×N Q×N 15 Q–Q2 and 16 B–Q4.

Now, however, White gains a clear positional advantage.

13 P–R5	B–B3

13 ... P–Q4 would have been answered by 14 B–N6 Q–B1 15 P–K5 N–K5 16 N×N P×N 17 P–B4.

14 B–N6	Q–N1

This appears logical: Black will force the bishop away by N–Q2, and then play P–QN4. But this plan is too slow, and 14 ... Q–Q2 was to be preferred, on which I was intending to continue 15 B–B3, preventing the freeing advance ... P–Q4.

15 Q–Q2	

This is the point. White indirectly defends his KP, and at the same time threatens to trap the knight at QN5 by 16 N–Q1 and 17 P–B3.

15 ...	P–Q4
16 P–K5	N–Q2

16 ... N–K5 17 N×N P×N 18 P–B4, with a possible 19 N–B5, looks terrible for Black.

17 B–Q4	P–QN4
18 B–N4	

Preparing P–B5, and preventing Black from advancing his BP by one or two squares. The apparently tempting continuation 18 P×P e.p. N×NP 19 P–B5 achieves nothing definite after 19 ... P×P 20 R×BP N–B5.

18 ...	P–KN3
19 QR–K1	

Black's pieces have ended up on the Q-side, and are completely unprepared for the defence of their king. Moreover, his rook is forced to vacate the square KB1 for his knight, which is essential for the defence.

19 ...   R–B1

20 P–B5

This decides the game.

20 ...   NP×P

20 ... KP×P is answered by 21 P–K6.

21 B×P   N–B1

On 21 ... P×B White again wins by 22 P–K6!.

22 Q–R6   N–N3

After 22 ... P×B White smashes open the black position by 23 P–K6 P–B3 24 R×P N×BP (24 ... B–K1 25 R×BP and 26 R–B7) 25 R–N5+ N–N3 26 R×N+ P×R 27 Q×P+ K–R1 28 B×P+ B×B 29 Q×B+ K–R2 30 R–K5.

In this variation there is also the entertaining continuation 30 N–Q4 (instead of 30 R–K5): 30 ... N×R (30 ... N×N 31 R–K3) 31 N–B5 R–R2 32 P–K7 R×P 33 Q×R+ K–N3 34 Q–K6+ K–N4 (34 ... K–R4 35 Q–R6+ K–N5 36 N–K3 mate) 35 P–R4+ K–N5 (35 ... K–R4 36 Q–R6+ K–N5 37 Q–N5 mate) 36 N–K3++ K–N6 (36 ... K–R4 37 Q–N4+ K–R3 38 N–B5+ K–R2 39 Q–N7 mate; 36 ... K×P 37 Q–N4 mate) 37 Q–N4+ K–B7 38 N(B3)–Q1 mate.

But let us go back. After 30 N–Q4 Black can defend against the mate by 30 ... R–B1, when after all White is forced into attempting to regain material.

23 B×N   RP×B

Cobo overlooks that after 24 ... B–B1 he loses control of the square KR4, and the white heavy pieces inevitably break through to his king along the KR-file. On 23 ... BP×B the immediate 24 R–B7 does not mate, since the black king has an escape route to the Q-side via K1 and Q2. I was therefore intending to play 24 Q–R3 B–Q2 25 R–B7 K×R 26 Q×RP+ K–K1 27 Q–N8+ B–B1 28 R–KB1 K–Q1 29 Q×B+ B–K1 (29 ... K–B2 30 Q–Q6+ K–N2 31 Q–N6 mate) 30 B–N6+ K–Q2 (30 ... R–B2 31 N–B5) 31 R–B7+ B×R 32 Q×B+ K–B3 33 N–Q4 mate.

24 R–K3	B–B1
25 Q–R4	B–KN2
26 R–R3	B–K1
27 Q–R7+	K–B1
28 Q×P	P–B3

If 28 ... B×P, then 29 Q×KP with an easy win, while after 28 ... N×P 29 R–R7 mate is inevitable.

29 R×P+   Resigns

Karpov–Enevoldsen
French Defence

1 P–K4	P–K3
2 P–Q4	P–Q4
3 N–Q2	

As I learned after the game, my Danish opponent had not expected this modest move (prior to this I had been playing 3 N–QB3). For this reason, although he normally plays quickly, he thought for some time, probably remembering the good old days, and perhaps his game with Tartakower. Finally he played...

3 ...   P–KB4

A continuation which occurs rarely in tournament practice. Theory considers that 4 P×BP P×P 5 Q–R5+ P–KN3 6 Q–K2+ Q–K2 7 N(2)–B3 assures White of an endgame advantage. Quite recently it has been decided that 4 P–K5 also gives White an advantage. I didn't wish to block the position, and it didn't suit me to go into an ending —I wanted a complicated game.

4 P×BP   P×P
N(2)–B3   N–KB3
6 B–KN5

An attempt to refute the variation in one move. Of course, the simple 6 B–Q3, N–K2 and 0–0 would have given White a solid positional advantage.

6 ...   B–K2

The only move, but an adequate one. White was threatening to check on the K-file with his queen and then capture on KB6. Now it was my turn to ponder: the early B–KN5 has not justified itself, and the development of White's K-side is retarded. I spent a long time calculating the consequences of the sacrifice of the QNP.

7 B–Q3   N–K5
8 B×B   Q×B
9 N–K2   Q–N5+

He has to hurry, otherwise after 10 0–0 White will get down seriously to the business

of exploiting the weak squares in his opponent's position.

10 P–B3   Q×NP
11 0–0   0–0

The acceptance of the second pawn sacrifice by 11 ... N×QBP was equivalent to suicide after 12 N×N Q×N 13 R–B1 and 14 R–K1+. Black's position is held together by his knight at K5, and he must maintain it there at all costs.

12 P–B4   P×P

After 12 ... P–B3 13 N–B4 Black was concerned about the weakness of his QP. He could have defended it by 13 ... N–B3 (13 ... P–KN4 is beautifully refuted by 14 B×N BP×B 15 N×NP R×N 16 Q–R5 Q×QP 17 Q×P+ K–B1 18 Q–QB7! with a double attack, while on 16 ... B–B4 there follows mate in two moves by 17 Q–B7+ K–R1 18 Q–B8 mate), but 14 R–B1 enables White to break through on the QB-file after exchanging on Q5.

13 B×P+   K–R1
14 R–N1

14 N–K5 would probably also have led to a win. 14 R–N1 is the first move of a variation which should have won the game by force.

14 ...   Q–R6
15 N–K5   P–KN3

The only defence against 16 N–N6+ and 17 R–N3, with mate on the KR-file.

16 R–N3   Q–K2
17 N–B4   K–N2
18 R–KR3!

With two threats: 19 R×P+ and 19 N(4)×P. Black has a defence—18 ... N–N4 but after 19 R–K3 Q–Q1 20 R(1)–K1 the intrusion of the white rooks down the K-file is inevitable.

18 ...   N–QB3
19 N(4)×P

An inaccuracy. White misses a beautiful win by 19 R×P+ K×R 20 N(4)×P (20 N(5)×P Q–Q3 21 N×R+ Q×N 22 Q–R5+ K–N2, and there is no mate) 20 ... Q–Q3 21 N×R+ K–N2 (21 ... Q×N loses to 22 Q–R5+ Q–R3 23 B–N8+ K–N2 24 Q–B7+ K–R1 25 N–N6+) 22 Q–R5 N×N 23 Q–R7+ K×N 24 P×N!. This is the move which I overlooked in my preliminary calculations, and which only came into my head several moves later—24 ... Q–Q2 (24 ... Q–K2 25 Q–N8 mate) 25 Q–N8+ K–K2 26 Q–B7+ K–Q1 27 Q–B8+ Q–K1 28 R–Q1+ B–Q2 29 Q×P, with the threat of P–K6.

19 ...   P×N
20 N×P   Q–B3!

Only this move maintains control of his KR1 square. White wins easily in the event of 20 ... Q–N4 21 N×R K×N 22 R–R8+ K–K2 23 R–K1.

21 N×R

21 N–B4 Q–N4 22 N–R5+ K–N3 23 B–Q3 (or 23 B–Q5) was tempting, but after 23 ... Q–Q7 there is no forced win.

21 ...   K×N
22 R–R7   N–K2?

Tired by the complicated calculations, my opponent failed to notice that on 22 ... N–N4 White cannot reply 23 R×P on account of 23 ... Q–Q3, when the rook is unexpectedly trapped. I was intending to answer 22 ... N–N4 with 23 R–R5 B–K3 24 B×B (Black can defend after 24 R×N B×B 25 Q–R5 N–K2, or 24 P–Q5 B–B2 25 P×N B×B 26 P×P R–N1 27 Q–B1 B×R 28 Q×P R×P 29 Q×R B–K7) 24 ... N×B 25 P–Q5 R–Q1 26 Q–N3 N(K3)–Q5 27 Q×P R×P 28 Q×BP, with a slight advantage.

23 R–K1

There was no point in winning the queen immediately by 23 R–B7+.

23 ...   Q–KN3
24 R–B7+   Q×R

Black also loses after 24 ... K–K1 25 P–B3 B–K3 26 B×B Q×B 27 R–R7.

25 B×Q	**K×B**
26 Q–R5+	**K–B1**
27 Q–R6+	**K–B2**
28 Q–R7+	**Resigns**

Bisguier–Karpov
English Opening

1 P–QB4	**P–QB4**
2 N–QB3	**P–KN3**
3 N–B3	**B–N2**
4 P–K3	

White avoids the symmetrical systems resulting after 4 P–KN3. The continuation chosen does not give him any chance of a serious advantage from the opening.

4 ...	N–KB3

The move order is important. In the event of 4 ... N–QB3 5 P–Q4 Black is unable to play 5 ... P×P 6 P×P P–Q4.

5 P–Q4	0–0
6 B–K2	P×P
7 P×P	P–Q4

As often happens, a distinctive opening transformation has occurred—from an English Opening we have reached one of the variations of the Grünfeld Defence.

8 0–0	N–B3
9 P–KR3	B–B4

This is probably better than the more usual 9 ... B–K3.

10 B–K3	P×P
11 B×P	R–B1
12 B–K2	B–K3

Black strengthens his control over the blockading square Q4, and at the same time prevents the active development of the white queen at QN3 (which could have occurred after 12 ... Q–R4 13 R–B1 KR–Q1 14 Q–N3).

13 Q–Q2	Q–R4

In general it is undesirable in such positions to allow the exchange of the fianchettoed bishop, but in this particular instance I did not object, since I was able to promptly step up my attack on the isolated QP.

14 B–KR6	KR–Q1
15 B×B	K×B
16 KR–Q1	R–Q3!

This way, since after 16 ... R–Q2 the pin by B–N5 is unpleasant in certain variations. The absence of the black-squared bishops allows the rook to occupy a black square at Q3; if 17 N–QN5, the white knight takes the square QN5 away from its bishop, so that 17 ... R–Q2 is then possible.

17 Q–K3	R(1)–Q1
18 P–R3	

The moves made up to this point have been of interest mainly as regards the opening. But now sharp tactical play begins, which I think the reader will find interesting.

18 ...	B–N6
19 R–Q2	

19 N–QN5 fails to 19 ... B×R 20 N×R B×B 21 N×NP Q–N3 22 N×R B×N.

19 ...	R–K3
20 Q–B4	N–Q4
21 N×N	R×N
22 P–N4	

White defends against the threat of 22 ... R–KB4 followed by 23 ... R×N and 24 ... Q×R. On 22 B–Q3 Black gains the advantage by 22 ... R–B3 23 Q–K3 R×N 24 P×R N×P, with the threat of 25 ... Q×R and 26 ... N×P+, when 25 B–K4 is refuted by the tactical blow 25 ... Q×R 26 B×R B×B! 27 Q–K5+ (27 Q×Q N×P+) 27 ... K–R3.

22 ...	P–KN4
23 Q–N3	R–B3
24 B–Q1	

After 24 R–Q3 White loses a pawn—24 ... B–B5 25 R–K3 B×B 26 R×B R×N! 27 Q×R N×P and 28 ... N×R+.

24 ...	B–B5

On 24 ... R×N there follows 25 Q×R Q×R 26 B×B, when the weakness of Black's KB2 is unexpectedly disclosed.

| 25 P–N3 | B–R3 |

I should have liked, of course, to capture the knight: 25 ... R×N 26 B×R Q×R, but then instead of the plausible intermediate move 27 R–Q1, which allows Black to bring the game to a fine conclusion—27 ... Q–B6 28 P×B R×P 29 R×R N×R 30 Q–K5+ K–R3!, White captures the bishop immediately: 27 P×B R×P 28 B×N P×B 29 Q–K5+, with a draw.

| 26 P–N4 | Q–Q1 |
| 27 B–N3 | |

The American grandmaster appears to be winning, but in fact Black has at his disposal a strong tactical stroke.

| 27 ... | N×QP |
| 28 R×N | |

Bisguier does not wish to lose slowly and painfully in an endgame a pawn down—28 B×R N×N+ 29 B×N Q×R 30 R–Q1 Q–B6, and instead rushes recklessly forward.

28 ...	R×R
29 N×P	R–Q6
30 Q–R4	P–R3
31 N×P	Q–Q5
32 R–K1	R×RP!
Resigns	

Karpov–Ungureanu
Sicilian Defence

1 P–K4 P–QB4 2 N–KB3 N–QB3 3 P–Q4 P×P 4 N×P N–B3 5 N–QB3 P–Q3 6 B–KN5 P–K3 7 Q–Q2 B–K2 8 0–0–0 0–0 9 P–B4 N×N 10 Q×N Q–R4 11 B–B4 B–Q2 12 P–K5 P×P 13 P×P B–B3 14 B–Q2 N–Q2 15 N–Q5 Q–Q1 16 N×B+ Q×N 17 KR–K1 KR–B1 18 Q–B4 P–QR4 19 K–N1 N–N3 20 B–Q3 N–Q4 21 Q–KN4 Q–B4 22 R–K4 P–QN4 23 Q–R3 N–N5

24 B–K3 B×R 25 B×B Q×KP 26 Q×RP+ K–B1 27 B×R K–K2 28 Q–K4 Q–B2 29 Q–N7 **Resigns**

SAN ANTONIO 1972

This was not the first major international tournament to he held in the USA (we are not, of course, talking about the New York battles of 1924 and 1927, but about more later times). Quite recently the famous musician Piatigorsky, whose wife had been Ladies' Chess Champion of the United States, organized at his own expense two first-class (remember Santa Monica!) events. Now the musician's place had been taken by businessmen. Here is what Tigran Petrosian had to say about this tournament, on returning from San Antonio:

"I will begin with the name of the tournament, which in the USSR has become known simply as the San Antonio Tournament, but which in America was called either the first Church International, or the 'Fried Chicken' Tournament. The point is that this event was held at the personal expense of a Texas businessman by the name of Church, who had grown rich on the selling of fried chickens, and who is now the owner of a firm controlling a large chain of restaurants, shops and filling stations. The San Antonio Tournament, although it did not become the greatest chess tournament in the history of America, as the organizers would have liked, was nevertheless a pretty significant event.

The route to the venue was long and tiring: London–New York–Dallas, and at last, San Antonio. In New York we could not rid ourselves of the feeling that we were at the bottom of a deep well, Dallas is still oppressed by painful memories of that distant tragic shot, but San Antonio was welcoming and quiet. From the plane we descended onto a carpet, and along a red nylon surface made our way to the airport building. It turns out that here there is a special 'red carpet' committee, which arranges the meeting of particularly welcome and honoured visitors.

I should like straight away to mention that, while still at the airport in Dallas, we sensed that the USA was experiencing something of a chess boom. In kiosks, alongside drinks and tobacco, amongst the souvenirs one could see magnetic travelling chess sets, and dozens of different chess books, both original and translated. The strongest European grandmasters and masters travel the country giving lectures and simultaneous displays. At Dallas we met up with an exhausted Lajos Portisch. He looked pretty awful, having just given a simultaneous display on sixty-five boards. Perhaps it was this that explained his more than modest start.

Why didn't Fischer play in the tournament? This question was answered half seriously, half jokingly, by one of the initiators of the 'Fried Chicken' Tournament, the American master Koltanowski: 'Because there was a danger that Bobby would demand as an appearance fee the whole of Mr Church's business, we decided not to invite him'.

If one takes account of the fact that our stay in San Antonio coincided with the USSR Championship and an important international tournament at Majorca in Spain, and that in England they were already preparing for the traditional Hastings tournament, the composition of our tournament was pretty imposing".

Anatoly Karpov elaborates on this:

"It is a pity, of course, that not only did Fischer not play, but that for some reason the other strongest American grandmasters were also absent. Robert Byrne, for instance, was replaced by his brother Donald (which caused certain incompetent journalists to make the usual errors in their reports)... But despite this, in its composition the event was an outstanding one—the participants included all, or nearly all the strongest European grandmasters at that time, with the exception of Hübner and perhaps Ljubojevic, who was already of considerable strength.

The playing conditions arranged in San Antonio were good. We lived in the 'Palasio del Rio'—one of the best hotels in this big Texas town, and the light and spacious playing hall, with its slightly raised stage, was within a hundred yards of the hotel.

This tournament, which was a class above the average event, was very important for me, if only because of the considerable prestige involved. At first I played very well, and gained a number of points—seven out of eight! At this stage only Bent Larsen, and then Paul Keres, were able to compete with me. Then at some point Larsen decided to 'play the fool'. He had the better game against Keres, failed to win it (although he evidently could have done), and adjourned with an extra pawn in a queen ending. Analysis revealed that Keres had sufficient drawing chances. And then, as often happens, with the analysis essentially concluded, we began to 'play about', looking at all sorts of unlikely continuations. We came across an amusing variation, in which Larsen could even lose, if he should carry on regardless, even when he could see that the game was drawn. Strange as it may seem, it was his extra pawn which would then prevent his king from breaking out of the mating net, into which he himself would have moved. Amusing, wouldn't you agree? But now imagine our astonishment when, after the start of the resumption, Petrosian and I went for a walk around the town, and then called in at the tournament hall. We saw that Larsen's king had climbed voluntarily into the mating net, and that it was time for the Dane to resign. After this blow Larsen could no longer recover".

Bent Larsen played in this tournament more flippantly than usual, and shared eighth to ninth place. For a player who each time fights for first place, and only first, this was a considerable failure. "To what extent was it accidental?"—Petrosian asks, and immediately answers the question himself: "The reason for Larsen's outstanding chess successes was revealed to me once at a tournament in Yugoslavia. It was in 1970. Larsen was playing Black against the well-known chess correspondent and international master Mario Bertok. The game was adjourned, and on resumption Larsen had to choose one of two continuations. The first, normal, one, which answered the needs of the position, led to a draw; the second was dubious, and after the correct reply by Bertok would have led to a loss for Larsen, but after a faulty reply—to a win for him. Larsen chose the second: Bertok made a mistake and lost. I asked Larsen on what basis he had come to this decision. He replied: 'Suppose I have three games against strong masters. If I play like you do—correctly—I will score one and a half points, but if I play like I do, I will perhaps be punished in one of them, but even then I will score two out of three, and that suits me better...'."

In the San Antonio tournament Larsen was severely punished: the two out of three didn't materialize.

"Regarding Keres", Petrosian continues, "it seems to me that he broke an important rule. A chess player, and indeed any person in general should be aware of his state of health, and should reckon with it and not ignore it. Keres' play was extravagantly young, and by about the sixth round he was 'exposed'. A deterioration in his play was inevitable. The unexpected point in his game with Larsen gave Keres new strength, but alas, not for long. Soon he lost to Portisch and to Evans, drew with Smith, and lost the chance of the high place his class deserved".

"And so, I took the lead", says Anatoly Karpov. "But then I too was let down by my game against Portisch, which I played very badly. At some point my opponent, who had White, lost his advantage, but in a good position I made an oversight, and immediately succumbed. It is curious that both Keres and I should make the identical psychological mistake in our games with the Hungarian grandmaster. Observing that the quality of Portisch's play in this tournament was not especially high, we aimed to exploit this and... were punished. After a poor start the Hungarian became the main rival of the Soviet grandmasters in the battle for first place, scoring nine points out of the last ten rounds(!)".

Tigran Petrosian once again joins the conversation: "Yes, it appeared that Portisch was not even thinking of fighting for first place, and this was most likely true. Even in the penultimate round, against Walter Browne, Portisch in a better position offered a draw. Browne declined, and they played on until there were virtually only the kings left, but the enthusiasm and persistence were displayed not by Portisch, but by Browne. Only a win in the last round over a depressed Larsen enabled Portisch to share first prize.

Anatoly Karpov made a particularly good showing in the tournament. He, more than anyone else, had the right to be the sole winner. He should not have lost to Portisch. The loss of this half point was unpleasant, but not irreparable. But then the fact that, two rounds before the end, tired by the strain of being leader, he was unable to win against Julio Kaplan, proved to be decisive. Instead of clear first place—a share with Portisch and myself of first to third. You ask, what about the short draw in the last round? This 'sin' was also shared by Karpov and myself. Towards the end of the tournament we were both very tired (I did not feel too well), and decided not to tempt fate, in view of the storming finish Portisch was making just behind us. Portisch's win over Larsen was to be expected. But the last round is different from all others, in that a mistake made in it can no longer be repaired. And each of us came independently to the same conclusion, especially since on this occasion a bird in the hand was to some extent the same as two in the bush".

"When I am involved in a chase, I normally play well at the finish. But when I am in the lead, towards the end I often tend for some reason to reduce speed", Karpov admits. "That was what happened to me in the last few rounds at San Antonio. On the very last day I had to play the Brazilian Henrique Mecking, while Petrosian was paired with the Canadian Duncan Suttles. We both had White (as did Portisch against Larsen), but decided—and I am no longer sure about the correctness of this decision—not to take any risks. And so, I went along intending to draw, which would guarantee me a share of first place. When we sat down at the board, Mecking looked at me like a badgered animal, although I could not understand why. For him the result of this game was of no significance—he had played poorly in the tournament. But it turned out that I was less nervous than Mecking—this was clear from his appearance. Then at some point he realized that I wanted a draw, whereupon he began to smile. But I thought that Mecking was the sort of person who would not agree to a truce. However, when shortly afterwards I offered a draw, he agreed without hesitation.

When playing against me, Mecking behaved quite correctly—here I have nothing to complain about. But both in Hastings, and in San Antonio, his behaviour in some of the games was simply criminal. Hear what Petrosian has to say".

And indeed, Tigran Petrosian had this complaint to make about the young Brazilian grandmaster: "On the organization of the event, the 'Fried Chickens' managed to cast their shadow. The chess boards were laid out on restaurant tables, covered with white table-cloths. And Mecking did not fail to exploit this. During the resumption of his adjourned game with me, where he had sealed a losing move, but where I was rather slow to exploit my advantage, Mecking began moving his elbows across the table-cloth, rocking the board from side to side, until this was noticed by the chief controller Golombek, who gave him a severe reprimand.

There was another episode in his game with Browne. Both were in time trouble, and Browne's flag was already raised, when Mecking committed another serious indiscretion. Browne made his move and pressed his clock, whereupon Mecking immediately started Browne's clock again, and began unhurriedly correcting the placing of a piece which was in any case correctly positioned. Browne was taken aback, grew agitated, blundered away a pawn, and lost".

It is for the undoubtedly talented Mecking to decide whether or not to be offended by Soviet players, who quite frequently criticise his behaviour in the press. But it is by no means a question of the top Soviet grandmasters wishing to somehow disparage a growing rival from the West. It will be readily noted that practically all USSR players speak with respect and affection about Lajos Portisch and Bent Larsen, Svetozar Gligoric and Wolfgang Uhlmann, Vlastimil Hort and Robert Hübner, Ljubomir Ljubojevic and Ulf Andersson, and many, many other top players from the West. And even with the hyper-eccentric—let's call him that—Bobby Fischer, it is by no means for his behaviour at the board that he is criticized by Soviet journalists and grandmasters. Certainly the former World Champion would never have permitted himself to do that which Anatoly Karpov told me about on his return from San Antonio:

"When at the start of the tournament my main rival was Larsen, the latter adjourned his game against Mecking in an inferior position. For some reason the game wasn't resumed straight away—I think that Mecking claimed he was ill, although he nevertheless played his game in the next round. Before the start of this next round Mecking came up and told me that he had an adjourned position against Larsen. "Yes, I know", I replied. "I have the advantage", he said cautiously. "Yes, I heard that, I know the approximate position". Then Mecking suggested that I help him analyse the position, so that I could thus rid myself of my rival, Larsen. Naturally I declined".

The reader may ask, why then did Karpov admit that he and Petrosian, together with Keres, had looked at the latter's adjourned position against Larsen? But here one must take account of several factors. Keres and Larsen were in an identical tournament position, and the Soviet players were not guided by any petty considerations. Keres was not only a compatriot of Karpov and Petrosian who had come to the tournament with them, but was also an old friend. They had been living together in the hotel, and Keres himself was always ready to assist with advice, or in the analysis of an adjourned position (as long as no extraordinary circumstances should prevent such co-operation). No one would have thought seriously about condemning one of the Western players for giving friendly advice to a colleague—if, for instance, Jan Timman, say, were suddenly to give help in analysis to that charming lad Ulf Andersson, his Swedish friend, with whom he had played together in many tournaments—one could give numerous such examples. But in the incident described by Anatoly Karpov, the young Brazilian grandmaster Henrique Mecking was guided by purely petty considerations. And Karpov was right to decline such an unsporting offer, even though it appeared advantageous to him.

To be fair, it should be mentioned that, according to several players, in recent years Mecking's behaviour would appear to have begun to change for the better. Some time later Karpov also remarked on this.

Going back to the San Antonio tournament, it is interesting to note that the then World Champion Bobby Fischer flew in there for the last round. He had acquired a new habit—now he was late not only for his own games, but also for other peoples'. The start of the last round was deferred, while the FIDE President Dr Max Euwe, despite the bad weather, awaited the "VIP" by the street entrance. It is significant that there then occurred the first meeting of Anatoly Karpov and Robert Fischer. Here is how Karpov himself describes this brief encounter:

"That day we were due to play the last round, when suddenly the start was deferred for some ten to fifteen minutes. I didn't understand what was happening, so I went over to Keres and asked him. He said that they were waiting for Fischer. I couldn't understand why it was necessary to hold back the start of the round on Fischer's account. We were supposed to start at two o'clock, we'd arrived, sat down, and it was now ten minutes past—why should we have to wait? He wasn't one of the tournament competitors! And if he had been a competitor, his clock would have been started, and that would be all: the round would have begun. But it

7

so happened that, as a mark of respect to the American Chess Federation, and to the tournament organisers, the players did not object. We sat and waited. Fischer appeared together with Euwe, and then Fischer came up on the stage and shook hands with each of the players. That is the sum total of my impressions. After this we began playing, and I didn't see Fischer again. It seems that he flew off again that evening. All I can say is that outwardly he made on me personally a favourable enough impression..."

Karpov–Browne
English Opening

1 P–QB4	P–QB4
2 P–QN3	N–KB3
3 B–N2	P–KN3
4 B×N!?	

An original idea: in exchange for giving up his bishop, White takes control over Q5. If Black does not like the position which arises after White's fourth move, he could have played 3 ... P–K3 instead of 3 ... P–KN3. This entire idea needs verifying and it is for this reason that this game is interesting from the theoretical point of view.

4 ...	P×B
5 N–QB3	B–N2
6 P–N3	N–B3
7 B–N2	P–B4

This advance, as it turns out, is hasty. On KB4, the pawn hems in the white-squared bishop. Possibly better was 7 ... P–Q3, so as on 8 P–K3 to reply 8 ... N–N5, retaining the possibility of finding an active spot for the white-squared bishop.

8 P–K3	0–0

Now it would have been thoughtless to continue 8 ... N–N5 inasmuch as the check on Q3 is not dangerous for White; he could play either 9 Q–N1, defending against 9 ... N–Q6+, or 9 KN–K2, allowing 9 ... N–Q6+.

9 KN–K2	P–QR3
10 R–QB1	

In order on 10 ... P–QN4 to have the possibility of 11 P–Q3 and on 11 ... P×P, of recapturing with the QP. 10 0–0 is also good.

10 ...	P–QN4
11 P–Q3	

Of course, dangerous was 11 P×P P×P 12 N×P R×P 13 R×P Q–R4 and on 14 N(5)–B3, there follows 14 ... R×P!

11 ...	B–N2
12 0–0	P–Q3
13 Q–Q2	Q–R4

Black is in serious difficulties. The QN pawn needed defending. It could only be defended by the queen, but that piece is not well placed on R4. On the other hand, both the exchange on QB5 and the advance 13 ... P–N5 were unpleasant for Black. Browne selected the lesser evil.

14 KR–Q1	QR–N1
15 N–Q5	Q×Q
16 R×Q	P–N5

Black must move the QN pawn, since to exchange it on QB5 serves no purpose and it is impossible to maintain the tension on the Q-side, for White threatened 17 P×P P×P 18 P–Q4 P×P 19 R×N B×R 20 N–K7+ and 21 N×B.

17 P–Q4

The game is strategically won: Q5 is firmly held. Black's pawns on the K-side have been stopped and White's extra pawn in the centre promises him all the winning chances.

17 ...   KR–Q1

Forced, inasmuch as after 17 ... P×P there would follow a massive exchange of pieces which would not be in Black's favour: 18 N×QP N×N 19 N–K7+ K–R1 20 P×N.

18 R(1)–Q1

An inaccuracy. White has an overwhelming advantage after 18 P×P P×P 19 R(1)–Q1, threatening 20 N–K7+.

18 ...   P×P
19 P×P   K–B1
20 P–B5?

A serious error, letting the lion's share of White's advantage slip. The quiet 20 N–K3 was much simpler and stronger, and found when my head was clear; but, during the game ...

20 ...   N–R2!

The point. The knight will have a wonderful post on QN4, from where it can go to QB6 and attack the QP. Any other move in this position would be much weaker.

21 N–K3

White gets nothing with 21 P×P B×N (worse is 21 ... R×P 22 N–K3 B×B 23 K×B and 24 P–Q5 with good prospects) 22 B×B R×P and 23 ... N–N4; also the simple 21 N×P does not work due to 21 ... B×B 22 N×P B–B6 23 N×R R×N. The

text was probably the only possibility of preserving the knight and fighting for a further advantage.

21 ...	B×B
22 K×B	P×P
23 P×P	R×R
24 R×R	R–B1

White has a clear theoretical advantage thanks to the presence of an extra passed pawn on the Q-side, but for the moment, he must tend to its defence. I decided to exchange the QB pawn for the QN pawn, loosening Black's hold on the strongpoint at his QB6. After 25 R–B2 N–N4, Black is on his way to seizing the initiative.

25 N–Q5	R×P
26 N×P	P–QR4
27 N–Q5	R–B3

This move and those following were made by Browne in time-pressure, and therefore I succeeded in increasing my advantage and winning. Of course, the normal result from this position would be a draw. This move is the first mistake. More precise was 27 ... N–B3, without fearing 28 N–N6.

28 N–K3	R–B4
29 N–KB4	B–R3
30 R–Q5	

White goes in for an exchange of pieces so that he can take advantage of his extra pawn on the Q-side.

| 30 ... | R×R |
| 31 N(4)×R | B×N? |

From this moment on White again has real winning chances. It was necessary to keep the bishop and continue 31 ... N–B3; then White's winning chances would be extremely problematical. Now both opponents, as is usually the case in endgames, bring their kings to the centre.

32 N×B	K–K2
33 N–B4	N–B3
34 K–B3	K–K3
35 K–K3	K–Q4
36 P–QR3	

Preparing the king's entry to Q3. Now 36 ... P–R5 is impossible due to 37 N–N6+.

36 ...	K–K3
37 K–Q3	K–Q4
38 P–B3	P–R3
39 K–B3	P–R4
40 K–Q3	P–B3
41 P–B4!	

Zugzwang. Black cannot move his king to QB4 due to 42 N×P and 43 P–QN4+; the knight cannot leave the defence of the QRP.

41 ...	P–N4
42 N–K3+	K–K3
43 P–KR4	

Blockading the pawns and guaranteeing the win.

43 ... P×RP 44 P×P N–K2 45 K–B4 N–N3 46 N–N2 K–Q3 47 K–N5 K–Q4 48 K×P K–K5 49 P–N4 K–B6 50 P–N5 K×N 51 P–N6 N–B1 52 K–N5 N–Q2 53 P–R4 N×P 54 K×N K–B6 55 P–R5 K×P 56 P–R6 K–K6 57 P–R7 P–B5 58 P–R8–Q P–B6 59 Q–K8+ Resigns

Karpov–Gligoric
Ruy Lopez

1 P–K4 P–K4 2 N–KB3 N–QB3 3 B–N5 P–QR3 4 B–R4 N–B3 5 0–0 B–K2 6 R–K1 P–QN4 7 B–N3 P–Q3 8 P–B3 0–0

9 P–KR3

Thus the Ruy Lopez—one of the oldest and most studied openings. Here it is difficult to devise something new in the very beginning of the game, so chess players spend much of their time in the opening choosing the variation with which to enter the middle game. In this game the players follow a classic pattern in one of the main variations.

9 ...	N–N1

9 ... N–QR4 leads to the so-called Tchigorin Defence.

10 P–Q3

The 9 ... N–N1 variation has recently become a frequent feature of international competition. 10 P–Q4 is considered the normal continuation. In that way White exerts pressure against the enemy centre, maintaining the initiative. With 10 P–Q3 White defers the start of active play for a while.

10 ...	QN–Q2
11 QN–Q2	B–N2
12 N–B1	N–B4
13 B–B2	R–K1
14 N–N3	B–KB1

This system is considered one of the best replies to the variation selected by White. Black has succeeded in regrouping his forces and is prepared for a battle in the centre.

15 P–QN4

This is the only way to drive away Black's knight. 15 P–Q4 is impossible because of the insufficient defence of White's K4.

15 ...	N(4)–Q2
16 P–Q4	P–R3
17 B–Q2	

Defending against the possibility of ... P-Q4

17 ...	N-N3

For some reason, Gligoric declines to play the known 17 ... P-QR4 which gives Black a completely equal game. Nevertheless, his move merits consideration.

18 B-Q3

This move blocks the incursion of Black's knight at White's QB4 and halts the advance of Black's QRP at the same time.

18 ...	R-B1
19 Q-B2!?	

At first glance a strange continuation— White places his queen on the same file as Black's rook. But the QB file will not in fact be opened, either by the immediate 19 ... P-B4 20 NP×P P×P 21 P-Q5, or after the preliminary exchange 19 ... P×P 20 P×P P-B4 21 NP×P P×P 22 P-Q5 with a very sharp position.

19 ...	Q-Q2

A lethargic move that will cost Black dearly. Not only does it lose an important tempo, but the queen has taken the Q2 square away from Black's knights, limiting their manoeuverability.

20 QR-Q1	Q-B3
21 B-K3	N-R5

This is the only way to gain time to defend against the threatened N-Q2-N3-R5. 21 ... N-B5 was impossible in view of 22 P-Q5 Q-Q2 23 B×N P×B 24 N-Q2 and 25 N×P.

22 R-QB1	N-N3
23 Q-N1	

Better is the immediate 23 N-Q2; then 23 ... P-Q4 is not dangerous since White's

K4 is safely defended, e.g. 24 QP×P R×P 25 B-Q4! (25 P-KB4? P×P with a winning position for Black) 25 ... P×P 26 N(2)×P. There is no defence against N-Q2-N3-R5.

23 ...	Q-Q2
24 N-Q2	P-B4

A forced action. Now White gets a strong, defended passed pawn on Q5.

25 NP×P	QP×P
26 P-Q5	N-R5
27 P-QB4	P-N5
28 R-B1	

Black's trouble is that he cannot find a satisfactory defence against the breakthrough P-B4, initiating a fearsome assault on the king's position. Q-side counter-play is hopelessly late.

28 ...	Q-B2
29 P-B4	N-Q2
30 Q-B2	N-B6

This advance of Black's knight loses a pawn by force after the transfer of White's bishop to Q2, but a retreat to N3 would be even gloomier.

31 P-B5	N-B3
32 N-K2?!	

Of course it would have been better to win the pawn by 32 N-B3, 33 B-Q2 and 34 B×N, but it seemed to me that Black was defenceless against a K-side pawn storm. However, it turns out that Black's king is able, a little at a time, to escape from its insecure refuge.

32 ...	N×N+
33 B×N	B-Q3
34 P-N4	K-B1
35 P-KR4	K-K2
36 P-N5	P×P

37 P×P	N–Q2
38 B–N4	

White's pieces have turned out to be unprepared for such a swift unfolding of events. The decisive thrust requires regrouping and the supplying of new pieces to the K-side.

38 ...	R–KN1

White was threatening 39 P–B6+ P×P 40 P×P+ N×P 41 B–N5. But without the advance P–B3, Black will hardly be able to manage. Thus 38 ... P–B3 was better here.

39 K–B2	R–KR1
40 R–KR1	QR–KN1

It is vital for the Black king to be able to escape to the Q-side without interference. Now White has an excellent chance to resolve the struggle in his favour by 41 P–R3 P–R4 42 Q–R4! N–N3 43 Q–N5! and Black cannot trap the queen since on 43 ... R×R 44 R×R R–QR1 there follows the deadly P–B6+, and Black has no time for P–B3 because of the manoeuvre N–N3 with attacks on Black's QR4 and QB4. But I bypassed this opportunity and made a not completely successful move.

41 Q–Q1	K–Q1

The sealed move. Gligoric, as previously, refrains from advancing P–B3. 41 ... N–N3

loses because of 42 P–B6+ P×P 43 Q–B3 N–Q2 44 N–N3 with the threats B×N and N×P. Also bad is 41 ... P–R4 42 Q–R4 N–N3 43 Q–N5.

42 Q–N1	N–N3
43 R–R2	Q–K2?

This is a serious mistake. It is necessary to push the Q-side pawns. White's knight immediately occupies QR5 and the game ends quickly.

44 N–N3	K–B2
45 K–B3	

Yet another little strategem; White's king move frees the second rank for his rooks and opens the KN1–QR7 diagonal for his queen.

45 ...	N–Q2
46 P–R3	P×P
47 R–R2	R–R5
48 R×P	R(1)–KR1
49 R–N1	

Black lacks the strength to defend all his weak points, and the game ends very quickly.

49 ...	R–QN1?

An error which does not change matters. All the same 49 ... P–B3 was more tenacious.

50 Q–K1	R×B

On 50 ... R(5)–R1 there would follow 51 Q–R5+ K–B1 52 P–B6 P×P 53 N×P.

51 K×R	B–B1
52 Q–R5+	Resigns

On 52 ... R–N3 decisive is 53 N×P B×N 54 R×R B×R 55 B×B+ N×B 56 P–B5.

MATCH-TOURNAMENT OF USSR TEAMS, MOSCOW 1973

One of the aims of this event was to provide practice for the top Soviet players prior to the coming Interzonal Tournaments in Leningrad and in the Brazilian town of Petropolis. Besides, it was interesting to see how the young players would fare in comparison with their older colleagues. The first and second teams were decided upon basically by choosing grandmasters with the biggest names, and the greatest successes in recent times. The third team, the youth team, was made up on an age principle, apart from anything else, since of course otherwise Anatoly Karpov would have been in the first team.

The two-cycle event was held in the enormous hall of the Soviet Army Central Sports Club. The playing area, where the boards were laid out, was bounded on two sides by stands for the numerous spectators. Along the other two sides of the enormous rectangle, demonstration boards were set up, so that the spectators could follow the course of the games not only by the faces of the players.

The results of the event, at first sight not very significant (1st Team—23½ points, Youth Team—18½, 2nd Team—18), showed, however, that worthy replacements for the leading grandmasters were developing. But certain individual results proved to be of exceptional importance, and, it would seem to me, influenced a great number of things. I am thinking in particular of the results of two famous Soviet grandmasters—Mikhail Tal and Anatoly Karpov. The Ex-World Champion, despite the pleas of his friends, flew to Moscow straight from hospital—in Riga he had just undergone a minor operation. After a record series of eighty-three tournament games without defeat, Tal lost twice to grandmaster Yury Balashov of the Youth Team. These defeats could not fail to affect Tal's general state prior to the Interzonal Tournament, although Tigran Petrosian thought that the defeats might prove beneficial: otherwise, he thought, Tal might altogether lose his sense of danger.

Exactly the opposite happened with Anatoly Karpov, who some six weeks before the Match-Tournament had taken second place in an international tournament in Budapest, where, hard as he tried, he was unable to catch grandmaster Efim Geller, who had played excellently. People had become accustomed to Karpov's victories, and this second place was regarded almost as a failure. Before the start of the Interzonal, Anatoly required a new burst of confidence, a new stimulus in his play. And he gained it, appearing on top board for the Youth Team.

In the first round, after sacrificing a pawn against Mark Taimanov, Karpov first positionally outplayed the experienced grandmaster, and then, literally out of nothing, developed an irresistible attack.

Taimanov–Karpov
Nimzo-Indian Defence

1 P–Q4 N–KB3 2 P–QB4 P–K3 3 N–QB3 B–N5 4 P–K3 P–B4 5 B–Q3 0–0 6 N–B3 P–Q4 7 0–0 P×BP 8 B×BP P×P 9 P×P P–QN3 10 Q–K2 B–N2 11 R–Q1 QN–Q2 12 B–Q2 R–B1 13 B–QR6 B×B 14 Q×B B×N 15 P×B R–B2 16 QR–B1 Q–B1

17 Q–R4 R–B5 18 Q×P Q–B3 19 Q–R3
R–B1 20 P–R3 P–R3 21 R–N1 R–R5 22 Q–N3
N–Q4 23 R(Q1)–QB1 R–B5 24 R–N2 P–B3
25 R–K1 K–B2 26 Q–Q1 N–B1 27 R–N3
N–N3 28 Q–N1 R–QR1 29 R–K4 R(5)–R5

30 R–N2 N–B1 31 Q–Q3 R–B5 32 R–K1
R–R6 33 Q–N1 N–N3 34 R–QB1 N×P
35 Q–Q3 N–K7+ 36 Q×N R×R+ 37
B×R Q×B+ 38 K–R2 (Diag.) 38 . . . R×N
39 P×R N–R5 40 White lost on time

When the players later analysed this game in the press centre, Karpov astonished all those around him with an abundance of beautiful, deeply-calculated and complicated variations. His friends had difficulty in dragging him away from the board, and almost forcibly took him home and soon put him to bed. Only those very close to him knew that he was quite ill that day, that he had severe tonsillitis and a high temperature . . .

A day later Karpov came up against "the" Boris Spassky. Thousands of chess fans came to watch this game. Karpov boldly sacrificed a rook for a bishop, his pieces developed incredible activity, and on move 32 an unexpected queen move provoked an ovation in the hall. For this brilliant victory Anatoly Karpov was awarded a special prize by the chess weekly *64*.

In the second cycle neither Taimanov nor Spassky tried to gain revenge. One gained the impression that both were happy to draw. Thus by scoring 3 points out of 4, Anatoly Karpov took first place among the leaders of the three teams. What was even more important was that he had managed to defeat one of the winners of the previous Interzonal stage, and also an Ex-World Champion, one of the favourites in the coming Candidates' event.

Anatoly Karpov admitted at the time:

"In the Moscow Match-Tournament I did not set myself the task of winning at all costs, but regarded the event simply as a stage of preparation towards the World Championship. There were various things that I wanted to clear up and test, in particular, certain opening schemes, which could later come in useful".

Yes, now he could look to the future with confidence—within a month the Interzonal Tournament was due to start! . . .

Karpov–Spassky
Ruy Lopez

1 P–K4	P–K4
2 N–KB3	N–QB3
3 B–N5	P–QR3
4 B–R4	N–B3
5 0–0	B–K2
6 R–K1	P–QN4
7 B–N3	P–Q3
8 P–B3	0–0
9 P–KR3	N–N1

Both players have long been devotees of the Ruy Lopez. They have adopted it in the most important of events, and have emerged successfully from theoretical duels. It is no surprise that on this occasion the object of discussion becomes the highly popular Breyer Variation.

10 P–Q3

The most critical continuation is of course 10 P–Q4. The continuation chosen is unlikely to give White any advantage, but on the other hand it leads to a prolonged and tense struggle.

10 ...	B–N2
11 QN–Q2	QN–Q2
12 N–B1	N–B4
13 B–B2	R–K1
14 N–N3	B–KB1
15 P–N4	N(4)–Q2
16 P–Q4	

All this had already occurred in several previous games. White is forced to advance his QP, otherwise Black will seize the initiative by the central freeing advance of his QP.

16 ...	P–R3
17 B–Q2	N–N3
18 B–Q3	P–N3

Spassky deviates from the game Karpov–Gligoric, San Antonio 1972, where 18 ... R–B1 was played.

19 Q–B2

White regroups his forces, vacating the square Q1 for a rook, at the same time defending once more his KP.

19 ...	N(B3)–Q2

Since White has overprotected his K4 square, Black must immediately organize pressure with his bishop from KN2 on the adjacent square—Q4.

20 QR–Q1	B–N2
21 P×P	

Here I thought for more than 30 minutes. Black has deployed his pieces very cleverly, and as a result it is not easy for White to obtain favourable play. The standard plans, where White attempts a K-side attack or undermines the centre by P–KB4, do not

work, since in each case Black has time to land a counter-blow in the centre—P–Q4. I came to the conclusion that White was virtually forced to make this exchange in the centre.

21 ...	P×P

This move can certainly not be termed a mistake, but perhaps Black should have exchanged knights?

22 P–B4

White has to hurry, as he has no time to prepare this advance. E.g. 22 B–K3 Q–K2 23 N–Q2 P–QB4, equalizing.

22 ...	P×P

On 22 ... P–QB4 there was the possibility of a piece sacrifice: 23 BP×P P–B5 24 B×BP R–QB1 25 B×BP+ K×B 26 Q–N3+.

23 B×BP	Q–K2

But this is definitely an inaccuracy. By leaving White's highly dangerous Spanish bishop alive, Black puts himself in great danger. 23 ... N×B 24 Q×N would have given equal chances.

24 B–N3!	P–B4
25 P–QR4	

Of course, in making this move I foresaw the coming exchange sacrifice and calculated its consequences. Strictly speaking, White decided on the sacrifice a move earlier, when he played 24 B–N3, and now there was no way, and indeed no reason, to go back on his decision.

| 25 ... | P–B5 |

25 ... P×P was bad in view of 26 P–R5 R–QB1 (25 ... R–QB1 26 P–R5 P×P comes to the same thing) 27 Q–R2 N–R1 28 B×NP!.

26 B–R2	B–QB3
27 P–R5	B–R5
28 Q–B1	N–QB1

Hardly any better for Black was 28 ... B×R 29 R×B N–R5 30 B×RP B×B 31 Q×B, when 31 ... N–B6 fails to 32 B×P with the threat of 33 Q×P+, while on 31 ... N–B1 White gains excellent attacking prospects by 32 R–QB1.

| 29 B×RP | B×R |
| 30 R×B | N–Q3? |

After this move comes a completely un-expected finish. Black also loses after 30 ... B×B 31 Q×B N–Q3 32 N–N5 N–KB1 33 N–R5 P×N 34 R×N QR–B1 35 R–KB6. Best is 30 ... R–R2, but in this case too White gains more than sufficient compensation after 31 B×B K×B 32 Q×P.

| 31 B×B | K×B |

32 Q–N5!

A surprise! White quite unexpectedly offers the exchange of queens, but Black cannot accept in view of the loss of a piece. Black would unexpectedly have won after 32 Q–Q2 QR–Q1 33 Q×N? N–B1.

| 32 ... | P–B3 |

32 ... QR–B1 merely prolongs the struggle, since after 33 R×N Q×Q 34 N×Q N–B3 35 N–K2 P–B6 36 B×P White is bound to realize his material advantage.

| 33 Q–N4 | K–R2 |

The only defence against 34 R×N and 35 N–B5+, but the position is already indefensible.

| 34 N–R4 | Resigns |

Resignation may seem slightly premature, but an examination of the following varia-tions shows that Black's position is complete-ly hopeless: 34 ... R–KN1 35 B×P R–N2 36 R×N Q×R 37 N(4)–B5, when mate can be averted only by giving up the queen by 37 ... Q–Q8+, or 34 ... N–KB1 35 N×P followed by 36 Q–R5+ and 37 R×N.

CHAPTER 3

On the approaches to Olympus

INTERZONAL TOURNAMENT, LENINGRAD 1973

The strength of the players in this event, as in every Interzonal, was highly uneven. Along with the personally invited top grandmasters, and the winners of the strongest FIDE Zones, were included representatives of countries where chess is as yet poorly developed. Bent Larsen, that normally fearless Viking, in a letter written before the tournament to the translator of his book into Russian, stated that he was most upset by the unequal division of the two Interzonal groups (in Leningrad and Brazil), and that in such a frame of mind it would be difficult for him to take one of the top places.

On examining the list of participants, Mikhail Tal remarked that the Leningrad goup contained a number of players who liked to, and had the ability to, play for an optimum result in any event. He anticipated a race along a bumpy road, where success goes not to the one who pedals slowly along, but to the one who holds tightly onto the handle-bars, pedals with all his might, while sitting confidently in the saddle, and not allowing himself to be dislodged from it by any vicissitudes of fate...

During a fairly important International Tournament in Tallinn which preceded the Interzonal, Tal was asked by a journalist to name the trio of probable winners in Leningrad. As the journalist listed the imposing names of the favourites, the Ex-World Champion nodded his head in agreement, and then suddenly remarked that one of the trio would definitely be a player who at that time was clearly under-estimated. Spassky, replying to the same question, confirmed this: "Two will be from among the favourites, and one will be Mr. X!" But who this mysterious Mr. X would be, and how he would fare in the Candidates' Matches, no one would venture to predict...

In the middle of the tournament "suspicion" fell on the Czech grandmaster Jan Šmejkal, and with good reason. It is true that in making his fortieth move in a winning position against the Argentinian Miguel Quinteros he failed to press his clock quickly enough, and suffered a highly vexing loss on time. But later on Šmejkal managed to win seven games in a row. Though constantly in time-trouble, this young, reserved man nevertheless joked: "I start to get worried only when my flag is raised".

Šmejkal was halted for the second time by the even younger West German grandmaster Robert Hübner (although it was only in the penultimate round, against Karpov, that Šmejkal's chances of reaching the Candidates finally disappeared). In the previous Interzonal Tournament, held on the Spanish island of Majorca, it was Hübner who had turned out to be this Mr. X, quite unexpectedly leaping out from behind the backs of several other likely candidates.

On watching his play at the Olympiad in the Yugoslav town of Skopje, where he came ahead of the top boards of all the other teams, not losing one of his 18 games and gaining 12 excellent wins, I was personally convinced that it was Hübner (together with Larsen) who could come between some of the Soviet grandmasters and success. But he arrived at Leningrad from Cologne after working on his university diploma, work which for nearly six months had not allowed him to spend any time on chess. Hübner insistently asked that he be seated at a table at the very back of the stage, where the noise of the thousands in the hall was less noticeable. At this table he acted extremely quietly, without zest, evidently playing himself in. Nevertheless, almost imperceptibly he stole up on the leaders.

Tigran Petrosian, who had studied Hübner well, (he had won a match, not without difficulty, against the German in the previous cycle) predicted that the West German player would be ultimately successful. But on the following day Hübner was easily beaten... by the totally inexperienced Cuban player Gilermo Estevez. Hübner should have paid heed to the words of this "hunter of grandmaster scalps", who called the mate he had inflicted on the great Tal a miracle, and the immediately added that if he could repeat this with one of the other grandmasters, he would consider his task for the tournament fulfilled.

In the final table, following the fourth-placed Šmejkal, Hübner shared fifth place with Bent Larsen. The Dane, in contrast to the West German grandmaster, had made a brilliant start—five wins, and only one draw, with the 21 year-old Filipino Eugenio Torre. Surprisingly, it was this lost half point which had a dispiriting effect on Larsen, and he literally ran away from the correspondents, with whom normally he was always so amiable. True, the Dane had already managed to "partly reveal himself" to one of them, in answering the question:

"What do you think you are lacking as a player?"

"Formerly", said Larsen, "I was lacking in objectivity in the assessment of a position and its possibilities, now I cannot make up for lost time."

It was sufficient for Larsen to suffer defeat in the first important encounter, when he "began to reel", and then soon fell back altogether. Karpov emphasizes the point: "I have come to the conclusion that, when the competition becomes more fierce, Larsen's nerves will simply not stand it."

And so it turned out that Mr. X was—Mr. Byrne. In Korchnoi's opinion he was more composed and more competitive than any of the others, and it was this in the main that enabled him to come ahead of Šmejkal, Hübner and Larsen. Robert Byrne had prepared this sensation. How else can one explain that which was said by the taciturn American at the very start of the tournament: "I think that I am capable of surprising a number of people". And he surprised them, this greying 45 year-old, whose concealed temperament, according to his friends, is only revealed in thunderous ovations at ballet performances with the participation of Maja Plisetska or Margot Fonteyn.

In the Leningrad hotel "Astoria", where the players lived and where they normally came together at the same time every day after dinner, I was talking to Byrne's second. Time and again my companion would anxiously look at his watch. His charge had not yet come down to dinner, and even without this there was already too little time left to prepare for the very important game with Tal. Finally the second excused himself, and went up to his grandmaster's room. He soon returned, and with a laugh explained: "Mr Byrne has asked not to be disturbed—he is writing a big article for the '*New York Times*'". In the bus, which took the players to the tournament hall, the grandmaster-journalist entered with a stack of typed sheets, which before the game he managed to send off by telex. After the game—which he drew— Byrne appeared in the press centre, and immediately began writing out some analysis.

...The reader will no doubt be asking: "But what about Mikhail Tal?" When during a game it is only the habit of fighting against illness (a "habit" which probably only he has) which enables you to keep sitting at the table, no other explanation is necessary. They try to persuade you to leave the tournament, but this means putting off your hopes for a minimum of three years, until the next Interzonal. And if you have already played half the number of games, and then you walk out—this means putting several "plusses" in the table (the same as wins) for those who are battling for a place in the first three, and thus creating unequal conditions. You use your last reserves of strength, and the first wins appear... Too late...

But it is not illness alone that explains Tal's major failure. There were also oversights of a competitive nature, associated, it would seem, with a somewhat erroneous assessment of his present-day possibilities. There was the psychological pressure of a series of recent triumphs, forcing him to battle not just for third, but definitely for first place. There was... However, one can't go into everything.

It was annoying, of course, that it was at the Interzonal Tournament that all this should happen. But after all, the chess doesn't end there, and Mikhail Tal has failed in not just one Interzonal Tournament...

Strange though it may seem, it is most difficult of all to talk about Anatoly Karpov. The idea that it helps to play on one's "home ground" is a dangerous one, if it is applied directly. In the hall are your friends and relations, who can sense your feelings almost in a physical sense. In addition, it must be agreed that in your home town it is more difficult to avoid distracting encounters with friends, invitations, and replies to questions by journalists, who consider you obliged to give only them an interview—you're one of them, from Leningrad. And the telephone calls! Autographs... All it needed was for Karpov to stop, and a dense crowd would form, from which he couldn't escape for a long time. At the age of twenty-two it is difficult to say "no" to a schoolboy, to say nothing of an elderly man. They'll start saying: "stardom has gone to his head". After one of the adjournment sessions, close to the end of the tournament, Karpov's mother and father, who had arrived in Leningrad from Tula, could not contain themselves: for the shy and considerate they themselves asked their son for his autograph.

Of course, at first sight all this may seem unimportant, but who knows, perhaps it was this complete concentration of all his physical, mental, and of course chess powers which enabled Anatoly to achieve such an exceptional result for an event of this class—13½ out of 17 possible points.

* * *

For Karpov the determining factor was his slogan: "The important thing is to remain one-self", after which he normally adds: "Strategy is dictated by the situation". But in these two statements, which at first sight do not tally very well, there is no contradiction. It is as if all the time the young grandmaster is disproving the Aristotle saying: "He who is young cannot remain calm". In the Match-Tournament of USSR Teams he scored three points out of four, relaxed and did some studying in Sochi, and then set off to Leningrad for the Interzonal. To a correspondent he calmly stated that in this three-year cycle Fischer would possibly remain Champion, but that in the following cycle one of the young players would beat him... Quiet courage is a rare quality, as is the character of a man who knows his own value, and does not allow himself to be distracted on the way to his goal.

Of course, Anatoly Karpov definitely wanted to be amongst the three winners of the Inter-zonal Tournament, and with every justification. True, he was not too happy with the pairings: it was essential to make a good start, and here he was with Black in the first game against the Cuban player Estevez. This game was adjourned in a position where Karpov had a certain advantage, but the opponent still had clear chances of a draw. Every day preceding the adjournment session, grandmaster Semion Furman and his assistant Yuri Razuvayev analysed the adjourned position. Then Karpov joined in, and after thinking for some forty seconds, decisively rejected the first move resulting from the lengthy analysis. Furman was even offended: "You straight away reject that which I've been working on for so long..." "No, even so I won't look at this continuation", Karpov stated categorically. The subsequent careful examination of the position, and the win on adjournment, showed that his unique intuitive flair had not let him down.

And now a few details of how some of Karpov's games went. Enormous efforts were required in the game with the "wounded Tal". All the time the Ex-World Champion had the advantage, and when the time for the sealed move arrived, it appeared that he had real winning chances. On adjourning the game, Karpov grimly searched for a draw, which would first appear, and then suddenly somehow vanish. Furman, who himself was down-hearted, tried to reassure Anatoly, pointing out that the resumption would not be for some days, and that there was still time to find a saving line. With the adjourned game on his mind, Karpov went to bed, but his sleep was troubled. And what happened was something which one encounters quite often with people whose work is with their brain; the solution, which depended on one unexpected move, was found... in his sleep. Afterwards, Karpov could remember the whole of his nocturnal discussion, except for this ill-fated move. And it was only just before the resumption itself that everything was established in full. However, Tal did not play the strongest line, and to attain a draw this strong study-like measure was not required. When Karpov gained this draw, Robert Byrne's second, international master B. Zukkerman exclaimed: "Well, if he can save a position like that, he must be altogether unbeatable!"

Tal–Karpov
Ruy Lopez

1 P–K4 P–K4 2 N–KB3 N–QB3 3 B–N5
P–QR3 4 B–R4 N–B3 5 0–0 B–K2 6 R–K1
P–QN4 7 B–N3 P–Q3 8 P–B3 0–0 9 P–KR3
N–N1 10 P–Q4 QN–Q2 11 QN–Q2 B–N2
12 B–B2 R–K1 13 P–QN4 B–KB1 14 B–N2
P–QR4 15 B–Q3 P–B3 16 P–R3 N–N3 17
R–QB1 P×QP 18 N×P KN–Q2 19 N(2)–N3
N–K4 20 N×RP R×N 21 P×R N(3)–B5
22 R–B2 Q×P 23 B–KB1 N×B 24 R×N
Q×BP 25 R–N3 Q–R4 26 Q–N1 Q–R2 27
R–Q1 N–Q2 28 N–B5 R–K3 29 N–Q4 R–K1
30 B×P P×B 31 N×P Q–B4 32 N×P
B×N 33 R×B(7) N–B3 34 Q–N3 B–B2

35 Q–N5 Q–B7 36 Q–N1 Q×Q 37 R(1)×Q
B–Q3 38 P–QR4 R×P 39 R–Q1 N–K1 40
P–R5 K–B1

41 P–R6 R–QR5 42 R–R7 P–N4 43 R–R8
B–K4 44 P–N3 K–K2 45 R–K1 P–B3 46
P–R7 N–B2 47 R–R8 R×P 48 **Drawn**

There were also other complications. In the game with Cuellar of Colombia, for instance. Such players, who realize beforehand the futility of trying for a high place in the tournament, see as their calling the taking of one or two notable scalps. Their names normally figure prominently in chess history, invested with the imposing titles of "threats to grandmasters". Who knows, perhaps it was this kind of fame that Cuellar envisaged, as he stared constantly at Karpov's castled position. During these moments the South American player acted in the style of North American Ice Hockey Professionals: just as the Canadians do with the puck, so he threw a pawn into "Karpov's zone", and after it sent several of his white pieces. It is always difficult defending against such forwards, especially if they not only like, but also know how to attack. In repulsing his opponent's clever threats, Karpov, who normally plays so quickly, got into time trouble, but nevertheless contrived to escape with an extra pawn.

This point cost both Karpov, and his trainer Furman, a great deal of nervous energy. They were late for the following round, when the car in which they were travelling swerved out into the middle of the road, and the driver began sounding his horn, so as to be let through. Furman, who was miles away, suddenly asked: "Who is that blowing his horn?" "It's us", Razuvayev answered with a laugh.

And so, Karpov had a lot of points, but his rivals also had no desire to fall behind. Nothing was settled until the penultimate round and the encounter with Šmejkal, for whom only a win would do. And if he should achieve this, Karpov's chances of reaching the Candidates, which not long before were so bright, would suddenly become problematic. So this was a really critical moment.

"My opponent", Anatoly Karpov relates, "surprised me by advancing his king's pawn on the first move. I decided to surprise him in return, and in the Sicilian Defence adopted an idea which had not been analysed in detail. Šmejkal worked things out excellently over the board, and by subtle play obtained a marked advantage. True, all this required of the Czech grandmaster a great deal of time, he failed to find a decisive continuation, and just before the adjournment even blundered away a pawn. At this point I felt genuinely sorry for him: after battling so bravely, his hopes were now dashed. Nevertheless, in the adjourned position I was by no means certain of a win. It was not without good reason that, in a conversation the previous day with a certain master, who was present at the tournament in the rôle of correspondent, Šmejkal had asserted that at any rate he wouldn't lose the game... I was late for the resumption, since the car I was travelling in broke down, and I had to continue by metro and then on foot. On entering the playing hall, I saw Šmejkal looking very downcast—he just couldn't forget that the previous day he had missed such a good chance of winning. On resumption my opponent nevertheless lost, and this meant that I was assured of at least a share of first place.

Šmejkal–Karpov
Sicilian Defence

1 P–K4 P–QB4 2 N–KB3 P–K3 3 P–Q4 P×P 4 N×P N–QB3 5 N–QB3 P–QR3 6 B–K2 Q–B2 7 0–0 N–B3 8 B–K3 B–N5 9 N–R4 0–0 10 N×N NP×N 11 N–N6 R–N1 12 N×B KR×N 13 B×P R–Q1 14 B–Q3 B–Q3 15 K–R1 B–K4 16 P–QB3 R×P 17 Q–B1 N–N5 18 P–KB4 N×B 19 Q×R B×KBP 20 Q–KB2 N×R 21 R×N P–K4 22 P–N3 Q–Q3 23 B–K2 B–N4 24 Q×P+ K–R1 25 P–QR4 B–K2 26 P–R5 R–KB1 27 Q–QB4 R×R+ 28 B×R Q–B3 29 K–N2 Q–B1 30 B–K2 B–B4 31 B–N4 Q–B7+ 32 K–R3 P–Q3 33 B–Q7 P–N3 34 B×P K–N2 35 B–N5 Q–QN7 36 P–R6 B–N8 37 Q–K2 Q×P 38 B–B4 Q–B8

B–Q5 44 B–Q5 B–B4 45 B–B6 B–Q5 46
B–N7 P–N4 47 K–N4 P–R4+ 48 K–B5
Q×P 49 K–K6 Q–B7 50 Q–N5 Q–B3+
51 K–Q5 P–N5 52 B–B8 Q–K2 53 B–B5
K–R3 54 Q–B1 Q–QB2 55 Q–K2 Q–B4+
56 K–K6 K–N4 57 Q–B1 Q–R6 58 Q–K2
B–B4 59 Q–Q2+ Q–K6 60 Q–R5 B–N3 61
Q–R2 Q–B7 62 Q–N1 P–N6 63 B–R3 K–R5
64 B–N2 Q–N8 65 Q×Q B×Q 66 K×P
B–Q5 67 P–R7 B×P 68 K×P K–N5 69

39 Q–B1 Q–R3+ 40 K–N2 Q×P+ 41
K–B3 Q–R4+ 42 K–N2 Q–R7+ 43 K–B3

K–Q5 P–R5 70 P–K5 P–R6 71 B×P+ K×B
72 P–K6 B–B4 73 Resigns

"I gained satisfaction", writes Karpov, "not only from my result in the Leningrad Interzonal Tournament, but also from the purely creative aspect of my play—a desirable combination for any player. I managed to go through the whole tournament without defeat, and played a number of good games, one of which was judged to be the best in the tournament. This was the game with Quinteros."

Since the subsequent Candidates' cycle was to make Korchnoi the main rival to Anatoly Karpov in the battle for the World Title, I think that it will be interesting to acquaint the reader with certain opinions which were expressed by him after the conclusion of the Interzonal Tournament in Leningrad (opinions which, to his misfortune, he himself was to disprove by losing the final Candidates' Match to Karpov).

And so, over to Korchnoi:

"It is unlikely that I will manage to win the Candidates' Cycle. Amongst my rivals there are some 'awkward' opponents. With my style, I prefer playing against those who take the initiative, rather than 'sit on the fence'. And in general I consider that the generation defeated by Fischer is no longer able to successfully compete with him. This is a task for the younger players. Will Karpov manage it? I don't know. Karpov's recent appearances have shown that, as a tournament fighter, he seems in no way inferior to Fischer..."

And later:

"Karpov is improving with every tournament. In one of my lectures I said that in this cycle no one can win against Fischer. To do this Karpov has as yet insufficient experience and knowledge. Perhaps Anatoly Karpov believed me when he said to the journalists that this was 'not his cycle'? Of course, Karpov's intention to battle for the highest possible place in the Interzonal was a surprise to no one. His play in this tournament was more mature than earlier. Karpov is growing into a great tournament fighter, he is not afraid to take risks, and is capable of playing to win in every game. At the same time he is highly practical, and does not commit blunders. His play now resembles that of Spassky in his best years—he is composed in every encounter, he plays each stage of the game equally well, without any obvious errors."

...Within a year the Candidates' Cycle was to show that Anatoly Karpov had grown not only into an outstanding tournament fighter, but also into a formidable match player...

Karpov–Quinteros
Sicilian Defence

1 P–K4	P–QB4
2 N–KB3	P–Q3
3 P–Q4	P×P
4 N×P	N–KB3
5 N–QB3	P–QR3
6 B–KN5	P–K3
7 P–B4	Q–N3

As Fischer frequently used to play.

8 N–N3

Of course, this is something of a concession to Black, but my good tournament position allowed me to avoid going in for the wild variations with the pawn sacrifice after 8 Q–Q2. To be fair, it should be mentioned that 8 Q–Q2 is the only way to fight for an opening advantage.

8 ...   B–K2

After 8 ... Q–K6+ 9 Q–K2 Q×Q+ 10 B×Q the ending is slightly better for White. I consider that 8 ... QN–Q2 is a more accurate move order, not determining for the moment the position of the black-squared bishop.

9 Q–B3	P–R3
10 B–R4	QN–Q2
11 0–0–0	Q–B2

Black prepares P–QN4 and B–N2. White, so as to utilize his lead in development, must initiate play in the centre as quickly as possible, and this is the aim of his next move.

12 B–N3	P–QN4
13 P–K5	B–N2
14 Q–K2	

14 ...   P×P

14 ... N–Q4 is much more promising, when White achieves nothing by 15 P×P N×N 16 P×Q N×Q+ 17 B×N R–QB1 18 P–B5 P–K4, or 15 N×N B×N 16 P×P Q×QP 17 P–B5 Q–N3. But there is a tempting exchange sacrifice: 15 N×N B×N 16 R×B P×R 17 P–K6 N–B3 (17 ... P×P is bad in view of 18 Q×KP) 18 P×P+ K×P 19 Q–B3 followed by B–Q3, B–B2, and a K-side pawn storm. The consequences of this sacrifice are very difficult to calculate.

15 P×P   N–R2

The knight is forced to make this sorry retreat to the edge of the board, since 15 ... N–Q4 fails to 16 N×N B×N 17 R×B P×R 18 P–K6.

16 N–K4

The knight heads for Q6, while incidentally preventing castling: 16 ... 0–0? 17 N–B6+ B×N 18 P×B, with a strong attack.

16 ...   B–N4+

Of course, 16 ... N×P is dangerous on account of 17 N(4)–B5, while on 16 ... N–N4 I was intending to play 17 N–B6+ P×N 18 P×P Q–QB5 19 Q×Q P×Q 20 N–R5, with a clear advantage.

17 K–N1	0–0
18 P–KR4	B–K2
19 N–Q6	B–Q4?

Black's position is unattractive. His pieces are disunited, and the knight at R2 is altogether cut off from the centre of events. But even so, by playing 19 ... B–QB3 or 19 ... QR–Q1, he could have put up a defence.

After the move played, White sacrifices the exchange to obtain a decisive attack on the king.

| 20 R×B | P×R |
| 21 N–KB5 | |

Threatening both 22 N×B+ and 22 P–K6. The reply is forced.

21 ...	Q–Q1
22 Q–N4	P–N3
23 N×P+	K–N2
24 N–KB5+	

White could have won more quickly by 24 N–Q4 K×N 25 P–R5 (the more showy 25 N–B5+ probably also wins: 25 ... P×N 26 B–KB4+ N–N4 27 P×N++ K–N2 28 Q×P R–R1 29 R–R6, with a mating attack): 25 ... P–N4 is answered by a pretty mate—26 N–B5, while on 25 ... K–N2 there follows 26 P×P P×P 27 N–K6+, or 26 ... N–N4 27 N–B5+ K–N1 28 P–N7.

| 24 ... | K–R1 |
| 25 B–Q3 | R–KN1 |

After 25 ... P×N 26 Q×P Black cannot avoid mate (26 ... N(R2)–B3 27 P×N N×P 28 B–K5).

| 26 N–R6 | R–N2 |
| 27 P–R5 | Q–K1 |

The only way of defending his KN3 square. On 27 ... N(Q2)–B1 there could have followed 28 P×P P×P 29 P–K6.

| 28 P–K6 | N(Q2)–B3 |
| 29 KP×P | Q–Q1 |

On 29 ... Q–KB1 White wins both by the simple 30 Q–Q4, as well as by the pretty 30 P×P! N×Q 31 N×N B–Q3 (defending against 32 B–K5) 32 N–B6 B×B 33 N×N Q–Q3 34 N–B6+ B–R7 35 N–K8! R×NP 36 B×R (pointed out by M. Tseitlin).

30 Q–Q4	N×P
31 B–K5	B–B3
32 R–K1	B×B
33 R×B	N(4)–B3
34 P–N4	Q–KB1
35 P–N5	N–K5
36 B×N	P×B
37 Q×P	Resigns

Tukmakov–Karpov
Ruy Lopez

1 P–K4	P–K4
2 N–KB3	N–QB3
3 B–N5	P–QR3
4 B–R4	N–B3
5 0–0	B–K2
6 R–K1	P–QN4
7 B–N3	P–Q3
8 P–B3	0–0
9 P–KR3	N–N1
10 P–Q4	QN–Q2

11 P–B4	P–B3
12 B–N5	

In the game between us from the Alekhine Memorial Tournament, 1971, Tukmakov continued 12 BP×P RP×P 13 N–B3 B–R3 14 P×P P×P 15 B–N5, but without achieving anything. He therefore decides to change his move order, but it is doubtful whether this innovation will find many followers.

12 ...	P–R3

The books state that Black also has a good game after 12 ... NP×P 13 B×P N×P 14 B×B Q×B 15 R×N P–Q4 16 R–K2 P×B. I think that 12 ... P–R3 is stronger, and even enables Black to gain a slight advantage.

13 B–KR4	N–R4!

The black-squared bishops are exchanged, and the knight establishes itself at ... KB5, from where it will worry the white king.

14 B×B	Q×B
15 BP×P	RP×P
16 N–B3	

And this is a serious inaccuracy, which allows Black to completely seize the initiative. White should have restricted himself to the modest 16 QN–Q2.

16 ...	P–N5
17 N–N1	

The knight would have been awkwardly placed at K2.

17 ...	N–B5
18 QN–Q2	P×P
19 N×P	N–K4!

Black's pieces have taken up ideal positions. The two knights in the centre control virtually the whole board. The white king is in danger, and the highly unpleasant 20 ... Q–N4 is threatened. With his next move White defends against this attack.

20 N(2)–B3	Q–B3
21 N×N	

White has to agree to the opening of the Q-file, since otherwise it is difficult for him to disentangle his group of pieces in the centre.

21 ...	P×N
22 N–B5	

Practically forced. 22 N–B3 is bad on account of 22 ... R–Q1 23 Q–B2 N×P+, while on 22 N–K2 there is the possibility of a knight sacrifice: 22 ... R–Q1 23 Q–B2 N×P+ 24 P×N Q–B6.

22 ...	B×N
23 P×B	QR–Q1

By winning a pawn (23 ... Q×P) Black would have lost the initiative, and after 24 Q–B3 he would have been faced with the lengthy process of realizing his extra pawn. I wanted more.

24 Q–B3	

8*

Any other move is answered by 24 ... Q–N4.

24 ...	R–Q7
25 R–K3	

White loses after 25 QR–B1 Q×P 26 R×BP? N×P+! 27 Q×N Q×P+ and 28 ... Q×R, while on 25 QR–Q1 Black can simply capture a pawn—25 ... R×NP. Tukmakov hopes for counter-play by attacking the KP.

25 ...	R×NP
26 QR–K1	R–K1
27 R–K4	N–Q4
28 Q–N3	N–B6
29 R×NP	

In the event of 29 R×KP White also loses the exchange: 29 ... N–K7+ (but not 29 ... R×R 30 Q×R) 30 R(1)×N R(7)×R.

29 ...	N–K7+
30 R×N	R×R
31 R–N7?	

White misses his last chance of fighting for a draw—31 Q–N6!.

31 ...	R–K2
32 R–N8+	K–R2
33 K–B1	

Of course, on 33 Q–N6+ Black must play 33 ... Q×Q, otherwise White has perpetual check.

33 ...	R–Q7

Avoiding the last trap: 33 ... R–N7 34 Q–N6+!! P×Q 35 B–N8+ K–R1 36 B–N3+ with perpetual check, or 34 ... Q×Q 35 P×Q+ K×P 36 B–B7+ K×B

37 R×R with a draw. On 33 ... R–K5 White again attains a draw: 34 Q–N6+!! Q×Q 35 P×Q+ K×P 36 B–B2.

34 White resigns

Karpov–Kuzmin
French Defence

1 P–K4	P–K3
2 P–Q4	P–Q4
3 N–Q2	

At present this continuation is supplanting the formerly popular 3 N–QB3. The point is that it leads to a slight, but lasting—I repeat: lasting—advantage for White.

3 ...	P–QB4
4 KP×P	KP×P
5 KN–B3	N–QB3
6 B–N5	B–Q3

On 6 ... P×P Black has to reckon with 7 Q–K2+, when the ending after 7 ... Q–K2 is in White's favour. He therefore wastes a tempo on 6 ... B–Q3, so as to be able to block on ... K2 with the knight.

7 P×P	

In the event of 7 0–0 P×P 8 N×P B×P+ Black has a good game.

7 ...	B×BP
8 0–0	KN–K2
9 N–N3	B–Q3

9 ... B–N3 also leads to a complicated position, with a slight advantage for White.

10 B–N5	

The bishop is to be transferred to KN3.

10 ...	0–0
11 B–KR4	Q–B2

A waste of time. Black should have begun a fight for the central squares by 11 ... B–KN5. I was intending to reply 12 B–N3 B×B 13 RP×B Q–N3 14 B–Q3, with the threat of 15 B×P+ K×B 16 N–N5+, while after 14 ... N–B4 15 B×N B×B 16 P–B3 White maintains a slight advantage.

12 B–N3	B×B

12 ... B–KN5 was again better.

13 RP×B	B–N5
14 R–K1	QR–Q1
15 P–B3	Q–N3
16 B–Q3	

The side with an isolated queen's pawn should aim either for an initiative on the K-side, or for the advance of this pawn. Here, since Black has no attack, there remains only one plan—to advance ... P–Q5. If he fails to achieve this, White will have a clear advantage.

16 ...	N–N3

16 ... P–Q5 would, of course, have been answered by 17 P–B4.

17 Q–B2	B×N
18 P×B	R–Q3

In the event of 18 ... P–Q5 19 P–KB4 (19 P–QB4? N–N5) 19 ... P×P 20 P×P an interesting position is reached, in which White's pawns restrict the black knights on both wings.

19 P–KB4	KR–Q1
20 P–R3!	

Now the advance of the QP is ruled out. White's plan is clear: he will transfer his knight to KB3, double his rooks on the K-file, and then, according to circumstances, advance his KBP and his Q-side pawns. By the advance of his KRP Black attempts to create counter-play, but without success.

20 ...	P–KR4
21 K–N2	P–R5
22 R–K2	N–B1
23 N–Q2	R–R3
24 N–B3	

What is Black to do with his KRP? If he advances it to ... R6, it will be surrounded. Its exchange leads to the opening of the file, which is dangerous for Black.

24 ...	P×P
25 P×P	N–Q2
26 QR–K1	K–B1

There is no other way of defending the back rank. Now the white pawns rush forward, and completely upset the co-ordination of the enemy pieces.

27 P–KN4	Q–B2
28 P–N5	R–KR1
29 K–N3	N–B4
30 B–B5	P–KN3
31 P–N4!	

Before retreating the bishop, the knight must be driven away from ... QB4.

31 ...	N–K5+

Totally bad is 31 ... P×B 32 P×N Q–Q2 33 R–R2 K–N2 34 N–R4, or 31 ... N–Q2 33 B×P P×B 34 Q×P, with an irresistible attack.

32 B×N	P×B
33 Q×P	K–N2
34 P–N5	N–R4
35 Q–K7!	

Forcibly transposing into a won ending, since 35 ... Q×QBP fails to 36 R–K3 Q–N7 37 R–K5.

35 ...	Q×Q
36 R×Q	R–Q6
37 R–B7	N–N6
38 K–N4	R–KB1
39 R(1)–K7	

Against the threats of 40 N–K5 and 40 R×BP+ R×R 41 R×R+ K×R 42 N–K5+ there is no defence.

39 ...	**Black resigns**

Karpov–Gligorić
Ruy Lopez

1 P–K4	P–K4
2 N–KB3	N–QB3
3 B–N5	P–QR3
4 B–R4	N–B3
5 0–0	B–K2
6 R–K1	P–QN4
7 B–N3	P–Q3
8 P–B3	0–0
9 P–KR3	N–N1
10 P–Q4	QN–Q2
11 QN–Q2	B–N2
12 B–B2	P–B4

Gligorić regularly employs this variation, which occurred in his games with Keres at San Antonio (1972) and with Tal in the Interzonal Tournament. Both Keres and Tal carried out the manoeuvre N–B1–N3. I decided to close the centre.

13 P–Q5	N–K1

Black plans to play ... P–B4 after ... P–N3 and ... N–N2.

14 N–B1	P–N3
15 B–R6	

After this, Black is unable to effect the advance ... P–B4.

15 ...	N–N2
16 N–K3	N–B3

Black's one possibility of counter-play is to somehow drive off the annoying bishop from KR6. Otherwise after P–KN4, K–R2 and R–KN1 White will prepare the standard 'Spanish attack' with N–B5.

17 P–QR4	K–R1
18 P–QN3	

I rejected the immediate 18 Q–K2 on account of 18 ... P–B5, when the besieging of the QBP would be a lengthy business, since undermining it by P–QN3 is not possible: the KP is attacked.

The move played is rather slow, but on the other hand it prevents ... P–QB5, and with it Black's Q-side counter-play.

18 ...	R–QN1

Otherwise it is difficult to defend the QNP.

19 Q–K2	B–B1

I would have preferred 19 ... Q–N3. It is true that this is not a normal 'Spanish' move, but there is no white bishop at K3, and therefore it is perfectly possible. It is important for Black not to allow an enemy rook onto the seventh rank.

20	P×P	P×P
21	R–R7	N–N1
22	B×N+	K×B
23	KR–R1	

While Black has been getting rid of the enemy bishop, White has taken firm control of the QR-file.

23	...	B–Q2
24	B–Q3	N–B3
25	Q–R2	

White plans by Q–R5 to offer the exchange of queens, after which his rooks would be able to 'plunder' along the seventh rank.

25	...	N–K1
26	Q–R6	

On 26 Q–R5 Black would have avoided the exchange by 26 ... Q–B1, and then evicted the white queen by ... B–Q1.

26	...	R–N3

Now White's positional advantage becomes threatening. Why did the Yugoslav grandmaster not play 26 ... N–B2 ? After 28 Q–R5 R–QR1 (28 ... R–B1 is bad in view of 28 Q–N6 followed by R–N7) both players had to appraise the following forced variation: 28 R×R Q×R 29 Q×N Q×R+ 30 K–R2 R–Q1 31 B×P B×B 32 Q×B R–Q2. White is the exchange down for a pawn. I thought that I would gain sufficient compensation: after 33 Q–N5 or 33 Q–R4 White has good prospects of an attack.

Gligorić avoided this variation on account of 33 N–B5+. However, this sacrifice gives White no more than perpetual check.

27	Q–R5	N–B3

The only move, since 28 R×B was threatened. The rook couldn't return to ... QN1, on account of the exchange of queens followed by 29 R–N7, winning the QNP.

28	N–N4	

Threatening 29 N×N and R×B. The rook at ... N3 is forced to retreat, thereby allowing the white pieces access to the square QB7.

28	...	R–QN1
29	N×N	

29 Q–B7 appears to be stronger, so as to answer 29 ... R–B1 with 30 Q×Q and 31 R–N7. But Black continues 29 ... B×N 30 P×B Q×Q 31 R×Q B–Q1, and after 32 R–B6 P–B5 33 P×P P×P 34 R×BP N×NP the weakness of White's KB2 square gives Black counter-play.

29	...	B×N

Taking with the king fails to 30 Q–B7.

30	Q–B7	Q×Q
31	R×Q	KR–Q1
32	R(1)–R7	B–K1

33 R(R7)–N7

Threatening 34 B×P B×B 35 R×KBP+, followed by R×R and the capture of one of the bishops.

| 33 ... | K–N1 |

Clearly the only move.

34 P–KN4

White's plan is to play P–N5, and, after driving the enemy bishop from the ... KR5–Q1 diagonal, to gain access to the square K7. The other possibility—that of restricting the black-squared bishop by P–R4 and P–N3—I rejected, since in certain variations the enemy bishop could emerge at ... KR3 after ... P–R4.

| 34 ... | P–R3 |
| 35 P–R4 | R×R |

Otherwise there follows 36 P–N5, when after 36 ... P×P 37 P×P B–N2 the manoeuvre N–R2–N4 wins for White. If Black does not exchange on ... N4, but retreats his bishop—36 ... B–N2, White himself exchanges on R6 and plays N–N5. After the forced ... B×N, Black cannot avoid the loss of his QNP. The move played also fails to save the game.

36 R×R	P–B5
37 P×P	P×P
38 B–K2	

38 B×P does not work on account of 38 ... B–Q2 39 P–N5 B–N5!, when after 40 P×B B×N 41 B–Q3 P–N4! the intrusion of the black rook becomes possible.

| 38 ... | R–R1 |

Now 38 ... B–Q2 is pointless, since on 39 P–N5 Black can no longer play 39 ... B–N5—the knight is defended, while 39 ... P×P 40 N×NP is quite unpromising for Black.

| 39 B×P | B–R5 |

In the tournament bulletin, and in other commentaries on this game, 39 ... R–B1 was recommended. I would have continued 40 B–K2, when Black has one possible reply—40 ... B–R5 (40 ... R×P? 41 R–N8 K–B1 42 P–N5!). Then comes 41 P–B4 B–B7 42 P–N5 P×P 43 N×NP B×N 44 P×B B×P 45 R–Q7, and Black is unable to defend his QP (on 45 ... R–R1 there follows 46 P–B3!, defending against the perpetual check). Thus after 39 ... R–B1 Black would have remained a pawn down, without obtaining adequate counter-play in return.

| 40 B–N3 | B×B |
| 41 R×B | R–QB1 |

The best chance. Black is obliged to keep control of his back rank, otherwise the white rook, after checking, will occupy the QB-file with decisive effect. 41 ... R–R5 fails to 42 R–N4 followed by R–B4.

42 K–N2

The sealed move.

| 42 ... | P–R4 |

In my analysis I did not consider this reply. After the game, Gligorić said that he, in turn, had not expected my sealed move. The Yugoslav grandmaster had only worked through the variations beginning with 42 P–R5, and had come to the conclusion that Black was lost.

However, 42 P–R5 would have allowed the enemy bishop some freedom, and therefore I preferred the solid 42 K–N2.

I assumed that Black was obliged to defend against R–N6, with the exchange of QBP for QP, which is advantageous for White. Since the QP cannot be defended by the rook on account of R–B6, the continuations which I analysed were 42 ... K–B1, 42 ... B–Q1 and 42 ... B–K2. The idea of this last move is to gain counter-play by ... P–B4. I planned to answer it by 43 K–N3 P–B4 44 NP×P P×P 45 N–Q2 K–B2 46 K–R3! (it is important that the black pawn should not advance to ... B5 with check!). In short, Black would not have gained any counter-play.

43 P×P

43 P–N5 is also possible, since Black can never play ... P–B3, on account of P×P followed by N–N5. Black would be unable to tolerate such a knight, while its exchange would lead to a won ending for White.

43 ...	P×P
44 R–N6	R×P
45 R×P	K–N2
46 R–B6	R–Q6

Black's desire to prevent the manoeuvre N–Q2–B4, and to somehow halt the advance of the QP, is readily understandable. But 46 ... R–Q6 meets with a forced refutation. 46 ... R–R6 or 44 ... R–N6 were the most tenacious moves, although with accurate play by White the game can no longer be

saved. On 46 ... R–N6, for instance, there could have followed 47 N–N5, and then P–B3 and K–N3, finally forcing Black into the unfavourable ending.

47 R–B7	K–N3

Otherwise comes 48 N–N5. But now if White captures the KP it will be with check. This is very important, since it does not allow Black to attack the white KP.

48 R–B8	B–N2
49 R–B6+	K–R2
50 N–N5+	K–N1
51 R–B8+	B–B1
52 R–B7	P–B3
53 N–K6	

It is now patently obvious that Black's position is hopeless.

53 ...	B–R3
54 R–Q7	

This ensures the advance of the QP. The bishop cannot leave ... R3 on account of 55 R–KN7+ and R–KB7, while the king has no move in view of 55 R–KB7. The rook, meanwhile, is obliged to keep an eye on the enemy QP.

54 ...	R–Q7
55 K–B1	R–Q8+
56 K–K2	R–Q7+
57 K–K1	R–B7

There are no more checks, there are similarly no moves with the other pieces, and the rook is forced to abandon the Q-file. Now White's passed pawn can advance.

58 P–Q6	R–B8+
59 K–K2	R–B7+
60 K–B1	R–B3
61 K–N2	

After this, apart from ... R–N3 and ... R–R3, Black has no move. The rook cannot leave the third rank on account of 62 R–K7, while on 61 ... B–Q7 White wins by 62 R–KN7+ K–R1 63 P–Q7 R–Q3 64 R–K7.

61 ...   R–N3

62 N–B7   R–N2

If 62 ... B–B1, then 63 N–K8. 62 ... B–Q7 is answered by 63 N–Q5, while if 62 ... K–B1, then 63 R–KR7 B–N2 64 P–Q7.

63 N–Q5   Resigns

41ST USSR CHAMPIONSHIP (PREMIER LEAGUE), MOSCOW 1973

For the first time the main tournament of the year in the Soviet Union—the USSR Championship—was held in two simultaneous stages—the Premier League and the First League. Those admitted into the Premier League included the fourteen Soviet competitors in the three-year World Championship cycle (the untimely death of Leonid Stein led to his place being taken by the then World Junior Champion Aleksandr Belyavsky), as well as the winners of the four semi-final tournaments. In the First League were grandmasters who had played relatively poorly in the semi-finals, and the strongest and most talented masters. The following year an "exchange" would take place between the two leagues: those who had done best in the First League would replace the failures from the Premier...

This reform of the system for holding the USSR Championship did not pass unnoticed in the chess world. It was discussed on the pages of the chess press in many countries, and the American journal *Chess Life and Review*, for instance, wrote: "We expect to see a powerful new generation of Soviet players, battling in conditions of increased rivalry". Evidently, such a pronouncement should be taken in the first instance as an admission of the fact that in the Soviet Union the number of strong players continues to increase.

The 41st USSR Championship—an outstandingly strong event—immediately received the name of "The Championship of Champions", since up till then there had never been such a strong one. Absolutely all the best players in the Soviet Union took part in the tournament. Nevertheless, it was by no means only the battle for the Champion's gold medal which excited chess fans. They were also highly pleased by the good form shown by the Soviet candidates for the World Chess Crown. Without forgetting for a moment about their coming Quarter-Final Matches, all the Candidates succeeded in finishing at the head of the tournament table, and once again demonstrated that it was they who were the most worthy representatives of Soviet chess players to contend for the World Championship.

The gold medal was won by Boris Spassky. After his victory over Tigran Petrosian in the 1969 World Championship Match, this was undoubtedly Spassky's greatest achievement. He had spent all his recent tournaments searching for his best form, which had so treacherously deserted him. During the USSR Championship the future winner's Second was grandmaster Igor Bondarevsky. The alliance, which had broken up not long before the match with Fischer in Reykjavik, was once again renewed, and many are inclined to attribute to Bondarevsky, a man of severe and demanding character, a considerable rôle in the success of Spassky, who clearly lacked the "firm hand" of an experienced Second. In the USSR Championship Spassky tried with all his might, took upon himself markedly greater stress, worked constantly and intensively at the board, and agreed to hardly any "bloodless" draws. At the end of the Championship the winner was extremely restrained, he endeavoured to avoid any public appearances, and wanted to go away as soon as possible to rest and to prepare for the Candidates' Matches. Spassky made just one exception, and gave a detailed interview to the chess publication with the highest circulation in the world—the "hundred thousand" weekly *'64'*. During this conversation one was struck by Spassky's tired appearance.

"And yet they say that victory in the Championship was attained easily . . ."

"Caruso also used to sing effortlessly, but it is said that during a concert he frequently had to change his shirt", Spassky replied without a smile.

This is what he had to say regarding Karpov's play in the tournament:

"Although Anatoly, as usual, played assiduously, I gained the impression that nevertheless he did not drive himself too hard. Perhaps this is associated with the fact that he had already used up a considerable amount of strength in previous events, but his play in the Championship lacked completeness. However, it is clear that he does possess this—potentially Karpov can without doubt play better than he did here".

And this is what Anatoly Karpov himself has to say:

"For the first time in the final of the USSR Championship I aimed for the title of Champion. The right to such a goal was provided by my consistently good results in a series of events, held since my last participation in the 39th USSR Championship in 1971—since then I had managed to finish ahead of many of the world's top players. But several factors combined to stop me taking first place in this, the 41st Championship. In particular, a certain 'split loyalty'. On the one hand, I wanted to win the Championship, but on the other hand I couldn't 'reveal myself' fully, since the Quarter-Final Candidates' Match with Polugayevsky lay ahead, and I had to economize both on my strength, and on . . . my openings.

I began the event, from the point of view of the points scored, better than ever before. And yet, even in those games which I won, against for instance Savon and Belyavsky, I could not rid myself of a feeling of a certain dissatisfaction with myself. I sensed that I was not in particularly good form. For the time being I had to simply try to 'master' myself and my opponents. That's what happened in the sixth round, when I won a tense game against Korchnoi.

Korchnoi–Karpov
Polish Defence

1 N–KB3 N–KB3 2 P–KN3 P–QN4 3 P–B3 B–N2 4 P–QR4 P–QR3 5 P–K3 N–B3 6 P–Q4 P–K3 7 P–QN4 B–K2 8 QN–Q2 N–R2 9 B–Q3 0–0 10 P–K4 P–Q3 11 0–0 P–B4 12 NP×P QP×P 13 B–N2 N–B3 14 P–K5 N–Q4 15 RP×P RP×P 16 Q–N1 P×P 17 P×P P–R3 18 B×P Q–N3 19 B–K2 R×R 20 B×R Q–R2 21 N–B4 R–N1 22 B–N2 B–R3 23 Q–B2 Q–N2 24 B–R1 N(3)–N5 25 Q–Q2 R–QB1 26 N–K3 N×N 27 Q×N B×B 28 Q×B R–B7 29 Q–Q1 Q–B3 30 P–R3 N–Q4 31 Q–Q3 Q–R5 32 N–Q2

R–R7 33 N–N3 N–N5 34 Q–N1 N–Q4 35 R–B1 Q–R1 36 R–B8+ Q×R 37 Q×R Q–B5 38 Q–N1 Q–K7

39 Q–QB1 B–N4 40 Q–B1 Q–B6 41 **P–R4 and White Resigned**

Incidentally, it was after this game that Korchnoi, as he himself put it, 'got angry', and, waving aside all prudent intentions, decided not to hold back any more before the Candidates' Matches, and played for all he was worth.

But the very next game, against Spassky, almost put me completely out of my stride. There I obtained a good, very good, perhaps even won position. But I did not win, and in fact very nearly lost. And then on top of everything I went and caught a cold. In the eighth round I quite unexpectedly lost to Petrosian. 'Unexpectedly', because I was in no mood for a fight, and anticipated a quick draw with Tigran Vartanovich, with whom I had always been on excellent friendly terms, and who I thought would have no desire to play for a win; 'unexpectedly', if only because before this game Petrosian had scored seven successive draws against opponents with whom the was on less friendly terms. This defeat was a good lesson to me for the future...

Realising that my form and physical condition left much to be desired, I did not overstrain myself, and did not and try to swim against the tide. For this reason, although I was not especially happy about my final placing, all the same I considered my result to be pretty good, especially since towards the end I nevertheless managed to overcome my depression. Although I scored less points at the finish than at the start, the quality of my play was higher".

Anatoly suddenly expressed a somewhat unexpected idea: "I think that Spassky's victory in the Championship was not as convincing and promising for him, as practically all the journalists hastened at that time to announce, as did the majority of the top players. They did not take into account the fact that the Ex-World Champion was lost against me, and had a difficult position against Kuzmin... If he had lost to either of us, the winner would have shared first place with him. And another thing. Look more closely at the tournament table—who in fact did Spassky beat? All those occupying the bottom places. He beat them using his 'old' knowledge: for instance, Rashkovsky and Tukmakov for some reason played against him different variations of the Sicilian Defence, which Spassky had prepared most carefully for his match with Fischer in Reykjavik. While the Chelyabinsk master Yevgeny Shvyeshnikov lost to the grandmaster in a variation which he constantly plays, and in which it was only against me that he didn't lose... No, I have no wish at all to cast doubts on the performance made by Boris Spassky—he might quite well have defeated these same opponents, thanks to the difference in class, even if he had played against them in their favourite schemes. I have said all this merely so that later the tactics chosen by me in my Semi-Final Match against Spassky should be more understandable, and so that the foreign reader should be able to learn more clearly the meaning of our somewhat sharp, but nevertheless apt saying: 'The devil is not so black as he is painted'.

There is probably one further factor which helped Spassky to become first. With all due respect to Robert Byrne, who at the age of 45 attained his greatest success, it can be assumed that, before his match with the American grandmaster, Spassky was much less afraid than his fellow-Candidates of disclosing his cards to his future opponent in the Quarter-Final Match. At any rate, three of the other Candidates for the World Championship acted with great caution.

It was just like in a bicycle race", jokes Karpov. "We were concerned only about the progress of the other Candidates, and avoided trying to move ahead, since otherwise we might suddenly get the 'wind in our face', as cyclists would say. We were not bothered about the other players, and this was probably how the improving grandmaster Gennady Kuzmin was able to edge his way into our group".

Lyev Polugayevsky made an interesting pronouncement immediately after the Championship:

"Karpov, my opponent in the forthcoming match, demonstrated his high class. He played, as I myself did, economically, without trying too hard, trying if possible to attain his goal by technical means, by punishing his opponents for the slightest errors. I think that we should both be happy that we finished up level in the table, and that from our appearances in the Championship neither of us gained any psychological advantage".

As you can see, the Premier League of the 41st USSR Championship is linked irrevocably with the coming Candidates' Matches.

Karpov–Spassky
Ruy Lopez

1 P–K4 P–K4 2 N–KB3 N–QB3 3 B–N5 P–QR3 4 B–R4 N–B3 5 0–0 B–K2 6 R–K1 P–QN4 7 B–N3 P–Q3 8 P–B3 0–0 9 P–KR3 N–QR4 10 B–B2 P–B4 11 P–Q4 Q–B2 12 QN–Q2 N–B3 13 P–Q5 N–Q1 14 P–QR4 R–N1

This variation occurred in the first game of the Spassky–Korchnoi match in 1968.

15 P×P

The immediate 15 P–QN4 is also good though the course chosen by White is not bad.

15 ...	P×P
16 P–QN4	P–B5
17 N–B1	N–K1

In my opinion this is an inaccuracy as it exposes Black's cards too soon, making his intentions clear. Also, it is not good to deprive the KR of the square K1 at such an early stage. In order to take advantage of this I managed to evolve a comparatively new plan involving the moves N(3)–R2 and P–B4.

18 N(3)–R2	**P–B3**

I believe that 18 ... B–B3 was better.

19 P–B4	N–B2
20 N–B3	

Here White has many varied possibilities. It looks natural to play 20 P–B5 P–N3 21 P–N4 N–N2 and then, by means of 22 B–K3, White obtains firm control of the QR-file. It remains unclear however, what benefit White could derive from control of the only open file.

20 ...	P–N3
21 P–B5	N–N2
22 P–N4	B–Q2
23 B–K3	R–R1
24 Q–Q2	

Evidently not the best move even though it forces Black's queen to move to QN2. More consistent was 24 R–B1 in order, after 24 ... R–R7, to chase the rook off the second rank by 25 B–N1 and only then to play 26 Q–Q2.

24 ...	Q–N2
25 QR–B1	

An important decision, conceding the QR-file to my opponent. But if I exchange even one pair of rooks I have little chance of success. If you want to play for a win give your opponent counter-play!

Spassky decides to accept my invitation and continues in the most natural way.

25 ...	R–R7
26 N–N3	KR–R1
27 P–R4	B–Q1
28 K–R1	B–N3
29 R–KN1	B×B
30 Q×B	Q–R2
31 Q–Q2	B–K1

I don't like this move. Black's pieces were already very passively placed. In covering the KN3 square yet again Black gives his opponent a completely free hand to attack his K-side.

It was better to manoeuvre the queen to Q1 via QN3.

32 P–N5	Q–K2
33 QR–B1	P×NP

Black had to reconcile himself to this exchange as otherwise White could deprive him of the opportunity altogether by 34 N–R2.

34 RP×P	Q–Q2
35 N–R2	

Simplest here was 35 R–B2, keeping in reserve the threat P–B6. This move would have set Black very difficult problems, particularly as Spassky only had four minutes left on the clock.

Instead of this strong continuation I played several ill-considered moves.

35 ...	Q–Q1
36 P–B6	

It seemed to me that after 36 P×P P×P 37 N–N4 Q×P 38 N–B6+ K–R1 39 Q–R2+ Q–R3 40 R–N2 (not distracting the other rook which may still come in useful on the KB-file) 40 ... R–R8 41 B–N1 Q×Q+ 42 R×Q+ N–R4 43 N(3)×N P×N, there is no forcing continuation to be seen and Black's position holds together.

If White plays 40 R–B2 (instead of 40 R–N2) then after 40 ... R–R8 41 Q×Q+ N×Q 42 R–R2 N–R4 43 N(3)×N P×N, Black's KN1 square is indirectly protected because White's rook is pinned.

It is true that in all cases Black's position remains extremely dubious and one must expect that White's play can be strengthened in one of the above variations. But at the time I succumbed to the temptation to win a piece.

36 ...	B–Q2

Black has nothing to lose and plays the best moves.

37 P×N	Q×P
38 Q–N2	

Stronger was 38 Q–B2, and after the forced reply 38 ... Q–B5 39 N–B5 it seems that White has a considerable advantage.

38 ...	R–N7
39 R–N1	

Even here 39 Q–B2 was better. It would have given rise to variations which I later analysed at home as they could have arisen from the adjourned position. For example, 39 ... Q–K2 40 N–B5 P×N 41 P×P R(1)–R7 (if 41 ... Q–B3 42 N–N4 Q–N4 43 R–N2 and White has a great advantage) 42 P–B6 Q–K1 43 R–B1 N–R3 44 R–N5 (preventing the assault ... B–B4) 44 ... Q–B2 45 K–N1 B–B4 (if 45 ... N–B4 46 N–N4 or 45 ... P–K5 46 Q–R4 Q×BP 47 R–B1) 46 Q–N6 (the tempting 46 R×B Q–N3+ 47 K–R1 N×R 48 B×N R×Q 49 B–K6+ Q–B2 50 N–N4 fails unfortunately to 47 ... R×R 48 R×R R–R8+). Evidently, in place of 45 ... B–B4, it is preferable to play 45 ... B–B1 46 N–B1 R×B 47 R×R R×R 48 Q×R Q×BP 49 R–N2 N–N5 50 N–K3

P–R4 (if 50 ... N×N 51 Q×P+ K×Q 52 P–N8 = Q+) 51 N×N B×N 52 Q–B2 K×P 53 Q–K3 and White's position is slightly better.

After 39 Q–B2, the move 39 ... Q–B5 (instead of 39 ... Q–K2) deserves investigation. Even in this case it seems to be possible to play 40 N–B5 Q×Q 41 R×Q P×N 42 P×P, and by means of a subsequent P–B6 White poses his opponent difficult problems. If Black tries to stop P–B6 the following piquant finish could occur: 42 ... R(1)–R7 43 N–N4 K×P 44 N–R6+ and all moves by the king lead to mate. If Black plays the immediate 40 ... R(1)–R7 then 41 N–K3 followed by N–B3–N5–K6 also gives White the advantage.

Of course I must allow myself the disclaimer that all the above variations are approximate and require thorough verification.

39 ...	R(7)–R7
40 Q–K2	Q–R5
41 QR–KB1	

The sealed move. In the adjourned position whatever advantage there is belongs to Black, despite White's extra piece.

41 ...	B–R6
42 R–B2	N–N4
43 Q–K3	B–N5

For move after move Black builds up threats forcing White to make the only possible replies.

| 44 R(1)–KB1 | K×P |
| 45 B–Q1 | |

I can find no other suitable reply.

45 ...	B×B
46 R×B	R–R8
47 R(1)–KB1	

47 R(2)–B1 is unsatisfactory because of 47 ... R(1)–R7, and 47 R(2)–Q2 for the same reason.

47 ...	R×R+
48 R×R	R–R7
49 R–B2	R–R8+
50 R–B1	R–R7
51 R–B2	R–R8+
52 R–B1	R×R+
53 N×R	Q×P+
54 K–N1	Q×Q+

An unnecessary exchange in my opinion. Black has the good move 54 ... Q–R5 (54 ... P–R3 55 Q–R7+ K–B3 is unsatisfactory because of 56 Q–Q7) with the idea of the manoeuvre N–R6–B5. White is practically forced to play 55 Q–R7+ K–R3 56 Q–K3.

However, the ending reached in the game is also favourable for Spassky.

55 N×Q	N–K5
56 N–Q1	N–B3
57 N–K3	P–R4

In my opinion it would have been better to play for the immediate penetration of the king (57 ... K–R3) before White's knight succeeded in creating a barrier.

| 58 N–B3 | N–K5 |
| 59 N–Q1 | Drawn |

The ending still contains some sharp play, e.g. 59 ... K–B3 60 N–K1 K–B4 61 N–QB2 N–B3 62 N–R3 or 59 ... P–N4 60 N–K1 N–B3 61 N–K3 K–N3 (if 61 ... N–K1 62 N–B3 K–N3 63 N–Q2 N–B3 64 N(2)×P P×N 65 P–N5 K–B2 66 P–N6 N–Q2 67 P–N7, and the black QP is lost after all) 62

N(1)–B2 N–K1 63 N–R3 (possibly more accurate is the immediate 63 N×P) 63 ... N–B2 64 K–N2 P–N5 65 N(K3)×BP P×N 66 P–N5 N×QP 67 N×P P–R5 68 N×P and although Black is naturally in no danger of losing, White's pawns can, in some cases, become dangerous.

AFTER THE 41ST USSR CHAMPIONSHIP AND BEFORE THE CANDIDATES' MATCHES

"A serious player", said Karpov during this period, "is often obliged to restrain his desire to play brilliantly. For the sake of what? For the sake of good results.

In the Premier League Spassky decided in one of his games to win brilliantly, although he could without much trouble have won the game by technical means. And he succeeded in winning brilliantly, although, as I was later told, Bondarevsky, who has once again become Spassky's trainer, sadly gave him up for lost when Spassky sacrificed something—after all, there was a safe and simple way he could have won. And here is another dismal example. Tal, with an overwhelming advantage in his game against Svyeshnikov, attempted all the time to sacrifice something brilliantly—and as a result drew with great difficulty. The player who goes in for irrational play, for brilliant combinations and wild complications, ends up losing a point—if only one out of ten. I, on the other hand, prefer to win ten games out of ten by technical means.

Of course, it is not all as simple as this. There may be times when the irrational player may come out higher than the rationalist. In that USSR Championship, I would say that Spassky, frankly speaking, played irrationally. I have in mind something quite apart from the above-mentioned game. The point is that Spassky revealed himself more than anyone else in the tournament. He revealed himself fully, avoided saving any theoretical discoveries for the Candidates' Matches, and liberally demonstrated his plans in a number of systems. But for this there is a serious explanation—before the Candidates' Matches it was necessary for Spassky to test his strength. All his performances in preceding international events, I would say, had been on a low level. He was possibly still affected by the depression following his match with Fischer. He had not yet been able to overcome the psychological trauma. And it is very good that Spassky should be able to find within himself the strength to stand up again. Yes, in revealing himself to such an extent in the Championship of the Country, Spassky acted irrationally, but in his position I would say that it was the most sensible course to take. Inwardly, psychologically, it was important for him to experience his strength, and the taste of genuine victory. The USSR Championship was Spassky's last rehearsal, and a very successful one, before his match with Byrne, in which I would give my unreserved preference to the Ex-World Champion.

For all the Candidates this Championship of the Country proved to be a very difficult tournament. We essentially have no tournaments at all in which it is possible to experiment. Suppose that I began experimenting—and from time to time it is necessary to do so—but that things didn't work out, and I did badly—they might find someone else to send to the next big tournament. So that one is forced to experiment, while keeping an eye on one's results. And even the USSR Championship Premier League, as you will know, had the character of an elimination event—the players had to do everything possible to finish in the first nine. And in general, the new system (of Premier League and First League), like any new system, still requires serious modification.

For Polugayevsky, my forthcoming opponent, this tournament was not necessary—he had forced his way into the Candidates' group later than the others. He was tired, and so in the USSR Championship played extremely rationally, although normally he puts into a game of chess all his strength, and all his knowledge. But here it was obvious that he was playing at half-power. I, to a certain extent, also played at half-power, but not because I did not need this tournament—in fact it was just what I needed—but because it turned out that I sensed that I was in poor form. Although, to a certain extent it could have been good that I was not yet in form, since the main tests were to begin after the Championship. And to try to force myself into form during the course of the tournament seemed pointless. Polugayevsky did not wish to reveal all that he knew about the openings, and neither did I. We rather watched each other during the course of the tournament. I in fact rarely stopped to look at his games, since I intended to examine them later, but he frequently came up to my board.

Petrosian too was of course only thinking of finishing in the first nine, and also of not falling too far behind the other Candidates. All the time his mind was on Portisch, his future opponent. The point is that the score in their previous games is strongly in favour of Portisch, although I do not consider that in a match this is of any great significance. What is perhaps slightly worse is that Petrosian has never yet beaten Portisch. This threatens to develop into something of a psychological barrier. Or it may work just the opposite way.

I thought that Korchnoi too would not reveal himself particularly. But he is of such an argumentative character, that at first he played at half-power, but then became depressed, especially after the defeat against me, and switched to 'full power', and worked in every game from beginning to end. He just worked and worked. I should like to point out that in chess (and in life too) with Korchnoi much depends on his mood. If he is in good form and in a good mood, he plays like a lion. But if he is out of form, Korchnoi is no longer the same Korchnoi. Then he plays merely for ambition, the moves come with colossal difficulty, and he torments others and seeks someone to blame.

I would think that he is not capable of winning three matches. One of these matches he will lose. All I can say is that, if Korchnoi is in his normal form and frame of mind, he will beat Mecking, but if his game does not go well, the very first match may prove very tense and unpleasant for him. Before the Interzonal Tournament in Brazil I would never have named Mecking among the list of future Candidates, although I had no doubt that he was a chess player of talent. But he has improved significantly, has done a great deal of work, and made a worthy appearance in the Interzonal Tournament.

I felt flattered, of course, to learn of Mecking's opinion, that only he or I can take the World Championship title away from Fischer. And I thought: it wouldn't indeed be bad to meet Mecking in the Final Candidates' Match... But I think that for the moment this will not happen, since both Mecking and I are as yet insufficiently mature players to reach the Candidates' Final. All my major international tournaments to date can be counted on the fingers of one hand. This, of course, is a very small number for a Candidate for the title of World Champion, which is what I am today. All my main rivals have played in many more events, and have much greater experience and knowledge of chess.

So do I nevertheless hope to become World Champion? I am pinning my hopes on the next three-year cycle. In that next cycle I will have a better chance, and for the following reasons.

9

Firstly, I hope to develop as a player, and to gain the necessary experience. Secondly, all the players of the older generation are approaching the critical age. By the age of forty one's success curve begins to dip. It is inevitable. It is a fact. And it must without doubt be youth that will dominate the next cycle...

I always want to be first. If I weren't a chess player, all the same I would aim to be first at something. Well, let's say, not first, but one of the best. And what about in chess? In chess— even more so. Otherwise it is stupid to play seriously. And besides, if you are not first, it means you have lost. And who enjoys losing? However, in chess anything can happen. The title of World Champion is played for once every three years. All sorts of unforeseen things can interfere. It is perfectly possible that I will not become World Champion—after all, in the entire history of chess there have only been eleven to date. But that is a possibility which I do not wish to analyse..."

MADRID 1973

The big international tournaments regularly organized in Spain at the end of the year are normally held in Palma—the main town on the Island of Majorca. In 1973 this event was held in Madrid, which was symbolic, in that it was here, almost four hundred years previously (in 1574), that the first international tournament in the history of chess had taken place, the contestants being the Italian masters Leonardo and Paolo Boi, and the Spaniards Ruy Lopez and Alfonso Ceron.

On this occasion the representatives of eleven countries arrived in Madrid, among whom were twelve top-class grandmasters—as regards the strength of the players it was an excellent tournament. The organizers awaited with particular interest two of the participants in the coming Candidates' Matches—Lajos Portisch and Anatoly Karpov. The Hungarian grand-master had been going to decline the invitation, but then, on the advice of a Doctor of Psychology, changed his mind and agreed to play. Portisch arrived in Spain (where a month after the tournament his match with Petrosian was due to start) together with his wife, intending to acclimatize well, and to test all aspects of his preparations. He tried to play very differently from normal, and this probably told on his result.

Well, and what about Karpov? It is quite well known that Ex-World Champion Mikhail Botvinnik was against Karpov's proposed appearance in Spain, since he considered that the better Karpov played in this tournament, the worse things would go for him in the Candidates' Matches. But Anatoly, as had already happened many times in his chess career, took the decision which he considered to be correct... Of course, in doing so he consulted with his permanent trainer Semion Furman, who, incidentally, also played in Madrid, and made an excellent showing. In connection with this it may be of interest to cite certain comments from the foreign press, which may not be familiar to the reader.

"With this pair everything is mysterious and unusual", wrote a correspondent from the Italian daily "*Panorama*" about Karpov and his trainer, "take their joint participation in one tournament, which is rather rare for a player and his second, and the Olympian calm which they both invariably maintain even in a difficult position, and even when in severe time trouble, (here the author evidently has the older player in mind, since Anatoly does not get into time trouble), and also the very nature of their collaboration, in the course of which not only does Furman help Karpov to play better, but Karpov also helps Furman."

And it is true that this instance gave a jolt to the opinion that taking up the work of trainer means virtually giving up success in practical play. "As a result of his association with Karpov", wrote the Swiss "*Nationale-Zeitung*", "Furman has acquired his second chess wind, and now demonstrates greater practical strength than ever before".

But let us return to the tournament itself, and to its winner. In what way was this event important for the future World Champion?

Anatoly Karpov emphasizes the following point:

"This was the first major international tournament where I managed to take first prize on my own, without sharing it with someone. Before this I had for a long time 'stuck' only to first place, but someone had invariably finished up alongside me. It is true that the 'co-authors' in my victories changed, whereas I remained there, but even so I was already rather tired of sharing first place. It was this that I was thinking about before the start of the tournament, although in the main it was nevertheless training goals that I set myself".

At first, when the Soviet grandmasters arrived in Madrid, it seemed that the Spanish Capital was in the grip of a really severe winter. But then, however, a thaw arrived from the Atlantic, and the temperature rose to about 15 °C. Play took place in one of the halls on the ground floor of the Castellano Hotel, in which all the competitors were accommodated. Before each round the organizers, who were concerned about the freshness of the air, thoroughly ventilated the room. So that during the opening it was cool, but then the small hall gradually filled up, and by the middlegame the temperature was normal. Towards the end of the round the spectators became excited, and despite a strict ban, began to smoke. The atmosphere thickened, it became stuffy, and in the endgame oversights occurred...

"However, the blunder in my first round game with the Spaniard Arturo Pomar was made nowhere near the endgame", relates Karpov. "All the time I had slightly the better of it, and I wanted to make more of it, whereas he didn't appear to want anything at all. I allowed my concentration to waver... I overlooked a fairly simple blow, and lost the exchange for

Karpov–Pomar
Caro Kann Defence

1 P–K4 P–QB3 2 N–QB3 P–Q4 3 N–B3 B–N5 4 P–KR3 B×N 5 Q×B P–K3 6 P–R3 P×P 7 N×P N–B3 8 N–B3 N–Q4 9 B–K2 N–Q2 10 0–0 Q–B3 11 Q×Q N(2)×Q 12 B–B3 B–Q3 13 P–Q3 0–0 14 P–KN3 KR–K1 15 R–K1 R–K2 16 N–N1 QR–K1 17 N–Q2 P–K4 18 P–N3 (Diag.) 18 ... P–K5 19 N×P B–K4 20 B–N5 B×R 21 R×B P–KR3 22 N×N N×N 23 B–Q2 N–Q2 24 P–QR4 N–K4 25 B–N2 P–QB4 26 B–K3 N–B3 27 B×N P×B 28 P–R5 R–K4 29 P–R6 R–Q4 30 K–B1 K–B1 31 K–K2 K–K2 32 K–Q2 K–Q2 33 P–QB4 R–R4 34 P–R4 K–B2 35 P–B4 R–B4 36 R–R5 P–N4 37 RP×P

P×P 38 P–QN4 NP×P 39 KNP×P K–N1 40 R×P R×R 41 B×R R–R1 42 K–B3 R–R8 43 P–N5 R–QN8 44 P×P K–B2 45 P–Q4 K×P 46 B×P R–QR8 47 P–Q5+ K–Q2 48 B–N8 R×P 49 P–QB5 R–R5 50 P–B6+ K–B1 51 B–Q6 P–B3 52 B–N4 K–B2 53 K–N3 R–R8 54 K–B4 K–N3 55 B–B5+ K–B2 56 K–N5 R–N8+ 57 B–N4 Resigns

9*

a pawn. Then I wanted to offer a draw, but since I wasn't risking a great deal, decided to play on a little, and... won".

Yes, for the greater part of the Madrid tournament Karpov played using his technique, without revealing himself much, remembering that his Candidates' Quarter-Final Match with Polugayevsky was imminent. Meanwhile the lead was assumed by the German grandmaster Wolfgang Uhlmann. After eleven rounds the leader was a whole point ahead of the Soviet trio and the Czech player Vlastimil Hort. At that time grandmaster Vladimir Tukmakov reported to Moscow by telephone:

"In my opinion, Anatoly Karpov has not yet begun to play at full strength in this tournament. It is true that the adjournment sessions have proved very successful for him, when thanks to his excellent technique he has managed to win from roughly equal positions. In the next round, the twelfth, one of the main encounters from the tournament is due to take place, between Karpov and Uhlmann... It is well known that Uhlmann's opening repertoire is well worked out, but highly restricted. This is particularly noticeable in his play as Black, when against 1 P–K4 he plays exclusively the French Defence. Uhlmann's success in a tournament depends to a great extent on how he fares with this opening. Up till now the French Defence has successfully stood the test. Will all these considerations be important in the central encounter from the twelfth round?"

Now we know that it was these considerations which played a considerable rôle in this vital and, one might say, decisive game of the Madrid tournament. Incidentally, this game was judged to be the best one in the entire event.

"In that twelfth round my compatriots also won, and we all three caught up with Uhlmann. The job was completed by my trainer, who on the following day, as it were 'receiving' my opponent from me, also defeated the German grandmaster", says Karpov. "Unfortunately, Furman then lost unexpectedly to the Spaniard Ricardo Calvo, which denied him a share of first place with me. I on the other hand finished well, for which I was awarded a special prize, and became, at last, the sole winner of a major international tournament. It is curious that, against the same Calvo in the thirteenth round, I succeeded in winning an amusing miniature game. On the whole I was satisfied with the quality of my play, and not without justification began looking optimistically to the future, since I considered that my dress rehearsal before the Candidates' Matches had gone successfully.

Of the non-chess impressions, I remember best of all the excursion to Escorial, the memorial palace of Spanish kings, which is situated some fifty kilometres from Madrid, in the Pyrenees. All the players went along, except Portisch, who had his own personal reasons for staying at home. All the way there Walter Browne was showing his games to Ulf Andersson and Julio Kaplan. The entrance to the inner part of the rectangular palace is not so easy to find, and everyone got out of the bus to look for the entrance, leaving only these three young players. The excursion proved to be exceptionally interesting, and from my point of view, beneficial in the educational sense... In a small café at the exit I spotted Browne, Andersson and Kaplan, drinking something, and listlessly moving the pieces on the chess board. 'Have you been in the palace?' I asked. 'No, we haven't'. 'Why did you come then? You could have stayed in the hotel to play chess', I said to them.

I have already said that the best young grandmasters from abroad devote a great deal of time to the study of chess, and to appearances in tournaments, and I consider that their Soviet contemporaries have something to learn from them in this respect. But I would never agree that there is nothing in the world, apart from chess, which is worth being interested in—this is the opposite extreme, and is even more harmful for a young person. Chess is my life, but not all of my life is chess.

In the hotel hall one evening, a list was put up of the best chess players of 1973, compiled from the results of a poll by chess journalists. My name stood at the head of the list! Strictly speaking, this was no great surprise to me, since on the results of the complete chess year such an outcome could have been predicted (however, what was clear to me was by no means obvious to certain other people: one journalist, for instance, on the list offered to him put me in... eleventh place). At the closing ceremony of the Madrid tournament, together with the first prize of this imposing event, I was also awarded the 'Chess Oscar', the prize for the best grandmaster of the year, nowadays perhaps the greatest honour after the gold medal of World Champion.

I glanced at the statuette (which depicts the coat-of-arms of Madrid)—an amusing little bear trying to climb up a big, solid tree—and thought about the Candidates' Matches awaiting me..."

Karpov–Uhlmann
French Defence

| 1 P–K4 | P–K3 |

The favourite opening in the repertoire of grandmaster Uhlmann, who is a faithful devotee of the French Defence (true, during my 1974 Final Candidates' Match I discovered that there is also another fervent follower of this defence).

| 2 P–Q4 | P–Q4 |
| 3 N–Q2 | P–QB4 |

It was this particular variation which had frequently occurred both in my games (with White), and in Uhlmann's games (with Black). Clearly, at home we had both prepared surprises for each other.

4 KP×P	KP×P
5 KN–B3	N–QB3
6 B–N5	B–Q3
7 P×P	

A small finesse. If 7 0–0, then 7 ... P×P, and White is practically forced to continue

8 N–N3 and then N(N3)×P, since 8 N×P involves an unclear pawn sacrifice (8 ... B×P+ 9 K×B Q–R5+ 10 K–N1 Q×N, as occurred in the game Geller–Ivkov, 1970). After the continuation in the game, White is by no means obliged to immediately occupy Q4 with a knight.

| 7 ... | B×BP |

The exchange of queens by 7 ... Q–K2+ 8 Q–K2 does little to assist Black in his battle for equality.

| 8 0–0 | KN–K2 |
| 9 N–N3 | B–Q3 |

The alternative is 9 ... B–N3; this has twice occurred in my games, and each time I managed to win. In the Championship of the Russian Republic (Kuybishev 1970), where I first met grandmaster Krogius (in the very first round of this tournament which was so important for me), I gained an advantage after 10 R–K1 0–0 11 B–K3 B–N5 12 B×B Q×B 13 B×N N×B 14 Q×P (cf. p. 45). The second game was against Vaganian (Budapest 1973).

10 B–N5	0–0
11 B–KR4	

The idea behind this move is fairly simple. The advantages of White's position are associated with the fact that his opponent has an isolated QP. In order to exploit this weakness he must attempt to simplify the position, by exchanging at least some of the minor pieces, and in particular—the enemy black-squared bishop, which is "covering the zone" around the QP.

In the game Bronstein–Furman (1949), where the plan of exchanging the black-squared bishops was first employed, Black did not appreciate the danger, and innocently played 11 ... Q–B2, which made things easy for White. (As the reader may already have seen, the attempt by Kuzmin to improve the variation for Black in the Interzonal Tournament (Leningrad 1973) did not prove successful (cf. p. 108).

11 ...	B–KN5

Uhlmann, in contrast, strives to battle actively for the central squares, by pinning the knight at KB3.

12 B–K2	B–R4
13 R–K1	Q–N3
14 N(B3)–Q4	

After releasing his knight at K2 from the pin, Black was intending to use it to attack the white bishop at KR4, and so White is forced to control his KB5 square.

14 ...	B–N3
15 P–QB3	KR–K1
16 B–B1	B–K5

Here the bishop does not occupy a particularly secure position (P–B3), but the square KN3 is needed by the knight at K2 in order to be switched to the centre. The routine 16 ... QR–Q1 would once again have created a pin along the KR4–Q8 diagonal.

17 B–N3	B×B
18 RP×B	P–QR4

Uhlmann must have underestimated the dangers facing him, otherwise he would have restricted himself to the simple 18 ... QR–Q1.

19 P–R4!	N×N
20 N×N!	

This is the whole point. The QNP is taboo, since 20 ... Q×P fails to 21 N–N5, with two threats: the obvious fork 22 N–B7, and the less noticeable but more terrible "trap"— 22 R–K2!.

20 ...	N–B3
21 B–N5	KR–Q1
22 P–KN4!!	

Such moves afford me the greatest satisfaction: White succeeds in seeing into the future. And in the immediate future the game transposes into a double-rook ending with white-squared bishops. The mobility of the black bishop is restricted by its own pawn at Q4, and now my pawn at KN4 will cramp it still further. It may be objected: but you are placing a pawn on a square of the colour of your own bishop! This is indeed so, but my bishop is 'working' along different diagonals.

| **22 ...** | **N×N** |

The preparatory 22 ... QR–B1 would have been technically better.

23 Q×N	**Q×Q**
24 P×Q	**QR–B1**
25 P–B3	**B–N3**

Here is the first consequence of the move 22 P–KN4. The bishop is forced to occupy an observation post at KN3 instead of a genuine working square at KB4.

| **26 R–K7** | **P–N3** |

It was probably time to decide on active measures with 26 ... R–B7, but the German grandmaster still hopes to hold on by passive defence.

| **27 QR–K1** | **P–R3** |
| **28 R–N7** | **R–Q3** |

But if now 28 ... R–B7, then very unpleasant for Black is 29 R–K2 R×R 30 B×R R–Q3 31 B–N5 followed by the advance of White's king to the centre, which enables him to achieve domination despite the limited material.

| **29 R(1)–K7** | **P–R4** |

Now after 29 ... R–B7 the following highly piquant variations are pleasant to calculate: 30 R–N8+ K–R2 31 R(7)–K8 R–B8+ (otherwise the bishop has no square to move to) 32 K–R2 B–N8 33 P–B4 B—K5

(33 ... P–B4 34 R–KR8+ K–N3 35 R(N8)–KB8, or 33 ... P–N3 34 P–N5!) 34 P–B5 P–N3 (34 ... P–N4 35 R–KR8+ K–N2 36 R(N8)–N8+ K–B3 37 R×RP+ K–K2 38 R–K8 mate) 35 P–B6 P–N4 36 R–N8! R×P 37 R–KR8+ K–N2 38 R(N8)–N8 mate. Black could have avoided all this 'brilliance' only by 33 ... K–N3, which would have forced me also to operate more prosaically...

| **30 P×P** | **B×P** |
| **31 P–KN4** | |

The fallen warriors are replaced by new ones.

| **31 ...** | **B–N3** |
| **32 P–B4** | |

With this move White appears to subject his king to unnecessary danger. But I had calculated that the rook at Q3 would not manage to come into play, whereas the two white rooks, dominating the seventh rank, would have time to carry out a mating attack.

32 ...	**R–B8+**
33 K–B2	**R–B7+**
34 K–K3	**B–K5**

34 ... R–K3+ 35 R×R P×R 36 R×QNP is equally hopeless.

| **35 R×BP** | **R–N3** |

The square KN2 has to be defended. In the subsequent play White succeeds in detaining this rook on the third rank, where its choice of square is highly restricted.

36 P–N5	K–R2
37 R(B7)–K7	R×QNP
38 B–K8	R–N6+
39 K–K2	R–N7+
40 K–K1	R–Q3

With his rook alone Black is unable to create any threats, and the king easily escapes the checks after 40 ... R–N8+ 41 K–Q2 R–N7+ 42 K–B3 R–QB7+ 43 K–N3.

41 R×KNP+	K–R1
42 R(KN7)–K7	Resigns

Karpov–Andersson
Queen's Indian Defence

1 P–Q4 N–KB3 2 P–QB4 P–K3 3 N–KB3 P–QN3 4 P–KN3 B–N5+ 5 QN–Q2 B–N2

6 B–N2 0–0 7 0–0 P–B4 8 P–QR3 B×N 9 B×B P×P 10 B–N4 R–K1 11 B–Q6 N–K5 12 Q×P N–R3 13 P–QN4 R–QB1 14 QR–B1 N×B 15 Q×N N–B2 16 KR–Q1 R–K2 17 Q–Q3 B×N 18 B×B N–K1

19 B–N7 R–B2 20 B–R6 R–B3 21 Q–N3 Q–N1 22 Q–R4 R–B2 23 Q–N5 N–B3 24 P–B3 P–Q4 25 P–B5 P–R4 26 P–QR4 R–K1 27 P×P P×P 28 P–R5 R×R 29 R×R Q–K4 30 Q×NP P–Q5 31 K–R1 Q–K6 32 R–B1 P–K4 33 B–Q3 P–R5 34 P×P Q–B5 35 R–KN1 Q×P(R5) 36 P–R6 P–N3 37 P–R7 K–N2 38 B×P Resigns

CANDIDATES' QUARTER-FINAL MATCH WITH LYEV POLUGAYEVSKY

"In preparing for the match with Polugayevsky, I anticipated a very hard fight", relates Anatoly Karpov. "I was concerned about my total lack of experience of match play, but nevertheless rated my chances more highly. In the press, Polugayevsky himself rated his chances in the match as a 'thirty-five per cent possibility of success', but I think that he was clearly being modest.

From the point of view of preparation, the event proved comparatively simple, since my opponent's opening repertoire is unusually limited and constant for such a class player. Polugayevsky decided to base his play on the use of opening preparations, which he had devised in accordance with games played earlier by me. Thus outwardly the match took the form of a clearly defined theoretical duel, as many of the experts had predicted. Of course, on the basis of these games it cannot be asserted that I succeeded in 'burying' the variation of the Sicilian Defence which occurred four times. But only one chink was needed—and it was this variation which proved to be the key to Polugayevsky. The point was that, in a detailed examination of my opponent's games, my trainer and I had established that Polugayevsky plays excellently in positions which demand exact and concrete calculation, but loses his way in positions where there is no specific plan, which demand that every move of the opponent must be taken into account, and where both sides have weaknesses, with fixed pawn structures".

"Before the match with Polugayevsky, Karpov already had a sufficiently deep, although perhaps not particularly extensive knowledge of the openings", adds Semion Furman. "The 'plan of campaign', in brief, was as follows: Polugayevsky likes positions which lend themselves to the calculation of variations—he must not be allowed to attain them on the board. The narrowness of the opponent's opening repertoire simplified our problem. After the match, many criticized Polugayevsky for the fact that he didn't play 'his own' game, but in fact this wasn't his 'fault', but the result of our efforts''.

...As you can see, everything was worked out beforehand. At the same time Polugayevsky continued to go his own way, further tempted by the fact that the positions he obtained out of the opening were perfectly good. However, he failed to take account of the fact that positions which were "in general" good, might not be so promising for him in particular, whereas Karpov felt very much at home in them. In addition, knowing beforehand that his opponent would adopt one and the same opening, Karpov gained the opportunity on each occasion to strengthen the variation still further. However, to be fair, it must be admitted that the start of the match appeared by no means so hopeless for Polugayevsky. This is explained by the fact that, on account of his lack of experience, Karpov did not immediately get into his stride, and also that, for instance, for the fourth game, Polugayevsky at home found an interesting opening idea, and gained an excellent position. It was here, during the fourth game, and later also the fifth, that the critical moment of the match occurred. It was here that psychology and the strength of the players' nerves came to the fore.

During the last hour of play, Polugayevsky, on account of his constant calculating of variations (and this was also taken into account by Karpov during his preparations), frequently runs short of time, becomes nervous, and makes mistakes. It was this that happened in the fourth game of the match—he began to lose his advantage, which had been gained at the cost of enormous effort. This "miraculous transformation" was not noticed by many of even the most eminent spectators. It is interesting that, in the press centre, many of the experts were puzzled as to why Karpov failed to exploit an opportunity to force a draw, which suddenly presented itself. And only the young grandmaster Yury Balashov, who knew Anatoly well, gave an accurate diagnosis with his customary calmness: "What does he want with a draw? For a long time now he's been playing for a win." And indeed, in the endgame Polugayevsky was completely outplayed.

According to Yury Razuvayev, on leaving the hall after this game had been adjourned, Karpov, looking a trifle surprised and embarrassed, said: "I seem to be winning now..." This was hard to believe, but when Razuvayev arrived the following morning at the "Moscow" hotel, where the all-night analysis of the adjourned position was still going on, he could see that the assessment given the previous day by Karpov was correct. Anatoly's enthusiasm and capacity for work created a terrific impression, and he did not cut short his examination of the position even when it was time to have if only a little sleep, and a bite to eat. And so, forgetting about food, Karpov set off for the resumption. And then came a surprise. Polugayevsky did not choose the strongest continuation, but on the other hand it was one which Karpov had hardly analysed. Many a player would be confused by such a "change of scene", but, despite his fatigue, Karpov at the board and in the limited time available found a subtle way to win.

4th Game
Karpov–Polugayevsky
Sicilian Defence

1 P–K4 P–QB4 2 N–KB3 P–Q3 3 P–Q4
P×P 4 N×P N–KB3 5 N–QB3 P–QR3 6
B–K2 P–K4 7 N–N3 B–K2 8 0–0 B–K3 9
P–B4 Q–B2 10 P–QR4 QN–Q2 11 K–R1 0–0
12 B–K3 P×P 13 R×P N–K4 14 N–Q4
QR–Q1 15 Q–KN1 R–Q2 16 R–Q1 R–K1
17 N–B5 B–Q1 18 N–Q4 N–N3 19
R(4)–B1 N–K4 20 B–KB4 Q–B4 21 N×B
Q×Q+ 22 R×Q R×N 23 B–B3 N(4)–N5
24 KR–B1 B–N3 25 R–Q2 B–K6 26 B×B
N×B 27 R–QN1 K–B1 28 K–N1 R–B2 29
K–B2 N–B5 30 R–Q3 P–KN4 31 P–R3
P–KR4 32 N–Q5 N×N 33 R×N N–K4

34 P–B3 P–R5 35 R(1)–Q1 K–K2 36 R(1)–Q4
P–B3 37 P–R5 R–B3 38 B–K2 K–Q1 39
P–B4 K–B2 40 P–QN4 N–N3 41 P–N5

... P×P 42 P×P R–B7 43 P–N6+ K–Q2
44 R–Q2 R×R 45 R×R R–K4 46 P–R6 K–B3
47 R–N2 N–B5 48 P–R7 R–R4 49 B–B4
Resigns

It is possible that all this exertion told at the start of the fifth game. Karpov looked unusually listless, and Polugayevsky (for the last time in the match) managed to put into operation another opening preparation. White gained an absolutely won position, and it was even good that Karpov was able to give up the exchange—otherwise he would simply have had to resign. What happened next was at first sight quite incredible, the sort of thing that those who are uninitiated in the secrets of chess, or who do not think deeply, sometimes call luck, or sometimes explain as hypnotism, or even more amusingly as "sorcery". Here, however, is what Mikhail Tal said, after he had just arrived in Moscow from an international tournament, and had appeared at that precise moment in the hall where the Karpov–Polugayevsky match was being played:

"I first went into the press centre, and glanced at the position", relates the Ex-World Champion. "I saw that Lyev was bound to win. I then went into the playing hall, looked at the stage and—couldn't believe my eyes: Karpov had such a self-confident air that you would have thought that it was he who was the exchange up, and had the winning chances. He was even smiling slightly at his own thoughts. Polugayevsky, meanwhile, was looking at the position in fright. Eh, I thought to myself, how easy it would be for him not to win this position. And that's exactly what happened—Lyev played on until a point where he must have been pleased to escape with a draw. It is very important to be able to keep a grip on oneself as Karpov did, in the most difficult of situations. The opponent always senses this..."

So what was it that took place on the stage at this point? Listen to Anatoly Karpov:

"At that moment there was a popular song going round and round in my head, with these words: 'Everything, like smoke, dispersed...' No doubt I subconsciously had in mind my lead in the match, gained with such difficulty in the previous game Nevertheless, this persistently recurring line from the song did something to calm me. I sat there as though there was nothing amiss, as if I could see that I had a perfectly respectable position. I did indeed see a great deal, but everything I saw appeared unpleasant for me. And it was probably at this point that Polugayevsky sensed that I was very calm...

It should be said that, in matches in general, somewhere around the third or fourth game you begin to sense your opponent, his mood, and even perhaps his desires. Sometimes you can guess his thoughts, or at any rate the direction along which his thoughts are working. Polugayevsky probably sensed that I was no longer concerned, that at heart I had already resigned this game, and was therefore absolutely calm. But as for him, he still had to gain the win, and, strange as it may seem, we were in an unequal situation: the psychological advantage —doesn't it sound amusing in such a situation?—was now on my side. And it was this that finished him!

Yury Razuvayev once told me", Anatoly goes on, "of a curious incident in which he was involved at a tournament in Yugoslavia. He was in desperate time trouble in a game against the Argentinian grandmaster Quinteros. The flag on his clock was already raised, and the position was extremely unclear; Quinteros similarly had little time left, but nevertheless, more than Razuvayev. The Argentinian quickly made his move, pressed his clock, and Razuvayev's flag began to climb higher. Here Yury picked up his coffee cup, very slowly began to take a sip, and. . . did not immediately make a move. On seeing all this, Quinteros became quite stupified, his hands even began shaking, and he ruined his game within three or four moves— such was the effect of his opponent's refusal to be hurried (but this was no deliberate psychological trick, but simply a delayed reaction on Yury's part).

Thus, in my opinion, in Moscow Polugayevsky found himself in a similar situation to that of Quinteros at that time in Yugoslavia. True, my opponent did not lose the game—to do that was simply impossible—but in the end he was almost happy to draw".

5th Game
Polugayevsky–Karpov
Nimzo-Indian Defence

1 P–Q4 N–KB3 2 P–QB4 P–K3 3 N–QB3 B–N5 4 P–K3 0–0 5 B–Q3 P–B4 6 N–B3 P–Q4 7 0–0 QP×P 8 B×BP N–B3 9 P–QR3 B–R4 10 B–R2 P–QR3 11 B–N1 B–N3 12 Q–B2 P–N3 13 P×P B×P 14 P–QN4 B–K2 15 B–N2 P–K4 16 R–Q1 Q–K1 17 P–N5 P×P 18 N×NP B–KB4 19 Q–K2 B×B 20 N–B7 Q–N1 21 N×R B–KB4 22 N–N6 P–K5 23 N–Q4 N×N 24 B×N B–KN5 25 P–B3 P×P 26 P×P B–K3 27 QR–B1 R–Q1 28 Q–QN2 N–K1 29 B–K5 B–Q3 30 B×B R×B

31 Q–N4 Q–Q1 32 R×R N×R 33 R–Q1 Q–N4+ 34 K–B2 N–B4 35 Q–KB4 Q–B3 36 N–R4 B–N6 37 R–Q2 P–KN4 38 Q–N8+ K–N2 39 N–N2 B–Q4 40 N–Q3 N–Q3 41 N–B4 P×N 42 R×B Q–N7+ 43 K–B1 P×P 44 R–KN5+ **Drawn**

The winner of the match was the first to score three wins, with a limit of fourteen games. It is not easy to adapt to playing to a fixed (in the Quarter-Finals, rather small) number of wins. The player who takes the lead gains a marked psychological advantage, as the other must all the time "keep a grip on himself", since one more defeat will leave him on the verge of catastrophe. After the match Polugayevsky admitted: "Now, with the benefit of hindsight,

I see very clearly the errors I made in preparing for the match. I devoted much time to purely chess work, and did not concentrate sufficiently on correct psychological preparation". After the match Karpov stated, very generously I would say, that the convincing score in no way reflected the genuine relative strengths, but more likely the psychological state of his opponent. This is possibly true, but the sixth game, the best in the match, showed that in the purely chess sense too, the future World Champion was clearly superior to his strong opponent.

As a resumé to this Candidates' Quarter-Final clash, I think it would be appropriate to present the conclusions drawn by grandmaster Aleksey Suetin:

"I do not wish to say that neither Polugayevsky's psychological condition, nor his opening repertoire, did not have any influence on the result of the match. Of course they did. But the main reason for such a crushing defeat was the play of the winner. Karpov has an amazing technique, which he utilizes in a sound, practical way. He plays effortlessly and quickly, and has an accurate positional sense, of which one gains the impression that it is more acute than that of his opponents. It has frequently been pointed out that Karpov has had little experience. This is true. But observe how quickly the grandmaster gains this experience. Karpov the student, while playing, is all the time learning. And the teacher, when he resigns, gives him a high mark.

The appearance of Anatoly Karpov among the four semi-finalists signifies that our famous musketeers have been joined by a young and skilful d'Artagnan".

6th Game
Karpov–Polugayevsky
Sicilian Defence

1 P–K4	P–QB4
2 N–KB3	P–Q3
3 P–Q4	P×P
4 N×P	N–KB3
5 N–QB3	P–QR3
6 B–K2	P–K4
7 N–N3	B–K2
8 0–0	B–K3
9 P–B4	Q–B2
10 P–QR4	QN–Q2
11 K–R1	0–0

against Bronstein. I also played this later, in the Leningrad Interzonal against Byrne, though this time without success.

12 B–K3

This idea is not new. It acquired a second wind 'at high level' after the game Geller–Ivkov, 1973.

White maintains the tension in the centre, not disclosing his intentions for the moment.

12 ...   P×P

This variation of the Sicilian Defence occurred each time in the match that Polugayevsky had Black. During our preparations for the match, my trainer, grandmaster Furman, and I had reckoned with this possibility, and had outlined the most expedient deployment of White's forces.

The usual continuation here is 12 P–B5. In 1971 I managed to win in this variation

13 R×P	N–K4
14 P–R5	

In the fourth game of the match I played the weaker 14 N–Q4, and after 14 ... QR–Q1 Black secured a good game.

14 ...	N(3)–Q2
15 R–KB1	B–B3

16 N–Q5	B×N
17 Q×B!?	

Here there is something I should like to explain. Certain chess commentators sometimes accuse me of being a dry, rational, careful player. It is true that I have a practical approach, and that my game is based to a great extent on technique. I attempt to play 'correct' chess, and never take risks as, say, Larsen does. As White, like everyone else, I aim for an advantage from the very start, but as Black I try first of all to equalize the position.

But when there is a choice of moves, I don't choose the simplest by any means, but rather the most expedient. If there are several equally good continuations, my choice depends to a great extent on my opponents. Against Tal, for instance, I prefer to go in for simple positions, which are not to his taste, whereas against Petrosian I try to make the play more complicated. But if I see one correct path, then whoever I am playing I go only along that one path. However, I sense that recently my style has been undergoing something of a change.

Let us return to the game. The sacrifice of two pawns which I offered against Polugayevsky would earlier, no doubt, not even have entered my head. Everyone thought that this was a prepared variation. But 'as God is my witness', this was pure improvisation at the board. Even today I find this a 'terrible' decision on my part. I could have played quietly—17 P×B, but after 17 ... N–B5 18 B×N Q×B White can only dream about the opening advantage that might have been.

17 ...	Q×BP

Polugayevsky spent more than an hour in uncertainty: to take or not to take? After all, he could have thought that, since I had sacrificed, it meant that everything had been worked out to the end beforehand. On the other hand, he simply couldn't find this forced loss for him, and so he looked for it over and over. In the event of Black declining the sacrifice, he would have come under heavy positional pressure.

18 N–Q4	Q×NP

As one says: 'In for a penny, in for a pound!'.

The attempt to limit himself to a small gain (if Black had even wanted to do this) would have led to a position with material equality and a marked positional advantage for White. E.g. 18 ... Q–B4 19 N–B5! Q×Q 20 P×Q, and Black's QP falls.

19 QR–N1	Q–B6

19 ... Q–R6 is weaker—the black queen would have been out of play on the edge of the board.

20 N–B5	

The aim of this move is to defend the bishop, without allowing Black's queen onto his QB4 square, which could have occurred after 20 R–N3 Q–B4 21 N–B5 Q×Q 22 P×Q N–B4, when Black can defend.

20 ...   Q–B7!

Polugayevsky manoeuvres excellently: this is the best move.

Any delay would have allowed White to co-ordinate his pieces: 21 B–Q4 Q–Q7 22 R–N2, or 21 KR–B1 Q–R6 22 R–R1 Q–N7 23 R–R2 Q–N5 24 B–Q2!, trapping the queen. By the move played, Black prevents this.

21 QR–K1

An inaccuracy. White would have had a big advantage after 21 KR–K1, whereas now Black finds a defence.

21 ...	**N–B4**
22 N×QP	**N(B4)–Q6**
23 B×N	**N×B**
24 R–Q1	**N–N5**

This is the important difference. If on my 21st move I had played KR–K1, the white rooks would now be standing at QN1 and Q1. Consequently, Black would have had only two possibilities: a) 24 ... N–B7+ 25 B×N Q×B 26 P–K5 B–K2 27 R–KB1, or b) 24 ... N–K4 25 N×NP—in both cases with the initiative for White.

25 Q×NP

Having been first two pawns down, and then one, perhaps my first subconscious aim was to eliminate this 'material deficiency'. But meanwhile, 25 Q–R5 would have created the threat of 26 R×B P×R 27 Q–N4+ K–R1 28 B–R6, which would not have been easy to meet (25 ... P–KN3 26 Q–QB5).

25 ...	**QR–N1**
26 Q–R7	**Q–B3**

The decisive mistake. Also bad was 26 ... N–B3 27 Q–B7 N–N5 28 Q×Q N×Q 29 B–N6, with advantage to White. But 26 ... Q–K7 would have given Black some counter-play, although even here the advantage is with White after 27 B–N6.

27 B–B4

Later I learned that, in the press centre at this point, Furman had shown that White could have won by the exchange sacrifice 27 R×B! P×R 28 B–R6 (threatening 29 Q–K3; on 28 ... N–Q6 there follows 29 B×R, and on 28 ... Q–B7—29 R–QB1 Q–Q6 30 Q–B5!). He was probably right, but this is not the only winning path. However, it is said that when I played 27 B–B4, with the threat of 28 P–K5, my trainer remarked contentedly: "that's also good". Indeed, the threat of P–K5 restricts Black's actions, and his knight finds itself out of play.

27 ...   R–R1

Defending against 28 P–K5.

28 Q–B2	**QR–Q1**
29 Q–N3!	

The threat is stronger than its execution! Strangely enough, this often is indeed the case. White does not hurry to advance P–K5, but increases the pressure.

29 ...	Q–B6
30 R–B3	Q–B7
31 R(1)–KB1	B–Q5

Otherwise comes P–K5 with a decisive attack. However, in any case the attack can no longer be halted.

32 B–R6

White directs his fire simultaneously against KB7 and KN7.

| 32 ... | N–B3 |

In the hope of complicating matters after 33 N×P Q–B5!

| 33 N–B5 | Q–N7 |

The game would have had an interesting finish in the event of 33 ... B–K4 34 B×P B×Q 35 R×B, when Black cannot avoid mate.

34 B–B1

White vacates the square KR6 for his knight with gain of tempo. There is no longer any defence.

34 ...	Q–N4
35 N–R6+	K–R1
36 N×P+	R×N

After 36 ... K–N1 Black is mated: 37 N–R6+ K–R1 38 R×R+.

37 R×R	B–B3
38 Q–B2	K–N1
39 R×B	P×R
40 Q×P	**Resigns**

C ANDIDATES' SEMI-FINAL MATCH WITH BORIS SPASSKY

Karpov's victory over Polugayevsky did not convince, it was not correctly understood by everyone. Botvinnik, it is true, said smilingly at that time: "In exactly the same 'incomprehensible' way he will also defeat Spassky". But this simply wasn't believed.

"Spassky's experience and chess strength will be opposed by the youthful ardour and ambition of his opponent, who is also now of considerable strength. I think that this Semi-Final will prove no less interesting than a clash between any one of the Candidates and Fischer." —this is what Tigran Petrosian had to say about the coming match between Anatoly Karpov and Boris Spassky.

As can be seen, in this pronouncement there is a complete absence of the dangerous element of forecasting. But that is Petrosian's nature. All (or almost all) the other experts and journalists, at all events, gave their preference to Spassky. Later, however, several of them extricated themselves quite well from the resulting situation, pleading that their work was similar to the art of a diplomat: having to predict what will happen tomorrow, and then being able to explain why it did not happen.

That before the match the weight of public opinion should be on the side of the Ex-World Champion is not at all surprising. As grandmaster Mark Taimanov can testify, the charm of the name of Boris Spassky in the hearts of his numerous supporters had not dimmed even after the shock in Reykjavik. His deep creative ability, harmonious style, chivalry at the board, and even, if you like, the elegance of his appearance, drew to Spassky the most widespread support. And his success in the very strong USSR Championship, together with his highly convincing victory in the Quarter-Final Match over Robert Byrne, were particularly weighty arguments in Spassky's favour when it came to making forecasts. Karpov, on the other hand, outwardly appeared less respectable on all counts. His somewhat drab style, rather rational approach, restrained temperament, and reticence, which journalists found so annoying, did not immediately win him widespread support.

When the FIDE President Max Euwe arrived in Leningrad for the start of the match, he was literally bombarded by questions from chess fans. At a press conference he was asked: "It is said that you give a certain preference to Spassky. Why?"

"From 1969 to 1972 Spassky appeared infrequently, and not very successfully", the President explained. "His play could in no way be compared with that which he demonstrated during the period of his highly interesting clashes with Petrosian. But now he has once again captured his earlier form. However",—here Euwe made a reservation—"in the development of talented young players, qualitative leaps can take place. It is difficult to guess whether Karpov will now make such a leap. If he does, then I do not rule out the possibility of him winning even the title of World Champion".

Later, Max Euwe characterized the chess style of Anatoly Karpov as follows:

"Perhaps, more than anyone, Karpov resembles Capablanca, although there is one important difference. When you play through Capablanca's games, you can't help thinking: oh, how simple it all is, I could play like that. Karpov's games, on the other hand, are startling in their strategy, which appears illogical, but it soon becomes clear that in fact his games contain a high degree of logic. The young Leningrad player, just like the Cuban, is especially tenacious in difficult positions; Capablanca and Karpov are linked by one more feature—the extreme rarity of their defeats. In Hungary, for instance, two books were published; 'Capablanca wins', and 'Capablanca loses'. The first is a highly weighty tome, while the second is a thin little brochure. I think that two similar books about Karpov would have the same appearance".

...Meanwhile, the time for the official opening of the match was approaching. A few hours before the ceremony, only those close to Karpov knew that he was not well, and would probably seek a postponement...

Why should he do this? In a match of the first to win four games out of a total possible number of twenty, the regulations allowed a player to take only two breaks on account of illness—and Karpov was intending to begin by using up one of these two postponements! But what was there to do, if Anatoly's temperature had jumped to 39 °C?! Only later, after the elapse of some considerable time, someone had an idea: why not defer the start of the match (the doctor would have allowed this). But for some reason no one thought of this at the time, and after the draw has been made it is no longer possible to be ill "without punishment"... In short, failing to take account of this subtlety, Karpov appeared at the opening of the match, and took part in the draw. He sat on the stage during the opening ceremony, and looked clearly unwell—many thought that he was nervous about the coming match against a formidable opponent. And only on the following day, when the first game was due to be played, it became known that, on account of illness, Karpov would be forced to start the match with... a postponement.

The following day, Boris Spassky, handsome and confident, appeared on the stage of the Dzerzhinsky Palace of Culture a few minutes before the start of the first game, and was immediately applauded by a thousand spectators. A native of Leningrad, he had then moved to Moscow, but had agreed to play this vital match in this his home town, which was now his opponent's permanent residence. Spassky sat down at the board, the controller started White's clock, but since Karpov had not yet arrived, Spassky soon retired into the wings. Then a new burst of applause—Anatoly Karpov had arrived. He sat down, quickly advanced his king's pawn, then again stood up and greeted his opponent with a handshake. And they sat down opposite each other—the one a thin, white-faced youth, not yet recovered from his indisposition, and constantly bringing a handkerchief to his nose, the other a man in the picture of health, handsome, and sun-tanned (he had just arrived back from a mountain resort)...

The first game in a match does not often give a definite result. As an example, in the ten matches Spassky had played prior to this one, he had twice begun with a win, twice lost, and six times drawn. In his eleventh starting game Spassky gained a fairly confident win, and what's more, with the black pieces, which in matches at such a high level is very important.

The reader should remember here the forecasts before the match, he should take into account the fact that Karpov's opponent was a highly experienced player, who before this, in the seven Candidates' Matches he had played, had scored seven impressive victories. Finally, it should be borne in mind that Karpov, who was not yet fully recovered from his illness, was meeting a grandmaster who for a number of years had been a standard, whose example he had followed. Taking all this into account, one can imagine the state of this young man, who had been defeated with the white pieces, and who now had to sit down again at the board and meet the onslaught of the popular favourite.

After the game had been lost on resumption, Furman was upset, but before going home managed to remind Karpov that Fischer had also lost the first game to Spassky, but had nevertheless gone on to win the match.

This is the appropriate place to relate how Karpov and his helpers had prepared beforehand an operation under the code name "blows from both hands". What did this mean? It had been noted that, as regards the openings, Spassky did not prepare very thoroughly for matches, and so it was decided to adopt against him as many different unexpected schemes as possible. In order to successfully adopt such tactics, Karpov had to undertake an enormous amount of preliminary work. It is sufficient to recall that Efim Geller, an openings expert, wrote: "As regards versatility, Anatoly Karpov is inferior to his opponent. This is noticeable, in particular, in his limited opening repertoire. As White Karpov plays only 1 P–K4, and as Black sticks to one or two defences..." At that time Geller had not yet become Karpov's second trainer, and could not have known that the young grandmaster was not at all what he appeared to be. Spassky judged Karpov exactly as Geller did—and was wrong.

It so happened that, for the second game, Mikhail Tal was roughly an hour late. By the entrance to the building where the match was being played, there was a crowd of fans, who had been unable to get tickets for the hall. An enormous demonstration board had been set up for them on the balcony. On glancing at it, Tal could not believe his eyes. "Surely they aren't demonstrating the second Semi-Final match from Odessa, with Petrosian again playing Black?" the grandmaster puzzled, for only with such a "combination" was it possible to have the position on the board, which was obviously from a Caro-Kann. But in fact everything was more real, and at the same more fantastic. The game being demonstrated was, as usual, from the Leningrad match. To 1 P–K4 Karpov had replied 1 ... P–QB3.

...We beg the reader's forgiveness, but we must for a short time return again to a description of the first game by Karpov himself, and for an explanation of what happened in the associated second game. And so, Anatoly Karpov relates:

"At the start of the first game I felt reasonably well. I had managed to get my temperature down, and my mind was working clearly. I chose a complicated line of play, since I reckoned that I could cope with any problems. Alas, I overestimated my strength. At the decisive point my thinking became confused, I made several obvious errors—and it was all over.

It is not by accident that I have dwelt in such detail on the events from the first game: it did Spassky a bad service. It was unlikely that he was hoping for an easy victory in the match, but after this easy win at the start, he evidently gained a false impression about my play in general.

Many failed to understand why in the second game the Ex-World Champion avoided any attempt to develop his initiative, and offered a draw as early as the seventeenth move. I can only suppose that Spassky, on seeing that I was not well, simply felt sorry for me. Sportsmanship has always been one of his distinguishing features. But there is also another, more probable, explanation. The Caro-Kann, which in the second game I adopted for the first time in my life, came as a complete surprise to Spassky, and he decided for the time being to avoid any active measures..."

That which happened with Spassky is not new in chess. After losing the title of World Champion in 1969, Tigran Petrosian quite unexpectedly admitted to me: "I will never forgive myself for having won the first game of the match against Spassky!" At the time this admission surprised me, and it was only later that I understood what Petrosian had in mind: the easy win* had deprived him of his vigilance, whereas it had geared up Spassky for a difficult fight. Something similar happened in the match we are describing. Karpov, who during the 1974 Football World Cup was astonished by the Dutch team ("See how they have all their pieces working!"), later had this to say about his loss in the first game to Spassky:

"He, like the Dutch in the Final against the West German team, was suddenly disarmed by scoring such an easy 'goal' in the very 'first minute' of the match".

In chess literature one often finds quoted the most characteristic words of this or that grandmaster. One can recall here Spassky's well-known pronouncement after he had lost the match to Karpov: "For me chess is first and foremost a game of justice. If you have made a mistake, not necessarily a chess mistake, but, say, a purely human one, such as showing contempt for your opponent, or being frivolous, then at the board you must definitely suffer retribution!..."

Before the match with Spassky, his young opponent was by no means confident of ultimate success. His confidence grew as the match progressed, and a big rôle in this was played first by the second game, and then by the third, which showed that the chosen "plan of campaign" was the only correct one. After winning a breathing space, and time to regain his health, and being convinced that everything was now going normally, Karpov began playing with his real strength. In general, Spassky has played an enormous rôle in the popularizing of the so-called "psychological approach" to chess. But here in Karpov he came up against a worthy successor, who in this respect had gone even further than his highly experienced opponent.

---

* Easy win?! Petrosian won only after Spassky had blundered on move 52. (K.P.N.)

Here it should be pointed out that Igor Bondarevsky, for many years Spassky's trainer, did a great deal towards creating the notion of the psychological stability of his "charge". Back in 1966, in their first Match for the World Championship, Petrosian had cast doubts on this assertion. For a long time after this no one was able to capitalize on this lesson, since psychology comes into effect only when the playing strengths of the opponents are roughly equal. Here Spassky was the stronger, and only in 1972, in the person of Fischer, did he meet a player who, while possessing tremendous practical strength, succeeded in finding the key to Spassky's by no means stable character. Rejecting, of course, Fischer's ugly methods of "psychological warfare", Karpov followed a similar path on the purely chess front: by changing his opening schemes, he did not allow his opponent to prepare properly at home, and caused him to get nervous.

In the third game Karpov quite unexpectedly played 1 P–Q4 and after a lively struggle levelled the score.

3rd Game
Karpov–Spassky
King's Indian Defence

1 P–Q4 N–KB3 2 P–QB4 P–KN3 3 N–QB3 B–N2 4 P–K4 P–Q3 5 N–B3 0–0 6 B–K2 P–B4 7 0–0 B–N5 8 P–Q5 QN–Q2 9 B–N5 P–QR3 10 P–QR4 Q–B2 11 Q–Q2 QR–K1 12 P–R3 B×N 13 B×B P–K3 14 P–QN3 K–R1 15 B–K3 N–KN1 16 B–K2 P–K4 17 P–KN4 Q–Q1 18 K–N2 Q–R5 19 P–B3 B–R3 20 P–N5 B–N2 21 B–B2 Q–B5 22 B–K3 Q–R5 23 Q–K1 Q×Q 24 KR×Q P–R3 25 P–R4 P×P 26 P×P N–K2 27 P–R5 P–B3 28 KR–QN1 P×P 29 P–N4 (Diag.) 29 . . . N–B4 30 B×NP N–Q5 31 P×P N×QBP 32 R–N6 B–B3 33 R–R1+ K–N2 34 B–R6+ K–N1 35 B×R R×B 36 R×QP

K–N2 37 B–Q1 B–K2 38 R–N6 B–Q1 39 R–QN1 R–B2 40 N–R4 N–Q6 41 N–N6 P–N4 42 N–B8 N–QB4 43 N–Q6 R–Q2 44 N–B5+ N×N 45 P×N P–K5 46 P×P N×P 47 B–R4 R–K2 48 R(N1)–K1 N–B4 49 R×R+ B×R 50 B–B2 B–Q1 51 R–R1 K–B3 52 P–Q6 N–Q2 53 R–QN1 K–K4 54 R–Q1 K–B5 55 R–K1 Resigns

Then came two tensely-fought draws, and a win as Black on the resumption of the sixth game . . . But it is time to hand over to Semion Furman, trainer of the young grandmaster: "I am pretty well acquainted with the style of play of the best players in the world. And this includes Spassky. It did not prove difficult for Karpov and me to form a correct impression of our opponent. It goes without saying that he is a strong player, talented and original, but his approach to chess, in my opinion, is not altogether correct. This refers in particular to the opening stage. Spassky used to think, and probably still thinks, that his strength in the middle-game and endgame is so great that he can afford to give his opponent a start in the opening. I consider the main cause of Spassky's defeat in the match with Fischer to be the fact that he was inferior to the American in the opening. The lessons from the Fischer–Spassky match were, of course, taken into account during our preparations for the Semi-Final Match between Karpov and Spassky. This explains the 'première' performance on the Leningrad stage of the Caro-Kann Defence, and the unexpected avoidance by Karpov in a number of games of 1 P–K4. We also had other things planned, but the match concluded long before the twentieth game. It turned out that Spassky, like Polugayevsky before him, was unable to obtain his favourite positions".

...However, that which Furman talks about here is only the overall scheme. In reality everything appeared much more complicated. After missing a draw on the resumption of the sixth game, a distressed Spassky was completely outplayed in the seventh. Either the closeness of the desired dénouement affected Karpov, or else—for the only time in the match!—his youth nevertheless told, but at one point he made an impulsive decision, and in the adjourned position there was no longer a win.

"I do not remember ever failing to win in such an overwhelming position", Karpov complains. "And when at home, after many hours of analysis, I became convinced that I would have to agree to a draw by perpetual check, I was really annoyed. I couldn't get to sleep, and right through till dawn tried to find something to occupy myself with. With Black in the eighth game, I came under a fierce attack. Tal stated that he didn't know whether he would have won this game as White, but that as Black he would certainly have lost it, and very rapidly. But I managed to save it. In the ninth game, one of the beautiful peculiarities of chess was revealed: the position of each piece, even if it be only in a variation, influences without fail the assessment of a position. But first, about my observations before this, the 9th game. As usual we shook hands, both by habit adjusted the pieces, and the controller started the clock. And I played 1 P–K4, returning to the move after which I had lost the first game. And suddenly Spassky, convulsively and with both hands, with a completely estranged look began adjusting, for the second time, his pieces, which were already accurately placed. Nerves...

In contrast to the Spassky–Fischer Match, where the American grandmaster changed his openings after a comparative failure", continues Karpov, "I, on the other hand, avoided schemes which had proved successful. Thus in the eleventh game with White I again reverted to 1 P–Q4. For Spassky it was probably quite difficult preparing for his games with me... It should, incidentally, be said that the relations between us remained invariably correct, although my suggestion after the first game of analysing it together in the playing hall was declined by Spassky. Later, it is true, we several times discussed the course taken by certain games, but without setting up the pieces on the board. It was pleasant for me when after the eleventh game, Spassky congratulated me most respectfully on my victory in the match."

* * *

...And so, the Semi-Final Match was over, but before we finally leave it, I would like to acquaint the reader with what Mikhail Tal said at that time in Leningrad, in answer to my question: "So why in fact were the oracles wrong?" This is how the Ex-World Champion saw this match:

"For a whole series of reasons, Karpov's victory over Spassky made a greater impression on me than Korchnoi's win against Petrosian. Earlier I remarked that, in the Odessa match, much would depend on who could seize the initiative, and thereby dictate the nature of the play. In the Leningrad clash I was primarily interested in the question of how Karpov, who is unaccustomed to noughts, would react to a first defeat.

And then came the very first game. It went on for quite a considerable number of moves, but during it Karpov was hardly seen; his faint silhouette showed up only at the end. Spassky won thanks to his obvious superiority. There was also that ill-fated cold, and the enforced postponement. To be honest, I thought that, despite all his affected outward calm, Karpov was beginning to 'crack up'. Nothing offensive is implied by the word 'affected'—Karpov is all the time on view, and this, believe me, is not easy. (I suspect, that when he said that the present World Championship Cycle would not be his, at heart he very much hoped that he was deceiving himself.)

I thought, well now, Karpov is a good defender, and will begin to dig his heels in, but even so, after such a defeat he will probably now lose the match. But now came the second game, and then the third... First the Caro-Kann Defence, and then 1 P–Q4. This was the action not of a boy, but of a man. I recall my 1965 Match with Spassky, when some time after the fifth game they tried to persuade me to give up my 1 P–K4, to change the tune, and to divert my opponent. But I was already too set in my ways. The present-day Karpov, although younger than the Tal of that time, did not allow himself to become set.

Karpov's opening repertoire is trained, like the voice of a good singer. And he looks after it. When he played against me in the last USSR Championship, he was probably afraid that I might play the Najdorf Variation of the Sicilian Defence (which I do quite often), and so he avoided 1 P–K4. There was a simple explanation: Karpov was faced with the Quarter-Final Match with Polugayevsky, in whose opening repertoire the Sicilian Defence is firmly established—so why disclose his intentions beforehand? Incidentally, he operated all the time in this way. In that game with Karpov I sank into thought as to what to play as Black, since in my preparations I had assumed that he would advance his king's pawn. In the end I decided on the Slav Defence. If he wants a draw, he can exchange on Q5, and if he doesn't... This was roughly the fifth time in my life I had played this variation (the last time, it would seem, was in 1952), while for him it would be the first. Karpov played the opening against me, just as Furman did against Kuzmin. And in general, many of his openings—Nimzo-Indian, King's Indian— remind one in all respects of the way that Furman plays them. In this stage of the game the young player believes his trainer quite unquestioningly. And not for nothing. Semion Furman has an exceptionally fine feel for the opening, and in his understanding of the game in general is a terrific chess player...

But what about Boris? In any elementary manual on psychology, it is stated that success breeds success. But not here! Spassky won the first game, but in the second—almost demonstratively avoided a fight. All right, the opponent played the Caro-Kann, which was probably a surprise. But surely there must be some way for White to attempt to seize the initiative, by himself avoiding the approved schemes. It was obvious that the Caro-Kann had not appeared accidentally in Karpov's repertoire, and it was obvious that he would have looked through Spassky's games, so the latter should have come to the conclusion to himself play something new. But Boris played such that Karpov, strictly speaking, did not have to find a single difficult to move, in order to equalize. And what about the way Spassky played the King's Indian Defence in the third game? Not at all how that variation should be played...

And here is something else of interest. At the start of the match with Polugayevsky, Karpov's play was uneven: at times it was successful, at others he missed things. The same happened against Spassky. And then came an explosive finish, which I am inclined to explain as being due to his increased belief in himself during the course of the match.

I was tremendously impressed by the finish to the ninth game. When a player finds the only saving move (when all other moves lose), he is given two exclamation marks. This is perfectly understandable: he deserves them. But what do you do when, out of several good moves, a player chooses one after which everything immediately becomes clear—this is it, the winning move! In the press centre we looked at a possible pawn sacrifice for Spassky, but found that it was insufficient, and that, after overcoming some difficulties, White should nevertheless win. But Karpov made a move after which Black had neither any sacrifices, nor anything at all, and after which there were no more questions. The finish of this ninth game creates a quite indelible impression. On the whole, it is rather difficult to surprise me. But Anatoly did this, spending on those eight or ten excellent concluding moves approximately five minutes.

I will not take it upon myself to comment on the tenth and eleventh games. Especially the latter. It is an exact copy of the twenty-first game from Spassky's Match with Fischer in Reykjavik. He tried and tried, but nothing came of it! No, it wasn't that he waved goodbye to the match—the waving happened of its own accord. Spassky most probably wanted to go on playing at full strength; he is one of those players who does not consciously resign. Here it happened sub-consciously...

Please excuse me these usual involuntary parallels and reminiscences, from which I cannot get away. But the state Spassky was in is familiar to me. It was in the twenty-first game of my Return Match with Botvinnik. When I sat down at the board, I thought that, with a bit of luck, I would win this, the twenty-first, then, with White, the twenty-second, and then we would suddenly be up to the twenty-third, and in the last game there would be something to play for. It could all have happened, except that I played that twenty-first game like a child, and met the deserved fate. No doubt if I had won it, I would have played the next game better. But it didn't work out! And it didn't work out for Spassky, either against Fischer, or against Karpov.

The present match was essentially over after the eighth game, when Spassky was unable to win it. Personally, I didn't doubt for a second that after Spassky had begun his attack with 24 P–R6, the game would soon come to a spectacular conclusion. But after the move 25 ... N–B3 (which Karpov made fairly quickly), there was no win to be found. Such a blow is more serious than any defeat. When you fail to win such positions, you begin to lose confidence, and your mind begins to fill with all sorts of devilish thoughts, such as: 'Is it possible to win against him at all?' "

8th Game
Spassky–Karpov
Caro-Kann Defence

1 P–K4 P–QB3 2 P–Q4 P–Q4 3 N–QB3
P×P 4 N×P B–B4 5 N–N3 B–N3 6 P–KR4
P–KR3 7 P–R5 B–R2 8 N–B3 N–Q2 9 B–Q3
B×B 10 Q×B KN–B3 11 B–Q2 Q–B2 12
P–B4 P–K3 13 Q–K2 B–Q3 14 N–B5 B–B5
15 B×B Q×B 16 N–K3 Q–B2 17 0–0–0
P–QN4 18 P×P P×P+ 19 K–N1 0–0
20 P–KN4 N–K5 21 KR–N1 N–N4 22 N×N
P×N 23 P–Q5

23 ... P–R3 24 P–R6 NP×P 25 R–R1
N–B3 26 R×P K–N2 27 R(6)–R1 QR–Q1

28 P×P P×P 29 N–B2 Q–KB5 30 P–B3 K–B2 31 P–R3 P–K4 32 N–N4 P–K5 33 P×P R×R+ 34 R×R R–K1 35 N×P Q×KP+ 36 Q×Q R×Q 37 N–B7 P–N5 38 P×P R×QNP 39 R–KB1 R–KB5 40 **Drawn**

9th Game
Karpov–Spassky
Sicilian Defence

I began the first game of the match with 1 P–K4, and lost. There were two reasons for this: Spassky's excellent play, and my indisposition that day. I then took a 'creative break' and began all of my subsequent 'White' games with 1 P–Q4. And here, at last, I returned to my earlier move.

1 P–K4	P–QB4
2 N–KB3	P–K3
3 P–Q4	P×P
4 N×P	N–KB3
5 N–QB3	P–Q3
6 B–K2	B–K2
7 0–0	0–0
8 P–B4	N–B3
9 B–K3	

Here, for the second time (the first time was after my first move), Spassky pondered: should he repeat, or not?

9 ...	B–Q2

In the first game of the match the Ex-World Champion adopted a comparatively new continuation, 9 ... P–K4. Here he decided to restrain his curiosity—what new move had his opponent prepared?—and played as is usual in the Scheveningen Variation.

10 N–N3	P–QR4?!

Although my opponent had decided to avoid the variation from the first game, he was still under the influence of his victory there. This is the probable explanation for his last, highly nervy move. The point is that he also made this same move in that first game, but here it is unfavourable, since it concedes White "eternal" use of his QN5 square, while Black gains nothing in return.

11 P–QR4	N–QN5
12 B–B3	B–B3

Of course, Black does not especially wish to allow the white knight to return to Q4, but it would be even more unpleasant to play 12 ... P–K4, reaching a position from the first game, but with the important difference that the black bishop stands passively at Q2, and not at K3.

13 N–Q4	P–KN3

In order to advance P–K4, Black has to weaken his king's position, otherwise the knight at Q4 can move to KB5.

14 R–B2	P–K4
15 N×B	

White probably also maintains his advantage in the event of 15 N(4)–N5.

15 ...	P×N
16 P×P	P×P

17 Q–KB1!

A battle is raging around the square QB4, which White hopes to occupy with one of his pieces. If Black were able to prevent this, his position would be by no means bad. There was no point in moving the rook off the KB-file (17 R–Q2), since it is not yet clear on which file its action will be needed.

17 ...	Q–B1
18 P–R3	

White naturally does not allow the exchange of knight for bishop (18 ... N–N5).

18 ...	N–Q2

In the event of 18 ... Q–K3 White has two ways of developing his initiative: either 19 R–B1 KR–Q1 20 B–K2 R–Q5 21 P–QN3 (establishing his bishop at QB4), or 19 P–N4 followed by P–N5 and B–N4.

19 B–N4	P–R4

This seriously weakens the position of the black king. The simple 19 ... Q–B2 was preferable, moving out of the pin, and uniting rooks along the back rank.

20 B×N	Q×B
21 Q–B4	

And so, the queen has nevertheless reached her appointed square.

21 ...	B–R5

Black has an unpleasant endgame after 21 ... Q–K3 22 Q×Q P×Q 23 QR–KB1.

22 R–Q2	Q–K2
23 R–KB1!	

I was not tempted by the prospect of winning the exchange: after 23 B–B5 Q–N4 24 R–Q7 N×P 25 B×R R×B Black has active counter-play.

The Q-file is not on its own a decisive factor, since the square Q8 is securely covered. White therefore has to direct his activities in other directions.

23 ...	KR–Q1

24 N–N1!

The clever point of this move is that White succeeds in choosing the most convenient moment for switching his knight to a more active position (this can happen particularly quickly, if Black should exchange rooks).

24 ...	Q–N2
25 K–R2!	

A rare instance of the mobility of an enemy bishop being restricted in the middlegame by the king itself.

25 ...	K–N2
26 P–B3	N–R3

The time had come to request the black knight to vacate its post.

27 R–K2!

But now White no longer intends to exchange rooks: he wishes to attack with his heavy pieces along the KB-file. At the same time a square is vacated for the knight, and there is also the threat of 28 P–KN3 B–B3 29 R(2)–KB2 R–Q3 30 B–N5.

27 ...	**R–KB1**
28 N–Q2	**B–Q1**
29 N–B3	**P–B3**

Black defends his KP, and simultaneously tries to block the KB-file. But White's attack is already irresistible.

30 R–Q2!

The 'hesitation' of the white rook may appear illogical. First it was about to occupy the Q-file, then it abandoned it, but now it returns and makes a decisive (this is the important thing!) intrusion along the open file.

30 ...	**B–K2**

On 30 ... N–N1 White wins immediately by 31 N–N5!. When Spassky made his move, I somehow lost my head a little. At first I thought that I was winning in all variations, but then suddenly I looked and couldn't see a win... Fortunately, this "black-out" lasted for only a few moments.

31 Q–K6	**QR–Q1**

This loses by force. Black could have prolonged the resistance only by 31 ... N–N1, as if setting up the pieces for a new game.

32 R×R	**B×R**

If 32 ... R×R, then 34 N×P Q–B2 35 Q–B7+ K–R1 36 Q×B Q×N+ 37 Q×Q P×Q 38 R–B6.

33 R–Q1

Material is level, and the black king appears to have avoided the immediate threats, but Spassky's position is deteriorating with every move. The point is that Black's pieces are disunited, and cannot come to each others' aid. Here, for instance, he cannot defend his second rank by 33 ... R–B2, because his bishop is 'hanging'.

33 ...	**N–N1**
34 B–B5	**R–R1**

35 R×B	**Resigns**

After 35 ... R×R White wins immediately—36 B–K7!.

POLUGAYEVSKY'S PREDICTION

Lyev Polugayevsky agreed to express his opinions only an hour before the conclusion of the last game of the Final Candidates' Match, when Korchnoi was still trying to break open the door shut securely by Karpov, but when it was already clear that the one going on to meet Fischer would be Karpov.

Under the very roof of the Estrada Theatre, the press centre of the match noisily and vainly lived out its last hour. Polugayevsky, who was already reconciled to the fact that he would have to return to his most unpleasant memory from the previous year, nevertheless said, with a slight smile, that perhaps it wasn't worth regretting it, that time would pass, he would become an old man, and would himself write a little book about how he played against Karpov... After being driven into the corner of the press centre, he asked only that everything he said should be recorded word for word, so that subsequently no false rumours should arise.

And so, Lyev Polugayevsky relates:

"I was upset when I learned that the pairings had drawn me up against Karpov. I realized that I was in for a very severe test—a match against a unique player. But, of course, I did not think that I had no chance. Before the match I saw that I had certain trumps. But during the course of play it turned out that I wasted my trumps—that, for instance, is what happened in the fourth and fifth games—whereas Karpov took everything that he was offered".

Within two months, Karpov came out again, this time against Spassky. The papers abounded with forecasts. *Soviet Sport* published Polugayevsky's opinion, in which he wrote about "Spassky's third birth", and about how the Ex-World Champion had managed to gear himself up for a long, hard fight. He also wrote that Karpov's results were astonishing, and that his natural self-possession was the envy of everyone. And he drew this conclusion: "Many grand-masters consider Spassky to be the stronger. And I think that Spassky is a deeper, more dynamic, and more versatile player than Karpov. But only in an abstract, chess sense, so to speak, without the clock ticking away alongside, without the match situation, and without the difference in age. And when all this is taken into account, I can't be so categorical about predicting the winner. I expect the match to be exceptionally difficult for both players, with an enormous rôle being played by those endless nuances, which are impossible to anticipate beforehand. The match is also particularly interesting for the fact that it sees a clash between two strong characters: the one acquired, the other inborn".

"Yes, in '*Soviet Sport*' I published an article in which I did not appear to express any preference for Karpov. It is true that there was no direct prediction in the article, but anyone who tried to look more deeply into my opinions could realize that, not only did I not rule out a win for Karpov, but rather even predicted it. And if it comes to that, my family and my trainer Vladimir Bagirov know that I even considered Karpov to have a big advantage. Why? The quality of Spassky's play in the USSR Championship, although he came first, to me personally seemed somewhat dubious. And in the match with Byrne, although Spassky again won, his play was far from faultless. Karpov, on the other hand, was improving from one tournament to the next. In addition I thought that Spassky was unlikely to be able to assess Karpov objectively—here you cannot trust what you see on the surface, and with Karpov everything is deeply hidden. Also, my match with Karpov did Spassky a bad service: he may have come to the conclusion that in certain games Karpov was saved only by a miracle...".

The certain contradictions that the niggling reader may see in the stand taken by Poluga-yevsky are explainable. Time brings its corrections—Karpov's class does indeed develop with amazing rapidity. And highly significant is the admission made by Polugayevsky, in the same *Soviet Sport*, now after the Final Candidates' Match: "On the whole it seems to me that all three of Karpov's match opponents, beginning with myself, underestimated the young grand-master".

It is interesting that Polugayevsky, while preparing for the match with Karpov, during which time he examined some two hundred and fifty of his games, found much in common between Fischer and Karpov. In the opening they both play "straightforward chess". What meaning does Polugayevsky attach to this definition of his? Both Fischer and Karpov are prepared to engage in a fundamental theoretical argument... when they believe in the correctness of their opening policy. And they believe in this almost always—they normally adopt only continuations which are thoroughly thought out and well-polished, in systems which are worked out beforehand. At the same time Fischer and Karpov both have an excellent technique, in which it is difficult to find any faults, although they both play perhaps more quickly than any other top grandmasters.

SPASSKY'S "SILENCE"

It is well known that after his 1972 match with Fischer, Spassky gave hardly any interviews. Before the start of the next Candidates' cycle, Spassky, who had just won the USSR Championship, had this to say: "I like Karpov very much. In particular, the way he plays so solidly. His play has a great deal of content, intensity, and completeness. Solidity... Solidity of chess thinking. There are bright stars that flicker, but he gives out a constant light".

And then just before his departure for Leningrad to the match with Karpov, in replying to a question about his opponent, he said: "I first met Anatoly Karpov at the chess board at the end of 1965, when grandmaster Igor Bondarevsky and I gave a simultaneous display against the youth team of the Russian Federation. The game with Tolya proved to be quite interesting, and ended in a draw. Karpov was then only fourteen years old, although in the quickness of his reactions he was markedly superior to his older colleagues. It is interesting that, in the way he built up his game, and in his subsequent play, even then one was struck by his solidity and seriousness, so unusual for his age. Nowadays many of the experts are associating the name of Anatoly Karpov with the future of our chess. The young grandmaster undoubtedly possesses great talent, and is distinguished among other rising stars by his consistent and excellent achievements. Karpov's play is always based on a sober assessment of the position—he is not tempted into trying for showy effects. One can add that he has a well thought-out opening repertoire". Later, after giving the prominent theorist, grandmaster Furman, his due, Spassky draws attention to the strong nerves and will-to-win of his opponent.

And to the question of whether or not he admitted to the possibility of failure in this match, Spassky replied as follows: "I am thinking least of all about the competitive aspect of the match. The main thing is to realize what Karpov constitutes as a pretender to the chess throne. If I see that he understands chess more deeply than I do, and calculates variations more accurately, then I will take any possible failure calmly. I will not feel any disappointment. Especially, since we must all be prepared to give up our places to talented young players. However, I hope to maintain my position for some five or six years. If I should succeed in winning the Candidate's event, I will approach the match for the World Championship in a different mood from that of two years ago. There I used up all my nervous energy before I even sat down at the board on the stage of the Exhibition Hall in Reykjavik. This time I will try not to repeat my old mistakes".

These opinions expressed earlier by Spassky enable us to understand a great deal, including the Ex-World Champion's conviction that he would defeat Karpov, whom at the same time he rates fairly highly. And of course, after winning against Karpov in the very first game, and already thinking about his coming match with Fischer, Spassky could in no way have thought that within a month it would all be over for him. And what is more, in summing up the results of the match, Mikhail Tal was to say that Karpov defeated Spassky certainly no less convincingly than Fischer had two years earlier. And indeed, in the creative sense this was Karpov's best match, and certainly his most mature one.

But after the match Spassky stopped making any public statements at all, as if he had taken a vow of silence. This is what I managed to glean from him on the telephone: "At present there is nothing I can reply. I don't know when I will reply".

* * *

Korchnoi—practically alone among the grandmasters—had no doubts about Karpov's victory over Spassky. Back on 23rd September 1973, immediately after the pairings had been made for the Candidates' Matches, he said "in secret" that within a year he would be meeting Karpov in the Final. Korchnoi's confidence in his own powers is well known. But how did he guess that it would be Karpov?!

When the Final Match with Karpov became a reality, Korchnoi, contrary to accepted tradition, decided to also predict the outcome of his own match. To do this he chose a rather original method: he, so he said, would do everything to prevent a match between Karpov and Fischer in 1975—the World Champion might inflict too strong a shock on the still young challenger, the Soviet hope. In the future, it would be a different matter...

But what did Karpov think after the Candidates' pairings had been made, after the USSR Championship Premier League? It will be recalled that at that time Anatoly said that he was as yet insufficiently mature as a player to get through to the Final Candidates' Match on this occasion, and that he was pinning his main hopes on the following cycle. And regarding Korchnoi, Karpov said at the time: "In his best years he didn't become World Champion, and now I think that he is not capable of winning three matches".

After beating Spassky, Karpov no longer wanted to wait for 1978 before throwing down the gauntlet to the World Champion.

And so, the confrontation in the Final took place between two players who each believed frantically in his own lucky star. That is why the struggle turned out to be stern, prolonged and nervy...

21ST OLYMPIAD, NICE 1974

We are in the Sports Training Base for USSR Olympic teams on the outskirts of Moscow... Conditions are strict, and even a journalist's identity card does not always allow one to enter the "holiest of holies". One of the "hosts", Gennady Kuzmin, holds up a finger to his lips (it is the "quiet period"!), and leads an excursion round the facilities. There is a swimming pool, a sauna, and an excellent sports hall...

"The chess players make use not only of these, but also the table games, which are on the first floor, and billiards... In short, it's great here", says Kuzmin, and he determinedly picks up a badminton racket.

Failing to find a worthy partner in this sport, Kuzmin does some jumping on... the trampoline. Then he explains:

"To be honest I did not really expect to be included in the Olympiad team. Now I have to show that the trainers were not wrong. However, I am well familiar with what an international team tournament is: I have played four times for our student team, and once in the European Team Championship."

Our conversation is joined by Tal:

"Gennady is making his debut in the team whereas I am already a veteran. Petrosian and I are the most experienced members, having first played back in 1958. How time flies. And now I have returned to 'my' customary board five", the Ex-World Champion remarks with a sad smile. But immediately he cheers up: "I love team events, meetings with old friends; I like to observe the influx of the 'new wave'..."

In a comfortable room we find the trainers, Efim Geller and Semion Furman. Geller himself has played six times in Olympiads, and was captain of the team in 1968 in Lugano. This is already the third time he is going as a trainer. He looks rather worried:

"We anticipate strong competition. In the first instance—from the Hungarians, Yugoslavs and Americans, especially if Fischer should play... And we have our difficulties. Our leaders Karpov and Korchnoi will be thinking about the fact that they soon have a decisive encounter with each other—will they be able to 'reveal' themselves? Will Spassky and Petrosian be able to throw off the burden of their recent failures? How will Tal's health be, will Kuzmin lose his head? Yes, there are plenty of questions..."

Semion Furman is going as trainer to the Olympiad team for the fourth time:

"Our team is, of course, very strong, but we also have our problems. The losing Candidates will probably feel out of sorts, while the winners may not show everything of which they are capable.

I think that Karpov will not find it easy on top board after his recent tense clashes, and with a further match before him, but I am sure that he will cope. I am hoping for the possibility in Nice of a game between him and Fischer: he will gain more by playing him once, than by hearing about him a hundred times."

Towards evening Karpov arrived at the training base. He had come direct by car from Tula, where he had been visiting his relatives. He had seen them for only a few days, before which he had caught a cold, and had even been ill on his birthday. Nevertheless, Anatoly looks cheerful, and, avoiding all the sports halls, challenges me to a game of billiards. During the game he says that he agrees with the opinion of the trainers, and has not asked to be withdrawn from top board, primarily because he wants if possible to meet Fischer. He becomes very absorbed in the billiards, and only a request for him to make an appearance in front of the USSR acrobatics team (which is also quartered here) drags him away.

It grows dark. Trees in the nearby forest are hardly visible. The players have to get up early—tomorrow morning they fly to France.

And here we are at Sheremetevo Airport. The grandmasters who have come from the training camp are joined here by the Muscovite members of the team—Spassky and Petrosian. Smyslov, who as usual is optimistic, remarks that a team of Ex-World Champions is travelling to Nice, and that it is probably as the most senior of these that he has been chosen as captain. Baturinsky, director of the USSR Central Chess Club, and leader of the departing delegation, gives his last instructions to his colleagues remaining in Moscow...

...Soon from Nice we began receiving laconic reports, like war resumés. The record number of teams—seventy-three—had on this occasion been divided into eight preliminary groups. Two teams from each such group went forward into each of the final sections. In its preliminary group the Soviet team encountered no problems—four matches were won with a "clean" score, in two the team dropped half a point, and in a further two—one point. Finishing eight points ahead of its nearest rivals, the USSR team confidently took first place.

In the previous Olympiad Finals the main rivals to the Soviet players in the battle for the gold medals had invariably been the Hungarian and Yugoslav teams. Here too it seemed that the Hungarians could prove serious rivals. However, this did not happen. It soon became clear that they could not withstand prolonged strain, and that their team operated highly impulsively. Their mood depended too frequently on Portisch's position: when he was winning, all the others also played with enthusiasm, but when he was losing they became visibly depressed. In the third round the Filipino Torre managed to beat Portisch—the Hungarian team as a whole lost, and right to the end was unable to recover from this unexpected blow. The Yugoslavs, in turn, lost to the Hungarians at the very start, and after this kept all the time at a respectful distance from the leaders, and made a fight only for second place.

The Soviet players, in contrast to their main rivals, on this occasion had no set-backs. Skilfully shuffling their uniform team, in which the reserves were not inferior to the main four, the USSR team drew further and further away from its rivals. Eight successive matches were won in the Final by the Soviet grandmasters, before the first drawn match occurred (with the Hungarian team). But by this time the USSR team already had a lead of four points.

It was just at this time, on the day of the next match against the Finnish team, that I, together with a group of Soviet players and journalists, flew in to Nice...

As soon as our "Caravelle" had landed a few dozen metres from the shore of the Mediterranean, we saw the smiling faces of Vasily Smyslov and Efim Geller. The wives of the Soviet team were also on the plane, and the team had "delegated" its captain and one of its trainers to meet us at the airport. The latest news was immediately exchanged. Everything was going well with our grandmasters, and just at that time they were winning against the Finns... However, the previous day the American players had almost spoiled the general good mood slightly, by protesting about the short draws in the USSR–Hungary match. (Later that evening the leader of the Soviet delegation told how the Americans themselves had withdrawn their protest, after an elementary calculation had shown that, in the USA–Hungary match, the draws had been the result of an even less intense fight.)

The weather at the world-famous resort was excellent, and after finishing their games, the players readily joined holiday-makers on the Côte d'Azure. From here came a mass of amusing stories. Among the constant spectators at the Olympiad, for instance, were the famous tennis player from the past, Pedro Gonzales, and the well-known actor Omar Sharif, who is also considered one of the strongest bridge players in the world. Against each other they played an endless series of chess matches, from which Gonzales emerged the clear winner. "I hope that you are now convinced that tennis has a much greater intellectual potential than bridge", he said to his partner on departure...

This is all very interesting, but we want to get to the scene of play as quickly as possible. Immediately inside the doors of the Exhibition Pavilion, among the numerous kiosks with chess literature and souvenirs, are several television screens. On one of them, Anatoly Karpov and the leader of the Finnish team, International master Heikki Westerinen, are analysing their recently-concluded game, the result of which, however, no one can tell us. Unexpectedly Karpov himself appears in this distinctive foyer. He has time only to tell us that he has won the game, and that he is now being taken to "another interview", from which he shortly returns. The popularity of the young grandmaster is so great, that even a simple handshake in front of the local officials (who incidentally, are very strict) is sufficient to gain one admission into the hall.

Karpov–Westerinen
Ruy Lopez

1 P–K4 P–K4 2 N–KB3 N–QB3 3 B–N5 P–QR3 4 B–R4 P–Q3 5 0–0 B–Q2 6 P–Q4 N–B3 7 P–B3 B–K2 8 QN–Q2 0–0 9 R–K1 R–K1 10 N–B1 P–R3 11 N–N3 B–KB1 12 B–Q2 P–QN4 13 B–B2 N–QR4 14 P–N3 P–B4 15 P–Q5 N–R2 16 P–KR3 B–K2 17 N–B5 N–N2 18 P–QR4 P×P (Diag.)
   19 P–QN4 P–QR4 20 B×QRP RP×P 21 P×P B–KB1 22 B–B6 Q–B2 23 P–N5 N–B3 24 Q–B2 KR–N1 25 N–K3 B–B1

26 N–B4 B–K2 27 P–N6 Q–Q1 28 R–R7 N–Q2 29 Q–R4 R×R 30 P×R R–R1 31 Q–R6 Q–B2 32 B×N(Q7) Q×B 33 N–N6 N–Q1 34 Q–R1 Resigns

Strictly speaking, it was difficult to call the central room of the Exhibition Pavilion a hall. It was more of an enormous covered stadium, with a green carpet which gave it an appearance similar to that of an extended football pitch. There, where in a stadium one of the smaller stands would be situated, was an enormous relief map of the world. And in the centre circle of this "football pitch", under a dome from which the numerous flags were lowered, rose a colossal white rook. When the Yugoslav grandmaster Ljubomir Ljubojevic first went into this tournament hall, he enthusiastically exclaimed: "If Fischer had seen where he was going to play, I'm sure he would have agreed to take part in the Olympiad!" The unanimous opinion of the competitors was that the hall where the event was held was ideal for play. Also happy with it were the spectators, who had the opportunity of following each game from a sufficiently close distance...

On the way to the hotel, Karpov remarked that he wasn't playing at all badly in Nice:

"In the preliminary group I won all four of my games fairly easily. In the first round of the Final, when Williams of Wales resigned against me, his colleagues considered the decision to be premature. 'Karpov would never have resigned in such a position, if he had been your place', one of them declared. 'If he had been in my place', retorted Williams, 'he would never have got into such a position as White!' And then 'by habit' I defeated Vlastimil Hort from Czechoslovakia; for some reason he generally finds it difficult playing against me... And then"—suddenly remembering the incredibly amusing accent of the West German grandmaster Wolfgang Unzicker, Karpov bursts out laughing: "after our game, he began, aloud and in Russian, to curse his position with its stupid black knights, which just couldn't jump out of their cage, and I nearly fell off my chair with surprise".

Williams–Karpov
Nimzo-Indian Defence

1 P–Q4 N–KB3 2 P–QB4 P–K3 3 N–QB3
B–N5 4 B–N5 P–KR3 5 B–R4 P–B4 6 P–Q5
P–Q3 7 P–K3 B×N+ 8 P×B P–K4 9 B–Q3
P–K5 10 B–B2 P–KN4 11 B–KN3 Q–K2 12
P–KR4 R–N1 13 P×P P×P 14 N–K2
QN–Q2 15 Q–N1 K–Q1 16 P–R4 P–R4 17
R–QR2 K–B2 18 R–R6 R–R3 19 Q–N5 K–N1
20 R–N2 K–R2 21 Q–N3 N–N5 22 R–R1
P–B4 23 K–Q1 R–QN3 24 Q–R2 R×R 25
Q×R P–N3 26 B–N3 B–R3 27 N–B1 N–B1
28 Q–K2 N–N3 29 K–Q2 N–B3 30 Q–Q1
P–B5 31 Resigns

Karpov–Hort
Pirc Defence

1 P–K4 P–Q3 2 P–Q4 N–KB3 3 N–QB3
P–KN3 4 N–B3 B–N2 5 B–K2 0–0 6 0–0 P–B3
7 P–KR3 P–QN4 8 P–K5 N–K1 9 N–K4
B–B4 10 N–N3 B–K3 11 P–QR4 P–N5 12
P–B4 P×P e.p. 13 P×P B–Q4 14 R–K1 N–Q2
15 B–KB4 P×P 16 N×P N×N 17 B×N
B×B 18 P×B Q–R4 19 Q–Q4 N–N2 20

P–QB4 B–K3 21 B–B3 QR–Q1 22 Q–R4 Q–B2
23 Q–K4 P–QB4 24 KR–Q1 R×R+ 25 R×R
R–N1 26 N–K2 R–N5 27 N–B4 N–B4 28
N×B P×N 29 B–N4 N–Q5 30 P–R4 K–N2
(Diag.)

31 P–KR5 R–N1 32 Q–K3 P×P 33 B×RP
N–B4 34 Q–B4 R–Q1 35 R–N1 K–R1 36 B–B7
Q–Q2 37 P–R5 K–N2 38 B–R5 Q–Q6 39
R–Q1 Q×R+ 40 B×Q R×B+ 41 K–R2
R–Q5 42 Q–B1 P–R4 43 Q–N5+ K–B1 44
Q–N6 N–N2 45 Q–N1 R–R5+ 46 K–N1 R×P
47 Q–N8+ K–B2 48 Q×P R–B8+ 49 K–R2
P–B5 50 Q–Q4 R–B7 51 Q–R1 N–K1 52
P–R6 N–B2 53 P–R7 R–Q7 54 Q–R5 R–Q2
55 Q–R4 Resigns

Karpov–Unzicker
Ruy Lopez

1 P–K4 P–K4 2 N–KB3 N–QB3 3 B–N5
P–QR3 4 B–R4 N–B3 5 0–0 B–K2 6 R–K1
P–QN4 7 B–N3 P–Q3 8 P–B3 0–0 9 P–KR3
N–QR4 10 B–B2 P–B4 11 P–Q4 Q–B2 12
QN–Q2 N–B3 13 P–Q5 N–Q1 14 P–QR4
R–N1 15 P×P P×P 16 P–QN4 N–N2 17
N–B1 B–Q2 18 B–K3 R–R1 19 Q–Q2 KR–B1
20 B–Q3 P–N3 21 N–N3 B–B1 22 R–R2 P–B5
23 B–N1 Q–Q1

24 B–R7 N–K1 25 B–B2 N–B2 26 R(1)–R1
Q–K2 27 B–N1 B–K1 28 N–K2 N–Q1 29
N–R2 B–N2 30 P–B4 P–B3 31 P–B5 P–N4
32 B–QB2 B–B2 33 N–N3 N–N2 34 B–Q1
P–R3 35 B–R5 Q–K1 36 Q–Q1 N–Q1 37
R–R3 K–B1 38 R(1)–R2 K–N1 39 N–N4 K–B1
40 N–K3 K–N1 41 B×B+ N×B 42 Q–R5
N–Q1 43 Q–N6 K–R1 44 N–R5 Resigns

...And so, no one even dreamed of contending with the Soviet team for the Olympiad gold medals and the prize offered by the President of France, Giscard d'Estaing. But for the silver and bronze medals a bitter fight took place. The Yugoslavs succeeded in demonstrating that they are rightly considered the second greatest chess power in the world. The Americans caught up with the Bulgarians, and on the number of victories won the battle for the bronze medals. For the USA team, who were appearing without Fischer, third place was an undoubted success.

...In 1974 the International Chess Federation (FIDE) celebrated its 50th anniversary. Thus it was a Jubilee FIDE Congress which was held in Nice at the same time as the Olympiad. And it so happened that, as regards the number of problems decided, it was one of the most important.

We must now dwell in some detail on the events which took place at the time of the Congress, and immediately after it, and on how the main question was decided—that of the coming match for the World Championship between Robert Fischer and the Soviet grandmaster who would win the Final Candidates' Match. It is necessary to do this, so that the reader will be able to understand better that which was to happen in 1975, when Fischer refused to defend his title, and the World Championship was awarded to Anatoly Karpov.

It is perhaps best to begin at the end, with how, on a quite wonderful night in a town park in Nice, the end of the Olympiad and the FIDE Congress were celebrated.

...Some one thousand top chess players, hundreds of delegates to the Congress, and numerous guests line the tables, where old and new acquaintances meet. There is a resonant thumping of the dancers' feet, and on the stages orchestras compete one with another. We hear the melodies of national French dances, and the rhythms of ultra-modern music. People are wearing posh suits, or provocative shorts and T-shirts with the autographs of famous grandmasters. There is conversation in a variety of languages.

The seventy-three-year-old FIDE President Dr Max Euwe is dancing jauntily with girls from the Paris television centre. Today he is just as confident as when I saw him recently in Holland, and then in Leningrad, and not at all the same man who met me in the Nice Exhibition Pavilion, when he was no longer confident of being re-elected. I remember that Euwe was alone, without his customary retinue, and that, smiling weakly at me, he had picturesquely drawn his palm across his throat. At that time it was expected that the Presidency would be taken over by a 37-year-old Puerto Rican, Rabell-Mendez, by no means a chess player (the elderly American chess patron I. Turover, in a conversation with me, angrily and wittily called this Candidate for the Presidency "mañana-banana"). But the FIDE Congress left Dr Euwe at the wheel of the International Chess Federation.

Wrapped up in their affairs, excited grandmasters walk hither and thither. The inseparable Ulf Andersson and Jan Timman do not think that World Champion Fischer will defend his title. The hope of Yugoslav chess L. Ljubojevic thinks that Fischer is afraid to sit down at the board, and that the Champion is evidently pursued by psychological uncertainty, by "starting nerves", as one might say. The American William Lombardy says: "If Fischer invites me again, as in Reykjavik, to be his second, I will of course accept. But possibly he won't play". Later, on the road to Paris, the veteran Argentinian grandmaster Najdorf wondered why, if Fischer was relinquishing his title, the Final Candidates' Match was being held this year, and not as laid down in the regulations regarding World Championship Matches.

On the background of general gaiety, one can make out a definite air of despair. Can it be that Fischer really won't play?!

11

Only Ex-World Champion Petrosian, who has seen it all, is calm. He says with a smile:

"These men do everthing that Bobby wishes, and he will sit down at the chess board on the conditions that he dictates to them".

Well, and here is Ed Edmondson, head of the USA Chess Federation. Tall and young-looking, he stands inside a wide circle of admirers, a glass of white wine in his hand. A former lieutenant-colonel in the United States Air Force, strong, clever and cunning, to the surprise of everyone he suddenly chose the career of a chess official. How vulnerable must be the position of World Champion Fischer, if, even with such a defender, he has lost the "lawsuit" at the FIDE Congress!

"What does the USA Chess Federation intend to do, so as no tto lose the title of World Champion without a fight?"

"Pray!", replies Edmondson, but the expression on his face is not at all pious. "Pray for Fischer, even though he let our team down, by not coming to the Olympiad. However, we are satisfied with third place, which could have been second, if your players had tried harder against our rivals. But then you will never write that down..."

Edmondson is friendly and courteous, but he won't give an interview.

Fred Cramer suddenly appears: a small man in glasses, with his tie awry. The American lawyer, a man who is close to the World Champion, is obviously merry.

"Just ask me, and I can give an answer to all your questions", he says, and immediately begins speaking very quickly: "This is a stupid Congress. They have killed the World Championship Match. I know grandmasters who have cried on account of the fact that they won't see Fischer at the board..."

"Is it your opinion that the match won't take place?"

"Fifty-fifty".

"You mean there is still a fifty per cent chance that Fischer will change his mind?"

"No. There is a half chance that the FIDE will reconsider its decision".

"But why doesn't the World Champion play at all? Perhaps he is ill?"

"Rubbish! Simply he is not given acceptable conditions. But physically, and chess-wise, he is in excellent condition. He plays tennis, and works a great deal at chess. He lives a full life. He has seven rooms, he receives guests... No, no, no..." Cramer suddenly stops himself, "Bobby would never forgive me if he found out that I had been talking about his personal life".

"The World Champion..."

"...Fischer is World Champion according to FIDE rules, but this he no longer considers himself."

This is the time to finally acquaint the reader with the content of the telegram which Robert James Fischer sent to the FIDE Congress, when he learned that his demands had not been supported by the delegates to the world chess forum.

"...I have been informed that my proposals have been rejected by a majority of votes. By doing so the FIDE has decided against my participation in the 1975 World Championship. I therefore resign my FIDE World Championship title".

Not simply World Champion, but "FIDE World Champion"! This nuance in Fischer's telegram was grasped by all who acquainted themselves with its word for word content. In short, the great grandmaster was unequivocably threatening to walk out of the International Chess Federation.

...The recommendation of the FIDE Central Committee, which met before the General Assembly, was precise, and again confirmed a decision taken earlier: "In the World Championship Match the winner will be the first to win six games, with an overall limit of thirty games; if on the expiry of the thirty games neither of the players has gained six wins, the winner will be the one who is leading at that point; in the event of an equal score after thirty games the World Champion keeps his title".

Shortly before the General Assembly began its work, Fischer sent his first "epistle to the congress". The telegram, which was not read out officially, contained, it is said, eighty-three words, and gave the Champion's position on a number of questions, mainly the regulations for the World Championship Match. The American delegates to the Congress scrupulously carried out their grandmaster's demands, and spoke out on literally every point. For example, Cramer insisted that the controller of the match, "who sees too much", should not have the right to appear in print as a journalist not only during the event, but even after it(!). The arbitrator was "saved" by a comment by one of the FIDE bureau members: "Mr Cramer will not stay quiet even for three minutes, and he wants the match controller to stay silent for his whole life".

But all this is mere detail. What were the main points that Fischer was striving for?

He wanted the match to continue until one of the players won ten games (and not six, as was decided earlier), with the total number of games played unlimited; with the score standing at nine wins each the World Champion would keep his title.

One doesn't need any special training in mathematics to realize that what Fischer wanted was an initial advantage of two points*. The point was that, under such "cunning" conditions, it would be impossible to win 10–9 against the Champion, but as a minimum only by 10–8. For a long time in chess there had been a parliament—the FIDE Congress, but here the chess king was trying to place himself above this parliament, or at any rate to gain the right to a "veto", which he would be able to use endlessly.

The Congress sittings took place in a more than democratic atmosphere, with each of the speakers speaking for a long time, and going out onto the platform several times. Each appearance on the platform by Edmondson was made somehow imperceptibly, and he moved about the stage as if he was in his own house:

"The next point on the agenda—whether to play the World Championship Match to six or to ten wins—will probably create a lot of discussion. I suggest we need a break, to have something to eat",—and the American headed for the exit.

Have you seen the trainer of a basketball or volleyball team, when he takes a postponement during a difficult match? The players gather round in a circle, and catch and remember each of the trainer's words—it is as if he wishes to embrace all his players, raise their spirits, calm the ardour of the over-excited... Edmondson, like a skilful trainer, went from one group of delegates to another. And then, when the break was over, he went along between the rows and, silently moving his lips, counted "his" votes.

So, six or ten? The voting takes place by country. The major chess powers, mainly European, say: six. The countries from the American Continent, and the representatives of Asia, where

---

* According to my mathematics, Fischer was asking for an initial advantage of *one* point. When World Championship matches were played over 24 games, the Champion enjoyed, in effect, a starting advantage of half a point, and thus Botvinnik was able to retain his title after drawing matches with Bronstein in 1951 and Smyslov in 1954. (K.P.N.)

11*

there are as yet few well-known players, and where it is not generally understood that the match may turn into an endurance test, they say: ten. The Chilean delegate gives an amusing reply: "Yes". "Yes what?" they ask him. "Ten, of course!". Cramer, contented, awards him top marks in the table which he keeps constantly in his hand.

Twenty-four delegates voted for play to go on up to six wins, while for ten wins there were twenty-six votes, with twelve abstentions. The proposal to play "without limit" came a cropper. A compromise was adopted—to play a match up to ten wins with a limit of thirty-six games. Otherwise the recommendations of the FIDE Central Committee given above remained in force.

...It was then that Fischer's second telegram arrived, the important part of which has already been cited. After this telegram was read out at one of the last sessions of the Congress, passions flared up with new strength. The Mexican delegate, as the representative of one of the countries which had offered to stage the match, tried to persuade the General Assembly to cede to Fischer's demands. "It will be very bad if the match for the World Championship is held outside the framework of the FIDE. Let us not forget that that chess and the FIDE are greatly indebted to Fischer for the growth in its popularity, and let us not limit the total number of games", this orator requested.

"But are you really sure that this will be the last concession to Fischer?", came a question from the hall, which remained unanswered.

The ultimatum by Fischer, who did not even bother to attend personally in Nice, stung many of the delegates to the quick. This is what a temperamental chap from the Dominican Republic had to say, unexpectedly affecting the mood of the representatives of Central and South American countries:

"I know that what I am about to say will reduce the number of my friends... I am a personal friend of Bobby, and I admire his intellect, and his constant determination to defend his principles. But today we, like Shakespeare's hero, are faced with a question: 'To be or not to be?'. My friend has indeed done much for chess, but now we have to decide: 'Either the FIDE, or Fischer?' ".

The debate was threatening to go on for ever. But Euwe, who was presiding over the meeting, was probably convinced by the words of the Tunisian delegate:

"If we decide to reconsider decisions which have just been taken, then today we should also elect a new FIDE President".

Even so, it was little Cramer who managed to be the last on to the platform. First he went into the hall, and from under one of the chairs took out a plastic stool, which had been secreted there beforehand. Climbing up on it, he now towered over the platform, and from there spent a long time asking that the point regarding the restriction of the total number of games be removed. On climbing down, in front of everyone Cramer tried to persuade certain delegates. Several nodded their heads in agreement, but later, when the vote came to be taken, for some reason they weren't in the hall. The result of this referendum (the last, as it then seemed) was: for the reconsideration of the previous decision—seventeen, against—thirty-five, abstentions—twelve. On the first vote, hardly anyone was for abolishing the limit. Now—seventeen...

Edmondson himself had the last word:

"Firstly, I think that we are all pretty tired, and it is time to put an end to all this. And now regarding the decision just taken. The USA's interests have not been supported, and we have suffered a defeat. I regret that the majority of votes went against us. But I wish to say to the lads from the Dominican Republic and other countries, who changed their earlier opinions: because of this they have not become our enemies".

The FIDE Congress sent Fischer a message, in which he was asked to reconsider his decision, and to fall in with the wishes of the millions in the chess world...

* * *

Noise normally has a bad effect on Karpov. Nevertheless in Nice, on the very edge of the Mediterranean Sea, in the hall where the winners of the Chess Olympiad were celebrating, where music rumbled and the voices of the entertainers from the Paris Television Centre never stopped, Karpov at first appeared completely uninhibited and genuinely merry. But as our hospitable hosts, with typical French spontaneity, made their publicity stunts more and more complicated, so the smile began to fade from Karpov's face. And when he and Spassky sat down at an unusual type of chess set, and some French beauty (Miss France 1972, it was said) attempted to place her silver slipper in the centre of the board, twenty-three-year-old Anatoly Karpov promptly hid himself completely behind his customary barrier of strict restraint. At the end of the evening he appeared to be asking himself—"what do I want with all this?".

Then he unexpectedly proposed: "Shall we go for a walk?". And, leaving a surprised group, quickly—he always hurries—he set off along the shore. It was some time before we found a vacant bench. Karpov sat in pensive silence, and then shrugged his shoulders: "It's so nice here, and you have to smoke!" After moving to the downwind side of him, I remarked that I had seen him dancing for the first time that evening.

"I still don't understand serious music", Karpov admitted. "But light music distracts me, and enables me to relax. The books that I choose now are also of a lighter nature; one can't always manage to get to the cinema or the theatre..."

"And what about stamps?"

"Oh, they more than anything divert me from chess, I leave time for them without fail". "How's university going?"

"What is this, an interview?", Karpov looks askance at me, but then gives a conciliatory laugh: "I've been having to take more time off. However, recently I passed in English Language. I probably shouldn't have studied it after the match with Spassky, and before the Olympiad and the Final Candidates' Match, but then English can come in useful at any time".

"Yes, at the Congress the comments about you were made mainly in English..."

Karpov's expression turns hard, his lips are proudly compressed, as in those photographs where he has refused to pose.

At the FIDE Congress Karpov spoke out determinedly against changing the rules for the holding of the World Championship. One of the delegates kept interrupting him, but the chairman did not support him, but, on the contrary, remarked that he was repeating what had been said before. Karpov blushed angrily, was silent for almost a whole minute, and then quite calmly added: "I consider these retorts as showing disrespect". And he went down into the hall, where he was applauded by some of those who had just then stopped him from finishing what he had to say.

"If I'd been in your place!..."

Karpov gives me such a look, that I immediately feel uncomfortable on account of my "lack of diplomacy".

It is already completely light—five o'clock in the morning. Time to sleep—a sportsman must stick to some sort of routine.

"Oh, never mind", Karpov waves his hand, "we're not playing tomorrow. And in general from childhood I've been used to going to bed late".

From the shore of the now choppy Mediterranean Sea the road turns towards our hotel with its romantic name of "Meridian." Glancing at the dancing neon lights, the grandmaster suddenly says quietly:

"My life is unsettled with all this travelling and preparation... Oh for some Ural ravioli—my mother makes delicious ones!"

It so happened that my next, real interview with Anatoly came only some several months later, before the start of the Final Candidates' Match...

CHAPTER 4

The Big Match

ASSESSMENTS AND FORECASTS

Alexander Alekhine said in his time that he knew many who were capable of playing for a win, but very few who were able to play for a draw. Later this ratio changed sharply—unfortunately, in favour of those who worshipped "his majesty the draw". But the logic of sport has normally allowed only those who play definitely for a win to reach the highest steps of the chess hierarchy. This has always been the case.

...Karpov, sober-minded and outwardly calm, spurns grandmaster draws:

"For me, chess is first and foremost a struggle. Therefore I consider competitive considerations to be of primary importance".

As we see, his aim is definitely to win. But what are the means of achieving this aim?

Viktor Malkin, a Doctor of Medical Sciences, who has frequently observed top chess players, states that they can be separated into people whose way of thinking is either intuitive or logical (analytical).

Karpov is much closer to the intuitive player. According to the scientist's definition: "intuitive thinking develops on the basis of subconscious generalization of accumulated experience". Subconscious! This is why brilliant intuition is demonstrated at times by child prodigies, who swiftly gain experience; many regarded Karpov as one. But nevertheless, one cannot call him a completely intuitive player—he quickly and accurately calculates, feels confident in complications, and, incidentally, quite consciously generalizes on his accumulated experience.

During the Olympiad in Nice, Jan Timman (Netherlands) mentioned that, as before, Korchnoi still gets into time trouble. Karpov, on the other hand, plays easily, with a big reserve on his clock, and never experiences time shortage. In the opinion of the Dutch grandmaster, this gives Anatoly Karpov the advantage. The Swede Ulf Andersson, as well as the Hungarian Lajos Portisch, considered the two players' chances to be roughly equal, while the Czech grandmaster Vlastimil Hort drew attention to Karpov's consistently good form (which, incidentally, was also confirmed at the Olympiad). But at the same time, Hort thought that in Nice Korchnoi husbanded his strength somewhat, on seeing that the Soviet team would be first, even without his "extra points". Hort declared that the Final Match would be a "war of nerves." The highly experienced Argentinian grandmaster Miguel Najdorf expressed his preference for Karpov... Many Soviet grandmasters, while readily assessing the strong points of both Candidates, were nevertheless cautious about expressing any definite conclusions. Lyev Polugayevsky noted that on Karpov's side were his age, consistency of results, and constant, steady progress ("He played considerably more strongly against Spassky than he did against me..."). Yevgeny Vasyukov saw an uncontestable advantage for Karpov in his constantly good form.

Eduard Gufeld: "Before each of Karpov's matches I have given preference to his highly-experienced opponents, and... have been wrong. Perhaps I will be wrong again". Mark Taimanov, while respecting the stability of Karpov's play and his growing strength, did not in general want to speak about a possible winner, and limited himself to this assertion: "In my opinion, sooner or later Karpov will be World Champion". Incidentally, this pronouncement was to a certain extent similar to the opinion expressed by the famous Dane, Bent Larsen—his sympathies were with Korchnoi, but the voice of reason told him: "Karpov".

David Bronstein thought that everything was already long-since determined by the comparative degree of preparation of the two players, about which nothing had been said. "Yes, the future is known best of all by the players in the match themselves, and after all Karpov has said that this will not be his cycle", remarked Ex-World Champion Vasily Smyslov with a smile. Mikhail Botvinnik, formerly so categorical in his assessments, declined to give a reply...

In no event had Anatoly Karpov suffered more than two defeats, and the Final Match was to be won by the first player to score five wins (true, the number of games was limited to 24). Karpov's success curve, which included only first places, or ones very close to first, had been steadily rising, whereas Korchnoi's was more of a sinusoid, signifying incredible variations in form. All the data from the "ratings tables" was fed into a computer at one of the Moscow Institutes. The computer, which is only able to calculate, "gave victory" to Karpov by a score of 5–2...

But besides arithmetic results, one must also take into account character, general physical condition, and many other things... Once Korchnoi won an international tournament with a record result, conceding only one draw. As usual, journalists asked him for an interview. In such instances the winner normally talks about the good weather, and about his excellent frame of mind. But Korchnoi angrily remarked that he had not played at all well, that he should have won the (one) game which ended in a draw, and to demonstrate his point began showering the journalists with variations, by which they were simply shocked. Prior to the Final Match, passers-by on the street asked him for his autograph, and when he had signed the bus route-map offered him, some boys timidly asked him who would win: he or Karpov. Korchnoi replied sharply and firmly: "I will!". This was the self-assertion of a person who was consciously strengthening his will and belief in himself. Not without reason did Mikhail Tal remark that he had never seen the temperamental Korchnoi so sober-minded as in that World Championship Cycle.

The aim of Karpov's life in chess is the World Champion's crown, and he has never attempted to hide this. Karpov's self-belief was no less than that of his opponent, but, as the reader has probably already noticed, the young grandmaster is much more reserved in character than his opponent. In the metro, three lads, on recognizing Karpov, requested his autograph, and asked him how he would fare in the final. "We'll see how it goes..." Karpov replied evasively. "We believe that you'll also beat Fischer!", one of the trio shouted after the grandmaster. Karpov smiled, but straight away became serious: "Oh, I don't like being the favourite. Everyone gives advice, offers their help..."

Most chess writers set themselves the rhetorical question: youth or experience? In the Roman army at the time of Julius Caesar, the soldiers chosen were between twenty-five and forty, which was considered the optimum age for heavy martial duties. Anatoly Karpov's determination, good sense, and amazing talent, had made him older than his years.

Both players were busy "arming themselves", and in this a far from minor role was played by general physical preparation. A great deal had been written earlier about how frail Karpov looks. But now in a leisure centre on the outskirts of Moscow, where Karpov was preparing for the match, he was stronger and healthier; he would enthusiastically swim in the lake and row quite professionally, while in his room, alongside a badminton racket, was a book by the great gymnast Shakhlin, with advice on how to get fit.

And at the same time, near Leningrad, Korchnoi, who had given up smoking for good, did his daily exercises and went cross-country running—this was not at all the same Korchnoi who had once lost consciousness while doing physical training.

HALF A MINUTE PER MOVE—
A VERBAL LIGHTNING CONTEST BEFORE THE START
OF THE FINAL MATCH

The conditions of this unusual event were as follows: both grandmasters were quickly given the most varied and fairly unexpected questions. At the same time the contestants in the "game" were warned that they were allowed not more than thirty seconds for a brief reply. If either of them should linger for more than half a minute, he would have overstepped the time limit, and, according to the rules of chess, would be given a loss in this particular question.

Karpov's out-of-town "residence" was situated some thirty kilometres from Moscow... The road ran through a little village, and then turned towards the forest. On the edge of an artificial lake stood a stone cottage. In this little house Karpov was to spend nearly three months...

On learning the latest city "news", Karpov hurried off to the sauna, while Furman, Geller, Bakh and their guest decided all the same to have something to eat. While Karpov was out, we even "risked" drinking the odd glass of cognac. Then Anatoly returned. The food was tasty and plentiful, and about chess—not a word, as was now customary. From a stereo record-player came the constant sound of music.

It was quiet and comfortable. We were all watching television together, while Karpov first played some harmless card game with his colleagues, and then took Geller on at a complicated variety of dominoes. Time passed and outside it had long-since grown dark, when Anatoly went out to speak to his parents, who had phoned from Tula. Geller laughed: "Anatoly never stops playing until he wins. But I also don't intend to lose..."

Karpov finally won some time after two o'clock in the morning... Unexpectedly he suggested doing a bit of work, and began answering questions. This was the night before the draw was made...

A few hours before the opening ceremony and the drawing of lots, I phoned Korchnoi's second, international master Vyacheslav Osnos at the "Sovyetskaya" hotel, and asked if he could put me through to Korchnoi. I have known Osnos for a long time, but on this occasion he replied firmly that Korchnoi was unlikely to want to chat to me before the start of the match, and that in any case he wasn't in Moscow—he was at present in a sanatorium outside the city... However, some ten minutes later the telephone rang at my home, and Korchnoi, instantly grasping the idea, requested me merely to ask him the questions, only as quickly as possible. He replied quickly, curtly, in a sharp, even slightly fierce voice. After taking a break for a meal, he soon rang again: "Well, where did we stop?" When it was all over, he asked whether Karpov had already been asked the questions, and then hastily added: "No, no, I on no account want to know what he said!"

On acquainting himself with the text of the conversation given below, Yury Zavadsky, chief director of the Mossovyet Theatre, declared that before him was a complete portrait of Karpov—an ultra-modern young man, endowed with rare self-possession and strength of purpose. Karpov, in his opinion, believes implicitly in his principles of life, as witnessed by the confident replies to the most intimate of questions.

It would be interesting to know whether the reader can also see that which the eminent director was able to discern in Anatoly Karpov's replies...

"Why do you like chess?"

Viktor Korchnoi: "It is my life".

Anatoly Karpov: "Well, what a question! For me it is—everything".

"At what age did you begin playing?"

Korchnoi: "Thirteen".

Karpov: "Somewhere between four and five. But it is only recently that chess has become everything for me. Even in 1969, when I was World Junior Champion, I didn't think that it would all turn out this way".

"Who is your ideal in chess?"

Korchnoi: "Emmanuel Lasker".

Karpov: "An ideal can only be a collective figure. The one who approaches most closely to it is probably Capablanca".

"What is more important during play—improvisation or analysis?"

Korchnoi: "What is important is a synthesis. The strength of a player depends on how harmoniously he combines these qualities".

Karpov: "It depends on the character of the position".

"Is it better to attack or to counter-attack?"

Korchnoi: "It is easier for the attacker, since his actions are, so to speak, primary, whereas a counter-attack is to a great extent the consequence of the opponent's actions".

Karpov: "At heart I am more of a counter-attacker, but if an attack turns up I do not avoid it".

"With which piece do you associate a secret weakness (not counting, of course, the king itself)?"

Korchnoi: "I don't think there is such a piece".

Karpov: "The one which looks best on the board".

"Does the spectre of time trouble bother you?"

Korchnoi: "Naturally, because it happens with me and leads to mistakes".

Karpov: "No, it doesn't".

"Do you believe in the problem of the difficult opponent?"

Korchnoi: "Yes, such a problem exists".

Karpov: "Not as yet".

"The happiest event in your life?"

Korchnoi: "My first victory in the USSR Championship—in 1960".

Karpov: "I hope that it still awaits me".

"Your biggest disappointment?"

Korchnoi: "My failure in the Final Candidates' Match with Spassky in 1968".

Karpov: "I don't remember... Such a question—and only thirty seconds to think about it... No, I don't remember. Let this, my first 'loss on time', be my last disappointment".

"What do you do after a loss?"

Korchnoi: "I go out alone for a long walk".

Karpov: "The same as after a win".

"And after a difficult win?"

Korchnoi: "It doesn't affect my normal behaviour".

Karpov: "I stay with the game for a little longer, and analyse it, but soon try without fail to get away from it completely".

"Your most difficult game in general?"

Korchnoi: "Possibly the first game of my recent Quarter-Final match with Mecking".

Karpov: "My game with the Filipino Torre in the elimination tournament for the Word Junior Championship in 1969. It decided whether or not I would be in the Final. At first the game went well for me, then not so well, then again well, then—badly, hopelessly so... During the second adjournment session I managed to gain the necessary draw".

"Imagine the situation: a decisive game is fixed for Monday the thirteenth, and a black cat crosses your path..."*

Korchnoi: "Monday the thirteenth suits me—it may prove unlucky for my opponent. And the cat I'll avoid".

Karpov: "The thirteenth is a lucky date for me—I have tested this on several occasions. I will avoid the cat, not because I am superstitious, but so as not to have to think about what will happen if I don't avoid it...".

"Do you believe in the element of chance in chess?"

Korchnoi: "Of course, otherwise I wouldn't have avoided the black cat".

Karpov: "Yes. And in play, especially at a high level, it can influence one's chess fate. However, one can and should fight against chance and fate".

"Do you dance?"

Korchnoi: "Yes, I like dancing".

Karpov: "I can, but badly. And I don't enjoy it".

"Do you smoke?"

Korchnoi: "I gave it up in February last year, the first time I have done so for a lengthy period".

Karpov: "No. Even in my youth I didn't try it, and I would advise others not to".

"Do you drink?"

Korchnoi: "Not any more!"

Karpov: "A little—on special holidays and on my birthday".

"Your favourite dish?"

Korchnoi: "Cottage cheese".

Karpov: "Ural ravioli, my mother makes delicious ones".

"Favourite season?"

Korchnoi: "Spring".

Karpov: "Winter and Summer. In the Urals, where I was born and grew up, the other seasons are short, hence the reason".

"Day of the week?"

Korchnoi: "Saturday: everyone relaxes, everyone is happy".

---

* The Russians consider it a sign of *bad* luck if a cat, particularly a black one, crosses their path. (K.P.N.)

Karpov: "Saturday: it comes before Sunday".

"And month?".

Korchnoi: "April—springtime".

Karpov: "May—there are numerous holidays, and also I was born in May".

"Which places do you like most of all?"

Korchnoi: "The Nyeva embankments".

Karpov: "Oh, there are many. Lake Turgoyak in the Chelyabinsk Region, where I used to go with my parents on free days; the countryside in the Urals is just as beautiful as on the outskirts of Moscow. And in towns—the Point on the St. Basil Island and Kirov Prospect in Leningrad, the Moscow Kremlin, unusual and incomparable Paris..."

"Which countries have you been to?"

Korchnoi: "Almost all".

Karpov: "I can say absolutely precisely—to fifteen".

"And where would you like to go?"

Korchnoi: "I said 'almost'... I've dreamed about going to Asia: Japan, Vietnam, the Philippines".

Karpov: "Anywhere where chess fate may take me, and where I have not yet been".

"Your happiest memory from your trips abroad?"

Korchnoi: "The New Year in Hastings between 1955 and 1956".

Karpov: "In 1971 in Puerto Rico the whole of our student team contrived to squeeze into a little Volkswagen, and we went to the beach. Imperceptibly, we all got sunburnt, so badly that we couldn't move. And the final was about to start. There were nine teams in the tournament—an odd number, which meant that in each round one of the teams would be free. I went to draw lots, and picked number one. Hurray! We're free tomorrow!"

"The academic subject, which was or has remained for you the most interesting?"

Korchnoi: "At school—history; later, at university—history of the ancient world".

Karpov: "At school—mathematics and geography; now—political-economics".

"What did you dream of becoming as a child?"

Korchnoi: "Probably a sailor—I'm from Leningrad".

Karpov: "According to my parents, a pilot, I promised to take everyone for a trip in an aeroplane".

"What would you have become, if you hadn't been a chess player?"

Korchnoi: "I was educated as a historian. And, most probably, my life would not be so interesting as it is now".

"Karpov: "I would have become... a chess player".

"What would you like to see your children become?".

Korchnoi: "Physicists".

Karpov: "Is it really worth thinking about it?".

"Name what is in your opinion the most highly-esteemed profession".

Korchnoi: "Scientist. He advances mankind".

Karpov: "Doctor".

"Your interests, hobbies?"

Korchnoi: "I love listening to verse. I like light music, and collect records and tapes".

Karpov: "I have many: philately, books, sports events, cinema, theatre—in short, everything that helps me to play chess well".

"Your favourite writer?"

Korchnoi: "O'Henry".

Karpov: "Lermontov".

"Film?"

Korchnoi: "Nights of Cabiria".

Karpov: "The epic 'The Liberation'".

"Singer?"

Korchnoi: "Beniamino Gigli".

Karpov: "More than anyone, Muslim Magomayev".

"And book?"

Korchnoi: "Victor Hugo's 'The man who laughs'".

Karpov: "Lermontov's romantic poems, and 'The twelve chairs' and 'The golden calf 'by Ilf and Petrov".

"Your favourite sport?"

Korchnoi: "Running".

Karpov: "As a spectator I like games. I myself enjoy gymnastics and running".

"Football?"

Korchnoi: "I only like high-standard football, but on the whole I am rather indifferent to it".

Karpov: "I don't have a favourite team; I support those that play well".

"An athlete who you like?"

Korchnoi: "The figure skater Aleksandr Zaitsev".

Karpov: "Brumel and Botvinnik—people who have time and again defeated not only their opponents, but also themselves".

"Does popularity bother you?"

Korchnoi: "Yes. The pestering of certain chess 'fans' simply gets on one's nerves".

Karpov: "In many cases, yes. One isn't allowed to relax".

"How many hours a day do you devote to chess?"

Korchnoi: "It depends on my mood, which in turn depends on what tournament lies in prospect. But on average—some three hours a day".

Karpov: "It depends how much time remains before an event. In general one can work fruitfully for up to a maximum of five hours a day; after that one is less efficient".

"Will you ever become a trainer?"

Korchnoi: "Yes, but not as zealous a one as some grandmasters are".

Karpov: "I am not sure. It is a difficult occupation. I do not make a very good teacher. Many things came easily to me, and I am probably unable to 'make sense' of a person who does not understand that which comes naturally to me".

"Does the reaction of the audience affect you during play?"

Korchnoi: "As a rule, no. But it can happen..."

Karpov: "And the behaviour of your opponent?"

Korchnoi: "Again, sometimes. At times certain opponents get on my nerves".

Karpov: "No, not particularly. Although if he behaves improperly, it can be unpleasant".

"What is your attitude to your opponent in the Candidates' Final Match?"

Korchnoi: "Karpov is a young and exceptionally talented player. But who knows, he may be spoiled by excessive fame".

Karpov: "Viktor Lvovich is older than me, and therefore my attitude to him depends upon his attitude to me".

"Do you have many friends?"

Korchnoi: "Despite my difficult character, 'for some reason' I have many friends".

Karpov: "It is not so easy to find friends, especially for a chess player. My friends are few, but I hope that they are all true, a thought which I try to reciprocate".

"What characteristics do you admire in people?"

Korchnoi: "In men—adherence to principles, in women—gentleness".

Karpov: "Sense of purpose and intelligent bravery, and in women—beauty combined with modesty".

"And the opposite: the characteristics which you find most unpleasant?"

Korchnoi: "Unscrupulousness, and lack of resolution".

Karpov: "Falsity and cowardice".

"Your favourite hero?"

Korchnoi: "Martin Eden".

Karpov: "The hero of our time".

TWENTY-FOUR ENCOUNTERS

The match was held in the best halls in Moscow; the venue was frequently moved, for which reason it was nicknamed "The match on wheels". The first part took place in the beautiful, white-marbled Hall of Columns of Trade Union House, which is situated right in the centre of the Soviet Capital. Interest in the meeting of the two popular grandmasters was so great, that at times the immediate vicinity of Trade Union House had to be closed to traffic. Even at the opening ceremony in the enormous Hall of Columns there were no empty seats. After some words of welcome, the chief controller, grandmaster Alberic O'Kelly from Belgium, announced in painstaking Russian the most important regulations, and then arranged the draw. Karpov, on picking out of an envelope the name of his opponent, thus gave Korchnoi the right to choose the colour. The latter, faced with a choice of one of two boxes offered him, began staring with exaggerated interest into the eyes of the controller, and . . . guessed correctly: in O'Kelly's left hand was the box with the white pawn. This meant that in the first and all the odd games, Korchnoi would have White.

. . . The press centre was linked to the stage by four television screens. Arranged in groups around the chess boards, grandmasters and journalists analysed the position, periodically glancing at the screens. At the start of the match (before his departure to the international tournament in Manila) perhaps the most popular figure in the press centre was Petrosian. The journalists would constantly turn to the Ex-World Champion: "Tigran Vartanovich, what should be played here?". "When I knew that, I was down on the stage, instead of up here", was Petrosian's joking reply.

After an extremely tense draw in the first game, Karpov gained a brilliant combinational win in the second encounter.

For all the arbitrary nature of many of the names in chess literature, they sometimes prove to be amazingly apt and witty. Thus the branch of the Sicilian Defence which was played in the second game of the match was long, long ago christened the Dragon Variation. And if you look at the peculiar form of the black pawn chain which arises immediately after the opening, you can make out directly the curved body of a hidden monster . . .

After the castling on opposite sides, everything or nearly everything is decided by the rapidity of the attacks on opposite wings. The Whites who did not number among its victims had already buried this variation several times, outstripping the opponent with the attack on the king. However, the "Dragon" again and again would come to life, painfully striking players who were excessively careless with its pawn tail in the centre and on the Q-side. And here grandmaster Vasyukov, an expert on this variation, on seeing Karpov going in for a forcing variation with pawn sacrifices, remarked: "Black will either beat off the attack and gradually win, or else he will lose quickly".

Karpov conducted the attack brilliantly, and this variety of the Dragon (the variation also occurs in other "subspecies") was, in the opinion of many, suppressed, seriously and for a long time.

...As soon as the journalists had sent in their reports, on the press centre television screens, which no larger displayed the empty stage, one caught glimpses of ice-hockey players. However, the voice of the commentator from distant Canada was constantly drowned by the chatter of the typewriter of New York Times correspondent, American grandmaster Robert Byrne, who was preparing his regular report.

After the brilliance of this second clash, the third game seemed somewhat insipid, but in it too one can clearly distinguish latent drama. And in general, many drawn, and at first sight undistinguished games from matches at high level are in fact full to the brim of hidden psychological meanings. And it is not even just a matter of the opponent's moves, but also his behaviour, and his reaction to what is happening around him. For example, Karpov was late for one of the adjournment sessions, for a perfectly valid reason: the car which was bringing him from the outskirts of Moscow began "spluttering" while still only at the city boundary. While the passengers watched the driver fix the fault, on the stage of Trade Union House Karpov's opponent painstakingly and demonstratively read his way through the magazine 'Youth'...

There was a new culminating point in the sixth game, when Korchnoi as Black adopted an insufficiently well-prepared variation of Petroff's Defence. While still in the opening he thought first for some forty minutes, and soon for a further fifty! The outcome of the game was decided, for to get into time trouble against Karpov is a hopeless matter. The spectators simply could not understand why Korchnoi was thinking over such obvious continuations. Incidentally, bewilderment regarding this was expressed by the famous ballet-master Igor Moiseyev, who was present at the sixth game. A passionate lover of chess, and himself a very strong player, he had put up his own personal prize for the winner of the match—a chess set of rare workmanship.

"Would you like me to tell you how I met Fischer?", asked Moiseyev, causing the journalists to burn with impatience.

"It was in 1958 during one of our first tours to New York. After one of the shows a young woman came up to me behind the stage, and, after thanking me for the performance, asked if I would like to meet her younger brother. "He's only fifteen', she said, "but he's already the strongest chess player in America". I was introduced to Bobby Fischer. I don't recall what I talked to him about, all I remember is that I suggested a game of chess. The boy agreed with a smile. Unfortunately, there wasn't a chess set to be found in the theatre. If only I had known what an opponent I was losing!", the famous ballet-master concluded his story.

But meanwhile, loud applause had already sounded from the packed hall—the score was 2–0 in Karpov's favour.

6th Game
Karpov–Korchnoi
Petroff Defence

1 P–K4 P–K4 2 N–KB3 N–KB3 3 N×P
P–Q3 4 N–KB3 N×P 5 P–Q4 P–Q4 6 B–Q3
B–K2 7 0–0 N–QB3 8 R–K1 B–KN5 9 P–B3
P–B4 10 Q–N3 0–0 11 QN–Q2 K–R1 12
P–KR3 B–R4 (Diag.)

13 Q×NP R–B3 14 Q–N3 R–N3 15 B–K2
B–R5 16 R–B1 B×N 17 N×B B×P+ 18
R×B N×R 19 K×N Q–Q3 20 N–N5
R–KB1 21 Q–R3 Q–Q1 22 B–KB4 P–KR3
23 N–B3 R–K1 24 B–Q3 R–K5 25 P–KN3
R–B3 26 Q–B5 P–N4 27 N×P P×N 28
B×NP R(5)–K3 29 R–K1 Q–KN1 30 P–KR4
R–N3 31 R×R **Black lost on time.**

How arbitrary are the characteristics which are sometimes attached to grandmasters! Before the start of the match, correspondents of the highest rank predicted with one voice that Korchnoi would aim for complicated 'power' play, and that Karpov would attempt to nullify this by his technical mastery. Oh, no! It all turned out the other way. On account of time trouble the older player committed inaccuracies in these complicated positions, and Karpov tried to keep pieces on the board. In short, the journalists had to make corrections during the course of their work, without again allotting the grandmasters their rehearsed rôles, even if they had been written by perfectly well-qualified script writers, but... written beforehand, without taking into account the particular situation.

With the seventh game began a long series of draws. They were far from peaceful ones, nor was the seventh game itself, the first of that outwardly depressing string of 'half points'. This is what Anatoly Karpov has to say:

"In both my previous matches—with Polugayevsky and with Spassky—it was the seventh game that had proved somewhat strange. With Polugayevsky, for instance, this game could have been the last in the match, since at the time I was leading by 2–0. I gradually outplayed my opponent, but in a position that was probably won, missed my chance. And then against Spassky. A more favourable position it is hard to imagine: an extra pawn, a positional advantage, and Black unable to move anything. But—again a draw! And then here, in the Final Match, I again obtained a marked advantage in the seventh game, but at the decisive moment victory again slipped from my grasp. Seven is said to be a lucky number. After this my belief is shaken.

Oh, that series of draws", sighs Anatoly Karpov. "The pain and suffering that it caused. But a match is not possible without these. There are not, and cannot be, chess players who are equal. If they did not commit inaccuracies, and did not miss chances, chess would long since have disappeared. But even so—ten draws in succession! And in this series there is also a game which stands out sharply from the others—the thirteenth. I consider it to be one of the best in the match. I was playing Black. Everything went well up to about the thirtieth move. My opponent chose an unfortunate plan, all the drawbacks of which I was able to demonstrate fairly accurately, and I obtained a promising position. But after move thirty we both ran short of time. I continued playing for a win, although there were no real prospects of success. I kept avoiding a draw. In a severe time scramble we gave up recording our moves, and made three or four more than necessary. It would seem that on the forty-third move I missed, for the last time, a variation which would have forced a draw. Or more correctly, I did not miss it, but again intentionally avoided it. It turned out, however, that I had assessed the position incorrectly (or, more likely, I was still under the influence of that which had been happening some fourteen to fifteen moves earlier), and the game was adjourned in a position that was very difficult for me. On the resumption I nevertheless managed to avoid defeat. Alas, this was one of the few games in the match which we analysed well. Here the first twelve moves after the adjournment followed our analysis. Korchnoi again got into time trouble (in this game he had difficulty with each of the time controls: as soon as the control was reached, his flag would fall, whereupon he would think for some thirty minutes over his next move, again run into time trouble, and so on right up to move ninety-six). And the positional draw which resulted came as a complete surprise to him. It was a very interesting position: Korchnoi had an extra pawn, all his pieces were active, and he had a passed pawn one move away from queening. And... there was no win. Without doubt a great disappointment for the attacker".

It was interesting to observe the press centre during the adjournment session of this game. The majority of those present thought that Korchnoi would win at any moment, and only Polugayevsky, on seeing how Karpov was defending, kept saying: "Terrific!". The time passed... In the hands of the remaining correspondents new scoresheets appeared (one such scoresheet is intended for eighty moves). The game seemed likely to break all records, and headlines were prepared of the type: "One hundred gone!", or "The 100-move war". But in the packed Central Chess Club (where the adjournment session was being held) they stopped reproducing the two Candidates' moves on the demonstration boards, and it struck ten o'clock in the evening. In the closed room where the game was being played, at exactly this point the controller approached the chess table, envelope in hand. Karpov was considering his ninety-sixth move. Since the time fixed for play had expired, he was asked to seal his next move.

"What a tremendous fight!", said Karpov after twelve hours of play, on emerging from the players' room.

"Has Black now achieved a 'fortress'?", I asked, a not altogether tactful question in such cases.

"Even if he has, it will take another forty moves or so to demonstrate it", Karpov smiled. "After all, my opponent is a pawn up".

However, a second adjournment session was not required. Korchnoi was obliged to agree to a draw.

13th Game
Korchnoi–Karpov
Queen's Indian Defence

1 N–KB3 N–KB3 2 P–Q4 P–K3 3 P–KN3 P–QN3 4 B–N2 B–N2 5 P–B4 B–K2 6 N–QB3 0–0 7 Q–Q3 P–Q4 8 P×P N×P 9 N×N P×N 10 0–0 N–Q2 11 R–Q1 R–K1 12 B–K3 B–Q3 13 QR–B1 P–QR4 14 Q–B2 P–QB3 15 N–K1 N–B3 16 B–B3 R–QB1 17 N–N2 P–R3 18 B–B4 P–B4 19 B×B Q×B 20 P×P R×BP 21 Q–Q2 N–K5 22 Q–B4 Q–QB3 23 R×R P×R 24 N–K3 P–Q5 25 N–B4 Q–R5 26 R–QB1 N–N4 27 Q–B5 N×B+ 28 P×N B–R3 29 N–Q6 R–K2 30 Q×QBP P–Q6 31 Q–Q5 Q–QN5 32 K–N2 Q×P 33 R–B6 Q–K4 34 Q×Q R×Q 35 N–K4 B–N4 36 R–Q6 P–B4 37 N–B3 B–B5 38 P–B4 R–B4 39 K–B3 K–B2 40 K–K3 K–K2 41 R–QN6

R–B1 42 R–N7+ K–B1 43 R–R7 R–B4 44
P–KR4 P–R4 45 P–R3 B–R3 46 K–Q2 R–B3
47 R–Q7 B–B5 48 N–Q1 B–N4 49 N–K3
P–N3 50 R–Q5 R–N3 51 N–Q1 K–B2 52
N–N2 B–R3 53 N–R4 R–QB3 54 R–B5
R–K3 55 R–K5 R–QB3 56 N–B5 B–B5 57
N–R4 B–R3 58 R–B5 R–K3 59 R–B7+ K–K1
60 N–B3 R–N3 61 N–Q1 R–K3 62 N–K3
R–N3 63 R–B5 R–N7+ 64 K–B3 R×P 65
R×RP B–N2 66 K×P R–B6 67 K–Q4 K–Q2
68 N–B4 R×NP 69 P–R4 K–B2 70 R–B5+
K–N1 71 N–K5 B–K5 72 R–B3 R–N8 73
K–B5 K–B2 74 P–R5 R–QR8 75 K–N5+
K–Q3 76 P–R6 R–QN8+ 77 K–R5 R–QR8+
78 K–N6 R–QN8+ 79 K–R7 K–Q4 80 R–B6
R–KB8 81 K–N6 K–Q5 82 R–B4+ K–K6

83 R–R4 B–R1 84 N×P K–B6 85 K–B7
R–Q8 86 P–R7 K–N5 87 R–R6 K–N6 88
R–R3+ K–N5 89 R–R5 R–QN8 90 R–R6
R–Q8 91 R–Q6 R–QR8 92 K–N8 B–K5 93
R–Q7 K–B6 94 R–KN7 R–R3 95 K–B8
K–N6 96 K–Q8 B–R1 97 **Drawn**

After a further three draws, Korchnoi in the seventeenth game chose a good plan, and gained an advantage. At this point his moves breathed energy, he boldly and abruptly placed his pieces on their best squares, almost screwing them into the board, and quickly and smartly pressed his clock. But suddenly he was as if caught by uncertainty, and he made a passive retreat. Subsequently, now in a position that was roughly level, perhaps very slightly favourable for Karpov, his opponent fell into a trap. He conceived an idea, but miscalculated in one of the variations, and on the forty-third move resigned in view of inevitable mate.

17th Games
Korchnoi–Karpov
Catalan Opening

1 P–Q4 N–KB3 2 P–QB4 P–K3 3 P–KN3
P–Q4 4 B–N2 P×P 5 N–KB3 P–B4 6 0–0
N–B3 7 Q–R4 B–Q2 8 Q×BP P×P 9 N×P
R–B1 10 N–QB3 Q–R4 11 R–Q1 B–K2
12 N–N3 Q–B2 13 N–N5 Q–N1 14 N–B5
P–QR3 15 N×B N×N 16 N–B3 N(2)–K4
17 Q–QR4 0–0 18 B–B4 Q–R2 19 B(4)×N
N×B 20 Q–K4 N–B3 21 R–Q7 B–B3 22
QR–Q1 Q–N3 23 Q–B2 N–R4 24 R(1)–Q3
P–R3 25 P–QR3 R–B2 26 P–QN4 R×R 27
R×R R–B1 28 R–Q3 N–B5 29 N–K4 Q–B2
(Diag.)

30 N–B5 N–K4 31 R–Q2 P–QN3 32
P–B4 P×N 33 P×N Q×P 34 B–N7 R–B2
35 Q–K4 Q–R8+ 36 K–N2 Q×P 37 P×P
R×P 38 R–Q3 Q–R4 39 Q–B3 Q–N3 40
R–Q7 R–B4 41 Q–N4 Q–B7+ 42 K–R3
P–N3 43 **Resigns**

3–0 in favour of Karpov. A draw in the eighteenth game 'from a position of strength'. Then the nineteenth game was adjourned in a position where, after prolonged analysis through the night, a correct diagnosis was made: on resumption the result should be a draw, although a certain accuracy was still required in the probable lengthy manoeuvring. Before the resumption

Karpov went off for a rest, and when he got up not long before they were due to depart, his seconds, after conferring amongst themselves, proposed to the young grandmaster a shorter, forced way to draw. There was no longer time to work through this variation thoroughly, and Karpov, after adopting the suggestion, went on to lose. Of course, he himself was also to blame for this defeat...

On either side of the Tchaikovsky Concert Hall, where the match had now moved to, the players were provided with a rest room. Korchnoi normally stayed on and relaxed there after the game, but after the twenty-first he quickly left. On the other side, Karpov sat alone in his room, after making a blunder in the opening.

"How could it be", he laughed bitterly. "In one of my opening notebooks Black's twelfth move is given an exclamation mark, and yet immediately after White's reply he has to resign! Once again I was too trusting... Well now, let that be a lesson to me".

Later both players explained why the last three games went the way they did. One can only say that, in this situation of widespread commotion and excitement, Karpov appeared absolutely calm. On making a move, he would go for a walk along the carpeted stage, apparently managing not only to assess the position on the board, but also to greet an acquaintance in the hall with a barely perceptible nod of the head. His opponent, on the other hand, would normally after a move go straight off to the back of the stage, where a special armchair had been placed for him, and, turning away from the hall, would fix the demonstration board with a tense stare, and mechanically recite prayers specially prepared for such moments. In these last three games they made even more of a contrast than usual, and their diametrically opposite natures were fully revealed.

And then came the very last game. The Estrada Theatre—on this stage from 1961 to 1969 four matches for the World Championship had been played... Making their way through the crowds of chess fans who had been unable to get tickets, came first Mikhail Tal, and then Boris Spassky... Moving through the foyer, they signed autographs, and gave interviews. Tal: "I don't recall a sharper and more nervy match from the psychological point of view". Spassky: "I feel for the players —after all, this is already their twenty-fourth game!".

To Karpov this hall was also familiar. In 1966, he, a fifteen-year-old, was here during the first match between Petrosian and Spassky, and to the amazement of the experts, guessed almost all the moves that were made on the stage. It is amusing that in 1969, at the second match between the same opponents, Karpov was unable to solve the same problem with such ease. I recall how grandmaster Lilienthal joked affectionately: "You've grown old, Tolya, you've grown old..."

So can it be that with experience it becomes more difficult to predict the future in chess? Just the opposite; knowing the past, it is much easier to do this. In recent chess history, there has probably not been a single instance when the last, deciding game of a high-level match has abruptly altered the result of the event. Many such clashes have taken an identical course: the player in the lead has chosen a very solid set-up, his opponent has attempted to breach it, and then, on finding himself in a difficult situation, has himself offered a draw; peace is then concluded, as they say, 'from a position of strength', in a position which is practically won for the leader. The Ex-World Champions Dr Euwe, President of the FIDE, and Petrosian predicted that in the present match too the last game would take such a course.

It will no doubt be of interest to recall that situations similar to the one described had already occurred in the eventful chess lives of both Euwe and Petrosian. Thus in 1935, before the start of the last game of his match with Alekhine, Euwe, who was leading, stated to his opponent that he would agree to a draw at any point. And this draw was later agreed when Euwe held an advantage, but even without having to realize this advantage the Dutch grandmaster became World Champion. Even more curious are two instances from Petrosian's chess life. The twenty-third game of his second match with Spassky was adjourned in a very difficult position for Petrosian. During the night of 16th to 17th June 1969, he came to the conclusion that there was no point in continuing the resistance, and thereby spoiling his fortieth birthday (17th June is his birthday). He could barely wait for the morning to come, whereupon he went to the telephone to announce that he was resigning the adjourned position, and would not be coming to resume it. However, Petrosian was forestalled by a 'counter'-ring—the chief controller O'Kelly told him that Spassky had offered a draw, which would assure him of the title of World Champion. And another instance. In the 1971 Candidates' Semi-Final Match, Petrosian was leading by a point against Korchnoi. Here Petrosian wrote down on his scoresheet a very strong move, and... offered a draw. Korchnoi declined. Petrosian then made this essentially winning move on the board. The time control was reached, and the game adjourned. Korchnoi thought and thought, and then asked: "Well, what will it be? A draw, or shall I resign?". Petrosian replied: "A draw".

In short, forecasters are helped by experience. In the region of the thirtieth move of the concluding game from the Final Match, Petrosian remarked: "Korchnoi, whatever he says, very much dislikes losing. He'll probably offer a draw now, and Karpov will not want to win". Literally a minute later the substantial walls of the press centre appeared to shake from the thunderous applause of the packed hall...

2nd Game

Karpov–Korchnoi

Sicilian Defence

1 P–K4	P–QB4
2 N–KB3	P–Q3
3 P–Q4	P×P
4 N×P	N–KB3
5 N–QB3	P–KN3

At the time, perhaps Korchnoi alone of the top players used to play the Dragon Variation. In particular, this opening twice occurred in his 1971 Candidates' Match with Geller, when Korchnoi succeeded in upholding the reputation of 'The Dragon'. In 1974 I naturally did not rule out the possibility of him employing this variation.

6 B–K3	B–N2
7 P–B3	N–B3

8 Q–Q2	0–0
9 B–QB4	B–Q2
10 P–KR4	R–B1
11 B–N3	N–K4
12 0–0–0	

The immediate 12 P–R5 is also possible.

12 ...	N–B5
13 B×N	R×B
14 P–R5	N×RP
15 P–KN4	N–B3

This position was reached in the fourth game of the afore-mentioned Geller–Korchnoi match, which continued: 16 B–R6 N×P 17 Q–K3 R×N(6) 18 P×R N–B3 19 B×B K×B 20 R–R2 Q–R4? 21 N–N3 Q×RP 22 Q×KP, with advantage to White.

16 N(4)–K2!

An attempt to support this move with variations was made by E. Chumak, a player from the town of Dnepropetrovsk, who in 1972 published an article on this topic.

The logical basis for the retreat of the knight from the centre is approximately as follows. The knight at QB3 is a highly important part of White's set-up, against which Black concentrates his attack. The characteristic exchange sacrifice (... R×N) frequently occurs on this square, when the opponent gains a strong attack (it is significant that, after the doubling of white pawns on the QB-file, Black's position is so rich in possibilities that even without an attack, in an endgame, he can maintain the balance—this was splendidly demonstrated in the games of the outstanding Soviet grandmaster Leonid Stein, whose death was so untimely). Thus the basic idea of 16 N(4)–K2 is to reinforce the position of the knight at QB3. In addition, from K2 the knight can easily be transferred for a direct attack on the hostile king. As the reader will already of course have noted, the two players, without worrying about loss of material, are mounting attacks on opposite wings—as normally happens in positions with castling on opposite sides.

After all these general considerations, one should not forget the concrete threat which White has created along the Q-file—17 P-K5 and 18 P–N5.

16 ...   Q–R4
17 B–R6

A typical device. In order to successfully develop his attack, White must definitely exchange off the bishop at KN2—the sole defender of the black squares around its king; besides, in some instances this bishop, like a long-range gun, can open fire on White's Q-side along the KR1–QR8 diagonal. Grandmaster Vladimir Simagin, who was generously endowed with rich creative fantasy, even devised in such positions a thematic exchange sacrifice for Black (B–R1), merely so as to preserve from exchange his favourite piece.

17 ...   B×B

17 ... KR–B1 18 B×B K×B 19 Q–R6+ K–N1 would have transposed.

18 Q×B   KR–B1
19 R–Q3!

Up till this point both players had been moving almost instantly. And here I played a move prepared beforehand, which caused Korchnoi to spend a long time deep in thought. And indeed, there was something for him to think about... It was established that the 'theoretical' continuation 19 R–Q5 does not gain White any real advantage. E.g. 19 ... Q–Q1 20 P–N5 N–R4 21 N–N3 Q–B1! 22 Q×Q+ R×Q! (earlier it was thought that Black had to take with the king, when White's position is a little better) 23 N×N P×N 24 R×RP P–B4!, and things are slightly more pleasant for Black. Or 20 P–K5 P×P 21 P–N5 N–R4 22 N–N3

Q–B1 23 R×N (23 N×N Q×Q 24 P×Q
B–B3!) 23 ... P×R 24 R×B Q×Q 25 P×Q,
and Black's outside passed pawn on the KR-
file gives him good counter-chances.

The innovation 19 R–Q3!, overprotecting
the knight at QB3, at the same time in a
number of variations frees the knight at K2
for the attack. If, without making this move,
White attempted to advance—19 P–N5 N–R4
20 N–N3, the unpleasant counter-blow
20 ... R×N would be awaiting him; now
this is no longer dangerous.

19 ...   R(5)–B4

When during our preparations for the
match we analysed 19 R–Q3, we came to the
conclusion that the best reply to it was 19 ...
R(1)–B4. It is highly probable that, after
36 minutes' thought during the game,
Korchnoi also came to the conclusion that it
was essential to secure himself against the
constantly threatening pawn thrusts—P–K5
and P–N5. I nevertheless consider that Black's
best practical chance was the retreat 19 ...
Q–Q1, as suggested by Botvinnik. Now,
after thinking for 18 minutes in search of a
refutation of 19 ... R(B5)–B4, I found a
fine forcing combination.

20 P–N5

The knights at QB3 and ... KB3 defend
their kings, and for this reason it is they
who are subject to the greatest danger (the
removal of the black knight from ... KB3
will almost immediately lead to White's
intrusion at Q5).

20 ... *see diagram next column* **R×P**

21 R–Q5!

Not, of course, 21 N–Q5 R×N!, when
Black's chief defender, his knight, remains
'alive'.

21 ...	R×R
22 N×R	R–K1

Here 22 ... Q–Q1 no longer works:
23 N(2)–B4 Q–B1 24 N×N+ P×N 25
Q×RP mate.

23 N(2)–B4   B–B3

White's Q5 square has to be attacked,
otherwise comes N×N+ followed by N–Q5,
and mates. On 23 ... B–K3 I was preparing
to play 24 N×B P×N 25 N×N+ P×N
28 Q×RP+ K–B1 27 Q×QNP Q–KN4+
28 K–N1 R–K2 29 Q–N8+ R–K1 30 Q×RP
(but definitely not 30 R–R8+?? K–N2!,
when it is Black, who threatens 31 ... Q–N8
mate, who wins) 30 ... R–K2 31 Q–N8+
R–K1 32 Q×P+—a rare and distinctive
type of 'windmill'.

24 P–K5!

Blocking that same fifth rank. There is a
dazzling array of spectacular possibilities, but

in fact this is the only decisive continuation. White fails to win by the straightforward 24 N×N+ P×N 25 N–R5 Q–KN4+ (this is the point!) 26 Q×Q P×Q 27 N–B6+ K–N2 28 N×R+ B×N.

24 ...	**B×N**

After 24 ... P×P 25 N×N+ P×N 26 N–R5, mate is inevitable.

25 P×N	**P×P**

In such positions the most important thing is—self-control! One would like, of course, to make a brilliant move as quickly as possible. But it was not yet too late to lose the game: 26 N–R5 (so as to answer 26 ... P×N with 27 R–N1+ and 28 Q–N7 mate) is met by the sobering 26 ... R–K8+.

26 Q×RP+	**K–B1**
27 Q–R8+	**Resigns**

If 27 ... K–K2, then 28 N×B+ Q×N 29 R–K1+.

AFTER THE BATTLE... THE WINNER SPEAKS

"Is there a sensation of happiness? Now, at this present moment, I don't particularly feel anything of the sort. Some time after the seventeenth game I thought: the match will soon be over now, things will be so much easier, and I will be uncommonly happy. But now—something of the feeling of a job well done. No, I do feel something else... I feel very, very good at heart that I have justified the hopes placed in me. It is very pleasant to see the happy faces of the fans, my relations and my friends... But a feeling of complete satisfaction, complete happiness, has not yet reached me.

Yes, at first I was not at all sure that I could win the Candidates' event. I did not think about whom in particular I would lose to, but I thought that at some level I would have insufficient experience. I began really to believe in the possibility of a meeting with Fischer when I learned that I had to play Korchnoi in the Final. If it had been a question of a tournament, I wouldn't have doubted for a moment that I was dealing with a highly dangerous rival. But not in a match, 'one against one'. But Korchnoi was one of the few who was firmly convinced that I would beat Spassky. It has to be admitted that, before our match, he 'understood' me better than I understood him. But from the very first few moves I realized that I had almost made an irreparable mistake, in not regarding him as my most dangerous rival...

After the Semi-Final Match with Boris Spassky, there was only just enough time to prepare for the Final: the Leningrad match finished in the middle of May, and in September the Final was due to start. And the Nice Olympiad, which lasted for the whole of June, also took a good deal of effort. To play for the USSR team is a great honour, especially on top board, and so I tried to put everything into my play. The result speaks for itself. But on the threshold of the Final Match this was not altogether rational.

And then, when at the beginning of July the Olympiad finished, I had to relax and do some training. I prepared with my trainers for a comparatively short period—only two months, and there was much that we didn't have time to do. In general, if it hadn't been for the good-quality and all-round preparations made for the match with Spassky, things would have been very, very difficult. I managed to utilize some unused 'material' in the Moscow match, so that the deficiences in my preparations for it were not so noticeable.

However, there was also a positive side to the fact that in July and August I did little studying of chess: I began the match in good spirits, and felt a great desire to play. And the first few games I played with particularly great enthusiasm.

I think that I should have won this match by a bigger score. Why do I think this? Because I myself know that at some point I weakened, at some point I played less well than I could have done. Regarding the nature of the course taken by the match, I would divide it into four basic parts: the first six games, the next eleven, the next four, and the last three.

I quickly got into my stride, took the lead, and, what is even more important, the initiative. And the fact that my opponent suffered only two defeats was fortunate for him. Then, in the second stage of the match (when there followed ten successive draws and my win in the seventeenth game), in trying to outplay my opponent in slightly better, but sometimes simply equal positions, I overstepped the mark, after which my troubles began. My tactics were based on a desire to drag my opponent into a protracted struggle, but, in overdoing things, I was forced myself to save some inferior positions, which cost me incredible effort. My play promptly deteriorated, and now I 'switched on' only when I found myself on the brink of the precipice.

Finally, in the seventeenth game, after my opponent had made a bad mistake in time trouble, I managed to extend my lead to 3–0. After this the match should have finished somewhere around the twentieth game... Why didn't this happen? It was all because of the 'seditious' thought that the match was essentially over,—so why all this additional effort, after all, all I have to do is to go along and sign the scoresheets of the last few games... In this, the third stage, I began, as bad footballers do when they are leading, to 'kick for touch', and was justly punished (although purely chess-wise my two defeats can be explained by blunders in analysis). Strange as it may seem, the second 'nought' had a beneficial effect on me. After making a sober assessment of the situation—the score was in my favour, and of the three remaining games I was White in two—I calmed down almost immediately, and began playing normal chess. In this, the fourth and concluding stage of the match, I was quite satisfied with my play; I as it were gained my second wind, whereas my opponent was exhausted both mentally and physically...

The length of the match, the enormous nervous tension, the sharpness of the competitive struggle, and the high goal we were both aiming for—of course, all this was bound to affect the creative side of the event. But our match—although rather drab and over-technical for certain chess fans—also had its undoubted virtues. Although we attempted to win against each other from level, and sometimes quite boring positions, and many of the games ended in draws, with virtually only the kings left on the board—nevertheless, despite this, in our match there were no bad mistakes, if you exclude those two analytical blunders in the nineteenth and twenty-first games, and there were much fewer inaccuracies than in similar events from the past. For instance, the 1972 Spassky–Fischer match in Reykjavik was more entertaining, but there were many more mistakes there than in our match, and the tenseness of the struggle was considerably lower.

Before the Semi-Final stage Korchnoi declared that his knowledge of opening theory was superior to that of the other three Candidates—Spassky, Petrosian and Karpov—but in the match with me he avoided sharp and topical variations, and did not engage in any theoretical discussions. As White he went from one little-known variation to another, thinking up new and dubious continuations and even entire openings, and caught me out only once, in the twenty-first game. As Black he literally 'slighted' me with his drawing tendencies in the French

Defence. Only in this opening did my trainers and I fail to cope with the problems we were set. The variation of the French Defence which is basic to my opponent's opening repertoire was analysed insufficiently accurately, and this was the main deficiency in our preparations. But also during the match itself we prepared insufficiently thoroughly for the games, with the result that in all the 'French encounters', with the exception perhaps of the eighteenth game, my opponent attained perfectly acceptable positions, and even equalized, literally on emerging from the opening. Thus I was essentially playing almost without the white pieces throughout the match, which once again emphasizes the unsatisfactory nature of my chess preparations for the event. On this occasion my home analytical work was also not particularly good, the direct result of which was those two absurd defeats.

The most important part of my preparation was, so to speak, psycho-physical, and while in the psychological sense some errors were made (for example, underestimation of my opponent), physically I was on this occasion excellently prepared. I did not catch even a single cold, which earlier used to happen fairly frequently with me. It is quite probable that the fact that I was able to keep in good physical shape was assisted by my residing constantly at an out-of-town *dacha*, where I lived on the edge of a lake in excellent conditions, periodically going for walks in the fresh air of the forest on losing my appetite for the game.

How is it, the reader may ask, that you say that you felt fine, and yet utilized all the post-ponements allowed in the match regulations 'for illness'? I utilized these days merely to regain my mood for play, to build up my 'chess appetite'. Incidentally, during one of my postpone-ments, on the invitation of my cosmonaut friend Pyotr Klimuk, I visited the cosmonaut's village on the outskirts of Moscow, and there made a detailed tour of the Yury Gagarin Museum...

I do not consider it necessary to hide the fact that the regulation, whereby the stipulated possible postponements can be taken only 'on account of illness', is in fact essentially fictitious. Much more logical was the previous regulation, whereby a player could take a break as he wished, for reasons known only to himself. After all, it is much simpler to stipulate a reason-able number of postponements, and leave it up to the players themselves to decide when to utilize them. In principle the match doctor is only needed for giving attention to the players in cases of necessity (and also if they don't have their own personal doctors). But the players themselves should control their own condition, for who else is as interested in this as they are?! And also because this should all the same remain a secret... I, for instance, would definitely not want it to happen that, say, during a match with Fischer, I was examined by some unknown doctor, who would thus acquire details of my state of health".

ROBERT BYRNE'S OPINION

It was at the closing ceremony of a major international tournament in the large hall of the USSR Central Chess Club... A balding, greying man with a young and unnaturally pale face, his eyes suddenly beginning to sparkle behind the glasses of his spectacles, he stood up in embarrassment to a storm of applause. His hand, holding a customary but on this occasion unlit cigarette, was propped up on the green table-cloth, and shook with emotion. Not far from Robert Byrne was an enormous, provocatively-smiling Russian souvenir doll—a present to the American grandmaster, who had made the best score among the foreign competitors in the Alekhine Memorial. In that same tournament, as Mikhail Botvinnik expressed it, a new chess star of the first magnitude had risen, and in that same tournament on 29th November 1971 the first meeting between Robert Byrne and Anatoly Karpov took place, and ended in a draw. A month later, on the last day but one of the departing year, they played again in Hastings, where this time Karpov won; later they played a draw in the Leningrad Interzonal Tournament. Byrne was able to observe Karpov's play both at the 20th Olympiad (in Yugoslavia), and at the 21st (in France). In short, Byrne is one of those few people—especially among foreign players—who is well acquainted both with Karpov and with Fischer. And for this reason I think that a talk with him will be of considerable interest...

Anatoly Karpov began and completed his Candidates' path in the presence of Robert Byrne. In the summer of 1973, Byrne, together with Karpov and Korchnoi, was successful in the Leningrad Interzonal Tournament, and in Autumn of the following year, after being eliminated from the Candidates, he came to Moscow for the Final Match as chess correspondent of the *New York Times*.

Both in Leningrad, sitting on the stage at the chess board, and in Moscow, sitting in the press centre at his typewriter (in all the Moscow halls where the match was played, the first thing Byrne did was to look for a socket where he could plug in his noiseless electric machine), he normally behaved impassively and even stiffly, but sometimes would suddenly reveal his uncontrollable temperament. Not for nothing did the students from the college in Indianapolis, where in the sixties professor Byrne gave a course in Classical German Philosophy, call him: "A snow-covered volcano".

And Robert Byrne began our conversation with some cold, sober judgements. Together with Pavlo Dembo, from '*Soviet Sport*', who was very friendly with Byrne, and Yury Zerchaninov from the popular magazine '*Youth*', I had gone to see him in the 'Intourist' Hotel. Byrne said that he was absolutely sure that Karpov would win, and that he was now observing him with interest in a new role—as a defender of difficult positions.

"In the Leningrad Interzonal Tournament", Byrne remarked, "Karpov was unable to display this quality—no one held an advantage against him".

"How highly did you rate Karpov's chances before the start of the Leningrad Tournament?"

"I thought that the three winning places would be contested in the main by Karpov, Tal, and Larsen*."

"In what order?"

"I did not think about the order, I merely singled out these four. And I thought that the Leningrad winners would have better chances in the subsequent matches than those from the second Interzonal—in Petropolis. This was based on the real strengths of the contenders."

"But did you consider then that it was Karpov who could become Fischer's opponent?"

"At that time I had practically no doubt that Fischer's future opponent would emerge from Leningrad—I thought that it would be Tal. And, as far as I remember, I wasn't the only one to put my money on Tal at that time".

"But Tal and Larsen 'cracked up', and together with Karpov and Korchnoi it was you who made up the trio..."

"I must say that Karpov's play in Leningrad was very convincing, but soon I was to experience Spassky's strength, when I lost the Quarter-Final Match to him, and I began to incline towards the thought that Karpov would only go as far as Spassky. And after the first

* and Korchnoi? (K.P.N.)

game of their match I even said that Spassky would again be playing against Fischer. I am afraid that Spassky too, on winning the first game against Karpov, began looking at the board while thinking already about Fischer. Outwardly Spassky appeared very calm, but in fact he was nervous. But here Karpov showed that he was not only outwardly, but also in general, very calm. He did not allow this first defeat to spoil his play. Karpov's rare calmness during play also enables him to practically avoid mistakes".

"Are you saying that your initial forecasts did not come true on account of the mistakes made by Tal and Spassky? Or was it simply difficult to foresee that Karpov would improve so much with each match?"

"But surely it's not just of small significance that Karpov emerged the strongest, because he did not make all those mistakes that the remaining Candidates made? And you are right, Karpov did indeed develop a lot during the time between the Interzonal Tournament and the match with Korchnoi. In this match, for instance, I became finally convinced that he has no weak spots in the opening".

"But perhaps the point is that Karpov, like no one else, has the ability to prepare?"

"This is so, but this isn't the first year I have been carefully following Karpov's progress, and he astonishes me with his knowledge of opening theory, where he now has no weak spots".

Byrne began quoting various games played by Karpov in USSR events. It is known to everyone that Byrne carefully follows games played by Soviet players, but it turned out that at any moment he could remember an enormous number of games by Karpov, Spassky, Polugayevsky... Gradually the conversation turned to Fischer. Both Byrne and Fischer were taught, although at different times (Byrne is fifteen years older than Fischer), in the same school. Now the main hall of this school displays portraits of both Roberts: the elder is a legend in the history of the school for his academic successes, while the younger, although he did not manage to finish school, became Champion of the World.

"Do you see anything in common between Karpov and Fischer?"

"As players, both are extremely rational. But knowing little about Karpov outside of chess, I wouldn't care to make any other comparisons. However, I hear that Karpov likes to work at night. Is this so?"

"Yes, he goes to bed late, and gets up late".

"Then they are also similar in that way. Once Fischer and I played tennis in Reykjavik at eleven o'clock at night. The next time Fischer said: 'Let's begin at three in the morning.' 'No', I said to him. 'You play, but I'm going to sleep'".

"Which of you won when you began at eleven o'clock at night?"

"Fischer won, but I was out of form. I smoked a great deal at that time, and I soon got tired out on the court. Now I can play for four hours at a stretch. At the moment I would probably beat Fischer".

"At tennis?"

Byrne laughed loudly. All his reservedness disappeared as soon as the conversation turned to his tennis duels with Fischer. He spoke excitedly, and soon returned to that late-night game of tennis in Reykjavik.

"Fischer saw that I could only play for twenty minutes, and for all these twenty minutes we merely warmed up. Then, noticing that I was already panting, he said: 'O.k., that's the end of the knock-up. Now we'll start playing'".

"Doesn't this tennis episode explain Fischer's desire to play against the challenger up to the first to win ten games?"

"Possibly. Although I think that Fischer overrates his physical possibilities. It is another matter that I see no equal to Fischer in his ability to concentrate at the board. He doesn't even need any assistance in the analysis of adjourned games. During his match with Petrosian, for instance, he didn't turn once to Evans, and the latter took offence and went off home. And in Reykjavik he only used Lombardy a few times. And even now, in 'hibernation', he maintains his strength—he works a great deal, and for him this takes the place of practical play. This is already the second time Fischer has carried out such a mad experiment, but the first time he disappeared from tournaments for a year and a half, this time it is already two and a half... But by constantly 'hibernating', he won't, of course, keep his chess crown. Karpov has won all his matches, and he is the present challenger. And if Fischer should try to avoid meeting him, it will be a really underhand action. In this case Karpov will become World Champion, and rightly so. But Fischer still has time to change his mind..." This is what Robert Byrne had to say during the Final Candidates' Match in Autumn 1974, and here is what he said after the match was over.

"In the match just finished, the majority of Americans favoured Karpov. He is young and talented. The competitive successes of this grandmaster, which are well known to millions of lovers of the ancient game, speak for themselves. And in general the public likes new names... American supporters of Karpov reckon that he plays splendidly, better than the 'old men'. Long before the finish of the Moscow match, in the USA the question began to be widely debated: "Fischer or Karpov?"."

Before my departure to Moscow I wrote an article about Fischer, in which I criticized his unsporting behaviour. I wanted the public to realize that the World Champion was putting up unacceptable conditions for the holding of the World Championship Match. A fortunate time was chosen for the publication of the article—there was a period of summery weather in New York, and the article was printed on the very day that I was on a plane heading for Moscow. I warned my wife: 'If the telephone rings at three in the morning, don't worry—it will be Fischer...'

On arriving for the match in Moscow, as a joke (and also seriously!) I bet a number of people a thousand dollars that Fischer would not play the match. No one would take me up. They were wrong not to! Now I myself am beginning to believe that the Fischer-Karpov encounter will take place...

I think that I will not be giving any secrets away, if I say that even now Fischer, despite his lengthy absence from tournament play, has maintained his great chess strength. I thought that he didn't want to play, because he was afraid of losing the title of Champion. And at the same time there is the temptation of being undefeated, of remaining in the eyes of the public the strongest player in the world, without officially having this title. This does not mean that he is afraid of some particular opponent. He is very afraid of chance mistakes... Fischer has a strongly developed fear of chance happenings. He perhaps foresees that in the forthcoming match for the World Championship the lead at the start will be assumed by the challenger, who has had a thorough training in events with other top grandmasters. Fischer, on the other hand, has had no practical experience in recent years. The World Champion probably considers that with an unlimited number of games he will be able to catch up... The chess world awaits with impatience the meeting between Robert Fischer and Anatoly Karpov. Their match must take place. I think that the times demand it".

KORCHNOI'S MONOLOGUE

The match is over. Over for everyone, except Korchnoi. In the 'Sovyetskaya' Hotel, with his ticket to Leningrad already ordered, he delivers an impassioned monologue. Time and again Korchnoi repeats, then contradicts himself, but remains true to himself—he remains Korchnoi. For him, competitive anger is like a stimulus on the way to the top.

"The match has concluded with the score 3–2 in favour of Karpov. But in the creative, chess, sense, in my opinion, I showed myself to better advantage than Karpov. The course of the match should have given a different result—3–2, 4–3 or 5–4 in my favour. But what turned out to be important was the stress factor. In my opinion, Karpov does not possess the powerful arsenal of other leading grandmasters, but he is a person of exceptional will-power, and is able to impose it during play. Karpov outplayed Polugayevsky, because Polugayevsky was overwhelmed by his will-power... I underestimated this strong-willed characteristic of Karpov, and it would have been better to overestimate it. But not to overestimate it as much as Polugayevsky did...

In the first half of the match Karpov as White played to win in every game. When I managed to equalise after the opening, I thought: well, the position is equal, a draw should now be agreed, since for both sides it is dangerous to take a risk. But here Karpov would sit, and after due thought, would find a way of complicating the position and of creating difficulties for me, forcing me to struggle on, and then after adjourning the game, would try to wear me out. Such an ability to force a struggle provoked in me, well, respect. This caused both Polugayevsky and Spassky a great deal of trouble—they were both overwhelmed by his will-power.

Probably before the match I, like Spassky, underestimated his strong-willed characteristics. If I had been fully aware of these characteristics of his, then perhaps I wouldn't have given him a 'start' at the beginning of the match, as I allowed myself to. At the start of the match I, almost intentionally, placed myself under attack. But at the beginning of the match I did not attach great significance to the results of individual games. Well, a point more, a point less, I thought, all the same it's the first to win five games. And so I allowed myself in the second game to play the extremely risky Dragon Variation, which I had analysed for several years, and which I knew was dubious. Perhaps if from the very start I had held onto him as tightly as he did me later, he would not have been himself. The mutual pressurizing began only when the score was 0–2, and until then the pressurizing had been all one way...

Before the match I paid particular attention to my physical preparation. And indeed, the match turned out to be long and nervy. As regards nervous strain, perhaps the only one to compare with it was the Spassky–Fischer match, in which there were no short draws. But even so, the average length of the games in our match was probably longer than in that one, and demanded greater physical exertion. And so, I paid attention to my physical preparation, and physically I was in the main able to last out. Although to be frank, by the twenty-second game, when I was close to levelling the score, my strength was nevertheless on the wane...

When in 1971 I played against Petrosian (that same Petrosian who does not allow you to make a fight of it), I was able to draw some conclusions, and I felt that I was now able to breach such a style. And here I came up against a similar style—Karpov would not allow a close-range fight—and again I failed to breach it, and only expended massive efforts on the approach.

I would divide the match into three parts. In the first part the young pretender did all the pressing, and this lasted roughly from the first to the tenth game. He pressed and pressed in each of these ten games. Then came the stage of fatigue, which perhaps affected my opponent more than me. It is no accident that between the eleventh and eighteenth games Karpov twice called for a postponement... And, finally, the third part of the match, when we were both tired, and although I began to catch up, I didn't have sufficient strength left. I repeat, although in the chess sense I had the advantage, I had insufficient strength to crack my opponent's resistance. The quality of his play at this point was very negative—anything, so long as he could keep me at bay. At any rate, that is the way it appeared to me, although perhaps from the side it appeared different.

Before the start of the match I assessed my chances as sixty—forty. Even now I would not change my opinion. Regarding my assertion that the match would only last seventeen games, in this there was, of course, an element of boasting. I thought that the struggle would be more lively.

Why did I lose the sixth game? On that day I was simply not in the mood for a fight. Every player has days when he is not in the mood. Fischer, during the most fighting stage of his match against Spassky, failed to win with an extra pawn in the seventh game. The only way I can explain this is that on that day he was not in the mood for a fight. In exactly the same way, on that day I would have lost any game, and I was lucky that I hadn't played the French, since then I would have been simply crushed in the match, by being deprived of my main opening weapon. On losing the sixth game I sensed that things were going to be difficult for me, and that I would be unable to win the match in seventeen games. I started to do the pressing, and held the advantage and winning chances in the tenth, eleventh, thirteenth, fifteenth and seventeenth games. But this only ended with me losing one game, and not winning any. The thirteenth was perhaps the turning point. Before that too things had been distressing. But then the thirteenth... When I failed to win it, I was visibly upset. After all, I had been pinning my hopes on the second half of the match, assuming that physically I was stronger than my opponent. But here I sensed that I myself was beginning to tire, and for the first time began to have doubts about the possibility of me winning. And when I lost the seventeenth game, I decided that the match was over, and that I didn't deserve any other result.

But even when I thought that the match was over, I did not give in. I managed to win a couple of games, but this did not change my conviction. I no longer had sufficient physical strength, and I was unable to make the decisive break-through. I was in low spirits, although I had not lost the will to win. I was further tired because in the middle of the match I had had to do a great deal of research work myself—I had been unable to persuade a single grandmaster to act as my second...

Yes, Karpov is a rare type of chess player, I would say. In his play first here and there one suddenly notices faults. But what enormous will-power! I have never seen in anyone such an ability to summon up his strength for a game. It's absolutely staggering! In a short space of time he puts in a colossal amount of work. With his will-power, one might say that he put a break on my play. This man is capable of putting into a game all that he possesses, all that he knows; he is a man who is able to impose his influence on an opponent. This demands enormous efforts on the part of he himself, and, as the example of Tal has shown, such a player may not last long. Karpov has given so much, and within six months will have given even more. I will once again cite the example of Tal. In the years when Tal was becoming World Champion, he had no understanding of chess. But how he could fight! Now he understands everything about chess, but he has not the same will-power...

I sensed the influence of Karpov's will on me during the course of the whole match. As time trouble approached I felt physically how he summoned up everything against me, strained himself to the utmost, and watched me ever so closely. In the sixteenth game he won a pawn in time trouble, and when the time scramble was over, I saw how he slackened the reins, as it were gave up the ghost, leaned back in his chair and relaxed for the twenty minutes that he spent over his sealed move, and—sealed the wrong one. But he would rarely relax in such a way...

And once Karpov read my thoughts! Yes, he actually read them. It was on the resumption of the nineteenth game, which was adjourned with advantage to me, but where I had been unable to find a win at home. And suddenly Karpov quickly and confidently gives up his rook for my bishop. Why does he sacrifice, why? Aha, no doubt he thinks that this way leads most quickly to a forced draw. But no, there is something wrong here. I begin to search for a mistake in his calculations, while alongside Karpov paces confidently up and down the carpeted stage. Here it is, here is the 'hole' in his analysis! I lift my eyes from the board, and see how my opponent begins to pace more slowly. He begins to have doubts, he returns to the board, and starts searching for what it is that I have found. I distinctly see how Karpov reads my thoughts, and follows exactly the same road along which I have just passed. He now sees everything that I have seen. On this occasion he saw that in his analysis he had committed a fatal error, and that now he was lost. But what, I wonder, did he see in other instances? This I don't know...

It turns out that it is the factor of will-power that now plays the determining rôle in chess. For this reason it was Karpov who emerged the winner. Although I still consider myself superior in the creative sense, as regards will-power he is clearly my superior. Karpov was able to inflict his will on me, and he won".

THE "SALIERI COMPLEX"

The World of chess is one of fierce competition and rivalry, with similarities to war, which makes certain analogies permissible. Not without reason is it said that chess is a war game...

Napoleon asserted, as is well known, that a man could become a real commander only if he possessed outstanding talent and an inflexible character. In applying this formula to chess, Botvinnik added two further components—fitness and special knowledge. Speaking in mathematical terms, chess strength is a kind of resultant force made up of four components, the values of which are variable. The first is natural talent. If you are not naturally talented, you cannot become a great player. It is curious that among players there is almost an unwritten agreement: not to discuss who is the most talented. This is considered almost indecent.

But nevertheless, the opinion currently held is that Tal is the greatest example of natural talent, that the most diverse chess arsenal among modern players is possessed by the universal player Spassky, and that for physical staying-power Smyslov has long had no equal. The player with the greatest will-power has also been found... Botvinnik does not appear in this list, and meanwhile it is he who in recent times has been World Champion for longer than anyone else. And can anyone answer the following question with any confidence and certainty: during the period of Fischer's best results, in which of the four components was he inferior to anyone?

The player who becomes Champion is the one who at the particular time has the greatest resultant chess strength. And it is a specific, chess talent to show that today you are the strongest. To be successful in match play, a player must be able to assess correctly the strong points of his opponent, attempt to neutralize them, and to utilize his own trumps. A classic example of this is still provided by the return match Tal–Botvinnik, when at the age of nearly fifty Botvinnik managed to extinguish the combinational fire of his young opponent. Polugayevsky admitted that he failed to utilize his trumps during his match with Karpov, while it would seem that Spassky lost his while still on the way to his match...

In their assessments, grandmasters nevertheless do not break the unwritten convention about great players, and do not touch upon the theme of natural talent. I, on the other hand, am not bound by this "convention", and would like to tell you an amusing story. Once, quite a long time ago now, I was playing friendly, "five-minute" games with a certain lad. We played and played, and I didn't manage to beat him once, but lost to him from inferior, equal, and superior positions. I thought to myself, what the devil, I do have the master title after all... Then the lad suddenly stood up, looked at me intently, and said with a slight smile: "Perhaps I'm simply the stronger player?" The lad was called Tolya Karpov...

In chess it is the strongest player who wins. But as to why Karpov wins—this question can be answered in various ways. Will-power, fitness, chess arsenal? But perhaps, nevertheless, an unusual natural talent.

For anyone who is closely acquainted with the modern chess élite, it is absolutely clear —independent of any personal sympathies—that amazing natural talent (and for some, one could possibly use an even stronger definition) is possessed by Vasily Smyslov, Mikhail Tal, Tigran Petrosian, Boris Spassky, Robert Fischer and Anatoly Karpov. All these, like rockets, burst swiftly into the world of chess, and then, utilizing their strongest qualities, became Champion. While giving Korchnoi his due as regards capacity for hard work, one nevertheless cannot place him on a par with these others. Years of intensive work, and the polishing of his professional ability, have made him into a very strong grandmaster, but it is always his qualities as a strong-willed competitor that have been most prominent, and never his supreme natural ability. That which came to Korchnoi with enormous difficulty was frequently surmounted with ease by the Champions, as if they were simply playing: they came, they saw, they conquered. He would devote all his strength to overcoming one, when another would appear... And now, when it appeared that he was close to his goal, a new star flashed onto the scene— Karpov.

If one makes a comparison between leading chess players and great musicians—Paganini, Tchaikovsky, Mozart, ... one cannot help but compare Korchnoi with Salieri. And it is by no means simply a matter of a kind of similarity in performance—in other instances too this would be highly conventional. The analogy is suggested more by the way that Salieri is depicted in Pushkin's drama, and by the way that Korchnoi reveals himself to us when he gets up from the chess board. When talking with Korchnoi after a game, one is staggered by his forthrightness and the way he reproaches himself. But it would be all right if that was all. He opens a valve for his prickly emotions, which he professionally restrains (though even so, less well than the majority of grandmasters) during a game, and gives vent to his lack of objectivity. And if it comes to talking about his young and highly-talented conqueror, Korchnoi rarely manages to conceal his envy, which takes the form of searching for the other's deficiencies. It may be objected that Salieri acknowledged Mozart's genius... At heart Korchnoi also acknowledges it, but outwardly disclaims it. And therefore we have an instance merely of a variety of the "Salieri Complex", augmented by non-objectivity.

Under modern (chess) conditions, the attempt to "take vengeance" on the opponent for his greater talent reduced itself to a belittling of this talent, and to a desire to change places with him—he is supposedly a player merely with will-power, whereas in the creative sense I am stronger.

What else could Korchnoi do? He couldn't do the same as Pushkin's character. So as loudly as possible he slammed the door.

After being sent by the USSR Chess Federation to the International Tournament in Amsterdam (July 1976), on the conclusion of the event grandmaster Korchnoi declined to return to the USSR.

The justification given by Korchnoi for his decision was that, in the USSR he was allegedly denied the opportunity to participate in events "according to his choice", and that he was subjected to "pressure" during the Final Candidates' Match and after it.

In reality, as was stated in a special announcement by the USSR Chess Federation, for more than a quarter of a century the Soviet Chess Organization had created for Korchnoi, as well as for other grandmasters, favourable conditions for the displaying of his talents, perfecting of his mastery, and the achieving of good results. Regarding his participation in events, Korchnoi travelled on numerous occasions to various countries of the world, and in the last few years alone had played in Great Britain, USA, West Germany, France, Spain, Yugoslavia...

Korchnoi's assertion that certain official organs or persons supposedly prevented him from winning, are simply ludicrous. In the history of the World Championship he is not the first player to resort to such dishonourable explanations as being the reason for his defeat.

Korchnoi's morbid pride, inordinate vanity, and self-assurance in his relations with his colleagues and opponents at the chess board were well-known, and were frequently pointed out to him. Each time Korchnoi repented, and promised to draw the necessary conclusions. During the Final Candidates' Match he made unjustified appeals, was rude both to the controller and his opponent, and after his defeat, in bitter and irresponsible interviews to the foreign press, spoke disrespectfully about the winner, and did everything possible to disparage his play and result of the event as a whole.

Such behaviour on the part of Korchnoi was unanimously condemned by the sporting public and by chess fans. In a letter to the paper "*Soviet Sport*" Korchnoi admitted that he was in the wrong, and apologized to his opponent. But, as we now know, this further 'confession' was merely the mask of an embittered individualist.

The USSR Chess Federation came to the following decision: for actions, unworthy of a Soviet sportsman, Korchnoi was disqualified and deprived of his titles of Honoured Master of Sport, Grandmaster and Master of Sport of the USSR.

This decision by the USSR Chess Federation was fully approved by more than thirty Soviet grandmasters, who in their letter to "*Soviet Sport*" wrote in particular:

"On meeting Korchnoi at the chess board, many of us encountered on several occasions his displays of conceit and tactlessness. Korchnoi was forgiven a great deal, his morbid vanity was tolerated, but this tolerance was evidently taken as a right. Now, after seeking protection with the Dutch Police from his imaginary pursuers, Korchnoi is attempting to raise his petty individual grievances to the level of international problems".

World Champion Anatoly Karpov also appeared in print:

"I am deeply surprised and distressed by the decision of Korchnoi to leave his motherland. I am surprised because, contrary to Korchnoi's present-day assertions, there were not, and could not have been, any hindrances to his chess playing in a country to which he owes everything, and which enabled him to fully reveal his talent.

On the contrary, it is known to everyone that for him, as for all Soviet sportsmen, conditions have been created, the like of which our colleagues in the West can merely dream about. To argue to the contrary is dishonest and dishonourable.

I am distressed, because the step taken by Korchnoi places in jeopardy his whole future career as a chess player.

Sharing the indignation of the Soviet public at Korchnoi's unworthy behaviour, I support the decision of the USSR Chess Federation to deprive him of his sports titles, and of the right to represent the Soviet Chess School in the World arena".

Thus after receiving a reprimand from the USSR Sports Committee, and being punished for his blatant tactlessness, although for which, incidentally, he was fairly soon forgiven, Korchnoi decided not to return to his motherland. At first this seemed improbable... The chess grandmaster had taken offence at criticism, and at the close supervision to which he was subjected, and this was sufficient to provoke such a fearful act on the part of a Party Member of ten years' standing?! Explanations were sought in the incredible impulsiveness which in general characterizes a number of Korchnoi's decisions. But then it became more and more clear that the ways of the grandmaster and of his Soviet colleagues had parted irrevocably. It was then that the declarations given above appeared in our press.

On finding himself in a situation where he was altogether unrestrained, Korchnoi began painting all and everything black. Anti-Soviet people on the fringe of chess skilfully assisted the development of the more unpleasant qualities in the emigrant's character. The "Salieri Complex" progressed, and Korchnoi declared war not only on his former compatriots. Roughly a year later the Yugoslav newspaper "*Sportske Novosti*", which is published in Zagreb, printed an article entitled "Korchnoi's book already has its opponents". In the article, it was stated that during an appearance at Zagreb University, the Danish grandmaster Bent Larsen had sharply criticized Korchnoi's autobiography, which had been published in Holland. In Larsen's words: "Certain people, who have involuntarily become actors in the performance staged by Korchnoi, are indignant at the rôles which he forces them to play, and at the script which he puts into their mouths". In this respect Larsen referred in particular to the highly talented young Dutch grandmaster Jan Timman. To the question as to what impression Korchnoi's book had made on him personally, Larsen replied: "It is by no means one of those books which one reads with keen interest, and therefore I limited myself to a cursory glance at it. I have to say that one thing which I found most repugnant was the attack made by Korchnoi on Mikhail Tal, which can only be called idiotic. However, everyone is perfectly well aware that Korchnoi 'crammed' into his book as many 'sensations' as possible, for the sake of money".

Unfortunately, competitive life is such that sometimes you have to sit down at the chess board against someone, with whom in normal life you would not want to shake hands...

But let us return to the end of 1974, and after the Karpov–Korchnoi match let us find out:

WHAT THE EX-WORLD CHAMPIONS HAD TO SAY

Max Euwe

"The Final Match just concluded was without doubt an encounter worthy of those seeking the title of World Champion. It took the course of a difficult, exhausting struggle. The match was interesting, in my opinion, in the sense of a psychological duel between two very evenly-matched opponents".

Mikhail Botvinnik

"Korchnoi probably displayed his maximum creative potential; Karpov has everything to look forward to".

Boris Spassky

(in the end he nevertheless broke his "vow of silence", and said a few words)

"This was Anatoly Karpov's cycle. All his matches—against Polugayevsky, against me, and against Korchnoi—he won well. At the present moment Karpov is objectively without doubt the strongest player.

In its duration the Final Karpov–Korchnoi Match was equivalent to previous matches for the World Championship. Karpov's play was, so to speak, technically powerful; he did not fully disclose his creative potential. Such a strategical plan appears to me to have been the correct one. It has to be borne in mind that it was Karpov who was the first to have to endure the increased strain of the new regulations for the selecting of the challenger."[*]

Tigran Petrosian

"I have taken part in many Candidates' events. I have also played matches for the World Championship. The experts and the players are normally of the opinion thatesuch high-level events do not justify the creative hopes expected of them. I think that one can make the following comparison: in studying and improving himself a player as it were accumulates capital, but when it comes to an event towards the World Championship, he only uses up this capital. There is nothing surprising about this. Everything is subordinated to one aim—that of attaining victory.

Someone said that the Karpov–Korchnoi match did not live up to its hopes in the creative sense, and was uninteresting. But this is a superficial point of view. There were a number of excellent games in the match. For instance, irrespective of whether Karpov found the variation at the board or whether it was the fruits of home analysis, the idea of the attack which he carried out in the second game, in the Dragon Variation, with its sacrifices on the fifth rank, could serve as a creative rehabilitation of the entire match. And to demand from grand-masters who are fighting for the World Championship that their games should be only creative discoveries, is unjust".

[*] The maximum number of games that might be played by a Candidate reaching the Final was increased from 32 in 1971 to 60 in 1974. (K.P.N.)

Mikhail Tal

"To me it seems incorrect to talk only about the results of the last match. The picture will be more complete if we examine the whole cycle of Candidates' Matches.

Against Polugayevsky we saw, despite his youth, a mature psychologist, able to subtly exploit the human weaknesses in his opponent's character. Knowing that his opponent, when he has a considerable advantage, is normally afraid to shed even the smallest part of it, he played so as to force the experienced grandmaster to shed it all. Knowing Polugayevsky's desire, in spite of everything, to demonstrate the irreproachable nature of his conceptions, he utilized this obstinacy to his own advantage.

Against Spassky we saw a really inspired player, equally formidable in attack and tenacious in defence. Chess-wise, the most impressive of Karpov's matches was the one against Spassky. True, the Ex-World Champion was not in form, and played no better than against Fischer (but probably also no worse!), but equally, Karpov's victory over him was no less convincing than Fischer's victory. While in the Match for the World Championship it was in the eleventh game that Spassky gained his second win (in the second game Fischer was defaulted for his failure to appear), by the eleventh game of his match with Karpov it was altogether all over.

Against Korchnoi this was no boy, but a man, able to endure an encounter which for its competitive intensity was unparalleled.

All the time Karpov is progressing, and is still far from his peak. I have no doubt that by the time of his match with Fischer he will be even stronger".

REARRANGEMENT OF THE COMPONENTS DOES NOT CHANGE THE SUM...

In the Final Match there were few tactical sacrifices or beautiful combinations, and it is these that normally delight large numbers of fans. The match was a competitive one. Korchnoi said that in the creative sense the match was a failure, and from this foreshortened point of view the winner appeared unconvincing. And indeed one frequently heard it said that Karpov had no real justification for being happy about "such" a win over Korchnoi, that the score was by no means crushing, and what about the quality of the games... Karpov was indeed not satisfied with the final result, and he himself said so. But the most surprising thing is that he was perfectly satisfied with the qualitative, creative side of the match, in which, in Karpov's opinion, there were fewer mistakes than in previous events at a similar level. Voices will be heard saying: there it is, complacency! But we will try to explain how this should be understood...

The reader may recall that after the Candidates' Semi-Final Matches were finished, Mikhail Tal remarked: "Karpov's opening repertoire is trained, like the voice of a good singer. And he looks after it". Now let us use this observation as an unusual epigraph to the following discussion...

On Karpov's own admission, it was only after reaching the Final Candidates' Match that he believed that he would emerge as Fischer's challenger. Before that he assumed that somewhere he was nevertheless bound to stumble, that somewhere he would be lacking in something —knowledge, experience, fortune... He had declared for all to hear: "this is not my cycle". (Many took this declaration to be a clever move, a "double insurance", which would allow him to play calmly and unhampered, but the young grandmaster was not pretending). In the Semi-Final Karpov came up against Spassky. The Ex-World Champion looked past his opponent —the blinkers which the thirst for revenge had placed on him allowed Spassky to see only Fischer. Neither he himself, nor the majority of the experts, expected to see Karpov as the winner at this stage, and Spassky lost his head. But how brilliantly Karpov played! "I was tremendously impressed...", "On the whole it is rather difficult to surprise me, but Anatoly did this..."—such were the assessments put forward by Tal at that time regarding Karpov's play. This was the admiration of a grandmaster whose depth of aesthetic feeling is second to none, and whom no one has ever reproached as having an uncreative approach to chess. Karpov defeated Spassky perhaps even more convincingly than Fischer had done so in 1972 in Reykjavik.

And now let us again go with Karpov along the second and third stages of the Final Match, and imagine this transition as he himself represents it: attempts to overcome the opponent by only technical means, tiredness setting in... And at the same time, with the score at 2–0 and 3–0 in Karpov's favour, let us switch on Tal's tape recording: "...trained, like the voice of a good singer. And he looks after it". And let us glance forward with the eyes of Karpov, who is afraid of "draughts" that might affect his voice, since the most difficult song lies ahead —ahead lies Fischer. This is not a justification for the tactics chosen by Karpov, but an elementary explanation of them.

Since we have already allowed ourselves so many conventionalities, we will permit ourselves one more. Suppose we exchange the points in time occupied by Karpov's matches against Korchnoi and Spassky. Since it is well-known that Karpov is constantly improving with time, in our conventional rearrangement there is nothing "illegal" (the sum has not changed!). After this logical operation let the sceptics, who have safeguarded themselves against the possibility of Karpov losing to Fischer, once again assess Karpov's creative potential.

CHAPTER 5

The Challenger Becomes Champion

"...Karpov has on his side the advantages of youth and an uninterrupted series of successes. Fischer, who is accustomed to the rôle of "child prodigy", feels psychologically rather uncomfortable in encounters with younger and ambitious opponents, who are afraid of nothing and no one".

(Messaggero, Rome)

Another one to assess Karpov's prospects quite highly was the chess correspondent of the London *Times*, international master Harry Golombek:

"Before the start of the cycle I thought that Fischer would defeat any of the eight Candidates, but now, bearing in mind Karpov's ability to improve constantly, and his skill in learning from his acquired experience, I am inclined to assess the chances of the participants in the 1975 World Championship Match (if, of course, such a match should take place) as roughly equal. But if I was nevertheless forced to choose a favourite, my choice would probably fall on Karpov".

It will be noted that Harry Golombek makes the proviso: if the match between Fischer and Karpov should take place. The point was that the FIDE Congress in Nice had not accepted all Fischer's demands regarding the revision of the World Championship Match regulations. When the Champion was denied an advantage of two points before the start of the match, he relieved himself "by telegram" of his distinguished title.

And so, there was a winner of the Candidates' Cycle—Anatoly Karpov, and there was Robert Fischer's unequivocal declaration by telegram to the Congress in Nice: "I divest myself of the title of FIDE World Champion". These were the facts. The question then was: who was the new World Champion?

If one follows the laws of formal logic, the answer is simple—Anatoly Karpov, the first pretender. But life does not always fit into syllogistic figures. Before everything was to reach its logical conclusion, numerous discussion drafts would be torn up, much ink would be shed, dozens of verbal waterfalls would be heard, and the most experienced chess diplomats would make the most complex underhand moves. We should not blame anyone severely for this. Forgetting for the moment the personal motives of some of the inspirers of that "historic boom", we will admit: the chess world was living in anticipation of a duel between two outstanding masters, and was hoping to witness a titanic struggle.

This hope was fated not to be realized. But the conscience of one of the two heroes of the unrealized match was clear: Karpov did everything possible to enable the match to take place.

You may recall that by no means all the points in the regulations adopted by the Congress in Nice seemed sensible to Karpov, but nevertheless he agreed to them. During the closing ceremony of the Final Match, he had this to say, addressing himself to the FIDE President:

"I should like to take advantage of the courteous attention you have paid our match by your presence here, to appeal to you, and in your person to the whole chess world. Before finding myself here in this highly esteemed rôle, I played sixty games in elimination events. These were the Interzonal Tournament, and the three Candidates' Matches against the top players of the time. In my opinion this is an extremely severe test, to which the strongest grandmasters in the world are quite unjustly subjected, especially since all sixty games were played during an incredibly short period.

During the course of the present three-year cycle, the regulations for the World Championship Match have already been changed, a fact which has undoubtedly provoked regret. But I would like to express the hope that, in the coming match with the World Champion Robert James Fischer, everything will be subordinated to the interests of chess."

Euwe was asked what he would do, if on the expiry of the stipulated time Fischer had not accepted the Pretender's challenge. The FIDE President replied:

"If by 1st April 1975 Fischer does not announce that he is accepting the challenge, I will interrupt my three-month tour of African countries, which is planned for the Spring, and will fly to Moscow to proclaim Karpov the twelfth Champion of the World".

...One must give Ed Edmondson his due. Perhaps, as he intended, he did indeed pray after the Congress in Nice that the chess crown would be retained by his country. But not all his time and effort was given over to prayer. He also had sufficient to become the initiator of a new, extraordinary Congress, and to recruit new followers in support of Fischer's demands.

Once again the chess world sank into a period of anxious waiting. But this time not for long. The first extraordinary Congress in the history of the FIDE was fixed for 17th March in Holland. On the agenda was one and the same question—the regulations for the World Championship Match (a match of which one of the participants was as before maintaining a deathly silence). Before the Congress began its business, Max Euwe was handed an open letter from Mikhail Botvinnik, of which the following were the most important points:

"Dear Professor, you and I are the last Mohicans from the tribe of Champions which was active in the first half of this century, and it is doubtful whether anyone understands better than we do the dangers now threatening the chess world...

I once happened to read the story by Mark Twain about the unfortunate bridegroom, who on the eve of his wedding invariably suffered an injury, which each time involved an amputation. Here a philosophical question arises: how much of a cripple should a man become before his fiancée (who loves him very dearly) finally refuses to marry him? In similar fashion one can ask: how many years should a Champion (for whose talent everyone has a high regard) not appear in any events, before the chess world finally realizes that general interests far outweigh any egotistical ones?

Formerly, when we sat opposite each other at the chess board, Professor, I was sometimes thrown into confusion by your unexpected moves. I hope that now too you will find a move which will meet with the approval of the chess world, and will regain for you the sympathy and confidence both of your colleagues, and of chess fans (including both Soviet, and American). In this just cause you can always count on the assistance of your old friend.

M. BOTVINNIK"

The Wijk aan Zee Congress, which was less representative than the one in Nice, abolished by a small majority the limitation on the number of games in the match for the World Championship, and by an equally small majority refused Fischer the last of his demands—that he should receive an advantage of two points even before the start of the event. It is characteristic that almost all the major and most influential chess federations, which number among their ranks the overwhelming majority of international grandmasters and masters, voted to reject the 'Fischer corrections'. Thus of the federations of the sixteen countries which made up the top group in the 21st Olympiad, only three—USA, Philippines and Wales—voted for the corrections; all the remainder were against.

As can be seen, although Edmondson did not achieve a hundred per cent success, his work was nevertheless not in vain. He exploited the imperfections in the structure of the FIDE to the utmost.

"We are all one family" is a splendid motto, but nothing should be taken to absurd lengths, otherwise it may threaten to turn into its antithesis. At the Wijk aan Zee Congress the lady delegate from the Virgin Islands was asked how many organised chess players she represented. It turned out to be sixty. This lady had two votes, since part of the islands belong to the English, and part to the Americans. In the USSR there are several million players and forty grandmasters, but our delegation had only one vote.

At all events, the resolution adopted by the Congress ran: "The winner of the match for the World Championship will be the first player to win ten games, the total number of games to be unlimited".

Holding its breath, the chess world followed the development of events before, during, and after the Congress. Into the orbit of chess passions—or more accurately, the fringes of chess—were drawn thousands of people, who not long before had been quite indifferent to the fate of the game. What can be said about the interested persons?

What was Anatoly Karpov doing, what was he saying, and about what was he thinking?

At the most tense moment he sensibly decided to rest his nerves, so he left Moscow and went and "hid" with his parents in Tula. There he was unexpectedly torn away from his favourite hobby—sorting out his enormous stamp collection—by the protracted ringing of the telephone.

"They've even found me here", said Karpov in annoyance, and then, covering the receiver with his hand and shrugging his shoulders in perplexity, he whispered:

"Belgrade. Who can this be?"

It was the Yugoslav grandmaster Svetozar Gligorić who had phoned, and Anatoly Karpov was heard to reply firmly to him: "I very much want to play the match, but I am not sure that this strong desire is shared by Fischer".

In 1972 a similar "Gligorić telephone mission", linking Fischer with Spassky, proved successful—then the American grandmaster evidently believed that he would win, and the match took place. But this time Fischer remained silent.

In this situation, which without exaggeration can be termed unique, Karpov, true to himself, did not once lose his head. He—and this was known to all—was against a match to ten wins without an unlimited number of games:

"I don't understand why Fischer is so keen to increase the number of games—clearly he is confident about his excellent physical condition. If he and I were to go out onto a wrestling mat, he would no doubt win, but whose chess endurance will prove to be the greater still has to be seen".

And he accepted the decision of the extraordinary congress to abolish the limit on the total number of games in the match.

Well, and wasn't he afraid of Fischer? How did he assess his own chances? Karpov's assessments convey the maturity of a man who knows his own worth:

"In my opinion, for a long time we underestimated Fischer, and said, just wait—when he comes up in a match against a real Soviet grandmaster, everything will be put in its place—Fischer will be beaten without fail. We then went to the opposite extreme. Even our strongest grandmasters would sometimes make statements to the effect that it would be a hopeless matter to try to defeat the World Champion, and they would merely estimate the score by which they would lose a match against Fischer. I am convinced that the truth lies somewhere in the middle. Against the present World Champion, as against any player, even the most outstanding, it is possible to put up a not unsuccessful fight. But only with genuine, all-round preparation. It is realized that this does not give any guarantee of victory, but it is essential to guarantee full mobilization of all one's powers".

It is strange, but true, that throughout this period of feverish activity the most interested person also remained the most calm and imperturbable. And the most practical. Karpov said:

"Well, the match with Fischer may not in fact take place. But all the same I will make very thorough preparations. Whatever happens this work will not be in vain. The study of Fischer's games will most likely enable me to improve and enrich my play".

"But are you nevertheless nervous?"

"What point is there in being nervous now? I had reason to be worried when the extraordinary congress had not yet been held, and I thought that absolutely all of Fischer's demands might be adopted there. If this had happened, I decided with myself, I would then simply not have had the moral right to play the match. But when I learned that the Congress had not proceeded at Fischer's bidding, I calmed down instantly. It was then clear that either the match would take place, or else I was immediately Champion of the World. What was there to worry about?"

Karpov spent the last few days of March at the training base on the outskirts of Moscow together with the USSR Ice-Hockey Team. After dispatching a telegram to the FIDE headquarters, he went off to look for the Ice-Hockey forward Vladimir Vikulov: before his departure Karpov had lost to him at billiards, and now, true to himself, he was seeking revenge. Only after satisfying his self-esteem did he join the rest who had gathered in the hall around a radio set: his trainer Semion Furman and the other ice-hockey players were awaiting the latest news—it was now the night of 1st April, and everyone was afraid of missing the announcement proclaiming the new World Champion. But there was no chess news...

Early next morning the Ice-Hockey Team were to fly off to their championship, and the players and Karpov began taking their leave, wishing each other good luck. Before going to bed, Anatoly breathed a sigh of relief:

"Well, all right, the waiting is over—tomorrow everything will be clear and settled".

He was wrong by one day.

Euwe deferred proclaiming the new World Champion until 3rd April, still hoping to hear from Fischer. But the latter refused to sit down at the board without first receiving a start of two points.

It is significant that the leading grandmasters in the world—Hort, Ivkov, Larsen, Matanović, Najdorf, Petrosian, Tal, Uhlmann, and many others—fully supported Karpov's position, whereas no one expressed support for Fischer's claims.

Miguel Najdorf: "Although he is an outstanding player, I think that even if the condition were accepted whereby with the score at 9–9 he remains World Champion, Fischer would all the same find a pretext for not playing".

Bent Larsen: "If Fischer wishes to leave the chess stage, he is free to do so, and others are free to express their assumptions as to the reasons for such a decision".

"It was not Karpov, but Fischer, who avoided the encounter. Karpov, on the other hand, demonstrated on more than one occasion his readiness to make a compromise for the sake of saving the match. The one thing that he was unable to do was to forcibly sit Fischer down at the board". (The Newspaper *Hörzu*, Hamburg)

"Anatoly Karpov", wrote the London *Times*, "is now the most worthy holder of the title of Champion".

From the Danish newspaper *Aktuelt*: "Of course, we all awaited with impatience the Fischer–Karpov match, but further attempts to 'save' the match at the cost of essentially allowing Fischer 'carte-blanche' would not only not have assisted the achievement of the aim, but would also have inevitably threatened the unity and integrity of the world chess movement".

The Belgian *La Cité* remarked wittily: "Fischer is sometimes compared with his great compatriot Paul Morphy. However, in at least one respect they are antipodes. Morphy, after demonstrating his superiority over his contemporaries, announced that he did not intend playing any more, without giving odds. Fischer, on the other hand, has let it be understood that he does not intend playing anyone, unless he receives odds".

And what is there to say if the World Champion's compatriots and former seconds, grandmasters William Lombardy, Robert Byrne, and Larry Evans, considered his demands to be unjust!

On 3rd April the International Chess Federation proclaimed Soviet grandmaster Anatoly Karpov the twelfth World Champion in the history of chess.

On 24th April 1975, in the Hall of Columns in Trade Union House, the official ceremony took place, as has already been described at the very beginning of this book. In his speech the FIDE President Dr Max Euwe said, among other things:

"I admire the composure of the new World Champion Anatoly Karpov, and the competitive qualities and the deep sense of respect which he has displayed throughout the time, almost a whole year, that this matter has lasted.

In the rules adopted in Nice, many of Fischer's wishes were granted, in particular that the match should be up to ten wins—an innovation which was not in the Challenger's favour. Karpov accepted it. In March of this year the Extraordinary Assembly once again met Fischer's demands, by abolishing the limit on the number of games. Karpov, being guided by the best competitive considerations, agreed to this also.

But, as you know, the Assembly rejected Fischer's last demand (the advantage of two points). With the final date for Fischer's reply drawing close, his friends did everything possible to try to persuade him to play, but without success. Fischer kept silent, and when this final date passed, a new World Champion was proclaimed. Anatoly Karpov, together with chess enthusiasts throughout the world, may regret that the match did not take place, and that he was unable to demonstrate in a competitive battle his right to the title, but Fischer had every opportunity to defend his crown. Both the venue for the match, and the controller, were chosen in accordance with his wishes. Fischer's obstinacy, or some other features of his character, which I, like many others, am unable to understand, prevented him from utilizing his right, and from fulfilling his duty to the chess world.

As regards Karpov, of this we are confident: he will be a worthy Champion, and will on many occasions demonstrate his strength in various events".

And these were Anatoly Karpov's words:

"...I am happy that the supreme chess title, or, as it is generally called, the 'chess crown', has returned to our country, which is rich in historical chess traditions, and is known worldwide for the depth of its chess culture. It was these traditions of the Soviet Chess School, which have been promoted by a whole series of World Champions, both male and female, that enabled me in a comparatively short time to acquire my chess mastery, and to achieve success in conditions of rivalry, more intense than ever before, between many top grandmasters.

...Of course, I realize perfectly well that my personal contribution to the treasury of world chess has been insignificant, perhaps for the reason that the number of years I have lived has not sufficed for more. The title of World Champion imposes on its bearer a high degree of responsibility, and great obligations. I will make every effort to fulfil them worthily. I am ready to collaborate with the FIDE as regards strengthening its unity and authority, and in the further development and propagation of chess in my own country and throughout the whole world.

I consider that one of the chief obligations of the World Champion is to be an active player, so that people of different countries can see the Champion at the chess board, and so that grandmasters and masters can measure their strength against his, and learn from him, and also teach him something. For this reason I firmly intend to appear systematically in USSR and international events".

Also of interest is the World Champion's point of view, expressed in less official circumstances:

"Fischer found himself in an unfavourable psychological situation. For him it would have been simpler to meet any one of his former opponents—since he had already defeated everyone apart from me, and they were all older than him, which is also significant. But as it was, everything turned out to be more complicated. We had never met at the board—we had never played in the same tournament, but had somehow missed each other. This meant that nowhere had he defeated me or finished ahead of me. I emerged on the world arena just at the time when he stopped playing in tournaments. There had been the 'Fischer years', but then it was I who began producing the best results, as I began winning tournament after tournament. This could not fail to make an impression, and the chess world became divided. Especially since fans are impressed by youth, and I am eight years younger than Fischer. This situation made a painful impression on Fischer. After all, he is accustomed to having everyone for him, and everyone supporting him. And perhaps it was this 'change of climate' that he was unable to cope with.

I don't know whose chess following was the larger, mine or his, but the general predictions were unfavourable for me. Fischer was bound to win—this was considered virtually an axiom. But I thought that I too had chances of winning. What they were in specific terms, I did not bother to assess, I simply decided that I had chances. And each day I improved them by working.

For my preparations for the match with Fischer, I had a great deal of material at hand. And I made a fairly good study of Fischer, if only in an indirect sense. I am talking not only about the purely chess side of the matter—in this respect the great American grandmaster had every right to be called the strongest. But a careful study of all the details of his previous matches showed that his thunderous victories by such impressive scores were the result not only of his chess superiority, but also of the psychological pressure which he exerted on his opponents. He constantly created a terribly nervy atmosphere, both before play, and during it, with his protests and demands... Apart from his marvellous works of chess art, Fischer also introduced into the chess world such commotion and confusion, that suddenly diplomats, orators and lawyers became required... Formerly players had been quite capable of agreeing amongst themselves, but now this became practically impossible, since now it became necessary to argue about what used to be such simple and obvious truths. I think, however, that much of this 'eccentricity' stemmed not from Fischer himself, but from his surroundings. It is quite possible that he rarely suspected what kind of a background was created by his entourage, or how purposefully and skilfully they worked on the nerves of his opponents, so as to distract them from the struggle on the chess board itself.

But whoever this stemmed from—I was prepared for this too.

The match itself promised to be interesting. I was intending to demonstrate in it everything of which I am capable, and I very much regret that it did not take place. It is difficult to overestimate what its significance for chess could have been. It could have produced a new explosion in the chess world, and the popularity of the game could have grown even more. True, with one proviso: that the match did not drag out. And there was a possibility of this happening—and an extremely drawn-out match threatened to cause harm to chess. Any big sporting event has a certain definite public appeal, the scale of which must be assessed in realistic terms. Thus no match is able to maintain interest in itself (I am not now talking about anything more than holding the public in suspense) over a period of six months. It must after all be possible to see the end: this lends perspective, and the approach of the finish promotes the excitation of emotions.

It is a great pity that the match did not take place. But this was not my fault, since there exist principles from which I am unable to deviate. But Fischer—and in this respect the fault was entirely his—proved to be sort of person who would not restrict himself to partial gains, but, if you will excuse me the sharp words, wanted to obtain things altogether unscrupulously. What did this lead to? After all, as it was practically all of his demands had been conceded. Who knows what further demands he would have put forward if his wishes had continued to be granted.

Since I was very keen to play this match and did nothing to prevent it, when I was proclaimed Champion I immediately announced that as before I was prepared to play Fischer. Naturally, not under conditions dictated by him, but under the most sensible conditions—ones which would be favourable to the holding of such a match, and would enable us both to demonstrate the best that we have in our chess arsenals. So that it would be really chess, and not a battle of endurance. I was prepared to meet Fischer personally, but received no answer to my telegram..."

CHAPTER 6

After the Match that Never Was

"As soon as it became clear that the match with Fischer was not going to take place, I decided that it wouldn't be a bad idea to play some chess. It is true that this represented a breaking of tradition. All my predecessors, on the threshold of becoming Champion, had promised not to curtail their appearances in tournaments, but on achieving their goal had not kept their word. It was as if they had promised to wait for three years—this being the period between matches for the World Championship. But I found myself in a special situation. The match with Fischer had not been held, but the inertia and the pre-match tension were enormous. I had to play, if only for prophylactic reasons—so as to 'let off steam'. And it wouldn't do any harm to test my preparations. I was in form, full of strength, and self-confident—so why indeed shouldn't I play?

I am sometimes asked whether I would have been so disposed if the match with Fischer had nevertheless taken place. The answer is no, of course I wouldn't! Grandmasters who have gone through this experience reckon that such a match takes several years off one's life. And these are no empty words. Without delving far back into history, it may be recalled how seriously the strain told on the participants in the match in Reykjavik. For some two years after this, Spassky was unrecognizable; only a shadow remained of the formerly self-confident fighter. And Fischer, possibly, has been engaged in regaining his strength... How would such a strain have affected me? I knew what was awaiting me, and I had prepared for it; I would certainly have been unable to return immediately to chess (especially if the match had dragged out), but in time I would without fail have done so. It is implied that this would have been as Champion—otherwise the reasoning loses its point.

After the lengthy and exhausting waiting for the match, I found it necessary to give myself a psychological break, if only a short one, so as to become accustomed to my new position, to take my bearings, and to calm myself.

My yearly norm corresponds to four or five tournaments. I wouldn't advise others to go by this, since each player has his own norm. For some, a condition for maintaining their form has to be constant participation in tournaments. But for me the criterion is my appetite for playing, and for chess."

On your marks! ✳ *Revenge in the first round* ✳ *Outsiders' tactics* ✳ *Inexhaustible possibilities of chess* ✳ *Yugoslav diary* ✳ *"Kar-pov! To-lya!"*

"And so, June arrived—time to go off to the Memorial Tournament for the eminent Yugoslav grandmaster Milan Vidmar, which was held in two towns, Portorož and Ljubljana. It was the first tournament I played in under my new title. Regarding the responsibility—there is no need to explain. And the atmosphere was far from easy; one might even say, psychologically difficult. On the one hand I was the lawful Champion, I had defeated the chess élite, and defeated them confidently enough... But I hadn't been able to demonstrate my superiority over the former Champion, and this had been Fischer, who for some personified a chess God. Here all words and explanations are hopeless. However much I said that it wasn't my fault, that I had done everything possible so that the match should take place (under reasonable conditions)—the words reached the minds of fans, but were not accepted by their hearts. But the fan is ruled by his heart, and so he stubbornly repeated: 'Even so, the match should have been held...' But did I ever want anything else?!

The ice could be melted, the alienation of a certain part of the chess public reversed, and general recognition won, by one thing alone—victories. Fresh victories..."

...In describing this, his first event as World Champion, we will glance at Anatoly Karpov's diary, or more accurately, the travel-notes which he made during his stay in Yugoslavia. From these cursory and rather fragmentary notes alone, the reader will be able to judge at what an intense and rapid tempo the life of a Soviet chess player proceeds during his foreign travels:

"Left Moscow at first light—on the very first plane. In Belgrade met by photographers and reporters. Accomodated in the 'Yugoslav', a new hotel on the banks of the Danube. A beautiful spot, but with one big drawback from the river—the pollution level of the water is many times higher than the established norm.

After a short rest we went to have breakfast with the Soviet Ambassador. He is a very likeable person, our Ambassador, and from him we learned a mass of useful and interesting information. And it was particularly pleasant for me to hear that in Yugoslavia I had many supporters, who called me simply 'Tolya'.

During the day we met the staff of a large printing organization (some two thousand people work in its printing works and publishing house), which publishes, in particular, the highly popular magazine '*Duga*'. We were then taken to a football match between Yugoslavia and Holland. The Dutch did not manage to field their strongest side—Cruyff did not play, and there were altogether only three of the squad which played in Munich. To the indescribable joy of their supporters, the Yugoslavs won 3-0.

On the same day, 31st May, we flew on to Ljubljana, where we were met by the President of the Slovenian Chess Federation, a kindly, respected man. During the war he had been in a concentration camp, and after the victory had worked as one of the advisers to the Head of the Republic. He was now retired, but was doing a great deal for chess, and was one of the organizers of the present international tournament.

The trip to Portorož took little more than an hour, so that by eleven o'clock in the evening we were already in the restaurant, where we were met by a terrible din—the last day of a television festival was coming to an end. Here this is a normal happening, since after all it is a well-known resort.

On the following day—a couple of interviews for radio and television, and then the drawing of lots. In the first round I was drawn straight away against Portisch, with White. Furman had noticed that he played the Slav Defence with a particular order of moves..."

Later, Semion Furman—not only trainer to the World Champion, but also a competitor in this same tournament—said smilingly:

"Portisch couldn't even understand where he had gone wrong. All the time he thought that everything was in order, but our assessment proved to be deeper and more accurate".

The testimony of grandmaster Ljubomir Ljubojević is also characteristic:

"Karpov conducted this game splendidly. At first I found some of his moves not altogether understandable, and only after careful analysis did I discover their hidden strength. Karpov defeated Portisch in grand style".

And here is an admission by Karpov himself:

"Naturally, when I sat down at the board I set myself the task of simply playing chess, and not of gaining revenge at all costs. But of course I hadn't forgotten that Portisch was one of the few remaining grandmasters who had inflicted an 'unanswered' defeat on me. (That defeat in 1972 at San Antonio cost me clear first place, and forced me to settle for a share of it.)"

Besides the players we have already named, Karpov, Furman, Portisch and Ljubojević, there were other strong grandmasters competing in the tournament: the Yugoslavs Gligorić, Velimirović and Parma, the Hungarian Ribli, Hort from Czechoslovakia... But it was by no means only they who presented a danger to the Champion in individual, 'personal' encounters.

"Yes", Karpov remarks, "here for the first time I sensed how complicated and difficult it is—both psychologically and physically—to play under the supreme title. Everyone knows the saying which with time and with use has become accepted: against the Champion everyone plays with particular enthusiasm. With constant repetition it does not become any less true. It is understandable that for a rival it is both honourable and, from the practical tournament point of view, valuable to score a point against the Champion. But as for the outsiders—they are doubly dangerous. A player who has begun a tournament badly, and has lost all hope of a respectable place in it, begins to play dispiritedly. Only not against me! He is ready to give up all the few points he has gained earlier on, for one alone—taken from the World Champion. For this point the unsuccessful player will sacrifice everything—for him it is virtually the only way of rehabilitating himself at a single stroke after all his previous omissions".

It is true that the tactics chosen by Karpov's relatively little-known opponents were not particularly diverse. At an early stage of the game the majority of them made a sacrifice (usually of a pawn), so as to attempt to take the game away from normal channels. When one comes to study these games, the gambit play of the World Champion's opponents does not appear to be very well-founded, but such an opinion is merely reached afterwards, under the impression of the convincing and simple way in which their plans are refuted.

Karpov–Barle
King's Indian Defence

1 P–QB4 N–KB3 2 N–QB3 P–KN3 3 P–K4 P–Q3 4 P–Q4 B–N2 5 P–B3 0–0 6 B–K3 (Diag.)

6 ... P–B4 7 P×P P×P 8 Q×Q R×Q 9 B×P N–B3 10 N–Q5 N×N 11 BP×N B×P 12 R–N1 B–B6+ 13 K–B2 P–N3 14 B–R3 N–K4 15 N–K2 B–Q7 16 B×P R–K1 17 B–B6 N–Q6+ 18 K–N3 B–Q2 19 R–Q1 B–K8+ 20 R×B N×R 21 N–Q4 QR–B1 22 B–QN5 B×B 23 N×B R–B8 24 P–Q6 Resigns

Karpov–S. Garcia
Sicilian Defence

1 P–K4 P–QB4 2 N–KB3 N–QB3 3 P–Q4
P×P 4 N×P P–KN3 5 N–QB3 B–N2
6 B–K3 N–B3 7 B–QB4 0–0 8 B–N3 P–Q3
9 P–B3 B–Q2 10 Q–Q2 Q–R4 11 P–KR4
KR–B1 12 0–0–0 N–K4 13 K–N1

13 ... P–QN4 14 N(3)×P Q–R3 15 N–B3
N–B5 16 Q–Q3 QR–N1 17 B–B1 R–N5
18 P–R5 Q–N2 19 P×P RP×P 20 B–R6
B×B 21 R×B K–N2 22 QR–R1 Q–N3 23
N(4)–K2 P–K3 24 P–N4 K–B1 25 R–R8+
K–K2 26 R×R N–K4 27 Q–Q1 B×R 28
P–N5 N(3)–Q2 29 P–R3 R×B 30 P×R
N×P 31 N–B4 Q–B7 32 N×NP+ P×N
33 R–R7+ K–Q1 34 Q×P Q–Q5 35 Q–K7+
Resigns

Karpov–Velimirović
Sicilian Defence

1 P–K4 P–QB4 2 N–KB3 P–Q3 3 P–Q4
P×P 4 N×P N–KB3 5 N–QB3 P–KN3
6 B–K3 B–N2 7 P–B3 0–0 8 Q–Q2 N–B3
9 B–QB4 B–Q2 10 0–0–0 Q–N1 11 B–N3
P–QR4 12 N(4)–N5

12 ... P–R5 13 B×RP R–B1 14 K–N1
N–QR4 15 B–N3 N–B5 16 Q–K2 N×B
17 Q×N R–B4 18 N–Q4 Q–R2 19 P–QR3
R–QR4 20 Q–Q2 N–K1 21 N–Q5 P–K3 22
N–N4 N–B2 23 P–B3 N–R3 24 N(Q4)–B2
N–B4 25 Q×P B–N4 26 B–R2 N–R5 27 Q–B7
B–K1 28 R–Q8 B–KB3 29 R×R Q×R 30
Q–KB4 Q–Q1 31 Q–K3 Q–B2 32 P–KB4 N–N3
33 P–K5 B–K2 34 N–Q4 N–B5 35 B×N
Q×B 36 R–Q1 B–QR5 37 Q–Q3 Q–B1 38
R–Q2 Q–B1 39 P–KN3 R–B4 40 Q–K4 R–B2
41 R–Q3 Q–B1 42 P–N4 B–Q2 43 N(N4)–B2
R–B4 44 Q–K1 Q–B2 45 P–KR4 P–R3 46
P–N5 P–R4 47 P–N4 R–B5 48 N–K3 R–B3
49 N×R B×N 50 R–Q4 **Resigns**

After the first half of the tournament, it moved from Portorož to Ljubljana. Leading was Karpov, with 6 points out of 8. At the new venue he immediately won a further two game', creating a big gap—and the battle for first place was decided. In second place, a point behinds came Gligorić. Only fatigue at the end of the tournament prevented the experienced Furman from finishing even higher that a share of third place with Ribli and Hort.

This is what Anatoly Karpov had to say at that time, in vindication of his basic assertion: "The possibilities of chess are endless".

"The art of chess is one of the best-studied manifestations of the human spirit. But here, as in other instances, a well-known rule is confirmed: the better you come to know the object of your study, the deeper you penetrate into its heart, and the greater the number of mysteries which you discover. And I sensed this very clearly at the last Olympiad, when twice I failed to gain an advantage from the opening with White, and twice I failed to equalize with Black. Such problems were encountered by Capablanca half a century ago, when opening theory was much less well worked out. For man, the possibilities in chess are boundless.

It is now more difficult than it was earlier to play successfully. Then there were a dozen players of extra-class, who were a head above all the others. Now the number of strong players has grown significantly, and to win even against an average master, maximum effort is required. But the demands which chess made on its players at the beginning of the century, and which it makes at the present time, are the same. In this respect nothing new has happened.

In order to reveal fully one's capabilities in chess, one must attain not only physical, but also intellectual maturity. Knowledge, artistry, and one's own creative creed—all this appears by the time one is approximately thirty. Nowadays it is not possible to study both chess and something else with an equal degree of success. But in order to display sufficient depth in one's purely chess thinking, one must also broaden one's general education. I study economics, and devote a considerable amount of time to improving myself in various spheres of knowledge. But my main thoughts are devoted to chess, and everything else is in the main of applicable significance.

What desires does a person experience when he succeeds in attaining his life's ambition? This question contains a very interesting paradox. How indeed do you create the psychological stimulus for further intensive efforts, if the main goal has been achieved? After all, to rest on one's laurels means to quickly go downhill. But in chess, for instance, competitive results are by no means everything. Of no less importance is the creative side of the matter, and here I am very far from the thought that I have achieved perfection".

Karpov's visit to Yugoslavia provoked enormous interest there, and he received numerous invitations from local chess organizations.

"I was intending to return home immediately after the tournament, so as to relax a little before the USSR Peoples' Spartakiad. But now I see that I will have to stay on for a few more days", the World Champion agreed.

Let us once again refer to the Karpov travel diary. Here are a few extracts:

"...The day began very early, at a half past four. We travelled quickly by car, but were nearly late arriving at Zagreb airport: the traffic was very heavy. The plane took us in 45 minutes to the town of Dubrovnik. Here we were met by grandmaster Čirič, against whom I drew in a simultaneous display during the European Junior Tournament in Gröningen in 1968. Now we looked round Dubrovnik together. A most beautiful place. An old fortress, narrow streets, something of a Turkish flavour, an enormous number of tourists, very hot. Some three hours later we went on further over mountainous and rocky terrain to the little town of Čapljina, where according to tradition, some two thousand years ago there was a 'bird capital'.

In this small town there are only six thousand inhabitants, but they managed to produce 25 fairly respectable participants in a simultaneous display against me, the same number against Furman, and some further 500 'observers'. (And before the start, some young musicians played two Russian folk songs in our honour, 'The Rowan-tree' and 'Kalinka'.) I was persuaded to accept a draw in the game with the director of the local confectionary factory, but after we had agreed the draw, the director kept on looking at the position—trying to find a win for me. Then he seriously asked me to analyse the position, and on being convinced that his position was hopeless, 'annulled' the result, and admitted defeat. I won there against a 12-year-old lad who not long before had beaten Gligorić in a simul; I beat him for educational reasons—so that he shouldn't become conceited.

Furman finished his display an hour later than I did, and then, together with a government representative, we went off to Počitel. This ancient Turkish fortress stands between Sarajevo and the sea in an exceptionally picturesque spot. Now there is a colony of artists there, who pay for their board and lodging with their paintings.

The following day we were at Mostar, where the main feature is an ancient hump-back bridge, 26 metres high. The river Neretva flows very swiftly here, and for the tourists, kids will jump into it from the bridge, 'for a fee'.

My simul here was again on 25 boards, and proved to be quite difficult (I lost 2 games, with 5 draws).

During the second half of the day we went to a partisan cemetery. A grandiose ensemble! During the war Mostar had its own partisan brigade, and several times practically the full brigade rested in the town, not fearing a raid. The partisans had excellent security, but nevertheless lost about a thousand men during those years.

In Sarajevo we were the guests of a publishing house which produces chess books. A crazy programme was arranged for us in the evening. Semion Furman gave a simul at a factory where buses and bicycles are made, while my main display was in a neighbouring town of miners and metallurgists at the sports festival of one of the major industrial enterprises. But first I had to travel with Furman to 'his' factory, and also play there on ten boards. Only then did I set off to 'my' festival, from where at one o'clock in the morning I returned tired, leaning on a souvenir walking-stick, made in the form of a miner's pick...

...We looked round one of the largest mosques in Yugoslavia. This happened to be on a Friday, when Muslims go to prayer. A crier stood on one of the top rings of a minaret, and, turning to each side in turn, called believers to the evening service. The floor of the mosque was completely covered in expensive carpets. The bare-footed Muslims pray sitting, always with their faces turned towards Mecca. The women do not normally take part in prayer, but if they do, they have definitely to take their place behind the men. The town of Sarajevo gained its name in Turkish times, from the caravanserai, as it served as a base for passing troops and transport. As regards denominations, it is heterogeneous: roughly 60 per cent of the inhabitants are Muslims, with the remainder Catholic or Orthodox believers. But what is curious is that there are no clashes on religious grounds.

The Turkish bazaar is a fascinating place, where one can buy practically everything, where in the direct presence of buyers the most diverse articles appear, and where before the eyes of the 'respectable public' are engraved plates, saucers and cups.

The simultaneous display was a prolonged one, because Furman and I each gave one at the same time. The point was that the organizers had arranged the tables rather awkwardly, making up an overall rectangle for Furman and myself: after making a move on each of the boards, it was necessary to walk 'idly' some 15–20 metres diagonally back to the first board. We still weren't finished after 3 hours, were late for the plane, and had to travel to Loznica by car.

We arrived in time for dinner, and were met by the local organizers, a representative of the Serbian Chess Federation (in Yugoslavia the Republic Federations are strong and highly independent), a second secretary from the USSR Embassy, and Soviet television staff, to whom straight after dinner I gave an interview for the programme 'Time' (what's more, the first time the equipment failed to function, and you can guess the mood I was in when it all had to be repeated).

The simultaneous display was staged in a large hall of the town's central cafe. What a fantastic reception! I had experienced the like of it, only perhaps after winning the Candidates' event, also during the 'coronation' in the Hall of Columns in Moscow, and then in Leningrad and Zlatoust. The participants and spectators gave a prolonged ovation, and chanted: 'Karpov! To-lya!'. We were presented with honorary medals of the town of Loznica.

Then I once again realized what is meant by the term micro-climate. We dined in an open-air restaurant, there was a slight breeze blowing, and it was very pleasant. But when we descended all of a few metres, into the park, we found the heat overpowering. Playing was difficult... At least one half of those who wanted to watch the display were locked outside—the large hall could not accommodate them all. Television used up the last resources of ventilation. It wasn't everyone who could stand it for long in such conditions—but in suit and tie I had to play for several hours. But even so I remained pleased with the evening...

The same Saturday we arrived in Belgrade at about midnight, and Sunday became for us a 'printing day': in the morning—an appearance in a journalists' editorial office, and then under the open sky in one of the central squares of the Capital—a simultaneous display for readers of the newspaper '*Evening News*'. It is difficult to overestimate the importance of such an event. Thousands of town people, strolling through the centre of Belgrade—and each, even if for only a moment, showed interest, looked at the boards, at the players, and finally at the World Champion. And, perhaps, on that day the army of chess players was reinforced by several dozen new recruits..."

The above description will possibly give the reader a better impression of the speed at which time races along during the foreign travels of the Soviet World Champion.

Karpov–Portisch
Slav Defence

| 1 N–KB3 | P–Q4 |
| 2 P–Q4 | |

Portisch is happy playing the positions resulting after 2 P–B4 P–Q5, hence my choice of move.

2 ...	N–KB3
3 P–B4	P–B3
4 N–B3	P×P
5 P–QR4	

With the clear intention of regaining the pawn without any trouble. This continuation assures White of a slight advantage, thanks to the freer positioning of his pieces. But account has to be taken of the fact that it has a very obvious and chronic defect—Black is given permanent control of his ... QN5 square.

| 5 ... | B–B4 |

The basic idea of the Slav Defence, which favourably distinguishes it from other variations of the Queen's Gambit—the ... QB1–KR6 diagonal is left open for the white-squared bishop, and it can be developed on any of the available squares.

6 P–K3	P–K3
7 B×P	B–QN5
8 0–0	0–0
9 N–R4	

Only in this way can White hope for an opening advantage. The black bishop becomes an object of attack, and sooner or later White will exchange his knight for it, thus gaining the celebrated advantage of the two bishops. In this case, it is true, this gives him only a slight advantage, in view of the closed nature of the position.

| 9 ... | B–N5 |
| 10 P–B3 | B–KR4 |

10 ... N–Q4 11 P×B Q×N is also played, and now 12 Q–B3 is the strongest, when White does not have to fear 12 ... N×N 13 P×N B×P 14 R–N1 and 15 B–R3. Black therefore has to restrain his ardour, and reconcile himself to 12 ... N–Q2 13 B–Q2 P–QR4.

By the move played Black draws the enemy fire, which is of course a double-edged decision: the white pawns will either restrict his pieces, or else they will become objects of attack.

| 11 P–N4 | B–N3 |
| 12 N×B | |

This exchange could also have been delayed —all the same the bishop had nowhere to go.

| 12 ... | RP×N |
| 13 Q–N3 | |

On this move, and on the series of moves following, depends not only the outcome of the opening stage, but also perhaps of the entire game. White's basic problem is associated with his queen's bishop. When considering the development of this bishop, White must not forget that his pawns are far-advanced, and that any counter-blow in the centre may have unpleasant consequences. Black's plans include the advance ... P–QB4, which will undermine the white centre, reinforce the bishop at ... QN5, and prepare the development of his knight on the active square ... QB3.

In the first instance White moves his queen away with gain of tempo, at the same time vacating the square Q1 for his rook. The bishop cannot retreat, since it is tied by the necessity to keep the QNP defended.

| 13 ... | Q–K2 |

13 ... Q–N3 is also possible, when there is no point in driving the bishop away immediately—14 N–R2?! B–K2, and on account of the time lost, White does not succeed in creating problems for Black in the ending. It is most sensible to play 14 R–Q1, defending once again the QP, and preparing the pawn advances P–N5 and P–K4.

14 P–N5

In order, after driving away the knight from ... KB3, to take control of his Q5 square, and in the event of ... P–QB4 (which is already practically prepared) to reply P–Q5.

| 14 ... | N–Q4 |

This forces matters. After 14 ... KN–Q2 15 P–K4 Black would not have been obliged to move his knight to ... QN3. Portisch was evidently afraid of the positional squeeze resulting from 15 P–B4, which after the move played is not at all dangerous for him.

| 15 P–K4 | N–N3 |

He doesn't wish to strengthen White's centre by 15 ... N×N 16 P×N.

16 N–R2!

In thinking over his previous move, Black had given main consideration to the retreat of the white bishop, allowing him to gain an important tempo which could have been used to play ... P–QB4. But White's intermediate move upsets all his plans. Black is obliged to retreat his bishop, since 16 ... N×B 17 N×B allows White a decisive gain of space.

16 ...   B–R4

After 16 ... B–Q3 17 B–K2 Black could not have prevented the further advance of the QRP, forcing back his knight.

17 B–K2   P–K4

The uneasy positioning of Black's minor pieces, which have become tangled up on the Q-side, forces him to adopt extreme measures. 17 ... P–QB4 does not produce the desired result, on account of the simple reply 18 P×P (the plausible 18 Q–N5 'misses the mark': 18 ... N–B3! 19 Q×P Q×Q 20 P×Q N×P, or 19 P×P P–R3!) 18 ... Q×BP 19 B–K3.

18 Q–B2!

Yet another intermediate move. The trapping of the bishop continues. While clearing the way for the QNP, the queen at the same time defends the second rank and the KP, and takes control of the square QB5.

18 ...   N(3)–Q2

The slight complications resulting after 18 ... P×P 19 P–N4! B×P 20 N×B Q×N 21 B–R3 Q–R4 22 B×R Q×NP+ (22 ... K×B 23 P–B4, and the advance of the pawns is crushing) 23 K–R1 K×B would have left

Black no better off—24 P–R5 N(3)–Q2 25 Q–N2 N–B4 26 Q×QP.

19 P×P   Q×KP
20 K–R1

A useful prophylactic move. The king was on the open QR7–KN1 diagonal, and to avoid dangerous intermediate checks retreats into the corner.

The subsequent play of both sides revolves around the threat of P–B4. White will all the time be preparing this advance, while Black will do everything possible to prevent it, making slight concessions on other parts of the board.

20 ...   R–K1
21 B–QB4

Q3 looks a more desirable square for the bishop, but it cannot be occupied immediately in view of 21 ... N–B4. In order to divert the knight, I devised a more serious threat— 22 Q–N3, to defend against which Portisch is forced for an instant to remove his attention from the square Q3, and this is sufficient.

21 ...   N–N3
22 B–Q3

In reply to the optimistic 22 ... N(1)–Q2 I had prepared an interesting tactical blow— 23 P–N4! Q×R 24 P×B N–QB1 (on 24 ... N×P White has the intermediate reply 25 B–K3 Q–N7 26 Q×N) 25 B–N2 Q×N 26 B–B4!, and the queen is trapped!

22 ...	N–R3

The threat is indeed stronger than its execution! So as to defend against P–B4 and P–N4, Black compromises his Q-side pawn formation. But here, of course, everything is by no means simple. As before it is not easy for White to settle on a post for his black-squared bishop, and for this reason he is also unable to develop his queen's rook. For the moment Black is better developed, and plans to exploit this in the most determined fashion.

23 B×N	P×B
24 R–Q1!	

A subtle, unobtrusive move. White had at his disposal a series of alternatives, but they are all markedly weaker. E.g. 24 R–QN1 P–QB4, and Black has nothing to worry about; 24 N–B3 blocks the queen's action along the QB-file, as a result of which 24 ... P–QB4 cannot be answered by 25 B–K3, on account of 25 ... N–B5. The bishop similarly cannot come into play immediately—24 B–K3? N–Q4!. The strength of the move played, apart from the fact that it takes control of the Q-file, lies mainly in the preparation of a counter-blow: 24 ... QR–Q1 25 B–K3 N–Q4 26 B–Q4!.

24 ...	P–QB4
25 B–K3	

Only now is it perfectly clear that White has solved all his problems, and has emerged from the opening with an advantage. But who would have thought that the game would last only another seven moves?!

25 ...	QR–B1
26 N–B3	

26 N–B1 also deserves consideration, so as to then transfer the knight to Q3 or K2, but White has his own idea—to control his Q5 square.

26 ...	N–B5
27 B–B1	

The bishop retreats, so as to then return. Shocked by the rapid and unexpected turn of events, on his following move Portisch commits a serious mistake, which loses the game.

27 ...	R–N1?

It is difficult to tell what Portisch was thinking about at this point, what variations he was calculating, and what he was hoping for. Possibly he simply overlooked that the square Q5 could be occupied not only by the rook (with gain of tempo), but also by the knight (with decisive effect). Meanwhile, after the essential 27 ... B×N the main battle would still have been to come—in a slightly inferior ending for Black: 28 Q×B Q×Q 29 P×Q.

Perhaps the Hungarian grandmaster was afraid of the *zwischenzug* 28 R–Q5, since after the retreat of the queen White gains a clear advantage (29 Q×B). Yes, if 28 R–Q5 had worked, then... but Black had an excellent rejoinder at his disposal: 28 ... Q×R! 29 P×Q R–K8+ 30 K–N2 B×P 31 Q×N B×R, with an unclear position. Therefore I was preparing to demonstrate my aspirations in the endgame.

28 N–Q5

Here Black could well have resigned. From inertia Portisch made a few more moves.

		29 B–B4	Q–K3
		30 KR–QN1	Q–R6
		31 B×R	R×B
28 ...	N×P	32 R×N	**Resigns**

In the Spartakiad programme ✻ The logic behind a sensation ✻
The twelfth defeats the tenth

On a July evening at Moscow's Sheremetevo Airport, crowds looked with interest at a rather slight, energetic young man, constantly hurrying his companion, who was shyly smiling, grey-haired, and economical in his movements. Returning from Yugoslavia were Anatoly Karpov, winner of an imposing International Tournament, and his trainer and prize-winner in the same event, Semion Furman. On landing at Moscow, they first of all enquired as to whether rail tickets had been booked for them, so that a day later they could dash on to Leningrad, not only to see their families, but also to meet up with their Spartakiad team. From there they had to hurry on to Riga.

The restoration of chess to the programme of the 6th USSR Peoples' Spartakiad was a great boost to the game: interest in it immediately rose in the Provinces, and Sports Directors could no longer wave aside the needs of chess players, as they had sometimes done in the past. The event brought together all the best players in the Soviet Union—25 grandmasters, 17 international masters and 72 Masters of Sport, representing the teams of all the Union Republics and the cities of Moscow and Leningrad. It was anticipated that those battling for first place would be the experienced Moscow team (Petrosian, Smyslov, Bronstein, Vasyukov...), the relatively young Ukrainian team (Belyavsky, Kuzmin, Savon, Tukmakov...), and the Russian Federation team (which included Spassky, and Polugayevsky, and Geller). I considered that Spartakiad medals could also quite possibly come the way of the Leningrad team. But made from which metal, that I did not know.

For our narrative, which is to a certain extent specific, the following moments were perhaps of the greatest significance: the performance of the World Champion himself ($5\frac{1}{2}$ points out of 7, first place among the team leaders), his fine creative achievement against Spassky, and also—paradoxical though it may seem—the crushing defeat inflicted by the Russian Federation team on the Moscow players. We will begin with the last-named point, since it was this match that in effect determined the overall winners of the USSR Peoples' Spartakiad. In addition, the Muscovites lost, such that the score of their defeat would remain for ever in the annals of team events. As one says, they were to go down in history...

When the Moscow team lost by a score of $\frac{1}{2}$–$8\frac{1}{2}$, certain specialists were inclined to assert that chess is first and foremost a game, and that in a game anything can happen. Replay this match, and perhaps... Of course, Spassky is not always bound to beat Petrosian. Naturally, it was not essential for it to be here that Smyslov should suffer his first defeat at the hands of Polugayevsky during their years of rivalry. And it is by no means certain that, playing Black, Krogius could overcome Balashov again. And Vasyukov, after refusing a draw, would be unlikely on another occasion to make such bad mistakes as he did in his game with Geller...

There must have been a dose of ill-fortune in a defeat of such dimensions, but there was also a degree of logic. To be precise, it was that for which journalists had already managed to find an elegant name—that of "logical sensation". Although the Moscow team had its big names, it was poorly prepared and badly organized. Despite all the efforts of its President Y. Vasilchuk, the work of the Capital's Chess Federation was disorganized, and was not helped by the city Sports Committee's indifferent attitude to chess. In short, the Muscovites had long been heading for such a "sensation".

The Leningrad team, headed by Karpov, managed to provide competition for the strong and harmonious Russian Federation team. Probably more than anyone, the World Champion needed to relax after his active appearances in Yugoslavia, and prior to the very important tournament in Milan. But realizing how much he was needed by his team, he did not permit himself to take postponements in any of the important matches. After a cleanly-won game against Kupreichik (White Russia), he admitted that he had been adversely affected by his opponent's long periods of thought, and that at these times he had particularly wanted to sleep (prior to this he had had to resume his games against Grigorian and Spassky after overnight analysis).

Karpov–Kupreichik
Slav Defence

1 P–Q4 P–Q4 2 P–QB4 P–QB3 3 N–QB3 N–B3 4 N–B3 P×P 5 P–QR4 B–B4 6 P–K3 P–K3 7 B×P B–QN5 8 0–0 0–0 9 N–KR4 B–N5 10 P–B3 N–Q4 11 P×B Q×N 12 Q–B3 N–Q2 13 B–Q2 P–QR4 14 QR–Q1 QR–Q1 15 B–N3 N(4)–B3 16 P–R3 P–B4 17 B–K1 Q–N4 18 B–N3 P×P 19 P×P P–K4 20 N–N5 P×P 21 N×P Q–QB4 22 B–KB2 Q–K4 23 B–N3 Q–QB4 24 Q–B5 Q–N3 25 K–R1 N–B4 26 B–QB2 QR–K1 27 R–B4 N(4)–Q2 28 R–B3 P–N3 29 Q–B4 B–B4

30 R–N3 B–N5 31 R–KB3 B–B4 32 N–N5 R–K7

33 B–Q3 R×QNP 34 Q–N5 K–N2 35 R–K1 Q–B3 36 Q–B1 R–R7 37 Q–QB4 R–Q7 38 B–B4 R–N7 39 Q–B3 R–N5 40 P–N5 B–Q5 41 Q×Q P×Q 42 N×B Resigns

...The Spartakiad competitors were provided with the fine halls of the Latvian Institute of Scientific-Technical Information and Propaganda—a splendid building, built alongside the famous Domkirk, and designed by G. Bosse, Professor at the St. Petersburg Academy of Art, and in which Aron Nimzowitsch, one-time contender for the World Championship and one of the classics of this form of art, had once played chess. And now in the Leningrad–Russian Federation match two World Champions clashed: the twelfth—Anatoly Karpov, and one of his predecessors, the tenth—Boris Spassky.

That day the majority of the competitors found it easier to breath—in both the direct and the figurative sense. The spectators were drawn, as if by a giant magnet, from the main hall to the special small hall where the match between the Leningrad and Russian Federation teams was being played. Apart from everything else, there was one further circumstance which irrepressibly attracted chess fans to that beautiful, isolated hall. On an eminence, which resembled an alcove from Tsarist times, and which was now transformed into a stage, two chess tables had been set up with the name-plates "A. Karpov–B. Spassky" and "L. Polugayevsky–V. Korchnoi". It was this eminence that was attacked by reporters, armed to the teeth with a variety of photographic equipment.

The inexorable controllers allowed into that hall only as many spectators as had gone out. Two places were saved for Karpov's parents, who, on noticing that the trainers of the Russian Federation team were reinforcing their players with chocolate, immediately asked that Anatoly be passed some berries which they had brought specially. Salo Flohr immediately joked: "If I were in Tolya's place, I would prefer that little black pawn at d5 to one of those berries".

Karpov, as if he had heard the experienced grandmaster's advice, began to lay siege to his opponent's isolated QP. Spassky's position began to give cause for alarm, and he sank deep into thought, allowing the Champion to make longer and longer circuits around the tables of the other competitors, which were arranged in a row. (Later, Anatoly said that on each occasion he returned to his place in a good frame of mind, since he very much liked his compatriots' positions: the Leningrad players had clearly seized the initiative in this very important match.)

After boldly capturing a pawn, the World Champion forced his opponent to set out on a sea of complications, no doubt already realizing that the latter would not "surface" again. And, being insufficiently loaded (due to an obvious lack of material), Spassky's ship began to sink. Karpov acted both accurately, and most elegantly. The Ex-World Champion offered a temporary queen sacrifice, which the Champion, with a fine rook move, forced to become permanent. The game was adjourned, but everyone realized that Black was merely putting off the decision to capitulate, and the applause in Karpov's honour was heard the following morning.

Nevertheless, analysis again had to be done at night—on the resumption of a game at such high level, nothing could be left to chance.

"Yes", says Karpov, "the Russian Federation team almost suffered a heavy defeat. At one point it seemed that we would win by 6–3 or even 7–2. In such events it frequently happens that losses by the leaders, especially those such as Spassky and Polugayevsky, can demoralize the remaining players, and then the whole team begins to 'collapse'. But chess players display their high class by not wasting their chances, and in the fifth hour of play the Leningrad players lost all their advantage, and the Russian Federation players succeeded in drawing the match.

In all team events (with the exception of this latest one) I had played for the Russian Federation team. And as soon as it became clear that Leningrad could no longer contend for first place, I began to support my old colleagues—the Russian Federation players, and was glad that they were able to win the title of Spartakiad Champions."

Karpov–Spassky
Queen's Indian Defence

Spassky doesn't normally play the Queen's Indian Defence as Black. Why he chose this opening, I can't imagine.

1 P–Q4	N–KB3
2 P–QB4	P–K3
3 N–KB3	P–QN3

4 P–KN3	B–N2
5 B–N2	B–K2
6 N–B3	0–0
7 Q–B2	P–Q4
8 P×P	N×P

Should the knights be exchanged, or not? On the one hand, such an exchange is favourable for Black, since with fewer pieces on the board it is easier for him to defend his cramped position. On the other hand, Black has to be prepared for a position with hanging pawns, where a greater number of pieces allows him better chances of fighting for the initiative. Therefore the choice of moves depends on a player's tastes.

9 0–0	**N–Q2**
10 N×N	

But now that Black has determined the position of his queen's knight, White can make this exchange.

10 ...	**P×N**

Capturing with the bishop is most 'uninteresting': 10 ... B×N 11 P–K4 B–N2 12 R–Q1, and White has a clear advantage.

11 R–Q1

The only active plan for Black involves the advance ... P–QB4. He can, of course, restrict himself to the more modest ... P–QB3—in this case Black's position will be markedly cramped, and although the possibility of him attaining a draw is not ruled out, he has a long and difficult defence in prospect. White's last move is directed against ... P–QB4.

11 ...	**N–B3**
12 N–K5	

But now the intrusion of the knight at QB6 is threatened, and the advance ... P–B4 is simply forced.

12 ...	**P–B4**
13 P×P	

Here Black was faced with a choice: with what should he recapture—bishop or pawn? In the event of 13 ... P×P White would have continued 14 B–N5, and although it appears that his pieces are rather insecurely placed, Black is unable to exploit this circumstance directly. At the same time, all Black's pieces are tied up: the bishop at KN5 has its sights trained on the one at ... K2, the same is true of the bishop at KN2 with respect to that at ... QN2, while the hanging pawns in the centre require constant defence. Nevertheless, the position after 13 ... P×P would remain tense and complicated, although I consider it more favourable for White.

13 ...	**B×P**
14 N–Q3	

In positions of this type, it is normally recommended that the knight be kept at Q4, so as to prevent the pawn advance ... P–Q5. If Black should succeed in effecting this advance, he obtains play against White's KP and a certain degree of freedom. But for the moment the QP cannot move on account of the pin on the long diagonal, and White utilizes the opportunity to drive away the bishop from ... QB4.

14 ...	**B–Q3**

After 14 ... R–B1 15 N×B R×N (15 ... P×N 16 B–N5 is totally bad) Black's position is only slightly inferior, but on the other hand... for the entire game.

15 B–B4

The exchange of black-squared bishops is one of White's best plans, since the isolated QP becomes even more vulnerable.

15 ...	**R–K1**

16 P–K3	N–K5
17 B×B	Q×B
18 N–B4	QR–B1

After this Black's position becomes very difficult, if not altogether lost. True, even the superior 18 ... QR–Q1 would have left White with a clear positional advantage.

19 Q–R4	Q–K2

When in positions of this type the move P–K3 has already been made, White's KB2 square frequently comes under attack. With the pawn still at K2 this square is less easily approachable, and besides, the white knight always has a safe square at Q3. But here a certain weakness of White's king position begins to make itself felt, and it is on this that Spassky plays.

Black threatens ... N×BP. This can be averted by 20 B×N Q×B 21 R–Q4 (essential, otherwise ... P–Q5) 21 ... Q–B7. Now White can probably win the QP, but whether he will win the game is not clear. The alternative is the sharp variations beginning with 20 Q×P. I thought over this move for quite a long time, and convinced myself that I would gain an advantage. White appears to take his queen away from the main theatre of events, but a more careful examination shows that it can soon be exchanged for its black opposite-number, which is situated on the same rank.

20 Q×P

Here White had to reckon with an interesting possibility—20 ... P–Q5, after which the long diagonal is opened, and ... N×BP is threatened. E.g. 21 R×P N×BP, and if 22 Q×B, then 22 ... Q×P, with a very strong attack. But 20 ... P–Q5 is refuted by 21 P×P N×BP 22 R–K1, and Black has two pieces 'hanging' simultaneously, whereas there are no dangers threatening White.

20 ...	N×BP
21 N×P	B×N
22 Q×Q	

If now Spassky had simply recaptured 22 ... R×Q, then after 23 R×B N–N5 White could have played to retain his extra pawn by 24 P–K4, or, even more strongly, continued 24 B–R3 N×KP 25 B×R N×R 26 R–Q1. The ending is very bad for Black—the bishop is certainly much stronger than the knight, while Black's king is a long way from the Q-side, where White has a pawn majority. Spassky therefore decides to sacrifice his queen.

22 ...	N×R
23 R–B1	

A fine move! Black's rook is driven off the QB-file, since his knight prevents him from capturing on ... QB8 with check. White, meanwhile, would capture on K8 not only with check, but also with mate.

23 ...	R–N1

If 23 ... R–R1, then 24 B×B R×Q 25 B×R R–K1 (mate on the back rank was threatened) 26 B–B6 R–Q1 27 P–K4, and Black's position is quite hopeless.

24 Q–N4

24 Q–Q7 was also possible, so as on 24 ...
B×B to make the intermediate move 25 R–B7
forcing the black rook to ... KB1. But one
should not expect too much of a good thing,
especially since in this variation it seemed
to me that White's pieces were slightly 'en-
tangled'.

24 ...	B×B
25 K×B	N×KP+
26 K–N1	R–K3

The material balance is in White's favour.
In addition, there is play taking place on
both wings, and the queen is stronger than
the rook and knight. Black's drawing chances
are associated with the insecure position
of the white king, and if he were able to
achieve co-ordination between his forces, it
might prove difficult for White to realize his
advantage. White therefore begins a forcing
variation, the aim of which is to exchange off
one of the black rooks. In this case the opponent's chances of resisting will be severely
reduced.

| 27 Q–KB4 | R–Q1 |

27 ... R(1)–K1 is bad in view of 28
R–B7, when the KBP is attacked. Advancing
the pawn is dangerous, as the king's position
is weakened, while 28 ... R–KB3, with the
hope of giving mate at ... KB8, is refuted
by 29 Q×N. Now White cannot play 28
R–B7, since the rook check at ... Q8 is highly
unpleasant.

28 Q–Q4	R(1)–K1
29 Q–Q7	N–N5
30 R–B8	

The forcing variation leads to the exchange
of rooks. It would appear that White has
weakened his rear-guard, and that the time
has come for Black to give a check at ... K8.
But this attempt at counter-attack would
merely have hastened Black's defeat: 30 ...
R–K8+ 31 K–N2 R–K7+ 32 K–R3 (but
not 32 K–B3 N×P+ 33 K–B4 R–K5+
34 K–B5 R–K4+ 35 K–B4 P–KN4 mate)
32 ... N–B7+ 33 K–R4 R–K5+ 34 P–KN4,
and 34 ... R×P+ fails to 35 Q×R, exploiting for the umpteenth time the weakness of
the back rank!

30 ...	N–B3
31 R×R+	R×R
32 Q–N7	R–K3
33 Q–N8+	N–K1

The position has clarified. Black's one hope
is to give up his knight and QNP for White's
Q-side pawns, and attempt to set up a fortress
on the opposite wing. But his pieces are so
badly placed that White has every right to
expect to gain at least a rook for his pawns.

34 P–QR4	P–N3
35 P–QN4	K–N2
36 Q–N7	P–R4
37 K–N2	K–B3
38 P–R3	

There is no reason to hurry, and White
can strengthen his position to the maximum
extent before commencing the advance of his
Q-side pawns.

38 ...	R–Q3
39 P–R5	P×P
40 P×P	R–K3
41 P–R6	N–B2
42 P–R7	

Of course, after 42 Q×N R×P Black is lost, but then the game would have dragged out, whereas I wanted to win cleanly.

42 ...	R–K2
43 Q–B6+	K–K4

43 ... K–N2 fails to 44 Q–Q6 K–B1 45 Q–Q8+.

44 K–B3

But now Black does not have a single move. E.g. 44 ... K–B4 45 Q–B5+ K–B3 46 Q–Q6+. Black's rook and knight are too close together, and get in each other's way. Spassky therefore resigned.

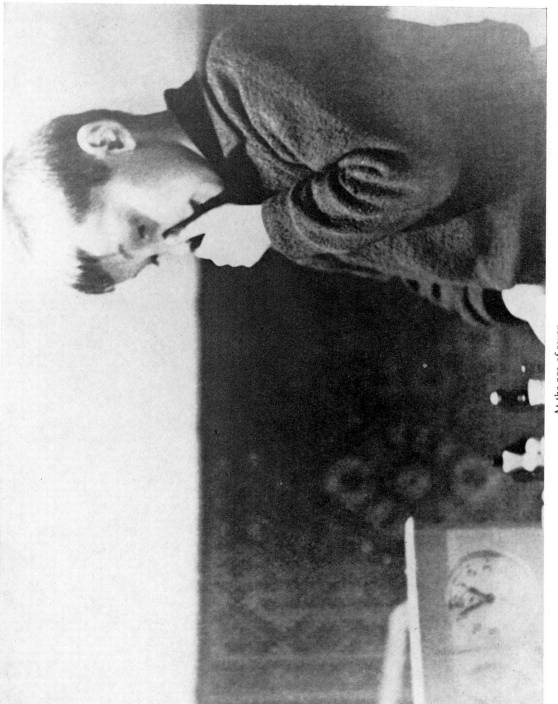

At the age of seven.

At the age of eight.

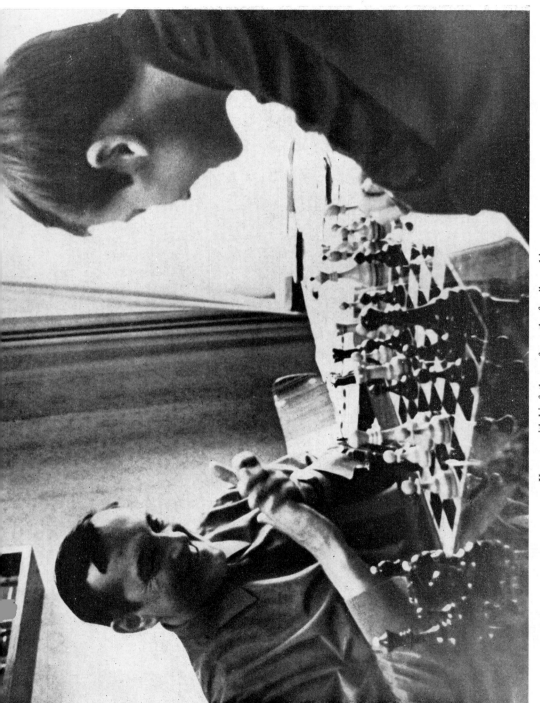

Karpov with his father —from the family archives.

During the Final Candidates' Match against Korchnoi. Moscow 1974.

Receiving the World Champion's medal from Dr Max Euwe. Moscow 1975.

The morning when Karpov became World Champion. Moscow 1975.

Karpov at his favourite relaxation. Moscow 1976.

With his niece Natasha. Tula 1975.

In The Hermitage. Leningrad 1976.

With his mother. Tula 1975.

Karpov's trainer, the late Semion Furman. Moscow 1976.

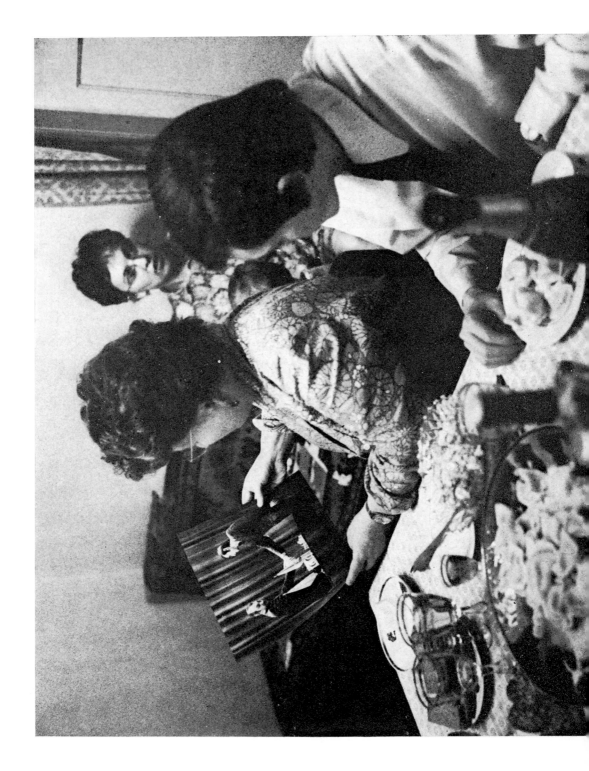

A successful catch. Plavinas (Lithuania) 1977.

Above and right: On holiday in Plavinas (Lithuania) 1977.

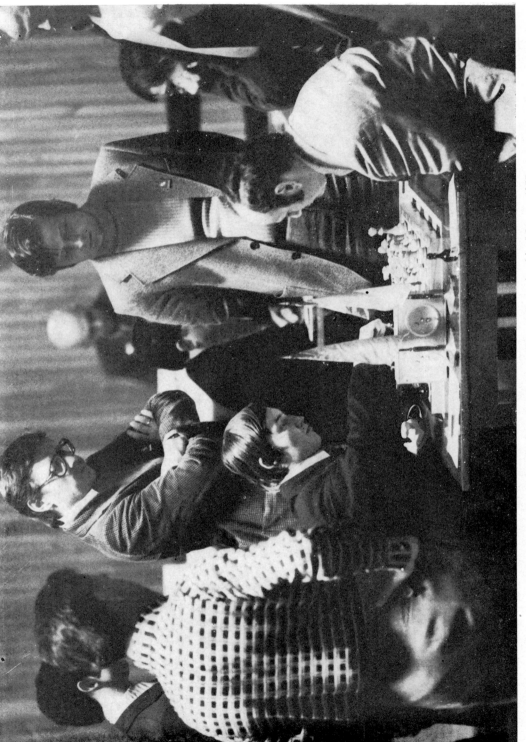

The Karpov–Portisch game from the European Team Championship. Moscow 1977.

Simultaneous display in Bugojno (Yugoslavia) 1978.

CHAPTER 7

Examination in Milan

One of the cities which contended for the Fischer–Karpov match was Milan. And although the match did not take place, in Italy they did not abandon the hope that they would play host to the best active players in the world. The match gave way to a tournament with 12 grandmasters, including some of the very strongest. The invitation list looked highly imposing. If the World Championship had been played on such a system, the Milan tournament would have been comparable to it. Also, the formula devised by the organizers was such that it repeated in miniature the stages of the three-year World Championship cycle. The tournament was not the end of the matter—the four winners made up two semi-final pairs, and then the winners of these matches met each other in the final.

Higher than the level of world standards ✳ Who is guilty? ✳ Chess suicide ✳ The red danger signal ✳ The Champion's first "I resign"

The one competitor without any impressive chess titles or significant achievements was Mariotti. But that is the unwritten law of all big tournaments—there must be at least one representative of the country in which the event is being held.

One thing that was striking was the efforts of the hosts to conduct the tournament on a level that was higher than world standards. A great deal of thought had gone into the organization of the grandmasters' every-day life—they lived and played in a complex of buildings, which together made up the "Leonardo da Vinci" hotel. The soft carpeting, covering all internal surfaces of the darkened tournament hall, which was situated deep below ground level, muffled all effects of noise. The atmosphere was that of a cinema during a performance, when the lights are switched off and the screen is lit up.

There were 700 places in the hall, and on the days of the most interesting rounds the number of seats was increased to 1000. The hall was almost always full, and this despite the high entrance fee: three thousand Italian lira (equivalent at the time to about five American dollars) was the price of an adult ticket, with a reduction for children.

What were Karpov's feelings before the start?

"On my own experience, I already knew that from the Champion only top results and only first places were demanded and expected. I also knew that the Champion did not receive, together with his laurel wreath, an insurance policy against misfortune, or any sort of magic wand, which would enable him, in contrast to mere mortals, to always be in top form. At the time, everything had gone well for me from this point of view. But I realized perfectly well that I couldn't hope to avoid failure. But only, I thought, not in Milan. Here I simply had to come first! On the one hand, it was such a grandiose tournament. So grandiose, that one might have thought that it had been devised to test the calibre of the new World Champion. On the other hand, the laurel wreath had not come to me as it had to its previous owners—there had been no match with the previous Champion, and the world still demanded proof of the legality of the new 'chess regime'. Milan would have to put the dot over the 'i'."

These words give the reader some idea of Karpov's frame of mind at that time. It becomes clearer why, in the Milan Tournament, the Champion's main problems were not creative, but purely competitive ones.

Karpov:

"I looked on the stages of this event as the components of one big tournament, and at each stage tried to decide a specific problem. In the first instance I had to end up among the four winners of the preliminary all-play-all tournament. In the second, semi-final stage, I had to either win the match of four games, or else draw it (in this case the player who had done better in the all-play-all tournament went through to the final). And only in the third, final stage, which consisted of six match games, was it essential to win. When one talks in terms of the necessity to be first, while playing 21 games in 25 days against very strong opponents, the creative aspect has to take second place.

Before the start we all tried to guess how many points would be needed to go through to the semi-final. It was agreed that 'plus three' would guarantee a place, but later it turned out that 'plus two' was sufficient.

The tournament had barely started, and Portisch and Ljubojević already had this 'plus two'. But while Portisch had defeated Mariotti and Gligorić in excellent style, Ljubojević had fortune to thank for both of his points. First he was quite outplayed by Andersson with Black. But, after obtaining a decisive advantage, and with every possibility of transforming it into a point in the remaining three minutes, the impractical Swede became so endeared with his position that he forgot all about his clock, and did not notice his flag falling. The following day the Yugoslav was given a 'present' by Larsen, who in his game with Ljubojević had better position, but then chose an unsound tactical path and lost.

I managed to catch the two successful starters by the fourth round. On the whole, I had no reason to feel unhappy: I had not allowed anyone to go ahead of me, this had not cost me any great effort, and I had won comparatively easily a 'drawn' ending against Ljubojević.

Ljubojević–Karpov
Ruy Lopez

1 P–K4 P–K4 2 N–KB3 N–QB3 3 B–N5 P–QR3 4 B–R4 N–B3 5 0–0 B–K2 6 P–Q4 P×P 7 P–K5 N–K5 8 N×P 0–0 9 N–B5 P–Q4 10 P×P e.p. B×N 11 P×B N×KP 12 B–N3 Q×Q 13 R×Q QR–Q1 14 R–K1 N–B4 15 N–B3 R–Q2 16 B–K3 N×B 17 BP×N KR–Q1 18 QR–Q1 P–KB3 19 R×R R×R 20 R–Q1 R×R 21 N×R N–Q4 22

B–Q2 B–N8 23 P–QR3 B–B7 24 N–K3 N×N 25 B×N B×P

26 P–B3 K–B2 27 B–B4 P–B3 28 B–Q6
K–K3 29 B–B8 P–N3 30 K–B2 P–QR4 31
K–K3 P–N3 32 P–KR4 P–QB4 33 P–N4 B–Q8
34 K–K4 P–R5 35 P–R5 P×P 36 P×P
P–B4+ 37 K–K3 K–Q4 38 P–R6 K–B5 39
P–B4 K–N6 40 B–N7 K–B7 41 B–K5 B–R4

42 B–B6 B–B2 43 B–K5 B–N6 44 B–N7 P–N4
45 B–B8 P–B5 46 B–N7 P–N5 47 K–Q4 P–B6
48 P×BP P×RP 49 P–B4 P–R7 50 K–B5
K–N8 51 K–N4 P–R8=Q 52 B×Q K×B 53
P–B5 K–N7 54 P–B6 P–R6 55 P–B7 B–K3
56 K–B5 P–R7 57 K–Q6 B–B1 58 **Resigns**

And on my game against Unzicker I had spent all of 15 minutes. Strictly speaking, the game lasted longer that this—one and a half hours, but, as the clocks at our table showed, the West German grandmaster had thought for one hour fifteen minutes, and I—for only a quarter of an hour. But what was interesting was the fact that we played a Ruy Lopez, and this opening, although it has been heavily analysed, with the variations given in the books going as far as move twenty, requires a special understanding. And Unzicker is in fact recognized as one of the experts on it. After this game Tal remarked wittily that I couldn't manage to win even a pawn against Unzicker: the latter succeeded in resigning in a position with complete material equality, and with the board almost completely full of pieces (this had happened at the Olympiad in Nice, and now again here in Milan).

Karpov–Unzicker
Ruy Lopez

1 P–K4 P–K4 2 N–KB3 N–QB3 3 B–N5
P–QR3 4 B–R4 N–B3 5 0–0 B–K2 6 R–K1
P–QN4 7 B–N3 P–Q3 8 P–B3 0–0 9 P–KR3
N–QR4 10 B–B2 P–B4 11 P–Q4 Q–B2 12
QN–Q2 B–Q2 13 N–B1 KR–K1 14 P–Q5
N–N2 15 N(3)–R2 P–N3 16 N–N3 P–B5
17 P–B4 P×P 18 B×P B–KB1 19 B–N5

B–K2 20 Q–Q2 B–QB1 21 R–KB1 N–Q2 22
N–N4 **Resigns**

The fifth round proved to be a peaceable one; all of the leaders scored half a point, and maintained their positions. Behind them came Browne and Šmejkal. Tal's position was still affected by the drama of the early rounds, when in two better positions he had suffered two defeats. For the time being Petrosian remained in the background, being content to draw.

When during a big tournament there happens to be a peaceable day, the annoyed spectators, on leaving for home, are not sparing in the offensive remarks they make regarding the 'guilty' grandmasters, while reporters give vent to their angry emotions on the pages of the press. It is as if we have in fact deliberately deprived the chess public of its right to attend a spectacle, performed with the utmost dramatic effect. On the whole, one can understand the public: the spectator who does not obtain from the film, performance or match that which he had hoped for, bears a grudge against the participants and the directors. Who else can he blame for an unsuccessful evening?

But in fact on such a day we, the players, frequently feel wrongly accused. The chess player goes along to a particular round, having planned his result beforehand. This plan depends upon many factors—on his tournament position, on the number of rounds remaining, on the comparative strengths of himself and his opponent, on his physical and nervous state that day... No one wishes to see himself beforehand as the loser. Some go along to the tournament hall with maximum pretensions, while others are happy to draw (and if the opportunity to earn a point should present itself, thanks very much). And these preliminary drafts, just like the players' moods and their opening plans, clash at the board. In some cases the flame of a heated struggle flares up and burns in long or short storms, but sometimes the clash does not produce even a spark. After all, it would be strange to demand that a grandmaster should squeeze out of a position more than is possible, merely to justify the demands of the public, and thereby sacrifice his tournament strategy, and with it the long months of hard work spent in preparing for tournaments. Of course, in saying all this I am disregarding 'agreed' draws...

In the peaceable fifth round, the flame did not begin burning at even one of the six tables. And this is no more than a coincidence. There was a coincidence of quite a different type in the following round, the sixth. Again each player went along to the hall, having determined his programme for the day—both optimum and minimum. Again each sat down at the board, not knowing the intentions of his opponent. But the 'coincidence' was that, for the majority of the competitors, the time had come to clear up their tournament positions. And straight away the play became interesting. On all six boards such battles developed that the hall that evening hummed and applauded, as if it were not a chess tournament, but a pop concert".

...A typical illustration of Karpov's apt comments is provided by the game between Larsen and Tal. In the previous round the Dane had moved up to the fifty per cent mark, and was hoping to continue his spurt. The Ex-World Champion, meanwhile, had only just brought this mark into view. Now a defeat for Tal was, as they say, equivalent to death (in this tournament), and defeat for Larsen was almost equally unbearable. These were the purely competitive considerations. Now picture to yourself in addition the psychological state of affairs between the two old rivals, who had already won whole matches against each other, and had reputations as uncompromising chess fighters. Fighters, but not gladiators, going to their deaths. Thus it was that they adopted identical tactics: knowing the opponent's character, each played cautiously, and carefully exchanged pieces, confident that sooner or later the opponent would lose patience, and in an unfavourable situation disturb the balance. Then an intent glance at the board revealed that the position was an almost certain draw. It was here that Larsen overreached himself. One incautious move by the Dane, and this proved sufficient for Tal to create an irresistible mating attack on the hostile king. And then, for the first time in the fashionable "Leonardo da Vinci" hotel, applause broke out in honour of a chess player.

Tal was even rather embarrassed by such an unlawful, as it were, win. As if in justification, he said: "I have regained with interest that which I lost in my game with Portisch". Incidentally, Portisch himself, who in a good position made a bad move, which led to his defeat at the hands of Andersson, joked gloomily, having in mind himself and Larsen: "The second chess suicide in one evening". And this is what Karpov had to say about his own game:

"In my game with Gligorić that evening, my position hung by a slender thread. And whether or not this thread broke depended much more on my opponent than on me. At first everything went easily and simply—we repeated the moves from our previous encounter in the tournament at Portorož. Only, my 17th move was a new one, improving the variation. Soon Gligorić was in a difficult position, and there were several ways I could have won. I made my choice, moved the piece, wrote down the move, and got up from the board. And suddenly, with some sort of sixth sense rather than a mental picture, I sensed that I had done something silly. Indeed, the move proved to be a terrible one: if my opponent found the correct plan, he could force me to seek salvation in perpetual check. Gligorić meanwhile was having a long think. The minutes dragged by unbearably slowly... "

...While Karpov was awaiting the verdict, I, together with the other journalists, experts and trainers, sat in the tournament hall, not knowing, not even suspecting the danger which hung over the World Champion. No one knew about this, apart from Karpov himself. Only later, when the game was finished, did he show everyone how Gligorić should have played, so as to avoid defeat. Only then did everyone gain a true idea of Karpov's self-restraint and strength of spirit. While awaiting his opponent's move, he remained absolutely imperturbable. Not a single muscle twitched on his face. He did not permit himself even a glimmer of a smile when he saw that Gligorić had not found the saving continuation, and the danger of losing an important half point passed. The game was adjourned, but on the following day, after the resumption, Karpov became the sole leader, with 4½ points out of 6.

The seventh day of play again proved to be a peaceable one. All the games ended in draws, with the exception only of the clash between the two Scandinavians—Larsen and Andersson. These two near-neighbours have long been regularly bashing one another. Not long before the Milan tournament, they had played an entire match together, which ended in a crushing defeat for the Dane by 2½–5½. Here he partially gained his revenge by defeating the Swede, who was quite unable to overcome the melancholy inertia resulting from his early misfortunes.

Then the calm was again replaced by a storm. The organizers of the Milan Tournament tried out the following innovation: when a player had less than five minutes left on his clock, a red plate was hung on the demonstration board, with the warning inscription: "Time trouble!". This inscription was something in the nature of a distress signal. In the eighth round the red signal burned on five of the six demonstration boards (Tal had quickly defeated Mariotti). At first the rate of play was slow, but as a result the tension increased, and was transmitted to the spectators... In the enormous hall there was such a silence, that at times one could even hear the jingling of teaspoons as the grandmasters stirred their coffee. And then, on all of the tables at once, time trouble sneaked up, and the punching of the clock buttons became quicker and quicker...

No, the World Champion did not share the lot of the others who were short of time. On the contrary, it was his opponent Andersson who ended up in this customary situation. Yet even so, Karpov, although not that evening, but after the adjournment, lost. He lost for the first time since becoming World Champion.

"It was a very interesting game. How I should play, I worked out beforehand. Andersson regularly runs short of time, and I played specially so as to give him food for thought. Everything worked out as planned. A position was reached which, though perhaps level, was very complicated, so that all the time it was necessary to calculate move by move: if I play here, he goes there, I do this, he does that... The position was full of hidden tricks, and gave rise to more and more possibilities which had to be assessed. Andersson began thinking for long periods—and ended up there, where I had pushed him.

Time trouble approached.

Andersson saw that if things should continue the same way, he would lose from an equal position simply through running out of time. He was no longer able to contain himself, and threw himself at me, sacrificing the exchange, for which however he gained inadequate compensation. I quickly extinguished his initiative. Was that all? It merely remained for me to win this 'won' game, to calmly play it out to its logical end.

But at that point I had something of a brainstorm: I felt that I had to win the game quickly. Why should I torment him, I thought, when he was already ready to be taken. He was in severe time trouble: no more than a minute or two for ten or more moves. A bad state of affairs! But I, the exchange up and with more than an hour on my clock, began playing, like a child, on his time trouble... Later I thought to myself: but couldn't I afford to do that? Without wishing to boast, I can say that I play blitz very well. And if Andersson and I were to sit down to play blitz, I would win any match against him. But here, in this one, single game, with the advantage of the exchange (true, not without some difficulties in realizing it), I lost... How did this happen? When a player is in time trouble, he is squeezed into a ball, and all his thoughts are concentrated on one thing: he tries to guess what move his opponent will make, and how he should answer it. The intensity of his thinking increases several times, and everything is worked out beforehand; at any rate, for each eventuality a reply is prepared. But for me, everything was just the opposite. Involuntarily you begin to weaken. You seem to be working with your former intensity, but your thinking begins to deteriorate: 'all right, let's make a couple more moves, there is no need to hurry, I'll still have plenty of time to think, to find something...' I made one 'simple move', a second 'simple move'—until I made what was at first sight an obvious move, but after it I thought for the entire remaining hour, without being able to think up anything—the position was lost..."

...During adjournment analysis, the diagnosis was confirmed: Karpov's position was lost. But not without reason did Portisch admit after the Milan tournament that he had never seen a player against whom it was so difficult to win. On the following day, a four-hour adjournment session did not suffice for Andersson to gain a win in a won position. A break for dinner was announced, after which play was to resume once again. To be honest, Karpov went off to the hall again, just so as to see whether his opponent would fall into the last drawing trap. After straying rather close to the trap, Andersson finally chose the correct path. When Karpov later showed the Swedish grandmaster what had been awaiting him, if he had chosen the other way, the latter was quite sincerely put out: "It would have been better if I had fallen into it. For such a brilliant finish I would not have grudged the half point!" In general, Ulf Andersson has a very fine appreciation of chess beauty, and in addition he is an excellent lad.

Anatoly Karpov:

"Andersson reacted quite calmly to his victory. He realized that a mishap had occurred and that his win had been fortuitous. I was annoyed, of course, but only by the absurdity of the defeat, and not because it was to Andersson that I had lost. If I had been told beforehand that I was fated to lose one game, and that I could choose the winner of it, then I would probably have chosen Andersson, because he is such a pleasant person. When a player loses, he suffers two thoughts: the first—he is angry with himself, how could he lose at all; the second—that he should lose to such a 'twit' (or unpleasant opponent). In the given instance this second thought was completely absent in me. I was angry only with myself: how did I manage to lose a won position?!

Karpov–Andersson
Sicilian Defence

1 P–K4 P–QB4 2 N–KB3 P–K3 3 P–Q4
P×P 4 N×P N–QB3 5 N–N5 P–Q3 6 P–QB4
N–B3 7 QN–B3 P–QR3 8 N–R3 B–K2 9
B–K2 0–0 10 0–0 P–QN3 11 B–K3 B–N2
12 R–B1 R–K1 13 Q–N3 N–Q2 14 KR–Q1
R–QB1 15 R–Q2 Q–B2 16 Q–Q1 Q–N1
17 P–B3 B–R1 18 Q–B1 N(3)–K4 19
N(R3)–N1 N–KB3 20 K–R1 P–R3 21
R(2)–Q1 B–B1 22 N–Q2 QR–Q1 23 Q–B2

N(4)–Q2 24 P–QR3 P–Q4 25 BP×P P×P
26 P×P B–Q3 27 N–B1 (Diag.)

27 ... R×B 28 N×R B×RP 29 N–B1
B–B5 30 R–B2 P–QN4 31 B–Q3 N–N3
32 B–K4 N–B5 33 P–R4 R–K1 34 P×P P×P
35 R–K2 B–K4 36 Q–B5 N–Q3 37 N–QR2
N(Q3)×B 38 P×N B–Q3 39 Q–QB2 R–K4
40 P–KN3 Q–K1 41 R(1)–K1 B–N2 42
K–N1 N–R2 43 N–B1 N–N4 44 N–Q2 B–N5
45 K–B2 B×N 46 R×B N×P+ 47 R×N
R×R 48 N–K2 B–B1 49 N–B3 R–K8 50 N–K2
R–QR8 51 R–Q4 Q–Q1 52 Q–B6 B–Q2 53
Q–Q6 Q–K1 54 Q–B4 Q–QB1 55 P–QN4
B–R6 56 Q–K4 B–B4 57 Q–K3 Q–B7 58 P–N4
B–Q2 59 Q–K4 Q–N6 60 Q–Q3 Q–N7
61 Q–K4 R–R1 62 Q–K3 R–R7 63 P–Q6
R–R1 64 R–K4 B–B3 65 Q–Q4 Q–N8 66
R–K7 Q–KR8 67 Q–KB4 Q–N7+ 68 K–K1
R–R8+ 69 K–Q2 Q–Q4+ 70 Q–Q4 R–R7+
71 K–B3 Q–B6+ 72 R–K3 R–R6+ 73 K–Q2
R–R7+ 74 K–K1 Q–R8+ 75 K–B2 Q–N7+
76 K–K1 Q–R8+ 77 K–B2 R–R8 78 R–QB3
Q–N7+ 79 K–K3 Q–B6+ 80 Resigns

Everyone was happy about my defeat. Andersson was not a contender for a place in the first four, who were to continue the battle in match encounters. If I had won, I would have been out of reach of the others, whereas now they were immediately alongside me, and while up till then everyone had been fighting for three vacant places, having almost automatically granted me one, now it suddenly turned out that again—as at the start—there were four. Everyone was happy!"

Karpov–Gligorić
Ruy Lopez

1 P–K4	P–K4
2 N–KB3	N–QB3
3 B–N5	P–QR3
4 B–R4	N–B3
5 0–0	B–K2
6 R–K1	P–QN4
7 B–N3	0–0
8 P–B3	P–Q3
9 P–KR3	N–N1

It has so happened that all the 'White' games I have played against Svetozar Gligorić have developed into 'Spanish duels'. And each time the Yugoslav grandmaster chooses the variation beginning with this move. It is a significant fact that this splendid player, a legend in Yugoslav chess and many times a Candidate for the World Championship, has as Black the narrowest opening repertoire of all leading present-day grandmasters, and perhaps of those from the past too. In reply to 1 P–K4 he has for many years now being playing only the Ruy Lopez, while to 1 P–Q4 he constantly adopts the King's Indian Defence.

10 P–Q4

In the first game between us at San Antonio 1972, I played the modest 10 P–Q3. At the Interzonal Tournament in Leningrad I varied, and played 10 P–Q4. In both games I succeeded in winning. We then played a draw in the International Tournament at Portorož in 1975 (incidentally, Gligorić played splendidly throughout that whole tournament, and took second place). Here my opponent was evidently not averse to repeating the variation. This meant that our intentions coincided.

10 ...	QN–Q2
11 QN–Q2	B–N2
12 B–B2	R–K1
13 N–B1	B–KB1
14 N–N3	P–N3
15 P–QR4	P–B4
16 P–Q5	N–N3

Everything tallies: this is what happened in Portorož. There I continued 17 N–Q2, but did not attain anything significant from the opening, and the game quickly ended in a draw. During that game I found an interesting idea—17 Q–K2, but decided to preserve it for some subsequent game that was more important in the competitive sense. It has to be admitted that many players operate in this way. By the time of my game with Gligorić in Portorož, I had practically

assured myself of first place, and was not aiming for a win. But in Milan we met at the point when the battle was at its fiercest for one of the top four places, which would allow one to go on and contend for overall victory in the tournament.

17 Q–K2!

An innovation! And a highly promising one. What is Black to do?

In the event of 17 ... P–B5 White has a very simple plan: B–K3 and N–Q2, followed by the doubling of rooks on the QR-file. For Black it will be very difficult to regroup his forces for counter-play on the Q-side, since without the exchange ... P×P his knight at KB3 cannot move to Q2 on account of P–R5, while this exchange of pawns creates chronic weaknesses on the Q-side.

The defence of the pawn by 17 ... Q–Q2 removes the attack from White's QR5 square, so that after 18 P–R5 the knight is forced now to move not to QB5, but to QB1.

The advance 17 ... P–N5 is not worth considering. One move remains, which, though rather unattractive, is perhaps the only possibility...

17 ...	N×RP
18 B×N	P×B
19 R×P	

Summing up the results of the opening battle, we must mention the following: White has a firm grip on the centre, and in the event of the undermining move ... P–KB4 his QP can be supported by P–QB4. An additional pawn island has appeared in Black's position—his QRP, and as a consequence his ... QR4 and ... QB5 squares are weak, and can successfully be occupied by a white knight (N–Q2–B4–R5). It is true that Black has the two bishops, but in the given position this is more of a drawback than an advantage. The black-squared bishop is blocked in 'à la King's Indian' by its own pawns, and in contrast to that opening it is much more difficult to make it active. The white-squared bishop is very necessary for Black, but more for the defence of his weak pawns and squares than for any activity, which is restricted by the powerful central wedge of white pawns.

White's immediate plans will include the doubling of rooks on the half-open QR-file, the transfer of his knight to QB4, and, possibly, the undermining of Black's strongly-supported QBP by P–QN4. Black has to regroup, and, by exerting pressure down the half-open QN-file, attempt either to advance his QRP, or else effect the standard counter ... P–KB4.

In 1977 at the European Team Championship I played a further game on this theme with the Czech grandmaster Jan Šmejkal, which developed as follows: 19 ... B–B1 20 P–N3 R–N1 21 R–R3 R–K2 22 P–B4 R(2)–N2 23 Q–B2, with a slight advantage to White.

19 ...   **B–N2**

In the present position this prophylactic move is a waste of time. Black should have proceeded straight away with his Q-side play, and in the first instance removed his bishop from the QN-file—19 ... B–B1!?.

20 P–B4

Black has wasted time, and so White succeeds in blockading the QRP. A subsequent P–QN4 will give him a pawn superiority in the centre, and will disclose the weakness of Black's QP.

20 ...	**B–QB1**
21 B–Q2	**R–N1**
22 R–N1	

Until White has brought up his knight, P–QN4 is premature. The alternative defence of the QNP—22 B–B3, would have given Black's bishop a slight degree of freedom after 22 ... B–R3.

22 ...   **R–K2**

Now Black is on the right track. The second rank is an excellent base for the rook, from where it can be quickly switched from one wing to the other.

23 N–K1

An inaccuracy. White should have played 23 P–N3, and then defended the pawn on this square either with his queen, or with his rook now at QR4. In the variation chosen by me, Black succeeds in blockading the QNP, and evicting the rook proves to be a much more difficult business that I at first imagined. From this point I began to lose the thread of the game, and the position began gradually to become level.

23 ...	**R(2)–N2**
24 N–Q3	**R–N6**
25 R(1)–R1	

The regrouping of White's pieces was hampered by the unprotected state of his rook at QN1. I now planned either to exchange one pair of rooks (which would be very useful for then playing P–QN4), or else to drive the rook out of ... QN6. Unfortunately, this plan demands considerable time, and Black succeeds in creating counter-play on the K-side.

25 ...	N–K1

With the clear intention of playing ... P–B4.

26 B–B3	Q–R5

27 N–QB1 was threatened, when the rook has no good retreat square. For this reason the immediate 26 ... P–B4 does not work. Black removes his queen from the ... Q1–QR4 diagonal, and at the same time puts White's KP under fire. 26 ... Q–K2 looks more passive.

27 R(4)–R3	P–B4
28 B–K1!	

The exchange can wait, and meanwhile the bishop sets up an ambush! The vis-à-vis positioning of the queen and bishop on the same diagonal makes P–B4 a possibility, and so the queen is forced to withdraw.

28 ...	Q–K2

28 ... P–B5 would have blocked the king's wing, and freed White's hands for the battle on the opposite flank. Black's pawn storm would come too late.

29 R×R	R×R
30 N–QB1	R–N1
31 N–Q3	

Convinced that without his knight it will be very difficult to effect P–QN4, White returns it to its initial position. Black's reply is forced in view of the threatened advance.

31 ...	R–N6
32 P–B3	

White has to find an alternative way of driving the rook away, but for the moment makes a stabilizing prophylactic pawn advance. At the same time he removes for ever the threat of a break-through by the KBP, which could have occurred after 32 Q–B2 R–N1 33 P–N4 P×P 34 B×P P–B5 35 N–KB1 P–B6!.

32 ...	Q–N4

The activation of Black's bishop by 32 ... B–R3 would not have prevented White from carrying out his strategic plan. The knight at KN3 is the one piece which is not engaged in the battle for space on the Q-side. My plans included an immediate switching of it via KB1 to Q2. In the event of this, it would have been dangerous for Black to give up his king's bishop for the knight, in view of the slightly open position of his king, and the weakness of the pawn wedge ... QB4/Q3/K4, which would have created the conditions for a piece sacrifice by White on QB5 or K5 (in the absence of the bishop).

With the move played, the black queen takes up an active position, and restrains White's bishop, which is tied to the defence of his knight, as well as the knight itself (33 N–KB1? P×P 34 P×P B×P). On the other hand, the black rook is in need of support, and in view of this 32 ... N–B3 deserved greater consideration, since it too prevents 33 N–KB1?—33 ... P×P 34 P×P N×KP 35 Q×N B–B4.

33 K–R2

The king fulfils two tasks simultaneously: firstly, it defends the knight, and secondly, it moves out of the pin. 34 Q–QB2 has now become inevitable, and Gligorić attempts to find counter-play on the K-side.

33 ...	N–B3
34 Q–QB2	R–N1
35 P–N4	

White at last carries out this long-awaited undermining pawn move, and threatens to break up Black's position in the centre. But Black, although he has lost the overall strategical battle, has in his turn succeeded in organizing counter-play directly against the white king. A new phase in the battle therefore begins—one which is purely tactical.

35 ...	P×KP

After 35 ... P×NP 36 B×P Black's position collapses.

36 N(N3)×P

It is advantageous for White to exchange one of Black's attacking pieces, especially such a dangerous knight.

36 ...	N×N
37 P×N	Q–K6
38 P×P	

This gives Black some practical chances. White could have gained by force a secure

advantage by 38 B–B2 Q×KP 39 R–K1 Q–B4 40 P–N4 Q–B6 41 R–K3 and 42 P×P.

38 ...	Q×KP

The only move. Of course, 38 ... P×P is bad in view of 39 B–B2 Q×KP 40 R–K1 Q–B4 41 P–N4 etc.

39 P×P	B–B4
40 R–R3	R–QB1
41 R–B3	B–B1
42 B–B2	

After 42 P–B5 Q×QP (not, of course, 42 ... B×QP? 43 P×B R×R 44 Q×R Q×N 45 Q×Q B×Q 46 P–Q7 and P–Q8 = Q) the white pawns are blockaded, and it is very difficult to advance them in view of the absence of the white-squared bishop. Therefore the pawns stand better at QB4 and Q5, even though they are further from the queening square. 42 P–N4!? also deserved consideration.

42 ...	B×QP
43 Q–R2?	

Fatigued by this long and tense game, I make a mistake which could have reduced my previous efforts to nought. Yes, this is chess! An excellently-played game, numerous interesting ideas, but then one incautious move and... an illogical result, on the basis of which many will draw hasty conclusions.

43 P–B5! was correct, when 43 ... Q×QP now loses (43 ... B×BP 44 B×B Q×QP 45 N–N4! is even worse): 44 P×B R×N 45 Q×R B×N 46 Q–B8+ K–N2 47 Q–B7+! K–R3 48 B–K3+. After 43 ... B–B1 44 Q–R2 a position is reached with similar ideas to the game, only by transposition of moves. Gligorić, who was also tired, failed to utilize this chance opportunity, and played

43 ...	P–QR4

Black had at his disposal the wonderful tactical possibility of 43 ... Q–Q5! 44 B×Q P×B+ 45 P–N3 (the retreat of the king to the back rank gives Black the chance in certain cases of creating mating threats) 45 ... P×R, and White is obliged to force a draw by 46 Q×P P–B7 47 Q×B B×N

48 Q–K6+ K–N2 49 Q–K7+ K–N1 50 Q–K6+ etc., since 46 N–B1 is dangerous in view of 46 ... R–N1!.

| 44 P–B5 | B–Q2 |
| 45 R–R3 | B–N4 |

The retreat of the bishop from Q3 is no better. After the move played there follows an elegant concluding combination (*see diagram*)

46 P×B	B×N
47 P–Q7	R–Q1
48 R×B!	Q×R
49 P–Q6+	K–R1
50 Q×P	Resigns

Strength and Belief ✳ *Sympathy of the 'Head of the City'* ✳ *Shadow of the patron Berger* ✳ *Petrosian content to draw* ✳ *Return of service* ✳ *Play over the whole field* ✳ *The end crowns all*

I must admit that, as the only Soviet correspondent at that tournament, I could not hide my disappointment after the World Champion's defeat. Anatoly immediately noticed this, similed, took me by the arm to one side, and said quietly but firmly:

"For goodness sake, don't worry. I'll still take first place."

I immediately believed him, and then others also began to believe... But about one thing even now I cannot agree—that many of those there were pleased about his defeat. In Italy there was a clear majority of supporters for Karpov. The Mayor of Milan came one day to the tournament. To the question, with which of the grandmasters his sympathies lay, the 'Head of the City', without much thought, replied that he naturally wished success to the Italian Sergio Mariotti and to the World Champion Anatoly Karpov. The point was that Karpov was from Leningrad, the Mayor emphasized, and that the towns of Milan and Leningrad were linked by a long history of friendship.

All this does not mean, of course, that the other grandmasters did not have their supporters. For instance, at that same time, after the eighth round, very many congratulated Portisch on catching up with Karpov by defeating Larsen. Out of the blue the Hungarian grandmaster suddenly turned to me, and in front of everyone began thanking me for my help. I had no idea what he was talking about, and completely lost my head. Then Portisch explained to those around:

"We live in the same hotel in adjacent rooms, and each morning I wake up to the sound of loud shouting as Roshal sends his report to Moscow at first light. Today he was quieter, so I had a good sleep, and with a clear head defeated Larsen."

Everyone around burst out laughing. Only Larsen remained sad. Later I asked him, perhaps not very tactfully:

"Bent, you recently celebrated your fortieth birthday. Do you feel that you are getting old?"

He replied:

"I feel it, when I play badly."

In the ninth round the Dane played Karpov. At first he had a good position, but then almost lost to the Champion, who had already regained his composure after the previous day's unpleasant adjournment session.

Before the last round, the number of contenders for the top four places was considerably greater than four. At this point, in preparing for the decisive battle, the grandmasters had to throw into the balance of their preliminary calculations the important factor of coefficients. This always happens when the demand for places exceeds the supply. It had already been stated that, according to the tournament regulations, in the event of contenders scoring an identical number of points, preference would be given to the one with the superior Berger coefficient. (In other words, to the one who did better against the leading competitors). So that quite unsuspectingly, and completely unknowingly, the deviser of the coefficient, Berger, was transformed into a friend and patron for some, and into an enemy for others. His shadow had been hovering over the tournament hall for days, and had now become apparent and tangible.

In order to assure himself of at least a share of first place, Karpov had to play for a win against Mariotti, but this meant opening up the position, which against such an opponent was just what he didn't want to do. However, even half a point (thanks to Berger!) assured Karpov not only of a 'place in the sun', but also allowed him, thanks to his superior coefficient, not to have to fear an equal score in the semi-final. And the World Champion himself offered a draw to his opponent, who thus didn't manage to win a single game in the tournament. However later, somewhat vexed, Karpov admitted:

"I would never have done this, if I had known beforehand that Browne would play so badly against Portisch."

The American Walter Browne, already in a difficult position, in time trouble engaged in digging a grave for his own king, in which he was clearly successful. The game was adjourned, but not resumed. Later that evening Browne learned of the strong move sealed by Portisch, and resigned. Thus sole first place in the preliminary event went to Lajos Portisch.

A place in the sun was also gained by Petrosian, who took up the challenge offered by Larsen to engage in a proper 'brawl', and after displaying his excellent chess and competitive qualities (about which one had then begun to forget), forced his opponent's resignation. Fourth on the table of coefficients came Ljubojević. Up to a certain point, Tal, for whom only a win would suffice, conducted his game excellently against the Yugoslav. But first he got his move order wrong, and then simply overlooked a double attack by Ljubojević's queen on his rook and bishop. Over a period of four hours on the adjournment day, the Ex-World Champion sought drawing chances with rare courage and genuinely Tal-like ingenuity, but there was no longer any way to save the game.

On the basis of these same coefficients, the semi-final pairings were determined: Portisch–Ljubojević and Karpov–Petrosian.

The next day, all four, with no time to shake off their fatigue, and so almost enviously glancing at their previous opponents who were preparing to leave for home, once again sat down at the board. However, any one of those preparing to depart would gladly have exchanged places with those remaining: who wouldn't want to be the winner of such a tournament?! Besides, there are players who, whatever their mood and state of health, simply cannot refuse a series of lightning games, should the opportunity present itself. On the first semi-final day some of the spectators were diverted from the main happenings by a blitz match between two grandmasters, who just the previous day had appeared dispirited and depressed by their tournament fate—Tal and Browne, the latter also an acknowledged master of lightning play.

On entering the main hall on the conclusion of 'his match', Tal, who had cheered up, glanced at the demonstration board, and said that the position in the Karpov–Petrosian game had already occurred seventeen years earlier in a game of his with Petrosian, who, it is true, had now varied on his fifteenth move.

However, this innovation did not unduly take Karpov aback, and on the 28th move, with virtually nothing left to play with, the players agreed a draw.

Karpov later gave a simple explanation of his semi-final tactics:

"A drawn result in the semi-final match gave me—thanks to my superior coefficient in the all-play-all tournament—the right to then contend for first place. Of course, if we had been playing a match of 8 or 10 games, such an advantage would have been of lesser significance. But when there are only four games (and if you divide them into Whites and Blacks, this leaves only two serious attempts to play for a win), the initial advantage has significant importance.

Fairly soon it became clear that Petrosian, true to his character, was not looking to complicate matters. Two further draws convinced everyone of this. Then came the last interval during this prolonged grandmaster event. And after two days free from matches, but full of lectures and simultaneous displays, the competitors once again sat down at the board. Karpov, who had returned from Vienna, where in 25 games against readers of the Austrian Communist Party newspaper *Volksstimme* he had scored four draws (winning the remainder, of course), also needed a draw in his last game with Petrosian. In the opening the knights straight away disappeared from the board, soon followed by the bishops... When on the thirtieth move Karpov stretched out for a white pawn so as to establish complete material equality, his hand was met by Petrosian's—the Ex-World Champion congratulated the Champion on reaching the final.

In similar circumstances, Ljubojević acted in completely different fashion to Petrosian. In the very first of his semi-final games he carried out a reconnaisance in force, and stole up so closely to Portisch's king that for a time the latter was close to defeat. Likeable Ljubo's next attempt came in the third game, but was punished by a nought. And in the fourth, playing White, he made a move in the Ruy Lopez which caused Karpov to exclaim: "I immediately wanted to resign to Petrosian, so as to then be able to play Ljubojević." The Yugoslav himself realized that he had played indifferently. "What sort of mood could I be in", he said, "when, irrespective of the result of this game, Portisch was already assured of a place in the final."

And so, in a match of six games, Anatoly Karpov was opposed by perhaps the strongest of the non-Soviet grandmasters competing—Lajos Portisch.

In chess, the right to make the first move is equivalent to the right to serve in tennis or volleyball. If it is well-practised, and the player sends the ball along a low trajectory into the very corner of the service area, the service becomes an attacking weapon. In chess such a weapon is in the hands of the player with the white pieces. More often that not his opponent is not concerned about winning the point. His immediate and basic aim is to achieve without disadvantage the 'return of serve'.

Karpov succeeded in doing this. All Portisch's attempts to seize the initiative were cut short, and he had to exchange the queens and agree to go into an ending.

...Just then, at any minute, Portisch was going to offer a draw. But first, for no apparent reason, out of inertia, he made one more move, with a pawn. It would have been possible to also reply with an unimportant move, without troubling to think for long, and extend a hand to the opponent... Perhaps no one in the hall, apart from Karpov himself, noticed what ideas were concealed behind this innocent move of a little foot-soldier. He didn't make 'any old move', but continued playing with clinical accuracy. Portisch's tactical manoeuvre, which was at the same time psychological, did not succeed.

Karpov made excellent use of his own service. In a Ruy Lopez he somewhat unexpectedly engaged in a rapid offensive on the K-side, advancing his infantry further and further forward, so as to force open a diagonal for his black-squared bishop, which was aimed at Portisch's castled position. The latter set up sound defensive lines, gathering for this purpose more and more pieces around his king. The remaining parts of the board inevitably became deserted. And when the defensive lines on one of these sectors became sufficiently stretched, Karpov made a break-through there...

Let us again resort to an analogy with another type of sport. Everywhere, especially in field sports, one sign of great mastery is the ability to utilize the entire area of the pitch. In football, this skill appears to be best perfected in the play of the Dutch team. This team became the originators of a style which was called 'total football'. And the fortunes of a modern football team depend to a great extent on how successful they are at total play—on how intensively all the 'pieces' operate over the whole pitch.

No one has yet succeeded in utilizing in a game all 64 squares of the chess board simultaneously. And, incidentally, there are special grounds for this. The outstanding Soviet study composer Kasparian, also a player of considerable practical strength, when giving tuition to young chess players, advised them to assemble their pieces in a 'striking force' on the wing where they were stronger, and to limit themselves merely to prophylactic measures on the opposite part of the board. When the more impatient listeners asked him: "Why isn't it possible to attack simultaneously on both flanks?", the teacher replied: "For that two sets of chess pieces would be required, but you have at your disposal only one."

...No, no one has yet succeeded in utilizing at the same time all the space on the chess board. But... the one who is closer than anyone to solving this extra-difficult problem obtains the greatest successes. An example of such a utilization of the majority of the squares on the chess board is provided by the second match game between Karpov and Portisch in Milan.

With each new move the white pieces took control of more and more space. Dangers threatened the black position from all sides. Threats followed one after another. Portisch went completely onto the defensive, and had not the opportunity even for a second to draw breath and take his bearings. Is it surprising that in such a situation he should suddenly stumble into a combinational trap, set for him by Karpov? Portisch adjourned the game with the hope of saving an endgame with opposite-coloured bishops. But Karpov's black-squared bishop had already carried out its destructive business, and the World Champion accurately brought the game to a successful conclusion.

Karpov–Portisch
2nd Match Game, Milan 1975
Ruy Lopez

1 P–K4 P–K4 2 N–KB3 N–QB3 3 B–N5
P–QR3 4 B–R4 P–Q3 5 0–0 B–K2 6 B×N+
P×B 7 P–Q4 P×P 8 N×P P–QB4 9 N–B6
Q–Q2 10 N–R5 B–B3 11 Q–Q3 N–K2 12
N–B3 R–QN1 13 R–N1 0–0 14 B–Q2 B×N
15 B×B N–B3 16 P–QR3 N×N 17 B×N
R–K1 18 KR–K1 R–K3 19 P–QB4 B–N2
20 P–B3 QR–K1 21 Q–Q2 B–B3 22 P–QN3
Q–K2 23 Q–B4 R–N1 24 B–B3 P–B3 25
K–B2 Q–B2 26 P–KR4 R(3)–K1 27 P–KN4
R–N2 28 R–N2 R(1)–N1 29 KR–QN1
R–KB1 30 R–N1 B–K1 31 Q–K3 Q–K3
32 Q–Q3 B–B3 (Diag.)

33 P–N4 P×P 34 P×P B–K1 35 R–Q2
R–N3 36 Q–Q4 Q–K4 37 Q×R Q–R7+
38 K–K1 Q×R(7)+ 39 K×Q P×Q 40

R–QR1 B–B2 41 R×P R–N1 42 K–Q3 P–R4
43 P–QN5 P×P 44 P×P R–QB1 45 R–R4
B–K3 46 P–N5 P–B4 47 P×P B×KBP+
48 K–Q4 K–B2 49 B–N4 K–K3 50 R–R6
R–QN1 51 P–R5 B–N5 52 P–R6 P×P 53
P×P B–B4 54 B–Q2 R–N1 55 B–B4 R–N1
56 R–R7 K–B3 57 R–KN7 B–K3 58 R–QB7
R–KR1 59 R–B6 R–KN1 60 R×QP K–B4
61 R×P R–N5 62 R×B K×R 63 K–K4
R–N8 64 P–N6 Resigns

The adjournment session was held in the morning, and the same evening the players met once again. Portisch, being unable to rest and pull himself together after his defeat, appeared somewhat depressed. One sensed that he was not himself, and was not prepared to take energetic command of the white pieces. Karpov easily equalized, and even began thinking of more, but his opponent did not commit any obvious errors, and after soberly assessing the situation on the board, the grandmasters thought it better not to tempt Providence. Just at this time a heavy thunderstorm broke over Milan, and this caused part of the public, who were out walking in the green surroundings of the hotel, to suddenly attempt to increase the number of spectators at the chess event. Two crowds of visitors ran into one another on the stairs leading down to the underground 'congress centre'—the one escaping from the rain and hastening below, the other already ascending to ground level...

And then came another short draw, in 26 moves. The state which was to a greater or lesser extent characteristic at that point of all four players in this marathon, working away in the hall of the 'Leonardo da Vinci' hotel, was expressed by Portisch:

"I don't know about Karpov, but I am terribly tired. To play at such an intensive tempo nineteen successive games against grandmasters... And what grandmasters! After such an event I will have to rest for some two months. I have already declined an invitation to a big tournament in the Philippines."

...Most probably it was also this fatigue which dulled Petrosian's so highly-developed sense of danger. On that day he disdained his customary caution, and played for a win as Black. Ljubojević, his opponent in the match for 3rd and 4th places, found an interesting queen move, which placed Petrosian on the verge of defeat. Then, it is true, the latter almost saved the game with his 'patent weapon'—a sacrifice of the exchange. But then—again, it would seem, nervous exhaustion played its part—he suddenly began playing at the same rapid speed as Ljubojević, blundered, and lost. Ljubojević thus levelled the score in their match. In the subsequent games the players took no more risks, and shared third and fourth prizes.

But let us return to the main match.

"In the fifth game we both played badly"—said Karpov about his penultimate encounter with Portisch. "A decline set in after the good play in the first few games of the match."

Whether the players played well or badly in the fifth game, it was the very last straw at which Portisch was obliged to clutch. For the last time he had White, and a win would give him hope: in the event of a draw after 'normal time', the match would continue until the first victory by either player.

Petrosian, who had already concluded his game with Ljubojević, glanced at the early middle-game position on the adjacent board, and remarked: "Anatoly has come under the same attack as Balashov did against me in the Moscow Team Tournament. How was it that I won there?" After an hour's thought Portisch had failed to find an answer to this question. True, he also chose a good plan, but Karpov defended against the immediate threats. Finally, the players went into an ending, which Portisch did not want, and adjourned the game. There was no resumption. On seeing the move sealed by Karpov, Portisch declined to make any further attempts to win the game.

That morning the Hungarian grandmaster looked absolutely exhausted. "Playing in such an event is impossible", he said when we met on the way to the hall. "I have this terrible thought that it could go on even longer, if I should suddenly win today."

His fears proved to be groundless. His optimum result in the last game turned out to be a draw...

Portisch as Black chose a variation for which Karpov and his trainer had not prepared specifically for this tournament. A sharp position arose on the board, and Karpov sank into thought. Furman, who was sitting next to me, suddenly grew nervous. "Most probably", I thought to myself, "the strain of such a long event is beginning to tell. Well, never mind, it will soon all be over." But the trainer, meanwhile, for the first time in many days, gave vent to his feelings:

"Surely he hasn't forgotten it all! We analysed this position once, and there is a sharp continuation leading by force to a big advantage. He's forgotten, he's forgotten..."

And then quite angrily:

"How can he remember, if he keeps in his head whole stamp catalogues, blast them! Even today before the game he was busy with his philately; he's driven himself completely round the bend."

"But perhaps..."—I timidly ventured to suggest...

The thought came to us both simultaneously. Furman, who instantly calmed down, formulated it precisely:

"You're right. There's no point in using a 'secret weapon', when everything is decided anyway."

A minute later he was looking at his pupil as fondly as before. And then he hastened to add: "Tolya asked me to fill in these first day covers." And with some philately envelopes in one hand, and the inevitable cigarette in the other, he went out to the foyer, where the post office workers were busy.

Karpov did not cede the initiative. Portisch, it was generally sensed, was no longer able to play at his normal standard. Several poor moves on his part, and it became clear that at any minute Karpov would gain a decisive advantage. But things didn't come to that: the Hungarian grandmaster managed, with a faint smile, to offer a draw.

This outstanding event was probably one of the most difficult in Karpov's career. It was also difficult for all the other grandmasters. But for no one was it so essential to take first place, as it was for Karpov. Only such a victory would add the necessary stamp to his Champion's diploma, a stamp which would finally certify that today he, and only he, was 'chess player No.1'. And this additional weight of responsibility complicated his position, and placed an additional burden on his shoulders. It is all the more remarkable, therefore, that over the whole of the marathon distance laid down by the organizers of the Milan event, Karpov neither doubted himself that he would be ultimately successful, nor did he shake the belief of others in himself. The nervous tension did not affect his sensible tournament strategy—he played evenly throughout the event, and in order to win he did as much as was necessary, and no more.

Such an approach was possible only in a person who was mature physically, spiritually and intellectually, a person approaching the height of his powers.

CHAPTER 8

Round the World with the Flying Man from the Urals

Portorož and Ljubljana, Riga, Milan... What more, it would seem, could be asked? The Champion was playing. And playing better than anyone.

But such is the way that the chess world is made up, that this meant little to it—it is demanding of its chosen ones. For three, four months Karpov's name did not appear in the lists of participants in International Tournaments, and the whisper began to go round: "Even the young Champion has not managed to avoid the inveterate champions' disease..."

But he was not sitting idle and resting on the laurels of his victories, which though fresh, were nevertheless in the past. He was erasing the fatigue accumulated during that difficult period when chess did not give him any free time, finishing University work, improving his fitness, and analysing his own games. In other words, he was again preparing for future tournaments.

After this period of non-participation, he was again eager to travel. "The winter sleep is over", joked Anatoly, "it is time to be on the move." And the 'flying man from the Urals' rushed off, along a route which is difficult even to imagine.

First—an International Tournament in the Yugoslav town of Skopje, and then—the USSR Cup in Tbilisi.

And then, even further: Leningrad–Moscow–Barcelona–Paris–Le Havre–La Rochelle –Moscow again–Leningrad (3 days at home)–Moscow–Krasnoyarsk–Yakutsk–Mirny–Ya-kutsk–Petropavlovsk-Kamchatsky–Khabarovsk–Moscow–Leningrad (3 days)–Moscow–Tokio –Manila–Moscow... All this within a space of two and a half months in 1976—from 10th May to 28th July. And what about those Siberian and Far-Eastern distances? The shortest flight— from Yakutsk to Mirny—was fifteen hundred kilometres. The habitual railway journey between Leningrad and Moscow was on the regular 'Red Arrow' service, all the rest was in the air—by Tupoliev and Boeing, Douglas and Ilyushin 18, Yakovlev 40, Antonov 24, Ilyushin 62, and even by helicopter.

And then by car—to the Vladimir District of the Russian Republic, and again by plane—to the province of Cordoba in Spain.

He finished the year 1976 in his own country, following his brilliant victory in the USSR Championship.

But let us return, however, to the beginning, to Karpov's Spring start...

AGAINST THE THEORY OF PROBABILITY

Echoes of the talk about a recurrence of the "champions' disease" reached Karpov. But as a person who since childhood had been sober in his assessments, he was little bothered by this talk. His reasoning was as follows:

"Champions are normally criticized for the fact that they rarely play. But what are they to do? After all, in any tournament they are expected to take only first place; second is already a failure, while third or fourth is virtually a fiasco. But this is just not possible—to win every tournament, one after another. This means that the only thing to do is not to play very often, and this is what my predecessors did. But I like playing, and I intend to play. And as regards first prizes... For four years in a row now I have been constantly taking first places. The one exception was the Premier League of the USSR Championship, where I shared second to sixth places. Now I also have working against me such a formidable opponent as the theory of probability. After each new tournament win, my chances of being first in the following one become smaller—in the end the theory of probability is bound to have its say! I'll be off form... I won't be well... There are plenty of tricks that life can play on a man, and you can't foresee them all. But now, with Milan behind me, this doesn't worry me too much. I will play."

And in the Spring Karpov set off to a strong tournament in the Yugoslav town of Skopje, a town which for him held vivid memories of his first chess Olympiad, a town which was destroyed by an earthquake and restored to life by the efforts of people from various countries. For this reason, the traditional meetings of chess players in the Macedonian Capital bear the name of the 'Solidarity Tournament'.

Karpov was accompanied to Skopje by another of our grandmasters, his contemporary and close colleague Rafael Vaganian, They have been friends since their school days, and since then have remained uncompromising opponents at the board. What's more—and this is not a particularly frequent occurrence in chess—the sharpness of their rivalry has not only not spoiled their relations, but rather has strengthened their former friendship. In Skopje, Vaganian, a rapidly improving player, was considered one of the favourites for first place, which meant that he numbered among Karpov's main rivals. The draw brought them together in the very first round. The battle, as usual, was most intense. Karpov won. And Vaganian, over-impressionable, was depressed by this initial misfortune, and was unable to forget about it and take part in the battle for the top places in the tournament.

Karpov relates:

"This game took too much nervous energy out of each of us, and in the subsequent rounds both Rafik and I played indifferently. I, it is true, managed to avoid any disasters. But the time came when it was necessary for both of us to improve our play. And when this happened, at last, Vaganian demonstrated his true class. He succeeded in scoring five and a half points out of six, and also 'on the way' shared first place in a very strong lightning tournament, which included all the participants in the 'Solidarity Tournament', with the exception of Ivkov and myself. But then Vaganian's luck deserted him. He left a piece *en prise* against a candidate master, which put him completely out of his stride. To crown all his misfortunes, he caught a cold, 'failing to notice' that snow fell in Skopje for a couple of days, and, now ill, blundered in a winning position into a mate in one against a not particularly strong master."

I have given Karpov's account of the tournament with practically stenographic accuracy. I recall how even then I was surprised that he should speak in such detail and with such fervour, which is in general rather uncharacteristic of him, about the vicissitudes of his colleague's tournament path, and so little about his own affairs and his victory. Among the traits of the Karpov character, sentimentality, if it is there at all, is very deeply hidden. He has equable relations with the majority of his colleagues or mere acquaintances, and the circle of those whom he numbers as his friends is very small. On the other hand, those in this circle are genuinely dear to him, and can rely on him; he is ready to help them in word and deed, and he takes to heart their joys and misfortunes. Incidentally, in valuing his relations with those close to him, he normally tries to choose them as his companions when he travels far from home, to tournaments abroad.

In the 'Solidarity Tournament', one of the participants was the veteran American grandmaster Reshevsky, whose religious beliefs and punctiliousness in following the practices of his faith are known to the whole chess world. It is also known that his religion forbids him from sitting down at the chess board on Friday evenings. For this reason it was agreed at a meeting of all the competitors that Reshevsky's games on that day of the week should be moved forward to the morning, so that they would finish before the onset of dusk. It so happened that the game between Reshevsky and Vaganian fell on a Friday. The latter regarded the prospect of a morning session with extreme calm, not to say indifference. Karpov grew alarmed: "Find out the exact starting time." Vaganian returned dismayed: "They say early, at ten." "On no account", said Karpov determinedly. "After all, you are used to getting up late. Don't even think of agreeing to anything earlier than midday. Eleven o'clock—that's the absolute limit, if your gentle character should not stand firm, and you begin to give way." And, this time together, they went off to see the organizers. Reshevsky argued, and threatened to leave Skopje, but all the other competitors condemned the American's behaviour (they were, after all, meeting him half way), and supported Karpov and Vaganian. This game, which began at eleven o'clock, was played brilliantly by Vaganian, and he immediately rushed into the hotel to thank Karpov, as if it were not he, Vaganian, but Karpov who had gained this rapid win, after carrying out a combination of rare beauty with the sacrifice of several pieces.

"Throughout the tournament, Uhlmann and I led by a fairly clear margin from all the others", said Karpov. "The rest were essentially never in contention for first place. Together we approached the last round with half a point separating us. It was then that the game between us took place; the draw had given the choice of weapon to the East German grandmaster—he had White. For Uhlmann, who was trailing by half a point, only a win would suffice.

On the day after the conclusion of the tournament, a number of papers printed a report by one of the press agencies: on the 20th move Karpov had offered Uhlmann a draw, the latter had refused and had gone on to lose. No one suspected that this might be an error. The situation appeared logical: it was sufficient for me to draw, which is what I offered. Uhlmann needed to win, so he played riskily, for which he was punished. But nevertheless the journalist was wrong. The draw was offered by Uhlmann, with White, and declined by me, with Black. I declined it, and then went on to win."

Uhlmann–Karpov
English Opening

1 P–QB4 N–KB3 2 N–QB3 P–K3 3 N–B3
P–QN3 4 P–K4 B–N2 5 Q–K2 B–N5 6 P–K5
N–N1 7 P–Q4 N–K2 8 Q–Q3 P–Q4 9 P×P
e.p. P×P 10 P–QR3 KB×N+ 11 Q×B
N–Q2 12 B–K2 R–QB1 13 0–0 0–0 14 B–N5
P–KR3 15 B–R4 Q–K1 16 B–N3 N–KB4
17 B–B4 P–QN4 18 B–Q3 Q–K2 19 B×N
P×B 20 KR–K1 Q–B3 21 P–Q5 R×P 22
Q×Q N×Q 23 B×QP KR–B1 24 B–K5
N×P 25 N–Q4 P–B3 26 N×BP P×B 27
N–Q6 (Diag.)

27 ... N–B5 28 N×B N–Q6 29 N–Q6
N×R 30 N×R(4) N–B7 31 N–Q6 R–Q1
32 N–N7 R–Q7 33 R–QB1 N–Q5 34 R–B8+
K–R2 35 P–KR4 R×NP 36 R–QR8 N–K7+
37 K–R2 N–B5 38 K–N1 N–Q6 39 N–Q6
N×P 40 R×P N–N5 41 P–N3 N–K6 42
K–R2 K–N3 43 R–N7 R–Q7 44 N×P N–B4
45 P–N4 N×P 46 K–N1 R–KN7+ 47 K–B1
R×P 48 R–R7 N–B4 49 P–R4 P–R4 50
P–R5 P–R5 51 R–R8 P–R6 52 Resigns

Remember Karpov's admission: "I play particularly well when I am involved in a chase, but when I am in the lead I often reduce speed." Does this mean that his words and actions do not coincide? No, it was simply that the Karpov playing in Skopje was not the same as the one who was responsible for these words. He had become slightly less rational at the board, but on the other hand much more aggressive and confident in his powers. He no longer considered it sufficient for him to simply take first place, and he did not want to avoid playing for a win in any game where there was a real chance of gaining one. And besides...

After the tournament, Karpov expressed to me a thought, which was a secret but which at the same time was straining to emerge, a thought which he did not want to pronounce for all to hear, but which at the same time was dear to him:

"Fischer once played here, in Skopje. He scored 13½ points out of 17. I have 12½ out of 15. As a percentage this is higher..."

The 'Solidarity Tournament' happened to fall at a time when a new word had begun appearing more and more frequently in the chess press—the word 'rating'. A system of individual coefficients, devised by the American Professor Élő, placed each player on a certain step of a hierarchal ladder, depending on his coefficient. This coefficient (which is the same as rating) was determined not by the number of first places in this or that tournament, but by the number of games won, or more precisely, by the number of points scored. True, Karpov himself always stated that he did not overrate the importance of a rating, but saw it merely as a kind of chess player's visiting-card. However, it could also be said that a visiting-card is no trifling thing... Be that as it may, but it was after the 'Solidarity Tournament' that the Champion's rating passed the 2700 mark. None of the other active grandmasters was even approaching this dizzy height.

Around this time Karpov gave an interview for a group of foreign journalists. As was usual in such conversations, the reporters again and again returned in one form or another to the same theme: "Who do you consider your most dangerous rival?" Karpov very much dislikes talking about this. He dislikes even more acting against his conscience. Tired of being diplomatic, the Champion finally uttered the phrase:

"I don't see anyone at the moment..."

A tasty morsel, wouldn't you agree, for anyone wishing to reproach the author of such a pronouncement of arrogance, conceit and self-reclamation? But the wisest and most far-seeing chess experts of the time were already aware of what sort of a player and what sort of a person the present World Champion was. A logical commentary on Karpov's pronouncement was given on the pages of the *New York Times* by Robert Byrne. "Karpov is noted for his extreme frankness and straightforwardness. He never puts on an act, and never resorts to diplomacy. So if he says that he does not see any dangerous rivals among the leading grandmasters in the world, the question for us is not to what extent these words reflect his authentic opinion, but to what extent they reflect the objective relative strengths."

Karpov–Vaganian
French Defence

1 P–K4	P–K3
2 P–Q4	P–Q4
3 N–Q2	

The opening was not unexpected for either of the two sides. The French is Vaganian's favourite defence, and I frequently employ the 3 N–Q2 system.

3 ...	P–QB4
4 KP×P	KP×P
5 KN–B3	P–QR3

A rarely-played continuation, by which Black prevents the development of the white bishop at QN5. In addition, he is ready in some cases to play ... P–QB5, when the advance ... P–QN4 is already prepared. It is also clear, however, that 5 ... P–QR3 does little to promote the development of his pieces.

6 P×P

This is apparently the simplest solution. It is considered, however, that 6 B–K2 leads to a more complex game, and gives White possibly even better prospects.

6 ...	B×P
7 N–N3	B–N3
8 B–Q3	N–K2
9 0–0	QN–B3
10 R–K1	B–N5

Both sides make 'their own' useful moves. The struggle revolves around the critical square Q4. If Black should succeed in advancing his central pawn to ... Q5, he will have a satisfactory game. But if White, on the other hand, gains this highly important square for his pieces, his opening advantage will be undisputed. In view of this, 11 B–K3 would be inaccurate here, on account of 11 ... P–Q5.

11 P–B3

There is no point in driving away the white-squared bishop immediately (11 P–KR3), since for the moment Black cannot castle in view of the check at KR7.

11 ...	P–R3
12 P–KR3	B–KR4
13 B–K3	0–0

The exchange of black-squared bishops is in principle unfavourable for Black, but in the event of, for instance, 13 ... B–B2, he would fall even further behind in development.

14 B×B	Q×B
15 Q–K2	

This does not appear altogether logical—placing the queen in front of the rook on the open file. Nevertheless, Black is unable to exploit this circumstance—after 15 ... KR–K1 his rook is defended only once.

15 ...	KR–Q1
16 QR–Q1	P–R4

Vaganian tries for active play on the Q-side, by driving the white knight away from QN3. He probably underestimated the following pawn sacrifice, after which the play takes on a forced aspect.

17 B–N1!

It will not be out of place to repeat that the basic idea of White's play is control of his Q4 square, over which a constant watch must be kept. Therefore the move Q–K3, which comes into White's plans, would be unsuccessful in this particular instance—17 Q–K3 Q×Q 18 R×Q B×N 19 R×B P–R5, and Black has everything in order.

17 ...	B×N

Black accepts the challenge, but otherwise there is insufficient justification for 16 ... P–QR4, which has weakened his Q-side.

18 Q×B	P–R5
19 N–Q4	Q×P

19 ... N×N 20 R×N(4) Q×P fails to 21 R–QN4, when Black loses a piece (the rook not only defends the bishop, but also blocks the QR3–KB8 diagonal).

20 N×N

Black's last piece is diverted from the defence of his king.

20 ...	N×N
21 Q–B5	P–KN3
22 Q–B6	

White's pieces are deployed most harmoniously; in particular, his queen not only defends the QBP, thereby excluding Black's most powerful piece from the game, but also creates the threat of the bishop sacrifice at KN6, with a subsequent mating attack.

22 ...	R–Q2

On 22 ... R–K1 I was intending to continue 23 B×P P×B 24 Q×P+ K–B1 25 Q×P+ K–N1 26 R–K6.

23 B–B5!

This is the whole point!

23 ...	R–K2

23 ... R–B2 would have been met by the simple 24 R×P. 23 ... P×B would also have lost, to 24 R–Q3 (it has to be this rook, blocking the QN1–KR7 diagonal; the other rook must control the K-file) 24 ... P–B5 (24 ... N–K2 25 R×N) 25 Q×BP Q–B7 (26 Q–KN4+ was threatened, but 25 ... P–B3 is more tenacious) 26 R–N3+ K–R2 27 Q–B6 R–KN1 28 R×R.

24 R×R

I could also have gained an advantage by 24 B×P P×B 25 R×R N×R 26 Q×N, but I wanted more.

24 ...	N×R
25 B–Q3	N–B4

The only move. The knight has no other square—25 ... N–B3 26 B×P. Also bad is 25 ... R–K1 26 R–K1 Q–R6 27 B–N5. And, finally, defending the knight with the king does not work—25 ... K–B1 26 R–N1 Q×RP 27 R×P, and now both 27 ... R–K1 and 27 ... Q–R6 are met by 28 B×P.

26 B×N	P×B
27 R–K1!	

Black's rook must not be allowed onto the third rank, otherwise after ... R–R3–KN3 and by giving up several pawns, he would gain good counter-chances with his dangerous passed QRP.

27 ...	Q×RP

A clever trap. Now the immediate 28 R–K3 suggests itself, but then Black has an interesting way to draw: 28 ... P–B5 29 Q×P(4) Q–N8+ 30 K–R2 P–R6! 31 R–N3+ Q–KN3 32 R×Q+ P×R. Here

White has no more than perpetual check, since his queen is unable to approach the black rook.

28 Q×RP	P–R6
29 Q–N5+	

The queen is transferred without loss of time to KB6.

29 ...	K–B1
30 Q–B6	K–N1
31 Q×P(5)	Q–Q7
32 R–K7!	

The final finesse. The black rook has to be diverted from the QR-file.

32 ...	R–KB1
33 Q–N4+	K–R2
34 R–K5	Q–R3
35 R–R5	R–QR1
36 Q–B5+	K–N2
37 R×Q	K×R
38 Q–B6+	K–R2
39 Q×P+	K–R1
40 Q×NP	Resigns

Karpov–Velimirović
King's Indian Defence

1 P–QB4	N–KB3
2 N–QB3	P–KN3
3 P–K4	

The move order chosen by White has its point. By leaving his pawn at Q2 for the moment, he can avoid the main variations of the Grünfeld Defence, and himself develop his pieces in accordance with the system chosen by Black. Here Black has two alternatives: either the King's Indian Defence, or else the Maróczy variation, resulting after

3 ... P–B4 4 N–B3 B–N2 5 P–Q4 P×P 6 N×P.

It should incidentally be said that in the given instance all White's trickery is unnecessary, since Velimirović is known to be a fervent follower of Indian set-ups.

3 ...	B–N2
4 P–Q4	P–Q3
5 P–B3	0–0
6 B–K3	P–K4

An old and forgotten variation. 6 ... P–B3 and 6 ... N–B3 have been more popular in the tournament practice of recent years.

7 P–Q5	N–R4
8 Q–Q2	Q–R5+

An idea discovered by Bronstein, and first employed by him in a game against Spassky. The point of the move is to sacrifice the queen for two bishops and two pawns. It is a clever idea, but that is all. At the time Bronstein did not find any followers, but now, 14 years later...

9 B–B2

Perhaps he'll change his mind?

9 ...	Q–B5

No. So the queen has to be won.

10 B–K3	Q–R5+

11 P–KN3	N×P
12 Q–KB2	

A pawn is lost after 12 B–B2 N×B 13 B×Q N×Q.

12 ...	N×B
13 Q×Q	N×B
14 K–K2	N×P
15 R–QB1!	

Stronger than 15 P–N3 N–R6, as chosen by Spassky in a similar situation. Instead of taking up a comfortable post at ... QR6, the knight will subsequently be driven back to ... QN3.

15 ...	N–R3
16 N–Q1!?	

The white knights take up ideal positions for an attack on the king. With the KN-file being half-open, the knight from K3 will be constantly threatening to move to KB5, while from KR3 the other knight will prevent Black from blocking the position by ... P–KN4.

16 ...	N–N3
17 N–R3	B–Q2
18 N–K3	P–KB3
19 KR–N1	QR–Q1

Velimirović prepares for active play in the centre, associated with the undermining move ... P–QB3. The rook supports the QP in advance, but it soon proves to be occupying a fatal square.

20 P–N3

The knight could have been sent on a distant raid via KN4 to KR6. But I had already noticed that although 20 N–B5? P×N 21 R×B+ K×R 22 R–KN1+ K–R1

23 N–N5 P×N 24 Q×NP B–N4+! 25 K–Q2 R–Q2 was ineffective at the moment, it would be very strong after ... P–B3, and so I decided to wait a little.

20 ...	P–B3
21 P×P	

The immediate 21 N–B5 would have shown inexcusable haste: 21 ... B×N! 22 P×B N×P 23 P×P P–R3!.

21 ...	P×P

Suspecting nothing, Black puts his head into the 'tiger's mouth'. This was his last chance to deviate—21 ... B×P.

22 N–B5!

A blow which shatters Black's defences. The sacrifice cannot be declined—the QP is directly attacked, but even more terrible is the threat of N–K7+.

22 ...	P×N

There is equally no salvation in 22 ... B×N 23 P×B P–N4 24 N×P! P×N 25 Q×NP R–Q2 26 P–B6.

23 R×B+	K×R
24 R–KN1+	

It turns out that if the rook at ... Q1 were on any other square, White's combina-

tion would be impossible, in view of 24 ... K–R1. But now this king move leads to an immediate mate after 25 N–N5! P×N 26 Q×NP R–B2 27 Q×R+, or 27 ... R–KN1 28 Q–B6+.

24 ...	K–B2
25 Q–R5+	

White also had excellent chances after 25 Q×RP+ K–K1 26 Q–R5+ (if 26 R–N7, then 26 ... R–B1, and the king runs away through the newly-opened escape square) 26 ... R–B2 27 R–N8+ K–K2 28 R×R P×P 29 R–KR8 P×P+ 30 K×P, and after the inevitable 31 R–R7 an unusual material balance would arise—queen against two minor pieces and two pawns, where the presence of the outside passed KRP must bring victory to the queen.

But I was attracted by another idea, and by other tactical strokes.

25 ...	K–K3
26 Q×BP+	

It is strange, but true, that after 26 P×P+ Black's king would be forced into the very centre (26 ... K–Q4) in front of his troops, but that White's queen, rook, knight and pawns would be unable to cause him any harm, in view of their remoteness and lack of co-ordination. E.g. 27 Q–N4 K–B4, and the king strolls fearlessly around the centre!

26 ...	K–B2

White wins easily after 26 ... K–K2? 27 R–N7+ R–B2 28 R×R+ K×R 29 N–N5+.

27 Q–R5+

As they say, testing Black's vigilance.

27 ...	K–K3
28 Q–B5+	K–B2
29 N–N5+	

Now that the pawn at ... KB4 has gone, White achieves nothing by 29 Q×RP+ K–K1 30 Q–R5+ R–B2 31 R–N8+ K–K2 32 R×R on account of 32 ... B×N.

29 ...	K–K1

After 29 ... K–K2 Black's position collapses rapidly: 30 Q×RP+ K–K1 31 Q–N6+ K–K2 32 Q–N7+ K–K1 33 N–R7 R–B2 34 N×P+ K–K2 35 N–N8+.

30 N–K6!

It was on this series of fine moves that I was pinning my hopes! The knight is pinned, but it cannot be taken.

30 ...	R–B2

Velimirović was relying on this defence, but in his preliminary calculations he underestimated the following manoeuvre by White. However, since the twenty-third move Black has made all the correct replies, and even if my opponent had seen everything, he would have been unable to deviate.

31 R–N7	R–QB1

The plausible 31 ... N–B4 leads to an interesting mating position: 32 N–B7+ K–B1 33 R×R+ K×R 34 Q×RP+ K–B1 35 Q–R8+ K–K2 36 Q–N7!.

32 R×R	K×R
33 N–N5+	K–K2
34 Q×RP+	K–Q1
35 Q–R8+	K–B2
36 Q×P	R–K1

First of all Black must safeguard the most vulnerable point in his position—... Q3.

37 P–KR4	N–B4
38 P–R5	N–K3
39 P–R6	

White gains no advantage by the exchange 39 N×N B×N (not 39 ... R×N 40 Q–N7, with good winning chances) 40 Q–N6! (40 P–R6 B–N1) 40 ... R–K2! (Black loses after either 40 ... K–Q1 41 P–R6 B–N1 42 Q×P+, or 40 ... K–Q2 41 P–R6 B–N1 42 Q–N7+ K–K3 43 Q×RP N–Q2 44 P–R4) 41 P–R6 N–Q2!, and the pawn is halted: 42 P–R7 N–B1 43 Q–B6 R×P 44 Q×N B–B1.

39 ...	N–KB1

The sacrifice is prepared, but White is in no hurry to accept it, and first makes all the useful moves available to him.

40 P–N4

While there is time, it is favourable for White to place his pawns on squares of opposite colour to the bishop, and at the same time to restrict Black's possibilities as regards the placing of his pawns.

40 ...	N–B1
41 K–Q2	N–K2
42 P–R7	

Now is the time to gain a material advantage. Black was already preparing to give up for the pawn his newly-arrived knight (... N–N1×P), and to retain his other, more active one.

42 ...	N×P
43 N×N	N–B1
44 N–B8	R–K2

The black pieces are cramped, but in view of the fact that the battle is being fought on one small part of the board only, and that it is difficult to advance pawns without them being exchanged, Black has created something of a fortress, which it is essential for White to break up.

45 P–R3	B–K1
46 N–K6+	K–Q2
47 N–N7	K–B2
48 N–B5	R–Q2

The only square for the rook. The fortress would have been shattered after either 48 ... R–R2 49 N–N7, or 48 ... R–B2? 49 Q–K6 R–B1 (49 ... K–Q1 50 K–K3 followed by N×P, but not 50 N×P? N×N 51 Q×N+? R–Q2) 50 N×P! N×N 51 Q–K7+, or 50 ... B–Q2 51 Q–R6.

49 P–R4

It is not by chance that I advance my pawns very cautiously. There are few remaining on the board, and the ill-judged placing of one pawn, and in particular a careless exchange, can lead to the win being missed. At this stage I was intending to take away the square ... QN3 from Black's king and knight.

49 ...	B–B2
50 K–B3	B–R7
51 P–R5	R–B2
52 Q–R6	R–Q2
53 P–B4	

The moment has arrived. White's pieces have taken up ideal positions, and it is now the turn of the pawns.

53 ...	P×P
54 Q×BP	R–B2
55 Q–R6	R–Q2
56 Q–R2	

An inaccuracy. On making this move I immediately noticed (as often happens with chess players) that by 56 N–Q4! I could have set my opponent very difficult problems, e.g.: 56 ... N–K2 (the only defence against the threat of P–K5) 57 Q–R8 N–B1 58 P–K5 P×P 59 Q×P+ N–Q3 (59 ... K–N2 loses to 60 P–R6+!) 60 N–B5 B–N8 (otherwise the king penetrates to QB5 via Q4) 61 N×N R×N 62 Q–QB5; or 57 ... R–Q1 58 Q–R2 B–N1 59 Q–N1, with the unpleasant threat of 60 N–B5, and in reply to 59 ... K–N2—60 Q–N7 R–Q2 61 Q–B8! B–R7 62 Q–K8 R–B2 (62 ... K–B2 63 Q–QR8) 63 Q–Q8 N–B1 64 N–B5; or 57 ... B–N1 58 N–B5 N×N 59 P×N B–Q4 60 Q–R8.

56 ...	B–K3
57 Q–R6	

I expected that with his sealed move Velimirovic would either return to the previous position (57 ... B–R7)—when I would no longer have missed my chance, or else play 57 ... B–B2, which is objectively stronger. In this case I would have had to prepare the break-through P–K5. I never thought for one moment that with his sealed move he would take such a highly-committing decision.

57 ...	B×N
58 P×B	P–Q4

The remainder is practically forced. White stretches his opponent's defences, combining the threat of advancing his passed KBP with attempts by his queen to break through to the black pawns, which in the end are decisive.

This loses immediately, but 62 ... R–B2 63 P–B6 similarly does not hold out any hope.

59 K–Q4	N–Q3
60 Q–B4	

Threatening 61 K–B5.

60 ...	K–N2
61 Q–K5	N–B2
62 Q–K8	K–B2

63 Q–QR8	K–Q3
64 Q–KB8+	K–B2
65 Q–B5	N–Q3

Or 65 ... K–N2 66 P–R6+.

66 Q×RP+	K–B1
67 Q–R6+	**Resigns**

THE STARS FAIL TO LIFT THE CUP

On the opening day of the team event for the USSR Cup, Anatoly Karpov gave an interview for Georgian radio and television. Appearing in the rôle of correspondent was Nana Alexandria.

"How do you rate the chances of your Central Army team?"

"Our team has often been in the battle for first place. But it was always lacking in something, and finished second (at any rate, in those events where I have participated). We would like to be first this time."

"Especially since your squad has been strengthened by a World Champion..." Alexandria added, having in mind the fact that Nona Gaprindashvili had recently transferred to the Army Club.

"By two World Champions, since I didn't have this title before", Karpov smiled.

After the competition for the Cup was over, an interview was given by Nona Gaprindashvili:

"I don't even believe it, I can't find words... Before the start of the tournament, we thought that second place for the Army team would be a failure... But not to finish among the prize-winners—it's just too much..."

The USSR Cup went to the strong and harmonious 'Burevestnik' team. The failure of the Army team confirmed once again an ancient truth: several stars do not necessarily make a team. We have already talked about this, when describing the 1972 World Olympiad and the 1975 USSR Peoples' Spartakiad. There will also be further occasion to talk about it. As regards Karpov, he was virtually the least to blame for the failure of the Army team.

These were his words:

"While still on the way to Tbilisi by train, I unexpectedly fell ill with tonsillitis, with a temperature of over a hundred. But on arrival it turned out that Vasyukov was also ill, and that Gipslis was not eager to play, i.e. the first board was vacant, so that against my wishes I had straight away to sit down and play Tal. I have an equal score against him. Although all of our games up till now have finished peaceably, they have by no means always been grandmaster draws. I recall how in the very first he tormented me for more than a hundred moves, and our encounters were no less complicated in the Interzonal Tournament, and in the USSR Championship. But in Tbilisi, Misha saw that I hardly had the strength to sit there, and did not insist on a hard fight. In the end I scored four draws and two wins—perfectly respectable for top board."

ONE HUNDRED YEARS BETWEEN THE TWO

After visits to Holland, Spain and France, the World Champion headed for Siberia and Kamchatka. He was in a hurry to go East, and for this reason his report was brief:

"The fourth Amsterdam Tournament proved to be a rather difficult one. Although it was over a short distance, things were made much more complicated by the unusual schedule: play from 13.00 to 18.00 hours, and adjournments from 20.00 to 22.00. The organizers had failed to provide for one small point—chess players also have to eat. In addition, during the event I became accustomed to sleeping very well, and so I had no time to prepare for individual games.

Perhaps only Walter Browne was happy about this schedule. Thus I learned about yet another peculiarity of the USA Champion—he likes to sit at the board hungry. But this did not help. In Amsterdam Browne at first played rather unsurely, and prior to the finish found himself in last place. In the last round but one he gained something of an advantage over Fridrik Olafsson, but was unable to find a win. Browne then went in for a highly risky operation. Olafsson ran short of time, and his flag fell when the American was already in a lost position. True, in the last round Browne won most convincingly against Jan Timman, and took second place.

I defeated Browne and Olafsson in our mini-matches, and had two fighting draws with Timman. But in the very first round Olafsson won against Timman, because the latter, after refusing the offer of a draw, then blundered. After this I was level with the Icelandic grandmaster for four rounds. In the deciding encounter I gained an advantage, but in my opponent's time trouble did not play quite exactly, and to a certain extent made the win more difficult. Nevertheless, I succeeded in defeating Olafsson...

On the conclusion of the tournament, I was presented with a replica of a Memorial Cup. The enormous glass pawn itself, commissioned in honour of Max Euwe's 75th birthday, remained in Amsterdam, where it was decided to hold further jubilee events in honour of the FIDE President.

My 25th birthday also coincided with the conclusion of the tournament in Holland, and when Professor Euwe and I appeared on T.V. together, the Dutch joked that it was the 'broadcast of the century'.

In Spain on 24th May I was ceremoniously awarded the 'Chess Oscar'. As in the previous year, it depicted a 'lady with an umbrella'—the symbol of Barcelona.

At the invitation of the France–USSR Society, I visited Paris, Le Havre and La Rochelle. It was very pleasant to receive from the Mayor of the French Capital the gold medal of Paris —the highest award there. However, I then had to 'pay for it': they sat down against me the strongest masters and candidate masters, and asked me to give a display on 22 boards. It was difficult work, the result being: $+13 -4 =5$.

"However", the World Champion smiled, "I do not expect that the tests awaiting me in the next few days will be any easier. I have a very intensive programme in Siberia and Kamchatka..."

Browne–Karpov
Ruy Lopez

1 P–K4 P–K4 2 N–KB3 N–QB3 3 B–N5
P–QR3 4 B–R4 N–B3 5 0–0 B–K2 6 R–K1
P–QN4 7 B–N3 0–0 8 P–B3 P–Q3 9 P–KR3
N–N1 10 P–Q4 QN–Q2 11 QN–Q2 B–N2
12 B–B2 R–K1 13 P–QN4 B–KB1 14 P–QR4
N–N3 15 P–R5 QN–Q2 16 B–N2 R–N1 17
R–N1 B–R1 18 B–R1 P–N3 19 P–B4 NP×P
20 P×P QN×P 21 N×N P×N 22 B–B3
B–B3 23 Q–K2 B–N4 24 N×P P–B4 25 P×P
R–B1 26 B–N3 R×P 27 B–N4 R–B3 28 B×B
R×B 29 Q–R2 B×N 30 B×B Q–B2 31
B–B1 R–Q1 32 R–N6 R(1)–Q3 33 R×R
R×R 34 B–Q3 (Diag.)

34 ... N–R4 35 P–N3 N–N2 36 R–N1
N–K3 37 K–N2 N–B4 38 B–B2 R–Q3 39
Q–B4 Q×P 40 R–N8+ K–N2 41 R–QB8
N–K3 42 Q–N3 R–Q1 43 Q–QB3 Q×Q 44
R×Q R–Q2 45 R–R3 N–B4 46 K–B3 K–B3 47
K–K3 K–K2 48 R–R5 K–Q3 49 B–Q3 R–R2
50 B–B4 K–B3 51 P–B4 P–B3 52 P×P P×P
53 B–Q5+ K–N3 54 R–R1 P–QR4 55
R–QN1+ K–B2 56 R–N5 N–Q2 57 K–Q3
P–R5 58 K–B2 R–R3 59 R–N7+ K–Q3 60
R–N1 P–R6 61 B–B4 R–R2 62 R–Q1+ K–B4
63 B–R2 N–B3 64 R–K1 K–Q5 65 P–N4
N×KP 66 R–Q1+ K–K6 67 R–K1+ K–B5
68 R–KB1+ K–N6 69 R–K1 N–N4 70 R×P
N×P 71 R–K3+ K–R5 72 K–N1 N–B7 73
B–K6 N×P 74 Resigns

ONLY A HELICOPTER CAN GET THERE...

During a period of eleven days in Siberia and on Kamchatka, grandmaster Karpov gave 13 simultaneous displays against the best local players, and read 20 lectures. He was the guest of engineering workers and river transport workers, machine operators and vegetable growers, corn-producers and fishermen, geologists and volcanists, students and young pioneers...

"Interest in sport in general, and in chess in particular, does not weaken the further away from the central regions you go, but rather just the opposite, it grows stronger. During appearances in some very big halls, I never saw any vacant seats. In Krasnoyarsk, one simultaneous display had even to be staged in a stadium, where the stands were filled with several thousand spectators. On account of the hot weather during the day, the display was switched to the evening. And it was here that the one mishap occurred, which could not have been avoided by the thoughtful and far-sighted hosts. A cold wind unexpectedly blew up from the Yenisey, forcing me to don an overcoat and then even to warm my hands before signing autographs. The display lasted for several hours, and all this time the spectators, dressed only in summer clothes, did not leave their seats, although they could perfectly well have utilized the services of television, which was arranging a transmission from the stadium. But they preferred to follow the course of the games from the demonstration boards erected around the football field. Among the eight of my opponents (out of twenty) who drew with me was an 11-year-old second category player I. Feygelson, to whom on behalf of the local Comsomol I made an award to mark the occasion.

They really play well over there! I found it especially difficult in a simultaneous display with clocks against a team from Krasnoyarsk. The overall score was 6½–1½, but by the regional Champion, V. Nikitin, I was, as they say, well and truly beaten. Incidentally, it so happened that I met this same player in all-Russian Republic events some eleven years earlier. I recall how even then he was a pretty strong candidate master, and of this I am sure: if the Siberians had more opportunities for contacts with masters, then Nikitin, and some of his colleagues, would long since have gained higher titles. In Krasnoyarsk I was asked to petition the Chess Federation of the Russian Republic for a tournament with the master norm to be held in Siberia. The local players very much want to test themselves in encounters with visiting opponents! (There the young candidate master L. Psakhis made an excellent impression on me.)

I also played in Divnogorsk, a town of engineering workers. Among the participants in this display I noticed two familiar faces—these were two proud candidate masters who had been defeated the previous day, and who had followed me from Krasnoyarsk. And both gained their revenge!

During the flight to Yakutsk, in the middle of the night our plane made a short stop at Bratsk. It was a most inappropriate time for autographs, but it was impossible to refuse a young lieutenant, who formulated his request as follows: 'Comrade Karpov, please sign here in this note-book, and put the date, I beg you! Otherwise my friend will not believe that I have met the World Champion. We spend all our free time playing chess.'

I was not grieved, but gladdened, by a loss in Yakutsk to 14-year-old Sergey Nikolayev, and I was also defeated by an experienced candidate master, 53-year-old A. Danilov. No, they are no weaker here than in Europe.

And, incidentally, the weather during my stay there—in June—was really hot, with temperatures in the thirties centigrade. And the white nights on the Lyena river are no less beautiful than those on the Nyeva. 'Rakyeta' hydrofoils speed along the great Siberian river, but with such distances the basic form of transport is nevertheless the aeroplane. It was by plane that we managed to reach the little town of Maya, and then visit a State farm, where Ekatarina Novgoroda, a Heroine of Soviet Labour and Deputy to the USSR Supreme Soviet, talked so passionately about the difficult work of Yakutsk vegetable growers. All around is permafrost, in which they had recently discovered a mammoth, which became a valuable exhibit at the museum of a Scientific Research Institute in Yakutsk.

In the town of Mirny, after a meeting with Party and Comsomol activists, I visited a magma quarry. The workers acquainted us with the process of ore enrichment, themselves asked numerous questions, and then enthusiastically took part—either as spectators or as my direct opponents—in a simultaneous display. That evening I returned to Yakutsk, and an hour later flew on to Kamchatka.

I spent four unforgettable days on the 'very edge of the world'. My chess career has already enabled me to see a great deal, and there will no doubt be much more of interest, but Kamchatka will remain in my heart for ever. It even seemed to me that we made friends with the most majestic natural feature of the area—a huge geyser, with an interval between eruptions of approximately five hours, gushed forth fifteen minutes after our helicopter had landed beside it. I, of course, joked that all this had been rather skilfully 'arranged' by the staff of the Volcanology Institute. They 'presented' to their guests one of the gems of Kamchatka—the amazingly beautiful crater of the Volcano Uzon. Inside the crater of the dormant volcano was a lake with hot sulphur springs. Let's have a bathe!..

Other things which stick in my memory are a visit to the town of Elizovo, in the centre of the region which provides Kamchatka's grain, a trip on a speed-boat with a fishing crew, and an appearance in the crowded hall of the fishermen's club in Petropavlovsk-Kamchatsky.

I have given many simultaneous displays, both in my country and abroad, but even so I found it very difficult combating the determination and energy of the Kamchatkans. I played one hundred games in displays on Kamchatka, and saw that chess enjoys great popularity there. Chess sections in sports schools for children and youths, young pioneers' chess clubs, serious propaganda work carried out by the press, radio and television—all this is a good foundation for future success. But Kamchatka needs a modern chess club—a centre for all the work with chess enthusiasts. In conversations with me, local officials firmly promised to help in the solving of this problem—just as they had done previously in Krasnoyarsk, Yakutsk, Mirny...

'Grandiose and fantastic!! Words are not enough!'—this was what I wrote in the visitors' book at the Krasnoyarsk Hydro-Electric Power Station. But how else do you convey an impression of the grand scale of Siberian power construction, and how do you describe the beauty of a valley of geysers on Kamchatka from on board a helicopter?!"

HOW MUCH IS ICE-CREAM IN MANILA

After a brief stay with his parents in Leningrad, Anatoly once again set off on his travels. This time the plane took him to the Philippines, where after the conclusion of the Interzonal Tournament there began a small but fairly interesting two-cycle event with four grandmasters. The participants, apart from the World Champion, were Walter Browne (USA), Ljubomir Ljubojević (Yugoslavia), and, of course, the idol of Philippine chess enthusiasts, Eugenio Torre.

Anatoly Karpov relates:

"The Philippines were contenders for the World Championship Match, then they managed to stage one of the Interzonal Tournaments of the following cycle. Immediately after this came our match-tournament...

The popularity of chess in this distant Asian country, which is made up of hundreds of islands, is enormous. In Manila I observed a street ice-cream vender, who tore himself away from the analysis of some chess game merely so as to ask each customer whether or not he was able to play. He received 'chess players' with open arms, and invariably proposed that they 'play for an ice-cream'.

I began the match-tournament with a defeat (with White!) at the hands of Torre, and even an excellent win over Ljubojević could not save me from second place in the event. The distance was too short, and besides, the 'local hero', my main rival, continued playing exceptionally successfully. I recall how in the press at that time—and not only the chess press—numerous voices were raised, asserting that my colleagues Ljubojević and Browne had deliberately allowed Torre to go ahead, by each losing one game to him, in order to become 'co-authors' in a sensation. And although these losses—especially from the excellent position that the American grandmaster had—appear somewhat absurd, even so I am not inclined to share the opinion which has gradually taken root regarding this. I am accustomed to the fact that both Browne and Ljubojević normally honour their competitive obligations. It is another matter that things can be influenced (and sometimes in the most unexpected and amusing fashion), by various extraneous factors, of which analysts, impassionately disecting other players' games, can have no knowledge.

Take, for instance, the last round. We played this out of town, in a splendid setting in the hills. Everything was excellently arranged. But the organizers failed to take into account one small factor, and it was this that influenced, strangely enough, the result, if not of the entire event, then definitely that of the last round. We began playing before dusk, and then the lights were incautiously switched on. Some thirty minutes later two enormous moths flew in, and for some reason went straight for Browne, the same Browne who, even without extraneous influences, is unable to sit quietly at the board. What didn't happen next! Observing this scene, and barely able to keep myself from laughing, I set up a positional fortress against Ljubojević, who, in his turn, speculated as to whether Browne could kill two moths in one blow. And throughout all this farce, only the aboriginal Torre remained absolutely imperturbable.

Browne, who had gained a winning position from the opening (a piece for two pawns), and had nevertheless only drawn the game, was terribly angry. "We both played badly here", I reassured him, "It's time that you and I left Manila." "And for good!" was the ready response from Browne, who is noted for his excessively categorical manner.

But I am not so categorical, and two years later again ended up in the Philippines—as a participant in a match for the World Championship . . ."

Ljubojević–Karpov
Ruy Lopez

1	P–K4	P–K4
2	N–KB3	N–QB3
3	B–N5	P–QR3
4	B–R4	N–B3
5	0–0	B–K2
6	R–K1	P–QN4
7	B–N3	P–Q3
8	P–B3	0–0
9	P–KR3	N–N1
10	P–Q4	QN–Q2

11	QN–Q2	B–N2
12	B–B2	R–K1
13	P–QN4	B–KB1
14	P–QR4	*see diagram*

The Ruy Lopez is one of the oldest of openings, but to this day it is constantly practised, and fully retains its attractiveness. Some of its variations have been studied thoroughly, while others require further research and practical testing. It has to be said that those players are wrong who consider that the Ruy Lopez does not deserve much attention, that it has been analysed through and through by many generations of chess players, and that it is impossible to find anything new in it. Even more mistaken are those who think that, after reading through and learning by heart the variations given in books, they can successfully employ them in tournament games. Grandmasters have a very serious approach to the study of this complex opening, and it is no accident that the great Capablanca considered the

Ruy Lopez to be a test of understanding of positional play.

Ljubojević adopts a continuation which came into practice after the Spassky–Fischer match (Reykjavik 1972).

14 ...   N–N3

This is what was played in the 10th game of the Fischer–Spassky match. Earlier I used to think that 14 ... P–QR4 was stronger, but after the improvement found for White—15 NP×P R×P 16 R–N1 B–R3 17 RP×P followed by 18 B–N3—my desire to defend Black's position faded of its own accord.

15 P–R5   N(N3)–Q2
16 B–N2   R–N1

In the afore-mentioned game 16 ... Q–N1 was played. The improvement was found by Spassky himself, and was employed by him after the match in a game with Planinc (Amsterdam 1973). Both continuations are directed against White's central break-through P–QB4, which would give him excellent chances.

17 Q–N1

A new move, associated with the familiar idea of pressure along the QR2–KN8 diagonal. 17 R–N1 is more usual.

17 ...   N–R4!?

White's queen has moved, and the indirect attack on KR5 has disappeared. The idea of this move is not only to occupy the strategically important square ... KB5 with the knight. Black is also preparing for the central counter-blow ... P–QB4, which did not work immediately: 17 ... P–B4 18 NP×P QP×P 19 P×KP QN×P 20 N×N R×N 21 P–QB4, with a clear advantage.

18 P–B4

In striving for the initiative, Ljubojević gets into difficulties. With the unpleasant vis-à-vis positioning of queen and rook on the QN-file, it is by no means favourable for White to initiate play in the centre. 18 N–B1 is quieter, although even in this case Black has no reason to fear 18 ... P–QB4 19 NP×P QP×P 20 P×KP (or 20 N×P N×N 21 P×N P–B5) in view of 20 ... P–B5 followed by 21 ... N×P.

18 ...   NP×P
19 N×BP

After the exchange 19 P×P P×P the QNP would be *en prise*.

19 ...   P×P!

Quite right! Black will not have a better opportunity to initiate counter-play.

20 B×P

The plausible 20 N×P runs up against 20 ... N–K4! 21 B–N3 (the knight is immune: 21 N×N P×N and 22 ... B×NP) 21 ... N–B5 with numerous threats, or 21 N–Q2 B–B1! with the obvious threat of 22 ... R×P, and the concealed one of 22 ... B×P.

20 ...   P–QB4

21 B–K3

Of course 21 P×P fails to 21 ... B×P, winning a pawn, while on 21 B–B3 the simple 21 ... B–B3 is unpleasant for White. Here Ljubojević thought up an interesting idea, which, however, meets with a combinational rejoinder.

21 ...   **P×P**

On the prosaic 21 ... B–B3, the queen vacates the QN-file with gain of tempo— 22 Q–Q1.

22 N–N6   **N(4)–B3**

Now that White has taken control of his KB4 square, it is time for this knight to return. The move played may appear very simple, but to find it at the board was rather difficult. It was only after lengthy reflection that I came to the conclusion that this 'return' was the most expedient move in the given position.

23 Q×P

Risky! But what is White to do? After all, it was possible that Black might hold on permanently to his extra pawn.

23 ...   **P–Q4**

23 ... B×P would have given Black an extra pawn, but would have lost a large part of his positional advantage.

24 Q–N3   **P×P**
25 N–N5

In choosing his continuations Ljubojević had of course calculated many moves ahead, but I managed to see a little further.

25 ...   **B–Q4**
26 Q–R4   **N×N**

Otherwise the extra pawn cannot be maintained. E.g. 26 ... P–R3 27 N×B N×N 28 N×KP R–N5 29 Q–R2 (the white queen is amusingly trapped in the variation 29 Q–B6 N–N1! 30 Q–R8 N–B2 31 Q–R7 N–B3!).

27 B×N

In the event of 27 P×N White's knight is caught—27 ... P–R3.

27 ...   **Q–K2!**

This was possibly the first surprise for White. The queen voluntarily moves onto the same file as the white rook, but it is not possible to exploit this circumstance.

28 P–B3

White similarly fails to regain his pawn in the event of 28 B×P B×B 29 N×B N×N 30 P–B3 R×B! 31 P×R Q–B4+ 32 K–R1 N–B7+ 33 K–R2 R–N1.

28 ...   **R×B!**

This sacrifice is nevertheless possible! It would be absurd to think that Ljubojević had overlooked this move. No, it was something later that he had not foreseen.

29 P×R   **Q–B4+**
30 K–R1   **B–B3!**

A simple but effective double attack—both the white queen and knight are *en prise*.

31 Q–R5

| **31 ...** | **P×P!** |

A surprise! White cannot exchange queens —the reason is obvious, but I should like nevertheless to give this mating finish: 32 Q×Q R×R+ 33 Q–N1 (33 R×R P×P+ 34 K–R2 B×Q with an easy win) 33 ... P×P+ 34 K–R2 B–Q3 mate.

| **32 N×P(3)** | **Q×B** |
| **33 Q×P** | |

33 QR–B1 R×R+ 34 Q×R Q–R5 merely prolongs the game.

| **33 ...** | **B×N** |

| **34 P×B** | **R×R+** |
| **35 R×R** | **N–R4!** |

With the unequivocable threat of 36 ... N–N6+ and 37 ... B–B4+. The knight also prevents the return of the queen to the defence via K2 or KB1. Incorrect was 35 ... Q–B7 36 R–KB1 Q–N6 37 Q–B8! N–Q4 38 P–N7 N–K6 39 R–KN1 Q×BP+ 40 K–R2 Q–B7+ 41 K–R1, when Black has only a draw.

36 R–K8

On 36 R–KN1 Black wins by 36 ... Q–B3, pinning the QNP and at the same time attacking the KBP.

| **36 ...** | **Q–B7** |

White's king is trapped in the corner, and there is no perpetual check. The remainder is all forced.

37 R×B+	**K×R**
38 Q–R3+	**K–K1**
39 Q–R4+	**K–K2**
40 Q–QN4+	**K–B3**
41 Q–Q6+	**K–N4**
42 Q–K5+	**K–R3**
43 Resigns	

IN THE VINE-GROWING REGION

Anatoly Karpov alternated most consistently his play in various events with appearances before the wide auditorium of chess enthusiasts. Thus almost immediately after the international tournament in the Philippines, and before his departure to Spain, he visited the Vladimir district...

"The venue for this appearance was not chosen by accident", says Anatoly, "since it already holds for me the most pleasant of memories. As a member of the Russian Federation Schoolboy Team, I frequently used to visit Vladimir—the strongest Russian youths had a kind of 'headquarters' here. And now I was able to observe with interest the Championships of the Republic, which were held in three groups: for youths, juniors and girls. I couldn't help remembering those same events in 1962 and 1965, when it happened that I took part. Now in the rôle of grandmaster I gave a series of simultaneous displays, and gave public lectures at an electrical appliance factory and in the regional Drama Theatre. I also have the pleasant memory of a visit to the town of Gus-Khrustalny, where famous Russian glass-blowers live and work."

And now this is Karpov in Spain:

"The little town of Montilla—whose population is all of some fifteen thousand—is situated on a picturesque hill, roughly an hour's drive from the ancient Spanish capital of Cordoba. This locality (Montilla means 'plateau') is known throughout the world for its famous 'Amontillado' wine, referred to in many songs and literary classics. Now its reputation has been further enhanced thanks to the international chess tournaments, traditionally organized by local vine-growers."

These tournaments normally comprise players of highly uneven strength; along with famous grandmasters, young Spanish players are also invited. This, together with the short distance, increases the rôle of chance, and transforms the event into something of a 'sprint with hurdles'. The sixth of these traditional tournaments provoked particular interest, because the World Champion himself was one of the starters. And it was the same Champion who, shortly before this, had, unusually for him, finished 'only' second in the Philippines.

In short, Karpov sensed the keen attention of colleagues and observers, and for this reason, of course, he tried very hard.

When Moscow was linked up to Montilla by telephone, Karpov said that it was quite by accident that they had found him in his hotel room, since for several days he had been spending nine hours a day in the tournament hall. The tight schedule did not allow any special days for adjournments (there were, it is true, free days, but only after the fourth and eighth rounds). 'Normal time' was from 16.00 to 21.00 hours, and adjournment sessions in the morning from 10.00 to 12.00, and in the evening (or more accurately, at night), from 23.00 to one o'clock in the morning.

"I have been suffering slightly from food poisoning, and have been placed on a strict diet. Willy-nilly I am forced to play from morning to night, so as not to have to go into the restaurant", joked Anatoly.

In the early rounds he set what was probably a record for the length of time at the board, spending altogether 32 hours on four games. Karpov made almost 300 moves in these games, and had it not been for a relatively 'short' draw with the Spaniard Calvo (in 42 moves), this record would almost certainly have become an absolute one.

By the seventh round the World Champion, who had dropped only half a point, had practically assured himself of first place. In the end, over the short 9-round distance, he finished a point and a half ahead of Calvo, the American grandmaster Kavalek, and the Englishman Stean, who reached the grandmaster norm. Then came Pfleger of West Germany, and the second representative of the USA—R. Byrne...

Without wishing at all to offend the participants in the Montilla tournament, it nevertheless has to be admitted that nearly all of them combined business with pleasure, playing chess and at the same time relaxing. In the later rounds, games quickly ended peaceably. The high percentage of draws in the final days of the event was also possibly influenced by the fact that the main question was completely settled—the winner was already known. The general pacification was also probably promoted by the atmosphere in the small hotel, which was, one might say, of the 'family-sporting' type. The hotel was situated some eight kilometres from Montilla, and the players naturally spent all their spare time together—either at a common dining table, on the tennis courts, or in the swimming pool... And all around for miles and miles there was nothing but vines...

...As regards Karpov, at the end of this event he decided to take a rest from the game, and not to play any more serious games before the USSR Championship. Before him was a highly important task—that of becoming Champion of his country.

But before we talk about the main tournament of 1976, it is necessary that we describe Anatoly Karpov's 'unofficial' meetings with his predecessor on the chess throne.

THE APPEARANCE OF FISCHER

Botvinnik, whom Karpov informed by telephone about his meetings with Fischer, was doubtful: "But are you sure that it was really him that you talked with, and not his double?" Yes, for everyone this appearance of the former Champion came as a complete surprise. And yet it was all perfectly logical and readily explainable.

Back in 1975, Smyslov, on returning from America, where he had been playing in the Lone Pine tournament, said that, according to the elderly grandmaster Kashdan, who was far from any diplomatic chess intrigues, Fischer was faced with a choice: either to take work as an unskilled labourer or to play chess. While everyone was talking about the fabulous wealth of the former Champion, his financial situation was in fact very bad, and the only way he could make a living was by playing chess. He was also no doubt missing his beloved game...

And then Fischer himself sought a meeting with Karpov. When, following the international tournament in Manila, the World Champion stopped off in Tokio, he was invited to dinner by the Filipino Florencio Campomanes. This energetic FIDE Vice-President, well-known for his friendship with Fischer, was not, as it turned out, in Tokio that day by accident. Hardly had Karpov entered his room in the Hilton Hotel, when Campomanes said: "I have a surprise for you"—and opened another door. On the threshold stood Robert James Fischer. The Ex-Champion was without his beard, about which so much had been written, and although he had put on a slight bit of weight, with his height this was not especially noticeable.

Matsumoto, a Japanese chess official who was present at that dinner, promised Fischer that he would say nothing to the press. But the very next day the foreign telegraph agencies reported the 'details' of the conversation between the Ex-Champion and the Champion. They had allegedly agreed to play a match together, and even wanted to play for a five million dollar prize fund. Later the *New York Times* corrected this figure—seven million dollars...

But what in fact had the conversation been about? Fischer said that he would like to play an unofficial match with Karpov. He didn't want to play against 'ordinary grandmasters', since he had already defeated them, and therefore he wouldn't be paid much for winning against them again. He added that he had reached the age of a businessman, and that he no longer wanted to 'play for nothing'. Karpov replied that he had agreed to play an unofficial match with Fischer, back at the time when he had just been proclaimed World Champion, that he was not concerned about the financial conditions, but that what was important was a sensible schedule for the event. The present year was already taken up: he was due to participate in an international tournament in Spain, followed by the USSR Championship in December. The match couldn't be held before then...

A month later, in Montilla, another tournament with Karpov's participation was drawing to a close, when Fischer flew in to Cordoba, the main town of this Spanish province. They once again met over dinner. The American grandmaster placed on the table his former cards: the number of games in the match should be unlimited, and the winner should be the first to win ten games (in a sub-variation of his 'project' he suggested that with the score standing at 9–9 they should play on to another three wins). Karpov asked with a smile how long such a match might go on. Fischer, after some thought, replied that there were two ways of looking at this. They both won frequently, so that the match could finish quickly. On the other hand, they rarely lost, so that it could also drag on. "But on average, if everything should go normally", Fischer summed up, "we should spend five to six months at the board." Evidently he was missing chess very much... Karpov spread his hands in disbelief: to play without a break for half a year, and against one and the same opponent, was simply not possible!

And then exactly at midnight on the eve of Karpov's departure from Madrid for Moscow, Fischer knocked on Karpov's door. He apologised for calling at such a late hour, and said to Anatoly that it had been a pleasure to make his acquaintance, and asked him not to be offended if he, Fischer, should begin playing against someone else. At that they parted.

CHAPTER 9

...In his Native Land

Karpov began the 44th USSR Championship with two colourless draws, which were followed by a defeat. After three rounds he was amongst those bringing up the rear of the tournament table...

Main tournament of the year ✳ *No respect for credentials*
✳ *All generals are equal* ✳ *Future heroes go ahead* ✳
In pursuit of form ✳ *Ten years after* ✳ *Error of the discontented*
✳ *The turning-point*

Chess events, like events in any type of sport, have numerous gradations, both official and unofficial. There is the degree of difficulty, the measure of responsibility, the title awarded to the winner, and many more. But there is one event with which others bear no comparison, which stands apart in its tension, its difficulty, and the special nature of the prestige which its winner immediately gains in the chess world. Without any exaggeration, this event can be called the 'tournament of tournaments'.

This tournament is the Chess Championship of the USSR.

But isn't there a degree of patriotism influencing our reasoning? Can we have forgotten about the Zonal and Interzonal Tournaments, where "the stake is higher than life itself"? Or the grandmaster tournaments such as the one in Milan, or that which was held somewhat earlier in San Antonio? And what about the Alekhine Memorial, and the traditional events in England, Holland and Spain?

All these tournaments, and many that have not been named, without doubt deserve the highest epithets as regards their complex, imposing and prestigious nature. The names of their heroes are recorded in chess history. A participant in many of those of recent years has been one of the authors of this book, and he knows from his own experience at what price victories are gained in them.

But we will not call just on personal impressions to demonstrate our point. Let us reason together.

In all the most important international events, Soviet players take part. And in all of them —with rare exceptions—they invariably occupy high places. It is these, the victors and prize-winners in various types of traditional grandmaster tournaments, memorial events and even Interzonal Tournaments, that the USSR Championship gathers together at the end of the year.

However, what we have said is not entirely correct. It does not apply to all of them. It is not everyone who manages to reach the Final, which since the early 70s has been called the

Premier League. In the paths of some stands the All-Union Elimination Tournament (and you have to get into that first!), in the paths of others, who have successfully completed this stage or are exempt from it thanks to their previous record, is the First League. This event possibly does not stand out among other tournaments being held in various corners of the globe, but at the same time it is little inferior to them. On the other hand, it is superior to the great majority in the evenness of its strength, and therefore in its bitter and uncompromising nature.

The number of interesting international events, although considerable, is nevertheless limited. Only a fraction of the representatives of our country, who are capable of making a worthy appearance there, can be delegated to such tournaments. These are, in the main, those who have proved themselves in the All-Union Championship. But there are plenty seeking these places, and each year new faces appear. They have one road to international fame—to break through the elimination net into the Championship Final of their enormous chess country. And this net catches not only the young and inexperienced, but also grandmasters of world renown.

But to break through into the Premier League is not so much a great piece of good fortune, but rather an enormous stimulus. One more step, a little more effort, and you are at the top, among the élite, in the narrow circle of the chosen few. And so a player will put in everything that he is capable of, plus a little more. He will not spare himself in striving for the slightest gain, for every little half point, realizing that the lack of such a half point can in the end squander the whole of his previous labours, and the gains achieved at such effort—without it, he may have to return to his starting position, and begin all over again.

Here we are bound to make one slight reservation. Tenacity can manifest itself in various ways: in cautious draws, when the players avoid the risk of losing an important game (in certain USSR Championships it has happened that there have been a number of such games), or else in full-blooded battles, when the players play for a win at all costs (such Championships are clearly in the majority).

...Even on the brilliant background of other USSR Championships, the 44th was distinguished as a unique event in at least one respect. Here is what grandmaster Mark Taimanov, the most experienced participant, had to say about it: "Twenty-two times I have played in the USSR Championship Final. I have, as they say, something to remember, something to compare. Therefore I can state with absolute conviction that there has never been a Championship that was so uncompromising, fighting, fascinating and, if you like, passionate. Not one uninteresting round, and 82 games with a decisive result out of 153! And this in the tournament which was the major one of all those played this year."

There were reasons for the 'uniqueness' of the 44th Championship. Or more precisely, there was one main reason, which overrides all others. Playing in it was the present World Champion.

We have already spoken on the theme that 'Champion' and 'active Champion' are concepts which are by no means identical. Usually it happens that, once a player gains the laurel wreath, he becomes a rare visitor to big tournaments. And about why this happens we have also spoken. And as for the World Champion being a participant in the Championship of his own country —this is an altogether exceptional phenomenon. This too can be explained. For anyone else, a place in the upper half of the results table is a worthy achievement, but for him, the Champion, there is no alternative: any place, apart from first, will be regarded by the public as a failure. But only once, in 1952, has there been an instance, when the World Champion—who was then Botvinnik—won the USSR Championship. He won it at the third attempt, after defeating Taimanov in a play-off match. (Before becoming World Champion, he had won the

All-Union Championship several times.) Holders of the chess crown preferred to avoid these tournaments, and for two decades no World Champion played in a USSR Championship. And always objective justification for this was found (and subjective reasons).

In short, a prophet has no honour in his own country.

Such is the set-up in the chess kingdom of our country—and in this lies our strength, in that nowhere else can the World Champion meet such a large number of rivals and colleagues from the path to the throne, than here, in the All-Union Championship. Certain of them, with all due respect to the leader, see him only as the first among equals, and consider him to be superior not so much in strength, as in fortune. Their memories obligingly provide one instance, a second, and a third, when some impulsive move stopped them from winning, when time trouble stole a decisive point, or when poor health forced them to choose an incorrect plan in a superior position. "If it hadn't been for this, or that, or the other", the former rival reasons to himself, "it could have been me sitting on the throne, and not him." And such reasoning is not altogether groundless. Equally logical, and therefore bound to spring to mind, is the following: "All right, perhaps then, at his celestial hour, he was stronger. Then, but not now. And today I have the chance to demonstrate that this former superiority has evaporated."

It cannot be denied that in the non-Soviet chess world there are a number of outstanding masters of their profession. But even so, no one will dispute the truth: no other chess army has in its ranks such a number—no, not of soldiers—but of generals, who carry the Field-Marshall's baton. And each who has failed to reach the summit in the previous cycle is eager to demonstrate the reality of his claims, by utilizing the rare opportunity of meeting the Champion, face to face, in the All-Union Championship. Of meeting and defeating him. And why not? Is such a task unreal? Hasn't it happened before? Here it isn't everyone who gives in to a young man who has grown up before their very eyes, and against whom they are confident that they know how to play.

"But surely many are afraid of you even here?"

"Chess is not a game for the faint-hearted. If anyone is in fact afraid, this only makes him work more assiduously: he prepares properly, and at the board re-calculates variations, checking both his moves and mine. For this reason their 'illness' does not make it easier for me, but harder", replies Karpov.

Abroad too they realize this: "I am impatiently awaiting this tournament", said the Brazilian Mecking on the eve of the USSR Championship. "For Karpov it is of particular significance, since the World Champion has never yet won the title of Champion of his own country. And this means that he will finally play all his trumps, and reveal all his secrets."

Yes, Karpov was the only Soviet World Champion who had not yet managed to become USSR Champion. All the others—although not during their years as Champion, but either before or after—had won this esteemed title.

. . . When the tournament was over, Karpov, assessing his play, had this to say:

"On account of a series of attendant circumstances, I was psychologically not altogether prepared for this difficult event. I began the Championship worse than ever before. . . I found it difficult playing, I wasted much time, and on occasions 'went to sleep' for half an hour, which formerly happened extremely rarely with me."

This 'series of attendant circumstances' was a lengthy one, and the circumstances were grave: his father fell seriously ill, then the same happened with his mother who had to go into hospital, and then Anatoly himself caught a cold.

All this explained, but by no means eased, Karpov's tournament position. And his loss to Geller in the third round was of the sort that can put anyone out of his stride for a long time.

After two draws, which Rashkovsky and Taimanov gained with him by accurate play, Karpov came up against one of the greatest experts on theory, and his recent consultant on opening questions. This last circumstance was most probably of decisive importance as regards Karpov's choice of opening: it wasn't easy to spring a surprise on Geller, who was excellently acquainted with Karpov's opening repertoire, and so he chose a variation of the French Defence, which he had never played before. But not without reason do they say that, in order to win in this defence, you must first lose a number of 'Frenches'. In short, the surprise did not come off. Geller, playing White, emerged from the opening with a marked positional advantage, and soon won a pawn.

After the game, Karpov said that neither of them had played the best way. But the decisive combination, carried out by Geller, was highly spectacular. Just when it seemed that Karpov had achieved his aim—that of forcing his opponent to exchange queens, Geller, in approaching time trouble, which seemed to focus his already sharp combinational vision, found a sacrifice of rare beauty of a queen for just one pawn. In the end White gained a material advantage, and although not without some adventures, won the game.

Geller–Karpov
French Defence

1 P–K4 P–K3 2 P–Q4 P–Q4 3 N–QB3 B–N5 4 P–K5 Q–Q2 5 N–B3 P–QN3 6 B–Q2 B–R3 7 B×B N×B 8 0–0 N–N1 9 N–K2 B–K2 10 R–B1 P–QN4 11 N–B4 P–KR4 12 P–QN3 B–R6 13 R–N1 P–R4 14 P–B4 P–QB3 15 P–B5 B–N5 16 B–B1 P–QR5 17 N–Q3 B–R4 18 P×P P×P 19 Q×P Q–R2 20 B–N5 B–B2 21 R×N+ Q×R 22 Q×P+ K–B1 23 N–B4 R–QR2 24 N–R4 Q–K1 (Diag.)
25 Q×KP P×Q 26 N(R4)–N6+ Q×N 27 N×Q+ K–K1 28 N×R R–R5 29 R–Q1 N–K2 30 B×N K×B 31 N–N6+ K–B2 32

N–B4 B×P 33 P×B R×N 34 R–QB1 K–K1 35 P–B6 K–Q1 36 P–B7+ K–B1 37 P–N3 R–QR5 38 R–B6 R×P 39 R×P P–N4 40 R–Q6 R–Q7 41 P–K6 K×P 42 P–K7 Resigns

That evening the fans in the, as usual, overcrowded hall of the Railwaymen's Central Club, where the tournament was being held, gave Geller an ovation.

Incidentally, the third round was marked by another sacrifice of the most powerful and formidable of the chess pieces. But Tal was more or less forced into doing this against Romanishin, in the illusory hope of saving the game. This hope was not realized. Along with the present Champion, the Ex-World Champion suffered his first defeat in the tournament.

At this point the tournament was headed by two of its future heroes—Yury Balashov, who within a month was to win the silver medal, and Iosef Dorfman, a young master from Lvov, who was destined in this Championship to gain his first grandmaster norm. The most highly titled players were keeping for the moment in the background. Among them were Petrosian and Polugayevsky—both participants in the Candidates' Matches which were to begin soon after the Championship. The unusual situation in which these venerable grandmasters found themselves made the tournament situation even more intriguing: the Candidates would have to reveal something, and what strategy would they choose prior to matches of such importance for them, how would they both appear on the threshold of these encounters? Lyev Polugayevsky later admitted: "To be honest, in my heart I had decided to try not to fully reveal myself. I am sure that Petrosian was also thinking the same. But soon the course of the tournament showed that to go the whole distance playing at half strength, and in doing so hope for a respectable result, would simply not be permitted by our opponents. And we were forced, as one says, to roll up our sleeves."

After four rounds, both Candidates had joined the leaders, who, it is true, apart from two and a half points, also had an adjourned game each. Petrosian was the first to disdain caution. He was paired against Gulko, and after the opening his prospects appeared far from bright. Then the position became slightly more level. And here, suddenly, almost out of the blue, Petrosian offered his young opponent a rook for a minor piece. The situation on the board changed sharply, mutual time trouble added further fuel to the fire, and Gulko was forced to convert his forwards into defenders, but even this did not save him from Petrosian's crushing and finely-conducted attack.

This game showed that Petrosian was in good form. As a highly experienced tournament fighter, he could only permit himself to go in for risky variations, rather uncharacteristic of his style, if he sensed his own strength. But for Karpov, such form had not yet come to him. In the fifth round they met, the World Champion and one of his probable rivals in the battle for this title. The game did not finish that evening. In a rook ending Petrosian had a big advantage.

Petrosian–Karpov
Queen's Indian Defence

1 N–KB3 N–KB3 2 P–QB4 P–QN3 3 P–KN3 B–N2 4 B–N2 P–K3 5 P–Q4 B–K2 6 0–0 0–0 7 N–B3 N–K5 8 Q–B2 N×N 9 Q×N P–QB4 10 R–Q1 P–Q3 11 P–N3 N–Q2 12 B–N2 N–B3 13 P–Q5 P–K4 14 N×P P×N 15 P–Q6 B×B 16 Q×P R–K1 17 P×B Q×P 18 Q×Q R×Q 19 K×B R×P 20 B×N P×B 21 R–Q7 R–N7 22 R–K1 R×RP 23 R(1)–K7 R–KB1 24 R×RP R×R 25 R×R R–Q1 26 R–N7 R–Q3 27 P–KN4 K–N2 28 P–B3 K–N3 29 K–N3 P–R4 30 P×P+ K×P 31 R×BP R–Q6 32 R×P R×NP 33 K–B4 R–N5 34 K–B5 R×P 35 R×P R–B8 36 R–QB6 P–B5 37 R–B8 K–R3

38 K–B6 K–R2 39 P–B4 R–B7 40 P–B5 P–B6 41 P–R3 R–B8

42 P–R4 R–B7 43 P–R5 R–B8 44 K–B7 R–B7 45 P–B6 R–B8 46 K–K7 P–B7 47 K–B7 K–R3 48 R–B5 K–R2 49 R–B6 K–R3 50 K–B8

K–R2 51 R–B7+ K–R1 52 P–B7 R–QR8   58 K–N3 R–R6+ 59 K–N2 K–N2 60 R–B2
53 R×P R–R1+ 54 K–K7 R–R2+ 55 K–B6   K–B1 61 R–B5 R–R3 62 K–N3 R–R3 63 K–N4
R–B3+ 56 K–N5 R–R4+ 57 K–N4 R–R5+   R–R2 64 Drawn

"On adjournment day I managed to find a study-like way to save this most difficult ending. To this half point I also added a whole one, at the same time halting the tournament leader Balashov. As it turned out, on the adjournment of our game from the fourth round he had sealed a bad move, and when the game was resumed he was still annoyed, and almost immediately, as if from inertia, he placed his queen *en prise*.

This first victory in the tournament enabled me to reach the fifty per cent mark—2½ points out of 5. But that was the very first swallow, which does not yet make a summer. I sensed that I was not yet on form. But I also knew what I had to do to regain this form—I had to battle in every game, however it developed, and to seek a fight with all my opponents, and especially with the main one—myself, my own sluggishness, and the inertia which was trying to rush me past difficult obstacles and steep barriers, instead of over them."

...Exactly ten years had passed since fate had first brought together at the board schoolboy Tolya Karpov and student Vladimir Kupreichik, far from home, at a tournament in Czechoslovakia. Remember the sheet from a school exercise book with an account of the tournament, and the heading 'Tolya Karpov's Victory'? At that time the student had been considered the senior, not only in age, but also in chess strength—he was a young, but already well-known master in chess circles. Now the rôles had changed. However, even ten years earlier, in Czechoslovakia, Kupreichik had lost to his young compatriot. And now Karpov, playing White, immediately forced his opponent to decide, one after another, a series of intricate problems. Up to a point Kupreichik was able to find successful replies to these questions, but even so he had to go into an inferior ending.

But here the hall became hushed. Karpov carried out an elegant combination. This was more like it—perhaps he had found his form? Now he would make a move, logically crowning all that had gone before, a move which the entire hall had seen. It had seen it, and was humming like an agitated bee-hive. But why was the World Champion suddenly pondering over such an obvious thing? Finally, Karpov picked up a piece and moved it. The same manoeuvre was repeated on the demonstration board. The hum grew louder—it wasn't the expected move. However, a minute later Kupreichik resigned: the continuation chosen by Karpov also led to a win.

Karpov–Kupreichik
Ruy Lopez

1 P–K4 P–K4 2 N–KB3 N–QB3 3 B–N5 N–Q5 5 N×N P×N 5 0–0 B–B4 6 P–Q3 P–QB3 7 B–R4 N–K2 8 N–Q2 P–Q4 9 P×P N×P 10 R–K1+ B–K3 11 N–K4 B–K2 12 B–N3 0–0 13 B–Q2 Q–Q2 14 Q–R5 P–B3 15 P–KR3 QR–K1 16 R–K2 P–QN3 17 QR–K1 B–B2 18 Q–B3 B–Q1 19 P–B3 P–KB4 20 N–N3 P×P 21 P×P P–N3 22 P–B4 N–B2 23 B–B3 P–B4 24 Q–N7 R×R 25 N×R Q×P 26 B–K5 Q–K5 27 Q×Q P×Q 28 N–B3 R–K1 29 R×P P–KN4 30 P–N4 R–K3 31 R–K3 K–B1 32 N–Q5 N×N 33 P×N R–R3

34 B–N8 P–R3 35 P–Q6 B×B 36 P×B
K–B2 37 B–B7 B×B 38 R–K7+ K–B1 39
P×B R–QB3 40 R×P K–K1 41 P–R4
Resigns

Isn't it all the same, which way you choose to reach your goal? As they say, it is the result that is important. But even so, this minute detail, this episode from one game, left open the question: had the Champion acquired that genuine 'Karpov strength', which was essential if he were to break through the solid ranks of his opponents, and leave them behind him?

The victory over Kupreichik brought him close up behind the leaders. Now, together with Geller and Petrosian, he had as many points as Dorfman and Balashov, but these two each had in reserve an adjourned game.

Awaiting him in the seventh round was Romanishin, a player of striking and original talent. Failures, when they occur, upset him, but on the other hand, when he is on top form he is not afraid of the devil himself. Each victory serves for him as an accumulation of strength, energy, and inspiration. He began the Championship with a distressing defeat, losing to his compatriot Dorfman, also from Lvov, the least experienced of the competitors, who at that time was not yet taken very seriously. Romanishin needed time to recover from the blow, and he fell behind everyone else. But then he won three games in a row. Now he had become especially dangerous, and besides, in the seventh round the draw had given him the white pieces.

Sacrificing a knight in the centre of the board against the World Champion, Romanishin rushed into the attack. Karpov defended, but his position appeared critical. Once again—as frequently happened in this tournament—it seemed to many that Karpov had missed something and that his replies could have been stronger. But here it was the discontented who were wrong. Karpov was already playing in his own special manner, in which only later, after an assessment of the entire course of the game, and not just isolated episodes, is his deep penetration into the position revealed. Few would venture to say at what point and after which move the position on the board became equal, and Karpov went onto the offensive. This seemed to happen of its own accord. When his opponent had made the stipulated number of moves before the time control, the Champion declined an offer of a draw.

This game was not resumed. After checking the correctness of the move sealed by Romanishin, Karpov agreed to a draw. But one already sensed that the turning point was imminent. This tense encounter showed that Karpov was ready in every game to fight to the utmost, and this was perhaps the most obvious indication of his form.

And the turning point arrived, on the very next day. After the Championship, Karpov was to say: "After the psychologically important win over Dorfman, things went much better..." Incidentally, one of those whom he singled out for his good result in the Championship was in fact 'that trouble-maker Dorfman'.

Curbing the obstinate ✳ Satisfaction from play ✳
Gauntlet thrown down at Tal ✳ Controllers go home ✳
At the head of the black army ✳ A draw—with his father ✳
Moral right ✳ Ever higher . . .

Before the tournament, the young master from Lvov was amongst the 'talented', and the 'hopefuls', but it was thought that he would be too afraid of the experienced players, the big names, and would come unstuck against them. That is possibly the way it was, but Dorfman, either before the tournament, or thanks to his successful start, had cured himself of this weakness. It is no mean feat to go ahead in such a tournament for seven rounds in a row!

Thus it so happened that the two of them—Karpov and Dorfman —had both rid themselves of their 'ailments' just at the time when they met each other. And for those who still had doubts about their 'recoveries', this game forced them to completely forget these doubts. This was a clash between two courageous and skilful chess duellists, which held the attention of the entire audience from the very first move until the 'lowering of the curtain'.

The Champion only had to force the tournament leader to retreat half a step, when the latter instantly replied with a clever counter-attack. While still in the opening, Karpov sacrificed a piece, and Dorfman without hesitation accepted the sacrifice. The grandmaster stopped the black king from castling, and attacked it in the centre, but the master did not even think of going totally onto the defensive. He sent his heavy pieces forward, trying to penetrate with them into the hostile position.

At one point it seemed that the smoke of this heated battle was about to disperse, and that Karpov would have to win back his piece and offer a draw. But he kept on fanning the flames. The tournament situation dictated his tactics—'all or nothing', while his fighting disposition and intuition suggested that his attacking resources were not exhausted. Deep and accurate calculation confirmed the correctness of this 'suggestion'.

When an ending came in sight, and they began 'licking their wounds', it turned out that the opponents were level on material. But Dorfman's king had not managed to reach shelter, and was now forced to set out on a lone voyage across the open board, while Karpov's rampant queen threatened to become extremely unpleasant. And this is what happened on resumption. The queen, which was also supported by a rook, carried out its destructive mission.

Now only one figure loomed ahead of Karpov—that of his long-standing friend Yury Balashov, whom, it is true, he was approaching not alone, but together with Petrosian and Rashkovsky.

When one recalls the battles of the 'forty-fourth', one feels the inclination to write about many games, and about every day of this unforgettable Championship. It gave so many examples of brilliant, uncompromising play, and there was such a number of excellent games, combinations and sacrifices, that they would have more than sufficed for several big tournaments. But we have no choice, since we are not writing a history of chess Championships, but have a different theme. Therefore we will restrict ourselves to authoritative comment, where a brief and at the same time accurate description of the 44th USSR Championship is given. This is what the well-known English master and chess journalist Harry Golombek wrote about it: "This year's Soviet Championship revived the splendid creative atmosphere of grandmaster tournaments at the beginning of the century when chess players thought more about the aesthetic side of the game, than about points. The 44th Championship confirmed a well-known truth, that the stronger the participants in a tournament, the greater the satisfaction they themselves gain from the game, and the greater the satisfaction they afford the spectators."

The extremely rare 'rests' which the competitors allowed themselves could not affect this assessment.

In the ninth round Karpov, who had worked like a Trojan in the preceding days, did not object to having a break. And Smyslov, the oldest of the competitors, who the previous day had also had to spend a long time on the analysis of an adjourned position, and on a difficult resumption, fell in with his wishes. By the time Karpov's car, travelling from outside the city to the Railwaymen's Club, had coped with the incredibly ice-bound Moscow roads, 25 minutes had elapsed since the start of play. In the tournament hall itself, the World Champion spent only a slightly longer time on his game with Smyslov. For Karpov this short draw was a kind of resting-place before the start of a long and decisive storm. (On the same day his companions in the tournament table met each other. Raskovsky was defeated—for the first time in nine rounds—by Petrosian, who together with Balashov was now half a step ahead of Karpov.)

However, the first attempt at a storm was not a complete success.

Tal numbers among those who is linked to Karpov by mutual admiration and by amicable feelings. But they have always played against each other with maximum effort. On this occasion a draw resulted after such a gripping and fascinating battle, that the spectators greeted it—for the first time the hall reacted in this way to a share of the point—with an ovation. Especially for this important game, the World Champion had prepared a clever opening innovation. Glancing at one point at the position, Semion Furman—half jokingly, half seriously—said to Alexandr Koblents, his old friend and Tal's long-standing trainer: "Don't be distressed, Misha will hang on for another thirty moves."

But 'Misha' found a clever rejoinder to his opponent's aggressive plan; he decided to give up his queen for rook and bishop. It was just this continuation to which Karpov had paid insufficient attention in his preliminary analysis, reassuring himself and his trainer that he would be able to work things out at the board during the game itself. But when, after spending some 40 minutes, he had 'worked things out', he realized that his position was not as good as had seemed to him at home. Convinced that for the queen Tal had more than sufficient compensation, Karpov changed course, and began peace negotiations. His opponent replied, however, that he would like to play on for a while. Neither of the players had much of an advantage at this point, but the pieces were still full of life, and it is not in Tal's nature to forget about a gauntlet thrown down to him at the start of a game. And here, almost immediately, Karpov committed a serious inaccuracy... It is difficult to convey what went on at that time in the hall and in the press-centre. Everyone kept finding wins for the Ex-World Champion. But on the board the Champion continued to come out unscathed. Tal played actively, although perhaps not quite accurately, and himself seemed surprised at the tenacity and ingenuity which Karpov displayed in the defence of a most difficult position. As a parting gesture, the Riga player set a trap, which was seen through by his opponent, and then to the applause of the spectators, himself offered a draw.

Karpov–Tal
Sicilian Defence

1 P–K4 P–QB4 2 N–KB3 P–Q3 3 P–Q4
P×P 4 N×P N–KB3 5 N–QB3 N–B3
6 B–KN5 P–K3 7 Q–Q2 P–QR3 8 0–0–0
B–Q2 9 P–B4 P–N4 10 N×N B×N 11 B–Q3
B–K2 12 KR–K1 0–0 13 P–K5 P×P 14
Q–B2 (Diag.)

14 ... P–R3 15 B×N B×B 16 P×P B–R5
17 P–KN3 B–N4+ 18 K–N1 Q–B2 19 P–KR4
B–K2 20 P–KN4 B–N5 21 P–N5 B×N
22 P×B P–KR4 23 Q–QB5 QR–B1 24 K–N2
Q–N2 25 B–K2 B–Q4 26 Q–K3 P–N5 27 P–B4
B×P 28 R–Q6 Q–N4 29 Q–K4 B×B 30
Q×B Q–B4 31 R×RP KR–Q1 32 K–N1
R–Q4 33 P–N6 P×P 34 R×P R(1)–Q1
35 R–QB1 Q–B6 36 R×P R×P 37 Q–B2
R(4)–Q4 38 Drawn

(It was at this time that the West German newspaper *Westdeutsche Allgemeine* wrote that, even at the most difficult point of the tournament, Karpov not only remained confident in his ultimate success, but also managed to instill this confidence in others.)

Now this most difficult part was behind him. Both mentally, and physically, the Champion was ready for take-off from the launching-pad which he had won back from his ailments, his sluggishness, and his lack of practice.

The Karpov finishing the tournament was quite different from the one who started it.

By scoring one and a half points in the next two rounds, he joined Balashov at the head of this gripping race.

Among the eighteen competitors, great interest was provoked by the play of the group of grandmasters belonging to the so-called new wave—those whose star had begun to ascend almost at the same time as Karpov's, and whose leader he was rightly considered. They were seen—and not without justification—as the future successors to the leading lights of the older and middle generations, and also as the main *dramatis personae* in future Candidates' cycles. And, little by little, one after another, they emerged onto the international arena, and began to make themselves known, from time to time justifying the claims made of them. They are players of varying styles, but all are related by the fresh and aggressive nature of their play, and they are all maximalists. This maximalism has sometimes been punished by a lack of points, and with it the loss of a high place in a tournament, but the young players remain faithful to their motto: 'all or nothing', and each failure only intensifies the thirst for revenge.

Two of them, who had performed excellently in the previous Championship in Yerevan, but who were now outside the first ten, and had not lost hope of improving matters towards the finish, were Vaganian and Gulko, Karpov's opponents in the next two rounds. Both had the advantage in the choice of weapon—against both the one, and the other, Karpov had Black.

Both games were adjourned. But while Gulko had to battle on against the World Champion already the exchange down, by the adjournment of the game with Vaganian Karpov had merely gained the initiative. This, it is true, is also a considerable advantage, but it was clear that numerous difficult obstacles, both seen and unseen, stood in the way of ultimate victory.

Before the adjournment session, Karpov quite seriously warned the controllers that he would probably also deprive them of their next free evening—he thought that the six hours allotted by the regulations for the settling of accounts in unfinished games would not be sufficient for him. But both he and the controllers were pleasantly surprised by events. After quickly disposing of the Muscovite, Karpov then broke with his heavy pieces into the position of the Yerevan grandmaster, who in trying to save the game, lost on time.

Vaganian–Karpov
Queen's Indian Defence

1 P–Q4 N–KB3 2 P–QB4 P–K3 3 N–KB3 P–QN3 4 P–KN3 B–N2 5 B–N2 B–K2 6 0–0 0–0 7 N–B3 N–K5 8 Q–B2 N×N 9 Q×N P–QB4 10 R–Q1 P–Q3 11 P–N3 B–KB3 12 B–N2 Q–K2 13 Q–B2 N–B3 14 P–K4 P–N3 15 P–Q5 N–N5 16 B×B Q×B 17 Q–Q2 P–K4 18 P–QR3 N–R3 19 N–K1 Q–N2 20 N–Q3 P–B4 21 P×P P×P 22 P–B4 P–K5 23 N–K1 R–B3 24 Q–B3 P–R4 25 N–B2 K–B2 26 K–B2 P–R5 27 R–KN1 R–KN1 28 B–R3 Q–R2 29 R–R1 R–R3 30 B–N2 N–B2 31 P–QN4 N–K1 32 P×BP NP×P 33 KR–QN1 K–B1 34 N–K3 R–N2 35 R–N2 Q–N3 36 N–B1 P×P 37 P×P R(3)–R2 38 R(1)–N1 R–K2 39 R–N3

R(R2)–N2 40 Q–N2 N–B3 41 K–N1

41 ... R–R2 42 R–K1 B–R3 43 R–N8+ K–B2 44 Q–B3 N–N5 45 R–Q8 R–R3 46 N–K3 N×N 47 R×N Q–N5 48 B–B1 Q–R4 49 K–B2 Q–R8 50 R–QN8 R–R7+ 51 K–K1 Q–N8 52 R–K2 R–R8 53 R–KB2 P–K6 **White lost on time**

Here we should single out one further factor. Karpov is a great lover of the white pieces, with which for a long time he has associated his hopes of gaining the majority of his points. He does not normally go "fortune-hunting" when his opponent has the right of first move. But here, even when the pairings gave him command of the black army, from the first move he played for a win, and only a win.

A round later Grigorian had White against him. He was another representative of the "new wave", and although he had not become a grandmaster, he was eager for the title, which his more fortunate contemporaries had already managed to attain. In addition, he was inspired by the victory he had just gained over one of these fortunate contemporaries, Gulko, a victory which had put him among the first ten, and thereby instilled hope of remaining in the Premier League the following year.

That day Grigorian played with amazing boldness, brilliance and inspiration, sacrificing first a pawn against the World Champion, and then a bishop, and, as in one of Visotsky's songs dedicated to chess: "even took off his jacket to make sure". The audience hummed with surprise and suspicion. "But instantly the hall became quiet" (again words from a song)—Karpov made his reply, got up from the board, and everyone saw how composed he was. And soon one of the controllers quietly brought his chair up to the table, and began carefully following the flag on Grigorian's clock, which was slowly rising. The flag did not fall, but in quick succession two white pawns fell, which was equivalent to the fall of the flag.

The previous day Karpov had drawn with Polugayevsky, and he now led the tournament with eleven points. Balashov was half a point behind, and Petrosian could catch him in the event of successful results in two favourable adjourned games (which, incidentally, he did not succeed in doing). Thus before the last round, only these three grandmasters, who were separated by minimal intervals, were contenders for the supreme title.

Closer than anyone to the gold medal was Karpov. And when play started and his pursuers quickly agreed draws—Balashov with Tal and Petrosian with Smyslov—the one and a half thousand spectators, who had somehow squeezed into a hall intended for nine hundred, prepared themselves for the normal finale in such cases: very soon the same result would be agreed between Karpov and Tseshkovsky. What was the point of playing on, if a draw would suffice for one of the players to become sole winner of the tournament, while the other desperately needed it, so as to retain a place in the First League? And the spectators prepared to applaud the new USSR Champion...

However, the ovation had to be delayed a little.

In a room behind the stage, where the players gathered on completion of their games, and into which journalists and seconds forced their way, applause was indeed heard. Someone went to congratulate Furman, but immediately realized his error—the clapping was coming from a television set, where they were applauding some performer. And Furman said:

"Don't be hasty; in such a position Tolya wouldn't offer even his own father a draw."

The trainer knew his pupil well. He knew that the present-day Karpov was different from the one of a few years ago, who would without thinking have cut short the battle, if he was in any case assured of success. But now he wouldn't concede even a half point to anyone, without first utilizing all the resources of the position to attain victory.

On learning of Furman's half-joking remark, Karpov retorted without a smile:

"Semion Abramovich is not altogether correct. My father I would have given a draw. But only him, and no one else..."

After the game he shared his feelings with me:

"At that point I even became rather angry, when I realized that a 'rational' solution to the problem was expected of me. Besides, the position was interesting, and I soon forgot all about points and half points, and began simply playing chess."

Thus the World Champion, now Champion of the USSR, won yet another excellent game. Only the threat of lowering the curtain enabled the controllers to save the hall from what would have been an explosively thunderous ovation.

Karpov–Tseshkovsky
Ruy Lopez

1 P–K4 P–K4 2 N–KB3 N–QB3 3 B–N5
P–QR3 4 B–R4 N–B3 5 0–0 P–QN4
6 B–N3 B–N2 7 R–K1 B–B4 8 P–B3 P–Q3
9 P–Q4 B–N3 10 B–N5 P–R3 11 B–R4 Q–Q2

12 P–R4 0–0–0 13 RP×P RP×P 14 N–R3 P–N4 15 B–N3 P×P 16 N×QNP QR–K1 17 N(5)×P(4) N×N 18 N×N N×P (Diag.) 19 B–QR4 P–QB3 20 B–B2 P–Q4 21 B×N R×B 22 R×R P×R 23 Q–N3 B–B2 24 Q–N4 B×B 25 RP×B P–K6 26 P×P R–K1 27 N–N3 R–K4 28 N–B5 Q–K2 29 R–R5 Resigns

...Then there was everything—speeches, congratulations, interviews, photographs in the papers, articles, selections of the opinions of the Soviet and foreign press, numerical computations, and analyses of individual games and of the overall tournament strategy of the Champion. Correspondents were not sparing in their brilliant epithets and superlatives. The most calm assessment of Karpov's performance was the one which he himself gave:

"Unfortunately, the World Champion is always restricted in the choice of his final aim in an event: first place—nothing else will do... This means that with my result I am satisfied. But in the creative sense I could have played better."

This was not affectation. Just as there was no boasting in that which he said in Skopje about his most dangerous rivals: "I don't see anyone at the moment". This was the same Karpovian sobriety of assessment, in which there is no place either for compliments to others, or for self-esteem, but a desire to express the essence of the matter. Anyone who wishes to read double meanings, hints, or superficiality into Karpov's words, is mistaken. This is not in his nature.

But only Karpov had the moral right to say this about himself. Both numerical indications, and an analysis of the games played (towards the end of the tournament) by him, confirmed this indisputable truth: today, on the sum of components which make up a chess player's class, he is superior to everyone.

Following Karpov's loss to Geller, he made a brilliant score—eight wins and six draws. At the same time, we should not forget that which we have already frequently talked about —for him, the World Champion, it was more difficult than for all the others. Karpov himself said:

"Many are agreeable in advance to draw with the Champion. But in order to come first in a tournament, it is necessary to win. This means that there are two problems to be solved: first to force the opponent to play, and then to outplay him."

He succeeded in solving these problems. And how he solved them! Of the eight games he won, four were with Black. These victories demonstrated the universal nature of his chess style. Against Vaganian, who the previous day had defeated Petrosian in excellent style, he acted contrary to the generally accepted laws of chess logic: while still in the opening, without first equalizing, he started a K-side offensive. Against Grigorian, on the other hand, he showed himself to be a highly skilful defender, as he worked everything out and repelled the storm.

This is all on the purely chess side of the matter. The Champion's physical preparation was well described by the Dutch grandmaster Donner: "One gains the impression that Karpov, for all his frail appearance, was the only competitor in this marathon who not only maintained his strength, but even continued to increase the tempo right up to the finish." In substantiating his point, Donner is not sparing in his epithets: "Karpov had to accomplish a whole series of competitive feats: first, in study-like fashion, he saved a difficult ending against Petrosian, and then defeated the two heroes of the start—Dorfman and Balashov. And finally, at the decisive moment, he won two complicated games with Black against Gulko and Vaganian."

And one further citation. Grandmaster Robert Byrne, chess correspondent of the *New York Times*, as it were supplemented and generalized the thoughts of his Dutch colleague. In summing up the outcome of the USSR Championship, which received big press coverage throughout the world, he wrote: "Karpov is in no respect inferior to his main rivals, and excells them in his ability to mobilize all his strength to the utmost at the decisive and most difficult moment."

This was the fourth USSR Championship in the career of Anatoly Karpov, then 25-years-old. In the first he shared 5th–7th places, in the second he finished one rung higher—fourth, and then came a share of 2nd–6th places. And now he had reached the summit. And this progress up the tournament staircase of the national Championships—first as a young grandmaster, then a Candidate for the world throne, and then World Champion—reflects with sufficient completeness his progress up the invisible staircase, not marked by definite steps, of his mastery of the ancient game.

Karpov–Dorfman
Sicilian Defence

1 P–K4	P–QB4
2 N–KB3	P–Q3
3 P–Q4	P×P
4 N×P	N–KB3
5 N–QB3	P–K3
6 P–KN4	

In those instances when victory is absolutely essential, I revert to this sharp variation devised by the unforgettable Paul Keres. And I was in fact meeting one of the tournament leaders...

6 ...	B–K2
7 P–N5	KN–Q2
8 P–KR4	

Many play 8 R–KN1, but 8 P–KR4 seems more resolute to me—all the same White must aim for a rapid pawn squeeze of Black's K-side.

8 ...	N–QB3
9 B–K3	P–QR3
10 Q–K2!	

Stronger, and at any rate more interesting than 10 Q–Q2, after which a black knight, after moving to ... K4, will constantly threaten to leap in at ... KB6 or ... QB5 (true, after B–K2 these danger squares are covered, but this is a quieter, more positional continuation). But now the queen stands on the same file as the black king, which creates conditions for the combinational thrusts N–Q5 and N–B5. Although the K-file is blocked by several pieces, it tends to clear quickly.

10 ...	Q–B2
11 0–0–0	P–N4

Black provokes his opponent into making a sacrifice, apparently not fearing its consequences. However, no other way of developing his pieces is apparent, since if he were to castle he would immediately come under a pawn storm.

Here I thought for a long time, trying to decide on the best way of sacrificing the piece. 12 N–B5 looks tempting, when 12 ... P×N is of course bad on account of 13 N–Q5 Q–Q1 14 P×P. But the *zwischenzug* 12 ... P–N5! leads to immense complications—13 N–Q5 P×N(4) 14 P×P N–K4!. It was also possible to wait a little (12 P–B4), so that my opponent should himself force me to give up the piece (12 ... P–N5 13 N–Q5). And even so, the most promising continuation seemed to be the one which occurred in the game.

12 N×N	Q×N
13 B–Q4!	P–N5

The only other way of defending the KNP was at the cost of a serious weakening of the important ... Q4 square (13 ... P–K4 14 B–K3).

14 N–Q5!   **P×N**

Now 15 P×P?? would be a bad blunder— 15 ... Q×QP 16 B×P Q×R(R8) 17 R–K1 N–K4 18 B×N P×B 19 Q×KP. It appears that White must win, since he threatens 20 Q×B mate, 20 B–N5+ and 20 Q×R+, but ... Black has not yet utilized his right to castle, and he unexpectedly wins—19 ... 0–0!.

15 B×P	R–KN1
16 P×P	Q–B2
17 B–B6	

In the event of 17 R–K1 N–K4 18 B×N P×B 19 P–KB4 P×P White does not have

the move 20 P–Q6, and it is just the presence or absence of this advance which particularly influences the decisions taken by White.

17 ...   N–K4

The only move, since 17 ... N–N3 loses after 18 R–K1 N×P 19 B–N2, and 17 ... N–B4—after 18 R–K1 R–R2 19 B–R3 B×B 20 R×B, when White now ties up the black bishop with a "triple knot" (by playing R–K3). In this last variation there is an amusing helpmate: 19 ... K–B1 20 B×B(8) B×B 21 Q–K8+ K–N2 22 P×B+ K–R1 23 Q×R+ K×Q 24 R–K8 mate.

18 B×N

18 ... B–N5 was threatened, so that there was no time for 18 P–KB4.

18 ...	P×B
19 P–KB4	B–KB4

19 ... P–K5 fails—to 20 P–Q6 B×QP 21 Q×KP+.

20 B–R3

This move provoked numerous arguments, since the continuation 20 P×P R–QB1 21 R–R2 B–B4 22 K–N1 is clearly advantageous to White. E.g. 22 ... B–N8 23 B–R3 (23 R–N2 Q–B4) 23 ... B×R 24 B×B Q×KP 25 Q×Q B×Q 26 B×R, although even here there are still technical difficulties to be overcome. What I was mainly concerned about was the continuation 21 ... Q–R4, since I did not want to play an ending of the type resulting after 22 Q×P Q×Q 23 B×Q R–B4. It may be objected that it is not essential to go into an ending, since there is the move 22 Q–B3 (after 21 ... Q–R4), attacking the bishop and gaining an important tempo. But then the battle flares up with new strength 22 ... P–N6! 23 Q×P (forced, since 23 Q×B

even loses—23 ... P×RP 24 Q×R+ B–Q1)
23 ... R–N3. I should incidentally remark
that an earlier 20 ... P–N6 is not dangerous
for White: 21 RP×P Q–R4 22 Q–B3 Q–R8+
(or 22 ... B–QN5 23 K–N1, and the white
bishop emerges with decisive effect on QB4,
blocking all the lines) 23 K–Q2 B–QN5+
24 K–K2.

I thought that I would achieve more by the
immediate exchange of bishops.

20 ...	B×B
21 R×B	R–QB1
22 P×P	

By playing 22 P–N3, I could have deprived
my opponent of his ... QB5 square—the
springboard for the transference of the black
pieces. In this case Black's only reply—22 ...
P–K5 (22 ... P–B3 loses to 23 NP×P B×P
24 P×P B×KP 25 R–K3 or 25 P–Q6) would
still not have enabled him to equalize after
23 Q×KP K–B1 24 P–B5.

22 ...   Q–B5!

This manoeuvre, which is closely linked
with the whole of Black's subsequent play,
is a tribute to Dorfman's ingenuity.

23 R(1)–Q3   Q–B5+!

Apart from this check, it was necessary to
examine at least two further possibilities:

I. 23 ... R×P 24 P×R Q×RP 25 P–Q6
(the exchange of blows—25 Q–N4 R–B5

26 R–Q4 B×P+! 27 Q×B R×R 28 Q–N8+
K–K2 29 Q–N5+ K–K1 30 Q–N8+—gives
White only a draw) 25 ... B×NP+ 26
R(R3)–K3 R–B5 27 Q–N2 (27 P–K6 does
not work—27 ... R–K5! 28 P–Q7+ K–Q1
29 Q–N2 B×R+ 30 R×B Q–R8+ 31 K–Q2
R–Q5+ 32 R–Q3 R×R+, and the threats
are parried. Besides, Black has a perpetual
check after 27 ... Q–R8+ 28 K–Q2 Q×P
29 P–Q7+ K–Q1 30 P–K7+ B×P 31 R×B
R×P+ 32 K–K1 R×Q+ 33 R×R Q–B8+
34 R–Q1 Q–B6+ 35 R(Q1)–Q2 Q–KN6+).
In view of the threats of 28 Q×B, 28 P–Q7+
and 28 Q–R8+, White has a big advantage.
Here is a possible variation: 27 ... B×R+
28 R×B Q–R8+ 29 K–Q2 R–Q5+ 30 R–Q3
etc. It should be added that on 26 ... R–B4
(instead of 26 ... R–B5) White can again
play 27 Q–N2.

White also has another possibility—25
R(R3)–N3 (instead of 25 P–Q6) 25 ...
Q–R8+ 26 K–Q2 Q×P 27 Q–Q1, and now:
a) 27 ... Q×KP 28 R(N3)–K3 Q–Q3
(28 ... B×P 29 K–K2!) 29 K–B1 with good
winning chances; b) 27 ... R–B5 28 P–Q6
B–Q1 29 P–K6, and White's advantage is
indisputable.

II. 23 ... Q×RP 24 P–Q6, and the black
rook on the QB-file is unable to escape from
the pursuit of the white queen: a) 24 ... R–B3
25 Q–K4 Q–B5 26 Q×Q R×Q 27 P×B,
with the advantage; b) 24 ... R–B4 25
Q–B2 followed by P×B; c) on 24 ... R–B5
White can play 25 P×B Q–R8+ 26 K–Q2
Q×P 27 R–Q8+ K–K2 28 R–Q7+! K×R
29 Q×R, with an irresistible attack.

24 K–N1   R–B5!

I repeat, I attach exclamation marks to the
entire plan of defence found by my opponent.

25 P–Q6	R–K5
26 R(R3)–K3	R×R

If Black had been tempted by 26 ...
R×NP, he could well have fallen into a very
pretty mate: 27 P×R B×NP 28 P–Q7+
K–Q1 29 R–Q1! R×R 30 Q×P, followed by
Q–B8+ and Q–K8 mate.

27 R×R   Q×RP

Something similar to that in the previous
note could have occurred after 27 ... R×P
28 P×R B×NP 29 P–Q7+ K–Q1 (29 ...
K–K2 30 Q–Q3) 30 Q×P.

28 Q–B3!   Q×P

The best of the three possible captures. The
other two were weaker: 28 ... R×P 29
Q–QB6+ K–B1 30 P×B+ K×P 31 P–R3!,
or 28 ... B×NP 29 P–K6 P×P 30 R×P+
K–Q1 (30 ... K–Q2 31 Q–B7+ K–B3 32
P–Q7+) 31 Q–QB6!, and Black does not
have a single check.

29 R–K1

White would have retained a certain
advantage after 29 Q–QB6+ K–B1 30
P×B+ Q×P 31 Q–R6+ R–N2, but I
wanted more, and so I "restricted" myself to
a quiet (but in fact risky) move.

29 ...   Q–N7

Also affected by the heat of the moment
was my opponent, who had at his disposal a
move which certainly deserved consideration—29 ... Q–N5!?. If White had 'taken
fright', he could have headed for a draw by
30 Q–QB6+ Q–Q2 31 Q×Q+ K×Q 32
P×B; if he wished to try to maintain his
initiative, there were two directions in which
it was worth searching: 30 Q–QB6+ Q–Q2
31 Q–K4 B–Q1 32 Q×RP R–B1, or 30
Q–Q3 followed by 31 Q×QRP.

30 Q–B5   R–N3

With the loss of a tempo, 30 ... Q–N5 is
no longer attractive—31 Q×RP B–R5 32
R–KB1 R–N2 (32 ... B–B7 33 P–K6!) 33
Q–Q3, winning at least one more pawn.
By bringing his rook out onto the third rank,
Black not only covers his KRP, but also
prevents the break-through by P–K6.

31 R–KB1   Q–Q4
32 P×B   K×P

The waiting move 32 ... P–QR4 fails to
33 Q–R5 P–R3 34 P–K6!! R–B3 (34 ...
Q×KP 35 Q×QRP, when the QNP falls,
and the black king remains exposed) 35
P×P+ Q×P (35 ... R×P 36 Q–N6 Q–K3!
37 Q–N8+ K×P 38 R–Q1, with a strong
attack) 36 Q–QN5+ K×P 37 Q–QB5+,
and the exposed state of his king makes
Black's position more than dangerous.

33 Q–B4!   P–QR4
34 Q–R4+   K–K1
35 Q×RP   Q–B6

The last attempt to exploit the weakness of
White's back rank.

36 Q–R8+   K–K2

36 ... K–Q2 is weaker, since then 37
P–K6+ completely exposes the king: 37 ...
R×P (37 ... K×P 38 R–K1+) 38 Q–Q4+
K–K1 39 R–Q1, or 37 ... P×P 38 Q–Q4+

Q–Q4 39 Q–R7+ K–Q3 40 Q–N6+ K–Q2
41 P–N3!, and Black has no useful move.

37 Q–R4+	K–K1
38 Q–QB4!	Q–N2
39 P–N3	

After at last making an escape square for
his king, White can now attack without
having to glance back so often at his rear-
guard.

39 ...	R–K3
40 R–N1	

I did not hesitate to give up the pawn,
since I was confident that Black's exposed
king would not be able to survive the attack.

40 ...	R×P
41 R–N8+	

It was this obvious move that I sealed.
Analysis showed that the position was won,
but that accurate play was required of White.

41 ...	K–K2
42 Q–R4+	K–Q2

If 42 ... K–K3, then 43 R–K8+.

43 Q–B6!

The first subtle point. 43 R–Q8+ was
tempting, when there are two possibilities to
consider:

I. 43 ... K–B3? 44 Q–R1+ K–N3 (44 ...
K–B2 45 R–Q7+) 45 R–Q6+ K–R2 46
Q–N1+ K–N1 47 Q–Q4 (not 47 R–QN6
R–K8+!), and it is doubtful whether Black
can save his queen.

II. 43 ... K–B2. White appears to win
immediately by 44 Q–Q4 R–K8+ (it is not
difficult to check that there is no other move)
45 K–N2 Q–B3 (again the only move) 46
R–Q5, when 46 ... Q–B6+ 47 Q×Q+
P×Q+ 48 K×P is bad for Black; everything
else is also bad, except 46 ... P–R5!, and
here White has an unenviable choice between
a queen or a rook ending with two pawns
against one:

a) 47 Q×P Q×R 48 Q×R P×P 49
RP×P; b) 47 P–R3 Q–B6+ (not 47 ...
NP×P+ 48 K×P R–QR8+ 49 K–N2
R–R7+ 50 K×R Q×P+ 51 Q–N2, and
White wins) 48 Q×Q+ P×Q+ 49 K×P
P×P 50 P×P, in each case with problematic
winning chances.

44 Q–B6 (44 Q–N5 P–B3!) looks dangerous
for Black, but here too he can transpose into
the above variations—44 ... Q–R8+ 45
K–N2 R–K3 46 Q–Q4 Q–B3.

43 ...	R–K2

The strongest. 43 ... Q–B2 loses quickly
to 44 Q×P+ K–B3 45 Q–B6+ K–B4 (or
45 ... K–N4) 46 Q–B1! Q–K2 47 Q–QB4+
K–Q3 48 Q–R6+ K–Q2 49 Q–B8+, or
48 ... K–B2 49 R–QB8+; 43 ... Q–R8+
is also weak in view of 44 K–N2 R–K2 45
Q–B5+ K–B3 46 Q×RP.

44 Q–B5+	K–Q3

On 44 ... K–B3 White should not be
enticed by checks—45 R–QB8+ K–Q3 46
Q–B5+ K–Q2, when his pieces have lost
their way in the opponent's position. 45
Q×RP is simpler, with very strong threats.

45 Q×RP

It's all very well checking, but a pawn is a pawn...

45 ...   R–K4

Black could have activated his queen—45 ... Q–K5 (45 ... Q–R8+ 46 K–N2 Q–K5 leads to similar variations) 46 Q–N6+ K–K4 47 Q–B5+ K–B5 48 R–N8 Q–K8+ 49 K–N2 Q–K4+ 50 Q×Q+ K×Q (White has an even easier win after 50 ... R×Q 51 R×P+ K–K6 52 P–R4 P–B4 53 R–N5, or 51 ... K–N4 52 R–N8 P–B4 53 R–N8+ K–R5 54 R–KB8) 51 R–N5+! K–B5 52 R×P+ K–N6 53 R–N5! (forcing the king to make a step backwards) 53 ... K–N5 54 R–N8 P–B4 55 R–N8+ K–B6 56 R–KB8 P–B5 57 P–R6 K–K6 58 P–R5 P–B6 59 P–N4 R–K5 60 P–B3 R–KB5 61 R×R K×R 62 P–R6 P–B7 63 P–R7 P–B8=Q 64 P–R8=Q Q–K7+ 65 K–R3, and White wins. Of course, there are numerous variations and possibilities in this position, especially for White. I have given only the main line, with what I consider to be the strongest moves for both sides.

46 Q–Q8+	K–K3
47 K–N2!	P–B3
48 R–B8	

The most accurate. White does not allow the black king the possibility of running away.

48 ...	Q–N2
49 Q–B8+	K–Q4
50 Q–B4+	Resigns

CHAPTER 10

On the Crest of a Wave

A few rounds before the end of the USSR Championship, a rather short, dark-complexioned man quietly took his seat in the third row of the auditorium. To many his appearance went unnoticed, but from the first row of tables on the stage, Karpov immediately saw Campomanes. He saw him, and was unable to conceal his anxiety. But, alas, the FIDE Vice-President had not brought any new proposals from Fischer, apart from a firm desire to play an unofficial match with the World Champion up to ten wins. And both of them—the active World Champion, and the Ex-Champion who had deserted the chess scene—remained in their positions...

Robert Fischer did not want to play against "ordinary grandmasters", and he silently declined to be included in the next World Championship cycle, thereby giving up his place in the Candidates' Quarter-Final Matches to Boris Spassky. As regards World Champion Anatoly Karpov, he had already made his plans for 1977, during which he intended taking part in five events.

But although he was on the crest of a wave, gaining quite phenomenal results, the Champion did not forget for one moment about the Candidates.

THE OUTSIDER SEES BETTER *(The Champion on the Candidates)*

The victor in the Hort–Spassky encounter was due to meet the winner of the Larsen–Portisch match. The other two semi-finalists would be provided by the winners of the two matches Mecking–Polugayevsky and Petrosian–Korchnoi. So how did Karpov initially rate the chances of the Candidates?

At first he wouldn't be drawn into this conversation, for the reason that such forecasts rarely prove correct, and that he does not like being wrong. But nevertheless I persuaded Karpov, and for a "starter" reminded him that three years previously he had predicted a more active emergence of young players into the leading rôles.

"Even now I can say", Karpov began, "that if the Interzonal Tournaments were replayed, Mecking would not be the only young player to make the Candidates. The young players did not perform at all badly. Who could have known that Hübner, who played better than anyone in Switzerland, would miss a forced mate in a few moves against Petrosian? Or that it would be in Manila that Ljubojević, who has had numerous successes lately, would prove to be so impressionable? They have lost three more years..."

"So who will win the quarter-final matches?"

"Hort has long been one of the strongest grandmasters in the world, but he has acquired ambition only comparatively recently, and not yet to the necessary degree. Vlastimil, whom

I genuinely like, is happy that he has made it to the Candidates, and I congratulate him from my heart on doing so. Even so, I think that he will lose his match, but lose it honourably.

Yes, in the match Hort–Spassky I give my preference to Spassky. I have always had an exceptionally high opinion of Spassky, and if he can get down to it as he used to, I can perfectly well see him being my opponent in the match for the World Championship. The Interzonal, it is true, undermined somewhat my faith in his chances, but that vast match experience... In short, the constancy of my faith is still sufficiently great.

Larsen, regarding his chances of success in his quarter-final match, said that he was now avoiding making forecasts, and that he would not even take it upon himself to name the winner in the coming match for the World Championship between Karpov and... Larsen...

I am absolutely convinced that those who are most happy with the pairings are Larsen and Portisch. Each of them already knows for sure that he will win. I should not like to argue with either of them, but since I have to give a definite answer, I will tip the Hungarian grandmaster. Portisch is the more serious in chess, as well as in life, although Larsen is no less talented. But the Dane plays too riskily, and his nerves may not stand up. Even in a tournament of uneven strength—and this used to be his forte—he can't last out. And don't go citing his victory in Switzerland—in Biel no one properly tested his nerves. In 1973, on the previous Interzonal, there was serious competition, and everyone remembers how that ended up for Larsen, who started with a series of wins. Talking about Larsen's nerves reminds me that Portisch also has lost his former composure. It more often happens that he is not on form, and he more and more rarely plays evenly and confidently... I make no secret of the fact that I see Spassky as the favourite among the first quartet.

The second quartet has turned out to be much stronger. It is difficult for me to talk about the Petrosian–Korchnoi match. By declining to return to his homeland after an international tournament abroad, my former opponent has severely compromised himself, and has lost much both as a person and as a chess player. This is bound to have its effect, and so I would not now give preference to him."

EASILY AND QUICKLY *(Bad Lauterberg: West German Open Championship)*

While the Candidates to his title were engaged in settling accounts with each other, the World Champion too did not wish to remain idle. And his next appearance, which coincided in time (March 1977) with the Candidates' Quarter-Final Matches, provoked chess correspondents—in the main from abroad—into making certain comparisons. This is what was written about Karpov by international master Mario Monticelli, who writes a chess column for the *Corriere della Sera* in Milan: "He tries to avoid unjustified risks during a game, but it is difficult to remember another Champion who would so readily take a risk when this seemed expedient. And now here, in a situation where the majority of his predecessors would have preferred to go into hiding and follow the course of events from the side, Karpov is taking part in an indirect creative competition with the Candidates."

In the West German Open Championship in the town of Bad Lauterberg, the competitors, apart from the World Champion, included virtually all of the strongest non-Soviet grandmasters not involved in the Candidates' Matches. Here is Anatoly Karpov's account of this highly interesting international tournament:

"The 'Aeroflot' plane landed in Frankfurt, from where we went on to Bad Lauterberg by car. The journey was not particularly interesting—it took place in fog, but also not tiring—thanks to the good roads and a talkative driver. He turned out to be Schultz, three-time boxing champion of West Germany, and a prize-winner at the Rome Olympic Games, who remembered very well the brilliant Soviet boxer Gennady Shatkov and... many of his passengers. He disclosed, with unfeigned pride, that in that very car he had driven Mohammed Ali, and Pelé, honoured guests at the Munich Olympiad, and even Rockefeller when he had been there on an official visit.

Bad Lauterberg is a smallish resort town, situated some fifteen kms from the East German border. Picturesque, mountainous countryside, and the absence of any major industry, are the chief virtues of this region. All of the permanent population (roughly 10,000) are engaged in the tourist trade. Chess, among other forms of cultural activity, occupies by no means last place. The local chess club was celebrating its 50th anniversary, and this, in combination with another date (the 100th anniversary festival in honour of Adolf Anderssen) were the grounds for organizing a chess event.

...The great number of guests included the directors of sport in West Germany. A speech by one of them ended in an appeal to the sports officials of individual districts to finance more actively the development of chess. I should add that, on the conclusion of the tournament, I gave some simultaneous displays, and saw for myself the substantial popularity of chess in the country, and also the considerable practical strength of the local enthusiasts. To a certain extent, a game against television viewers was another indication of this. Each move, made by me once a week, was first recorded (wherever I happened to be!) on film, which was sent off to West German T.V., and shown there on Fridays. The strongest West German players, or foreign grandmasters who happened to be in the country, commented on the moves made, and 'predicted' the further course of the game. When the tournament in Bad Lauterberg was drawing to a close, my opponents were considering their 29th move, and the position was approximately level...

But let us return to the tournament, which drew a strong entry (13 grandmasters and 3 German masters), and proved highly interesting. At the drawing of lots Semion Furman and I picked numbers one and two, but in contrast to my trainer this did not afford me much joy: I was faced with Black against Hübner, Olafsson, Andersson, Gligorić, Torre... However, a battle for first place essentially did not result—at the start I managed to win five games out of six. Soon it proved that I had been wrong to complain about the pairings—with White I scored 7½ out of 8. And over the entire tournament I had, it would seem, only one inferior position (against Csom), and two genuinely tense games (with Olafsson and Hübner).

At first Robert Hübner appeared to be my main rival, but he created a two-fold impression. He is becoming less of a professional chess player, as he absorbs himself in the study of papyrus manuscripts and, as far as I know, achieves more and more success in this science. At the same time it is noticeable that he enjoys playing chess, but the results of the last Interzonal Tournament made an indelible impression on him. In one interview Hübner even stated that as before he wants to play chess, and that he gains satisfaction from it. But as soon as he remembers his tragic game with Petrosian from the Interzonal Tournament, where he failed to see a forced mate, he becomes completely down-hearted.

At any event, Hübner played well in the first half of the tournament, and for a long time was in second place. Then came our meeting. Hübner had no noticeable advantage, but he avoided

19

a draw. Then, evidently deciding that he had 'got worked up', he began peace negotiations, which I turned down. Twice he had to play on this game in the evening—from 22.00 to 24.00, and once in the morning—from 10.00 until 12.00. What's more, for the morning session he arrived without having had a good sleep. (Normally, as Hübner himself stated, he gets up much earlier, but during a tournament he finds morning play very difficult.) The West German grandmaster nevertheless drew against me, but then, fatigued, he lost first to Timman, with whom he immediately exchanged places in the table, and then also to Miles from England.

In his game against the Englishman, Hübner adopted in the opening an idea of our own Oleg Romanishin, but failed to take into account the fact that Black had developed his bishop at b4 instead of his knight at f6. This game did not finish as quickly as it should have done, merely on account of technical errors by Miles.

Talking about the strongest present-day English player, we should remember that he is one of the youngest grandmasters in the world, and that therefore he naturally attracts attention. Tony Miles is a nervy kind of person, in which he resembles Henrique Mecking. But, just like the Brazilian, when he finds himself in a difficult position he forgets about everything else, clasps his head in his hands, and behaves at the board quite normally... At any rate, this is how they have both played against me. Miles' lack of experience, plus his as yet not particularly good technique, are to a certain extent compensated for by a well-prepared opening repertoire, and his ingenuity in double-edged positions.

Before the finish Jan Timman won five games in a row (which, incidentally, he had done not long before this in the International Tournament at Wijk aan Zee). In general, the Dutch grandmaster is, as they say, a player of moods. On this occasion he was in an excellent frame of mind, since tournament fortune was with him, and smiled especially kindly on him in clearly lost positions against Gligorić and Olafsson. The result was clear second place, although two points behind me.

I will not take it upon myself to describe all the participants, but I should nevertheless like to say something about the powerful and confident play of Fridrik Olafsson. He is an exceptionally determined player, which in combination with his tenacity (he fought for 95 moves in his game against me, and succeeded in saving it), makes him a dangerous rival in any event. And, on the other hand, a complete contrast to Olafsson in this tournament was Ulf Andersson. Right since the time of our appearance together in the 1969 Junior World Championship, I have had a great affection for the Swedish player. And this makes it all the more distressing to see the metamorphosis which has occurred with Ulf in recent times. Andersson plays as if he were an old man, who knows everything and fears everything. All the time he plays the same positions, and both as White and as Black rarely advances his pieces beyond the third rank. Yes, as before he rarely loses, but... he has completely stopped winning. Fourteen draws and one defeat (in his favourite set-up) is of course a pitiful result.

Naturally, I cannot avoid talking about my trainer, who was also my rival at the Bad Lauterberg tournament. When he used to play, Semion Furman needed, even more than I do, to have a person close to him alongside. It is not every middle-aged person who is able to adjust rapidly to constantly-changing companions in his chess travels. I, on the other hand, find it easier to get on with new people, since as a last resort I am able, if one can put it this way, to abstract myself.

On this occasion, Furman and I as it were acted as trainer to each other, although there was very little time for this (six rounds, a free day, eight rounds, another free day, and then the last round). The experienced grandmaster played splendidly (it is sufficient to recall his brilliant win over Gligorić), and only tired towards the finish, losing with White to Torre. But on the other hand, for instance, in his game against another young grandmaster, Miles, Furman gave a demonstration of how to play a typical position with an isolated queen's pawn. Furman's third place was absolutely merited.

The tournament was a fighting one; draws were agreed only after a full-blooded struggle. The organizers were equal to almost every occasion, except when it came to exclusively chess matters. However, it isn't always possible not to reproach them. Here is a typical example. During a severe mutual time scramble (it would have been even worse if only one of the players had been short of time) one of the controllers was recording the game. Forty moves had been made, but the players did not know this, and were feverishly seeking the best continuations. Suddenly the controller, without waiting for the fall of one of the players' flags, called play to a halt with the announcement that the control had been reached. When the astonished grandmasters drew attention to this (the incident described occurred in a game between two of the German masters), the controller declared that such a regulation had very recently been adopted by Congress into the FIDE rules. I think that this was simply a misunderstanding—there just can't be such a regulation!

There is one further question to which I should perhaps reply, concerning my game from the last round against Torre. Many supposed that I wanted without fail to gain revenge against the Filipino grandmaster for my defeat in the tournament at Manila, and that therefore I played for a win when I was already assured of first place. There was, of course, some justification for such a supposition. But without wishing to offend at all Eugenio Torre, who is a talented player, I should remark that as yet he does not number among the players fighting for the world crown, and there was no particular necessity to demonstrate my superiority over him. I was simply playing chess…"

Karpov–Sosonko
Sicilian Defence

1 P–K4 P–QB4 2 N–KB3 P–Q3 3 P–Q4 P×P 4 N×P N–KB3 5 N–QB3 P–KN3 6 B–K2 B–N2 7 0–0 N–B3 8 N–N3 0–0 9 B–KN5 B–K3 10 K–R1 P–QR4 11 P–QR4 N–Q2 12 P–B4 N–N3 13 P–B5 B–B5 14 B×B N×B 15 Q–K2 N–N3 16 Q–N5 N–Q5 17 N×N B×N 18 QR–Q1 B–N2 19 B–K3 N–Q2 20 N–Q5 R–K1 21 P–B3 B–K4 (Diag.)

22 B–N6 N×B 23 N×N R–R3 24 N–B4 Q–N1 25 N×RP R–QB1 26 N–B4 B×RP 27 N–N6 R×N 28 Q×R B–K4 29 P–R5 R–B3 30 Q–K3 Q–B2 31 R–Q5 R–R3 32 Q–Q3 K–N2 33 R–N5 P–N4 34 Q–Q5 R–R2 35 P–KN4 Q–B1 36 K–N2 Q–Q2 37 P–B4 Q–K1 38 P–N3 Q–Q1 39 Q–Q2 P–B3 40 R–KR1 B–B5 41 Q–B3 Q–KR1 42 Q–R3 P–R4 43 Q×P Q×Q 44 R×Q B–Q7 45 P–N4 **Resigns**

Karpov–Miles
Sicilian Defence

1 P–K4 P–QB4 2 N–KB3 P–Q3 3 P–Q4
P×P 4 N×P N–KB3 5 N–QB3 P–KN3 6
B–K2 B–N2 7 0–0 0–0 8 B–KN5 N–B3 9
N–N3 B–K3 10 K–R1 Q–B1 11 P–B4 R–Q1
12 B–B3 B–B5 13 R–B2 P–K3 14 R–Q2 Q–B2
15 Q–K1 P–KR3 16 B–R4 R–Q2 17 QR–Q1
P–K4

18 B×N B×B 19 B–N4 P×P 20 B×R
Q×B 21 R×P Q–K2 22 R–Q7 Q–K4 23
N–Q2 B–K3 24 N–B3 Q–N1 25 R(7)–Q6
B–K2 26 R(6)–Q2 B–B3 27 N–Q5 B–N2
28 P–B3 P–KN4 29 Q–B2 N–K4 30 Q–B5
B–N5 31 R–KB1 P–N3 32 Q–N5 Q–N2 33
N–Q4 B–Q2 34 Q–N3 Q–R3 35 Q–Q1 B–N5
36 Q–N1 N–B5 37 Q–Q3 P–N4 38 R(2)–
KB2 Q–N2 39 P–QN3 N–Q3 40 N–B5 N×N
41 P×N R–Q1 42 P–B4 K–R1 43 P–KR3
B–R4 44 R–K1 Resigns

Karpov–Liberzon
Sicilian Defence

1 P–K4 P–QB4 2 N–KB3 N–QB3 3 P–Q4
P×P 4 N×P N–KB3 5 N–QB3 P–Q3 6
B–KN5 P–K3 7 Q–Q2 P–QR3 8 0–0–0 B–Q2
9 P–B4 B–K2 10 N–B3 P–N4 11 B×N P×B
12 K–N1 Q–N3 13 P–B5 0–0–0 14 P–KN3
K–N1 15 P×P P×P 16 B–R3 B–QB1 17
Q–K1 KR–K1 18 N–K2 Q–B4 19 N(3)–Q4
N×N 20 N×N B–B1 21 R–KB1 P–Q4 22
N–N3 Q–B2 23 B–N2 P×P 24 Q×P B–QN2
25 R×R+ R×R 26 Q×B+ Q×Q 27 B×Q
K×B 28 P–B3 B–K2 29 N–Q4 P–K4 30
N–B5 B–B4 31 K–B2 P–QR4 32 P–KN4
K–B3 33 N–N3 B–K2 34 R–B5 R–KN1 35
P–KR3 K–Q4 36 K–Q3 P–R5 37 N–K4 K–K3
38 R–R5 R–Q1+ 39 K–K2 P–R6 40 P–N4
K–Q4 41 K–Q3 K–K3+ 42 K–B2 R–QB1 43
K–N3 K–Q4 44 N–N3 B–Q3 45 R×RP P–K5
46 N–B5 R–Q1 47 R–R7 B–B5 48 K–B2 K–B5

49 R–QB7+ K–Q4 50 R–B5+ K–K3 51
N–Q4+ K–B2 52 R×P B–K6 53 R–N7+
K–N1 54 N–B5 R–Q7+ 55 K–N3 Resigns

* * *

On the conclusion of the Bad Lauterberg tournament, Tony Miles shared his impressions
of the World Champion's play on the pages of the London weekly *The New Statesman:*

"I was particularly struck by the rapidity and ease with which Karpov plays comparatively
simple technical positions. On his game with Keene, which lasted 57 moves, he spent only one
and a half hours, as opposed to three and a half hours by his opponent. In his game with
Olafsson the difference in times was even more striking. When I last compared the clocks,
Karpov's read 2½ hours, and Olafsson's—5½, and after this I think that the difference continued
to increase."...

TEAM CHESS (Moscow: The European Team Championship)

"For me the European Team Championship was virtually a continuation of the international tournament in West Germany—here too I was in good form. True, it was difficult even to imagine that I would achieve such a performance in Moscow..."

Pupils from the Suvorov Military School, dressed in ceremonial uniforms, announced with a fanfare the beginning of the festivities, and invited the envoys from eight European countries into the circular arena of the "Wings of the Soviets" Sports Palace in Moscow. Spectators in the packed stands greeted with applause the foreign and Soviet grandmasters. Bread and salt, symbols of hospitality, were presented to the guests on embroidered cloths by girls in Russian national costumes. The traditionally business-like atmosphere of the official opening ceremony was enlivened by a display of "live chess". The following words are from a popular song about chess: "There is a great deal of art on a small chess square". On this occasion the art was demonstrated by young soloists from a dance ensemble, who performed the rôles of living chess pieces. At the finish of the display, a lone pawn gained a draw for the Whites (who were directed by a Moscow young Pioneer) against a queen, bishop and knight of the Blacks (to them the microphone commands were given by grandmaster Yury Balashov).

In conclusion, a "musical drawing of lots" was held. To the strains of an accordion, a little lad darted out on a painted toy horse, followed by girls dressed up as Russian dolls. Each of the team captains was invited to choose the girl who appealed to him, and she in turn presented him with his number in the starting table.

In the first round, eight grandmasters of the USSR team met the Czechs. In the first game to finish, Geller had to be content with a draw against Lechtynsky. Then the same result was agreed in a tense encounter between Jansa and Petrosian, in which White won a pawn, but had insufficient time left to realize his advantage.

Karpov, leader of the Soviet team, seized the position of Jan Šmejkal in a vice-like grip, and the Czech grandmaster had to give up the exchange. When the gong announcing the end of the session sounded, the World Champion had maintained his advantage, although the position on his board had become much sharper.

Furman, Karpov's constant second, and also fulfilling here the duties of trainer to the Soviet team, remarked anxiously: "Our lads have adjourned several of their games; we'll be up working all night." The fruits of this work were seen the following morning, when one after another, Karpov, Polugayevsky, Tal, Balashov and Romanishin each brought their team a point... The score in the USSR–Czechoslovakia match became 6–1, with one game still unfinished, where Tseshkovsky held the advantage.

Karpov–Šmejkal
Ruy Lopez

1 P–K4 P–K4 2 N–KB3 N–QB3 3 B–N5 P–QR3 4 B–R4 N–B3 5 0–0 B–K2 6 R–K1 P–QN4 7 B–N3 P–Q3 8 P–B3 0–0 9 P–KR3 N–N1 10 P–Q4 QN–Q2 11 QN–Q2 B–N2 12 B–B2 R–K1 13 N–B1 B–KB1 14 N–N3 P–N3 15 P–QR4 P–B4 16 P–Q5 N–N3 17 Q–K2 N×RP 18 B×N P×B 19 R×P B–B1 20 P–N3 R–N1 21 R–R3 R–K2 22 P–B4 R(2)–N2 23 Q–B2 N–K1 24 B–Q2 N–N2 25 N–R2 P–B4 26 R–N1 R–KB2 27 P–N4 P×NP 28 B×P R(2)–N2 29 R(3)–N3

Q–N3 30 R(3)–N2 P–QR4 31 B–R3 Q–Q5
32 R×R R×R 33 R–Q1 Q–N3 34 N–B3
Q–N6 35 Q–B1 Q–R5 36 R–Q3 R–B2 37
R–B3 B–R3 38 N–Q2 P–B5 39 N(3)–B1
N–K1 40 B–N2 N–B3 (Diag.)
　41 R–R3 Q–N5 42 B–B3 R×P 43 N×R
Q×N 44 N–Q2 Q–K7 45 R×P B–Q6 46
B–N4 B×P 47 N×B N×N 48 B–K1 N–B4
49 Q–Q2 Q–B5 50 R–R7 Q–K5 51 Q–R5
P–N4 52 B–N4 Black lost on time.

You should have seen how adjourned games were analysed. Analysis went on through the night in the "Moskva" Hotel. Most of the players who did not have a game to resume the following morning normally also took part in the analysis. This was expected of the trainers, but no one would have condemned a player, who, tired out after his game, had gone off to sleep. Oh no! Dorfman, who made a successful debut for his country's team, admitted that when he resumed his game against the Rumanian Ungureanu, he made 14 moves exactly according to analysis, the main rôle in which had been played by Karpov. After his own game, the Champion spent five hours during the night at the board of one of his team colleagues!

Yes, yes, there is such a concept in chess—the team player. He comprises a great many things. These include concern for his colleagues, a readiness to give up a higher board or to "concede" an easier opponent or the white pieces to his neighbour, or to replace a tired colleague who has played conscientiously in all his preceding matches, without permitting himself short draws, which are equivalent to additional rest days. In short, a team player is a person who is fully endowed with competitive integrity.

Special demands are made on the team captain (who happened in this case to be Karpov). In the navy there is the rank of Lieutenant-Commander. During the 6th European Team Championship, Karpov could well have been awarded the rank of "Champion-Commander", if such a one existed. And all these qualities did not arise by chance. Remember how the trainer of the USSR Youth Team A. Bikhovsky related earlier how Karpov had cemented together so well the student teams of 1971 and 1972...

Concern for the team... Tseshkovsky, for instance, was much less upset about the fact that he could find no way of winning his adjourned game against the Czech player, that his colleagues were apparently not doing so well in their next match—with the Yugoslavs. He sat sullenly "on the substitutes' bench", but soon cheered up: on the top boards the USSR players had seized the initiative. Like true team leaders, at the most dangerous moment of the event they acted confidently and calmly. Karpov completely outplayed his very strong opponent, Ljubojević, Polugayevsky defeated the experienced Matanović, and Tal outwitted the energetic Velimirović...

All the games by the World Champion in this event were full of interest, and all were on different tactical levels. Here, for instance, is what he himself had to say about his encounter with Florian Gheorghiu:

"The Rumanian player is not one of the leading grandmasters in the world, but those who are well acquainted with our branch of sport will long-since have noticed that it is difficult to win against him. And during our game, many expected that at any moment a draw would be agreed..."

And here is a short description of his game with the strongest non-Soviet grandmaster, Lajos Portisch:

"This, in contrast, was quite a dramatic game. The position reached on the board was unusual, not to Portisch's taste. On the seventh move I managed to find a new continuation, and as Black, did not experience any difficulties at all. Then my position became slightly better, and my opponent overlooked a tactical blow."

When play on the other boards was still in full swing, and in the overcrowded hall the applause in honour of Karpov was gradually dying down, a reporter asked Portisch for his opinion of Karpov's play.

"You are asking me a question with a forced reply", the Hungarian grandmaster smiled, "A question, to which everyone knows the answer."

An amusing, and to some extent symbolic episode occurred in the fifth round, when the trainers of the USSR team laid on the table alongside each Soviet player a beautiful box containing a medal. According to Karpov, grandmaster Raymond Keene, who was sitting opposite him, reacted unusually to this:

"I've never seen the gold medals being awarded before the end of an event."

It had to be explained to the Englishman that these awards were not for winning, but for taking part, and that memorial medals were being awarded to all the participants in the European Championship. The medals for Great Britain and other countries had been passed on to their trainers and representatives, and they would not doubt soon be distributed among the players.

This explanation was not the only one to be made that evening on the top board of the USSR–Great Britain match. The point was that the lighting in the "Wings of the Soviets" Hall was not entirely suitable for the needs of chess players, and, being uneven in places, made it inconvenient playing in certain parts of the sports arena. The squares of the varnished chess tables caused inconvenient reflections, and so some of the grandmasters placed on their tables duller, non-reflecting boards. This was done, for instance, by Petrosian, Polugayevsky and Portisch, who look after their sight, and always attempt to remove any hindrance to their play. Karpov suggested to his opponent that they do the same. But Keene suddenly declined, and what's more, did so in a categorical and provocative manner. In the end the conflict was resolved by the controllers, who by moving the table around the sports arena, found a place where the light no longer played peculiar tricks on the varnished chess squares.

Keene lost this game. But prior to it, he did not miss any opportunity to proudly remind everyone that, not long before in Bad Lauterberg, he had been the only one who managed to draw with Black against Karpov. Here, incidentally, is what Keene wrote at that time:

"After the tournament in Bad Lauterberg, I interviewed Karpov for *'The Spectator'*. He said that he would be perfectly satisfied if he were able to retain his title of World Champion for 6–9 years. However, I do not believe that during this period anyone will be able to match Karpov for practical strength, or in his quickness of reaction and the incredible rapidity of his play. Even so, it would be interesting to know whether or not the winner of the Candidates' event will be able to set Karpov any serious psychological problems in the match for the supreme title."

A significant and revealing opinion. So, according to Keene, first and foremost one must set

Karpov "psychological problems". Was it for this reason that the English grandmaster behaved in such a fashion during his game with the World Champion in the European Team Championship? At that time Keene, it is true, was not yet Korchnoi's second, and only became this before the Final Candidates' Match*, which, as is now known, was held in an atmosphere of genuine psychological warfare...

When the European Championship was over, everyone involuntarily compared Karpov's play with the standard displayed by the participants in the Candidates' Quarter-Final Matches. International Judge and grandmaster Miroslav Filip, Captain of the Czech team, stated:

"If I hadn't seen the Portisch–Karpov game, I would never have believed that it was possible to win in 23 moves as Black against a player of such class as the Hungarian grandmaster."

Botvinnik once said that nowadays it is more and more difficult for the World Champion to attain a marked superiority over top-class grandmasters, and that he can only be considered the first among equals. It seems to me that such a position in the chess world does not altogether suit Karpov—the present World Champion tries to be not only the first among equals, but also unconditionally the strongest.

Here is a more official point of view. At the closing ceremony of the 6th European Team Championship, the FIDE President Max Euwe made a speech, in which he stressed that the victory of the USSR team had been expected by everyone, but that the style in which this victory had been attained was admirable. The President remarked especially on the brilliant result of the Soviet team leader Anatoly Karpov—5 points in 5 games against the best foreign grandmasters.

"During the two years that have elapsed since I had the honour of crowning Karpov, the present World Champion has played more often, and more successfully, than any of the Champions before him", Dr Euwe emphasized.

And, finally, the last word to Anatoly Karpov:

"In the competitive sense, the USSR team played exceptionally well: we finished ahead of our nearest rivals, the Hungarians, by ten and a half points. We also won first prize on practically all of the individual boards (only on board two did we have to concede). In my opinion, Polugayevsky and Tal played excellently, Balashov and Romanishin performed diligently, while Tsheshkovsky, Dorfman and Svyeshnikov all made successful debuts in the collective.

I emphasize the word collective, since in my opinion team events cannot exist without such a concept. Essential features of it are the joint analysis of adjourned positions, preparations for subsequent games, and discussions on the composition of the team for the next match. As Captain, I am bound to say that, although as a whole things went well for us, there were players who did not fit in. Unfortunately, this refers to the most experienced, whom it is the most difficult to influence, and whose advice to the team can at times prove highly useful. But nevertheless, the main thing is the collective. If it is healthy, it can manage perfectly well without the activity of one or two of the participants. At all events, we played well and confidently right through the Championship of Europe.

The Yugoslavs, it would appear, have nearly caught up with us as regards the number of active grandmasters. The Hungarian team was also composed entirely of grandmasters. In such a situation it is especially pleasing that our leading players are still the strongest, and that new faces have already begun to join this leading group.

---

* In fact, Keene became Korchnoi's second before the Semi-Final Match with Polugayevsky. (K.P.N.)

Many were interested as to why I didn't play in the last two rounds. For the team this was not necessary, since we had already played our strongest rivals, and were effectively already assured of first place. And I do not especially like playing when the game has no competitive significance. Besides, I needed to rest a little: ahead was another important event—in Las Palmas

Portisch–Karpov
King's Indian Attack

1 N–KB3	N–KB3
2 P–KN3	P–QN3
3 B–N2	B–N2
4 0–0	P–K3
5 P–Q3	P–Q4
6 QN–Q2	QN–Q2

This would appear to be a new move. An entertaining game was played in the First League of the USSR Championship in 1976: 6 ... B–K2 7 P–K4 P×P 8 P×P N×P? 9 N–K5, and Black resigned, since on 9 ... N–Q3 there follows 10 B×B N×B 11 Q–B3, with a double attack—on QN7 and KB7 (Kochiev–Ivanov).

7 R–K1	B–B4

But this is certainly a new idea. Black has solved all his opening problems.

8 P–B4	0–0
9 P×P	P×P
10 N–N3	

It is understandable that the bishop at ... QB4 should be playing on White's nerves, but on QN3 the knight will be badly placed.

10 ...	B–N5

Weaker was 10 ... B–Q3 11 N(N3)–Q4 R–K1 12 N–QN5.

11 B–Q2	P–QR4

Black gains a slight advantage after 11 ... B×B 12 Q×B P–B4, but I was aiming for a more complicated game.

12 N(N3)–Q4	R–K1

There is no point in immediately driving away the knight (12 ... P–B4). The move ... R–K1 is useful, and White has nothing better than to 'force' the advance of the QBP.

13 R–QB1	P–B4
14 N–B5	N–B1
15 P–Q4?	

A risky decision, since Black is better prepared for a clash in the centre.

15 ...	N–K5
16 P×P?	

This move is associated with an oversight in the resulting complications. Perhaps Portisch simply overlooked Black's 17th move? However, White was already in some difficulty over his choice of continuation. If, for instance, 16 P–QR3, then 16 ... B×B 17 N×B Q–B3, and from being an active piece, the knight at KB5 becomes highly vulnerable.

| 16 ... | N×B |
| 17 N×N | Q–N4! |

All of a sudden both knights are 'hanging'. 18 N–K3 loses immediately to 18 ... R×N 19 P×R Q×KP+ and 20 ... B×N, so there is no choice.

| 18 N–Q6 | B×N |

Here, on the other hand, White has a wide choice, but... of evils. We will begin by examining 19 P–KR4: 19 ... Q–R3 20 N×R (20 N–B5 Q–KB3, and White remains a piece down) 20 ... R×N 21 P–B6 B–R3. More interesting is 20 N×B, and if Black replies 20 ... B×R(K8), then after 21 Q×B R×P 22 Q×R Q×R+ 23 K–R2 (the king has an escape square—an important contrast to that which occurs in the game) 23 ... P×P 24 B×P, White gains some counter-play. The whole point is, however, that after 19 P–KR4 Q–R3 20 N×B Black captures the other rook—20 ... B×R(B8) 21 Q×B R×P, with a quick win.

There is also the move 19 P–B6. Then comes 19 ... B–R3 20 P–B4 (20 N×R R×N) 20 ... Q–K2 (this is better than the immediate 20 ... B–K6+, on which there can follow 21 K–R1 Q–K2 22 B×P), and on 21 N×R Black has the *zwischenzug* 21 ... Q–K6+!.

19 N×B	B×R(K8)
20 Q×B	R×P
21 Q×R	Q×R+
22 Q–B1	Q–Q7!
23 P×P	

In the event of 23 P–B6 Black wins by 23 ... R–B1 24 Q–N5 Q–B8+ and 25 ... Q×BP.

| 23 ... | R–B1 |
| **White resigns** | |

He either loses his queen, or gets mated—24 Q–N5 R–B7!.

Karpov–Keene
Pirc Defence

1 P–K4 P–KN3 2 P–Q4 B–N2 3 N–KB3 P–Q3 4 N–B3 N–KB3 5 B–K2 0–0 6 0–0 B–N5 7 B–K3 N–B3 8 Q–Q2 P–K4 9 P–Q5 N–K2 10 QR–Q1 K–R1 11 P–KR3 B×N 12 B×B N–Q2 13 B–K2 P–KB4 14 P–B4

14 ... P–KN4 15 P×NP P–B5 16 B–B2 P–KR3 17 P×P B×P 18 B–N4 N–KB3 19 Q–K2 R–KN1 20 B–K6 R–N2 21 K–R1 N–N3 22 R–KN1 Q–K2 23 R–Q3 R–R2 24 B–KB5 R–KN1 25 P–KN3 R(2)–N2 26 Q–K1 P–R3 27 P–QR4 P–N3 28 Q–KB1 N–R4 29 P–KN4 N–N6+ 30 B×N P×B 31 R(3)×P B–B5 32 R–B3 N–R5 33 R–Q3 Q–N4 34 Q–B2 Q–R3 35 B–K6 R–KB1 36 N–K2 N–N3 37 B–B5 B–N4 38 P–R5 P×P 39 R–R1 N–R5 40 R×P N×B 41 NP×N B–R5 42 Q–K3 Q–R4 43 Q–B3 Q–R3 44 R–R1 R(1)–KN1 **Black Resigns**

Ljubojević–Karpov
Queen's Indian Defence

1 P–QB4

Ljubojević normally begins his games against me with 1 P–K4, but apparently my opponent was not very satisfied with the results of our previous encounters, or in particular with the course taken by the games.

1 ...	N–KB3
2 N–KB3	P–QN3
3 P–KN3	B–N2
4 B–N2	P–K3

The Queen's Indian Defence occurs frequently in my games. This defence does not allow Black much hope of seizing the initiative at an early stage, but if White is to gain an opening advantage, he is required to demonstrate a deep understanding of positional play.

5 0–0	B–K2
6 N–B3	0–0
7 R–K1	

A deviation from the schemes resulting after 7 P–Q4. The rook supports the KP, so that it can be advanced on the following move. In the event of 7 ... N–K5 8 N×N B×N 9 P–Q3 B–N2 10 P–Q4 White gains a tempo in comparison with normal positions.

7 ...	P–Q4

Preventing the advance of White's KP. By attacking the centre, Black lets it be known that he does not object to having hanging pawns.

8 P×P	P×P
9 P–Q4	P–B4
10 B–B4	N–R3!?

A tribute to the fashion of recent years. The knight used to be developed at ... Q2, where it frequently prevented the other forces from being deployed as well as possible, and cramped the movements of the queen, and with it the rooks. On ... QR3 the knight has quite good prospects, since a route is already prepared for it via ... QB2 to ... K3.

11 N–Q2?

A fanciful idea. The place for this knight is in the centre, at K5. But Ljubojević plans to transfer it to K3, with the aim of developing imaginary pressure on Black's QP.

11 ...	Q–Q2

Simple and good. Black prepares to develop his rooks on the central files. It is clear that after 11 ... P×P? 12 N–N5 White would easily regain his pawn, and would favourably occupy his Q4 square.

12 N–B1	KR–Q1
13 P–KR3	

Unexpectedly it turns out that the knight cannot go to K3 immediately, in view of 13 ... P×P 14 Q×P B–B4 followed by 15 ... P–Q5, when White loses a piece.

13 ...	QR–B1
14 R–B1	P×P

White should have defended his QP with his bishop, but instead he preferred to bring a rook to the centre. Utilizing a favourable opportunity, Black creates for himself an isolated pawn. The point of the exchange is that the black pieces are excellently developed, and require new squares in the centre. In addition, the 'isolani' does not stop still, but moves irresistibly forward, dislodging the white pieces from their positions.

15 Q×P	R–B5

15 ... B–B4 would be a perfectly good
move, were it not for 16 Q–R4, when transposing into the endgame is not particularly
favourable, and otherwise White gains an
important tempo.

16 Q–Q1

The queen has to go back home, since other
retreats would have exposed it to further
attacks.

16 ...	P–Q5

This allows a clever rejoinder on White's
part. Immediately afterwards, the highly
interesting idea of 16 ... N–R4 came to
mind. Now 17 N–K3 fails to 17 ... R×B
18 P×R P–Q5. The bishop has to move—
17 B–K5 (on 17 P–K3 there follows 17 ...
N×B 18 KP×N P–Q5, with advantage)
17 ... P–Q5 (with great effect) 18 B×B Q×B
19 N–N5 R–B4 20 R×R P×R 21 Q–R4
P–B3, and White has to play 22 B–B4.

In passing, I should mention that in reply
to 16 ... N–R4, 17 B×P is bad in view of
17 ... N×B!.

17 B×B	Q×B
18 N–K4!	

Ljubojević displays his customary resourcefulness! The knight leaps into the centre
where it is twice attacked, but it cannot be
taken—the rook is *en prise!*

18 ...	R×R
19 N×N+	B×N
20 Q×R	Q–Q4
21 Q–N1	

White is cramped, and any pawn advance
leads to a weakening of his position, but of
course Black's advantage would have been
considerably greater, had not Ljubojević
found that original way of exchanging knights
on move 18.

21 ...	N–B4
22 N–R2	

The knight tries unsuccessfully to return
to that square which it left voluntarily on the
11th move.

22 ...	P–KR4

Besides controlling his ... KN5 square,
Black creates an escape square for his king.

23 P–KR4

23 N–B3 was impossible, on account of 23
... P–Q6, with numerous threats.

23 ...	P–Q6?!

Another over-hasty move, which almost
loses Black his advantage; he should have
maintained the tension in the centre. He had
at his disposal the excellent move 23 ...
P–R4, securing the post of his knight at
... QB4 (24 B–B7 fails to 24 ... R–Q2 25
B×P N–R5, and the bishop is trapped).

24 P×P	N×P
25 R–Q1	

And here I had thought from afar that I
would win easily by...

25 ...	Q–QN4

White's bishop and QNP are both under attack (and what's more, the pawn is attacked three times), but once again my opponent demonstrates his amazing tactical ingenuity.

26 B–N5   **B×B**

It is not difficult to see that the QNP is 'poisoned'.

27 P×B   **Q–KB4**

Now it becomes essential to block in White's knight, and to attempt to exploit the weakening of his king's position. The pin along the Q-file prevents active play on Black's part.

28 R–Q2   **R–Q5**
29 Q–B2

Avoiding a standard trap: 29 Q–Q1 N×BP!.

29 ...   **P–R5**

30 P×P

White cannot ignore the presence of this pawn, and is forced to expose his king.

30 ...   **Q–R6**
31 Q–B6

The only defence against the threats of 31 ... N–K8, 31 ... N–B5 and 31 ... R×P,

since 31 P–B3 would prove to be a decisive weakening: 31 ... Q–N6+ 32 R–N2 (32 K–B1? Q–K8+ 33 K–N2 N–B5 mate!) 32 ... Q–K8+ 33 N–B1, and now not 33 ... N–B5 34 Q–B8+ K–R2 35 Q–KB5+, but 33 ... N–K4.

31 ...   **R×P**

For reasons already given, 31 ... Q×P is weak in view of 32 Q–B8+ K–R2 33 Q–KB5+.

32 Q–N2   **Q–B4**

Black could also have attempted to win the ending resulting after 32 ... N–B5 33 Q–N3 (weaker is 33 Q×Q N×Q+ 34 K–N2 N×NP) 33 ... N–K3 34 R–Q3 Q×Q (34 ... N×P? loses to 35 Q–N8+) 35 R×Q R–QB5.

33 Q–N3   **R–Q5**
34 P–N6

White sensibly gets rid of his weak pawn. In the subsequent play he must aim for the exchange of queens (his king is exposed), whereas Black must try to retain all the pieces, or as a last resort go in for the exchange of rooks.

34 ...   **P×P**
35 Q–K3   **R–Q4**
36 N–B1   **N–B5**
37 Q×N?

This move involves an oversight. Ljubo-jević hopes to set up a fortress, but overlooks that after the check on ... KN5 he is unable to co-ordinate his remaining pieces. After 37 N–N3 Q–B2, or 37 R×R N×R, Black would have had to demonstrate excellent technique in order to realize his minimal material and positional advantage.

37 ...   **Q×Q**
38 R×R   **Q–KN5+**

It was this check that Ljubojević underestimated. He had reckoned only with 38 ... Q–B5, when after 39 R–Q8+ K–B2 40 P–N3 he does indeed obtain a fortress.

Further resistance is already a hopeless matter.

39	N–N3	Q–QB5
40	R–Q8+	K–R2
41	P–N3	Q–B7

Now one of the Q-side pawns is inevitably lost.

42	K–N2	P–KN4

However, Black is not obliged to hurry. First of all it is best to free his own king.

43	R–Q6	Q×RP
44	N–K4	Q–R4
45	K–B3	Q–KB4+
46	K–K3	Q–N4
47	K–Q4	P–N5
48	K–K3	Q×P+
49	K–B4	Q–KB6+
50	K–K5	Q–B1
51	N–N5+	K–N1
52	N–K4	P–QN4
53	R–K6	P–N5
	Resigns	

TWO EXCLAMATION MARKS *(Las Palmas: a spectacular victory)*

It was a warm spring evening at the end of April. In the town of Balashikha hundreds of chess enthusiasts clung to the enormous windows of a crowded hall, and people stood on the balconies of neighbouring houses... In the hall the opening ceremony of an international tournament was being held, the crowning event of a "Moscow evenings" festival, in which a total of one hundred thousand people had taken part at various stages!

Among those greeting the participants was Anatoly Karpov. The World Champion made the first moves in a simultaneous display, and then "passed the baton" to grandmasters R. Knaak (East Germany) and N. Kirov (Bulgaria), who continued the battle against local young Pioneers. Karpov himself hurried off home to his family in Leningrad—after the May Day festivities he had to fly to a tournament in Spain, and the last few days had been very hectic—after his brilliant performance in the European Team Championship, he had taken part in a plenary session of the Comsomol Central Committee, and had met chess enthusiasts in Zelenograd...

A further week passed. Karpov and Tal, good friends in life and rivals at the chess board, after staying at the Cosmonaut's village, set off for Las Palmas in the Canary Islands.

By that time the World Champion's individual rating had reached the amazing figure of 2725, and in order to maintain it at this exceptionally high level—as his status demanded!—in the event about to start Karpov had to score not less than 12 points out of 15. To be honest, the fulfilling of such a "norm" in the company of such prominent grandmasters appeared to be a super-human task.

...If applause breaks out in the tournament hall, the spectator who has been momentarily distracted will immediately look for the demonstration board on which a fine piece sacrifice has been made, or else a manoeuvre leading to victory for one of the players. But it sometimes happens that applause is heard in honour of a player who by stubborn defence has gained a draw. This was how Jan Timman was saluted in Las Palmas after his game with Karpov. And by no means because the Dutch grandmaster was more popular there than the Soviet World Champion. The point was that, by drawing with Karpov in the seventh round, it was Timman who had succeeded in halting a run of thirteen successive wins, gained by the Champion in international events (2—at the finish in Bad Lauterberg, 5—in the European Team Championship, and 6—here in Las Palmas). But the very next day the World Champion forced his next opponent to capitulate—the hitherto undefeated Hungarian, Adorjan—and now led the tournament with 7½ points out of 8!

As we have already spoken about popularity, it must be said that, in general, Soviet players in Spain are always the centre of attention. Ten years previously, Mikhail Tal had been literally forced to take part in... a bull-fight. The grandmaster was armed with sword and red cloth, and dramatic music began to play. However, it must be admitted that against the Ex-World Champion they were evidently afraid of sending out the usual bull, and the animal which appeared in the arena was more like a cow in temperament. Perhaps Tal hypnotized the attacker, or perhaps the bull's attention was distracted by the brightly-dressed photographer who was preparing to immortalize the "historic moment"—at any event, the animal turned in the direction of the photographer, and chess enthusiasts will never now see this picture...

Another photograph which in all probability has not been preserved is one recording the first kick in a football match in the Spanish League between the teams of Las Palmas and "Salamanca". Karpov was asked to make this kick on a day free from chess, and Anatoly, who was heartily sick of reporters, most professionally directed the ball at the lens of the camera trained on him.

Our two grandmasters spent all their other free days in the company of their compatriots: in such a major oceanic port there were many Soviet sailors, and they constantly invited the chess players to visit their ships. In their turn, the sailors came and supported Karpov and Tal in the tournament hall.

According to Tal, in the international tournament at Las Palmas the World Champion played "quite brilliantly":

"As I observed how he conducted an offensive with pawns and pieces on the position of the Spanish grandmaster Pomar, suddenly I remembered for some reason the name of a book I once read: 'The tanks move in diamond formation', and similar associations were provoked by the way in which, soon after the opening, he enveloped and then began to squeeze the Englishman Miles' position. Many of Karpov's intentions become understandable to his opponents only when salvation is no longer possible. For Anatoly, absolutely everything worked out well. Even when he overrated his chances somewhat, and found himself in a complex position against Browne. The Champion was faced with a dilemma: whether to play for a draw, or to provoke complications, which objectively were in his opponent's favour. Karpov knit his brows, sat motionless for some twenty minutes, and then rushed into a hand-to-hand fight. In time trouble the American grandmaster blundered and lost. On the conclusion of the game everyone asserted: 'Browne should have won', but Karpov in reply showed such amazingly long and beautiful variations that those of us around could only stand and marvel. On that occasion I admired both these variations, and the startlingly competitive nature of his character."

But Karpov was especially successful in his game against the Italian player Tatai, whose play was affected by a recurrence of that most widespread chess disease—"pawn-grabbing in the opening". In pursuing a trivial material gain, Tatai wasted time when he should have been developing his pieces, and conceded the Soviet grandmaster a great deal of space. With all his forces Black bore down on the position of the white king, which had not succeeded in castling, and then the World Champion made a spectacular, although temporary sacrifice of his queen...

When he dictated this game to Moscow by telephone, the normally reserved Karpov gaily exclaimed: "Notice that his king is quite bare!".

Tatai–Karpov
English Opening

1 N–KB3 P–QB4 2 P–B4 N–KB3 3 N–B3 P–Q4 4 P×P N×P 5 P–KN3 P–KN3 6 B–N2 B–N2 7 Q–R4+ N–QB3 8 N–KN5 P–K3 9 KN–K4 N–N3 10 Q–N5 P–B5 11 N–R4 0–0 12 N×N P×N 13 Q×BP P–K4 14 Q–B2 N–Q5 15 Q–N1 P–B4 16 N–B3 P–K5 17 P–Q3 P–QN4 18 B–K3 P–N5 19 N–Q1 R–K1 20 P×P P×P 21 B×N Q×B 22 P–QR3 B–N5 23 Q–B2

23 ... Q–Q6 24 P×Q P×P+ 25 K–Q2 R–K7+ 26 K×P R–Q1+ 27 K–B4 R×Q+ 28 K×P R(7)–Q7 29 P–B3 B–KB1+ 30 K–R5 B–Q2 31 Resigns

Later, in the traditional poll held by the chess publication *"Informator"*, and also by the Yugoslav newspaper *"Politika Express"*, the game Tatai–Karpov was voted the very best of those played in the first half of 1977. The opinion expressed by the expert grandmaster jury was confirmed by a special poll among the readers.

This superb win as it were put a full stop (or more correctly, two exclamation marks—the highest assessment in chess) to the battle for first place in the tournament at Las Palmas. With two rounds still to go before the finish, Karpov was out of reach of his rivals. In the penultimate round he again won, and in the final game drew with Tal. As a result—an amazing score: 13½ out of 15 (only three draws), two and a half points ahead of the second prize-winner. His individual rating reached the figure of 2740.

After an excellent start, relative misfortune overtook Tal—he shared fourth place, allowing past him not only the World Champion, but also Larsen and Timman. The Ex-Champion considers that he was let down by his desire to keep up with Karpov at all costs. Regarding this, the reader will no doubt be interested in the winner's point of view, which, incidentally, testifies to his chess respect for any opponent, and to a considerable extent gives an answer to the question as to why the World Champion drops points extremely rarely in encounters with lesser-known opponents.

"I must mention that the chess strength of so-called outsiders is normally underestimated both by the public at large, and by many fairly strong players. For the latter this is especially dangerous, since on finding themselves in the rôles of participants, they may fail to gain anticipated points. For example, the masters in the tournament at Las Palmas managed, in varying degrees, to surprise more than one of the favourites.

The play of the Argentinian Debarnot and of the Cuban representative Hernandez deserves particular recognition. The first reached the IM norm, while the second achieved a full grandmaster result. Hernandez began the tournament with three noughts. This 'Q-side castling'.

as chess players joke, enabled him to hide his king so far away that he did not then lose a single game. But, joking aside, Hernandez, who in addition defeated Larsen and Tal, once again showed that masters of his class are worthy of respect.

The reader may think that I am leading him towards a conclusion about the reasons for Tal's relative failure. This is not quite so. The Ex-World Champion always respects his opponents, but, in my opinion, he does not adopt altogether correct tactics in his games with some of them. In attempting to force matters in the opening itself, he sometimes forgets about the very deep theoretical knowledge of many masters, about their fairly sharp tactical vision, and about the fact that many of them have broad international experience, and so are afraid of virtually no one. After defeating Larsen in an interesting though by no means faultless game, the Riga player began playing excellently, but after coming unstuck in a game with Visier, became quite unrecognizable. Right at the finish, when Tal still had chances of third place, he was annoyed by the drawing tendency of a game with Garcia, and committed an irreparable mistake in a pawn ending. We must hope that the grandmaster tournament in Leningrad will return Tal his confidence, especially since no masters, outsiders, are expected to take part..."

As always, the observations and conclusions made by Karpov regarding chess life abroad are highly interesting:

"The Danish grandmaster Larsen lives almost permanently in Las Palmas, and his example has been followed by the Argentinian Debarnot. Both of them have done much to promote the popularity of chess on the Canary Islands, where now there is even the regular publication of an independent chess periodical. The team from these islands is now the strongest in Spain, and the spacious local chess club, which is maintained in perfect order and has numerous special rooms, is undoubtedly one of the best in Europe. On the conclusion of the tournament, a mass simultaneous display by the participants in the international tournament was held for several hundred school children in the central square of Las Palmas. It is significant that the popularity of chess is growing not only in this province, but also over the whole country."

After taking a last bathe in the ocean, the World Champion set off to the ancient town of Barcelona, to receive his fourth "Chess Oscar". This was the award to the best player of the previous year, 1976. And in 1977 he had succeeded by that time in winning 26 games, with 9 draws. 30½ points in games against 35 players, of whom twenty-four had the grandmaster title—at no time and by no one had such a fantastic showing been made!

"What an amusing coincidence", the World Champion remarked, when he was told of these figures. "The number of games won—26—corresponds to the number of the birthday I have just celebrated during the tournament. I thank all those who congratulated me on my birthday and on my victory in the tournament, and I admit that I was happy with the result, with my physical condition, and, most important, with the content of the games played. I can only hope for similar form in other events."

Karpov–Pomar
Queen's Indian Defence

1 P–QB4 P–K3 2 P–Q4 N–KB3 3 N–KB3 P–QN3 4 P–KN3 B–N2 5 B–N2 B–K2 6 0–0 0–0 7 N–B3 N–K5 8 Q–B2 N×N 9 Q×N P–QB4 10 R–Q1 P–Q3 11 P–N3 Q–B2 12 B–N2 B–B3 13 Q–B2 N–Q2 14 P–K4 KR–Q1 15 Q–K2 QR–B1 16 R–Q2 Q–B3 17 R–K1 R–K1 18 Q–Q1 QR–Q1

19 P–KR4 P–QR3 20 P–KN4 P–N3 21 P–N5 B–N2 22 P–Q5 P×P 23 KP×P Q–B1 24 B×B K×B 25 R(2)–K2 K–B1 26 Q–R1 K–N1 27 Q–N2 N–B1 28 Q–B6 N–Q2 29 Q×QP N–K4 30 R×N Resigns

Karpov–Miles
1 ... P–QN3

1 P–QB4 P–QN3 2 P–Q4 B–N2 3 P–Q5 P–K3 4 P–QR3 N–KB3 5 N–QB3 B–Q3 6 N–B3 P×P 7 P×P 0–0 8 B–N5 R–K1 9 P–K3 B–K2 10 B–QB4 P–KR3 11 B–B4 N–R4 12 B–K5 B–KB3 13 B–Q4 B–R3 14 KB×B N×B 15 0–0 P–B4 16 B×B N×B 17 Q–Q3 Q–B1 18 N–Q2 P–Q3 19 N–B4 R–Q1 20 P–K4 N–B2 21 P–QN4 N–R3 22 P–N5 N–B2 23 P–QR4 Q–Q2 24 P–B4 R–K1 25 QR–Q1 QR–Q1 26 P–R3 Q–K2 27 P–K5 P×P 28 P–Q6 Q–B1 29 P×P N–R2 30 Q–B3 N–K3 31 Q–N7 R–R1 32 N–Q5 P–N3 33 N–K7+ K–N2 34 N–B6 Resigns (Diag.)

Browne–Karpov
Queen's Indian Defence

1 N–KB3 N–KB3 2 P–B4 P–K3 3 P–Q4 P–QN3 4 P–KN3 B–N2 5 B–N2 B–K2 6 0–0 0–0 7 N–B3 P–Q4 8 N–K5 N–R3 9 B–B4 P–B4 10 R–B1 N–K5 11 BP×P KP×P 12 B–K3 Q–Q3 13 N–B4 Q–K3 14 N×N P×N(K5) 15 P×P N×P 16 Q–B2 QR–B1 17 Q–N1 KR–Q1 18 P–N3 P–B4 19 R–B2 N–R3 20 R–Q1 B–Q4 21 N–N2 N–N5 22 R(2)–Q2 N–B3 23 N–R4 B–B3

24 B×NP P×B 25 N×P N–N5 26 N×R B–B6 27 P–QR3 B×R 28 R×B P–K6 29 R–Q4 P×P+ 30 K×P R×N 31 R×N B×B 32 K×B Q×KP+ 33 K–R3 R–B7 34 Q–KR1 R–Q7 35 R–N8+ K–B2 36 R–N4 K–N3 37 Q–B6+ K–N4 38 Q–R1 Q–N5+ Resigns

CHAPTER 11

"That Way it's More Human"

"We have all gathered here, so as to mark in the language of chess a great event in the life of our country", said grandmaster Mark Taimanov, speaking for the people of Leningrad at the Opening Ceremony of the International Tournament dedicated to the 60th Anniversary of the Great October Revolution.

"Bridges hang over the waters..." ✳ *First defeat of the year*
✳ *In the room behind the stage* ✳ *A law is a law* ✳
Drama of 1001 mistakes

The crowded hall greeted with applause each well-known name in the chess (and not only the chess) world, thus as it were expressing an "advance of confidence" in the guests and hosts of the tournament. The Director of the USSR Central Chess Club, V. Baturinsky, made the point that the composition of the Jubilee Tournament was especially interesting, in that it included the best representatives of all the generations of chess players who had been fostered during the years of Soviet power. Among the participants were the 56-year-old Ex-World Champion Vasily Smyslov, still a formidable player, the 40-year-old Ex-World Champion Mikhail Tal, once again on the upgrade, Yury Balashov, who had completed his higher education and was now gathering strength, ambitious grandmasters from the USSR Students' Team headed by Oleg Romanishin and Rafael Vaganian, and one of the Leningrad hosts, Alexandr Kochiev, born in 1956, who was included in the tournament at the last minute, formally as an international master, but who had in fact already reached the GM norm. Appearing for the first time as World Champion before his demanding Leningrad compatriots was Anatoly Karpov...

To a tournament dedicated to the Anniversary of the October Revolution, it was logical to invite, in the main, representatives of Socialist Countries who had achieved major successes in the international chess arena. During the drawing of lots, the grandmasters one after another went up to the controllers' desk, and selected colourful albums which contained views of the river Nyeva, and on which were inscribed "Bridges hang over the waters...".* These words of Pushkin sounded as a symbol of friendship between players from the different countries.

In our major cities there are concert halls which are particularly ready to open their doors for chess spectacles. In Moscow, for instance, there is the Railwaymen's Central Cultural Club, and in Leningrad—the Dzerzhinsky Palace of Culture. Chess fans filled it during the 1973

* A line from Pushkin's "The Bronze Horseman" (K.P.N.).

Interzonal Tournament, and also the Semi-Final Candidates' Match between Karpov and Spassky; here too the USSR Championship Premier League was held in 1974.

There were a thousand places in the hall, but, as it turned out, not enough tickets for everyone who wanted to watch. This no doubt goes to explain the cunning of some so-called enthusiasts. Thus during the very first round some forged tickets were discovered. Another manifestation, by no means criminal, of the chess boom is autograph-hunting. However, this has already become something of a special tradition. R. Plyatt, a National Artist of the USSR, relates:

"Something similar occurred during the Moscow International Tournament of 1925. I myself remember how I stuck so closely to the famous grandmasters, that to this day I seem to be able to feel with my fingers the quality of the material of Capablanca's suit."

Rostislav Plyatt happened to be in Leningrad on theatrical business, and on his first free evening he hurried along to the tournament together with the well-known playwright Leonid Zorin. For exactly five hours neither of them moved from their seats, but constantly followed the play of the actors on the stage. "There is something I don't quite understand about the Karpov–Taimanov game", Plyatt admitted. "It isn't always essential to understand the beautiful, it is sufficient simply to be delighted by it", Zorin, a first category player, remarked with a smile, when in the central game of the first round Black carried out an unexpected and most spectacular combination.

One can explain Karpov's defeat in purely chess terms. After gaining an advantage in space, he forced his opponent to give up a pawn. But Taimanov cleverly contrived to compensate for this material deficiency by the immediate activation of his pieces. White, somewhat mechanically pushing a passed pawn on the Q-side, weakened his vigilance on the opposite flank...

Karpov–Taimanov
Sicilian Defence

1 P–K4 P–QB4 2 N–KB3 N–QB3 3 P–Q4 P×P 4 N×P P–QR3 5 P–QB4 P–K4 6 N–N3 N–B3 7 N–B3 B–N5 8 P–B3 0–0 9 B–K3 P–Q3 10 R–B1 P–QN3 11 B–Q3 B–QB4 12 Q–Q2 B–K3 13 N×B NP×N 14 0–0 N–Q5 15 N–Q5 N–Q2 16 P–B4 R–N1 17 P–B5 B×N 18 BP×B Q–N3 19 R–KB2 P–B3 20 R–QB4 P–QR4 21 R–R4 R–R1 22 Q–K1 R–R2 23 P–QN3 KR–R1 24 R–N2 Q–B2 25 B–Q2 N–N3 26 R×P P–B5 27 B–KB1 R×R 28 B×R Q–B4 29 B×N Q×B 30 K–R1

P×P 31 P×P P–N3 32 P×P P×P 33 P–QN4 K–N2 34 P–N5 P–B4 35 P×P N×BP 36 R–N3 Q–Q5 37 P–N6 R–R8 38 R–N1

38 ... N–N6+ 39 Resigns

But one can also regard what happened in a different light. By virtually everyone, Karpov's defeat (incidentally, his only one up till then in 1977) was called a sensation, which demanded an immediate explanation.

And straight away everyone forgot that the World Champion, despite having gained victory after victory, was also only a mere mortal. However, he himself was "guilty" of causing this to be forgotten.

Karpov's defeat upset, more than anyone, Kochiev, who was due to play him in the second round, and who with some justification was afraid of the angry Champion. The young player took all the measures necessary from his point of view: playing White, he did not object to repeating moves, and accurately and methodically exchanged pieces, which left the board almost completely deserted. It seemed to me personally that these "scorched board" tactics angered Karpov still further, and with special efforts he attempted to breath life into a drawn position. At all events, by the adjournment the Champion had managed to gather some barely noticeable advantages, but on resumption they proved insufficient for a win.

In the third round the spectators again saw the usual Karpov—calm, confident, and, if it is permissible to express it so, competitively cunning.

The Champion's opponent, Jan Šmejkal, well-known for his exceptional chess strength and constant... time troubles, seemed to have taken himself in hand, for he began the game at a fairly rapid tempo. It was this haste that betrayed the Czech grandmaster: Karpov realized perfectly well that Šmejkal was incapable in one day of curing himself of his chronic chess disease.

By intricate manoeuvring the World Champion skilfully maintained the tension on the board, and meanwhile his opponent began more and more frequently to sink deeper and deeper into thought. The crisis arrived when the minute hand on Šmejkal's clock had approached right up to his flag. It was at this point—no sooner, and no later—that Karpov gave the signal for his pieces to begin surrounding the enemy king.

Karpov–Šmejkal
Pirc Defence

1 P–K4 P–KN3 2 P–Q4 B–N2 3 N–QB3 P–Q3 4 N–B3 N–KB3 5 B–K2 0–0 6 0–0 B–N5 7 B–K3 N–B3 8 Q–Q2 P–K4 9 P–Q5 N–K2 10 QR–Q1 K–R1 11 P–KR3 B×N 12 B×B N–Q2 13 B–K2 P–KB4 14 P–B4 P–QR3 15 BP×P N×KP 16 R–B2 Q–Q2 17 QR–KB1 P×P 18 N×P R×R 19 B×R P–R3 20 P–QN3 R–KB1 21 P–B4 P–KN4 22 N–N3 N(2)–N3 23 B–K3 R×R+ 24 B×R Q–B2 25 Q–QB2 N–R5 26 B–K2 N(4)–N3

27 B–Q3 B–K4 28 B–B2 N–B5 29 B–K4 Q–B3 30 Q–Q1 P–N3

31 Q–N4 K–N2 32 B–K3 K–B2 33 Q–B8 Q–K2 34 B–R7 N×RP+ 35 Q×N Resigns

When, in the room behind the stage, the grandmasters analysed the concluded game, and Karpov demonstrated one variation after another, Šmejkal, bewitched by the thin and rapid fingers flying over the board, whispered loudly:

"I felt that my position was inferior, but I didn't realize that it was so bad."

This was followed by a draw with Vaganian.

Then came the most dramatic game of the entire tournament, and perhaps not only of this tournament.

Who hasn't seen a chess clock? There are two mechanisms, linked internally by a metal arm. Make a move, press the button on the top panel of the clock, the second button on the opposite side springs up, and now your opponent's minute hand renews its race around the dial in the direction of the control flag hanging over the figure "12". From master-standard tournaments upwards, the rate of play is normally forty moves in 2 hours 30 minutes (and then on resumption sixteen moves in each hour).

The clock had never let Karpov down; easiness and rapidity are enviable features of his play. This makes all the more astonishing the incident which occurred in the fifth round of the jubilee event in Leningrad.

Any photographer who had managed to take this unique picture would, in my opinion, have been able to count on a prize in any competition. Face to face were Karpov, his face turned slightly pale and stoney, and his astonished opponent—Belyavsky. The World Champion's hand, which had only just left the clock button and which he had not had time to lower, and, perpendicular to it, the hand of the controller (or of fate*), made as it were the sign of the cross over this chess game. But while journalists and spectators were trying to grasp what had happened, Karpov had time to glance askance at his clock, and with a handshake, as is customary, thank his opponent for the game.

It turned out that Anatoly, after making his move, heard—as sometimes happens—his flag falling, and immediately understood everything. The two minutes which he had had left for one move had passed imperceptibly. In chess terms, where "a few seconds are not to be sneezed at", two minutes is quite a long time. But a law is a law: the last, fortieth, move is considered completed only when not only the move has been made, but also the clock button pressed; if the opposite is the case, and the flag falls—the game is lost.

On this last move White had either to move his king, or else to block a check. Karpov had played the game well, won a pawn, and now had to choose between these two possibilities. As was discovered immediately after the game, the first path would have won by force. And on the second road, which the World Champion chose, success also awaited him—Karpov definitely convinced himself of this, only at home, late at night, whereupon he finally put the chess pieces away.

This dramatic incident will go down in the annals of chess, and for a long time to come will serve as a warning. In this tournament the grandmasters began glancing warily at their clocks long before the control. Thus a position in the game Šmejkal–Ribli promised excitement. The Czech grandmaster cleverly sacrificed the exchange and seized the initiative. Black seemed to be lost. But to Ribli's assistance came the hand on Šmejkal's clock: 10 minutes—for 16 moves, 5 minutes—for 15, 4 minutes—for 13 . . . Exactly like the launching of a space ship, except that that which was preparing to lift off was no rocket, but the flag on a chess clock. And, perhaps (this at any rate is what they would write in a novel) it was at this instant that Jan Šmejkal remembered his entire chess life. There flashed before his eyes dozens of wonderful positions, built up by hours of painstaking effort, and destroyed in seconds by time trouble hurricanes. At this terrible vision Jan even screwed up his eyes, and pronounced mechanically: "Are you playing for a win?". And immediately he heard the kindly voice of his Hungarian friend: "No".

---

* In the Russian there is a play on words here: Sudyi and Sudbi. (K.P.N.)

"How many times has my flag fallen in winning positions, but only when I have already made a dozen instant moves. Here there was no time trouble, no haste. Incredible!", exclaimed Šmejkal, time and again returning to the incident from the Karpov–Belyavsky game.

The eminent grandmaster and acknowledged humorist Savielly Tartakower once called chess a comedy of 1001 mistakes. But the players themselves don't do much laughing, and even the winner, to say nothing of the loser, experiences serious anxiety each time. And therefore I should like to suggest a correction to the formulation given above: it is a question not of a comedy, but of a drama of 1001 mistakes. How many dramas are played out in every tournament!... But that which happened to Karpov can definitely be regarded as a "record".

The following day the World Champion took something of a risk by provoking an attack on himself. But Lothar Vogt, a young East German master, shielded his guns, and with a steady hand directed his chess ship directly into a peaceful harbour.

Strength and weakness of the "isolani" ✳ Fare for gourmets ✳ When home advantage does not help ✳ The last defensive line ✳ Grandmaster memory

An eternal problem—that of the isolated queen's pawn—was discussed in the game Karpov–Kuzmin. Such a pawn is a considerable force in the middlegame, controlling very important squares and promoting the activity of its senior colleagues in the team. But it becomes a weakness in the endgame, when the recent defenders, no longer concerned over their king, become bolder, and secretly begin to molest the orphan pawn.

"The next time I will probably do better to give up two pawns, than to have an isolated one", Kuzmin grinned, after losing a typical such position to Karpov.

Karpov–Kuzmin
Sicilian Defence

1 P–K4 P–QB4 2 N–KB3 N–QB3 3 P–Q4 P×P 4 N×P N–KB3 5 N–QB3 P–K3 6 N(4)–N5 B–N5 7 P–QR3 B×N+ 8 N×B P–Q4 9 P×P P×P 10 B–Q3 P–Q5 11 N–K2 B–B4 12 0–0 B×B 13 Q×B 0–0 14 B–N5 P–KR3 15 B–R4 R–K1 16 QR–Q1 R–QB1 17 KR–K1 R–K3 18 K–B1 Q–B2 19 B–N3 Q–N3 20 P–N4 P–R3 21 N–B4 R(3)–K1

22 R×R+ R×R 23 N–K2 R–Q1 24 B–R4 N–K4 25 Q–B5 P–Q6 26 P×P N–B5 27 N–B3 N×P 28 N–K4 Q–K3 29 N×N+ P×N 30 Q–B3 R–K1 31 B×P K–R2 32 P–Q4 **Resigns**

This game recalled the best achievements of the World Champion, who exchanged off what he considered to be his opponent's superfluous pieces, blockaded and surrounded the "isolani", and then himself contrived to launch an attack on the black king. The finale was highly spectacular.

We have already said that, in chess tournaments, one day is different from the next. There are rounds which, for a long time later, need only a single mention of them to cause enthusiasts to raise their thumbs in admiration. And there are also long series of rounds which are remembered only in the results table of the event.

If you had failed to arrive for the very beginning of one such round, you could have met Vasily Smyslov on the Nyevsky Prospect. It was not yet evening, and in the rays of the sun which had finally emerged from behind a cloud, the Ex-World Champion was returning on foot and in a good mood to his hotel. As Black he had gained "his half point" against Taimanov, and now, glancing at his watch, he advised the correspondent he had just met to hurry, since he knew how events were developing in the other games. He knew that Karpov's play had not worked out against Zoltán Ribli, the second-strongest Hungarian grandmaster (after Portisch), and that the World Champion had had to agree to a draw. But for chess gourmets there was still fare remaining... And in connection with this we must talk in more detail about the game between Oleg Romanishin and Guilermo Garcia. It is worth doing this, for the added reason that today they are virtually the most promising grandmasters in their respective countries (Garcia is undoubtedly the strongest Cuban player since the time of the great Capablanca).

Both young grandmasters arrived in Leningrad directly by air. They had just shared first place in the Capablanca Memorial Tournament in Cienfuegos. Formally (by the table of coefficients) Romanishin was considered the winner of this important international event. But in their individual encounter Garcia had defeated the visitor. And two further circumstances added special colour to this new encounter between Romanishin and Garcia. At that point the Lvov player was the sole leader, and was playing White, with which up till then he had won all his games.

At first it seemed that White, who seized the initiative, would also win on this occasion. But then two knights, which had been prancing impressively around a beseiged black pawn, suddenly lost their way and, after almost perishing, started back home, now separately, having lost touch with each other. One returned. The second knight was trapped *en route* in the vicinity of the black king. Romanishin was forced to sacrifice a pawn to stop Garcia "killing off" the now virtually hobbling prisoner. In time trouble the Lvov grandmaster succeeded in making the stipulated number of moves, but in the adjourned position he was in a bad way. As they say, the unpleasantness was merely delayed.

There was a curious psychological connotation to the Šmejkal–Tal game. Black began sizing up his opponent's position. His rook, which had mounted the spring-board at e6, began to loosen up on this square and prepare to make a dive. But on looking ahead more closely, he perceived a number of underwater rocks, and so descended from the spring-board and warned his colleagues against running up against the reef of white pawns. Tal had little time left on his clock, so he sounded the retreat ("look before you leap"), and agreed a draw with Šmejkal. Yes, the Ex-World Champion has become much more prudent than of old. (A fact from his biography: in Yugoslavia many years ago, Tal, who couldn't swim, "for no particular reason" jumped off a high board.)

After the eighth round Taimanov and Tal had joined Romanishin on five points. With the second half of the event beginning, Karpov had four points.

Tal, after declining a draw, promptly lost to Vaganian, but then defeated Belyavsky. Romanishin adjourned one game in an inferior position, although before that he won against Gheorghiu. The Rumanian grandmaster, in turn, inflicted a defeat on Taimanov, who correctly captured one piece sacrificed by his opponent, and then, hurrying in his opponent's time trouble, captured a second. And then a black bishop, which had seemed to be dreaming away at the side, suddenly woke up and quietly stepped from one square to another. And its owner—Florian Gheorghiu—stood up from the board, and, paying no further attention to the hateful clock face, proudly looked around at the surrounding crowd of players. However much Taimanov thought now, mate to his king was inevitable.

In short, there was no grandmaster in the tournament to whom a well-known chess saying could be applied: "as lucky as the first prize-winner". And it was in this situation that Karpov had to make his spurt, a spurt which everyone was expecting of him. For everyone remembered how he had been able to master his tournament fate in the 1976 USSR Championship. But what's this? A draw with the Yugoslav M. Knežević, and then two barely noticeable inaccuracies, letting slip a clear win in the game with I. Radulov from Bulgaria...

On the conclusion of the tournament, both the winners, and other experts, in one voice explained the World Champion's modest placing as being due to fatigue after his several tournament victories prior to the jubilee event. This is correct. But no one knew of the other reasons why Karpov did not achieve an extended spurt during the second half of the event. To have talked about this during the tournament or immediately after it would have signified an attempt at justification. But now we can mention it. In the first instance, he caught his customary cold. And although this may sound strange, treating this proved difficult because of the very fact that he was living at home. There was no mother at home: she was seriously ill, and had been taken to hospital, where her son visited her practically every day. His father was also not feeling well, and Anatoly did not want to leave him alone. So Semion Furman went to the Karpov home to help prepare for each game, and then before play they would go off to eat... It was one instance when playing on one's home ground was not an advantage. But about all these complications no one even guessed.

"Do you notice how calm Karpov is?", remarked the observant Plyatt. "His play is clearly not going well, but he shows no sign of it. In his place others would have become nervous and fussy. But he is showing rare self-possession."

After a win, at last, over the Italian Mariotti, Karpov met Tal. As Black the Ex-World Champion adopted a variation which was fashionable several years ago, when Karpov was not yet the strongest player in the world. The Champion, however, proved to be in the know, and achieved some advantage at the cost of an isolated but passed pawn. Supported by the other pieces, this pawn pesistently advanced, like a battering-ram. Tal, in time trouble, feverishly erected one new barrier after another in the path of this audacious and dangerous pawn, while Karpov thoughtfully and methodically cleared the way for it. At the last defensive line the stubborn pawn encountered a black rook, behind which was now only the Ex-World Champion himself, his chest pressed against the edge of the table, and his eyes hypnotically fixed on the uninvited guest... Karpov moved in with his queen first on one side, then on the other... Tal did not give in. Karpov then began regrouping his forces... It was this that he was engaged in when the end of the session sounded.

In the adjourned position many quite justifiably thought that Karpov would gain a badly-needed point...

After a short draw in the 13th round, Tal was making a farewell "cruise" around the stage when he stopped by the board where Balashov and Karpov were playing. The Ex-World Champion knit his brow and raised his eyebrows, like a man recalling something, and walked slowly to the exit. Later Balashov told me that exactly the same position had occurred roughly a year earlier in one of his lightning games with Tal... The memories of these grandmasters!

The variation also proved perfectly suitable for a serious game with the World Champion himself. At any rate, White won a pawn, and Karpov was forced onto the defensive. He defended actively. Balashov could find no way of strengthening his position, since his extra pawn required constant surveillance. The Muscovite decided to exchange this pawn for another, but the presence on the board of opposite-coloured bishops led all the same to a draw.

Touch—move ✳ *Smyslov blocks the goal* ✳ *Secret in the envelope* ✳ *From the pages of Jack London* ✳ *When the bridges are raised...* ✳ *Adjournment day* ✳ *The last round, like a Première* ✳ *Exception to the rule*

That same day Romanishin, after acknowledging the congratulations on his win over Šmejkal, went off to resign his adjourned game from two rounds earlier against Taimanov. However, he told the chief controller V. Mikenas of his decision, rather than the Leningrad player himself—at that time it was better not to approach Taimanov even with good news...

While still in the opening, Taimanov had won a pawn against Kochiev, and everyone hastened to count the sum of points which would bring the experienced grandmaster close to one of his major successes. Taimanov himself did likewise. He impulsively picked up a bishop, and immediately sensed, rather than saw, that he had done something irreparable. Despairingly twisting the piece round on its square, Taimanov heard the voice of his opponent: "You have to move the bishop!.." By one of the three ways open to him, Kochiev coolly captured a piece.

In a popular ice-hockey song they sing about the magnificent five and the goalkeeper. After the thirteenth round it was suddenly noticed that six players were contending for the top places in the tournament, among whom, with a "clean" score, was the goalkeeper Smyslov, who had not conceded a single "goal"—he was the only undefeated participant.

It was precisely at this time that the encounter took place between the two World Champions—past and present. Karpov probably knew that the opening would be a Ruy Lopez, but possibly did not expect the Open Variation. Smyslov did not play quite exactly in the opening, which had been prepared specially for this highly important encounter. However, it was not only this inaccuracy, but to a greater extent the tournament situation, which forced Karpov to decline in an apologetic voice the draw offered by his respectful opponent.

Gradually Karpov gained complete control over the central squares, and on the K-side he prepared to throw a terrible pawn under the legs of a rather insecurely placed black knight. The commentators unanimously assessed Smyslov's position as strategically lost.

But here Karpov hastened to capture a pawn which had been left undefended by his opponent—and this was in fact a trap set by Smyslov. The black pieces, which hitherto had been tied down, became more and more active, and the assessment of the adjourned position came to depend upon the move sealed by the Ex-World Champion.

For the following round Smyslov arrived in excellent spirits, which was immediately noticed by everyone. The Ex-World Champion does not number among the chess tricksters, and is not one to put on an act. It followed, the observers reasonably assumed, that Smyslov had sealed the best move in his adjourned game against Karpov the previous day, and now the World

Champion was faced with a difficult defence on resumption. In the fifteenth round Smyslov drew fairly quickly as White with Ribli...

That whole evening, Tal played on the nerves of the spectators—there is no other way of putting it—after earlier beginning, with a victory over Knežević, his finishing spurt. He kept catching his opponent Radulov's king in a mating net, and then letting it out. Finally, the "Odyssey of the black king" ended in its death.

Romanishin drew with Belyavsky, but had "in reserve" a won position against Vaganian.

But the World Champion had not yet given up the fight for first place. Curious associations were suddenly provoked by the Garcia–Karpov game. In 1925 one of the players in the first Moscow International Tournament was the Mexican Carlos Torre. Adopting his favourite opening, he gained a very fine and sensational win over the great Emanuel Lasker. Now among the players in the Leningrad International Tournament was Guilermo Garcia, who many of the spectators immediately recognized as resembling the hero of Jack London's well-known story "The Mexican". And it was Torre's Opening (such a name has now become perfectly official) that Garcia employed against World Champion Karpov. The Cuban grandmaster sacrificed a pawn, and "requested" the black king to remain in the centre. Considerable skill was demanded of the present Champion for him, in contrast to Lasker, not to lose, but to win. Karpov played equally strongly in this game as he had in most of the game against Smyslov. On this occasion, however, he did not commit any inaccuracies towards the end, but himself switched to counter-attack, won the exchange, and adjourned the game with a marked advantage.

Then, meeting Gheorghiu, he gained another win. And for Karpov the whole weight of his tournament fate fell on the adjournment day. Or more precisely, on his two unfinished games —against Tal and Smyslov (the result against Garcia was obvious).

Along with the International Tournament, the season of White Nights was drawing to a close in Leningrad. In this wonderful city there was a markedly smaller number of those visitors who only a few days previously had been flocking in vast crowds to the Nyeva to watch the night-time raising of the bridges. Tourists began going to bed early. But the chess players had come to Leningrad not for a holiday, and so lights burned in certain windows of the "Moskva" Hotel until day-break. A light was also burning in the Karpovs' flat.

"What was the sealed move?" asked Yevgeny Stepanovich Karpov on the adjournment day, as he entered the Palace of Culture. He didn't know that the game had already finished...

Smyslov had sealed the best move. Karpov thought that the question of capitulation was just a matter of time. That would have been the case, had the Ex-World Champion not grown nervous and made a mistake. It would seem that Karpov should have been pleased, that he had "escaped with slight shock"; more than that, he had gained half a point, instead of losing a whole one. But this was only at first sight.

Imagine to yourself the state of a man who, a few moves before the adjournment, had an indisputable advantage against Smyslov, a rival and one of the strongest participants. The state of a man who had not simply relinquished his advantage, but who was now even forced (each day, before his other games) to painstakingly carry out what was almost certainly futile work, analysing all the possible continuations, with the feeling that his opponent had sealed the strongest move, after which a vexing and therefore doubly-painful defeat was inevitable. For several days Karpov was in such a state, but he managed to pull himself together and win two games. The relaxation set in at the very moment when he drew with Smyslov. Fifteen minutes later the resumption began of his long-adjourned game with Tal (the opponent had been ill, and it had twice been postponed). During that quarter of an hour Karpov was unable to "restore himself", and for this reason he was also unable to win this adjourned game.

Karpov–Tal

English Opening

1 P–QB4 N–KB3 2 N–QB3 P–B4 3 N–B3 P–K3 4 P–KN3 P–Q4 5 P×P N×P 6 B–N2 N–QB3 7 0–0 B–K2 8 P–Q4 0–0 9 P–K4 N–N3 10 P–Q5 P×P 11 P×P N–N5 12 N–K5 B–Q3 13 N–Q3 B–N5 14 Q×B N×N

15 B–N5 B–K2 16 B×B Q×B 17 QR–N1 QR–Q1 18 KR–Q1 N–K4 19 Q–K2 KR–K1 20 R–K1 Q–Q2 21 P–N3 P–B5 22 Q–Q2 P×P 23 P×P Q–B4 24 R–K3 N–N5 25 R×R+ R×R 26 R–Q1 R–Q1 (Diag.)

27 P–Q6 N–B1 28 N–K4 N–B3 29 N×N+ P×N 30 Q–N4 P–N3 31 B–N7 K–N2 32 B×N Q×B 33 P–Q7 Q–B4 34 Q–N4+ Q–KN4 35 Q–B3 Q–K4 36 Q–N7 Q–K7 37 R–Q6 Q–K4 38 R–Q3 Q–K7 39 Q–Q5 Q–K4 40 Q–B3 Q–K3 41 Q–Q1 Q–K4 42 R–Q2 P–QR4 43 R–Q5 Q–K5 44 P–KN4 Q–KB5 45 P–R3 P–R3 46 R–Q4 Q–K4 47 Q–Q2 Q–KN4 48 Q–Q1 Q–K4 49 R–Q5 Q–B5 50 K–N2 K–B1 51 R–Q4 Q–K4 52 Q–Q3 K–N2 53 R–Q6 Q–QB4 54 Q–Q2 P–N4 55 R–Q5 Q–B3 56 K–N3 P–R5 57 P×P P×P 58 Q–Q4 Q–K3 59 P–N5 P–R6 60 P×RP+ K–R2 **Drawn**

Prior to the last round he had missed his last chance of first place: Romanishin had 10½ points, Tal had 10, and Vaganian, Karpov and Smyslov—all 9½.

In Leningrad, if you turn off the Nyevsky Prospect into Kharkov Street, you see a road sign which is familiar to all drivers—the "No Entry" sign. It hangs not far from the Dzerzhinsky Palace of Culture. Why is it forbidden to drive through here? It was so that vehicle noise did not penetrate through the open windows of the tournament hall. The far-sighted organizers had been concerned for the players, even at the distant approaches, so to speak, of the outer defences. This measure proved especially useful during the last round.

The last round of this long and difficult event had the appearance of a gripping theatrical Première. With the difference that in theatres not absolutely all of the standing room is taken, and none of the audience have to stand on tip-toe, leaning on their neighbours' shoulders between the wide-open doors. And another thing. In the theatre the audience sometimes knows how even the best detective play is going to end.

Romanishin later explained how he tuned up psychologically for his game with Karpov:

"In principle, I considered that I would be happy with a draw. After all, it was difficult to imagine that Tal would win his fourth game in a row. But on no account had I to concede Karpov a psychological initiative—he exploits this better than anyone else. This meant that, to gain a draw, especially with White, it had to be done by active play. In a slow, quiet, 'hundred-move' game the Champion would have a moral advantage, since I might possibly begin gradually to fear for the capital accumulated over the tournament as a whole."

Romanishin played actively, and after an inaccuracy by his opponent, gained good prospects. Then he failed to take into account a manoeuvre by Karpov, but did not end up in an inferior position, and therefore was able to offer a draw with a clear conscience.

After this offer had been accepted, Tal stopped coming over to the neighbouring table. And only once, quickly strolling around the practically deserted stage, the Ex-World Champion bumped into Radulov, and learned from him that the other Ex-World Champion had declined the Bulgarian grandmaster's offer of a draw. This meant that in one of the possible variations (Smyslov wins, Tal loses) Smyslov could overtake him. But it wasn't this variation that Tal was thinking about when he returned to his table—even without this in the position on the board there was plenty to ponder over.

With practically all of his forces, Kuzmin—who also didn't want a draw—advanced against White's K-side. Only a single black knight was left "grazing" somewhere to one side. It was his very "one horse-power" that Kuzmin was lacking to successfully conclude his attack, in certain variations of which he managed to drive the white king between the lines of his own and the enemy pieces, but just couldn't manage to mate it. And when Tal's opponent began to sacrifice, it seemed to me from where I was sitting that a faint smile flickered across the Ex-World Champion's face (later he said that he had gained genuine satisfaction from this "real game" the like of which he had been yearning for). At any event, in this amazing game, which several times drew applause from the hall, it was White who supplied the combinational full stop. Under the threat of mate or loss of his queen, Kuzmin resigned.

Later, in the players' room, which had been invaded by dozens of spectators, Tal simply couldn't settle down to analyse the game—people were constantly shaking his hand. With enormous difficulty his happy trainer Aleksandr Koblentz pushed his way through: "Incredible! What a game!"

And so, first and second places were shared by Romanishin and Tal with 11 points. Third came Smyslov on 10½. By scoring 10 points, Karpov shared fourth and fifth places with Vaganian.

Then, replying to the congratulations, Mikhail Tal said:

"I have been watching the games of Vasily Vasilievich for some thirty years now. For twenty years I have known him personally. But never have I seen such 'youthful' play. Smyslov is undoubtedly one of the three main heroes of the tournament. The other two are Oleg Romanishin and Anatoly Karpov."

Later Tal wrote: "One of the heroes of the tournament was Karpov... In a recent appearance on Central T.V., the World Champion half-jokingly complained that the fans demand of him only victories, only first places. Well, one can understand the fans: Karpov has greatly spoiled them, and now it is thought that the World Champion must always invariably win. But this is a delusion. Without making any historical analogies, I can say that nowadays such an outcome is an exception to the rule. And what is astonishing is the fact that, over a period of six months, Karpov has succeeded in taking first place in four major events. He could of course have done better in Leningrad, but I think that he was extremely tired.

At the start he unexpectedly suffered two reverses, one of which was particularly distressing. To lose accidentally on time in a won position!... Despite all his misfortunes, Karpov found the strength to battle right to the last round, and towards the finish played several quite excellent games. The World Champion has kept his 'powder dry', and—of this I am absolutely convinced—in the next few months will gladden his supporters."

Vasily Smyslov: "I don't think at all that Karpov played badly. After all, there are two aspects to the game—the competitive and the creative. In the creative sense the World Champion's games were on a sufficiently high level, but this was not reflected in his result. That's sport."

Oleg Romanishin didn't consider it in order for him to assess the World Champion's performance. But on the other hand, he expressed an interesting opinion on a more "general question": "Each player has his own chess 'patents'. With Karpov, for instance, this is technique. In this he has no equals. It has been said of the great footballer Pelé that he has perfect ball control. When moving about the field, he sees the entire playing area, and merely has to decide where to move to or whom to pass the ball to. About the ball itself he doesn't have to worry at all: it is as if attached to his foot, and obediently obeys his will. Karpov's relationship with his chess pieces is the same. For him there is only one problem—where to transfer this or that piece. But how to transfer it—he already knows. And it is this that constitutes his extremely fine technique."

It may be objected that it was errors of technique which prevented Karpov from winning in the deciding games against Smyslov and Tal. If citation of the banal formula "Man is only human" is insufficiently convincing, then let us quote an incident from the realms of music.

The eminent pianist Artur Rubinstein was once making a recording of a Chopin Polonaise. To general amazement he went wrong in a bravura passage. The remainder of the performance was impeccable. Afterwards it was suggested that he re-record the unsuccessful part.

"Let it stay as it is", the maestro replied, "That way it's more human."

G. Garcia–Karpov
Torre Attack

1 P–Q4 N–KB3 2 N–KB3 P–K3 3 B–N5 P–B4 4 P–K3 Q–N3 5 B×N P×B 6 QN–Q2 Q×P 7 B–K2 P×P 8 N×P P–QR3 9 0–0 Q–N3 10 R–N1 Q–B2 11 B–R5 R–N1 12 Q–B3 B–K2 13 Q–R3 N–B3 14 N×N NP×N 15 P–KB4 P–Q4 16 P–K4 Q–R4 17 QR–Q1 Q–B4+ 18 K–R1 P–R4 19 P–B4 K–B1 20 KP×P KP×P 21 Q–Q3 R–N2 22 KR–K1 B–R3 23 Q–KR3 P–R5 24 R–K2 B–B1 25 Q–R4 B–K3 26 N–B3 B–B4 27 P×P P×P 28 R(1)–K1 B–K5

29 P–B5 Q–B5 30 Q–R3 B–N5 31 N–Q2 Q–Q5 32 N×B B×R 33 N×P Q×N 34 R×B R–N4 35 B–N4 P–R4 36 Q–R3+ K–N2 37 B–R3 P–Q5 38 R–Q1 R–QB1 39 Q×P P–Q6 40 Q–KB4 R–B7 41 Q–K3 P–Q7 42 K–N1 R–B6 43 Resigns

CHAPTER 12

His Powder Remains Dry

After his unaccustomed placing of equal fourth in the Leningrad Tournament, it might not have been easy for Karpov to "recuperate" quickly. But unexpectedly to his aid came... British Television. At a most opportune moment—and at great benefit to itself—the BBC organized a small international event, of a light, almost diversionary nature.

The eight participants were divided into two groups: Karpov (USSR), Pfleger (West Germany), Hartston (England) and Hug (Switzerland), and Larsen (Denmark), Miles (England), Schmid (West Germany) and Donner (Holland). The intention of the organizers was that the knock-out system should ensure a meeting in the final between Karpov and Larsen—the favourites, who had been seeded in different halves of the tournament.

Each player was initially allotted two hours for the first forty moves, with the usual rate thereafter, but then (in the event of a draw) the time for thinking was reduced. In a second game, each player was allowed only half an hour, and in a third game (if one should be required) the time control was cut right down to 15 minutes each for the whole game. The results of the event weer kept strictly secret: the BBC was preparing a special programme, and wanted to keep viewers in suspense from August until November—when chess and chess players would appear on the screen. At the same time, all the players were required to make detailed comments on their games, with a frank account of those thoughts, even fairly abstract ones, which came into their heads during the game.

This was the first international event of this nature. A year earlier, the BBC had staged a similar tournament with some of the strongest British masters. On that occasion Michael Stean had drawn applause from all those in the T.V. studio, when he made the following comment on his game with William Hartston: "My position is collapsing more rapidly than the British Economy. Besides, in contrast to the Treasury, which has the possibility of printing new paper money, I am forced to make do with what is on the board..."

"On this occasion the commentary, at any rate in the chess sense, was certainly deeper", relates Anatoly Karpov. "After the game we explained our ideas, which were later dubbed on, and we repeated the moves themselves the following day in front of the T.V. cameras. At times, however, this led to curious happenings...

Miles and I were repeating for the T.V. recording our fifteen-minute game. Exactly as in the tournament game itself, we both—deliberately, of course—got into incredible time trouble. And here Miles left open a mate in one move—in his haste he moved his king to the wrong square. What was I to do? I decided nevertheless to drive the lone king, with my queen, onto the same square where it had perished during the actual game. In the game itself, Miles had not resigned, as he was hoping I would lose on time; this was our third game in the final, after two earlier draws, and the time allotted to us had been considerably decreased. Before that I defeated Hug at the first attempt, and Pfleger—at the second."

While one of the finalists, the World Champion, had immediately been guessed correctly by everyone, hardly any "suspicion" had fallen on Miles, since everyone expected the representative in the final from the second quartet to be Larsen. But meanwhile, Tony Miles had managed in his twenty-one years to develop into a very strong grandmaster. True, he did admit: "Unfortunately, at present I find it very difficult playing against Karpov. The trouble is that, whereas he determines without any difficulty my intentions at the board, for me his moves and plans are often totally incomprehensible."

This admission was recalled soon afterwards at a serious international tournament, where both the top prize-winners showed that the "television training" had not done them any harm at all.

* * *

In the small Dutch town of Tilburg, the Interpolis Insurance Company organized an international tournament. The players comprised strong grandmasters only, and the complete absence of outsiders made for an extremely high average Elo coefficient for the event—2582. At any rate, the experts on "chess mathematics" could not recall even a single such tournament (of twelve competitors) of the 14th category of difficulty on the special scale introduced by the FIDE. Such imposing grandmaster names naturally provoked great interest, both in themselves, and due to the fact that one of them—Anatoly Karpov, had recently finished behind the winners in the Leningrad tournament, and that the match for the World Championship was not so far away...

Karpov considered that the rather unusual, "two-tier" procedure for the drawing of lots was not only the most objective, but also proved highly entertaining for the public. The FIDE General Secretary Ineke Bakker first took out from a basket beautiful boxes with the players' names, and as each player was called he went up to the controllers' desk to choose his number.

The organizers also introduced another innovation. The competitors played in a spacious, and at the same time comfortable room, while the spectators were accomodated in a neighbouring demonstration hall, with places for one thousand. The games were demonstrated by T.V., and were commented on by Dutch masters.

When it became known that Viktor Korchnoi, one of the finalists in the Candidates' Matches, was intending to visit the tournament, and wished without fail to watch directly in the isolated playing hall, practically all of the players made a joint declaration protesting against the anticipated visit. And Korchnoi did not appear at the tournament...

Rumours to the effect that Karpov allegedly got into a difficult position in his first round game against Timman proved to be strongly exaggerated. In fact the World Champion attacked his opponent, and even sacrificed a piece. The Dutch grandmaster defended excellently, and for one move his position even became better. But only for one move... And in the end the result was a draw.

In the drawing of lots, the number one fell to Karpov, and the number two—to Miles. This meant that they were to meet in the second round, and later it turned out that this was the order in which they would finish in the final table. In their individual encounter the Englishman's nerve failed him, and he sacrificed a rook, but lost the game.

Karpov–Miles
English Opening

1 P–QB4 P–QB4 2 N–KB3 N–KB3 3 N–B3
N–B3 4 P–Q4 P×P 5 N×P P–K3 6 P–KN3
Q–N3 7 N–N3 N–K4 8 P–K4 B–N5 9 Q–K2
P–QR4 10 B–K3 Q–B3 11 P–B3 0–0 12 N–Q4
Q–R3 13 N–N5 (Diag.)

13 ... P–Q4 14 N–B7 Q–Q3 15 N×R
P×KP 16 P×P N×KP 17 R–Q1 Q–B3
18 B–N2 N×BP 19 B–Q4 B×N 20 P×B

N×B R×N 24 B×P Q–B4+ 25 B–Q4
Resigns

P–B4 21 0–0 N(B5)–Q3 22 N–N6 P–K4 23

...As the foreign newspapers described, in the restaurant where the participants in the Tilburg Tournament dined, the menu consisted of 12 special dishes, bearing the names of the 12 grandmasters: "Smyslov Entrecôte", "Whipped cream with chocolate à la Miles" etc. There was also a dish named after Karpov, a dish which, incidentally, Miles took a liking to. "I'll have the chess crown", the Englishman joked. "Isn't it a little early?", maliciously enquired G. Bruckner, correspondent of the Vienna paper *Kurier*. "After all, in your individual encounters with the World Champion you haven't as yet put up much of a resistance against him." "Don't you understand", Miles retorted in the same spirit, "that Karpov plays particularly strongly against me, since he sees me as his most dangerous rival."

A joke is a joke, but it was he who proved to be essentially Karpov's only rival in the Tilburg Tournament. In the fourth round Tony Miles began a series of four wins, which "took in" Soviet grandmasters Smyslov and Balashov. In this Interpolis Tournament, one of the youngest grandmasters in the world achieved his biggest success to date, and, according to Balashov, showed himself to be an exceptionally bold and fighting player, who had succeeded in finding "his" style. Even his manner of sitting at the board shows that Miles is always intent only on winning. He normally offers a draw only in an inferior position.

The middle stage of the tournament was marked by intense competition between Karpov and Miles. And it was only after the ninth round that the World Champion drew half a point ahead of his determined rival. In the penultimate, tenth round, Karpov defeated Andersson, and Miles—Olafsson. During the last round, the Swede Andersson, a player of exceptional practical strength, but who is at times too peaceable, kept on saying: "I seem to be losing...", but then he took himself in hand and inflicted a defeat on Miles. As a result, Karpov, with 8 out of 11 (without defeat) finished a point ahead of the Englishman. A point further behind was a whole group of famous names: Vlastimil Hort, Ljubomir Ljubojević, Jan Timman and Robert Hübner.

Vasily Smyslov and Yury Balashov did not make particularly successful appearances, but all the games between the Soviet players struck a serious blow at the idle talk about constant draws between our representatives. The most tense game in the whole event was without doubt that between Karpov and Smyslov, which after a lengthy adjournment session the Ex-World Champion managed to save. This is how grandmaster Balashov described Karpov's play in Tilburg:

"In my opinion, this appearance by Karpov can be regarded as one of his best tournament achievements. The point is not even that the winner achieved such a fine score: Karpov's play at the grandmaster tournament in Holland showed that the creative side of his game is continuing to develop. The World Champion convincingly refuted the opinion of those who predicted that after the Leningrad Jubilee Tournament he wouldn't manage to quickly regain his form. Perhaps at the start of the Interpolis Tournament the Leningrad grandmaster did not play quite as easily as, for instance, in Bad Lauterberg or Las Palmas, but he played excellently during the second half of the event: five points out of six games with grandmasters speaks for itself. In these games Karpov once again demonstrated his characteristic rapid and irreproachably accurate calculation of variations, and his ability to immediately detect in a position its latent possibilities."

Hübner–Karpov
English Opening

1 P–QB4	P–QB4
2 N–KB3	N–KB3
3 N–B3	P–Q4

One of the possibilities available to Black, leading to an immediate clash in the centre. The game frequently transposes into one of the variations of the Grünfeld Defence. At the same time, it should be noted that it is only with this order of moves that Black can develop his bishop at KN2, while avoiding a Maróczy bind set-up.

4 P×P	N×P
5 P–KN3	

White could have transposed into a position from the Queen's Gambit (5 P–Q4 P–K3 6 P–K4 N×N 7 P×N P×P B–N5+), or from the Grünfeld Defence (5 P–Q4 N×N 6 P×N P–KN3).

5 ...	P–KN3
6 P–Q3	

6 B–N2 B–N2 7 0–0 0–0 8 P–Q3 is the more usual move order, but evidently Hübner decides to first develop his Q-side pieces.

6 ...	B–N2
7 B–Q2	P–N3!?

An interesting idea! Black fearlessly opens the ... QR1–KR8 diagonal, and in addition is not afraid of checks on the QR4–K8 diagonal. His plan is, firstly, to defend in advance his QBP, which is usually highly vulnerable, and secondly, to develop his bishop on the long diagonal, which is not normally possible when White develops his bishop at KN2 at an early stage. A straightforward calculation demonstrates the correctness of Black's plan.

8 Q–R4+

This attempt to exploit the position of the black king in the centre proves unsuccessful. In the event of the quiet 8 N×N Q×N 9 B–N2 B–N2, or 8 B–N2 B–N2, Black's position is again satisfactory.

8 ...	B–Q2
9 Q–R4	B–QB3

The immediate 9 ... P–K3 was also possible.

10 B–N2

10 B–R6 would have been premature, since the knight at QB3 is left inadequately defend-

ed, and after 10 ... B–B3 White has only one reply—11 B–N5.

10 ...   P–K3

Black is in no hurry to castle, since after the exchange of queens his king will be more needed in the centre.

11 Q×Q+

In the event of 11 B–N5 Black easily attains a satisfactory position: 11 ... P–B3 12 B–R6 0–0.

11 ...   K×Q
12 R–QB1

White vacates the QR1–KR8 diagonal, with the aim of preparing P–QN4, and at the same time takes up a position vis-à-vis the bishop on the QB-file. The immediate exchange on Q5 could hardly have satisfied White, since then there could have followed 12 N×N P×N! 13 B–B3 P–Q5 14 B–Q2 P–QR4!, with a big spatial advantage for Black.

12 ...   N–R3!?

A knight on the edge of the board!.. Many 'quote' Tarrasch, stating that a knight on the edge of the board is always bad. But there is no rule without an exception. In the given specific position the knight is better placed at QR3 than in the centre at Q2. The work being carried out by this piece is considerable: firstly, it overprotects the QBP in the event of P–QN4 by White; secondly, it allows Black to comfortably deploy his remaining pieces on the QB-file, and thirdly, it is ready at any moment to give additional protection to the square ... Q4.

13 N×N

White can no longer delay this exchange, since otherwise (after, say, 13 0–0) Black

plays 13 ... R–QB1, and after 14 N×N he can recapture with the pawn.

13 ...   B×N

Here the capture with the pawn would be ill-advised, since after 14 P–QN4 the bishop at QB3 is undefended.

14 B–B3

By offering this exchange, White hopes to equalize and gain a draw, but I was aiming for a different result...

14 ...	**P–B3**
15 P–QR3	**K–K2**
16 0–0	**KR–QB1**
17 N–Q2	**N–B2**

Black's positional superiority gradually takes shape. Realizing that if the game continues to follow a quiet course he will be faced with nothing but defensive problems, Hübner decides to escape from Black's positional grip, and attempts to break out on the Q-side. This idea meets with an unusual refutation.

18 P–QN4	**B×B**

An essential interim move, which has the aim of luring the white king to KN2.

19 K×B	**P×P**
20 B×NP+	**K–Q2**

Following the rules of the endgame, the king moves to the centre, and itself covers the weaknesses along the open file.

21 B–B3

This leads by force to a very difficult position for White. Better was 21 N–B4 (21 N–K4 is weaker in view of 21 ... N–Q4 22 B–Q2 P–B4) 21 ... N–Q4 22 B–Q2 P–QN4 23 N–R5 P–B4, although in this case too Black's Q-side pawn majority gives him a clear advantage in the ending.

**21 ...   N–Q4
22 B–N2**

After 22 N–K4 N×B 23 N×N P–B4 Black attains a won position, but now misfortune strikes from the other side.

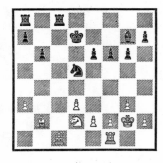

**22 ...   B–R3!
22 P–K3**

There is no other was of blocking the QB1–KR6 diagonal. 23 KR–Q1 loses quickly to 23 ... R×R 24 B×R N–B6 25 R–K1 N–R7 26 N–N3 (26 P–K3 also fails, to 26 ... R–QB1 27 B–N2 R–B7!) 26 ... N×B 27 N×N R–QB1.

23 ...   B×P!

A simple combination, leading by force to an ending where Black has a rook and two pawns for two minor pieces.

24 P×B	**N×P+**
25 K–B3	**N×R**
26 N×N	**R×R**
27 B×R	**R–QB1**

A very important gain of tempo. Without this White would have time to place his bishop at QN2 and his knight at K3, and thereby defend all squares along the QB-file against intrusion by the black rook. Of course, even then the advantage would have remained with Black, but its realization would have involved considerable difficulties.

28 B–N2   R–B7!

The most determined move. Black exchanges his KBP for the white QRP, and obtains two connected passed pawns on the Q-side. The fact that his pawn formation in the centre and on the K-side is spoiled is not important, since White requires too much time to exploit the resulting weaknesses.

29 B×P	**R–R7**
30 K–K3	**R×QRP**
31 N–Q2	

After lengthy consideration, White finds the best way of deploying his forces: his king defends the QP and attempts to approach the opponent's passed pawns, his bishop operates along the long diagonal, and his knight heads for K4. The harmony of Whyte's pieces is complete, and only the material balance is not in his favour.

31 ...	**P–QN4**
32 N–K4	**P–N5?**

Over-hasty. Black allows his opponent use of the square QB4, and restricts the action of his own rook. 32 ... P–QR4 was more accurate.

33 K–Q4	P–QR4
34 K–B4	

With the highly unpleasant threat of 35 B–N2 R–R7 36 K–N3, trapping the rook.

34 ...	R–R7
35 P–R4	K–B3
36 B–Q4	

White has achieved something resembling a fortress. By occupying the central squares with his pieces, he has stopped the further advance of the passed pawns, and has prevented the approach of the black king. And all this as a result of a single inaccuracy! Everything could have been so much simpler if Black had not advanced his QNP so hastily.

36 ...	R–K7

Here I managed to find a clear-cut plan. Firstly, the rook has to be transferred to a more active position on the eighth rank, from where it can disturb the white king. Secondly, for the time being the rook must keep an eye on the actions of the white knight, which cannot move for the moment in view of 37 ... P–K4.

37 B–K5	R–K8
38 B–B6	R–QN8

Threatening to advance his QNP.

39 B–K7

The only defence, since if White attempts to drive away the rook by 39 N–Q2, then 39 ... R–QB8+ 40 K–N3 K–N4, and White's whole set-up collapses.

39 ...	P–K4

At last the KP advances and blocks the long diagonal. The main point is that now, after a check at ... QB8, the white king has only one retreat square—QN3. But then Black's king goes the other way, and breaks through on the Q-file.

40 P–N4	R–QB8+
41 K–N3	K–Q4
42 B–N5	

Black wins by force after 42 B–Q8 K–Q5 43 B×P K×P 44 N–B6 R–QN8+ 45 K–R2 K–B7.

42 ...	R–QN8+

Before the rook is moved away, the white king must first be driven back.

43 K–B2	R–KR8
44 K–N3	R–R6!

This rook is unusually energetic.

45 N–B6+	K–Q5
46 N×P	R×QP+
47 K–B2	P–R5
48 B–K7	R–QB6+
49 K–N1	R–B2
Resigns	

Olafsson–Karpov
King's Indian Attack

1 N–KB3 N–KB3 2 P–KN3 P–QN3 3 B–N2 B–N2 4 0–0 P–K3 5 P–Q3 P–Q4 6 QN–Q2 QN–Q2 7 P–B3 B–K2 8 Q–B2 0–0 9 P–K4

P–B4 10 R–K1 Q–B2 11 P–B4 P×KP 12
P×P QR–Q1 13 P–KR3 B–Q3 14 P–N3
B–K4 15 R–N1 P–KR3 16 N–B1 B–Q5 17
B–B4 P–K4 18 B–B1 N–N1 19 N–R4 N–B3
20 P–R3 P–R3 21 N–B5 P–QN4 22 B–Q2
P–N5 23 P×P N×NP 24 B×N P×B 25
N(1)–K3 B–B6 26 KR–Q1 P–QR4 27 N–Q5
B×N 28 KP×B K–R1 29 R–Q3 P–R5 30
P–Q6 Q–B4 31 R×B P×R 32 Q×P P×P
33 R×P R–N1 34 Q–K3 Q×BP 35 R–Q3
KR–Q1 36 N–K7 P–K5 37 R–Q4 Q–K3 38
Q–B4 R–N3 39 N–B5 P–N4 40 Q–B1 Q×N
41 Resigns

Karpov–Smyslov
Ruy Lopez

1 P–K4   P–K4

Smyslov is a constant and faithful admirer
of the Ruy Lopez. There is probably no
variation, no branch of this opening, that
has not been tried by the Ex-World Champion in his extensive tournament experience.

2 N–KB3	N–QB3
3 B–N5	P–QR3
4 B–R4	N–B3
5 0–0	N×P

The Open Variation has relatively recently
become the favourite of my opponent, but
the fact that Smyslov chose it was not at all
unexpected for me; our game from the
Leningrad International Tournament of 1977
developed in exactly the same way.

6 P–Q4	P–QN4
7 B–N3	P–Q4
8 P×P	B–K3
9 P–B3	B–QB4
10 QN–Q2	0–0
11 B–B2	B–B4
12 N–N3	B–KN5
13 N×B	N×N

14 R–K1	R–K1
15 B–B4	

In the well-known game Fischer–Larsen
(Santa-Monica 1966) White carried out a
different idea: 15 B–K3 N–K3 16 Q–Q3
P–N3 17 B–R6. But in reply to 15 B–K3,
Black now more often continues 15 ...
N–K5, as occurred, for instance, in the game
Geller–Tseshkovsky (44th USSR Champion-
ship).

15 ...   B–R4

Recommended by Keres. In the event of
15 ... N–K3 a position from the afore-
mentioned Fischer–Larsen game can arise
after 16 Q–Q3 P–N3 (bad, of course, is 16 ...
N×B 17 Q×RP+ K–B1 18 Q–R8+ K–K2
19 Q–R4+ and 20 Q×B) 17 B–R6.

16 B–KN3   N–K3

This is better than 16 ... B–N3, as played
by Smyslov in our game in Leningrad, when
after 17 N–Q4 White gained a clear advantage.

17 Q–Q2

White frees himself from the pin, and is not
afraid of the doubled pawns on the KB-file
(after 17 ... B×N), since in this case the
front KBP will be useful for breaking up the
black king's position.

17 ...   N–K2
18 N–R4!

An excellent idea. Now the knight can keep a watch on the black bishop, while the KBP is granted complete freedom of movement. In the future it will be very important to control the square KB5, and for this reason 18 N–Q4 is weaker, since by 18 ... P–QB4 Black forces his opponent to decide on his subsequent plan, and neither 19 N×N P×N, nor 19 N–B5 N×N 20 B×N B–N3, is at all promising.

18 ...   **P–Q5**

Black initiates play in the centre, and indirectly prevents the advance of the KBP—19 P–KB4 P×P 20 Q×P Q–Q5+, with the exchange of queens, and good counter-chances.

19 B–K4   **P–QB3**

Effectively the only reply. On 19 ... R–QB1 there could have followed 20 Q–B2 B–N3 21 QR–Q1 P–QB4 22 P–KB4.

20 Q–B2

White also maintains his advantage after 20 N–B3, which forces the exchange of Black's bishop. The move played leads to a more complicated game.

20 ...   **B–N3**

Otherwise the bishop remains out of play.

21 QR–Q1   **Q–N3**

22 P–KB4!

White is not afraid of ghosts: the discovered check is not dangerous.

22 ...	**P–Q6+**
23 Q–B2	**Q×Q+**
24 K×Q	**B×B**
25 R×B	**N–QB4**

Weaker is 25 ... QR–Q1 26 R–K3 N–QB4 27 P–N4. Now White cannot reply 26 R–K3, in view of 26 ... N–Q4, when the rook comes under attack.

26 R–Q4	**QR–Q1**
27 K–B3	

Of course, nothing is achieved by 27 P–N4, in view of 27 ... R×R 28 P×R N–K5+ 29 K–N3 N–B6, when Black has dangerous counter-play. White chooses perhaps the most logical plan for strengthening his position, which naturally required him to foresee the possible course of events.

27 ...   **P–R3**

This creates the natural threat of trapping the knight, and at first sight it is not clear how White is to disentangle his group of pieces on the K-side. But nevertheless there is a way: the best form of defence is—attack!

28 B–B2

With an indirect, but nevertheless very obvious attack on the knight at ... QB4.

28 ...   **N–K3**

White would have had an undisputed advantage after 28 ... R×R 29 P×R N–R5 30 P–QN3 N–B6 31 R×P N×P 32 K–K4. It is natural therefore that Black should try to get rid of the most active enemy piece.

29 R(4)×P!

As before, White does not intend to concern himself over the defence of his knight. His basic idea in this game is to keep the initiative, despite possible loss of material.

29 ...   R×R

The advance of the KNP does not win a piece: 29 ... P–N4 30 R×R R×R 31 R×R N×R 32 B–B5, and the square ... QB3, which would otherwise link Black's two knights, is occupied by his own pawn.

30 R×R   P–N4

Black loses a pawn after 30 ... N×P 31 K×N P–N4+ 32 K–K4 P×N 33 B×P. But why should he consider such variations, when the white knight can be attacked directly?

31 P–B5   N–B5

Smyslov later said that he had overrated his chances, and that he should have played more cautiously—31 ... N–KB1. He then gave only the variation 32 P–B6 N(2)–N3 33 N×N N×N 34 B–N3 N×P+ 35 B×N R×B 36 R–Q6 R–QB4, and although White retains a certain advantage, to realise it would be difficult. But the whole point is that in the event of 31 ... N–KB1 I was intending to sacrifice a piece—32 R–Q6 P×N 33 K–K4

N–R2 34 R×RP, or 33 ... N–Q4 34 R×BP —with excellent winning chances.

32 R–Q6

First of all Black has had to allow the rook to take up an active position.

32 ...   N(2)–Q4
33 B–Q4   P×N
34 R×BP

The black knights are deprived of their last strong point in the centre, and are left 'hanging'. As a result of his combination, White has gained two pawns for the piece. But in the endgame—and this should never be forgotten—the king is often transformed into a formidable force.

34 ...   P–B3

Black's only chance, which surprisingly proves successful.

35 P–K6

To this day I am perplexed as to why it was that my hand stretched out to this pawn, and advanced it one square—after the natural 35 P×P White gains a third pawn for his piece, with the pawn at KB6 constantly threatening to give check and queen. Of course, the move played does not yet relinquish the win, but this first inaccuracy is unfortunately followed by others.

35 ...   N–R4

With the position blocked it is easier for Black to co-ordinate his pieces, and in all variations White is just one move away from a clearly won position.

36 R×P   N–N2

37 K–K4	N–K2
38 B×P	N(N2)×P

The cavalry is reunited! Black's QNP is indirectly defended by the knight at ... KB4, in view of the possible fork at ... Q3.

39 P–R4

Since the attack on the QNP gets nowhere, I decided to exchange it, so as to clear the way for the two connected passed pawns on the QN- and QB-files.

39 ...	P×P
40 R×P	R–Q1?!

An attempt to break free with the rook, which should have ended in catastrophe. Black should have tried to improve the position of his king by 40 ... K–R2, although even then after 41 K–K5 White has excellent winning chances.

41 R–R7!

Once again White is not afraid of anything.

41 ...	K–B1

There is no alternative. In his preliminary calculations Black had clearly made an oversight; on 41 ... N–Q3+ White has the excellent reply 42 K–Q3, and on his next move blocks the Q-file with his rook, defending against any possible discovered check.

42 R–Q7?

Now it is White's turn to go wrong. He should have immediately advanced his QBP, taking away squares from the black knights.

42 ...	R–B1
43 P–QN4	

A further inaccuracy, after which the win is perhaps no longer possible. More exact was 43 P–QN3, intending to advance the QBP.

43 ...	K–K1
44 R–R7	

White has to return his rook to its former post, thus admitting the inaccuracies committed. Now Black has the possibility of a forcing continuation, which Smyslov, a master of defence, promptly finds.

44 ...	N–Q3+
45 K–Q3	N–Q4
46 B–K5	N–N4
47 R–R7	R–B3!

The only move, but quite sufficient.

48 R×P	N(N4)×P
49 R×P	N–R7

Having sensed the possibility of saving the game, Smyslov plays with amazing tenacity. He is not afraid to allow the advance of the QNP, since the KP represents the chief danger.

50 P–N5	R×P
51 R–R5	

Here, for perhaps the last time, White could have fought for an advantage by 51 B–Q4.

51 ...	R–KN3

The final subtlety: Black halts the advance of the enemy K-side pawns. The remainder of the game is not of any great interest, as it gradually heads towards a draw.

52 B–N3	R–N5
53 K–B2	N(7)–N5+
54 K–N3	R–Q5

55 B–B2	R–Q6+	60 R–QN5	R–Q7
56 K–R4	R–Q8	61 R–N3	R×P
57 P–N6	N–QB3	62 K–N5	R–Q7
58 P–N7	K–Q2	63 P–R4	N–B4
59 B–N3	N(4)–K2	Drawn	

CHAPTER 13

What was Decided in Caracas

The Central Committee of the International Chess Federation is composed in the main of members of the FIDE Bureau: the President and General Secretary, three Vice-Presidents —from Europe, Asia and America, two long-serving delegates from the major federations— USSR and USA, and an equal number of officials of the chess movements which enjoy the greatest authority. The Committee also naturally includes the World Champion and the Lady World Champion, and the Presidents of all the eleven zones into which the chess world is divided. Once every four years the FIDE Congress, in choosing its leaders, names a further eight to ten representatives of the most important commissions, or simply the most active congressmen.

For a long time, congresses were held yearly. But in 1974, in Nice, the decision was taken to meet every other year, and in the intervening year, when there was no congress, to hold a meeting of the FIDE Central Committee. It is significant that this decision proved merely to be a formal one, since the problems arising all the same required the calling of an Extraordinary Congress in the "intermediate" years—in 1975 in Bergen regarding the match for the World Championship, and in 1977 in Lucerne on the question of excluding the South African Federation from the FIDE for discrimination against chess players—the native inhabitants of this racist State.

But before reporting on the meeting of the FIDE Central Committee in the Autumn of 1977 in the Venezuelan Capital, and on the highly important decisions taken there, we should perhaps first make a short excursion into the recent past, and touch, as it is customary to say, on the "history of the question". In the capacity of "guide" we have invited the Director of the USSR Central Chess Club, V. Baturinsky, at the same time an eminent professional lawyer, who took part in the solution of this question at various stages of its discussion. And so:

AN EXCURSION INTO HISTORY

"In February 1976, in the FIDE's Amsterdam head-quarters, the first session of the special commission for the drawing-up of the rules for the next World Championship match was held. Eight members of this committee took part in the work, among them Anatoly Karpov and myself, as representatives of the chess organization of our country", Baturinsky relates. "The difference in behaviour between the present and the former World Champion was immediately noticeable: while Fischer limited himself to telegram ultimata addressed to the similar committee during the previous World Championship cycle, Karpov readily joined in the work himself, and together with all the other members attempted to find an acceptable and just formula.

Here, incidentally, is what Karpov said at the time: 'The hullabaloo surrounding the abortive match with Fischer has subsided, and one must suppose that the American player's former supporters have come to realize the total inexpediency of his proposal to play a match up to ten wins by one of the players, without any limitation on the total number of games. This is equivalent to asking an athlete to run a marathon, without restricting the length of it beforehand."

The essence of the Soviet proposal was to introduce the former limit on the total number of games—24 (or at most 30)—and to play to six wins by one of the contestants. If neither of them had won six games by the time the limit was reached, the Champion was to be the one who was leading at that point. In the event of an equal score the Champion was to remain Champion.

However, it very soon became clear that the majority—and in particular the FIDE President Dr Euwe—were already set on an 'unlimited' match. The basic argument put forward for this was that, if the match is a limited one, the player who is leading has the opportunity to draw one game after another, 'sitting it out', as it were, until the fixed number of games expires. And for the chess world, such a match, it is alleged, ceases to be of interest. But after all, the chess world has already witnessed an unlimited match, in 1927, when Capablanca and Alekhine played 25 draws in 34 games, and isn't that why, starting in 1935 when Alekhine and Euwe met, matches with a fixed number of games have been played?* In short, the argument reached deadlock...

And then Euwe—one must give him his due—found an interesting way out. A limit should not be fixed, but the match should be to six wins (and not ten, as Fischer insisted in his time). With a score of 5–5, the President proposed, the World Champion should keep his title, but... And it was here that a highly important addition was made: 'the Challenger receives the right to a new match with the Champion within a period of one year'.

In the almost hopeless situation which had arisen, this appeared to be a reasonable compromise, and the Soviet representatives, wishing to put an end to differences of opinion, agreed to it. At the same time, Karpov nevertheless requested that his particular opinion be recorded: 'As before, I consider that the best solution is to limit the total number of games, but I will go along with the majority'. This was the degree of 'unanimity' that was achieved.

After the recommendations of the special committee had been announced, articles appeared in the foreign press, in which it was asserted that the formula adopted did not differ essentially from Fischer's demands that he be given a start of two points, and that now Karpov was receiving a similar advantage. For some reason the authors of these publications forgot about the big step made in the Challenger's favour: the possibility of the right to a return match. Then Euwe made another half step: the second match, if it should be necessary, would be played with a limited number of games.

But even so", said Baturinsky, summing up this excursion into the past, "it was not felt that the solution was the 'final one, and would not be appealed against'. It was clear that at the meeting in Caracas in the Autumn of 1977 the FIDE Central Committee would still have to return to the question of the World Championship Match."

THE DISCOVERY OF AMERICA

Without having received their American transit visas, the Soviet delegation set off on the long journey to Caracas, where by that time the sessions of the leaders of the International

---

* In Alekhine's matches with Bogolyubov in 1929 and 1934 there was a limited number of games. (K.P.N .)

Chess Federation were already beginning. The flight by the route Moscow–Brussels–Amsterdam–Zurich–Lisbon–Caracas occupied, including changes, more than twenty-four hours, and confused completely our concept of day and night, since the time zones, as well as the airlines and the types of plane, changed several times. And so it happened that, when in one of the aircraft flying over the ocean they showed a film, almost all of the passengers—with the exception perhaps of only the World Champion, the Lady World Champion and the journalist sitting between them—were already soundly asleep.

During that time, the film "Ali the Greatest" told of the life and sporting achievements of the famous boxer Cassius Clay. The film, although rather naïve, proved highly entertaining, but far too frightening. To go to sleep after watching it proved to be no easy task—before one's eyes there constantly appeared pictures of professional boxing turned inside out, with the faces of sportsmen distorted with malice, and with blood in the ring and outside of it.

When we emerged from the plane, at first it seemed that we had landed not on the Western Coast of the Atlantic Ocean, but somewhere on the Black Sea coast of the Caucasus—there were the same mountains, and similar vegetation. On emerging in our car from a 2 km-long tunnel, we discerned on either side of the road pitiful hovels alternating with large modern buildings. The staff from the Soviet Embassy, who had obligingly met us at the airport, told us that Caracas is a city of contrasts (nowhere can you get away from this apt cliché!), where almost two and a half million inhabitants share the stylish central avenues and, shrouded in smoke and mist, the slopes of the surrounding mountains and hills. Oil is helping Venezuela to grow fat, but nevertheless this, virtually the most flourishing country in South America, does not yet have any real industrial muscle.

All around could be heard typical Spanish music: it was a public holiday in Venezuela, commemorating the discovery of America. It was on this day many years ago that Columbus had landed here, and so on this day now no one works. Only the leaders of the International Chess Federation were in session, in the best hotel in Caracas, where they were also living. So did we go from the aeroplane straight to festivities? No, since immediately we had to join in the work of the "Little Congress", as the Central Committee of the FIDE is called here; we had to join in the chess life of Caracas.

The work of the governing organ of the International Federation was held in two sessions: morning and afternoon. For this reason, Anatoly Karpov and Nona Gaprindashvili were unable to reach the Club of Venezuelan–Soviet Friendship until late in the evening! Hundreds of chess fans, in the main young people, greeted the World Champions from the USSR. Among those present at this festive and stirring meeting were the General Secretary of the Venezuelan Communist Party, and the Soviet Ambassador V. N. Kazamirov. At the Friendship Club, a chess club named after Karpov was opened.

In a simultaneous display, Nona Gaprindashvili defeated all her male opponents, and conceded only one draw—to the University Lady Champion E. Rosa, a member of the Venezuelan team. The hosts put out very strong opposition against Karpov, including members of the national team which had just competed successfully in the World Student Olympiad. The master A. Palsios, a former Champion of Venezuela, defeated Karpov, but in the remaining 24 games the grandmaster, who was stung to the quick, conceded only two draws.

The simultaneous display by the world Champion in the club bearing his name finished at one o'clock in the morning, and then early the next morning the chess congressmen were received by the Venezuelan President C. A. Perez.

(It so happened that later, by the time we were due to leave for home, the authorities in the USA decided after all to grant a visa to the World Champion and one of his companions, and I was able to witness friendly meetings with Soviet citizens working there, and with North American chess enthusiasts. But it was not only this that we had in mind, when we called this section "The discovery of America". This refers to the events which took place at the "Little Congress" in Caracas.)

It was anticipated that at least two most "punctilious" questions—on the attitude of the FIDE to the Rhodesian Chess Federation, and on the match for the men's World Championship—would provoke heated discussion. However, in the words of the Lady World Champion Nona Gaprindashvili, "suddenly the FIDE Congressmen with astonishment discovered for themselves America*, realizing that everything could be decided in a business-like, calm and benevolent atmosphere". Many associated the creation of such an atmosphere with the behaviour of the authoritative Soviet delegation.

It all began with the striking off the agenda of the question regarding the restoration of the rights of the Rhodesian Chess Federation. Those who practise apartheid in their country could not find any advocates, and no one wished to defend a matter which was doomed beforehand to failure. While "documents" sent to Caracas in fact testified—and did not refute at all—the presence of discrimination with regard to the black majority of Rhodesian chess players.

As the reader will already know, for a long time it had not proved possible to regulate strictly the rules for World Championship Matches, and the search for a solution to this question remained one of the FIDE's most difficult problems. Now such a solution was found, thanks, to a great extent, to the clear-cut and realistic position adopted by the World Champion.

A FORMULA WHICH SUITED EVERYONE

There was no lack of possible variations... A clear majority supported the idea of a match to a definite number of wins by one of the players, without any limit on the total number of games. At the same time, everyone realized that the World Champion would either have to be granted an advantage of two points, (as Fischer had demanded) or else he would be deprived altogether of any traditional advantage. Immediately, many began talking about the possibility of a return match. Naturally, the congressmen were not governed by the interests of Karpov...

The Champion took the floor:

"I came to this splendid, but alas, very distant city of Caracas straight from a tournament in Holland. I mention this not so as to remind you of this latest success of mine, but to emphasize that I decided to come, without resting after this difficult tournament, so as to be able to participate in the work of this respected committee. Especially, since the question raised today affects me directly. Here, however, I must also emphasize that to no lesser extent it affects the entire chess world, since nothing influences the development of our game more than matches at the highest level. It will be recalled, for instance, what a boost was given to world chess by the Spassky–Fischer match. I regret that my match with Fischer in 1975 did not take place

* "To discover America" is a Russian idiom, with the meaning here of "to state or find out something that is already obvious". (K.P.N.)

I think that at the time I showed that I wanted to play, and, in spite of everything, was ready to agree to a compromise. Now too I am prepared to demonstrate my desire not to be obstinate over debatable questions. And there are still plenty of such questions, and in the proposals made here there are several variations.

It has to be said that a match of a limited number of games by no means foreshadows a long series of draws. But many talk about this, and wish to see something new. All right, I am prepared to play an unlimited match even after having played such a number of games in tournaments. Some are against the World Champion having a draw 'in reserve'—I also agree with them. I hope that I will not be required to play a return match. But if it should happen that way, that the Challenger wins, then together with him the whole chess world will win too: the millions of chess enthusiasts will receive a new stimulus towards the popularization of our game in the form of a highly interesting return match. I am prepared to support this compromise. And now it is the turn of the other delegates to speak."

During Karpov's speech the other delegates made attempts to applaud him. Only Euwe began talking somewhat uncertainly about granting the Champion the right to a return match only in the event of him losing by 5–6, but evidently he himself immediately sensed that he was on his own. Others, in contrast, suggested corrections "in favour of the Champion". Karpov, who speaks English fairly well, responded without waiting for a translation:

"No, I don't insist on having White in the first game. The drawing of lots is in itself a highly interesting procedure during the Opening Ceremony of a match—why deprive the spectators of this pleasure..."

The return match was to begin not later than a year after the conclusion of the first match... The regulations? They were to remain the same...

The decision was adopted unanimously. The match for the World Championship would be played up to six wins by one of the players, with no limit on the overall number of games; in the event of the World Champion losing, he would have the right to a return match within a year under the same conditions.

Everyone, without exception, applauded. The American Ed Edmondson, who at one time had spoken rather disrespectfully about Karpov, now himself approached this Soviet journalist, and, tapping expressively with his finger-nail on my note-book, asked me to write down the following, word for word:

"Anatoly Karpov has convincingly demonstrated that he is not only the undisputed World Champion, but also a real gentleman. I publicly retract my previous words, and declare that he is the genuine king of chess."

CHAPTER 14

Super-Tournament in Bugojno:
Both Performance and Rehearsal

Between Tilburg and Bugojno five whole months elapsed—a break, the like of which there had not been in Karpov's tournament practice for five years, since 1973.

"I needed this break so as to relax (I had, after all, played a great deal), to look back, and finally, to look more closely ahead—the Final Candidates' Match was over, and it was time to study the games of my future opponent. It is difficult to convey the difficult nature of my appearance in Bugojno. I couldn't disclose my plans before the match for the World Championship, but it was essential to gain some good practical training; it wasn't worth showing my cards, but I very much wanted to occupy a high place in one of the most representative international tournaments in chess history. In short, as Tal so aptly expressed it, it was simultaneously both a performance, and a rehearsal.

(In the following exposition, Anatoly Karpov's account of the event in Bugojno will be supplemented, as it were, by the impressions of Mikhail Tal.)

How the idea became reality ✳ *A successful opening but a hitch in the middlegame* ✳ *Tal, the 'peaceable Hussar'* ✳ *Balashov's birthday* ✳ *Beware: fortieth is fatal* ✳ *On the edge of the abyss* ✳ *An encounter, similar to two others* ✳ *'Hat-tricks' by the rivals* ✳ *Pawns loosen the position* ✳ *Spassky's useful training*

The idea of staging this "super-tournament" was conceived not long before, and not many believed that it would be realized. The point is that the world's top grandmasters plan their appearances in advance, and have everything worked out for almost a year ahead. There is a definite chess élite, whom everyone knows, and the substitution of even one grandmaster from it is always very noticeable. Thus chess enthusiasts in one voice drew attention to the presence among the sixteen participants of the "home players" E. Bukić and M. Vukić. Both are perfectly respectable grandmasters, and have excellent theoretical knowledge in particular, but in Bugojno each of their opponents "planned" in his games against them to score at least one and a half points. Yes, in the world of chess everything is relative... Even such a well-known, experienced and strong grandmaster as another of the Yugoslavs—Borislav Ivkov, insured himself here: "The tournament is very suitable for me—I have the fourteenth-highest rating, so even if I should end up thirteenth, I will not be too upset."

And so, the idea of holding the super-tournament became a reality, thanks to the efforts of the organizers and the fervour of the participants themselves. Robert Hübner had been in the United States for a long time, studying his favourite speciality after finishing University, but he couldn't resist the temptation to play. Very shortly before, Lajos Portisch had successfully concluded the tournament in Wijk aan Zee, where he had come ahead of Korchnoi, but he too did not want to miss out.

Boris Spassky cut short a holiday after the Final Candidates' Match. Bent Larsen and Tony Miles came direct from the tournament in Reykjavik. And only Vlastimil Hort, who had also been playing in Iceland, hesitated at the last minute, and sent a telegram, saying that he was unwell. But he too was persuaded to recover...

The chief controller of the tournament was also well matched with the participants. For prestige, popularity and, if you like, colourfulness, it is difficult to compare the celebrated Argentinian grandmaster Miguel Najdorf with other controllers, who are normally solid and reserved people, decorously installed in their places. Najdorf, armed with a pocket set, would circle rapidly round the tables, and then get down to analysis. He is 68 years old, and virtually all the moves he suggests, according to Tal, are the best.

"The Soviet delegation's journey to the tournament began with a lengthy delay at Moscow Airport: on account of bad weather our flight was not accepted by Belgrade. We eventually made the flight towards evening on 23rd February, and in the Yugoslav Capital went directly to a reception dedicated to the 60th anniversary of the Soviet Army. The following day we made the 5-hour car journey to Bugojno—a small town in Bosna with three industrial firms. A typewriter factory together with the town council financed the grandmaster tournament. The organizers did everything that was in their power, caught literally every word of their guests, and carried out their every desire. Only, the stage of the largest hall in the town proved rather cramped for the sixteen players, as well as the controllers and demonstrators. For the spectators there were quite insufficient places, since interest in the tournament was so great that chess enthusiasts totally choked the hotels in Bugojno and its surroundings... I began the tournament with a win over Larsen, against whom up till then all my games had ended in draws. After three rounds I had 2½ points..."

Tal fills in some of the details:

"Karpov once lost a game to Ivkov. As is well-known, the World Champion does not like 'being in debt', but on this occasion this enviable quality almost let him down. Playing White, the Yugoslav grandmaster did not aim for complications, and the Champion himself had to assume the rôle of 'trouble-maker'. At some point Anatoly overshot the mark, and lost a pawn, but by stubborn defence saved the game on resumption. Karpov also had to adjourn his third game—against Miles. The English grandmaster was outplayed in an ending which many thought to be practically drawn. This endgame made a great impression on the spectators, who filled the hall just as tightly during the adjournment session as during 'normal time', And it is worth mentioning that the adjournment session went on until half past midnight..."

Karpov–Miles
1 ... P–QN3

1 P–QB4 P–QN3 2 P–Q4 P–K3 3 P–Q5 Q–R5 4 N–QB3 B–N5 5 B–Q2 N–KB3 6 P–K3 B×N 7 B×B N–K5 8 Q–B2 N×B 9 Q×N 0–0 10 P–KN3 Q–K5 11 P–B3 Q–N3 12 N–K2 B–N2 13 0–0–0 P–Q3 14 P–KN4 N–Q2 15 P–KR4 Q–B3 16 Q×Q N×Q 17 P–K4 N–Q2 18 N–B3 N–K4 19 B–K2 N–N3 20 K–Q2 N–B5 21 B–Q3 B–R3 22

K–K3 N–N7+ 23 K–Q2 N–B5 24 R–R2 QR–K1 25 P–N3 R–K2 26 K–K3 P–K4 27 N–K2 N×B 28 R×N R–R1 29 N–N3 B–B1

30 P–N4 P–QR4 31 P–R3 P×P 32 P×P R–R5 33 R–QN2 R–K1 34 R–B3 B–Q2 35 P–B5 R(1)–R1 36 P×QP P×P (Diag.)

37 N–B5 B×N 38 NP×B R–R6 39 R–QB2 K–B1 40 R×R R×R+ 41 K–B2 R–N6 42 R–B6 R×NP 43 R×QP K–K2 44 R–QB6 K–Q2 45 P–R5 R–N7+ 46 K–N3 R–N8 47 P–R6 P–N3 48 P×P RP×P 49 R–B2 R–N8+ 50 R–KN2 R–QR8 51 R–KR2 R–R1 52 K–N4 P–B3 53 R–QN2 K–B2 54 R–QB2+ K–N2 55 P–Q6 P–QN4 56 P–Q7 **Resigns**

"There then followed a 'hitch': a postponed game against Balashov, who was unwell, and then a loss to Timman. The Dutch grandmaster played well, whereas I felt indisposed, and the quality of my play was poor. Depression set in... Against Gligorić I failed to win a game in which for a long time I was close to victory, but finally ended up in an inferior position. Then came short draws with Hübner and Tal, and a fighting one with Spassky. In this series there was, it is true, a draw which should perhaps be mentioned particularly...

Yury Balashov fell quite seriously ill, and his enforced 'absenteeism'—the schedule was fairly tight—almost caused him to have to withdraw from the tournament. When it appeared that the illness had been overcome, his temperature again jumped up. In such a situation Mikhail Tal and I considered it not altogether sporting to attempt to defeat our colleague, and by agreeing draws with Balashov I think that we enabled him to gain an essential breathing-space. However, for the Ex-World Champion in this tournament a draw became the normal result in virtually every encounter."

Tal relates:

"Yugoslav journalists were, in their time, the first to supply me with all kinds of nicknames ('The luckiest of them all', The pirate from Riga', and such like). On this occasion they replenished their collection with yet another one—'The peaceable Hussar'. I cannot say that I was particularly pleased with this version, but one can't argue with figures. The fact that for the first time in several years I went through a tournament without defeat served only as formal consolation. I couldn't manage to break this stodgy series of half points, even though at times I resorted to strong measures—my blows proved to be insufficiently firm. My one win in the second half of the tournament (and in the tournament as a whole I only scored two) was gained, one might say, in the cinema."

The point was that, in the small hall of the town's Cultural Centre, half an hour before the start of the adjournment session, the players who were free used to sit down to watch films (such as "Spartacus", "Ivan Vasilievich changes profession", and others). Tal and Balashov decided to watch a film for a short while before beginning the resumption of their unfinished games. Yury was more fortunate, but only slightly: of the fact that Vukić was resigning to him without playing on, Balashov learned while on the way to the Cultural Centre, while Tal learned of Gligorić's capitulation only when he was already in the cinema.

Balashov's birthday—on 12th March he celebrated his 29th—turned out to be very happy for the grandmaster. It is known that many do not like playing on such a day, but for him everything went amazingly well. The day before, he had prepared a first present for himself by completely outplaying Vukić. And what's more, Balashov, who is renowned for his amazing memory, recalled that he had been born at exactly the same time that he wrote down on his scoresheet the winning move. There is no mistake here. Yury after all is a native of Shadrinsk, beyond the Urals, and in all his calculations he took account of the differences of the time zones. On the following day, when his birthday was formally celebrated, Balashov won a quite splendid game against Miles. This, incidentally, enabled him after all his troubles to reach the fifty per cent level.

But what about the World Champion?

"To be honest, I didn't consider myself obliged without fail to take first place, but even so it was time to put in a finishing spurt. Incidentally, the players I was due to meet were those against whom I am normally successful. The first in line was Ljubomir Ljubojević, against whom, it is true, I had not yet won on Yugoslav soil. On this occasion we both played for a win; I was attempting to join the leading group, which Ljubojević was already in, alongside Timman, chasing after Spassky..."

Here it is probably worth describing an instructive incident which occurred in Bugojno, and which, incidentally, influenced Ljubojević's high placing in the tournament. He was provided with a considerable boost by his game with Bukić. After outplaying his opponent, Enver Bukić obtained an overwhelming position. At this point, move forty had been filled in on both scoresheets—both White's and Black's. The demonstrator also indicated that the control move had been made. Bukić could easily have won by any natural move, but to make sure he decided to think about it. When some three minutes later he moved one of his pieces, the flag on his clock had already fallen. It was then that an error was discovered: it was in fact this move that was the control move, the fortieth. It is difficult to convey how upset Bukić was... But a rule is a rule: he was judged to have lost on time, and the appeal jury (Najdorf, Karpov and Larsen) upheld the controller's decision.

A lively battle developed in the Karpov–Ljubojević game, when it suddenly transpired that in an apparently quiet position Black was losing a piece. Following this victory came a game against Vukić with Black...

To catch the leaders in a tournament of such even strength is always difficult. After all, it means that one has to win to order, so to speak, both with White and with Black. And while with White this may work out, with Black against opponents who do not wish to progress, but have sufficient class to hold their own, it is difficult to attain a lively game. And it is doubly difficult when you can't disclose the whole of your arsenal, which is needed for a subsequent, most important matter—a match for the World Championship.

"My desire to win at all costs with Black against Milan Vukić, who planned his tactics cleverly, nearly ended in a major disaster for me. In this, probably the most crucial game of the tournament for me, I was in a losing position for some twenty moves. By desperate manoeuvres I managed to stay on the edge of the abyss, and when at last the Yugoslav grandmaster offered a draw, Black even had a slight advantage, although this was only symbolic in character. But then in my following game, against Vlastimil Hort, I succeeded in winning in highly spectacular style..."

This game has its prehistory. In 1970 Karpov won from a similar position in the Championship of the Russian Federation against the late grandmaster A. Zaitsev. Then a young master, Karpov had suffered much anxiety before gaining the win: later, at home, he tried to find an improvement in this variation. And now here, Hort went and chose this very variation. It is true that he later deviated, but the continuation he chose was known to be unpromising. By an elegant queen manoeuvre, followed by the switching of his rook to the third rank (reminding one of a similar rook manoeuvre by Karpov in a well-known game between the same opponents from the 1971 Alekhine Memorial Tournament), the World Champion forced his opponent's resignation.

Karpov–Hort
Caro-Kann Defence

1 P–K4 P–QB3 2 P–Q4 P–Q4 3 N–Q2 P×P 4 N×P N–Q2 5 N–KB3 KN–B3 6 N×N+ N×N 7 N–K5 B–B4 8 P–QB3 P–K3 9 P–KN4 B–N3 10 P–KR4 P–KR4 11 P–N5 N–Q4 12 N×B P×N (Diag.)

13 Q–B2 K–B2 14 R–R3 N–K2 15 B–QB4 N–B4 16 R–B3 Q–Q2 17 R×N+ P×R 18 Q×P+ K–K2 19 Q–K4 R–K1 20 B–B4 K–Q1 21 Q–K5 R–N1 22 0–0–0 P–KN3 23 R–K1 B–N2 24 Q–N8+ K–K2 25 R×P+ Resigns

Hort began the tournament excellently, for almost two thirds of the distance was in contention for one of the very top places, and even recorded a "hat-trick"—three wins in a row. But then... Then he crashed, and during an almost hour-long T.V. broadcast (such broadcasts devoted to the Bugojno tournament were made each day) he half-jokingly, half-seriously "complained" about Spassky, saying that he simply couldn't play well when they were in the same event. It seems that Spassky is like a bad omen for him, constantly crossing his path. Of course Vlastimil immediately added that he had nothing against Boris personally, and that he even found the Ex-World Champion very likeable.

Yes, in tournaments of such high class it is not often that "hat-tricks" occur. But meanwhile Spassky also gained three wins in a row. To this it may be added that, after a draw with Portisch, the Ex-World Champion won another game, against his customary opponent, Larsen. In the middle of the tournament the Dane suffered a series of serious reversals. Sensing that he was not on form, he adopted against Spassky the resilient Caro-Kann Defence, but the reputation of this opening alone proved insufficient for a successful battle against his constant "conquerer".

"There is an explanation as to why Larsen's play against Spassky is so totally undistinguished. Here the psychological incompatibility of the two players takes effect; the Danish grandmaster is quite unable to maintain his composure in his encounters with the Ex-World Champion. This is why the overall score between them is crushingly in Spassky's favour. After his win over Larsen in Bugojno, Spassky played a series of draws, and the tempo of his advance was curtailed. This allowed me to close up on him, and when, after drawing with Byrne, I managed to defeat Bukić, I drew level with the long-standing leader."

...Grandmaster David Bronstein once half-jokingly "disclosed" the secret of Karpov's victories: "He plays the opening, and then moves pawns backwards and forwards until he wins." And although pawns, as is known, cannot move backwards, and Bronstein's search for originality occasionally leads him onto the wrong track, nevertheless, according to Tal, the formula given above can be applied to the game between Karpov and Bukić. For a long time the Yugoslav grandmaster put up a tenacious defence, but White so "shook" his position, first from one side, and then from the other, that in the end Bukić lost his bearings and overlooked a decisive blow.

Karpov–Bukić
Sicilian Defence

1 P–K4 P–QB4 2 N–KB3 P–Q3 3 P–Q4 P×P 4 N×P N–KB3 5 N–QB3 P–QR3 6 B–K2 P–K4 7 N–N3 B–K2 8 0–0 0–0 9 P–QR4 N–B3 10 K–R1 B–K3 11 P–B4 N–QN5 12 P–B5 B–Q2 13 B–KN5 B–B3 14 B–B3 R–B1 15 Q–K2 P–R3 16 B–R4 P–N3 17 KR–Q1 Q–B2 18 B–N3 B–N2 19 R–Q2 KR–Q1 20 QR–Q1 N–K1 21 P–R4 N–KB3 22 B–B2 N–Q2 23 P–N3 K–B1 24 N–B1 Q–B5 25 Q–K1 Q–B2 26 Q–N1 N–B4 27 N(1)–K2 B–QB3 28 P–N3 Q–N2 29 Q–N2 Q–B2 30 B–K3 B–B3 31 K–R2 Q–K2

32 Q–B2 B–N2 33 B–N2 K–N1 34 Q–B3 K–R2

35 Q–R5 Q–B1 36 R–KB1 N–Q2 37 R–B1 R–B3 38 N–Q5 N×N 39 P×N R(3)–B1 40 B–K4 N–B4 41 B×N R×B 42 P–KN4 **Resigns**

"In the last round, Spassky was playing White against Miles, while I had Black against Portisch. For a player of his class, Portisch made a very poor showing in Bugojno, and at no point was he over the fifty per cent mark. Striving at the last minute to improve his tournament position, Portisch played for a win as White, which suited me, since in turn it enabled me to hope for a win in a full-blooded struggle. After all, I thought that Spassky had real chances of beating Miles; otherwise I might perhaps have been content to draw...

Spassky did not gain any advantage, and, as he later admitted, was prepared to settle for a draw, but then noticed in time the position in my game with Portisch. Seeing that I held an advantage, he returned to his board, and tried to complicate things for Miles. After I had won against Portisch, Spassky in fact succeeded in outwitting his opponent. We thus finished level and shared first place.

When Spassky had lost somewhat submissively to Ljubojević in the first round, one gained the impression that an unenviable rôle was in store for him in this strong company. But very soon it became clear that he had run into excellent form, and that his play was fresh and interesting. And at the end everyone was joking: 'Spassky used the Final Candidates' Match as training, so as to make a successful appearance in Bugojno'."

Portisch–Karpov
Nimzo-Indian Defence

1 P–Q4 N–KB3 2 P–QB4 P–K3 3 N–QB3
B–N5 4 P–K3 0–0 5 B–Q3 P–B4 6 N–B3
P–Q4 7 0–0 P×P 8 B×BP P×P 9 P×P
P–QN3 10 B–KN5 B–N2 11 R–K1 QN–Q2
12 R–QB1 R–B1 13 B–Q3 KB×N 14 P×B
Q–B2 15 P–B4 KR–K1 16 Q–K2 P–KR3
17 B–Q2 B×N 18 Q×B P–K4 (Diag.)
19 Q–N3 P×P 20 R×R+ N×R 21 B–B4
Q–B3 22 B–B5 R–Q1 23 P–KR3 N–B4 24
R–Q1 Q–B3 25 B–N1 Q–K3 26 K–R2 K–B1
27 B–K5 Q×BP 28 Q–B4 N–K3 29 Q–K4

Q–Q4 30 Q–K2 N–Q3 31 P–QR4 N–QB5
32 B–N3 N–B4 33 B–R2 P–Q6 34 Q–K1 Q–Q5
35 P–B3 N–K6 36 R–Q2 R–K1 37 Q–QB1
N×RP 38 K–R1 N–QB4 39 B–B2 Q–K4
40 B–QN1 K–N1 Resigns

* * *

Karpov's success in Bugojno, in one of the most representative tournaments in the history of chess, was reinforced, if one can so express it, by his first place in the "Unofficial Lightning World Championship" (that at any rate is what the Yugoslav press named this event in the town of Mostar). At first it was planned to make this tournament, in which 14 grandmasters took part, a double-round event, but it proved impossible for Karpov to participate in a second cycle, and he flew off urgently to Leningrad...

CHAPTER 15

Looking Ahead

FIDE NAMES THE PHILIPPINES

"I have already spoken about that which complicated my task in the Yugoslav Super-Tournament, but there were also other problems of a psychological nature. On 2nd March, when the event in Bugojno was in full swing, the date expired by which time both participants in the match for the World Championship had to send in their demands, indicating the venue where they would like the match to be played, and it is quite natural that during those days my thoughts wandered away from Yugoslavia. Dr Euwe, the FIDE President, had no reason to hurry, after receiving the two telegrams—according to the agreement in force, he had two whole weeks in which to announce his final decision. Besides, following the telegrams, the participants in the match were required to send 'confirming' letters. But when on 2nd March I went to the Post Office to send off my letter, there was news already awaiting me there: the International Chess Federation had named the town of Baguio in the Philippines as the venue for the coming match. From a legal point of view, Euwe was correct, since Korchnoi's request had named, in order of preference, Austria, the Philippines and Holland, while the telegram sent by the Soviet Chess Federation had given West Germany and the Philippines, and thus the 'desires coincided' at the second choice—the Philippines. But why didn't Euwe want to wait for my letter? What if it had not confirmed the telegram from the USSR Chess Federation, or had not been sent at all? After all, then the FIDE President could have found himself in an extremely ticklish situation...

I nevertheless sent my letter, and of course it corresponded fully with the request sent by the Soviet Chess Federation. Immediately there came a joint proposal from the chess organizations of West Germany and Austria, who were both prepared to stage part of the match in each of these two European countries. (Incidentally, since 1927, matches for the World Champion had been held only in Europe, with its temperate climate). However, everything remained unchanged—the 1978 match was to be held in the Philippines, in the town of Baguio, which is situated 250 kms from the Capital of the country, Manila...

At the time that this decision was taken, I didn't yet know that my constant trainer and old friend would not be with me in the Philippines, and that only a few days later we would be accompanying Semion Abramovich Furman on his last journey...

A LIFE WITHOUT AN ENDING (The story of a trainer, the work of whom continues)

Well-known Soviet grandmaster, outstanding chess theorist, wonderful trainer—these words will stand alongside his name and the dates of his life (1920–1978).

Behind these words lie years of successful appearances in events of the most varied class: from competitions in workers' collectives, when 18-year-old Leningrad metal-worker Semion Furman really became fascinated by chess, to Championships of his country and major international tournaments.

He only needed to touch the pieces once, whereupon inspiration took possession of his whole being, and he worked ecstatically at chess. It is difficult to find a branch of opening theory which escaped his attention. What a worker he was! Whole regions of opening theory (Ruy Lopez, Queen's Gambit, Nimzo-Indian, Grünfeld Defence—no, one can't list them all) he worked on for years, scrupulously and fundamentally.

And he generously shared the fruits of his labour. When before an important match any of the top players began to have doubts, Furman would extract from the reserves of his phenomenal memory another "sacred" variation, and in a calm quiet voice would pronounce his piece: "Yes I've done some work on that. . ." And in the USSR team, for which he worked as trainer, any player, even one of world renown, was prepared to follow his advice—such was the "guarantee of quality". Why, if he was so generous, did he never exhaust his reserves; why, if he was giving away, did he nevertheless become richer? Because he continued working!

In the tournament at the West German town of Bad Lauterberg, Furman won a brilliant game against Gligorić. The Yugoslav grandmaster, an acknowledged specialist on the opening, was distressed: "Surely I haven't been playing a bad variation of the King's Indian Defence all these years?!" Furman merely smiled enigmatically, and later explained:

"I lost to him once in a USSR–Yugoslavia Match, and since then have been dreaming of revenge. At last it happened that I had to play Gligorić with White. . ."

The right of the first move in his hands was a weapon of destructive power. While he was still a master, it was written of him: "If Furman played all his games with White, he would be comparable with the World Champions." A collection of Furman's games has not yet appeared, and this is a gap which would be worth filling, if only because such a collection would in itself be a splendid text book of chess. Perhaps it would be opened by his spectacular game against Smyslov, which won the brilliancy prize in the 1949 USSR Championship? Or perhaps some other game, a positional one, against some other outstanding grandmaster?

Players will learn from his games, without even knowing that when he played many of them he was unwell. Just as his opponents did not know. Once, in a winning position against Tal, he moved his pieces so slowly in time trouble, that for no obvious reason he lost on time. Only very recently we learned from his family that his hand was numb from neuralgia. But it also happened that sometimes his opponents knew. . . He began one tournament very badly, fell ill, and lost several games in a row. An old friend came up to him. They had prepared together for tournaments, had notebooks on opening theory in common, and did not hide their weak points from each other, as a result of which they would normally draw their games. Not looking Furman in the eye, the grandmaster warned that the following day he was going to play for a win against him. Furman nodded, as if to say "I understand". The following day, he gave of his all, and won. He won in this one game alone.

He became a grandmaster in 1966, when he took first place in the Open Championship of Czechoslovakia in the town of Harrachov. Immediately after this he rushed off to a USSR Championship Semi-Final, from where, after he had suffered four defeats in a row and lost 17 kilos in weight, he underwent a very serious operation. Many years later, this incurable disease with its absurd name was to return and overcome this exceptionally life-loving person.

But at that time he was restored to health in 1967, and won a strong tournament at the Polish town of Polanica-Zdroj.

According to a widely-held opinion, a player who is constantly engaged in training work deteriorates as a practical player. Furman, an honoured trainer of the USSR, did much to strengthen the position of the supporters of the opposite point of view, of which formerly there were very few. Madrid (1973), Portorož and Ljubljana (1975), Bad Lauterberg (1977) —in all these major international tournaments, where the winner was Anatoly Karpov, the third prize-winner was Semion Furman (the second prize-winners varied).

Chess correspondents remarked on the unusual nature of their collaboration: not only did Furman help Karpov with his play, but there was also a reverse connection—as a result of his association with Karpov, Furman himself gained his second wind, and he showed greater practical strength than before.

While agreeing with this in principle, Furman once admitted:

"When Karpov is there, I mobilize myself to the full, and play better. You see, if I play badly I won't have the same authority. How can I then start giving him advice?"

As regards authority, his doubts were unnecessary. Here are the World Champion's words:

"I often heard questions being asked about the rôle of a trainer in that period when, as they say, the pupil surpassed his teacher. But it is naïve to suppose that in an imaginary match with Furman I would have won easily. This is demonstrated by Semion Abramovich's highly successful appearances when he was well over fifty. And as regards theoretical knowledge, here Furman was superior to the majority of world-famous grandmasters."

Words which do honour both to the Champion, and to his trainer.

Furman, although good-natured, was, strangely enough, a very quiet man. It is said that when he first accompanied home his future wife, to whom he had just been introduced, Semion Abramovich did not utter a single word. The girl enquired as to the reason for his silence. In reply he automatically said: "Ask me some questions". He was accustomed to preparing only for lectures, and to constantly answering all sorts of questions about chess. Furman rarely gave interviews on so-called general topics, and I was highly astonished when on one occasion abroad he said to a journalist that he had two sons. After enjoying the impact he had made, he explained seriously: "It is true that they have different surnames—Aleksandr Furman and Anatoly Karpov." He loved both lads whole-heartedly.

But when he used to watch Anatoly playing, he would keep his feelings deeply concealed. I can recall perhaps only that one instance in Milan, when he did not contain himself, but expressed aloud his anxiety during the last game of Karpov's match with Portisch.

Although methodical and slightly deliberate, he was, to coin a phrase, absolutely non-standard. Frequently it was simply impossible to guess his next step, since he in no way corresponded to his outward stereotype of an accurate and reserved person, from whom one could expect a banal decision.

Furman was surrounded by young people, who were drawn towards this radiant person. He was respected for his warmth, his knowledge, and his seniority. But, being extremely enthusiastic, even venturesome, among young people he did not look out of place. We were once fixing our bait before going fishing on a lake. The waves began to get up, and we wondered whether we ought to go out in boats in such bad conditions. But he was the first to the oars, ahead even of a physical training instructor.

He constantly took upon himself a big work load ("Until we finish, no one is going home!"). Karpov alone could attempt to stop him, because in life, in contrast to chess, the teacher and pupil exchanged places—the junior became the senior. In Karpov's diary we read: "Yesterday Sema (this is what Karpov sometimes called his trainer—in his absence, of course—A.R.) again deceived me: he sat up until four a.m. It is becoming simply agony for him to get up in the morning, and he is totally unconcerned for his health. I gave him a severe telling-off." This entry was made during a USSR team tournament, when everyone came and consulted with Furman, asked him to "have a look at this adjourned position", or simply wanted to enjoy his pleasant company... And he, being so kind, was unable to refuse anyone...

But he could also be angry. At the Final Candidates' Match in Belgrade, Furman went along to size up the play and behaviour of Karpov's future opponent. As is well-known, the match was held in an atmosphere where sportsmanship did not take even second place. A foreign reporter incautiously asked Furman how he, as the Champion's trainer, would have reacted, if similar psychological pressure had been put on Karpov. You should have seen Furman at that moment! He clenched the fingers on both hands, and drew in sharply: "I would, I would..." Then he breathed out, and surprisingly calmly rapped out: "We wouldn't have allowed this."

Full of ideas and specific plans, Furman hurried off home, to Karpov—to continue their preparations. He was stopped by the doctors. He didn't give in ("You've got the wrong man"). But doctors are stronger than a patient. And as yet this disease is stronger than doctors...

He caught the news from Yugoslavia of the grandmaster tournament in Bugojno from a radio, which he kept by him in hospital. Prior to the last round he managed to be happy for a while. "Well done, Tolya! You've saved your openings, not given away our plans, and made an excellent showing." He didn't separate himself from Karpov, and as usual said: "We... Our..." His feelings and his awareness of duty always lived inseparably in him.

The grievous news arrived during the Closing Ceremony of the International Tournament in Bugojno. The grandmasters at once stood up in memory of their colleague. But one could re-alize fully what had happened only by glancing at the World Champion—in this moment of silence his eyes said everything.

...Semion Abramovich Furman couldn't bear being alone, and used to mock himself:

"I am like an isolated pawn—my strength is in the middlegame, when there are many pieces around, and all together we embark on an attack. But in the endgame the board becomes deserted, and they attempt to get rid of the weak, lone pawn."

But in his life there was no ending, around him it was never deserted, and the game did not end. The game which he considered the main vocation in his life. The game, which continues...

MYSTERIES OF THE CHESS COEFFICIENT

In recent years, the organizers of some international tournaments have been trying to assemble events consisting solely of grandmasters (seeing that the number of holders of the title is constantly on the increase...).

Milan 1975, Leningrad 1977, Tilburg 1977, Bugojno 1977. In each of these tournaments only grandmasters played, and three of the events were of the 14th category of difficulty on the FIDE scale. In all these "super-tournaments" Anatoly Karpov took part, and only once did he fail to reach the finishing tape ahead of the others.

The average ratings of the events listed were very high: Milan—2599, Leningrad—2551, Tilburg—2582, and Bugojno—2588.

All systems of individual coefficients are based on not particularly complicated formulae, which take account of some initial level of the participants in a tournament, the composition of the event, the number and results of the games played, and in the end give, in some arbitrary mathematical form, the present practical strengths of the players. This at first sight highly laborious calculating operation does not occupy a great deal of time. Professor Árpád Élő, who is in charge of FIDE rating questions, has said that on the computation by his formulae of 220 major tournaments, and the compilation of a list of individual coefficients, or rating-list, for 1300 top players, he spent 160 hours (it will be understood that this is mainly preparatory work, since the actual "machine time" of a computer is much less).

The word "rating" in English has several meanings, of which for us the most appropriate is "appraisal", or even "technical power", or, if you wish, "individual coefficient". Once a year, Prof. Élő publishes a rating list of the leading players in the world, in which account is taken of international tournaments, as well as the most important national tournaments. In the USSR we have also begun to calculate individual coefficients—specially for Soviet players.

Why, you may ask, calculate individual coefficients separately for Soviet players, when Prof. Élő already does the same in parallel? For the basic reason that Prof. Élő is concerned with grandmasters, but by no means with all players of master strength. In our rating list, account is taken of all serious tournaments held in the USSR, which is especially important for talented young players, for the reason that their basic training ground is Soviet events. Moreover, the most important tournaments in our country (and often, incidentally, abroad) are held at the very end of the year, and for twelve whole months players "carry" a coefficient which does not correspond to their present-day practical strength: Prof. Élő produces his rating list, rounded off to the nearest five, in January, and is normally able to include only events finishing before 31st October.

The system of individual coefficients has its drawbacks, of course. There is a certain time lag—a player can raise his rating, and then play rarely, but nevertheless remain among the élite. The importance of the event is not taken into account—the weighting of games played in the World Championship cycle should somehow be increased. The battle for first place in a tournament should also be reflected (and also, particularly, in a match)—after all, a player who wishes to be successful may adopt special tactics so as simply to finish ahead of a rival, rather than gain the maximum number of points—in short, first place is first place. But these are now problems for mathematicians. In general, the introduction of a system of individual coefficients is undoubtedly a progressive step.

The few remaining opponents of the new system usually put forward a sort of moral argument: they say that the assignment of such figures, like inventory items, may offend such creative people as chess players ("Tell me your rating, and I'll tell you who you are"). But didn't our antediluvian classification system, with its unsavoury "confirmed" and "unconfirmed" titles, also offend?! Incidentally, the system of individual coefficients should by its very nature assist in the battle against colourless draws, since at the board a player will want to raise his coefficient and at the same time lower that of his rival—after all, it may happen that, by ratings, teams begin to be picked, and the right granted to participate in international tournaments, etc. etc. (Here it is worth recalling one further interpretation of the English word "rating"—"reprimand", or "scolding"). More soundly-based and objective criteria may therefore come to take the place of subjective appraisals.

In Professor Élő's system of coefficients, it has so happened that boundaries, approximate of course, have begun to take shape. 2400 is a fairly strong master, 2500 and above is a grandmaster, and 2600 is a top-class grandmaster. All this, however, is very arbitrary... And nowadays the excessively increasing number of bearers of the highest titles demands a toughening of the criteria. But there is another positive feature of the system—if so desired, it allows for the classification norms to be regulated.

A sprinter who today runs a hundred metres in 10.2 seconds will, for instance, be expected tomorrow to produce a result nearer to ten seconds dead. But it is harder for him to "discard" one tenth of a second, than it is for a sprinter who has covered the same distance in 11.2 seconds to discard half a second. Exactly the same happens with the individual coefficients of chess players. The mathematical formula by which they are calculated demands of someone with a rating of 2700 that he produce constant and excessively high "points" results. The higher a grandmaster rises, the more difficult it is for him to achieve each new (and maintain the old—remember: "reprimand"!) 5–10 points of his rating.

The record here belongs to Fischer—2780, a fantastic figure, which was attained after his outstanding victories in successive matches over Taimanov, Larsen, Petrosian and Spassky. The point is that Prof. Élő calculated Fischer's rating over a period of a whole year, wholesale, so to speak. But after all, that Fischer who defeated Taimanov by a score of 6–0 was then bound to defeat Larsen by something like 5–1, and after his "clean" score against Larsen he was simply obliged to win against Petrosian by roughly that score which in fact occurred— $6\frac{1}{2}$–$2\frac{1}{2}$. And if Fischer's coefficient had been calculated after each successive match, when new and higher demands would have been put forward, it is unlikely that he would have attained the summit of 2780. But mathematics gave a "piece bonus" to that Fischer who was only just embarking on his swift ascent, and did not take account of the fact that at each stage of the ascent the "target" should have been raised.

Karpov's personal record is 2740 (this was his coefficient calculated after the tournament in Las Palmas). All other players have stopped at a respectful distance from the 2700 mark...

"I am not hypnotized by my Élő coefficient, and I by no means consider that I am obliged to increase it in every tournament. The individual coefficient is not a stimulus, but a visiting card—and that's all! It is another matter that a visiting card should be as imposing as possible. And even so, it seems to me much more important to gather a bigger collection of 'Chess Oscars' that Fischer has."

THE TRANSFORMATION OF "UNCLE OSCAR"

On the whole, chess journalists consider their occupation to be almost as ancient as the game itself, about which they write. And for this reason the ways of popularizing the game used to change as rarely as the rules of chess. But the spirit of the times has affected even journalists writing on chess themes, and following the example of their colleagues in sport, they have also begun marking the departing year by voting for the best grandmasters...

In the Spanish town of Palma, the capital of the Balearic Islands, and situated on the largest of them—Mallorca, at the end of the year top international tournaments used to be held, the strong composition of which would draw the attention of the sporting press. In December

1967 the permanent director of these tournaments, Jorge Puig, called a meeting of the correspondents who had gathered there, and under his chairmanship they chose the best player of the departing year. He was named as Bent Larsen, who was awarded the "Chess Oscar".

Why Oscar? Chess players borrowed the name of the prize from film makers, who themselves tell a rather amusing story with regard to its name. It appears that when a statuette, which was about to be awarded for an outstanding film production, was first displayed in a hall of the American Academy of Art, it—the statuette, which depicted a man—was seen by a certain actress. "Good heavens, he's just like my Uncle Oscar!", she exclaimed. Things went on from there, until they finally reached chess players.

Incidentally, at first the "Chess Oscar" itself corresponded in some way to its name, in that it depicted a small male figure seated on a mule. Many associated this portrayal with Sancho Panza, although, strictly speaking, the peasant on a mule appeared in Spanish history long before the heroes of Cervantes.

In 1968 and 1969 the "Chess Oscar" was awarded to Boris Spassky (and starting at this time, journalists began determining not only the very best grandmaster, but also the "top ten" of the year). In 1970, 1971 and 1972 the silver award went to Robert Fischer. Note, incidentally, that these grandmasters became the prize-winners just at the time when they had the most ambitious intentions, when they were eying the chess throne. But as soon as they became World Champion, the triumphant years changed into "the years of the quiet sun"...

The association of journalists writing on chess topics has been recognized by the International Chess Federation. For ten years the association was headed by Jorge Puig, then came a change of leadership, but the President—now honorary—as before sends questionnaires out to the most authoritative journalists from various countries. These questionnaires give the results of 25 leading players. It is stipulated that the list does not include any player who in that year has won less than 12 games against grandmasters, and account is taken not only of the percentage of points scored, but also of the standard of the tournament.

Those who are unfamiliar with these essential conditions risk finding themselves in a curious situation. One "general-sports" journalist wrote knowledgeably: "In chess periodicals, for instance, I happened to come across rather superficial opinions on the foreign opponents of our leading grandmasters... Was this why in 1969 we placed Fischer last among the ten strongest players in the world?" "We" did not put Fischer on the list at all, since at that time he was not taking part in any major events. There were not many journalists who failed to adhere to the voting conditions, but those who did so certainly didn't put the American grandmaster in last place—it was for this reason that the total number of votes cast for Fischer was sufficient only to place him (and this against the rules) in the first ten.

...International tournaments, for all their desire to become traditional, rarely manage to maintain their residence permits in one town. Since 1973 the tournaments on the island of Mallorca have, unfortunately, "departed this life". And, as has already been said, Anatoly Karpov was awarded his first "Chess Oscar" at the tournament in Madrid. It was then that an outward transformation of "Uncle Oscar" took place: the prize depicted the coat-of-arms of the Spanish Capital—a little bear, clambering up a tree. Subsequent "Oscars" have symbolized the coat-of-arms of Barcelona, the town which has taken upon itself the organizational bother of determining the best chess player of the year. Its statuette depicts... a lady with an umbrella.

When World Champion Anatoly Karpov received his fourth "Oscar" in a row, he said:

"I think that public opinion was considerably influenced by the results of the USSR Championship—the main tournament of the past year, 1976. I am happy that I was able to win that tournament, and happy that I have been able to surpass the achievement of American grandmaster Robert Fischer, three-time winner of the 'Oscar'."

On becoming World Champion, Anatoly Karpov remained the best and most popular grandmaster in the world. One might even perhaps propose a new form of name for the "Oscar": "The Karpov Benevolent Society".

News of the award of the fifth successive "Chess Oscar" (it so happened that Soviet journalists did not take part in this poll) came just at the time when Anatoly was defending his diploma project in the Economics Faculty of Leningrad University.

In Place of an Epilogue

ON THREE PILLARS

One of the directors of the Leningrad State University once said: "Karpov is noted for his terrific sense of purpose, capacity for hard work, and self-discipline. These are qualities which are needed by young people, and Anatoly's example is exceptionally necessary and useful. Futurologists call Economics the science of the 21st century, and I hope that this final-year student, who at the beginning of the next century will be at the height of his creative powers, will in science too achieve significant success."

Karpov is indeed very fond of Economics:

"When I changed Universities from Moscow to Leningrad, I considered very seriously my choice of Faculty. I was attracted by Economics, which enables one to lean on mankind's common experience, and on the sum of knowledge accumulated by whole generations. Besides, there is a very important similarity between Economics and Mathematics—both fields of activity demand strict logic. There is another similarity in the search for optimal solutions. '

Value and importance of spare time ✳ *All forms of study* ✳
Chess is life, but life is not only chess ✳ *Rome holiday* ✳
Support of the State

Anatoly Karpov's diploma thesis was entitled: "Spare time and its economic significance under Socialism". There it is stated, among other things, that: "...ways of increasing spare time have on the whole been studied in sufficient detail. But the problems of filling it, or, as it is customary to say, using it effectively, remain a 'sealed secret'."

At the defence of his diploma thesis, to a rather unexpected question by his opponent as to how the grandmaster himself solved such problems in his every-day life, Anatoly Karpov replied:

"Since for me personally it is difficult to increase the amount of my spare time, I attempt to utilize it in the most rational way."

And so that this reply should not appear to be a mere witticism, we give a further quotation from his thesis:

"Activity is measured in time, but also, time is measured in activity. In other words, the degree of saturation of spare time is an important social and moral category. A person's psychological satisfaction (or, on the contrary, dissatisfaction) depends to a great extent on the genuine fullness of his hours and minutes (including, of course, his spare time), as does the 'economic value' of his activity and its social worth."

"But nevertheless, time is not elastic, it cannot be stretched. So in that case where do you hide your 'psychological dissatisfaction?' "—this was the question now of a journalist.

"That is not a simple question to answer. In our time a person must overcome a number of temptations on the road to finding himself. It frequently happens that, straight from youth, there is a mass of things which at first sight seem important and absorbing. Many events occur in the world around you, and what's more, they are highly interesting. You don't want to miss anything, and you hope to have time for everything. This is self-deception, of which it is essential to rid oneself as soon as possible. It is here that the inner voice of reason must operate. You must choose what for you is the most important. I would even go as far as to say: the most vitally essential."

"Excuse me, but you yourself said that your life is chess."

"That's true. Chess is my life, but you know, my life is not only chess, and I don't live alone in the world. I think", Karpov continued with a smile, "that I have found an optimum solution for myself in the philosophy of the ancients, who considered that their world was supported on three pillars.* My entire life is the same: education, public service, and of course, chess."

"Education is becoming the decisive factor, determining the place of a person in the system of production, and in the life of society"—again an extract from the diploma thesis. And further on: "...the assimilation and utilization of cultural values. This relates to all forms of study, reading, listening to the radio and watching television, and visits to the cinema, the theatre and museums. The aim of this is the enrichment and development of personality." The reader should not be confused by the fact that "all forms of study" are placed alongside, for instance, the cinema: Karpov has in mind study in the broadest sense of the word—on attainment of a higher education diploma, or any other sort, the education of a person does not come to an end. Further on we read: "...creativity (scientific, technological, artistic, sporting) social work... Through these the self-assertion and self-realization of an individual are fulfilled, a new type of person is formed, and his creative potential is developed and realized."

...I have always been astonished by the furiously rapid tempo at which he lives, as he constantly hurries somewhere and greedily soaks in the surrounding world.

I cannot forget how, after the strong and lengthy Milan International Tournament, the obliging hosts organized a week-long tour of Italy. The idea was that the "Milan examination" should be followed by the "Rome holiday". But Karpov turned this holiday into a genuine race for new impressions. During an event he considers it essential to sleep well, but here every day at first light he would rouse his tired companions and urge them: "Come on, hurry up, or we won't have time to see anything." And he himself found time to go everywhere. The Coliseum and St. Peter's Cathedral, the Vatican Museum and the famous leaning tower of Pisa, the Florence Picture Galleries... And this is what happens all the time, wherever he is.

On returning from Venezuela through the United States of America, he managed in just a few days to give a simultaneous display and public lectures in Washington, to visit the Aeronautics and Space Museum, the Arlington Cemetery, the Capitol (at a session of the Senate), and the White House. He also met many interesting people, and spent time in the company of a group of distinguished Soviet international correspondents, among whom he already had old friends and supporters—V. Zorin, M. Sturua and others... He learned many interesting and instructive facts from a conversation with the Soviet Ambassador A. F. Dobrinin, who,

* Literally 'on three whales', from Russian mythology. (K.P.N.)

incidentally, is a connoisseur and fine judge of chess. After an evening at which Andrey Voz-
nesensky, who was also in the USA, read some of his verse, the Ambassador's wife noticed
the excited but clearly fatigued appearance of Anatoly Karpov, and advised him to relax,
if only for a short time, at the Soviet Embassy's country house. After thanking her, the World
Champion promptly enquired as to whether it wouldn't be possible to utilize this time for an
excursion to Philadelphia—the Rodin Museum was there—and besides, the town lay only
"very slightly" off our route to New York. Dobrinin, who was unable to restrain a smile, asked
the Cultural Advisor to make the appropriate arrangements, and presented Karpov with a
splendidly produced album of reproductions from the American National Gallery. Anatoly
did not put this album down throughout the several hours of the journey, managing, however,
to enquire about anything of interest that was flying past the windows of our car.

"In Washington we saw the splendid monument to the Marines, didn't we? Well in Philadelphia we will shortly see several Rodin originals—among them 'The Burghers of Calais'.
How is it that you aren't interested in how this museum of the great French sculptor came to
be in America, and is now barely inferior to his Paris Museum?", Karpov asked in surprise,
whereupon he related its highly interesting history.

On our very first night in New York, when legs were collapsing and eyes closing, he climbed
to the 107th floor of the highest building of the biggest city in the world, and then began dis-
covering how from the engineering point of view one explains a 5-metre oscillation of the top
of this building...

Anatoly Karpov knows the specific nature of the conditions of life in many countries of the
world, and is interested in their customs and laws. He has met many prominent public officials
from abroad, and has conversed with the heads of a number of States... But nevertheless,
the main thing remains his contact with ordinary people. Through television he has played
against German chess enthusiasts, and scored instructive victories in the tournament specially
organized and filmed for English T.V.. Anatoly Karpov has represented our country at numerous press conferences, and at festivities held by the newspapers *Volksstimme*, *L'Unità*, *L'Huma-
nité*"... At these and similar press conferences he is asked the most varied questions, and the
World Champion's replies invariably provoke the same reaction—laughter and applause.

"Radio Canada": "From where did you acquire such talent?" Reply: "As has already been
stated here,—from the Urals".

"Belgian Television": "In the sporting world a virtual 'personality cult' has been built up
around you. What do you think of this?" Reply: "I realize that this cult, as you have deigned
to call it, will disappear when my victories come to a halt. But the support of my State will all
the same remain."

Le Monde (Paris): "At your age you are constantly having to represent an enormous country.
Don't you find this too heavy a burden?" Reply: "Every real person living in Soviet society is
prepared for this."

> *Meeting with Comrade Brezhnev* ✳ *Ambassador of the Soviet Union*
> ✳ *Most important present* ✳ *We are all related from childhood* ✳
> *Story of a certain correction* ✳ *The echo must not be late*

Here now is a question asked by a correspondent from our magazine *Student Meridian*:
"Your life is extremely full. And even so, there must be events which you have experienced
with particular happiness and enthusiasm?"

"The high spots? Yes, my life is pretty full, and there are plenty of events. And one of the chief such events does not even relate directly to chess. I am thinking of the meeting I had with Leonid Ilyich Brezhnev, whom I visited as a member of the Komsomol Central Committee. The conversation that we had made a great impression on me. As a chess player I was happy to learn that Leonid Ilyich is familiar with our chess problems and events. In this I saw a further indication of that deep attention which is given to the development of chess in our country.

Another event was the adoption of the new USSR Constitution. At that time I was a long way from home, in Venezuela. But even there, all of us Soviet people carefully followed announcements in the press. Chess players from other countries are usually apolitical, and are not normally concerned either about international relations, or about the events inside their own country. But here, even among them, interest was aroused. And this inspired pride in our great motherland."

During one of his triumphal tours through the countries of Western Europe, he was awarded the Gold Medal of Paris, and the Medals of Le Havre and La Rochelle. The leaders of the French Chess Federation all became members of the Franco–USSR Society. At that time the Executive President of the Franco–USSR Society, Guy Desson, stated: "If others were to follow his example in devoting so much attention to the problems of strengthening friendship and mutual understanding between peoples, the cause of peace would gain significantly. Anatoly Karpov is a wonderful ambassador for the Soviet Union."

But he is not only an ambassador, he is first and foremost a citizen of the Soviet Union. Both at home, in Leningrad, and on his trips across the country, Karpov frequently gives lectures in factories and to students; he has been to the Urals, to the Vladimir Region, to Armenia and Georgia... Especially memorable was his visit to Siberia and Kamchatka. As a genuinely public-spirited person, he not only played chess and talked about it; Karpov also took notice of other things: "I must say that I was very struck by the concern shown for visitors to the beautifully-built and lovingly-looked-after Central Komsomol Stadium in Krasnoyarsk. For this it is sufficient to see the genuine museum-like cleanliness and exemplary order which reign in all the buildings of this stadium."

In the Pioneers' Palace in Petropavlovsk–Kamchatsky, a big event was being held: the 17th Regional Pioneers' Rally. The best of the best gathered here from all over Kamchatka. The motto of the large Assembly read: "We take our example from the Communists". The children were delighted to receive the news that they would be visited by "the" Karpov. In one of the Kamchatka newspapers at the time, it was written: "The World Champion has left us with a most important present—a yearly mass tournament for the Anatoly Karpov Prize", and in another it was reported that the World Champion, together with a third-year pupil, had cut the ribbon at the opening of a new chess club named after him.

The organization of events for chess enthusiasts, the opening of new clubs—in conversations with the local authorities he always brings up these questions. He works enthusiastically on the editorial boards of "*Student Meridian*" and the weekly "*64*". He endeavours to stress the importance of chess culture on the pages of newspapers, particularly "*Pravda*" and "*Leningrad Pravda*", for which he frequently writes in his rôle as chess correspondent. Here is what he wrote in "*Pravda*", in one of the articles which played a highly important part in solving a most serious problem for our chess movement: "Specialized literature is produced in too small numbers, and is not always what chess players want. I received a letter recently from a certain lover of the ancient game. He stated that he had wanted to acquire a book on chess, but that he had been told in a shop that the particular book was in short supply, and was being sold only to experienced players; for them, it was supposedly more necessary. But how does one attain mastery without the use of books? We end up with a vicious circle... I have deliberately not named the town where this happened, since everywhere there is a shortage of chess literature."

In that same article Karpov wrote: "It is gratifying that the Sports Committee of the USSR and the Komsomol Central Committee are devoting considerable attention to chess, and especially to the rising generation. The Komsomol sponsors events in Pioneers' Palaces, as well as the 'White Rook' Competition... The results have not been long in showing—more and more children are being introduced to chess, and their mastery is growing."

As the French writer Saint-Exupery said, we are all related from childhood.

...The fine hall of the Moscow Pioneers' Palace is crowded. Several hundreds of hushed children are listening to the great Mikhail Botvinnik.

"Soon the computer will be playing very strongly, and by no means everyone will be able to compete successfully with it..."

A little pioneer puts his hand up in the air. His question is full of entreaty:

"Comrade grandmaster, but will people be allowed to play chess?"

There comes a relieved sigh from the entire hall: "Yes!!"

The enchanting world of chess attracts youngsters. But somewhere nearby the thumping of a football is heard, pressing them to go out onto the street, the hollow blows of the ice-hockey puck ring out, and even on T.V. one can hear the clinking of the figure-skaters. And, encouraged by parents, other things have begun to appear, apparently strict and severe, but also interesting, if one looks more closely: mathematics, physics, various languages, music... A "competition of interests" is beginning.

An emotional lady spectator, looking around the enormous tournament hall and the festively dressed public, keeps on repeating that she would like to see her boy on the chess stage, open to the whole world. The dramatic outcome of a game causes her to sigh sorrowfully: "No, it's too hard a life, this chess playing". But in chess, tragedy for one of the players almost invariably means triumph for the other. And perhaps a few moments later this mother will again change her mind, when she sees how the hall gives a thunderous ovation in honour of the Champion, and how an enthusiastic admirer runs out to the happy winner with a bouquet of flowers.

This is, so to speak, canvassing by personal example.

Anatoly Karpov, who has been a delegate at two Komsomol Congresses, and is now a member of the Central Committee, has twice received awards "For active work in the Komsomol". What does this work consist of?

"I consider my most important duty to be the propaganda of chess among young people. After all, it is in the continuity of generations, and the constant concern of experienced players for the young, that the strength of the Soviet Chess School lies."

In the yearly competitions for the prize of Soviet World Champions held under the motto of the "White Rook", Pioneer teams made up of pupils from classes three to seven participate, and they take in thousands and thousands of schools from all over the Soviet Union. The newspaper "*Komsomolskaya Pravda*" stages another highly interesting event for Pioneers' Palaces. Each team in the final is represented not only by six schoolboys and one schoolgirl, but also by a "famous captain"—a grandmaster and former pupil from a Pioneers' Palace. The grandmasters give simultaneous displays with clocks against all the teams (except their own, of course). The points scored by the children against the other captains are added to the points gained by their own captain. Chess players rarely remember their games from child-hood. But each of the young players will undoubtedly remember for their whole lives these games against outstanding grandmasters. A display with clocks by a great master is a lesson which you can then describe to your young compatriots, when you return to your home town...

At the first such tournament in 1972, Anatoly Karpov gladly accepted an invitation to be captain of the team from the Chelyabinsk Pioneers' Palace. Like Mikhail Tal with his compatriots from Riga, Karpov lived in the hotel with his team, and spent all his spare time with the children, who were only some six to seven years younger than him—a hardly noticeable difference, if you take into account his outwardly youthful appearance.

There was an interesting episode which caught the attention of those present at the Closing Ceremony. In many respects it was a revealing incident.

The tournament is over. Photographers quickly line up the children in front of their various cameras, efficiently bringing forward the smallest onto the front row. And suddenly there is a hitch. A dark-haired little boy in enormous glasses and red scarf stubbornly hides behind his friends, who are embarrassed and can't do anything with him. When Misha Moskovich is forcibly dragged to the front, he bursts into tears...

Ex-World Champion Mikhail Tal, captain of the Riga team, is confused. Little Misha bitterly complains to his bigger namesake: "The grandmasters incorrectly gave me a nought..."

Smyslov had not participated in the adjudication of his adjourned position with the lad, but Tal himself was absolutely in agreement with the chief controller.

"Mishenka, your position is quite lost", Tal tries to persuade the lad. "As soon as the white knight reaches e5..."

They began playing blindfold. The one, wiping away his tears, entered into this unjust adult world, while the other stood helplessly, like a kind father, smiling. They were cut short by the bells hurrying people along to the Closing Ceremony. In short, they were in time trouble. At the final bell Tal looked around uneasily and said:

"I think that the wrong position has been adjudicated. Where are the controllers, if it's not too late?"

Behind the curtains of the stage, Tal quickly went up to Botvinnik:

"Mikhail Moiseevich, you remember the knight which went from f3 to e5; well it should be at g1."

The latter understood immediately. Both looked carefully at one another, as if their match for the World Championship was still continuing. Then Botvinnik, thinking his own thoughts, said severely that the incorrect position had been given to him by... by... well, who had given it to him? Tal was more decisive than in the return match—whoever had given it in, the lad wasn't to blame. Voices were heard:

"Let's get started, one half point won't alter anything in the table."

"That's no argument for a lad", Tal insisted.

In the hall the mischievous clapping of the children could be heard, urging the curtain to be lifted, while on the stage, shifting their chairs and bending over like conspirators, the grand-masters were in thought. No one had a pocket set, so one of the World Champions took a piece of paper and began drawing out a board on it. Someone helped to draw the kings, and others began calculating variations.

The officials of the Komsomol Central Committee and the USSR Sports Committee waited patiently, observing with interest the grandmasters, who were cut off from the entire world and linked by this one, single position, created by a young pioneer from Riga.

"No, this won't do", said Botvinnik, who was the first to come to his senses. "We won't decide anything this way."

Did this mean that the controller was to leave in force the previous decision?

The answer was soon given: announcing the final results of the event, the punctilious and intractable Botvinnik added that "for technical reasons, one game had not been adjudicated". From the platform the speeches began, and the hall started applauding, but in the honorary praesidium the seasoned grandmasters continued looking at the piece of paper with the chess diagram drawn on it.

A symbol of friendship between the different generations was provided by red carnations: the schoolboys presented them to their teachers. Misha Moskovich proudly and ceremoniously presented his carnation to Botvinnik, and said something to him. The adults standing alongside began shaking with laughter. Almost crying, Tal spread his hands:

"What can we do with him? He's asking for a win now!"

For boldness and determination displayed in the saving of a difficult position, the boy was given a draw. The tables had to be altered, and the Soviet Union Telegraph Agency reported the corrected final results of the first tournament of Pioneers' Palaces, dedicated to the 50th Anniversary of the Lenin All-Union Pioneers' Organization, and to the half-century Jubilee of the foundation of the USSR.

This is the Soviet School of Chess; this is the attention enjoyed by young players in the Soviet Union. The echo of the great chess achievements of our grandmasters is not too late. But then an echo can't be late...

INFORMATION FOR REFLECTION

"Information, even the most valuable, cannot guarantee success; depth of thought and a broad education are also required. The modern chess player has to make all-round preparations, which should include both independent research, and the study of the chess classics.

The latter is particularly fruitful. Here you cannot limit yourself by saying: 'I already know that'. Every reading provides new insight. Thus after studying 'Yevgeny Oniegin' at school, I considered that I knew and remembered it fairly well, but on looking at the novel some two to three years later, I discovered for myself completely new sensations and thoughts, and entered into a new world. I have no doubt that if I were to read the novel today it would again be an enriching experience.

In exactly the same way, I have this desire inside me to go through the whole of Capablanca. I know all his games, but from a long time ago—it was from them that I learned to play chess, and later I returned to certain of his games—but now I should like to go logically through his life and career, and understand at the board the reasons and consequences of the changes in his ideas and opinions.

Lasker and Alekhine demand the same kind of attention. And in general, it is not possible to say today about one of the classics: 'he has aged and is no longer needed', because each of them was original in his own way. The games of, for instance, Morphy, an artist so distant from our era and our kind of chess, are instructive for the reason that he sensed the harmony of the pieces and objects of attack, and his ability to switch from attack to positional play was tremendous, even by today's standards. He would attack, gain an advantage, and then transform it into a win by non-combinational means. This is a very important feature, which distinguishes him from his contemporaries. From him one can study the brilliant thread of the initiative, for which he was ready to give up pieces, to say nothing of pawns.

During Anderssen's time romantic chess flourished: the sacrifice was seen as the main element of beauty, and to decline a sacrifice was regarded as cowardice. In essence, the rule of draughts also existed, unwritten, in chess: if I sacrifice, the opponent is obliged to take. Chess was then purely a game. But when Steinitz appeared, bringing new depth to the game, and working out the laws of positional play and displaying its beauty, the character of chess changed. Next came the change outlined by Alekhine, but instilled and developed by Botvinnik—the scientific approach to chess.

The earlier kings—Lasker, and particularly Capablanca—hardly studied the opening at all. They were such genii—and knew it—that they were able to cope at the board with any unpleasantness. And they demonstrated this in practice. The most striking example: when Capablanca encountered at the board Marshall's brilliant invention—his counter-attack in the Ruy Lopez—he worked out the subtleties and made a move which even today is not considered bad.

But Alekhine worked a great deal at home. A whole series of his well-known games were won straight from the opening, by seizing his opponent in a vice prepared beforehand. And his grip was strong: once he had seized a victim, he did not let him go.

It was in this direction that Botvinnik began working. His scientific approach to chess gradually became established in the forefront. I think that he did not study at home such questions as, say, a new move or a new idea somewhere about the fifteenth move in some variation. He worked out entire new systems. In this he was fortunate: chess was still to a considerable extent virgin land, and he went along it with the 'first plough'. But today we have to be satisfied with innovations on the twelfth to fifteenth moves. And even that we can't always manage!

Botvinnik could permit himself long breaks, when he wouldn't play for a long time, but would leave chess for, say, a year, and carry out scientific work. And altogether he didn't play a great deal. Nowadays a player can't permit himself this. Sifting through information and making one's own searchings are one thing, but if you don't play for half a year, you begin to sense a deterioration. You acquire the feeling of something having been lost, and you lose confidence in yourself, as if you have to begin studying something, but what and how is not clear. For this reason a player endeavours to compete in events more or less regularly. Everyone works at home, but this is now no longer enough.

Botvinnik also laid the foundations of a serious competitive approach to chess. What does this signify? In former times the play was according to a rather simple scheme: a player thought up an idea and put it into practice, whereupon his opponent thought up a counter-idea; and then it was revealed whose idea had worked, and who had made a fool of himself, at the same time it was revealed who was the winner and who the loser. The essence of the matter was: the idea didn't work, so the game was lost. Nowadays this appears rather ridiculous, and nowadays no one has to be taught that, if one idea does not work, one must promptly think up another, and play on—but formerly that's how things appeared. Our players were the first to display tenacity in defence. On obtaining an inferior position they continued to battle on; if they carried out some idea, but the position became even worse—even so they battled on, until the opponent dealt the final blow. . . This sharpening of the struggle demanded of players special preparation, so as to be able to endure the physical and nervous demands which formerly were absent.

I think that the competitive side in chess will continue to prevail very slightly over the creative. And here an enormous rôle is played by the availability of information.

After Botvinnik, chess needed a Tal—and he appeared, as an enormous, striking artist. He rushed by like a devastating hurricane, clearing the way for his antithesis Petrosian. The chess swings were balanced by Spassky—the integral and completely universal player. He was equally good at attacking and defending, and at accumulating positional advantages. It was he who created the fashion of universalism, which is alive to this day.

While for Tal, in order to become Champion, it was sufficient to frighten his opponents, by sacrificing and sacrificing (Petrosian also had the ability to make combinations, but he suppressed this gift, and played purely positionally), nowadays, in order to attain big successes, this is not nearly enough. You must be able to do everything fairly well (with no obvious defects), and in addition you must be able to do something exceptionally well.

Under Petrosian and Spassky, chess became 'softer'. Players allowed themselves breaks both during a game and during an event. And then Fischer appeared and forced them to play as had been the case in Botvinnik's time (only at a higher level), to which they had become unaccustomed: all five hours in a highly intensive struggle. They didn't expect this. Perhaps this is the main explanation for the crushing defeats which eminent players suffered at the hands of Fischer.

Fischer returned the sharpness to chess, made it tougher, and carried the competitive aspect to the limit, battling on until only the 'bare kings' remained. He raised universalism even higher, demonstrating amazing technique in the realization of an advantage, splendid combinational and positional play, a feel for the initiative, and an ability to attack. But most characteristic of him was his competitive nature: his exploitation in a battle of every chance to the last.

Nowadays chess is developing even more quickly. The numerous tournaments give a vast amount of material for analysis. Material is not just being accumulated, but also interpreted. Reassessments of variations and entire systems take place before our very eyes. Formerly one could play one set of variations, but then chess theory advanced, and it turned out that it was no longer a simple matter to employ one's favourite schemes; for instance, Black had learned to equalize in what were previously thought to be hopeless positions, while in others, where Black used to feel very comfortable, he now found it so difficult that it was better not to attempt to play them. Therefore players are all the time forced to seek something new, and to change their favourite systems and variations.

The element of psychology in chess has become very important, especially in matches. You have to understand yourself, seek the key to your opponent, and have the ability to utilize this knowledge both of yourself and of your opponent in specific situations at the board. You may deviate at some point from the strongest continuation, but on the other hand drive your opponent into a position which he doesn't like playing. And the further you go, the greater the weight in chess that this ability will acquire."

* * *

The Soviet chess "pyramid" is enormous. At the base of it are the popular All-Union events for Pioneers and schoolchildren. We know how to teach chess as a science and as an art. But perhaps it is time to put the accent on the third aspect? It is not only a science and an art, but also a sport. This means courage, determination, tenacity and industry—these are the characteristics which have to be instilled in our children, along with the teaching of the "sight of the board" and the calculation of variations. So that later, when they emerge onto the level of world chess, their country can be proud of them. And rely on them.

Tournament and Match Results

Results of Anatoly Karpov's appearances, from the time when he was awarded the master title.

Year	Event	Place	+	=	−
1966	'Masters against candidate masters'		5	10	0
	USSR Junior Team Tournament	Board one in lower age-group	5	3	0
	USSR-Scandinavia Junior Team Match	Board six	1	1	0
1966/7	Trinec	1st	9	4	0
1967	RSRSF Spartakiad	Board two	4	1	2
	Elimination Tournament for the World Junior Championship	5th	3	1	3
	USSR Schools' Spartakiad	Board two	5	4	0
1967/8	Groningen	1st	6	8	0
1968	USSR–Yugoslavia	2nd Junior Board	3	1	0
	USSR–Scandinavia Junior Team Match	Board two	0	1	1
	Moscow University Championship	1st	7	6	0
	USSR Team Championship	1st Junior Board	9	2	0
1969	Elimination Match-Tournament for the World Junior Championship	1st	5	5	2
	USSR–Yugoslavia Junior Team Match	Board three	2	2	0
	Tournament of Eastern Bloc Armies (Warsaw)	Reserve	1	0	0

Year	Event	Place	Result +	Result =	Result −
1969	USSR Armed Forces Team Championship	Board two	5	1	1
	World Junior Championship (Stockholm)	1st	12	5	0
	Hungary–RSFSR (Budapest)	Junior Board	0	2	2
1970	RSFSR Championship (Kuybishev)	1st	8	9	0
	Caracas	4th–6th	8	7	2
	38th USSR Championship (Riga)	5th–7th	5	14	2
1971	Training Match v Korchnoi		2	2	2
	Semi-Final 39th USSR Championship (Daugavpils)	1st	9	8	0
	18th Student Olympiad (Puerto Rico)	Board three	7	1	0
	USSR Armed Forces Team Championship	Board one	2	4	1
	USSR Team Championship (Rostov-on-Don)	Junior Board	6	1	0
	39th USSR Championship (Leningrad)	4th	7	12	2
	Alekhine Memorial (Moscow)	1st–2nd	5	12	0
1971/2	Hastings	1st–2nd	8	6	1
1972	USSR Olympiad (Moscow)	Board two	4	3	2
	19th Student Olympiad (Graz)	Board one	5	4	0
	20th FIDE Olympiad (Skopje)	1st Reserve	12	2	1
	San Antonio	1st–3rd	7	7	1
1973	Budapest	2nd	4	11	0
	Match-Tournament of USSR Teams (Moscow)	Board one	2	2	0
	Interzonal Tournament (Leningrad)	1st–2nd	10	7	0
	European Team Championship (Bath)	Board four	4	2	0
	41st USSR Championship (Moscow)	2nd–6th	5	11	1
	Madrid	1st	7	8	0
1974	Candidates' Quarter-Final v. Polugayevsky (Moscow)		3	5	0

Year	Event	Place	Result +	=	−
1974	Candidates' Semi-Final v. Spassky (Leningrad)		4	6	1
	21st FIDE Olympiad (Nice)	Board one	10	4	0
	Candidates' Final v. Korchnoi (Moscow)		3	19	2
1975	Ljubljana/Portorož	1st	7	8	0
	USSR Spartakiad	Board one	4	3	0
	Milan: Preliminary Tournament	2nd–4th	3	7	1
	Semi-Final v. Petrosian		0	4	0
	Final v. Portisch		1	5	0
1976	Skopje	1st	10	5	0
	USSR Team Cup	Board one	2	4	0
	Amsterdam	1st	2	4	0
	Manila	2nd	1	4	1
	Montilla	1st	5	4	0
	44th USSR Championship (Moscow)	1st	8	8	1
1977	Bad Lauterberg	1st	9	6	0
	European Team Championship (Moscow)	Board one	5	0	0
	Las Palmas	1st	12	3	0
	Leningrad	4th–5th	5	10	2
	Tilburg	1st	6	8	1
1978	Bugojno	1st–2nd	6	8	1
	Match for the World Championship v. Korchnoi (Baguio)		6	21	5

Index of openings

(Numbers refer to pages)

* Indicates an annotated game (all notes are by Karpov himself).

Index of opponents

(Numbers refer to pages)